"I cannot say that I am in the slightest degree impressed by your bigness, or your material resources as such. Size is not grandeur, and territory does not make a nation. The great issue, about which hangs a true sublimity and the terror of overhanging fate, is what are you going to do with all these things?"

—SIR THOMAS HUXLEY

# Our Recent Past

Our

**Prentice-Hall, Inc.**    Englewood Cliffs, N.J.

THOMAS NEVILLE BONNER

# Recent Past

AMERICAN CIVILIZATION

IN THE TWENTIETH CENTURY

*For* RAY ALLEN BILLINGTON

*Indulgent teacher, untiring scholar, and generous friend*

*—whose example has inspired us all*

### Our Recent Past

AMERICAN CIVILIZATION IN THE TWENTIETH CENTURY

*Thomas N. Bonner*

© *Copyright 1963 by* PRENTICE-HALL, INC.,
*Englewood Cliffs, New Jersey*

*Library of Congress Catalog Card No.: 63–11091*

*Printed in the United States of America*

*Designed by Walter Behnke*

C

# Preface

This is an interpretive account of recent American history that assumes at least an elementary knowledge of our nation's past. I have always felt that a book intended for use in a course in recent American history, which is normally taught in the upper-division, should differ in approach and level of analysis from the books used in the basic survey course. I have tried to avoid that excessive factualism that Toynbee has called "the one damned thing after another school of history." At the same time I have not forgotten altogether that some who read this book will need refreshing on the events and forces that molded our recent past.

In interpreting that recent past I have looked for themes and unifying ideas that cut across the usual boundaries between our political, intellectual, social, and economic lives. The past is always more meaningful, I believe, when woven into larger patterns of interpretation than when examined inch-by-inch outside those patterns. This book represents what might be called the "civilization approach" to the study of history as opposed to narratives that are more exclusively political, social, or economic. In each period covered by the book—the eighteen-nineties, the progressive years, the World War I era, the twenties, the New Deal, World War II, and the times since—I have tried to point out the interrelationships be-

tween events in different areas of our national life.

Although I have been mindful of Sir Walter Raleigh's warning that "whosoever in writing a moderne History, shall follow truth too neare the heeles, it may haply strike out his teeth," I have nonetheless dealt with very recent events, believing that modern history must treat, however tentatively, of the events of only yesterday. Indeed, the proportions of this book were determined on the assumption that the years since 1945 are at least as important to the century's story as the years before 1920.

I am aware of the very real problems facing an historian who tries to write a brief, interpretive, and yet integrated account of our recent history. I hope that my colleagues, many of whom like myself have asked for this kind of book for use in Recent American History courses, will be charitable in judging its shortcomings.

Many persons have helped in the creation of this book. I should like to thank Dr. Milo Bail of the University of Omaha for a reduction in teaching load and financial assistance to meet typing costs of the manuscript. Miss Mae Donne did an unusually conscientious job of typing, while Miss Ellen Lord, Librarian of the University, was unfailing in her warmth and kindness toward the project. A number of my colleagues read portions of the manuscript, and three of them—Dean Robert Harper, Professor Frederick Adrian, and Professor Roy Robbins—read all of the chapters. My good friend William H. Harbaugh improved considerably the first four chapters by his careful job of criticism. Last but not least among those who rendered notable encouragement and assistance are Mr. Edgar P. Thomas and Mr. Ronald Nelson of Prentice-Hall.

*Thomas N. Bonner*

# Acknowledgments

### Picture Credits

Page 2, Brown Brothers.   Page 34, New-York Historical Society.   Page 78, U.S. Signal Corps, in the National Archives.   Page 108, Underwood and Underwood.   Page 138, Underwood and Underwood.   Page 182, Culver Pictures.   Page 208, United Press.   Page 246, United Press. Page 274, United Press.   Page 310, United Press.   Page 338, United Press.   Page 378, United Press.   Page 412, Wide World Photos.   Page 440, Wide World Photos.

### Quotation Credits

Page 35, *The Autobiography of W. Allen White* (New York: Macmillan, 1946).   Page 139, Sinclair Lewis, *Babbitt* (New York: Harcourt, Brace & World, 1922).   Page 183, *The New York Times,* July 9, 1932.   Page 247, *Memoirs of Herbert Hoover,* v. 2 (New York: Macmillan, 1953).   Page 275, Reprinted by permission of the publishers, The Vanguard Press, from *Shall Not Perish from the Earth* by Ralph Barton Perry. Copyright 1941 by The Vanguard Press, Inc. Page 379, *Wall Street Journal,* April 29, 1955.   Page 441, From "Burnt Norton" in *Four Quartets,* Copyright 1943 by T. S. Eliot. Reprinted by permission of Harcourt, Brace & World.

# Contents

# The Axis
# of the Nineties

CHAPTER ONE

Electrical building, Chicago World's Fair, 1893.

# THE MOOD OF THE TIMES

"All hail the Twentieth Century! . . . Altruism is displacing selfishness as a social force. A century of honor lies behind us. . . . If war still exists it is not waged as it was in the eighteenth century. Prisoners are not put to death, nor are they made to suffer in property or person. . . . There is a deep-seated and ineradicable conviction that "war is hell"; and that its horrors not only must be mitigated, but that eternal peace must be established. . . .

"It falls to the lot of each generation to inspire its successors; to each century to create the enthusiasm that shall kindle the manhood of the next. What are we to do for the Twentieth Century? Can we write a second Declaration of Independence? Socially great questions are sure of being solved just ahead. Equitable distribution is coming in the form of a living wage, co-operative industries, old age pensions, and a relief of taxation that falls upon the poor. . . . It is getting to be a universal social conception that we must, whether we will or not, bear each other's burdens.

"We are now, in our higher civilization, inaugurating a change . . . fully equal to that from feudalism to centralism. The control, which for three centuries has been concentrating in the hands of the middle class is now passing into the hands of differentiated educated masses. . . . They now have the ballot as well as the school. It is impossible to withhold sympathy from those who work in the belief that society can be so ameliorated that there shall be an end of wars, and of standing armies; and an equalization of the products of industry that shall essentially banish poverty and its vices. It is our sublime aim to infuse the Twentieth Century with a purpose superior to that of the nineteenth—a humanity broader, a hope higher, a will more rational."

—THE INDEPENDENT, January 3, 1900

# A CENTURY'S HERITAGE

The editor of *The Independent*, like Americans generally in 1900, knew that the old century had been kind to the United States. To compare the outlook and prospects of the country in 1800 with those of 1900 was to see the difference. In 1800, the five million Americans who greeted the census-taker had known far less reason for confidence. Hemmed in by mountains and discouraged from venturing beyond them by the ruggedness of transportation, two of every three Americans still lived within fifty miles of the sound of rolling surf. It took travelers three days to pass from Boston to New York, while no road could be counted on south of Baltimore, especially in rainy weather. The daily rounds of toil and rural chores, the crude housing and cruder diet of the American of 1800 made his life scarcely better than the lot of fortunate peasants in Saxon Britain a thousand years before. His politics, it is true, were far in advance of anything known in Europe, but they were rooted in principles whose truth few Europeans would accept as proven. The political capital of the new nation was still an ambitious village in 1800, and the Capitol itself stood bleakly, half-finished, overlooking a dismal swamp. The western boundary of the rude republic stood at the Mississippi whose waters rolled southward largely unnoticed by human eye.

The great impulses that were to create modern America—industrialism, urbanism, mass immigration, the massive westward movement—throbbed feebly in the current of American life in 1800. It would have taken a prescient observer indeed to have seen the promise of American industrial growth in the household industries of New England in 1800, or the later runaway growth of American cities in the halting population advance of New York and Boston. America was already a mixture of European nationalities, but as yet there was no sign of the great flood of migrants that was to pour in later in the century. Even the great westward trek of the American people, so long a central feature of the nation's history, had not yet reached the thunderous pitch that would cause later writers to liken it to the great movements of peoples across the face of Roman Europe.

## Portrait of a Nineteenth-Century American

Yet if we look away from the physical conditions of an American's life in 1800 to the American himself, we notice an interesting thing. For although the setting of life was sharply different from that of the country now, the characteristics of the average citizen of that day bear a striking resemblance to those of his descendants. We have been taught in recent years to be wary of portraying the qualities of an entire people—and rightly so—but there seems little doubt that the nineteenth-century American, even in 1800, possessed a cluster of culture patterns, attitudes, and traits that we have come to think of as "characteristically American."

From the beginning, life in America tended to center in the individual. The forces pulling him away from settled routine always tended to leave him isolated, independent: initially a New World that drew him away from an ordered society; then a beckoning Western frontier that threw him back again on his own resources; and, throughout, a new political experiment that bid him renounce tradition and the authority of the past. The individual seemed always to be on his own, as often by circumstance as by choice. Though he joined with his neighbors in barn-raising, Indian fighting, and other communal undertakings, he faced most of the major responsibilities of life alone. In America there was no established church in the European sense, no respected upper class, no hallowed tradition to provide the cement of social custom and accepted ways. The American's world was particularistic, cut into a thousand differing patterns of religious, political, and community loyalties, that were united only in what had been left behind or rejected in 1776.

A New World meant new dreams. The American was not only an individualist thrown into a wilderness by the social revolutions of his European motherland; he was very early an optimist in his assessment of future prospects. Forced to rely on his own experience, he discovered a power and a confidence that enabled him to face the future with an almost eager expectancy. The flood of American opportunities, the very surplus of material abundance, made it easy for him to believe in the future and its promise. Daily he saw old dreams fulfilled and new hopes launched. Because his own experience was good, he was ready to believe in all instances that "experience is the best guide."

If America seemed a modern "land of plenty," it is not surprising that American values should have been materialistic. Life was attuned to success, to the spaciousness of the western Eden, to the social mobility encouraged by unsettled class lines. Though there was much to praise in the functional simplicity of his crafts and architecture, the American's materialism and practical approach to life were often condemned by European visitors. Dickens thought the Americans totally "money-mad," while the Polish novelist Sienkiewicz put it more politely when he wrote: "The American people are extraordinarily matter-of-fact. No one troubles himself about things which have no connection with reality or material benefits or which cannot be grasped and calculated." This American fascination with numbers, with size, with the purely quantitative, has continued to attract the attention of foreigners into our own time.

The great enemy of success was idleness. Americans hated idleness as fiercely as they admired industry and perseverance. A generation taught to read by the famous McGuffey readers did not soon forget the familiar injunction to "Try, try again; If you find your task is hard, try, try, again." And to fail, to be poor in a rich country, was a stigma not lightly borne. It indicated some signal weakness in the individual himself. Being poor in nineteenth-century America, Professor Bremner tells us, was thought of as "a self-inflicted mortification." *

The nineteenth-century American thus worked hard, made a fetish of progress, worshipped success, and zealously guarded the conditions and the system which he believed responsible for his

---

* R. Bremner, *From the Depths* (New York: New York University Press, 1956), p. 70.

good fortune. His faith in democratic government was in fact a conviction that the political and social system evolving in America was the one most likely to guarantee his continued happiness and welfare. There was little abstract about it. His political ideas, especially his confidence in self-government, his belief in the right of all men to freedom, and his conviction that the United States possessed a unique destiny, grew out of the evolving culture of nineteenth-century America. The rights which he enjoyed he usually held to be *natural* rights arising from the processes of nature or the design of God himself. Once gained by free men, these rights were, he thought, invulnerable to recapture by a despot. He was free because that was his natural condition; it was God's intention that he should be so. He had a right and a duty to govern himself because no free man could ever consent to be ruled by another. And it was his further duty—indeed, his mandate—to carry the message of self-government around the world.

By the end of the nineteenth century, the American had succeeded in creating his own "national style." He had a characteristic way of looking at life and approaching problems, a hard-headed practicality in his daily life, a unique political system, and a strong faith in himself and his mission in the world. The abundance of the American economy enabled him to escape the want and misery that oppressed so much of Europe. His isolation from close contacts with that continent protected him from continued exploitation during the nation's infancy. His historical experience made him a cheerful and smiling individual by any comparative human standard. The editor of *The Independent* was expressing only a normal American sentiment in his optimistic prediction that the progress of the old century would continue and even accelerate in the new.

## The Changing Eden

The crucible in which these basic American traits and outlook were formed was the special cultural and social environment of the United States in the nineteenth century. Basically, this environment was rural. Nineteenth-century America was a land of small farms, sprawling plantations, scattered population, county towns, and slow communications. Agriculture dominated its economic interests until well after the Civil War. Politics, too, tended to revolve around the shifting concerns of the agrarian population. Rural ideals of family relationships, religious loyalties, and community life exerted a profound attraction throughout the nation.

American traits reflected their rural origin. The intense individualism of Americans suited a land of few people, little tradition, and much opportunity; their optimism looked to a continuation of the same kind of open, free society they had known; even their practicality, their self-reliance, and their coarseness of manner were traceable to their experience in creating life anew in a wilderness; and their political ideas, like their political practice, were rooted in their unique historical experience.

What would Americans do if that experience were to change? How would they react in crisis? What if the economic environment no longer favored the cult of individualism? Would the ideals forged by farmers in a small nation hugging the East Coast be applicable to a time of great cities, bustling factories, and continental domain? Did Americans have a usable past? Only after confronting these questions could Americans hope to answer the query of the philosopher Santayana "whether materialism or idealism lies at the base of [the American's] character."

Out of these questions and the answers given by Americans come the materials for a history of the United States in the twentieth century. The great problems of the twentieth century were fashioned in the nineteenth: problems created by the coming of the machine and the march to the cities, by expansion to the Pacific and the closing of the frontier, by the heritage of the Civil War and the questions it left unsolved, by the waves of immigrants pouring into Eastern ports, by the scientific revolution that shook the foundations of religion and established patterns of thought, and by the titanic surge in American power that thrust her at century's end onto the stage of world politics.

### The Advance of the Factory

No single change in American life in the nineteenth century was so fraught with significance as the steady intrusion of industrialism into the nation's economy. Everywhere the factory appeared, it brought a new atmosphere that affected not only the American's patterns of work and his standard of living, but even his recreations, his worship, and his modes of thought. A whole new social structure began to emerge. For industrialism was more than a new way of producing goods. In America, as earlier in Britain, it meant an increase and concentration of population, a vastly expanded trade, and a rise in importance of the middle classes, who make business and industry their province. These changes, in turn, produced abundance and want, comfort and misery, pride and jealousy in the affected classes of society. In the wake of industrialism a fleet of new social tensions and strains arrived to be weighed against the eventual improvement in levels of living and increased leisure time of the average industrial worker and his family.

The change-over in America from an almost wholly agrarian society to a heavily industrialized one was swift and overwhelming. In 1865 nearly all the great resources that were stored under American soil—coal, iron, oil, and the rest—lay undiscovered and unexploited. Of the rich natural treasures only the forests and the land itself had been put to extensive use. Yet only thirty years later, the United States would pace the world in the exploitation of its resources and the output of its manufacturing industries.

The growth of the American industrial plant in the 1870's and 1880's almost beggars description. No other country, not even the Soviet Union, has industrialized completely in so short a time. American manufacturers enjoyed the benefit of the British experience as well as British capital; and abundant resources of good coking coal and high-grade iron ore combined with a never-failing supply of immigrant labor to make their task easier. A huge domestic market without internal tariff barriers encouraged risk, initiative, and investment. And the American's practicality and ingenuity, nourished in an agrarian age, found new outlets. Nor did America lack imaginative business leaders—such as the great steelmaker Andrew Carnegie, who caught a vision of the future role of steel in the nation's and the world's economy; John D. Rockefeller, who controlled the flow of crude oil to an oil-hungry nation; and the railroad builders like Jim Hill and E. H. Harriman, who pushed 200,000 miles of track across the continent in only fifty years. By 1894 the United States had emerged as the foremost industrial nation.

What did all this mean? What was the significance of so volcanic an upheaval in the lives of ordinary men and women? What new vistas were opened by the wholesale substitution of machinery for laborious human toil? What were the new problems? And what did the far-reaching changes in daily life purport for those American ideals and characteristics nourished in an earlier, simpler time? Before attempting an answer to these questions,

With industrialism came far-reaching changes in the tempo of everyday life. Machine shop, West Lynn, Massachusetts, 1896. (Brown Brothers.)

we must first look at the other social impulses that the nineteenth century bequeathed to the twentieth.

### The Surge to the Cities

The same generation that witnessed the industrialization of the United States saw the birth of its modern, dynamic, urban culture. Rural America, in the historian Arthur Schlesinger's picturesque phrase, was like a stag at bay, making its last desperate stand against the domination of the urban Northeast. But the fight it fought, although it had its heroes and colorful moments, was doomed to failure. Inexorably the lure of city jobs and city attractions drew the young, the hopeful, and the adventurous along with the newcomers from Europe. According to census figures, there were only 141 cities of 8,000 persons or more in the United States in 1860, compared with 545 in 1900. Five of every six Americans lived in a community of fewer than 2,500 people in 1860, but by 1890 one of these persons had gone to the city and by 1910 still another had turned his back on rural life. Small cities grew large and the large cities became even larger. New York leaped from 1,500,000 in 1860 to 2,500,-000 in 1890 and to about 5,000,000 in 1915. Chicago grew even faster. Number-

ing only 100,000 inhabitants in 1860, this sprawling midwestern giant increased tenfold, to 1,000,000, by 1890 and twenty-five fold, to 2,500,000, by 1915.

To rural America, the city had always been evil incarnate, a place of idleness, sin, and crime. Country ministers inveighed against big cities, cursing them as "immense accumulations of ignorance and error, vice and crime." Editors of farm journals urged young men seeking their fortunes not to sacrifice their individuality in the city, where they must "cringe and flatter, and . . . attend upon the wishes of every painted and padded form of humanity." From the printing press came such lurid books as *Vampires of New York, Tricks and Traps of Chicago,* and a host of others.

The rural animus against urban ways declined somewhat as the surge to the cities continued, though suspicion remained. For cities were becoming a national phenomenon and could no longer be identified exclusively with a distant and suspect East. Midwestern as well as East and West Coast towns swelled with the expansion of industrialism. Of the fifty principal American cities in 1890, twelve were in the Middle West. Urbanization was clearly becoming a controlling force in American history. A new way of life for Americans was taking shape. Walt Whitman, poet of the new urban democracy, could write of the "splendor, picturesqueness, and oceanic amplitude and rush of these great cities." But the clergyman Lyman Abbott voiced a more common attitude, rooted deep in the American rural past, when he queried: "What shall we do with our great cities? What will our great cities do with us? These are the two problems which confront every thoughtful American. For the question involved in these two problems does not concern the city alone. The whole country is affected, if indeed its character and history are not determined, by the condition of its great cities."

## The Eclipse
## of the Rural Frontier

The move to the cities coincided in time with the last burst of settlement on the western frontier. The last frontier was passing away over the lonely, sprawling plains of western Kansas, Nebraska, the Dakotas, and Montana. Never had the drawbacks of rural life been felt so keenly. Now, not only the drudgery and monotony of the farm itself but also the comparison with the lot of the city-dweller made the farmer discontented. Farm women, in particular, could contrast the bleakness of their existence with the appealing photographs and stories of city women appearing in the new ladies' magazines. This social frustration probably played as large a role in inspiring the farmers' protest movements of the 1880's and 1890's as did their economic grievances about low prices, railroad abuses, and high interest rates.

No one who has read the moving story by Ole Rölvaag of the struggles of Per Hansa and his gentle wife, Beret, in the Dakota Territory in this period can doubt the suffering, overwork, loneliness, and spiritual starvation of these "Giants in the Earth." Per Hansa learned that farming in

The end of the nineteenth century saw the passing of the frontier. Purcell, Oklahoma, in 1894. (Standard Oil Company, N. J.)

America, like manufacturing, was becoming a business. More and more, the American farmer turned his back on simple self-sufficiency and threw his energies into raising a cash crop. And he used his proceeds from his crop to buy the necessities and luxuries of life being produced in the industrial centers. Like any businessman, he invested heavily in his venture and sought to turn his investment in land and machinery to profit; like him, too, he offered his product on a free market in competition with other producers. And just as producers in other lines of business enterprise sought to achieve peak efficiency by installing machinery and tapping new sources of power, so did the farmer try to mechanize his ancient operations.

But the farmer suffered peculiar disadvantages as a capitalist. He depended heavily on the haphazardness of nature for the safety and growth of his crop. He competed with thousands of small producers like himself who shared his individualistic traditions and distrusted cooperative action. In moving his crop, he was often at the mercy of a single railroad whose rates mirrored the lack of competition. In selling, he bid in an open market against producers in Canada, Australia, and Russia, as well as other Americans, while he bought at prices inflated in many instances by tariffs guarding the manufacturer from competitors abroad. For his credit and currency he looked to the resources of great metropolitan banks whose control he often thought lay in Wall Street. Small wonder that the western and southern farmer acquired what Russel Nye has called a "colonial complex" in his dealings with eastern business and banking houses.*

The urban and industrial pressures on rural America seemed to intensify with the end of the moving frontier, a turning

* R. Nye, *Midwestern Progressive Politics* (East Lansing: Michigan State College Press, 1951), pp. 4-9.

point revealed by the report of the Superintendent of the Census in 1890. No longer was there a clear line of demarcation between the settled and unsettled areas of the United States. To many, the nation seemed smaller and the temperature in the urban-industrial cauldron seemed to rise with the realization that the old escape valve to the West was closed. "Across the plains where once there roamed the Indian and the Scout," ran a later melancholy couplet, "The Swede with alcoholic breath sets rows of cabbages out."

As a memory, the frontier with its emotional associations of independence and individualism was perhaps more powerful than as an actual fact. A number of voices were raised in the 1890's—Theodore Roosevelt's and the historian Frederick Jackson Turner's among them—to express fear that the end of the frontier meant the end of the old American virtues. As John Steinbeck put it years later in *The Red Pony*, "No, no place to go. . . . Every place is taken. But that's not the worst—no, not the worst. Westering has died out of the people. Westering isn't a hunger any more. It's all done."

### The South in Transition

No section of the nation felt so keenly the turmoil of the quarter-century following Appomattox as the South. Decimated and impoverished by war, humiliated in defeat, the former Confederacy had no time to brace itself to the economic, social, and intellectual storms of the postwar era. As late as 1880 the region still seemed hopelessly crushed, sunk in poverty, its economy infirm, its mood despondent, its people still nursing the wounds of war. Politically, the conservative white Southerners had accomplished the two great objectives that had stirred them during the hated Reconstruction days—to crush Negro aspirations and oust the hated carpetbaggers. Ancient cleavages between sections and classes in the South, though far from healed, were submerged for the time in the common cause of white supremacy. The Republicans gave up their hope of becoming a national party. "Our straight Republican, carpetbag, Negro governments," pronounced William Chandler, a member of President Arthur's cabinet, "have been destroyed and cannot be revived. . . ."

The disfranchisement and segregation of the one-time slaves did not follow immediately on the heels of Reconstruction, however. A full fifteen years or more passed in most of the former Confederate states before the discriminatory patterns familiar to twentieth-century Americans were imposed. A number of contemporary reports on race relations by Northern observers, both Negro and white, point to a period of relative freedom for the Negro in the enjoyment of his personal rights during the late 1870's and 1880's. The Populist agitation of the nineties, however, threatened the political solidarity of the South and held out the prospect of a two-party competition in many states. Native whites were faced with the choice of asking for the Negro's vote or taking it away from him. Beginning in Mississippi, the latter course was chosen in state after state. Ben Tillman of South Carolina boasted later on the floor of the United States Senate that "We took the government away. We stuffed ballot boxes. We shot them. . . . [then] we got tired. . . . So we called a constitutional convention, and we eliminated . . . all the colored people whom we could."

The swing of the South toward extremism in its treatment of the Negro was accompanied by a decline of Northern liberal interest in him. Northerners by this time were more interested in the economic promise of the section than in the ancient problem of Negro rights. Early in the 1880's a remarkable transformation of the whole Southern economy was ini-tiated, as large amounts of Northern and English capital made their way into the stream of commerce. A new class of Southern industrialists seized the unusual opportunities open to talent and ambition and began the creation of what came to be known as the New South. First in railroads, then swiftly in iron, tobacco, and textile manufacturing, Southerners showed that they knew the route that could lead them out of their economic slough to prosperity and self-respect. "If John D. Rockefeller can do what he is doing for oil," cried James Buchanan Duke, "why should I not do it in tobacco?" Only by rejecting their agrarian past, painful, as this was, and creating new industries, new jobs, and new opportunities could Southerners hope to share in the rising standards of living in the nation.

### The Uprooted

The South largely escaped the brunt of one of the important forces remaking nineteenth-century America. The great flow of European immigrants into the Atlantic ports and thence by rail to the iron, milling, packing, steel, and refining centers to the West skirted the South almost altogether. No one has described with greater feeling than the historian Oscar Handlin how these "uprooted" Europeans, torn by disaster and calamity, forced to the agonizing decision to abandon home and village, endured the prolonged crisis of the crossing to make a fresh start in a strange and terrifying land. That they found the physical conditions in America hostile to their customs and traditions and became islands of stubborn resistance to the currents of American life was not surprising. The foreign ghettos of the larger American cities were somber and depressing, filled with biting poverty, alive with the tensions of tenement life. And there was always the terrible crowding. Family ties loosened as the well-defined roles of family members began to lose their meaning in the baffling new homeland. Democracy especially puzzled the immigrant. To whom should be look for leadership and authority? Often he identified democratic politics with the local "boss" who took his part when he became embroiled in the maze of American laws. Yet native reformers, he learned, were opposed to this one group of men in America that aided and befriended him. That older Americans found the immigrant's attitudes strange, his poverty appalling, and his "clannishness"—a protective coloration in an alien and often unfriendly society —un-American is easy to understand.

To believe the newcomers un-American became easier as the sources of immigration from Europe shifted in the 1880's. The great bulk of immigrants heretofore had set sail from Great Britain, Ireland, Germany, and Scandinavia, the very lands the first American colonists themselves had left. The later arrivals from northern Europe simply enlarged the numbers, without greatly altering the proportions, of these groups in the American population. Their appearance, customs, languages, traditions, and religion all found some echo in the composite American nationality of the nineteenth century. But the 1880's brought a significant change. For the first time peoples from southern and eastern Europe—Italy, Russia, Poland, Austria-Hungary—joined the procession from the Old World. Few at first, their number grew swiftly—12,000 Italians in 1880, 52,000 in 1890, 100,000 in 1900; 5,000 Russians in 1880, 100,000 in 1900; 17,000 from Austria-Hungary in 1880, 115,000 in 1900. By 1900 the proportion of northwest Europeans in the American population was cut from 90 per cent to less than 75 per cent and it was to drop still further.

What did it mean? To the "old" American these recent immigrants sometimes seemed to represent a new and threaten-ing element in his civilization. He was normally Protestant; they were chiefly Catholic or Jewish. He was usually literate; they, often as not, could neither read nor write. He had been raised in freedom under democratic institutions; they had known little but subservience and autocracy. His was a land of plenty; theirs had spawned lives of grinding poverty. His manners and customs reflected an open, mobile society; theirs mirrored the class-bound, limited vistas of their lands of origin. To the native American the immigrants revealed all the tough, angular features of an alien peasantry. They were strangers among friends. They were "different"—and unwanted.

The alienation of the immigrant was furthered by the mobilization of native Americans against him. Disturbed by turbulent changes in their own lives, many Americans found outlet for some of their anxiety and frustration in denouncing the new arrivals' strange conduct and ways. "No Christian culture lies behind them," warned the Reverend S. L. Loomis in 1887; "they have never breathed a Christian atmosphere. Ideas with which all Americans, whether of pious parentage or not, have been familiar from childhood, are strange to them." Newcomers were often blamed for fostering labor unrest and bringing radical ideas into the country, particularly after Chicago anarchists of foreign birth were convicted of throwing a bomb into the police ranks in 1886. "These people," wrote one editor, "are not Americans, but the very scum and offal of Europe." Another decried the "rag-tag and bob-tail cutthroats of Beelzebub from the Rhine, the Danube, the Vistula, and the Elbe."

Even though recent immigrants were in truth usually highly conservative, they became the target of natives concerned about their growth and influence. New movements got underway. In Boston, an Immigration Restriction League was

Family of Bohemian cigarmakers, lower east side, New York City, about 1900. Photographed by Jacob Riis. Victimized by tenement owners who controlled the work, immigrants often labored 14 to 17 hours a day, 7 days a week. (Jacob A. Riis Collection, Museum of the City of New York.)

formed in 1894 to work for a limitation on immigration, especially from the "less desirable" areas outside northwest Europe. Earlier, in Clinton, Iowa, an American Protective Association was organized to fight the rising Catholic influence in American political and economic life. Every recruit to the A.P.A. swore never to vote for a Catholic, never to hire one when a Protestant could be had, and never to go on strike with Catholics. Though much of this "nativism" was aimed indiscriminately at all foreigners, it was the "new" immigrants who came more and more to bear the onus of anti-foreign and anti-Catholic feeling in the country. This blaming of the newer arrivals for the country's ills brought a playful rejoinder from the Irish-American humorist Finley Peter Dunne, who had his bartending "Mr. Dooley" comment: "As a pilgrim father that missed th' first boats, I must raise me Claryon voice again' th' invasion iv this fair land be th' paupers an' arnychists iv effete Europe. Ye bet I must—because I'm here first. . . ."

### The Darwinian Impact

A generation that knew such changes as those just recounted might be supposed to be exempt from further anxiety of mind and spirit. But in truth the most serious adjustment in the human condition between 1850 and 1890

came not from industrialism, immigration, or the other forces that so deeply affected daily life. It was rather a subtle yet profound shift in the way men thought —the way they looked at the old verities of religion, their views on morals, their approach to life's problems and ultimate concerns.

The revolution in thought had been centuries in the making but it struck the post-Civil War generation with peculiar force. One cluster of ideas in particular dramatized for this generation the slow change-over from a static, fixed view of life and matter to the dynamic modern concepts of growth, movement, and change. The writings of an English naturalist, Charles Darwin, expressed a new theory of the development of life in language that any ordinary man of intelligence could understand. "I am aware," Darwin wrote in *The Descent of Man* (1871), "that the conclusions arrived at in this work will be denounced as highly irreligious; but he who denounces them is bound to show why it is more irreligious to explain the origin of man as a distinct species by descent from some lower form . . . than to explain the birth of the individual through the laws of ordinary reproduction."

What were these conclusions of Darwin's? In this book and in his earlier *The Origin of Species* (1859), he offered a pic-

13

ture of living organisms everywhere in competition for food and the other necessities of survival. In this struggle for existence those organisms that are best adapted to get plenty of food and to avoid other predatory creatures tend to survive, to find suitable mates, and to reproduce. What determines which organisms are lucky enough to be born with the superior capabilities for surviving? Basically, Darwin said, it is pure chance. Since life began, most organisms have reproduced in large quantity and their offspring have varied slightly in height, strength, fleetness, and other traits important to survival. Those variations ("sports" Darwin called them) that were particularly useful for protection or the acquisition of food tended to be perpetuated since their lucky possessors were more likely to remain alive to produce offspring. Thus did a particular "sport," a line of development, a species become established. The chain of life, strung on these two great principles of *chance variation* and *natural selection,* led from the simplest organism through the various species to man himself. Man's brainpower and facility at communication give him a favored position in the struggle for existence but he is nevertheless a part of the natural history of all living things.

Darwin's enemies raised two vital questions: (1) What happened to God in this evolutionary scheme; and (2) what purpose could there be to human life if it evolved out of nothing toward a future equally obscure? To the first, Darwin's champions in the United States, notably John Fiske and Edward Livingston Youmans, replied that there was no real conflict between evolutionary theory and religion. Evolution was but one further evidence of the infinite subtlety of God in working out His purposes in the world. "What else is Evolution," asked Professor James T. Bixby, "but the secular name for the Divine Indwelling?" Had not the

course of evolution led steadily and progressively upward—striving toward that perfection which was God's own nature? Darwin's theory explained only the development, not the source of life. Gradually the churches retreated from their initial stance of hostility to Darwinism. The universe was now seen as an unfolding revelation in which the Divine purpose was becoming progressively more clear. Evolution was headed toward some definite end known only to God, but which promised even more glorious progress for humankind in the future. The second question now answered itself. Life had as much meaning as ever in the buoyant, optimistic context in which Darwin's early interpreters placed evolution. The churches had seemingly snatched victory from the very jaws of defeat.

But what about morals? What support could be found in the new theory for man's moral ideas, based as they were on Christian concepts of life and the universe? John Fiske provided the clue. "We see that the distinction between right and wrong is rooted in the deepest foundations of the universe," he told a great audience assembled to honor Darwin's English interpreter, Herbert Spencer: "we see that the very same forces . . . which brought upon the scene the primal germs of life and caused them to unfold . . . have wrought into the very fibres of the universe those principles of right living which it is man's highest function to put into practice." Fiske concluded his speech with the assurance that Darwin's theory had given morality a sanction more "powerful than has ever been assigned in any philosophy of ethics."

Not all Americans were satisfied, of course, with the easy optimism of Fiske, as the conflicts of the nineties were to make clear. Some saw real danger to their faith and morals in Darwinism. A number saw a devastating threat to the "Rock of Ages" in the age of rocks, as it was put by one speaker, while many clung to a literal and fundamental faith in the doctrines of traditional Christianity. Catholics were generally less disturbed than Protestants by the change in outlook, primarily because of their greater reliance on sources other than the Bible for religious support.

But among all ranks and faiths the new scientific approach to life symbolized in Darwinism brought a jarring realization of new forces afoot that threatened the security of comfortable opinions and ancient beliefs.

## YEARS OF TRANSITION: THE TURBULENT NINETIES

The generation that came to terms with Darwinism was destined to live between two worlds. In their own lives they experienced the impact of the dynamic forces creating modern America. They had seen the filling out of the country, the mushrooming of cities and factories, the rounding out of the western frontier, the revival of the South, the coming of the immigrant, and still other changes not recounted here. But they still knew, too, the America of the small farm and the crossroads village, of local enterprise and slower-paced life, of religious orthodoxy and the traveling Chautauqua.

**Indian Summer?**

The great themes of the twentieth century were already on the horizon but the concerns of the nineteenth had not yet faded from sight. Politicians still wrangled over the tariff, taxes, currency, honesty in government, and the South's responsibility for the War. The Monroe Doctrine and the traditions of American isolation still ruled the nation's thinking about foreign relations. Vast economic changes had overtaken the country but they were discussed largely in the agrarian context of a half-century before. So the prevailing mood of the nineties, except for the unemployed and a few sensitive literary men, suggested that of *The Independent's* editor—roseate optimism and unbounded confidence. The wars, economic crises, and social cataclysms of the

twentieth century still lay ahead.

Yet the 1890's were shaken by premonitory tremors of the earthquakes to come. Labor violence flared on a scale hitherto unknown in the relations between employers and workers. The severest depression of the century awoke many to the existence of poverty and misery in the United States. A hotly contested election in 1896 was filled with appeals to class interest and with denunciations of Wall Street and the new capitalists. Reformers and politicians called openly now for an end to traditional freedom of enterprise and for governmental powers to discipline big business. Both Christianity and Darwinism were put to work on behalf of the proponents as well as the opponents of change. American writers discovered European pessimism and some rejected the "see no evil, speak no evil" tradition of American literature. And as the century drew to a close, the United States, buoyed up by a wave of expansionist national sentiment, reversed its isolationist traditions and started to acquire an overseas empire.

Professor Fred Pattee has described the nineties as an "Indian Summer," an "equinox between two creative periods," a moment's pause between two epochs of history.* It was an era bright with the colors of the past, yet alive with the vital

* F. Pattee, *The New American Literature, 1890-1930* (New York: The Century Company, 1930), p. 3.

forces of the future. To some they were the "Gay Nineties," dreamy with the memories of a slower-paced life, small towns, the horse and carriage, fast bicycles, church suppers, romantic novels, the "splendid little war" with Spain, or the great Chicago Exposition of 1893. The songs of the era would have a permanent nostalgia, even for those born after 1900— "The Bowery," "The Rosary," "The Sidewalks of New York," "On the Banks of the Wabash," and "After the Ball is Over."

To others, the 1890's would seem gay only in retrospect if at all. Four years of deep depression left their mark on farmers, workers, and businessmen. To Ray Stannard Baker, then a cub reporter, the contrast between the gaiety of the Chicago Exposition and the sight of a nation in distress a few months later was startling: "What a spectacle! What a human down-fall after the magnificence and prodigality of the World's Fair. . . . Heights of splendor, pride, exaltation in one month; depths of wretchedness, suffering, hunger, cold, in the next."

### Industrial Violence

The industrial workers made jobless by the depression of 1893 to 1897 felt particularly the disproportion between the promise of the new industrial order and its actualities. Most of them lived close to the margin of subsistence, even when employed, but loss of their jobs brought acute distress and near panic. Their wages of four to five hundred dollars a year did not permit them to set much aside for emergencies, and even these wages were slashed as the depression neared.

It was a fight over wages that precipitated the brutal steel strike at Homestead,

"By the beautiful sea." The closing years of the nineteenth century were, for some, rich with memories of the past and with promise of the future. Ocean Grove, New Jersey, about 1900. (Library of Congress, Detroit Publishing Company Collection.)

Pennsylvania, in 1892. The strike pitted the powerful Amalgamated Association of Iron and Steel Workers, perhaps the strongest union in the country, against the Carnegie Steel Company, one of the world's greatest steel manufactories. With Carnegie out of the country, the management of the company's forces fell to Henry Clay Frick. At stake was a proposed reduction in the rate and minimum pay for piecework. When negotiations became stalemated, Frick shut down part of the plant and barred some 800 men from their jobs. The union's reply was a full-scale strike. Frick had already requested 300 armed guards from the Pinkerton Detective Agency, and when the hated "Pinkertons" arrived by boat the strikers attacked with cannon shot, dynamite, and rifle fire. The "battle" ended with the capitulation of the Pinkertons. At Frick's request the governor now sent troops to Homestead and the city became an armed camp. For five months the strikers held out, until exhaustion, poverty, and public opinion forced their surrender. An anarchist unconnected with the strike tried to assassinate Frick, which further harmed the strikers' cause.

The violence and hatreds unleashed at Homestead opened the eyes of Americans reared in the pre-industrial era. Then, only two years later, came another serious outburst of violence, this time in Chicago, which forced Americans to awake even more fully to the changes that had come over the country. The Pullman Company of Chicago, hard hit by the depression, laid off a number of its men and sharply cut the wages of the remaining workers. Five times in all, wages were reduced in the year before the strike. Most of the men lived in a "model" village built by Pullman, where rents and prices were not cut with the wage slashes. In protest the men left their jobs. Only the support of the American Railway Union, led by Eugene Debs, enabled the strikers to hold

out. Debs, soon to be a leader of the Socialist movement, called a boycott against the handling of Pullman cars by his union members, which resulted in the dismissal of a number of railroad workers. The strike spread. Violence erupted against railroad officials and equipment and traffic around the rail hub of Chicago was paralyzed. At this critical point President Cleveland did an unprecedented thing. He ordered federal troops to Chicago to permit the movement of the United States mails. Debs was jailed and the strike collapsed. Governor Altgeld of Illinois, sympathetic with the strikers, was incensed at Cleveland's action and denounced it as unconstitutional. But the strike was broken—and by the use of federal troops.

### The Response to a New Order

The uprisings at Chicago and Homestead were part of the laboring man's response to new social order being created by the machine and the city. "Organize or perish" was fast becoming the slogan of workers as well as farmers and businessmen caught up in the maelstrom of change. The old faith in individual action grew weaker as the individual was pushed farther and farther from the mainsprings of power. What could a worker do to ensure justice for himself against the Carnegie Steel Company? Could a lone farmer force the Union Pacific Railroad to grant fairer rates on its cars or in its freight elevators? What of the small businessman—could he compete in markets increasingly dominated by such giants as Carnegie, Rockefeller, Harriman, or Morgan? What, in short, was the proper role of the individual in a modern industrial society?

No one knew the answer but few denied the validity of the question. The central issue of the new era became the proper response to these great, swift changes in American life. Everyone was caught up in the uncertainty and insecurity. No wonder the burgeoning working class sought in organization some release for its sense of impotence in dealing with the masters of capital, or that farm agitators clamored for united action against railroads, money lenders, and manufacturers. Other groups, too, felt powerless and lost amid the rush of change. City dwellers, transplanted in large numbers from their rural origins, began to experience the anonymity and impersonality of urban life. Immigrants, most of them congregated in cities, felt uncomfortable amid the growing xenophobia, while they themselves added to the overpowering impression of a changing America.

Businessmen, too, were bewildered by the tempo and extent of change. The insecurity of business conditions in the 1880's and 1890's has often been forgotten by those anxious to focus attention on the few conspicuous business successes. Failures, though, were far more numerous than the notable successes. Indeed, as Edward Kirkland has reminded us, fourteen of the twenty-five years between 1873 and 1897 were, to those who lived through them, times of business "recession" or "depression." The general price index fell from a high of 129 in 1864 to a low of 71 in 1894. The businessman, like Americans in other fields of endeavor, fought against these economic upheavals and tried to control them. For no more than the worker or the farmer did he relish the constant worry, the dread uncertainty, which each new day brought.*

Like them, too, he looked to organization for protection of his interests. By controlling competition he might hope to lessen the more drastic exigencies of a market economy. In railroading in the eighties, for instance, the competition grew so fierce that five lines were compet-

---

* E. Kirkland, *Dream and Thought in the Business Community, 1860-1900* (Ithaca: Cornell University Press, 1956), pp. 7-10.

ing for traffic between New York and Chicago and the passenger fare was forced down to the ruinous rate of one dollar. Plainly, to limit such cut-throat and wasteful competition seemed the sensible course. It was the operators themselves, rather than the government, who moved first to limit competition by pooling agreements on markets, freight, and rates. In the oil industry the frugal John D. Rockefeller carried the process further by organizing the first trust, an arrangement to bring separate companies under unified management and control by exchanging their stock for trust certificates issued by the Rockefeller group. Outlawed in 1890 by the Sherman Act, which forbade "combinations in restraint of trade," the trust gave way to the holding company, still another way of checking competition, this time by allowing a company formed for the purpose in New Jersey (and later other states) to "hold" and vote the stock of formerly competing firms.

## Laissez-Faire or Positive State?

Ought government itself perhaps be used to discipline the rampant economic tendencies of the time? There were some who thought so, though in the nineties their number was never large. Strong government meant weak liberties to most Americans, and despite the tremendous changes in American life they still looked to the lessons that Jefferson taught in the agrarian republic of a century earlier. "The object of government is not to make laws," wrote one lawyer in 1899; "the object of government is to avoid making laws."

*The Liberal Tradition.* This suspicion of government ran deep in the liberal tradition. In the political catechism of the nineteenth-century American, individual rights, including the right to use one's property as one saw fit, were sacred. No community or government could know better than the individual himself what was best for him. Governments should properly restrict themselves to the preservation of law and order. Economic liberties like political liberties were anchored to faith in a natural law that governed economic as well as other kinds of activity. The law of supply and demand, for example, operated always to produce the fairest price because it was in accord with the truths of nature. To go against a law of nature by controlling prices or wages or competition was to invite disaster. "Oh, those grand immutable, all-wise laws of natural forces," cried Andrew Carnegie, "how perfectly they work if human legislators would only let them alone!"

*The Gospel of Wealth.* Was Carnegie insincere? Some critics thought so, but there is evidence that both Carnegie and his generation believed the doctrines they preached. Thomas Cochran has shown in his study of nineteenth-century railroad leaders that the public and private attitudes of these men were not in sharp conflict. Certainly Carnegie followed his own "Gospel of Wealth" in working hard, living simply, and administering his great fortune as a public trust. He apparently believed that the sons of the rich were more to be pitied than envied. He once likened them to the "fat, useless pug-dogs which young women drag wheezing about at the end of strings." His rules for success were stringent: thrift, hard work, no vacations, no gambling or market speculation, no drinking (except possibly at meals), and disdain for luxury. It was only men leading such puritanical lives, said Carnegie, who would achieve great wealth. This was the theme of the Horatio Alger novels which the rising generation was reading. It was also the theme of many a Protestant preacher, such as Bishop William Lawrence, who declared that "it is only to the man of morality that wealth comes."

The rich man was God's trustee. So the money he earned through right living did not really belong to him. He had a duty to protect it, enlarge it, and use it for philanthropic works. Philanthropy, though, was different from charity. While the latter provided only relief, philanthropy was aimed at the underlying causes of great social evils. The man of wealth, Carnegie claimed, was "the mere agent and trustee for his poorer brethren, bringing to their service his superior wisdom, experience, and ability to administer." To some, of course, this seemed pure hypocrisy. Mr. Dooley doubtless echoed their sentiments when he said of Rockefeller, whose justification of wealth was similar to Carnegie's, that "he's a custojien iv money appinted be himself. He looks afther his own money an' th' money iv other people. He takes it and puts it where it won't hurt thim and they won't spoil it. He's a kind iv a society f'r th' previntion iv croolty to money."

*Social Darwinism.* Carnegie, more than most business leaders of the day, took a keen interest in the literary and intellectual currents of his age. Upon reading Darwin and Spencer, he recalled later, "I remember that light came in as a flood and all was clear." Evolution seemed to him to prove the progress of mankind; growth, after all, was written into the very blueprints of the cosmos. "All is well since all grows better" became the Scotsman's cheery motto.

Why did Carnegie and other business spokesmen find Darwinism as preached by Spencer so exciting? Primarily because Spencer insisted that evolutionary forces were at work in society as well as biology. All life was a struggle in which the fittest endured. This was as true of social life as of animal existence. Did not laborers compete for bread, businessmen for profits, farmers for markets, in a ruthless battle to survive? Who did not know of the hundreds of poor and hungry men who trooped disconsolately each morning to the factory gates so that a handful of the strongest might be selected for work? The survivors of the fierce economic conflicts of the eighties and nineties, especially the great industrial tycoons, could well believe that their own fitness had been proven, and that it was futile for government to interfere. Progress, too, was as inevitable in social as in animal evolution but reformers could do nothing to expedite it. It was a matter of law, determined by forces beyond human control. Amidst the great social upheavals of the nineties it was not hard to believe that the individual was powerless to arrest or alter this natural course of events. In Spencer's hands, the new science of Darwin seemed to give further sanction to the old doctrine of laissez faire.

Of the American "Social Darwinists" who followed Spencer, William Graham Sumner of Yale was easily the most influential. In a little book entitled *What Social Classes Owe to Each Other* (1883), Sumner argued that government had only two major tasks: to protect the property of men and the honor of women. The state, which some reformers called on for aid, he defined as merely an abstraction for All-of-us. The real question then was what ought All-of-us to do for Some-of-us? But since Some-of-us are included in All-of-us, the final question was what ought Some-of-us to do for Others-of-us? Sumner's answer was clear: nothing. The ills of the human condition were natural ones, part of the struggle for existence, for which one's fellow-men could not be blamed. The "forgotten man" in American life, to use Sumner's phrase, was the industrious, prudent, dutiful man who was forced to take on additional responsibility in looking out for his weak, negligent, inefficient, and intemperate neighbors. It was not the duty of the state—of All-of-us—to make these unfortunates happy but only to see that the competition of life was fair and open. A free man owed to his fellow citizens only respect, courtesy, and good will.

*The Call to Reform.*   Not all business and professional men were converts to Social Darwinism, though. Even those who accepted Sumner's conclusions could find such pre-Darwinian authorities as the Bible and Benjamin Franklin to support their preference for self-help and individual responsibility. And many who praised Sumner adopted only those of his precepts that fitted their conservative beliefs and ignored, for example, his low-tariff views.

There were still others, moreover, who claimed to see in Darwinism the precise opposite of what Sumner saw. The sociologist Lester Ward, for one, read his Darwin in a vastly different light. In *The Psychic Factors of Civilization* (1893), Ward flatly denied that the fittest necessarily survive in the competition of social life. Competition, in fact, involves enormous waste and "prevents maximum development, since the best that can be attained under its influence is far inferior to that which is easily attained by the artificial . . . removal of that influence." He asked his readers to consider fruit trees and domestic animals, species whose protection from competition had enabled them to survive and flourish. Why should not man likewise use his intelligence to plan his own social life? Government he defended as a product of human intelligence and sharply criticized those who would use Darwinism to prop up the ancient doctrine of laissez faire.

Ward and others worked out much of the theory of the positive state in the nineties, well before twentieth century progressives turned it to use. The democratic state was not an evil force, they insisted, but an instrument that reformers must turn to good use. "We regard the state as an agency whose positive assistance is one of the indispensable conditions of human progress," read the platform of the newly formed American Economics Association in 1885. This platform was the work of a group of young economists led by Richard T. Ely, who unhesitatingly described economics as a "moral science." Among sociologists, E. A. Ross and Albion Small followed Ward in rejecting Social Darwinism and demanding that the state play a larger role in American life.

Outside the Ivory Tower, other reformers pressed for an end to do-nothing government. By the close of the century, Henry George's single-tax movement, aimed at abolishing poverty through ending the "tyranny" of private ownership of land, had gained thousands of followers. Another well-known reformer was Edward Bellamy, whose Utopian novel, *Looking Backward* (1888), made him one of the most celebrated Americans in the nineties. Bellamy thundered against the prevailing economic system as "radically wrong in morals and preposterous economically." The much-vaunted competition in business life was, he said, no more than a "brutal and cowardly slaughter of the unarmed and overmatched by bullies in armor." Like Ward and George, he attacked the laissez-faire theory of the state, advocating strong governmental action to nationalize basic industries and restore economic equality.

*How the Other Half Lives.* The cry for reform, lost in the general acclaim for laissez-faire ideas in the nineties, was embittered by the realization of terrible conditions in the depressed areas of the nation. In the severe winter of 1893-1894 more than two million men were idle and the problem of how to care for them and their families proved staggering. Out of Massillon, Ohio, in 1894 came the tragi-comic march on Washington of General Jacob S. Coxey's Army, demanding that the unemployed be put to work on the public roads. But Coxey's ragged marchers were stopped at the Capital steps and their leader was ignominiously convicted of walking on the grass.

A number of other reformers tried to rouse the conscience of the nation to the pressing problems of unemployment, want, and tenement life. Benjamin Flower in the pages of *The Arena*, Florence Kelly in her investigations of living and working conditions in Illinois, and Jacob Riis in his photographs and pen portraits of slum life in New York alerted Americans to the seriousness of affairs. Riis, a police reporter, entitled his book *How the Other Half Lives* and by doing so coined a phrase that was to outlast his own reform career. The power of Riis's impassioned appeal is suggested by the following description of a tenement hallway:

Cherry Street. Be a little careful please! The hall is dark and you might stumble over the children pitching pennies back there. Not that it would hurt them; kicks and cuffs are their daily diet. They have little else. Here where the hall turns and dives into utter darkness is a step, and another, another. A flight of stairs. You can feel your way, if you cannot see it. Close? Yes! What would you have? All the fresh air that ever enters these stairs comes from the hall-door that is forever slamming, and from the windows of dark bedrooms that in turn receive from the stairs their sole supply of the elements God meant to be free, but man deals out with such a niggardly hand.

*The Social Gospel.* The ranks of the reformers were enlarged in the final decades of the century by a small band of clergymen. In the name of Christian ideals they joined in the denunciation of extreme laissez faire and urged the government to act. Rather than the ancient gospel of the salvation of the individual they proposed that a new gospel of the salvation of society be given a higher priority in the crisis of the times. Christians could best save themselves by working for the regeneration of their fellow men.

And what kind of society did the preachers of the Social Gospel see about them? In their view it was brutally selfish, fiercely competitive, lacking in brotherly

ment of business prosperity. Blame for the farmer's ills was heaped on the heads of the reigning railroad and industrial magnates. Farmers looked back nostalgically to the rural age of their birth and many came to hate the forces creating modern America. An older America spoke in their distrust of factories, cities, immigrants, and intellectuals. They lamented the passing of the frontier and castigated the "money power" for the decline of American opportunity. They blamed foreigners and sometimes Jews for their money troubles (Mary Lease called President Cleveland "the agent of Jewish bankers and British gold"). They clung to their fundamentalist religious beliefs and condemned the city ministers who made weak compromises with atheistic evolution. Theirs was a Holy Crusade on behalf of an older America and its values against the forces of modernism. The call to battle was sounded by Ignatius Donnelly in his pessimistic book, *Caesar's Column*:

. . . life is a dark and wretched failure for the great mass of mankind. The many are plundered to enrich the few. Vast combinations depress the price of labor and increase the cost of the necessaries of existence. The rich, as a rule, despise the poor; and the poor are coming to hate the rich. The face of labor grows sullen; the old tender Christian love is gone; standing armies are found on one side, and great communistic organizations on the other; society divides itself into two hostile camps; no white flags pass from the one to the other. They wait only for the drumbeat and the trumpet to summon them to armed conflict.

Donnelly drew up the platform for the new Populist Party, which met in Omaha on July 4, 1892. Defiantly he turned his back on laissez faire and presented the most far-reaching program of governmental intervention advocated by any major political group in the nineteenth century.

The platform approved by the convention called for such reforms as (1) free silver at the ratio sixteen to one, (2) a graduated income tax, (3) a "subtreasury plan" that would enable farmers to borrow against their crops, (4) government ownership of railroads and telegraph lines, (5) restriction of immigration, (6) direct election of senators, and (7) the initiative and referendum.

The first plank was to be a club against monetary deflation. As debtors, farmers were acutely interested in increasing the supply of currency. In the late seventies many had supported the Greenback movement to issue unbacked paper currency; but since the early eighties inflationists had turned more and more to silver as a medium of devaluation. The explanation was quite simple. New silver discoveries had made that metal plentiful in relation to gold. Both were acceptable as currency but the official rate of exchange of the two metals at the government mint—sixteen to one—now overvalued silver. This made silver the ideal tool for inflating the currency, provided that the government would coin all of that metal brought to its mints at this favorable ratio. An expanded money supply, it was believed, would bring the hoped-for rise in the prices of farm commodities.

The silver inflationists almost reached their goal in 1890, when Congress, under pressure from drought and depression-ridden farmers, passed the Sherman Silver Purchase Act providing for the purchase by the federal government of virtually the entire silver output of the country. But the Act proved powerless to halt a new downward spiral of prices in the early nineties. By the time of Grover Cleveland's second inauguration in 1893 the stage was set for the terrible depression whose effects have already been described. No inflationist, Cleveland pressured Congress into a repeal of the

Sherman Act in the belief that it had contributed to the financial panic that set off the depression.

Revolt now flared among southern and western Democrats whose ardor for free silver rose with their distress. The President further antagonized his rural following by an arrangement with Wall Street bankers to keep the nation on the gold standard. The events of 1894 and 1895—Coxey's Army, the Pullman strike, a new failure at tariff reform, farm drought, and the relentless fall of farm prices—pointed ominously to a showdown in the election year of 1896.

*Year of Decision: 1896.* In that critical year furious Democrats from the South and West repudiated Cleveland, adopted free silver, and nominated William Jennings Bryan of Nebraska as their standard-bearer. The peroration of Bryan's famous speech—"You shall not crucify mankind upon a cross of gold"—closed an appeal in which he rang every change in the Populist register. "Burn down your cities and leave our farms," he cried in defiance of the industrial East, "and your cities will spring up again as if by magic; but destroy our farms and the grass will grow in the streets of every city in the country." And pointing his finger dramatically to the West, he praised the hardy pioneers who had forsaken city comforts to "rear their children near to Nature's heart, where they can mingle their voices with the voices of the birds."

To the Populists the temptation of Bryan and free silver, offered by the Democrats, proved irresistible. They now endorsed Bryan for President but substituted the fiery Tom Watson, a Georgia Populist, as their vice-presidential nominee in place of the Eastern banker, Arthur Sewall, the Democratic candidate. The Republicans chose William McKinley, a self-educated, dignified, and capable Ohioan long identified with the high-tariff policies of his party. With his

shrewd campaign manager and close personal friend, Mark Hanna, he organized the Republican forces for victory. To the endless procession of visitors who trooped to the famous "front porch" in Canton, Ohio, McKinley explained that free silver did not mean free dollars for the masses; only that the mints of the federal government would be thrown open freely to the owners of silver bullion. These gentlemen would get a dollar for fifty-three cents worth of silver, said McKinley, while their fellow-citizens would have to accept it as a full dollar in payment for goods and services. Thus did he appeal to the hard-money instincts of the working class. Only the gold standard, he told the many delegations of wage-earners from eastern cities, offered justice to all classes.

Bryan's campaign was stupendous—18,000 miles, 600 speeches, 5,000,000 auditors. But his single-minded concentration on the silver issue offered little hope to disaffected laborers and others whose support was vital if Bryan was to win. A correspondent of the *Cleveland Plain Dealer*—a free-silver paper—commented

William Jennings Bryan, delivering his "Cross of Gold" speech, which won him the presidential nomination at the Democratic Convention in Chicago in 1896. (Underwood & Underwood.)

"What are you crying about now, Willie?"
"Little Johnny Hay and I are playing imperialism, and Billy Bryan, next door, is squirting water on us." McKinley was the butt of cartoonists who looked upon him as the pawn of big business and of political boss Mark Hanna. (New York Public Library.)

on the genuine enthusiasm of the wage earners for McKinley and his pledges of business and labor prosperity. Many an old Populist, too, was certain that Bryan was leading the rural rebels down a blind alley with his crusade for silver.

McKinley's triumph at the polls was complete. He had spoken for the new America—the America of booming factories, big cities, and expanding capitalism. He had identified his political future not with the wealthy and privileged alone —these had few votes—but with the rank and file of the middle class, the businessman, merchant, and professional man, as well as the workingman who hoped to get ahead. Bryan had given his heart and his magnificent voice to the cause of rural America—and he had lost. He had divided the American people along geographical and class lines in the most sharply sectional election since 1860, and the entire South and the plains and

mountain West had followed him down to defeat. Bryan's fight was not entirely in vain, however. He had raised issues that would affect American politics for decades to come. He called the campaign of 1896 "The First Battle" and would live himself to see not only his own party but the Republicans adopt many of the planks in the old Populist platform. "His cause is not lost," said the Populist *Augusta Chronicle* following the election; "his victory is but deferred."

### The Changing Intellectual Climate

The sense of alienation from the newer America that drove Bryan's followers into revolt was shared by other Americans—city workers of rural origin, older businessmen, recent immigrants, and a number of writers and intellectuals. By the nineties the older literary generation was passing—Bancroft died in 1891, Whitman in 1892, Parkman in 1893, Oliver Wendell Holmes in 1894 —and a new generation of writers born in the years of rapid change struggled for recognition. "Our modern literature," Alfred Kazin has written in a brilliant synthesis,

was rooted in those dark and still little-understood years of the 1880's and 1890's when all America stood suddenly, as it were, between one society and another, one moral order and another, and the sense of impending change became almost oppressive in its vividness. It was rooted in the drift to the new world of factories and cities, with their dissolution of old standards and faiths; in the emergence of the metropolitan culture that was to dominate the literature of the new period; in the Populists who raised their voices against the domineering new plutocracy in the East and gave so much of their bitterness to the literature of protest rising out of the West . . .*

* A. Kazin, *On Native Grounds* (New York: Reynal and Hitchcock, 1942), pp. viii-ix.

*The Naturalistic Revolt.* One writer who gave much of his bitterness to the literature of rural protest was Hamlin Garland. No one who has read his *Main Traveled Roads* (1891) will regard the farmer's life on the old Middle Border as a pastoral idyll. Endless monotony, drudgery, ugliness, and hopelessness are the farmer's lot in Garland's stories—a soldier comes home from war to find no trumpets or flags but only a chance to eke out a miserable living on his farm; a newcomer burns up his life to improve some rented land, only to be exploited by its owner; a patronizing brother from the great city comes home to a surly welcome from his rural family.

Garland and his generation rejected the older "genteel tradition" in literature that had ignored the evils and vulgarities of American life. "You could not write about life as it was," complained the young Theodore Dreiser, "you had to write about it as somebody else thought it was, the ministers and farmers and dullards of the home. Yet . . . this sweetness-and-light code, this idea of a perfect world which contained neither sin nor shame for any save vile outcasts, criminals and vagrants, was the trashiest lie that was ever foisted upon an all too human world."

Dreiser wrote of the city in the same vein that Garland had written of the country. The city was a place of crowded, scummy tenements, of stifling summer streets, of drunkenness, fighting, and poverty, of overpowering forces too great for the individual to control. In his first novel, *Sister Carrie* (1900), he wrote of a simple country girl, fond of pretty things, who becomes the mistress of several men, one of whom she marries only to drive him to bankruptcy and ruin. She finally reaches success on the stage while her former husband, forced into destitution, takes his own life. Significantly, the novel was not released in an era when the reigning fa-

vorites were *Beside the Bonnie Brier Bush, Penelope's Progress,* and *When Knighthood Was in Flower.*

Garland and Dreiser shared a sense that the times were out of joint, that the old order of society was doomed, and that the promise of American life had lost its glitter. But Dreiser more fully represented what came to be called the "naturalistic" school of fiction. This school departed from the realism of Garland in its whole-hearted espousal of the pessimistic strain in the Darwin-Spencer tradition. To the pessimistic naturalist, the significant thing in the Darwinian view of evolution was the neutral, impersonal role of the environment. It was environment—the forces of nature—that selected those variations with survival value and ruthlessly crushed all others. Nature was harsh, cruel, indifferent to life. It alone determined the success or failure of all efforts, all innovations, all human strivings. Man was no more than a superior animal spurred on by the same elemental physiological drives as his animal kin. Human responsibility and human ideals lost much of their old meaning. In such books as Ambrose Bierce's *Can Such Things Be* (1893) and Stephen Crane's *Maggie, a Girl of the Streets* (1892), the mood is dark and brooding, a complete reversal of American optimism.

Garland's meliorism struck deeper roots in the American tradition. Though imbued with naturalistic themes, his writing, and frequently that of Frank Norris and Jack London, looked to an improvement in the conditions of American life. They found it hard to hold to the depressing conviction that men were only "human insects." They were "soft" naturalists, unwilling to close the door finally on human choice. Whether consciously or not, they drew on a different strain in Darwinism—the importance of spontaneous "chance" variations that defied a completely controlled or "determined" view of the development of life. While Norris and London wrote darkly of "the law of claw and fang" and of men as "pawns of circumstance," their very concern often betrayed a predilection for an open universe and a belief that men had in fact some choices to make. In *The Octopus* (1901), Norris struck the reformer's note frequently in his hatred of the Southern Pacific Railroad, while Jack London, as we shall notice in the next chapter, often preached the call to reform the world.

*The Birth of Pragmatism.* The same forces that beat in upon the world of Norris and London stirred the whole intellectual universe. In every field of thought and endeavor men were learning to cope with the moral and intellectual implications of Darwinism and the urban-industrial revolution. As early as the 1870's, in Cambridge, Massachusetts, an informal gathering of Harvard lecturers found reason to uphold American individualism and optimism against the determinism preached by many of Darwin's interpreters. William James, a leading spirit, argued that random variations in the evolutionary process gave as much scientific backing to the idea of free will as environmental forces acting on these variations gave to determinism. To some degree at least, there was uncertainty and hence freedom in the universe.

James's whole career was devoted to the rescue of the idea of human responsibility from the determinists, Social Darwinists, and naturalists who sought to prove that human will and purpose played no part in the unfolding social drama. Neither evolution, nor for that matter the law of diminishing energy in physics, according to James, determine man's fate or predestine him to a helpless role in a closed universe. To James, the whole drama of life lay in its alternate possibilities, in the "zone of insecurity in

human affairs." He took a functional view of mind in his *Principles of Psychology* (1890), expressing the belief "that the knower is not simply a mirror floating with no foot-hold anywhere, and passively reflecting an order that he comes upon and finds simply existing. The knower is an actor, and co-efficient of truth on one side, whilst on the other he registers the truth which he helps to create."

His lecture on pragmatism in 1898 at the University of California formally launched the pragmatist movement. In this and other lectures and essays he worked out the ideas now associated with his name: Philosophical concepts must be judged by their practical consequences; a view of the world that makes no allowance for faith will never be accepted; the right to believe on incomplete evidence— to exercise the *will* to believe—is a basic human need; truth is a property of ideas or beliefs, the quality that makes them "agree with" the mind that holds them. "I am well aware how odd it must seem," said James in 1907, "to hear me say that an idea is 'true' so long as to believe it is profitable to our lives. . . . Let me now say only this, that truth is *one species of good*, and not, as is usually supposed, a category distinct from good, and co-ordinate with it. *The true is the name of whatever process proves itself to be good in the way of belief, and good, too, for definite, assignable reasons.*"

James and the other founders of pragmatism left as their legacy to the new century a humanistic fact-mindedness, a preference for the historical approach to the study of institutions, a relativistic approach to truth and morals, and a view of scientific law that stressed probabilities rather than mechanical certainty. The legacy was testimony enough to the survival in an age of change of historic American optimism, practicality, and faith in the individual. Out of this legacy the next generation—John Dewey, Thorstein Veblen, Charles Beard, and others—would con- struct a philosophy for the Progressive Movement of the twentieth century.

## THE NINETEENTH CENTURY: FINAL CURTAIN

We have by no means exhausted the theme of the nineties as a time of transition. New movements were also afoot in *fin de siècle* painting as Winslow Homer, Albert Pinkham Ryder, and Thomas Eakins pushed beyond the objective formalism of academic nineteenth-century art to look unblinkingly at nature; in architecture, Henry Hobson Richardson and Louis Sullivan were pointing the way to twentieth-century functionalism in building and house design; in sculpture, Daniel Chester French and Augustus St. Gaudens began to break away from the stereotypes of neoclassicism; in medicine, modern concepts of disease causation and treatment were beginning to gain popular acceptance; and in journalism, the social sciences, and still other arts and sciences the mood of the nineties was distinctly transitional.

Through all the din and tumult of these years of upheaval, however, Americans remained remarkably steadfast to the ideals nourished in their national infancy. Faith in the democratic system and in America's mission to carry it abroad was not perceptibly weaker in 1900 than in 1850; liberty was still hailed as the central feature of the American scheme of government and social organization; and individualism, for all the attacks on it, continued to find greater defense in America than in most other countries. There was little slackening, either, of that national optimism that had so impressed De Tocqueville earlier in the century, and American confidence in the future

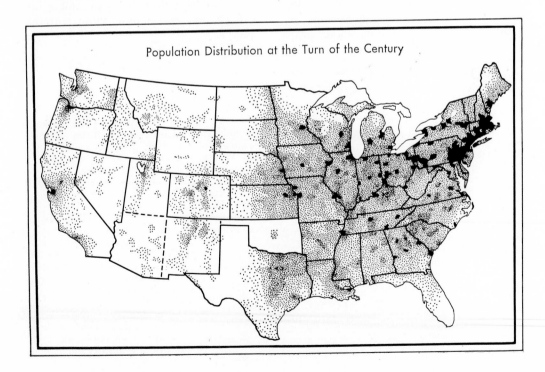

Population Distribution at the Turn of the Century

seemed undaunted by the troubles of the nineties.

The final years of the old century were filled with a buoyant optimism as prosperity returned, farm prices rose, and the "wild talk of the nineties," as one paper termed it, was pushed into memory. The brief war with Spain contributed to the exuberant mood—what better tonic for national morale than a war of easy victories, few casualties, and much martial glory? Even the xenophobia of the nineties seemed to collapse with the return of prosperity.

The greatest of centuries was drawing to a close but the prospects for the new century seemed equally good. The population of the country stood at a towering seventy-six million in 1900, fifteen times what it had been in 1800. The automobile had been invented; air travel was being freely predicted; mass production was around the corner; and the farmer, thanks to foreign crop failures, new gold discoveries, and the growing urban market, was entering the Golden Age of American Agriculture. Well might the Reverend Newell Hillis of New York exclaim in 1900: "Laws are becoming more just,

rulers humane; music is becoming sweeter and books wiser; homes are happier, and the individual heart becoming at once more just and more gentle."

The nation would need such optimism before the new century was far advanced. Across the threshold of the twentieth century lay the crises and cataclysms of our own recollection—two murderous wars, terrifying depression, menacing totalitarianism, weapons capable of snuffing out all human life, the endless sense of anxiety and tension. In their blissful ignorance Americans of 1900, asked by a newspaper to predict the greatest menace of the new century, named such evils as alcohol, the sensational press, or Oriental competition with American labor. The great social upheavals of their own time they had not yet recognized as "problems." Out of the tensions produced by industrialism and labor unrest, Darwinism and modern skepticism, immigration and racial tensions, Marxism and radical movements, grew the historical patterns of the present fearful era in world history. It was not long after 1900 that Americans realized how threatening those patterns could be.

## FOR FURTHER STUDY

### General Accounts

H. Faulkner, *Politics, Reform and Expansion, 1890-1900* (New York: Harpers, 1959). The best general survey of the decade of the nineties.

S. Fine, *Laissez-Faire and the General-Welfare State* (Ann Arbor: U. of Michigan Press, 1956). An important analysis of the conflict between these two critical ideas in American thought from 1865 to 1901.

R. Gabriel, *The Course of American Democratic Thought* (New York: Ronald, second edition, 1956). By all odds the most stimulating analysis of American democratic ideas in the nineteenth century.

* E. Goldman, *Rendezvous with Destiny* (New York: Knopf, 1952). A sprightly interpretation of the currents of reform from the Civil War to the New Deal.

* S. Hays, *The Response to Industrialism, 1885-1914* (Chicago: U. of Chicago Press, 1957). A recent treatment of these three decades in brief compass.

### Special Studies

A. Abell, *The Urban Impact on American Protestantism 1865-1900* (Cambridge: Harvard U. Press, 1943). The standard

* Starred books are available in paperbound editions.

work on the subject.

* H. Adams, *The United States in 1800* (Ithaca: Cornell U. Press, 1955). A reissue of the famous six opening chapters of Adams' great *History*.

R. Bremner, *From the Depths* (New York: New York U. Press, 1956). How Americans discovered poverty in the United States in the nineteenth century.

* D. Brogan, *The American Character* (New York: Knopf, 1944). A well-known modern interpretation of the American character by a Britisher.

V. Brooks, *The Confident Years: 1885-1915* (New York: Dutton, 1952). A famous literary critic's impressionistic treatment of the nineties and beyond.

W. Bryan, *The First Battle* (Chicago: W. B. Conkey Company, 1896). Bryan's own account of the campaign of 1896.

A. Carnegie, *Autobiography* (Boston: Houghton Mifflin, 1920). The steelmaker's reminiscences of his career and associates.

* T. Cochran and W. Miller, *The Age of Enterprise* (New York: Macmillan, 1942). A pioneering attempt at a social history of industrial America.

T. Cochran, *Railroad Leaders, 1845-1890* (Cambridge: Harvard U. Press, 1953). A new approach to the business mind through an intensive examination of railroad presidents' correspondence.

* H. Commager, *The American Mind* (New Haven: Yale U. Press, 1950). The opening two chapters are a brilliant examination of the nineteenth-century American and the watershed of the nineties.

J. Fiske, *Excursions of an Evolutionist* (Boston: Houghton Mifflin, 1887). Essays and addresses of an early American Darwinist.

R. Ginger, *Altgeld's America* (New York: Funk and Wagnalls Company, 1958). The author contends that the rural ideals of Lincoln's day needed readjustment to the harsh realities of the nineties.

* O. Handlin, *The Uprooted* (Boston: Little, Brown, 1951). Already a classic among the histories of immigration.

* J. Hicks, *The Populist Revolt* (Minneapolis: U. of Minnesota Press, 1931). Long the best general history of the farmers' revolt.

J. Higham, *Strangers in the Land* (New Brunswick: Rutgers U. Press, 1955). A thorough, imaginative treatment of the nativist movement, 1860 to 1925.

* R. Hofstadter, *The Age of Reform* (New York: Knopf, 1955). A much-discussed reinterpretation of the reform movement of the nineties and after.

* ———, *Social Darwinism in American Thought* (Philadelphia: U. of Pennsylvania Press, 1944). A pioneer work on Social Darwinism.

* W. James, *Essays in Pragmatism* (New York: Hafner Publishing Company, 1948). A good collection of some of William James's basic papers and essays, including "The Will to Believe" and "What Pragmatism Means."

* H. Jones, *Guide to American Literature and Its Backgrounds since 1890* (Cambridge: Harvard U. Press, 1953). A brief but valuable classification of titles, with commentary.

* M. Josephson, *The Robber Barons* (New York: Harcourt, Brace, 1934). The title suggests the theme of this history of the great American capitalists from 1861 to 1901.

* A. Kazin, *On Native Grounds* (New York: Reynal and Hitchcock, 1942). Perhaps the most incisive treatment of American literature since the 1890's.

* G. Kennedy (ed.), *Democracy and the Gospel of Wealth* (Boston: Heath, 1949). Was Godliness in league with riches? The pros and cons of the Gospel of Wealth doctrine.

E. Kirkland, *Dream and Thought in the Business Community, 1860-1900* (Ithaca: Cornell U. Press, 1956). A thoughtful rejoinder to the "Robber Barons" school of interpretation of this period.

M. Leech, *In the Days of McKinley* (New York: Harper, 1959). A sympathetic and well written reassessment of the McKinley career.

H. May, *Protestant Churches and Industrial America* (New York: Harper, 1949). A scholarly analysis of the sources of the Social Gospel movement.

A. Nevins, *Study in Power: John D. Rockefeller*, two volumes (New York: Scribner's, 1953). This is a superior biography of the great oil magnate.

R. Nye, *Midwestern Progressive Politics* (East Lansing: Michigan State College Press, 1951). Good treatment of the midwestern problem, the Populist movement, and the farmers' political struggle to 1950.

F. Pattee, *The New American Literature, 1890-1930* (New York: The Century Company, 1930). Though dated somewhat, this book still contains a number of useful insights.

S. Persons (ed.), *Evolutionary Thought in America* (New Haven: Yale U. Press, 1950). The most satisfactory book on this difficult and complicated subject.

* D. Potter, *People of Plenty* (Chicago: U. of Chicago Press, 1954). The first two chapters contain the best analysis yet made of the problems involved in studying national character.

* J. Riis, *How the Other Half Lives* (New York: Scribner's, 1890). A classic in the social reform movement.

* G. Santayana, *Character and Opinion in the United States* (New York: Scribner's, 1920). Chapter 6 is a well-known description of the American character and ideals by this famous philosopher and friend of William James.

A. Schlesinger, *The Rise of the City, 1878-1898* (New York: Macmillan, 1933). Indispensable to the student of American urbanism.

F. Shannon, *The Farmer's Last Frontier* (New York: Farrar and Rinehart, 1945). A well-regarded history of American agriculture from 1860 to 1897.

* W. Sumner, *What Social Classes Owe to Each Other* (New York: Harper, 1883). An inexpensive reprint by the Caxton Printers makes this important book available once more.

F. Weisenburger, *Ordeal of Faith* (New York: Philosophical Library, 1959). The subtitle indicates the theme: "The Crisis of Church-Going America, 1865-1900."

* G. Whicher (ed.), *William Jennings Bryan and the Campaign of 1896* (Boston: Heath, 1953). A good selection of materials, pro and con, on the Bryan campaign.

P. Wiener, *Evolution and the Founders of Pragmatism* (Cambridge: Harvard U. Press, 1949). This volume gives a clear exposition of the ideas of Peirce, Wright, James, and others, as well as their relationship to evolution.

* C. Wittke, *We Who Built America* (Englewood Cliffs: Prentice-Hall, 1939). A good, comprehensive history of the immigration movement.

C. Woodward, *Origins of the New South 1877-1913* (Baton Rouge: Louisiana State U. Press, 1951). Without doubt the best survey of this troubled period in the history of the South.

* ———, *The Strange Career of Jim Crow* (New York: Oxford U. Press, 1955). An important reinterpretation of the history of racial segregation in the Southern states.

I. Wyllie, *The Self-Made Man in America* (New Brunswick: Rutgers U. Press, 1954). An interesting little book that corrects the impression that all American businessmen looked to Social Darwinism for their justification.

## Fiction

* S. Crane, *Maggie: a Girl of the Streets* (New York: Modern Library, 1933). First published in 1892, this novel was a landmark in the naturalistic revolt.

I. Donnelly, *Caesar's Column* (Cambridge: Harvard U., 1960). A reissue of this famous anti-Utopian novel by the Minnesota Populist leader.

* T. Dreiser, *Sister Carrie* (New York: Modern Library, 1932). When Mrs. Doubleday first read this in 1900, she refused to let her husband release it for publication.

* H. Frederic, *The Damnation of Theron Ware* (New York: Stone and Kimball, 1896). This story of a Methodist preacher who falls in love with his red-haired organist shocked the generation of the nineties.

* H. Garland, *Main-Traveled Roads* (New York: Harper, 1922). Dedicated to Garland's parents "whose half-century pilgrimage on the main-traveled roads of life has brought them only toil and deprivation."

O. Rölvaag, *Giants in the Earth* (New York: Harper, 1927). A moving story of Norwegian immigrants in the grip of the natural furies of an untamed Dakota.

* E. Stone (ed.), *What Was Naturalism?* (New York: Appleton-Century-Crofts, 1959). A useful little source-book of excerpts from Darwin, Spencer, Crane, London, Norris, Dreiser, and others.

## Films and Records

*Age of Reform* (National Educational Television, 29 minutes, sound, black and white). Discussion of the thesis of Hofstadter's book cited above.

*The Case for Darwin* (National Educational Television, 30 minutes, sound, black and white). Presentation of the arguments and evidence for Darwin's momentous theory.

*The Gay Nineties Live Again* (United World Films, 10 minutes, sound, black and white). A re-editing of original film negatives of the nineties.

*Industrialism on the March* (National Educational Television, 29 minutes, sound, black and white). How industry grew after 1865.

*The Living Past #1* (Film Classic Exchange, 15 minutes, sound, black and white). Shots of the McKinley-Bryan campaign, McKinley's inauguration, the Rough Riders, and other events of the nineties.

*Our Nation's Roots* (National Educational Television, 26 separate films, 29 minutes each, sound, black and white). A series of kinescoped programs on immigration of which numbers 19 (seeds of nativism), 21 (immigrants and the labor movement), and 22 (the "new" immigration) will be of special interest.

*The Realists* (Coronet, 11 minutes, sound, black and white). A film examination of the import of the writings of Dreiser, Garland, Crane, London, and others.

*Settling the Great Plains* (McGraw-Hill, 12 minutes, sound, black and white, or color). The adjustment of the homesteaders to the difficulties they found in the Great Plains environment.

1900-1914

# The Progressive Temper

CHAPTER TWO

President Roosevelt, Yellowstone Park, 1903.

THE MOOD OF THE TIMES

"I did not know at the time how completely I was a product of my environment. If I was a young cocksure reactionary in the nineties, it was because my kind and class were that, and I fear sadly that I must confess that unconsciously I took the protective intellectual, political and social color of my time in the first decade. So we all went together down to the road of reform to progress, Bryan, LaFollette, Roosevelt; scores of leaders in scores of states—little Bryans, little LaFollettes, little Roosevelts appeared in scores of statehouses and countless city halls. . . .

"They were leaders who were led. Some way, into the hearts of the dominant middle class of this country, had come a sense that their civilization needed recasting, that their government had fallen into the hands of self-seekers, that a new relation should be established between the haves and the have-nots, not primarily because the have-nots were loyal, humble, worthy and oppressed— Heaven knows we knew that the underdog had fleas, mange and a bad disposition—but rather because we felt that to bathe and feed the underdog would release the burden of injustice on our own conscience. We should do it even unto the least of these.

"We were not maudlin, as I recollect it. We were joyous, eager, happily determined to make life more fair and lovely for ourselves by doing such approximate justice as we could to those who obviously were living in the swamps, morasses, deserts, and wildernesses of this world. It was not religious—at least not pious— this progressive movement. It was profoundly spiritual. And the insurgents, who were later called progressives, had the crusaders' ardor, and felt for one another the crusaders' fellowship. They sang songs, carried banners, marched in parades, created heroes out of their own ideals. It was an evangelical uprising without an accredited Messiah."

—WILLIAM ALLEN WHITE, *Autobiography*

# WHAT WAS PROGRESSIVISM?

These words of William Allen White strike deep to the core of the progressive mentality. For progressivism was basically a change of mood, of temper, of national spirit in response to the strange new world of industrialism and the city. It was a recovery of conscience after the frustrations and vain protests of the nineties, a reinvigoration of the reform spirit as the new century dawned. The change in temper swept through a score of otherwise unrelated political and social movements; it made reform the order of the day on the local, state, and national levels; it challenged the cherished ideal of limited government; it infused intellectuals with new visions of the promise of American life; it cast up new leaders to fight for these visions; it caused newspapers like White's *Emporia Gazette* in Kansas to expose fraud and injustice; and it gave to the American people a deep and rewarding sense of participation in great and exciting events.

Not quite all the people, however. The appeal of progressivism, as Will White says, was greatest among the middle classes—teachers, editors, small businessmen, professional men, and white-collar workers. Workingmen showed little interest, except for particular reforms, in the goals of progressivism and were rarely themselves the first beneficiaries of its achievements. The newcomers from Eu-

36

rope, who made up a large proportion of the unskilled labor force, were likewise normally beyond the range of progressive interest, though they did experience in this era a welcome lessening of the nativistic pressures that had bedeviled them earlier. And during the hey-day of the progressive reformers one group of Americans actually suffered a deterioration in its political and social status—American Negroes. The Southern Negro, in particular, felt the bonds of social segregation draw tighter, saw his Populist champions of the nineties turn against him, and finally lost a grip on the voting and other civil rights given him by the Fourteenth and Fifteenth Amendments.

## New Wine and Old Bottles

What of the farmer? Agrarian spokesmen, long embittered by monopoly, corruption, and governmental indifference to their problems, did not hesitate to join the new battle against the forces of privilege. In Wisconsin, Minnesota, Kansas, and other farm states, new leaders raised another reform organization on the ashes of the old Populist protest. To a considerable extent, the progressive movement in the Middle West was a renaissance of the old Populist spirit, which had been temporarily submerged by prosperity and the Spanish-American War.

But progressivism was something more than warmed-over Populism. Otherwise, how can we explain why Populism failed in the troubled nineties and progressivism succeeded in the prosperous years after 1900? And why such men as Theodore Roosevelt, Woodrow Wilson, Robert La-Follette, and Will White, all of whom feared Bryan in the nineties, became leaders of the new protest movement in the Progressive Era? Nor can we ignore the national character of the progressive movement in contrast with the sectional impulse behind the farmers' revolt.

Undoubtedly, there were vital links between Populism and progressivism. The new reform movement after 1900 drew heavily on the Populist experience for its ideas, support, and, in some instances, leaders. Agrarian crusaders whose careers spanned both epochs saw little difference in fighting for reform under a progressive or under a Populist banner. Yet the progressives clearly built on a broader foundation than the Populists had: Their appeal was diffused more widely through the urban masses, they aimed their reforms as much at businessmen as at farmers, and their methods and vocabulary were far less radical than those of the Bryan crusaders.

What Richard Hofstadter has called the "status revolution" also played a role in driving many of the Bryan-hating middle class into revolt after 1900. Populism was a defensive reaction of desperate farmers to their changing status in an urban-industrial world; progressivism, according to Hofstadter, was a similar reaction on the part of individualistic lawyers, doctors, teachers, merchants, clerks, and other members of the middle class to the realization that they, too, were losing their former importance to new groups and organizations cast up by the urban-industrial revolution. The business corporation, the labor union, the farm cooperative were all major responses to the "organize or perish" dictate of modern capitalism. But what could the individual merchant or lawyer do to rescue his dwindling status from the chain stores and law factories rising in the larger cities? In their own way, by decrying big business, by urging government to discipline unfair competitors, by defending an older America against the forces that were remaking it, these middle-class reformers were traveling the same road the Populists had taken a decade before. But unlike the Populists, they insisted that their revolt be moderate, respectable, and conservative. "Populism," in Will White's memorable phrase, had "shaved its whiskers, washed its shirt, put on a derby, and moved up into the middle of the class—the upper middle class."

A host of new organizations provided the middle classes with instruments for social and political reform. The strength of progressivism, as Samuel Hays has stressed, lay in its organizations. Leagues to protect consumers, church groups working for reform, associations agitating for labor legislation, committees against child labor, fellowships of university scholars, new professional fraternities, and federations of women's clubs joined in the fight against the *status quo*.

Women, anxious to improve their own status, threw themselves into politics and reform movements. In 1900 women could vote in only five states, had equal guardianship of children in but seven states, and were sharply limited everywhere in career opportunities. Often barred from the man's world of business and the professions, educated women from the upper classes founded settlement houses in the slums, championed women's rights, worked for labor legislation, and otherwise battled for social justice. Such women as Jane Addams, Florence Kelley, Julia Lathrop, and Lillian Wald through their example and their influence on women's clubs across the country had an unmistakable impact on the reform movement. The new president of the powerful General Federation of Women's Clubs, Sarah Decker, sounded a clarion call for a change in the direction of women's interests in 1904 when she remarked, "Ladies, you have chosen me as your leader. Well, I have an important piece of news for you. Dante is dead. He has been dead for several centuries, and I think it is time we dropped the study of his inferno, and turned attention to our own."

### Profile of a Progressive

The ladies, at least some of them, did turn their attention to such progressive concerns as municipal corruption, food adulteration, child labor, working women, and the power of big business. Having grown up in a time of rapid change, they adjusted easily to a political philosophy that called for innovation.

The progressive woman, like the progressive man, was frequently young, city-bred, college-educated, middle-class in origin, North European in extraction, Protestant in religion (especially Congregationalist, Unitarian, and Presbyterian), and newly come to the reform movement.

Not only did the progressive leader usually fit these patterns, but, according to George Mowry's study of the California progressives, he tended to work at one of a relatively small number of occupations. (A high proportion of the progressive leaders in California were attorneys, journalists, independent businessmen, doctors, and bankers, only a tiny fraction of whom had any connection with a large industrial or financial corporation.) Though a man (or woman) of good education, he was all but excluded from politics unless he accepted the domination of the corporation (notably the Southern Pacific

American women had spoken out for their political rights even before the Civil War. Later, groups like the National Woman Suffrage Association took up the fight. Front row, second from left, Susan B. Anthony; fourth from left, Elizabeth Cady Stanton. (Culver Pictures, Inc.)

Railroad) or the labor union. And though often wealthy, his wealth counted for little against the great aggregations of capital wielded by the new giants of industry and finance. He was devoted to capitalism and free enterprise, but he was determined to crush out the inequalities and abuses that free capitalism had engendered.

## The Faith of a Progressive

His approach to reform was moral and political—and to the progressive both words meant essentially the same things. He was suspicious of the class-consciousness of the Populists and repulsed by the revolutionary doctrines of the socialists. Looking to older American traditions of equality of opportunity, opposition to monopoly, faith in self-government, and humanitarian concern for one's fellow man, he sought to make Jeffersonian and Jacksonian ideas relevant to the problems of an industrial society. He clung fervently to the old triad of American values—representative democracy, individualism, and freedom—in the face of powerful changes that seemed to some to have made them irrelevant. Accordingly, as a reformer, he stood for piecemeal change and partial solutions—he would tinker with the economic machine to get it to run better, but he was steadfastly opposed to a drastic overhaul. He was a practical man, interested in performance, conservative in temper, imbued with tradition, yet aware of the need for change; and his pragmatic approach to reform left a deep mark on twentieth-century reform movements in the United States. From Theodore Roosevelt and Woodrow Wilson to Franklin Roosevelt, Harry Truman, and John Kennedy, the liberal tradition in this century has been to limit change, to solve specific problems, to avoid the Scylla of doctrinaire socialism and the Charybdis of standpat conservatism.

The moral basis of progressivism was made clear by the religious (or "spiritual," as White calls it) cast of much of its thought. The progressive leader was usually a religious man or woman, immersed in problems of morality, ready with an apt Biblical allusion for each new situation. Giving the impression of moral certainty, of knowing what his values were, he seemed to act more often from motives of personal responsibility than from abstract notions of social justice. His support of the reform movement put him on God's side in the eternal struggle between good and evil. In characterizing the settlement-house movement, Jane Addams characteristically ascribed it to "a bent to express in social service and in terms of action the spirit of Christ." And the muckraking movement in journalism, Lincoln Steffens tells us, was likewise aimed at the Christian sense of responsibility for one's brothers and sisters. Even Socialists, according to David Shannon, "joined the party because capitalism had offended their Judeo-Christian ethics rather than because of any exposure to dialectical materialism." Most Socialists, he assures us, "were in a sense Christian Socialists."* It is probably no coincidence that a number of strong-minded progressive leaders, including Woodrow Wilson and Charles Evans Hughes, were ministers' sons. "Religious zeal and moral fervor," writes Hughes' biographer, "infused all his early education."† In Wilson's case, the stamp of his Calvinistic background remained on his personality for all his days.

## The Religious Impulse

Progressivism has been called a secular version of Social Gospellism. Both shared a faith in the dignity and worth of man, the gradual perfection

* D. Shannon, *The Socialist Party of America* (New York: The Macmillan Company, 1955), p. 59.
† M. Pusey, *Charles Evans Hughes*, 2 volumes (New York: The Macmillan Company, 1951), I, p. 7.

of human society, and the social derivation of evil. According to Walter Rauschenbusch, the greatest prophet of the matured Social Gospel, sin was a social force that ran from man to man along the lines of social intercourse. The conditions of modern social life turned brother against brother, made selfishness a moral principle, and pitted man against immoral society in a one-sided gladiatorial combat without quarter or mercy. Modern capitalism, wrote Rauschenbusch in his most famous book, *Christianity and the Social Crisis* (1907), "makes Ishmaels of our best men and teaches them that their hand must be against every man, since every man's hand is against them." What was needed was positive social action on behalf of the laboring man, the working child, the exploited female, the slum-dweller, and all those unable to protect themselves.

The victory of the Social Gospel in American Protestantism was signaled by the adoption in the major denominations of vigorous platforms of social reform. Thus, in 1908 the General Conference of the Methodist Church took an unequivocal stand in favor of abolishing child labor, regulating working conditions for women, suppressing the "sweating system," reducing the hours of labor, and raising wages to the highest level that each industry could afford. That same year the newly organized Federal Council of the Churches of Christ in America, representing thirty Protestant denominations, approved an almost identical statement and appealed for its support "to the toilers of America and . . . those who by organized effort are seeking to lift the crushing burdens of the poor, and to reduce the hardships and uphold the dignity of labor."

Catholics were no less concerned over the social problems that accompanied the rise of industrialism. Catholic parishioners were, in fact, likely to be more urbanized, less affluent, and more recently arrived in America than their Protestant neighbors. In the memorable encyclical *Rerum Novarum* (1891), Pope Leo XIII condemned the prevailing economic ideology of laissez faire as heartless and unchristian. Laborers were more than a commodity to be bought and sold, he asserted. They were entitled to humane treatment, a just wage, and the right to organize themselves. Not class struggle but class cooperation should mark the life of a Christian community. Of American Catholic exponents of social action, Father John Ryan was the most effective and best known. Minnesota-born, he had grown up in the stormy Populist era, attended St. Paul Seminary, and then gone on to graduate studies at Catholic University in Washington, D. C. His doctoral dissertation, *A Living Wage*, was published in 1906 with an introduction by Richard Ely, long-time proponent of an ethical approach to economics. "The laborer's right to a living wage," Father Ryan affirmed in good Social Gospel fashion, "is like all other moral rights, based on his intrinsic worth as a person. . . ." All his life Father Ryan worked in the cause of social justice and played a significant role in winning support for new economic and social legislation.

The Social Gospel, like progressivism in politics, was primarily an urban movement. Rural churchgoers were indifferent to many of the demands of their city brethren. But one reform they could and did support with enthusiasm—the ancient campaign against Demon Rum. To many a country-bred Protestant( whether he remained in the country or not), drinking was a city habit linked to other city sins and to free-drinking immigrants. Spurred by the Women's Christian Temperance Union (1874) and the militant Anti-Saloon League (1893), the forces of prohibition moved into state and local politics and won a series of spectacular victories.

State after state closed up its saloons. By 1917, three-fourths of the states had some ordinance restricting the sale of liquor, and thirteen states were bone dry. The union of temperance and social justice objectives can be seen in the Declaration of Principles of the W.C.T.U. (1902), in which, besides pledging themselves to work against the traffic in alcohol, members declared for a living wage and the eight-hour day.

## Intellectual Progressivism

The absorption of the progressive generation in what the Social Gospelers called the "social crisis" carried over to intellectual and artistic circles as well. "In the world of thought," wrote Rauschenbusch, "all the young and serious minds are absorbed in the solution of the social problems. Even literature and art point like compass-needles to the magnetic pole of all our thought."

Most intellectuals accepted not only the need for reform but also the framework of values on which progressives and Social Gospelers built their case. As yet, few American scholars or writers doubted the existence of basic moral absolutes, the purposefulness of human life, or the certainty of social progress. The mood of Victorian optimism, marred only slightly by the doubts arising from Darwinism, flooded into the new century. For most educated Americans the words "freedom," "justice," and "truth" still had objective, if not altogether precise, connotations. And their faith in the future of democracy and freedom was as strong as ever.

Typically, the progressive intellectual sought new justifications for believing in the old realities. He agreed with Sumner that natural law made little sense in a dynamic, changing, Darwinian universe and found James's questioning of all absolutistic doctrines unanswerable. Yet he continued to be cheerful, optimistic, and progressive in temper. He was critical of Social Darwinism and all defenders of the *status quo*, refused to believe that freedom, democracy, and individualism were just accidents of historical experience, and searched the records of history, law, economics, and social life for new grounds on which to take a hopeful stand.

And he found them. He discovered the writings of the unpredictable Thorstein Veblen, whose *Theory of the Leisure Class* (1899) was fast becoming a textbook for unorthodox economists. This sardonic son of a Norwegian immigrant, educated at Carleton College, Minnesota, and at Yale, scandalized his contemporaries by rejecting outright the doctrines of classical economics and by demanding that economics be made an evolutionary science. No longer should defenders of the business system be allowed to cling to exploded concepts of natural laws, he argued; the study of economic institutions must start anew from a disinterested, scientific, anthropological point of view. Veblen sought to show by erudite allusions to anthropological lore that the modern businessman was a lineal descendant of the barbaric warrior and the feudal noble. Like his prototypes, the businessman was savage, exploitative, and materialistic. His ostentatious manner of living, his habits, dress, manners, and education were all part of a vulgar ritual that bore witness to the degeneration of a strong, primitive culture. With delicious irony he traced the family tree of modern industrialists to barbarians skilled at predatory fraud. Worst of all, from the standpoint of furious critics, he pretended to draw no moral judgment from his work—this was not for the "scientific" observer to do; he was simply presenting the unvarnished anthropological facts for all the world to see.

Veblen's writings were welcomed by scholars and intellectuals who were already probing for weaknesses in the armor of defenders of the *status quo*. Students of economics, he seemed to be saying, must study economic institutions—actual economic behavior—rather than abstract theories that rested on outmoded notions of natural law. Progressives were certain that what Veblen's followers found would confirm their view that the defective business system was responsible for most of the ills of society.

Besides traditional economics another intellectual bulwark of conservatism to be stormed was the mysterious science of the law. Beyond all man-made law, nineteenth-century jurists had proclaimed, was an eternal and immutable law that man did not make. This law, screened through the imperfect reason and logic of fallible men, undergirded the statutory law found in the constitutions and enactments of legislative bodies. Gradually the Constitution and the lawyers on the Supreme Court who interpreted it had come to be regarded by conservatives as the true keepers of the American tradition, defenders of the eternal against the onslaughts of subversive radicals and windy reformers. For a quarter-century after 1890 the Court moved to suppress scores

of federal and state actions levying an income tax (*Pollock* vs. *Farmers' Loan and Trust*, 1894), enforcing the Sherman Act (*United States* vs. *E. C. Knight Company*, 1895), limiting hours of labor (*Lochner* vs. *New York*, 1905), and regulating the employment of women and children (*People* vs. *Williams*, 1907), all on the ground that these actions deprived someone of his property or his liberty without due process of law.

The progressive attack on the conservatives' use of the law and the Constitution was led by a distinguished jurist, Oliver Wendell Holmes, Jr., and a brilliant historian, Charles A. Beard. Appointed to the Supreme Court in 1902 by Theodore Roosevelt, Holmes was for the next thirty years a judicial champion of skeptical humanitarianism. "When we study law," Holmes once wrote, "we are not studying a mystery but a well-known profession." The life of law, he remarked in a famous sentence, had not been logic, but experience. Like Veblen and Beard, he believed in the importance of historical study, since history—the record of past experience—was the source of all knowledge of the law. Law was not derived from God or

Gallery of the progressive era. John Dewey, educator; Robert LaFollette, legislator; Ida Tarbell, author; Washington Gladden, clergyman. (First left, Culver Pictures, Inc.; others, Brown Brothers.)

Nature—not from "some brooding omniscience in the sky," as he once put it—but from the actions of lawgivers, whether princes or legislators. And what motives inspired the lawgiver? Not an abstract ideal of doing justice, but a pragmatic search for what was expedient for the community concerned. "The felt necessities of the time," Holmes had written in *The Common Law* (1881), his most famous book, "even the prejudices which judges share with their fellow-men, have had a good deal more to do than the syllogism in determining the rules by which men should be governed."

While Holmes was warning the Court against using the Constitution "to prevent the making of experiments that an important part of the community desires," Charles Beard turned his historical researches on the Constitution itself. In 1913 he published *An Economic Interpretation of the Constitution*, a landmark in American historical scholarship. If economic biographies of all the men who shared in some way in the adoption of the Constitution were available, Beard wrote in the opening chapter, the theory of economic determinism as it applied to American history could be tested. This was not possible, he admitted, but he

proceeded nevertheless to pile up fact after fact concerning the economic holdings of the framers of the Constitution. His conclusion was clear—it was not some vague concern for justice or the general welfare that had driven the Founding Fathers, but the selfish economic advantages each would enjoy under a stronger government. The Constitution, therefore, "was not created by 'the whole people' as the jurists have said; neither was it created by 'the states' as Southern nullifiers long contended; but it was the work of a consolidated group whose interests knew no state boundaries. . . ."

If the Constitution was a class document that represented the interests of only a small group, then the whole conservative position was undermined. This was realized by a number of progressives who now welcomed Beard, as they had Veblen, into the reformers' camp. Economic determinism was, like pragmatism and the new concept of law, a method— a new way of looking at history and applying it to contemporary affairs. It, too, seemed like a liberating shift from conservatism to reform, from logic to experience, from absolutes to relatives. It substituted the dynamic, changing outlook on life of Darwin for the static, unvarying universe of Newton. Nothing is more characteristic of the modern temper than this progressive habit of viewing things dynamically, of imagining them always growing, always becoming, always emerging from something else.

This shift in attitudes was often no more than intellectual muckraking—the sweeping out of the cobwebs of ancient dogmas and seemingly discredited creeds, the preference for the new because it was new, an affectation of an *avant-garde* skepticism that withered old faiths while disdaining to notice whether new ones would be along to replace them. But a good many progressive intellectuals did crave positive values, and for these they

looked to John Dewey. It was Dewey who made the serious seekers after truth feel at home in a rootless, random universe, who raised action to the dignity of a philosophy, and who converted pragmatism from a philosophy of individualism to a national program of social action.

Dewey was forty-one years old, with a distinguished career of teaching, writing, and educational reform behind him, when the new century opened. Yet his period of greatest influence was still to come. For Dewey was to be the real spokesman for intellectual America in the Progressive Era. As one scholar put it, "We were all Deweyites before we read Dewey and we were all the more effective reformers after we had read him." He showed Americans how an enormously sophisticated intelligence could be put to work on behalf of social justice and humane reform. He taught his generation three things of transcendent importance in the intellectual outlook of progressives: (1) faith in the potentialities of human intelligence, (2) confidence in ordinary experience as a substitute for the old absolutes, and (3) the revolutionary possibilities of the schoolroom in creating a new social order.

Dewey's educational ideas fitted hand-in-glove into his whole philosophy. The traditional separation by philosophers of mind and body was untenable in the post-Darwinian world, Dewey believed, and so was the time-honored distinction derived from it between liberal and vocational education. The old curriculum was organized rationally and logically, along the lines of progressive difficulty of subject matter; yet through experience the child learned what was most meaningful to him. Studies in the traditional school were impersonal and objective, based on general and eternal truths, whereas the child's world was intensely personal and confused, based on partial insights into his experience. In the typical classroom, teacher-pupil relations were autocratic, yet the child was expected to learn how to live in a democracy. Properly understood, education, in Dewey's view, was both a psychological and a social process. The teacher must begin with the child as he finds him, bubbling with the contradictions of his individual impulses and experiences. Still, he must also introduce the child to the social world and its processes, which have already begun to mold his character and his fortune by the time he enters school. The teacher must recognize and seek to harmonize this relationship between individual impulse and social good. The schoolroom must become a miniature of the real world (that is, the progressive, democratic world) outside the classroom. School and society, according to Dewey, are really one.

Like James, Dewey assigned a creative role to intelligence and would not accept the idea of a universe of completely blind chance. Unlike James, Dewey put intelligence to work in the cause of social reform. For several decades Dewey's voice was heard on behalf of dozens of reform movements, civil-liberties campaigns, educational battles, and political crusades. He believed all his life that the great task of philosophy, as of all creative intelligence, was "to face the great social and moral defects and troubles from which humanity suffers, to concentrate its attention upon clearing up the causes and exact nature of those evils and upon developing a clear idea of better social possibilities. . . ." Like Thoreau, he taught that philosophers "should not *play* life or *study* it merely . . . but earnestly *live* it."

The same rebellion against formalism and tradition that stirred in Dewey, Veblen, Holmes, and Beard was felt in literature and the arts. While the dominant note in literature continued to be one of buoyant optimism, as echoed in novels of

historical romance and adventurous action, a muffled beat of questioning of traditional values grew louder as the First
World War approached. The fictional
Mrs. Wiggs might proclaim from her
Cabbage Patch that "ever'thing in the
world comes right, if we jes' wait long
enough," but Jack London, Upton Sinclair, and other socialist novelists were
unwilling to wait. Stephen Crane and
Frank Norris, vigorous dissenters to the
genteel tradition in the nineties, were
dead by 1902, but London and Dreiser
were more active than ever. In *The Iron
Heel* (1908), London tells the story of a
premature socialist uprising in Chicago as
"the people of the abyss, mad with drink
and wrong, . . . snarling and growling,
carnivorous, drunk with hatred, drunk
with lust for blood" turn on their capitalist masters. But they are methodically
slaughtered and a reign of terror is inaugurated.

More popular than London's tract was
the novel of a younger socialist writer,
Upton Sinclair, whose *The Jungle* (1906)
was for a time the most talked-about book
in America. *The Jungle* describes the descent of a husky Lithuanian immigrant,
Jurgis Rudkus, into the pit of the Chicago stockyards. Happily married, he
watches the strength and morale of his
young bride, Ona, fail in the continual
fight against disease, cold, layoffs, bad
food, and cruelty. Then his strength, too,
falters and he is forced to take the vilest
job in the fertilizer plant. Ona is then
forcibly seduced by her boss; Jurgis attacks him and is sent to jail; he returns
penniless to find his family evicted and
Ona dying in childbirth. Brought to despair by his jungle-like environment, Jurgis
discovers socialism and welcomes its doctrines as the only hope for the future. The
book created a sensation, not so much for
its outspoken socialism, as for its realistic
descriptions of the horribly unsanitary
conditions in the packinghouses. "I aimed
at the public's heart and by accident I hit
it in the stomach" was Sinclair's sardonic
reaction.

In the arts, the revolt against formalism
made considerable headway by 1914. To
a number of sensitive souls the times
seemed out of joint; it was increasingly
difficult to express the disparate forces at
work in modern society through the
medium of the fine arts. For one, architecture, influenced by Louis Sullivan and
Daniel Burnham, was moving into the
modern era of light construction, vertical
lines, and steel framework in the design
of public buildings; and Frank Lloyd
Wright was seeking to relate form to function in private dwellings as well. "Here is
no body of culture evolving through centuries of time," said Wright of Sullivan's
work, "but an Individual working away in
the poetry-crushing environment of a
more cruel materialism than any seen
since the days of the brutal Romans."

Modern painting, too, was evidencing
a mood of chronic alienation from
norms and standards. American painters
had been slow to adopt the methods and
techniques of the French impressionists
in the old century; and despite such pioneers in realism as Eakins, they had
grown even more conservative, stylized,
and impatient of new departures in the
early years of the twentieth century. But
here as elsewhere in American life new
impulses gathered force beneath the surface. These impulses erupted first in 1908,
when a group of artists calling themselves
"the Eight" staged an exhibition at the
Macbeth Gallery in New York, and again
in 1913 at the famous Armory Show. The
paintings of Robert Henri, John Sloan,
and other members of "the Eight"
shocked a large segment of the viewing
public, primarily because of their subject
matter: drunkards and prizefighters, peddlers and prostitutes, alleys and bar-

rooms—the "Ash Can School" some derisive critics called it. Five years later came the Armory Show. Here most of the pioneer American modernists were represented as well as a number of the French school, including Van Gogh, Cézanne, Rouault, and Gauguin. For many visitors, perhaps most, the Armory experience came as a blow: Picasso's cubism, the highly colored, child-like work of the Fauves, even postimpressionism were totally strange. Of contemporary observers, Walter Lippmann seemed best to catch the meaning of the new art when he wrote that the modern artist finds "the world so complex that he can't find common experiences and common aspirations to deal with. . . . He has to be satisfied with a cult. . . . but in his heart he is unsatisfied with his work, and so he develops a habit of chronic rebellion. . . . I venture to suggest that what the rebels are rebelling against is not a classical authority: none exists today that has any compelling force. They are in rebellion against something within themselves; there are conflicts in their souls for which they have found no solution. . . ." *

## Journalistic Crusaders

The tornado of resentment of things as they were that swept across the world of art and intellect touched

* W. Lippmann, *Drift and Mastery* (New York: Mitchell Kennerley, 1914), pp. 194-195.

"McSorley's Bar" by John Sloan. (Detroit Institute of Arts.)

down at many other points in American life, but nowhere with greater force than in journalism. If it was the intellectuals who moved the minds of the progressives, it was the journalists who moved their hearts. The roots of the journalistic crusade for reform lay back in the nineties with the advent of such newspaper innovations as banner headlines, Sunday supplements, and the free use of pictures. These changes were aimed at a new clientele—the urban masses. The modern metropolitan daily with its foreign correspondents, single editorial page, colored supplements, comic strips, sports pages, women's section, extensive advertising, and bannering of sensational news was born in the quarter-century ending with World War I. As advertising and circulation figures rose, newspapers became big business and editors fought for the mass market with all manner of features—puzzles, baby shows, kitchen recipes, contests—to appeal to every shade of interest. By 1914 a number of the more enterprising publishers—William Randolph Hearst, E. W. Scripps, Frank A. Munsey—had acquired extensive newspaper chains.

Magazine publishers, Hearst and Munsey among them, were also seeking a mass audience for their publications. Suddenly, almost inadvertently, a number of these publishers stumbled onto the widespread public interest in the social and economic evils of the day. The muckraking crusade began. "I did not intend to be a muckraker," wrote Lincoln Steffens, author of a devastating series of articles on municipal corruption in 1902 and 1903 in McClure's Magazine; "I did not know that I was one till President Roosevelt picked the name out of Bunyan's Pilgrim's Progress and pinned it on us. . . ." Steffens, greatest of the muckrakers, explained that his whole purpose was "to see if the shameful facts, spread out in all their shame, would not burn through our civic shamelessness and set fire to American pride."

"Set fire to American pride"—this was the aim of the muckraking articles published in McClure's, Cosmopolitan, Collier's, Everybody's, and the other magazines. Ida Tarbell wrote a factual series on the growth of Rockefeller's Standard Oil Company that was printed side-by-side with Steffens' exposures of the corrupt alliances between businessmen and political bosses in a half-dozen cities. Both were careful to build their cases slowly, factually, without naming villains, making it clear that it was the system rather than individual culprits they sought to indict. Others turned to the meatpacking industry (Charles Edward Russell), the railroads (Ray Stannard Baker), the insurance companies (Burton J. Hendrick), and the "frenzied finance" of stock market manipulators (Thomas Lawson). The "system," wrote the millionaire Lawson, "has taken from the millions of our people billions of dollars and given them over to a score or two of men with power to use and enjoy them. . . ."

By 1905 muckraking was at its peak and the public was treated to hair-raising accounts of food and drug adulteration (which played a significant role in the adoption of the Pure Food and Drug Act of 1906), corruption and murder by state political machines (with Steffens again leading the attack), and (in 1906) treason in the United States Senate itself! The novelist David Graham Phillips made the last charge in a lurid and poorly substantiated series of articles in Cosmopolitan which began with these words: "The treason of the Senate! Treason is a strong word, but not too strong, rather too weak, to characterize the situation in which the Senate is the eager, resourceful, indefatigable agent of interests as hostile to the American people as any invading army could be, and vastly more dangerous. . . ."

A whole spectrum separated Phillips' yellow journalism of 1906 from Ida Tarbell's scholarly and restrained articles of 1902. Though there was much truth in Phillips' charge that some senators were mere tools of special interests, the tone of his writing and the unfairness of his language brought savage denunciations down on his head. Phillips' attack divided the whole muckraking movement. Some charged that sensationalism would harm the whole reform program; others felt that in attacking the Senate he was weakening federal authority at a time when popular confidence in it was needed. What-

ever the justice of these criticisms, it should be noted that seven years after Phillips' articles the Seventeenth Amendment, providing for the popular election of senators, was adopted by the nation. After 1906 the sensational note became dominant in the literature of muckraking and by 1908 the movement was clearly on the wane. Steffens sounded the death knell in the latter year in his description of the average American's sentiment: "I'm tired of exposure. I know something is wrong; something big. But what is it? Don't go on proving the evil over and over again. Tell us what to do about it."

## THE PASSING OF LAISSEZ FAIRE

Steffens did not know what to do about it, but there were others who thought they did. For more than a decade the clamor for governmental intervention in the nation's economic affairs had been rising—from Populists, socialists, professors, reformers, muckrakers, social workers, labor leaders, businessmen, and a growing number of politicians. The ideal of laissez faire began to weaken as group after group jumped on the bandwagon of the positive state. Each group, to be sure, had a different motive and a different goal in climbing aboard, but all were agreed that the American tradition of limited government must be modified in confronting the crises raised by industrialism. This was the most notable political change of the Progressive Era: the victory of the idea that both state and federal governments had a broad responsibility to regulate and control the nation's economic life.

The aura of radicalism about governmental intervention faded as each group surveyed its own needs—whatever was necessary could hardly be radical. This pragmatic attitude quieted the doubts of the labor leader seeking workman's com-

pensation laws or safety legislation, the social worker fighting to outlaw child labor, or the businessman interested in tariff protection or antitrust action against his large competitors. The foremost champions of strong government were those groups that hoped to benefit from increased governmental activity.

### Businessmen Organize

Laissez faire was in fact already doomed before government began to move vigorously into American economic life. For the growth of monopolies, of huge financial-industrial aggregations, of labor unions, of farm cooperatives was a clear signal that competition in the old sense was dead. The rise of bigness in business was in large part a response to economic factors that rewarded size and efficiency and penalized individual enterprise.

In the factories of the city, mechanization had proceeded swiftly. New cutting machinery, larger drills and presses, swift communications, mechanized office equipment, standardized parts, and new and cheaper sources of power all contributed to the decline of small enterprise.

Assembly line in Ford plant, early 1900's. The success of the auto industry resulted largely from the mass-production methods popularized by Henry Ford. (Ford Motor Company.)

Organization was now the key to industrial success. The ablest shoe manager could no longer make a pair of shoes alone—but he knew how to organize men, materials, machinery, and production schedules. This tendency to combine advantages and mass human labor was irresistible. A great domestic market lay open to any man who could organize his resources so as to make a cheaper, a better, or a newer product. Inevitably, the small entrepreneur found the going more difficult as he lagged behind the leaders in mechanization, specialization, research, and the employment of new talent. In the industries dominated by big business —especially steel, oil refining, farm machinery, railroading, and electrical supplies—small businesses made little headway. According to the 1910 census, one per cent of America's industrial firms were responsible for 44 per cent of the nation's manufacturing output.

The drive toward bigness was furthered by financial mergers planned by J. P. Morgan, who organized the United States Steel Company in 1901, and other giants of high finance. The center of gravity of American business and industrial life moved definitely toward Wall Street in the first decade of the twentieth century. Through holding companies, stock purchases, and interlocking boards of directors, the Morgan partners had a hand in hundreds of American industries, many of which they had never seen. By 1915, according to the Commission on Industrial Relations, "the final control of American industry rests . . . in the hands of a small number of wealthy and powerful financiers."

What to do about it? This was the rub. Most progressives, like the Populists earlier, wanted to smash the trusts, restore competition, set the clocks back, and go on living as they had before big business had reared its ugly head. Their sympathies clearly lay with the small businessman, the expectant capitalist, what Woodrow Wilson called "the man on the make." But was it possible to reverse the mighty surge toward monopoly? Was it desirable? Was bigness in itself an evil? Wilson thought so and staked his political life in 1912 on his belief in competition. But Theodore Roosevelt, city-bred, disillusioned with his own trustbusting, came to speak for another wing of progressivism in accepting the inevitability of business combination and calling for increased governmental powers to control it. Not bigness, but underhanded methods and chronic wrongdoing, said Roosevelt, should be the concern of government. Wilson drew his inspiration from the past, from the anticapitalist traditions of Jefferson, Jackson, and the Populists; Roosevelt looked to the future and anticipated the strong government philosophy of his distant cousin's New Deal.

### Workers Organize

Both Wilson and Roosevelt were progressives. Both were typically believers in private enterprise, suspicious of trusts, conservative in background, and latecomers to the reform movement. And both were fearful of the mass labor and radical movements engendered by modern industrialism. Like most progressives they adopted a hesitant, skeptical attitude toward labor's attempt to unionize itself against the pressures of big business and to gain admission to the inner councils of industrial decision.

Clearly, organization was proving the key to greater security for workingmen as it had for industrialists and financiers. Although it had been laid low in the late eighties and nineties by the public reaction to the bitter Haymarket episode, the collapse of the Knights of Labor, and the defeats suffered at Homestead and in the Pullman strike, the union movement now rallied, grew militant, and waxed strong in the reform atmosphere of the progressive years. Union membership shot up 500 per cent between 1898 and 1914. As one evidence of this growing strength, three times as many strikes were called in 1902 as in 1898.

The American Federation of Labor, founded in 1881, was the chief beneficiary of the rise in union membership. From 278,000 members in affiliated craft unions in 1898, AFL rolls swelled in 1914 to 2,021,000, a figure that comprised three-fourths of all unionized workers in the United States. At the head of the AFL was Samuel Gompers, son of Dutch-Jewish parents, who was born in London in 1850, emigrated to America in 1863, and early became a convert to unionism. "In my religion," Gompers wrote, "I am a workingman. In politics, I am a workingman, and in every nerve, in every fiber, in every aspiration, I am on the side which will advance the interests of my fellow workingmen." Indifferent, in fact, to politics, he insisted that the trade union movement must concentrate on simple economic objectives: the eight-hour day, more wages, better working conditions. A pragmatic, fact-minded man, he had no use for sweeping theories or revolutionary manifestoes. "We must build our program upon fact," he said on numerous occasions, "and not theories." He believed that the bargaining table was the best instrument yet devised for raising the laboring class out of its misery. He had no real social philosophy other than the conviction and will to seek a better life for the working class. Indeed, when asked by a Congressional committee to explain his union's philosophy, he replied, "It works along the line of least resistance and endeavors to accomplish the best results in improving the condition of the working people, men, women, and children, today and tomorrow, and each day making it a better day than the one that has gone before."

Gompers, like spokesmen for farm and business groups, preached organization as the only recourse of the individual against the social chaos left by the industrial upheaval. The world of individual craftsmen and employers who could negotiate over wages and working conditions as equal bargainers was forever gone. Laissez faire was dead. So workers must be prepared to defend their interests before state and federal lawmakers or face an avalanche of unfriendly legislation inspired by employers' organizations. The National Association of Manufacturers, which had been founded to increase foreign trade, turned in 1903 to a country-wide campaign against closed shops, strikes, the eight-hour day, and protective labor legislation. It rallied thousands of small and medium-size employers, who felt harassed by unions on one side and new labor laws on the other, and stiffened their resistance to labor's gains. The measure of the NAM's success was indicated by a speech in 1906 of its president, David M. Parry, wherein he boasted that "a change has come and this Association is largely responsible for it. The strike is no longer popular. . . . When an independent workman, a 'scab,' if you please, is mysteriously assaulted the police are much more active than formerly in running down his assailant. When lawmakers are threatened with political death unless they vote for semisocialistic legislation they discuss the matter and look up the Constitution. . . . What has brought about these changes? The question can be answered in one word—Organization."

The employers' counteroffensive slowed the advance of unionization but did not halt it. Gompers openly threw his support to the Democrats in 1908 and again in 1912 when they seemed to promise relief from the employers' constant use of legal injunctions against unions under the Sherman Act. Some grew impatient with the slowness of the AFL advance, however, especially its indifference to the mass of unskilled immigrant workers, and drifted into the more militant Industrial Workers of the World or the socialist movement.

The IWW was born in 1905 of a union of dissident AFL and socialist unions with "Big Bill" Haywood's belligerent Western Federation of Miners. Severely condemning the AFL for skimming the aristocracy of skilled craft workers off the top of the labor movement, Haywood, an erratic Marxist revolutionary, issued a manifesto calling for "one big union," the overthrow of capitalism, and "direct action" to achieve these goals. The IWW's violent preachments and colorful leaders appealed strongly to lumberjacks, migratory workers, and Western miners. But the "Wobblies," as IWW members were called, were soon torn by internal dissension and lost much of their original strength as union after union seceded. Reckless, combative, violent in speech, resorting to sabotage on occasion, the IWW staged spectacular "sit down" strikes in Akron rubber plants and Michigan lumber camps, then moved east in 1912 to conduct a widely publicized strike in the textile mills of Lawrence, Massachusetts. The organization's greatest appeal was always to the unskilled, the unsettled, and the immigrant laborer. At peak strength about 1910 the Wobblies probably numbered 60,000 but their power dissipated rapidly, collapsing altogether during the First World War.

The political counterpart of the IWW was the Socialist Party of America. A coalition of almost all the small Marxist parties of the late nineteenth century, the Socialist Party, organized in 1901, depended for much of its political support on such native radical traditions as Populism and on Edward Bellamy's Nationalist clubs. Its leader was Eugene V. Debs, a fervent, dedicated, but moderate socialist who had led the American Railway Union in the ill-fated Pullman strike. Five times he ran for President of the United States on the Socialist ticket and the steady rise in his vote is one indication of the growing appeal of the socialist movement. He received 95,000 votes in 1900, 402,000 in 1904, 421,000 in 1908, 897,-000 in 1912, and 920,000 in 1920. In the 1912 election, which was prior to the adoption of the women's suffrage amendment, Debs received 6 per cent of all votes cast. Socialist influence can also be seen in the party's control of such cities as Milwaukee, Berkeley, and Butte during these years. Largely a federation of regional groups with different, even conflicting, views, the party's greatest strength lay in New York City, Pennsylvania, Chicago, Milwaukee, Oklahoma, and the Mountain West (home of the Western Federation of Miners). Its methods were evolutionary rather than revolutionary, its appeal was to the ballot box rather than the barricade. Like the IWW, though, it was torn by the bitter issues raised up by the First World War—whether to support an "imperialist" war and how to stand on the Bolshevik Revolution—and had difficulty surviving the war.

Whatever their influence, labor movements, radical or conservative, accounted for but a fraction of the total labor force in the country between 1900 and 1914. In all, close to 37 million Americans worked for some kind of wage in 1910, about a third of them on farms, the rest chiefly in business or industrial employment of some kind. About two million of these workers were fifteen years of age or younger. The average wage for all industrial employment that year was twenty-nine cents per hour and the number of work hours per week averaged close to fifty-five. A Census Bureau report of 1904 revealed that almost 100,000 grown men earned less than three dollars a week, over a million earned under eight dollars weekly, and at least two and a half million had an income of less than twelve dollars each week. Even this last amount was, in the view of many social workers, inadequate to sustain life if a man were married and had a family. Other observers put the number living at or below the level of subsistence at ten million persons or even higher. If we add unemployment and industrial hazards to this picture of life among the underpaid, it is easy to understand the contemporary vogue of Edwin Markham's *Man with the Hoe* with its characterization of the brutalized toiler "Bowed by the weight of centuries . . .

the emptiness of ages in his face, and on his back the burden of the world. . . ."

## Government Acts

Public intervention on behalf of the laboring class was largely a state rather than a federal movement during the Progressive Era. Federal action was held back by the laissez-faire tradition, unfavorable court decisions, and fear of the labor movement on the part of progressive leaders. Even state legislation was often regarded as a matter of social justice, rather than a concession to labor's growing demands.

Most successful of all the reform drives on behalf of labor were the campaigns to limit child labor, protect women in industry, and enact workmen's compensation laws in individual states. The first issue appealed to humanitarian and moral sentiments in all classes of the population. "This great nation in its commercial madness devours its babes," cried John Spargo in *The Bitter Cry of the Children* (1906). The indomitable Jane Addams, founder of Hull House and veteran of a score of humanitarian crusades, charged that Americans had "come to think that a bolt of cheap cotton is more to be prized than a child properly nourished, educated, and prepared to take his place in life." A National Child Labor Committee, formed in 1904, gathered evidence, drew up model bills, and lobbied at state legislatures. Its program seemed modest enough —a minimum age of fourteen in manufacturing and sixteen in mining, a maximum of eight hours per working day, and the prohibition of night work—yet no state met these requirements in 1904. Some states did have statutes regulating child labor, but they were poorly enforced and easily circumvented, and they usually applied only to factory employment. New York State, for instance, had 400,000 children working as bootblacks, peddlers, newsboys, and messengers in 1901, none of them covered by existing laws.

This situation changed radically during the progressive years. In 1903 New York enacted a child labor statute that extended to the jobs just noted. State after state moved to bar minors from hazardous occupations, night work, and excessive hours. Then in 1909 Delaware became the first state to ban the employment of all children under fourteen. By the outbreak of World War I, 47 states had set a minimum age limit, usually fourteen, and most had gone far beyond this in protective legislation. Even a federal child labor bill, introduced into Congress in 1914, was passed two years later with Wilson's support, only to be invalidated later by the Supreme Court.

State laws regulating the hours of women also ran afoul of the courts. Not until the Supreme Court's decision in *Muller* vs. *Oregon* (1908) was the green light finally given to efforts of state legislatures to limit the length of the working day for women. In this famous case, the Court upheld the constitutionality of an Oregon statute limiting the hours of women in industry to ten per day. The case was argued before the Court by Louis D. Brandeis, who ignored the usual array of legal precedents, and presented instead a sheaf of expert testimony that long hours were dangerous to women's health and morals. In ruling that the Oregon law did not violate the freedom of contract protected by the Fourteenth Amendment, the Court inaugurated the important precedent of examining the pertinent sociological facts in determining the reasonableness or unreasonableness of social legislation.

Messenger boys pose with policeman, City Hall Park, New York, 1903. Widespread abuses—long hours, arduous tasks, dangerous working conditions, lack of time for schooling—led to the need for child labor laws. (Culver Pictures, Inc.)

Attempts to regulate the hours of women in industry appealed particularly to women's organizations, though they were also supported by organized labor because of the depressing effect that long hours and low wages for women had on the whole labor movement. The real champion of labor laws for women was Florence Kelley, former Hull House resident and chief factory inspector of Illinois, who used her post as general secretary of the National Consumers' League to work for reform. Following the Court's decision in the Oregon case, progress was swift. By 1917, 39 states had enacted laws limiting the hours of women, usually to eight, and many had barred night work as well.

Women's wages were also the subject of special legislation. It was customary in many industries to pay women only a fraction of the male wage on the ground that women worked only for "pin money" and not to support themselves. This notion was exploded by a survey of working women in Pittsburgh conducted by Elizabeth Beardsley Butler in 1910. There was public indignation, too, at the revelation during a strike at the Triangle Waist Company in New York that some of the girls working seventy hours a week were getting only four or five dollars for their labor. This indignation turned to wrath when a fire broke out in March, 1911, in the crowded upstairs quarters of the Company, killing 148 workers—mostly young girls—as they scrambled madly to reach blocked or nonexistent fire exits. A Massachusetts law of 1912 created a commission to make wage recommendations for women and a number of western states followed with more stringent legislation in the next few years. In all, nine states had enacted minimum wage laws for women by 1914.

More popular than the movement to regulate women's wages was the campaign for workmen's compensation laws. The introduction of high-speed machinery had brought with it a corresponding heightening of danger to life and limb, yet existing laws threw most of the responsibility of proving an employer's liability for injury or death on the worker or his family. Drawing on European, particularly German, models, American reformers recommended legislation to replace the doctrine of employers' negligence—always difficult to prove—with a contributory system of state insurance in cases of industrial injury or death. Ten states passed compensation laws in 1911 after earlier laws in Maryland (1902) and Montana (1909) had been thrown out by the courts. By the end of 1917 some 40 states and territories had acted similarly, and the Supreme Court had upheld the principle of workmen's compensation. Some students of labor history regard these laws as the greatest achievement of the whole progressive period.

## FIGHTING THE POLITICAL MACHINES

The use of governmental power, however hesitant, in the cause of social justice betokened a continuing belief in the potentialities of democratic government. Close to the progressive heart lay a faith in enlightened self-government as the medicine for most of mankind's ills. This faith, far from being smothered by Steffens's revelations of far-reaching corruption in our political life, now blazed forth in a crusade for more democracy as the remedy for the nation's troubles. The American people, so the argument ran, had lost control of their representative institutions to greedy monopolists and venal politicians. City, state, even federal lawmakers were in corrupt alliance with the business community. The remedy? Give the government back to the people. Permit them to introduce legislation directly (the initiative), vote on crucial issues (the referendum), nominate their own candidates (the direct primary), elect their senators directly, recall unfaithful officials—and give women the precious right to vote. "Cure the ills of democracy with more democracy"—this was the second great political theme of the progressive reformers.

## The Changing Meaning
## of Democracy

Had the people ever actually controlled the government? Few doubted that ultimate sovereignty lay with the great body of citizens, but how was public will translated into public policy?* The Fathers of the Constitution had been vague on the matter, though they clearly distrusted sudden, popular change. And the nineteenth century had done little to clarify the mystery. Most republican theorists of the early period had spoken warmly of the intermediary role of representative institutions in refining the "raw materials" of political life. A legislature, it was held, was a bulwark of reason and caution against the raw passions of a changeable majority. Representative government meant not so much popular government as deliberate government, one that was orderly and disciplined, and was conducted according to due processes of law.

But it was precisely these representative institutions that had gone sour. City after city, state after state, Steffens had shown, were in the grip of special interests, of racketeers, and of political bosses. Some reformers charged that the United States Senate itself was likewise only a panel of puppets whose strings were pulled by bosses or plutocrats. So, defensively, the progressive reformers substituted a broader but more ambiguous meaning of democracy for the older representative one. Government was now held to be *directly* responsible to the people, not only in periodic elections, but in an immediate, ongoing sense. Democracy was more than a political system; it was synonomous with a whole way of life. The "people" were idealized: all were held to be intelligent, responsible, and public-spirited like the progressives themselves. Drive out the corrupt lawmakers, it was argued, and an enlightened people would see to it that honesty and justice were again enthroned in political and social life. Public opinion was to be valued as never before. And so in hundreds of American communities and states political reforms aimed at bringing government closer to the people became the order of the day.

Conservatives were skeptical. Henry Cabot Lodge, senator from Massachusetts and close friend of Theodore Roosevelt, argued that while government should be responsive to public opinion, that opinion, to be heeded, must be informed. Government must, of course, make provision for the discussion of great public issues. But the direct democracy of the progressives, he charged, thrust a ballot or a petition into the public's hands without informing the public what the real issues were. Consequently, representative institutions would be undermined and a strong executive would emerge to provide the leadership and stability which the new democracy could never give. Other critics struck deeper. For one, A. Lawrence Lowell, political scientist and Harvard president, questioned the assumption of man's rationality upon which democratic processes rested. Drawing on new psychological concepts of man's prejudices, drives, and subconscious feelings, Lowell predicted that

* I am indebted for a number of ideas in this section to Stow Person's *American Minds* (New York: Henry Holt and Company, 1958), pp. 363-374.

direct democracy would magnify these by encouraging offhand impressions and thoughtless predilections. True public opinion, in contrast, was informed and temperate; it made use of expert judgment; it came filtered through representative bodies. Politics in a democracy, said Lowell, existed to clarify public issues and make possible a simple, clear-cut choice.

Ignoring conservative doubts, the progressives pushed ahead with their reforms. The secret ballot, a practice that was borrowed from Australia, was victorious everywhere by 1910; by that year, too, many states had adopted corrupt-practices legislation to limit the amounts and uses of funds donated to political campaigns; the direct primary was in use in thirteen states by 1912; the initiative and referendum were on the statute books in twelve states, the recall in seven, by the end of the same year. In choosing senators, over half the states were voting directly for their candidates by 1912, when a reluctant Senate finally approved the Seventeenth Amendment making it mandatory for all states. And women's suffrage had become a reality in thirteen states by 1914, well before the ratification of the Nineteenth Amendment in 1920.

### City and State Reformers

Most of these reforms were designed to break the hold of machine politicians over municipal and state affairs. Since the rapid growth of American cities had thrown waves of new settlers, immigrants included, helter-skelter into communities bursting with new wealth, new industries, and new opportunities, the temptations to corruption proved irresistible. City after city fell prey to grafting politicians who built imposing empires on public indifference and the lust of businessmen for franchises and special privileges.

A few colorful reform mayors had appeared on the scene in the nineties, nota-

bly the redoubtable Samuel ("Golden Rule") Jones of Toledo. Something of a Christian Socialist, Jones had left his profitable and well-run factory to head up a reform administration that repudiated the boodlers, fought the granting of franchises to the special interests, and championed the idea of civil service and municipal ownership of utilities. This eccentric but beloved man offered free sleigh rides to the city's children, took clubs away from his policemen, and turned his salary over to charity. When local ministers proposed that prostitutes be driven from the city, Jones suggested instead that the fallen women be taken into the pastors' homes for Christian rehabilitation. The Golden Rule was his rule of life in politics as in his private affairs. "Love," he once remarked, "is the only regenerative force."

Jones was followed by more effective, if less spectacular, champions of municipal reform. In Cleveland, the hard-driving Tom Johnson fought bribery and privilege and made his city what Steffens called "the best governed city in America." In his campaigns he argued strongly for equal taxation, home rule for Cleveland, and municipal ownership of utilities. His example was followed by reform-minded mayors in Denver, Milwaukee, New York, St. Louis, Kansas City, and other cities.

The trail of corruption and "invisible government" led straight from the courthouse to the statehouse. City machines were frequently found to be geared to state machines, either as minor cogs or occasionally as the main spring. Both Jones and Johnson carried their battles to the state arena in Ohio, but with indifferent success. Ohio, like Missouri, New Jersey, and other states to greater or less degree, was in the grip of railroad and corporate interests that operated through party caucuses or behind them. In New Jersey, the railroad interests were said to have appointed the attorney general, chief justice, commissioner of banking and insurance, and other high officials of the state. In New York, on the other hand, the politicians seemed to be in the driver's seat. In a well-known speech, Elihu Root, a prominent conservative, complained that the real rulers of New York had been the political bosses: "I don't know how many years Mr. Roscoe Conkling was the supreme ruler in this State. . . . Then Mr. Thomas Platt ruled the State; for nigh unto twenty years he ruled it. It was not the Governor; it was not the Legislature; it was not any elected officers; it was Mr. Platt."

Most widely known of the state reform leaders was Wisconsin's Robert M. La-Follette, whose name became synonomous with progressivism to many Americans during the reform era. Elected governor in 1900 on a platform of railroad regulation and the direct primary, he was at first thwarted by conservative Republicans in his own party. Fighting back hard, he got control of the legislature and enacted the most complete program of progressive reforms in any state. Not only the direct primary and a railroad rate commission, but also civil service, conservation measures, antilobbying legislation, a high corporation tax, and ultimately a state income tax became part of the "Wisconsin idea." He surrounded himself with a number of expert advisers and intellectuals of high integrity, many of them professors at the University of Wisconsin. Ambitious, highly principled, a product of big-city reform as well as rural discontent, LaFol-lette left Wisconsin in 1906 for a stormy career in the United States Senate.

From Wisconsin the reform impulse moved to Iowa, Minnesota, Missouri, South Dakota, and other midwestern states. Able leaders—Albert B. Cummins, Joseph Folk, Coe Crawford—followed La-Follette in fighting monopolies and railroads, instituting direct democracy, backing social legislation, employing university experts, and dismantling their predecessors' machines. In the East, Charles Evans Hughes in New York and Woodrow Wilson in New Jersey battled for many of the same reforms as the midwestern progressives, while on the West Coast, the movements led by Hiram Johnson in California and William U'Ren in Oregon testified to the national character of the progressive drive. It was largely because of U'Ren that Oregon pioneered in enacting the initiative and referendum (1902), the direct primary (1904), and the recall (1910).

By the end of the era, no state was untouched by the many-sided program of the progressive reformers. To be sure, the problems that inspired the movement had by no means been solved—political corruption, alas, survived the Progressive Era and corporate power remained formidable. Yet the average progressive's conclusion that government was somewhat more honest, big business under closer check, and social justice a little nearer to realization than at the beginning of the period only a perfectionist would deny.

## THE FIRST ROOSEVELT

The assassin's bullet that cut down William McKinley in Buffalo in September, 1901, brought a fateful change in the national administration. The popular McKinley had beaten Bryan a second time the preceding November in an election that had added imperialism to the issues of 1896. To replace Garret Hobart, who had died in office, the Republicans had nominated young Theodore Roosevelt of New York for the vice presidency. "Don't any of you realize," Mark Hanna is reputed to

have said, "that there's only one life between that madman and the Presidency?"

### Enter "Teddy"

Now Roosevelt was presi-
dent. His years in the White House
(1901-1909) coincided with the hey-day
of progressivism in the states and cities,
the rise and decline of the muckraking
movement, and the launching of the many
crusades for social justice. His own administration provided outlets at the national level for some of the same reform
impulses that moved LaFollette, Steffens,
Jane Addams, and other progressive figures. He gave the progressive movement
a national cast and dramatized progressive sentiments and ideas. At home and
abroad he became the symbol of the new
philosophy of positive government and
vigorous leadership. He left his own stamp
—moral, cautious, colorful—on the entire
era. To some, he was progressivism incarnate; others questioned his sincerity or
his actual accomplishments. Yet few
doubted that his administration marked a
new turning in American political and diplomatic history, a turning that befitted a
new century.

What a curious, complex man was
Roosevelt! Born to moderate wealth and
educated privately and at Harvard, he had
overcome poor health, gone into Republican politics in 1881 at age 23, roped
cattle in the Dakotas, and made a national reputation before he was 40. Struck
by double tragedy in 1884, when his wife
and mother died the same day, he sought
solace in ranching, writing, and politics.
That year, too, he refused to follow the
Mugwumps in their revolt against the
spoilsman Blaine and was rewarded when
Blaine got him an appointment to the
new Civil Service Commission. He threw
his immense energies into this seemingly
insignificant post, dramatizing his exploits
with colorful newspaper interviews and
charges. "The only trouble I ever had

with managing him," President Harrison
said later, "was that he wanted to put an
end to all the evil in the world between
sunrise and sunset." From his civil service
job Roosevelt moved to the presidency of
the New York City police board in 1895.
Again he allied himself with the forces of
reform, enforcing saloon laws, fighting
Tammany corruption, and prowling New
York's streets after dark concealed by a
swirling cape and cap pulled over his
eyes. Everywhere he left a trail of lively
controversy, broken careers, and splutter-
ing obloquies against wrongdoers.

Theodore Roosevelt (1858–1919). Roosevelt's
personality was scarcely less striking than his
career. He was extraordinarily quick in grasp-
ing ideas, keenly interested in all manner of
subjects, and a wholehearted scorner of the
insincere. (Brown Brothers.)

His strong and effective support of Mc-
Kinley in 1896 got him an appointment as
Assistant Secretary of the Navy under
John D. Long. Once more he made a
minor post into a rostrum for leadership
as he readied the Navy for war and

plumped for intervention against Spain in Cuba. He dispatched a famous telegram to Admiral Dewey in Hong Kong, ordering him to coal his ships and be prepared to move on the Spanish fleet if war broke out. When the war did come, Roosevelt raised a volunteer regiment of Rough Riders, embarked for Cuba, and won lasting glory through his personal bravery in the charge on San Juan Hill. What followed seemed an anticlimax: a hero's return, a term as governor of New York, and then the honorific but normally dull job as vice president.

Nothing about Roosevelt was dull, however. Overflowing with energy, he charged the most commonplace actions with high drama. John Burroughs tells of sitting with President and Mrs. Roosevelt in their little cabin in Virginia when "Suddenly Roosevelt's hand came down on the table with such a bang that it made us both jump, and Mrs. Roosevelt exclaimed, in a slightly nettled tone, 'Why, my dear, what *is* the matter?' He had killed a mosquito with a blow that would almost have demolished an African lion." Another writer commented later that Roosevelt often "killed mosquitoes as if they were lions, and lions as if they were mosquitoes." A big-game hunter, an amateur biologist, an historian and author of a half-dozen books, he lived life to its strenuous hilt and fascinated the American people in the process. He made the White House exciting for the first time since Jackson, by branding a well-known naturalist a "nature faker," by attacking birth control as "race suicide," by seeking to abolish the motto "In God We Trust," by fighting Congress over a system of simplified spelling, and by inviting poets, scholars, prizefighters, and explorers to 1600 Pennsylvania Avenue.

### "His Accidency"

Roosevelt did not forget that he was president by accident. "I

wish to state," he announced publicly, "that it will be my aim to continue, absolutely unbroken, the policy of President McKinley for the peace, the prosperity, and the honor of our beloved country." Yet his very first message to Congress revealed signs that TR's administration would have a velocity, if not yet a direction, of its own. Though advising caution in approaching the problem of trusts, he nevertheless argued that more regulation of corporations doing interstate business, along with full publicity concerning their actions, might halt the trend toward monopoly. Mr. Dooley caught exactly the President's divided temper with his comment: "Th' trusts, says he, are heejoous monsthers built up be . . . enlightened intherprise. . . . On wan hand I wud stamp thim undher fut; on th' other hand not so fast."

When TR did move against the trusts, he did so suddenly and without warning. On February 19, 1902, Attorney General Knox startled Wall Street by announcing he would begin suit against the Northern Securities Company, a holding company for three important northwestern railroads. A stunned J. P. Morgan, his interests heavily affected, went to Washington and told the President, "If we have done anything wrong, send your man to my man and they can fix it up." But Roosevelt refused to deal and would not even guarantee that other Morgan interests would not be attacked. The case was successfully prosecuted and the government's action was eventually upheld by the Supreme Court in a five-to-four decision.

The fact of TR's action was as important as its results. He insisted that he was not against big business, only opposed to its unfair practices. He was not against wealth, only the "malefactors of great wealth." In all, the government began 44 such antitrust actions during Roosevelt's administration, including suits against the Standard Oil Company, the American Tobacco Company, and the DuPont Company. Ironically, though known to history as the great trust-buster, Roosevelt never viewed antitrust suits as the final answer to business consolidation. His own preference, more and more, was for governmental regulation rather than dissolution. One step in this direction was taken in 1903 with the creation of a Bureau of Corporations to collect and publicize information about the business activities of great corporations.

Aside from the Northern Securities action, the most radical departure from past policy in TR's first term was his role in the great coal strike of 1902. The strike began in May when John Mitchell of the United Mine Workers led his union members out of the mines of northeastern Pennsylvania. The coal operators held firm as summer and fall passed. With winter coming on, the situation became desperate as the coal shortage grew acute. Public sympathy for the miners ran high, especially after the publication of a letter by George F. Baer, a leading spokesman for the operators, who warned that "The rights and interests of the laboring men will be protected and cared for not by the labor agitators, but by the Christian men to whom God in his infinite wisdom has given the control of the property interests of the country."

Roosevelt finally intervened. He summoned the coal-mine owners and Mitchell to the White House. Mitchell offered to submit the issue to arbitration but the operators refused. Instead they proposed that Roosevelt use troops against the strikers and end the work stoppage. Disgusted with the "arrogant stupidity" of the operators, the President toyed with the idea of seizing the coalfields. But a compromise was finally reached at the White House on October 13th between Roosevelt and representatives of J. P. Morgan, who agreed to put pressure on the operators. There was to be a commis-

sion of arbitration to include various interests excepting the union. When the operators proved adamant in their opposition to his appointing a union representative, Roosevelt designated the President of the Brotherhood of Railroad Conductors as the "eminent sociologist" called for in the original agreement. The commission subsequently awarded the miners a 10 per cent raise in pay and a reduction in working hours.

### "My Policies"

All during his first term, Roosevelt built his strength toward 1904 and the day he would be president in his own right. Gradually he asserted his control over the party machinery previously run by Mark Hanna in McKinley's interest. He built up his party following in the South through a wise use of the federal patronage and an appearance of championing the Negro, and he played his hand carefully in the key states of New York and Pennsylvania. By the early months of the critical election year, Roosevelt was in sure command. Then, his only rival, Hanna himself, died before the Republican convention met. The Democrats cooperated by naming a weak conservative, Judge Alton B. Parker of New York, as their candidate.

In selecting Parker, the Democrats were fishing for conservative votes. A brief but sharp financial panic in 1903 had caused some financial leaders to speculate publicly that Roosevelt's unfriendly policies toward business had provoked the slump. But the Democrats miscalculated. Far from attracting conservative votes, Parker's nomination only pushed a number of progressive Democrats into the Roosevelt camp. Election day found 7,623,000 Roosevelt supporters trooping to the polls versus 5,077,000 Parker voters. Indeed, every state outside the Solid South was Roosevelt's. Victory was complete. On election night, all his ambitions now realized, he issued a fateful statement: "Under no circumstances will I be a candidate for or accept another nomination."

In his second term, TR turned to problems of railroad rates and food adulteration, and spent much time in developing his conservation policies. On the first of these issues, he demanded of Congress effective rate regulation through the Interstate Commerce Commission. The Hepburn bill, introduced for this purpose, became deadlocked in the Senate, which was sharply divided between conservative and progressive Republicans. Senator Nelson W. Aldrich, leader of the conservatives, maneuvered to remove the teeth from the bill, which had the President's support. In particular, the conservatives sought broad powers for the courts to pass on the reasonableness of rates. After trying to line up a coalition of Democrats and progressive Republicans behind a strong bill, Roosevelt finally agreed to compromise. The Hepburn Act (1906) gave the ICC power over railroad rates when a shipper made complaint, but subjected the Commission's rulings to review by the courts. District courts might issue temporary injunctions halting the implementation of ICC decisions, but provision was made for speedy appeal to higher courts, where presumption was to be in favor of the ICC. This satisfied neither the progressives, who wanted much more power for the Commission, nor the conservatives who wanted no further regulation at all. Had Roosevelt not intervened, however, it is almost certain that no bill would have passed.

While the Senate was wrangling over the Hepburn bill, Upton Sinclair was writing *The Jungle*. Its publication gave a strong momentum to the efforts of Senators Beveridge, Hepburn, and others to get a food and drug act through Congress. TR read the book and according to Mr. Dooley he "suddenly . . . rose from th' table, an' cryin': 'I'm pizened,'

began throwin' sausages out iv th' window." He ordered a new investigation of the meatpacking industry and held the resulting "hideous" report over the heads of recalcitrant Congressmen. When Congress failed to move swiftly enough, he released part of the report. Hesitation now gave way to haste and Congress quickly approved the Pure Food and Drug Act (1906) and, a week later, the Meat Inspection Act. The former measure was directed against the sale of adulterated, misbranded, or dangerous foods and drugs, while the meatpacking law required that federal inspectors enforce sanitary standards in the slaughter houses.

Less dramatic but much more important was Roosevelt's leadership of the conservation movement. During his two terms in office he set aside almost 150 million acres of public timber land in the states and some 85 million acres of mineral lands in Alaska, supported reclamation and irrigation projects, created forest reserves and national parks, and made possible the great Roosevelt Dam in Arizona. He backed the Newlands Act (1902), which provided that revenue from western land sales should go toward the building of dams and irrigation projects. He withdrew numerous waterpower sites from public sale or lease and vetoed a bill that would have granted to private interests the right to exploit the power potentialities at Muscle Shoals, Alabama, the future site of TVA. He spoke out constantly, too, on the need to conserve the nation's forest resources, to prevent the depletion of valuable mineral deposits, and to protect the fertility of the soil. "We are prone to speak of the resources of this country as inexhaustible," he warned Congress in 1907, [but] this is not so. The mineral wealth of the country, the coal, iron, oil, gas, and the like, does not reproduce itself . . . and wastefulness in dealing with it today means that our descendants will feel the exhaustion a generation or two before they otherwise would." Other forms of waste, he advised, could be stopped entirely, especially the loss of topsoil through erosion, and the denuding of the nation's forests through failure to preserve or replace this great resource.

In 1908 he called a conference of governors, congressmen, cabinet members, and Supreme Court justices to review the work of conservation and to plan for the future. Out of this conference came 36 state conservation commissions, a federal conservation commission, and a pledge to halt the plunder of America's great natural wealth. This work of Roosevelt's in conserving America's natural resources was in many ways his most significant and enduring contribution to the nation.

Roosevelt's last two years in the White House were marked by stormy controversy. His conservation program exasperated a number of westerners who had been profiting from the lax policies governing the national domain. His battle for simplified spelling in the government departments, for all its comic aspects, stirred some heated opposition. His discharge of three companies of Negro soldiers who refused to inform on a fellow soldier who had killed a citizen of Brownsville, Texas, provoked a hornet's nest of criticism. But the greatest controversy was aroused by his increasingly outspoken progressivism as the time came nearer for him to return to private life. He assailed the business community for intensifying the financial panic of 1907 in order to lay the blame for it at his door, when the government had actually cooperated closely with Morgan in staving off disaster on Wall Street, although the President had refused to make a conciliatory statement of his intentions "just for the effect on the stock market." His messages to Congress in December, 1907, and the following month were the most radical of his entire administration. In them he seemed to reflect the growing dominance of the reform spirit in all areas of American life. They foreshadowed the coming conflicts of the Taft and Wilson era in demands for an income tax, a postal savings system, an end to the free use of injunctions against labor unions, and national controls over big business and the stock market. His tone and language grew increasingly bitter as he turned on concentrated wealth and its guardians in the courts. More and more, he aligned himself with the progressives in their drive to capture the Republican party for the cause of reform. As a result, he left a party and a Congress hopelessly divided by controversy he had sown. And his chosen successor, William Howard Taft of Ohio, would reap the harvest.

## TAFT AND THE GREAT SCHISM

Two men more unlike than Roosevelt and Taft would be hard to conceive. No man enjoyed the presidency more than TR; few laid down its burdens with greater relief than Taft. By nature Roosevelt was restless, impulsive, fun-loving, and enamored of attention and the limelight; Taft was retiring, reflective, serious, and apprehensive of the public spectacles that politics demands. "I should like to have stayed on in the Presidency," TR wrote in 1908, "and I make no pretense that I am glad to be relieved of my official duties." Taft's mother, on the other hand, accurately appraised her son's feelings about public life when she predicted in a letter to him in 1907 that "the malice of politics [will] make you miserable."

In choosing Taft, Roosevelt had passed over Elihu Root, who he felt was too closely tied to Wall Street, and Charles

Evans Hughes, whom Roosevelt seems not to have liked. Like Root, Taft had been a member of the Roosevelt cabinet as Secretary of War, after being the first governor of the Philippine Islands. Despite his conservatism and love of the judiciary, Taft was regarded by Roosevelt as the man most likely to carry on "my policies." His Democratic opponent in 1908 was William Jennings Bryan, destined for a third time to see the presidency elude his grasp. As the campaign warmed up, Roosevelt urged Taft on— "Do not *answer* Bryan; attack him!"— but partisanship came hard for Taft. Fortunately it was not really needed. Bryan's campaign faltered well before the end and Taft won handily in November, though his margin was only half that of Roosevelt's in 1904.

### Year of Trouble

The outcome showed one disturbing sign. The Democrats had registered significant gains along with the progressive Midwestern wing of the Republican party. This promised trouble for Taft, and it was not long in making its appearance. Both Democrats and progressive Republicans were committed to a downward revision of the tariff, which the Republican platform of 1908 seemed to promise, and to breaking the dictatorial grip of speaker Joe Cannon over the legislative machinery of the House of Representatives. Taft was known to be in sympathy with both these objectives. Yet after Taft had called Congress into special session to revise the tariff, he gave confusing signals to his lieutenants on Capitol Hill and complacently signed the resulting Payne-Aldrich bill (1909), which actually raised duties on hundreds of commodities. The Old Guard, shrewdly led by Senator Aldrich, had won the day. The bill included a pioneering one per cent tax on corporation profits and added hides, sea moss, hog bristles, canary bird seed, and other items—"prac-

tically ivrything nicissry to existence," said Mr. Dooley—to the free list. To make matters worse, Taft defended the bill publicly, even going so far as to call it, in a speech at Winona, Minnesota, "the best tariff act" ever passed.

Taft grew closer to Aldrich and softened his attitude toward Cannon at the very time that progressive fury was rising against the President's failure to lead in the tariff debate. In March, 1910, George Norris of Nebraska, at the head of a combination of Democrats and Republican insurgents, staged a revolt against "Cannonism." Once more, Taft deserted the progressives, though he had written privately of his hostility to Cannon and what he stood for. In heated, lengthy sessions, Norris's forces stripped away Cannon's power to appoint the all-important Rules Committee and with it the ability to decide what bills might come before the House. Standpat conservatism had lost an important fortress and sentiment was hardening against Taft.

The most violent quarrel of Taft's troubled first year in the White House concerned conservation. It centered on the policies of Taft's Secretary of the Interior, Richard A. Ballinger. Convinced that TR had stretched the law in withdrawing from private exploitation a large number of waterpower sites in the Northwest, Ballinger returned over a million acres of land to the public domain. Certain coal lands in Alaska, in which the Morgan-Guggenheim syndicate was interested, were also turned back for possible private use. Roosevelt's champions, notably Gifford Pinchot, Chief of the Forestry Bureau, rose in indignation at this apparent reversal of their former chief's policies. Pinchot publicly accused Ballinger of conspiring with Morgan, Guggenheim, and other interests to overthrow Roosevelt's conservation policies. In the ensuing contretemps Taft upheld Ballinger and dismissed Pinchot. Though a Congressional investigation conducted by a committee friendly to the Administration cleared Ballinger of charges of corruption, the odor of "give-away" hung over the transactions. And although historians have since testified to Taft's support of the conservation movement and Ballinger's innocence of the insurgents' charges, the incident contributed heavily to the growing rift between Taft and the progressives, many of whom looked forward with eager expectancy to Roosevelt's return from an extended hunting trip in Africa.

For all the progressive attacks, however, Taft was no hidebound reactionary. His blunders arose as much from mistakes of political strategy and a personal disinclination to lead as from blind opposition to reform. He broke more trusts than Roosevelt, supported the move to strengthen the Hepburn Act, proposed the strategy that led to the adoption of the income tax amendment, backed the creation of a postal savings system, and achieved a number of lesser progressive reforms between 1910 and 1913. But these gains were not enough. Powerful forces were driving for more sweeping change, dividing the Republican party, and pointing toward 1912 as the most crucial election year since 1896.

### The Conquering Hero Returns

"It is hard to bring back the sense of excitement, almost of tumult, that was in the air over this land in the summer and autumn of 1910," William Allen White wrote years later. "It was revolutionary." From the moment TR left the jungle, the finger of fate nudged him back into the center of controversy. Pinchot rushed to meet him in Italy, carrying letters from insurgent Republicans denouncing the President. Even before he reached home, Root had advised him personally of the political situation, and he had a letter from Taft charging the insurgents with seeking to disrupt the party. "I have had a hard time," Taft complained to his former chief, "I do not know that I have had harder luck than other Presidents, but I do know that thus far I have succeeded far less than have others."

If Roosevelt had been less volatile, it would have been difficult for him to stay out of the battle-royal that was shaping up; as he was, it was inevitable that he was drawn in. After trying hard to heal the breach in his party, he gradually abandoned the position of impartiality. He received most of Taft's enemies at Oyster Bay while refusing an invitation to come to the White House. He allowed himself to become embroiled in the New York primary, then journeyed into the South and West during the summer and fall of 1910. At Osawatomie, Kansas, he embraced the philosophy of the "New Nationalism" preached by Herbert Croly in *The Promise of American Life* (1909) and adumbrated in his own last messages as President. The New Nationalism was a call for positive government in the national interest. Since laissez faire was outmoded, federal power must be used to regulate corporate power, tax wealth, protect the nation's resources, and restore sovereignty to the people. "The National Government belongs to the whole American people," TR asserted, "and where the whole American people are interested, that interest can be guarded effectively only by the National Government." Finally, as the provocations and pressures to declare his intentions mounted, Roosevelt announced in February, 1912, that he would be a candidate for President once more.

### Crossroads: 1912

The rupture of the Republican Party was complete. The insurgents, now dominant throughout the West, vowed not to accept Taft again in

1912; the eastern conservatives would have no one else. But the breakup was even more complex. For a while, before Roosevelt's intentions were clear, many progressives had pushed LaFollette for the nomination; now he was deserted by all but a handful, leaving intense bitterness in the LaFollette camp. Roosevelt fought desperately in the primaries, his only hope for the nomination, and swept to victory in state after state, including Taft's home state of Ohio. In all, he won more than 75 per cent of the delegates in the states where Republicans had a chance to elect their representatives. But to no avail. Taft controlled the big eastern delegations, the patronage-fed southern deputies, and the strategic National Committee which organized the convention. Impotent, Roosevelt watched the convention's deliberations with mounting rage, castigating the "saturnalia of fraud and larceny" as the "doomed and passion-drunk" credentials committee awarded the contested seats to Taft men. Humiliated by impending defeat, he and his followers bolted the convention and announced plans for an independent party.

The Progressive Party convention of 1912 was fired with a religious passion. Senator Beveridge, the keynoter, rang all the changes on the now familiar progressive themes. His perfervid oration ended with the whispered words, "Mine eyes have seen the glory of the coming of the Lord." The convention responded with the moving stanzas of the *Battle Hymn of the Republic*. Roosevelt himself took the platform to deliver a "Confession of Faith" aimed at all directions of liberal and radical support. Gesturing vigorously, he went down a long list of changes he advocated: women's suffrage, the direct election of senators, preferential presidential primaries, the initiative and referendum, a national commission to regulate all interstate business, tariff reform and a permanent tariff commission, minimum wages and maximum hours, unemployment insurance, old age pensions, and, most radical of all, the recall of judicial decisions. He closed with the ringing challenge: "We stand at Armageddon and battle for the Lord!"

The Democrats met in more hopeful if less heated temper. After all, Roosevelt's bolt virtually threw the election into their lap. The leading contenders for the nomination were Woodrow Wilson, the reform governor of New Jersey, and Champ Clark of Missouri, Speaker of the House of Representatives. Wilson had worked hard for the nomination, traveling, speaking, planning, while Clark had done little to advance his candidacy. But Clark enjoyed the support of most of Bryan's old following in the Middle and Far West and had come off well in the primaries and state conventions. By convention time he had some 436 delegates pledged to him against 248 for Wilson; in addition, Oscar Underwood, Congressman from Alabama, bit deeply into Wilson's Southern support. The irrepressible Bryan proposed at the outset that no candidate be named who was subservient to "J. P. Morgan, Thomas Fortune Ryan, August Belmont, or any member of the privilege-hunting and favor-seeking class." Not unexpectedly, the early balloting went in Clark's favor. Already in the lead, he seemed on the verge of victory when the Tammany boss, Charles Murphy, brought New York's heavy vote into Clark's column. At that point he had a majority of convention votes but not yet the two-thirds required for nomination. Then the tide turned to Wilson. Bryan himself went over on the fourteenth ballot. But it was Wilson's successful courting of the Underwood bloc and the big Northern delegations that ultimately brought him victory.

Taft surrendered early in the campaign. The real fight was between Roosevelt and Wilson for the progressive vote. To Roosevelt's New Nationalism Wilson opposed his New Freedom, promising a return to Jeffersonian individualism and equality of opportunity. Fortified by the arguments of Louis D. Brandeis, lawyer and champion of small business, Wilson struck hard at Roosevelt's proposals for federal control of corporations. All semblance of privilege, he argued, must be destroyed; businessmen must be forced to be efficient and competitive; monopolies could not grow without government aid or collusion. Reduce the tariff, break up the monster trusts, and there would be no need for federal regulation. "Consciously or unconsciously," Wilson was to tell Congress later, "we have built up a set of privileges and exemptions from competition behind which it is easy for any, even the crudest, forms of combination to organize monopoly. . . ." In contrast, Roosevelt continued to believe that the best way to deal with monopoly was to regulate it by federal action before it grew too powerful. He advocated with his customary vigor a federal commission to control and regulate all big combinations, by advising them of illegal practices before they committed them, by moving swiftly against all infringements of the law, and by encouraging honest businesses regardless of size. "Draw the line on conduct and not on size" would be a fair summary of Roosevelt's position.

Wilson also assailed Roosevelt's strong stand on behalf of federal social legislation. He ridiculed the reforms called for by Roosevelt as "paternalistic" and "collectivist." Yet Wilson's own reform record in New Jersey and his attitude toward monopoly and special privilege stamped

him as a progressive. More and more, as the campaign wore on, Wilson identified his own interests with the rank and file of the people, clothing his principles in the most moving language heard in American political life since Lincoln.

## 1912 Election

| | Popular Vote | Electoral Vote |
|---|---|---|
| Wilson (D) | 6,293,454 | 435 |
| Taft (R) | 3,484,980 | 8 |
| Roosevelt (P) | 4,119,538 | 88 |
| Other | 1,135,697 | 0 |

Since all the candidates—Wilson, Roosevelt, Taft, and Debs, the Socialist—were, in fact, progressive by comparison with Cleveland or McKinley, the outcome was a revelation of the extent of the progressive revolt since 1900. Wilson won 6,293,454 votes, Roosevelt 4,119,538, Taft 3,484,980, and Debs 897,011. Roosevelt captured the Republican progressives but Wilson held on to the progressives in his party; some deserted both for Debs. Taft explained that "I got . . . the irreducible minimum of the Republican party that was left after Roosevelt got through with it. . . ." Wilson was a minority president, despite his overwhelming electoral victory, and his political future like that of his party hung on what he would do in the next four years.

# WILSON AND THE NEW FREEDOM

## Roundsman of the Lord

The new President's personality was scarcely less complex than Roosevelt's. Cold and reserved on the outside, he burned within with an intense conviction and a firm sense of purpose. A Calvinistic feeling of duty and moral righteousness flowed early into his life—there were Presbyterian ministers on both sides of his family—and endowed his character and bearing with a hard, granitic quality. Men never loved Wilson as they loved the ebullient TR, yet they followed him in places where Roosevelt could not have taken them. He radiated strength, conviction, certainty. He clung to his convictions and ideals with a stubborn tenacity that infuriated friends as well as foes. No president was ever more sure of himself, none less willing to compromise his principles or tolerate basic disagreement. Intuition rather than logic guided his thought processes, and argument could not dent a conviction based on moral feeling. "With him," wrote Robert Lansing in his diary, "it was a matter of conviction formed without weighing evidence and without going through the process of rational deduction. His judgments were always right in his own mind, because he knew that they were right. How did he know that they were right? Why he *knew* it and that was the best reason in the world. No other was necessary."

Wilson's star had risen rapidly. Virginia-born, he grew up in the Reconstruction South, graduated from Princeton, tried law, and then took a doctoral degree in history and political science at The Johns Hopkins University. After teaching briefly at Bryn Mawr College and Wesleyan University, he went to Princeton in 1890, where he gained fame as an outstanding teacher and scholar. In 1902 he became president of Princeton and immediately launched a series of reforms that caught the eyes of educators all over the nation. Two of his reforms ended disastrously, yet sharpened the image of Wilson as a spokesman for democratic aspirations. The first was a proposal to abolish Princeton's exclusive eating clubs and substitute a quadrangle system of colleges where students might eat and work together. Wilson went down to defeat amid a storm of alumni and faculty protest. His second humiliation came after a bitter struggle over the site and administrative control of a proposed graduate college. Wilson wanted the college located near the center of university life and under his personal control. But his chief opponent, Dean Andrew F. West, won the day for his own view of a graduate college peripherally located under his own direction. West's victory was made possible by Wilson's obstinacy, his refusal to compromise, and the Dean's own ability to raise money for the kind of school he wanted. The behavior of Wilson in this academic quarrel gave a foretaste of what he would do in his later political career.

He welcomed the opportunity to escape from his dilemma at Princeton to the larger world of politics. Offered the nomination for the governorship by the Democratic machine in New Jersey, Wilson accepted, then turned on the bosses. As at Princeton, he began with a hurricane of activity, reorganizing the statehouse, supporting direct primaries to end the boss system, getting public-utilities legislation enacted, and fighting for protective labor laws. Then, as opposition mounted, Wilson's campaign slowed; once more he showed his inability to work with men whose personal loyalty to him was not complete. Indeed, he reached the nadir of his career in Jersey politics shortly before the Baltimore convention offered him new opportunities for service to his ideals.

## Battles with Congress, 1913-1914

Wilson's view of the presidency, like Roosevelt's, was a larger one than that which had prevailed since Reconstruction days. The president, Roosevelt had said, was a "steward of the people," bound to do all he could for the people within broad constitutional and legislative limits. Wilson, too, had written of the president's office as "anything he has the sagacity and force to make it." A strong president must be a strong party leader, managing Congress in the interest of the whole people. For he alone spoke for the nation. And his ultimate strength was the people, whose champion he was. Wilson's own faith in the people was complete, an enduring source of strength during his White House years.

The wall between president and Congress, Wilson had said in his first and best-known book, *Congressional Government* (1885), must come down if the American system was to work effectively. As president, he sought to accomplish this through frequent meetings with congressional leaders, personal representatives on Capitol Hill, and special messages to Congress. He broke precedent by becoming the first president since John Adams to address the Congress in person. He demanded and usually got party responsibility. He sought to lead his party and, through his party, the Congress and nation. "The offices of President and Vice-

President," said Wilson in his eloquent inaugural address, "have been put into the hands of Democrats. What does the change mean? . . . The success of a party means little except when the Nation is using that party for a large and definite purpose."

No one could mistake, Wilson declared, the purposes for which the Nation was using the Democratic Party. The people must be freed from the domination of the special interests. Tariff duties must come down and business made to compete once more; the antiquated banking and currency system must be overhauled, new antitrust laws passed, and conservation measures extended. Government must be put at the service of humanity in protecting the victims of great industrial and social processes. "The Nation has been deeply stirred," Wilson said in describing the progressive mood, "stirred by a solemn passion, stirred by the knowledge of wrong, of ideals lost, of government too often debauched and made an instrument of evil. The feelings with which we face this new age of right and opportunity sweep across our heartstrings like some air out of God's own presence, where justice and mercy are reconciled and the judge and the brother are one."

The "new age of right" began with a special session of Congress called to deal with the tariff. Wilson was at the peak of his influence and effectiveness as he molded public opinion and pressured congressmen toward the goal of downward revision. Taft had failed to exercise leadership in his tariff fight and had thereby disrupted his party; Wilson commanded his forces from first to last and emerged from his battle with a united, stronger party. He met frequently with his lieutenants, wrote to wavering congressmen, appealed to party loyalty, and worked incessantly to keep his Democratic majority united behind the bill introduced by Oscar Underwood in the House. The bill passed the House but ran into trouble in the Senate. Again he urged his followers to stand firm, especially those from the wool and sugar states, who were under tremendous pressures from interests at home to exempt these commodities from the free list. Confident of victory, Wilson refused to compromise and struck out instead at the many lobbyists who had flocked to Washington to convert their representatives. "Washington has seldom seen so numerous, so industrious, or so insidious a lobby," the President declared, yet the people at large had no lobby except their senators and representatives. Wilson's victory was overwhelming. The Underwood-Simmons Act lowered duties to 29 per cent from an average of 40 per cent under the Payne-Aldrich tariff of 1909 and added a long list of important commodities to the free list. To replace the loss in customs revenue, the first income tax under the Sixteenth Amendment was imposed, calling for a one per cent tax on all incomes over $4,000, with the surtax rising to 3 per cent on incomes over $100,000. The income tax was the symbol of a new age, in which wealth was coming to be viewed as a social as well as an individual product.

A tired Congress groaned at the news that Wilson wanted it to stay in special session to consider his plan for banking reform. Few denied the need for change, though, for the banking problem was old and infinitely difficult. Currency was notoriously inelastic; it piled up in New York and other eastern cities when unneeded, and flowed out seasonally to pay for western grain or cattle. Bank reserves were often immobile; only a J. P. Morgan could rescue the financial world from its recurrent panics and even he was not omnipotent. Everyone agreed that more central direction, more governmental control was needed. But how

much? The extreme progressives wanted complete federal control over banking and currency, whereas conservatives and banking interests favored a large measure of private direction. The Aldrich plan, approved by the American Bankers' Association, called for one great national bank with branches spread about the country. Though government would be represented, the direction of the system would rest essentially with private bankers. Wilson took his stand behind the proposals of Congressman Carter Glass of Virginia for a decentralized system of reserve banks, controlled by member banks, but subject to general supervision by a national board. Progressive Democrats, Bryan at their helm, would have none of the Glass bill, which they saw as a surrender to the private banking interests. Wilson finally arranged a compromise: a decentralized Federal Reserve system with a supervisory Federal Reserve Board to be appointed by the government. After a final round of skirmishes and amendments, the Federal Reserve bill became law two days before Christmas. It was probably the most important law passed in the Wilson administration. Indeed, its fundamental plan—twelve Federal Reserve banks, controlled by private interests, yet closely supervised by the government-appointed Federal Reserve Board—became the basic design of the American banking structure.

All through 1914 Congress and the administration wrestled with the third major plank of the New Freedom: the promise to deal effectively with big business. Much of Wilson's campaign had hung on his pledge to crush monopoly and restore competition. Most Democrats thought that the Sherman Act needed only to be amended and clarified. But how could this be done without incurring progressive charges of naïveté? Wilson's answer was the Clayton bill, named for the chairman of the House Judiciary

Committee, which specified unfair trade practices and banned interlocking directorates. A separate bill provided for a new trade commission to replace Roosevelt's Bureau of Corporations and to gather information for antitrust actions. A long period of turmoil and controversy followed the introduction of the Clayton bill. Labor was particularly aroused by Wilson's failure to include a specific exemption of unions from antitrust suits. Under pressure Wilson made some concessions but not enough to satisfy the labor leaders. The final version of the Clayton Act held that labor was not to be considered a commodity and that antitrust laws did not outlaw unions. But it stopped short of labor's demand for an end to employers' use of injunctions against unions. Nevertheless, Gompers hailed the Act as labor's "Magna Charta."

Sometime during the debate over the Clayton bill, Wilson seems to have grasped for the first time the strength of the old Roosevelt arguments for a powerful trade commission to advise and regulate rather than destroy the great corporations. He now backed the creation of a stronger Federal Trade Commission, which was empowered to issue "cease and desist" orders to any firm found guilty of unfair methods of competition as defined in the Clayton Act. Under heavy pressure, this bill passed while the Clayton bill was allowed to flounder in the Senate, assailed by a series of weakening amendments. As finally passed, the Clayton Act banned unfair competition (especially interlocking directorates), the acquisition of a competing firm's stock, and price discrimination, but the language and force of the original bill were gone.

## Farewell to Reform

The reform impulse grew feeble toward the end of 1914. Wilson's own indecision and the outbreak of war in Europe slowed the feverish tempo of change. The president did sign the Smith-Lever Act (1914), which provided federal support for agricultural education, and approved without much enthusiasm the LaFollette seamen's bill (1915), which established new safety standards for maritime vessels and freed sailors entering American ports from bondage to labor contracts. But the strong leadership he had given the reform movement in his early months of office seemed lacking. He seems for a while to have regarded the progressive goals as fulfilled by the legislation of his first eighteen months in office. At the state level by 1914, a large part of the progressive program had been enacted and the Sixteenth and Seventeenth Amendments had been approved.

But progressivism was to have one last gasp before being submerged in the concerns of war and its aftermath. This last bundle of reform measures was a response to the multiple pressures of a new political campaign, the mounting defense emergency, and Wilson's own change in thinking since 1912. Wilson had never abandoned the laissez-faire postulates which guided his debate with Roosevelt, and he had pointedly ignored progressive demands for federal social measures. He now reversed himself. With his support, Congress pushed through in 1916 the long-blocked plan for a system of federal farm-loan banks, adopted a workmen's compensation law for federal employees, and embraced the Keating-Owen federal child-labor statute. Further, to stave off a threatened railroad strike in a time of national emergency, Wilson backed legislation calling for an eight-hour day for railroad workers and for the right to force railroads to operate their trains for defense purposes. The Adamson Act, approved in early September, 1916, went part-way with Wilson in granting the eight-hour day, but it established a commission to consider the rest of the railroad problem. Finally, in 1917, he signed the Smith-Hughes Act, which gave new impetus to vocational education in the nation's schools.

The ebbing of progressivism left the domestic scene quiet after more than a decade of continual excitement. A procession of strong and colorful leaders—Wilson, Roosevelt, LaFollette, Bryan—had dramatized on the national stage the deep and confused yearnings of a people responding to great social change. The problems they faced were complex and insistent. To say that these leaders were ineffective, or superficial, or moralistic in their solutions is to miss the real significance of the movement they led. Their reforms were deliberately superficial because they believed deeply in the rightness of the American system; their approach was moral because they knew no other way to give meaning to their protests. That they were often ineffective seems clear in retrospect. Their reforms did not stop the growth of business combination nor wipe out the stain of polit-ical corruption; their regulatory commissions were often staffed with men out of sympathy with progressive objectives; and their social vision did not extend equally to all groups in the population. But they did demonstrate that business could be regulated by the government, that good laws might lighten the burdens of those most adversely affected by industrialism, and that morality and conscience still counted for something in even a bureaucratic age. The progressive movement, moreover, brought a sharp and revealing reversal in business attitudes. Thrown on the defensive then, business leaders have ever since concerned themselves with public opinion and offered concessions to employees and the community without always being forced to it. A socially responsible capitalism was born in the progressive age, an age that finally saw the advent of the positive state in America. By the close of the era, most Americans were convinced that strong government was not an evil if used wisely for the public good.

## PROGRESSIVE AMERICA, 1900–1914

During all these years of progressive excitement, important changes were taking place in the social scene as well. If the world of business and politics was in constant turmoil in the first decade and a half of the twentieth century, so were the everyday lives of millions of Americans. For the Americans who lived through the Progressive Era were a growing, mobile, and prosperous people. The population soared from 76 to 92 million in the decade after 1900 and probably reached 100 million by 1915. Of this last number, one in ten was a Negro, one in seven was born in a foreign country, and one in two lived in a community of 2500 persons or more. Most were relatively prosperous, as even farmers saw their produce double in value since the dark days of the nineties.

### Still on the Move

But there were fewer farmers to enjoy the unprecedented prosperity. The mechanization of farm life, the temptation of high prices for land, and the lure of the city combined to draw many farm folk out of the countryside. Iowa, for instance, suffered an absolute drop in population in the first decade of the century. The move to the cities seemed irresistible. Urban population rose 39 per cent between 1900 and 1910 compared with a 9 per cent increase in rural places. Immigrants continued to flock into the eastern cities, more and more of them from southern and eastern Europe. In the first decade of the twentieth century, over six million came from this part of Europe compared with less than two million from the old sources. According to the census of 1910, more than a million foreign-born Italians and a similar number of Russians were residents of the United States.

Americans were still on the move. In general, the population movements of the era were from town to city, from east to west, and from south to north. The westward movement, despite the end of the old frontier, was by no means dead. Over five million Americans born east of the Mississippi River were living west of it in 1910, the new states in the Southwest, along with California, showing the greatest increase. The immigration northward was largely a response of Southern Negroes to local pressures and beckoning opportunities. Over a million Negroes lived in the northeastern and north central states before World War I and this figure rose sharply with the increase in wartime jobs. Most of the Negro migrants headed for jobs in industrial cities, particularly New York, Chicago, and Detroit.

### The Color Line

They left behind them a South where the caste boundary between the races was hardening into seemingly final rigidity. Negro inferiority was the assumption lying under the strict etiquette of race relations that banned Negroes from any contact with whites except in a servile capacity. Streetcars, restaurants, hotels, parks, bathing beaches, and railroad stations were now required by law to discriminate between the races. The ballot was wrenched away from the Negro in state after state through literacy tests, poll taxes, and outright intimidation. A thousand lynchings between 1900 and 1914 warned the Negro of the price of violating racial taboos.

Little room was made for Negro rights under the progressive banner. Many progressives were white Southerners; under their influence, Wilson's administration markedly extended segregation in the federal offices. And those progressives who did speak out would normally endorse the efforts of Booker T. Washington to win Negro acquiescence to the social pattern of the dominant whites. Born a slave, Washington had raised himself by heroic efforts to the leadership of his race. He had won over the South to his program of industrial and practical education for Negroes at Tuskegee Institute, which he founded in 1881. To the Negro he preached the need to become useful to the whites, thereby winning good will and support from the dominant race. In Atlanta he made a famous speech at the Cotton States Exposition in 1895, expressing his love for the South and his understanding of its customs. He renounced northern support and asserted that "reforms in the South are to come from within." The Negro, he assured his white listeners, was more concerned with economic opportunities than with political or social privileges.

This counsel of acquiescence, sometimes called the "Atlanta Compromise," told Negroes in effect to make the best of a situation they could not change. It appealed to the leaders of the New South, who needed a supply of docile semiskilled workers, and to conservatives who looked back to the untroubled race relations of antebellum days. It did not appeal to young W. E. Burghart DuBois, a brilliant Negro graduate of Harvard, who was winning acclaim as a scholar and writer. He assailed Washington's program for creating "a voteless herd to run the machines and wash the dishes for the new aristocracy. Negroes would be educated enough to be useful but not enough, or not in the right way, to be able to assert self-respect." At Niagara Falls, in 1905, DuBois launched a drive for Negro rights among Negro leaders, and the following year a conference was held at Harper's Ferry in West Virginia. "We shall not be satisfied with less than our full manhood rights," read the manifesto from the scene of John Brown's raid. "We want our manhood suffrage and we want it now. Second, we want discrimination in public accommodations to cease. Third, we claim the right to associate with such people as wish to associate with us." DuBois's campaign struck a spark in the North among liberal whites, especially after a bloody race riot in Springfield, Illinois, less than a block from Lincoln's home. These liberals now joined with DuBois and some of his associates in the Niagara Movement to create the National Association for the Advancement of Colored People in 1909. The new organization, with DuBois as editor of its journal and director of publicity, now began an intensive campaign against lynching, segregation, and the disfranchisement of the Negro. Significantly, the N.A.A.C.P. took the position that these suppressive tactics were not Negro but American problems.

## Signs of the Modern Age

To the average citizen, white or Negro, who lived through the progressive years, the most momentous changes affecting his daily existence seemed far away from the world of politics and social conflict. Neither civil rights, nor progressive politics, nor direct democracy, but a far-reaching scientific and technological revolution had the most to do with upsetting the time-worn routines and expectations of everyday life. Modern medicine was born in the half-century ending in 1900 and a host of new

medical discoveries and events competed for the public's attention. At the end of the century came sensational reports from France of the work of Pasteur in developing immunization against hydrophobia and anthrax, from Germany of Koch's discovery of the bacillus of tuberculosis, and from England of the brilliant antiseptic surgery of Joseph Lister and his school. The "reign of the microbes" had begun. Between 1880 and 1900 the germs responsible for diphtheria, bubonic plague, typhoid fever, cholera, and dozens of other diseases were identified. These rapid-fire events inspired a tremendous burst of pioneering in surgery, provided a new and broader basis for public health work, and opened up a new world of protection against illness through immunization. In America, by World War I, most infectious diseases had been brought under control, Walter Reed and the Yellow Fever Commission had performed their brilliant mission in Cuba, and the Rockefeller Commission had largely succeeded in eradicating hookworm in the southern states. In addition, American medical education, long backward by European standards, was immensely stimulated by the example of The Johns Hopkins University in founding a quality school and by the influential report of Abraham Flexner on medical schools given to the Carnegie Foundation for the Advancement of Teaching in 1910.

In this era, the average American's life was affected by hundreds of new inventions that altered his diet, habits, amusements, transportation, and communication. The telephone came into common use in the Progressive Era. Invented by Alexander Graham Bell in 1876, it was still a luxury confined to 1,355,900 homes and businesses in 1900. Fifteen years later more than nine million telephones were in use in the American Telephone and Telegraph Company's system alone. The motion picture was also developed during the progressive period. From being merely a popular novelty at the beginning of the century, the motion picture moved into the nickelodeon and finally the movie palace in these years. By World War I, Hollywood had produced *The Birth of a Nation* at a cost of $100,000, and such stars as Tom Mix, Mary Pickford, and Pearl White were known to millions of movie-goers.

Automobiles and airplanes, however, still belonged more in the category of daredevil amusements than means of transportation during much of the progressive period. Learned scientists were still debating whether an airship was possible in 1903 when Orville Wright lay down in his starched collar and business suit to make the first powered flight at Kitty Hawk, North Carolina. "NO BALLOON ATTACHED TO AID IT" read the explanatory headline of the event in the Norfolk *Virginian-Pilot,* the only newspaper to learn of it. Five years later the world was still ignorant of the existence, let alone the significance, of the Wrights' flying machine. Then a secret observer, who witnessed one of the Wright brothers' flights, wrote that "we were paralyzed and dumb with the wonder of it all. It is something that few mortals had believed to be within the scope of possibility. . . . There was something weird, almost uncanny, about the whole thing. Here on this lonely beach was being performed the greatest act of the ages, but there were no spectators and no applause save the booming of the surf and the startled cries of the sea birds." The reporter scurried back to break the news to the world, toning it down as he knew he would be accused of fakery. Yet,

Wright bi-plane in flight. The first successful motor-driven airplane was tested on December 17, 1903, at Kitty Hawk, North Carolina, by the Wright Brothers. The longest of four free flights lasted 59 seconds and attained a speed of 30 miles per hour. (Brown Brothers.)

by World War I, the airplane was sufficiently developed to be used in aerial bombardment and spectacular mid-air dogfights. The realization of its commercial possibilities, however, still lay a decade or more in the future.

The automobile, though familiar on some city streets in 1900, was still regarded as a badge of wealth and sporting instinct. As late as 1907 Wilson referred to motoring as "a picture of the arrogance of wealth, with all its independence and carelessness." It was Henry Ford who put the automobile within reach of the middle classes and ultimately of the laboring man. A half-million Fords, largely the famous Model-T, had rolled off his assembly line by 1912. In all, more than a million cars were registered by 1913, over half of them foreign-made. The Lincoln Highway Association was formed that same year to work for "a continuous improved highway from the Atlantic to the Pacific, open to lawful traffic of all description without toll charges." Roads were still incredibly bad, and night and winter driving were dared only in emergencies. But the basic advances had been made by 1914: automatic assembly, interchangeable parts, improved tires, electric headlights, and especially the self-starter. Probably no invention in history has ever been improved so rapidly as was the automobile during the years from 1900 to 1914. What the automobile has meant to every phase of modern life, no man or woman living in the 1960's will need to be told.

## FOR FURTHER STUDY

*The books by Cochran and Miller, Goldman, Hays, Hofstadter, Nye, and Woodward cited at the end of Chapter I continue to be especially useful for the topics dealt with in this chapter.*

### General Accounts

* F. Allen, *The Big Change* (New York: Harper, 1952). A delightfully written interpretation of the social and political transformation of America since 1900.

H. Faulkner, *The Decline of Laissez-Faire, 1897-1917* (New York: Rinehart, 1951). The most comprehensive history of the economic changes of the Progressive era.

————, *The Quest for Social Justice, 1898-1914* (New York: Macmillan, 1931). Deals with such topics as labor's growth, changes in transportation, women's and children's rights, religion, science, and recreation.

* L. Filler, *Crusaders for American Liberalism* (Yellow Springs, Ohio: The Antioch

* Starred books are available in paperbound editions.

Press, 1950). A new edition of a provocative treatment of the reformers of the Progressive Era.

A. Link, *Woodrow Wilson and the Progressive Era, 1910-1917* (New York: Harper, 1954). The best general account of these years.

G. Mowry, *The Era of Theodore Roosevelt, 1900-1912* (New York: Harper, 1958). An outstanding general introduction to the Progressive Era.

### Special Studies

J. Blum, *The Republican Roosevelt* (Cambridge: Harvard U., 1954). A brief but stimulating interpretation.

————, *Woodrow Wilson and the Politics of Morality* (Boston: Little, Brown, 1956). A succinct biography concentrating on Wilson's presidential years.

* M. Borden (ed.), *America's*

*Ten Greatest Presidents* (Chicago: Rand, McNally, 1961). Includes good essays on TR and Wilson.

J. Commons (ed.), *History of Labor in the United States*, 4 volumes (New York: Macmillan, 1918-1935). Volumes 3 and 4 of this work have not been surpassed for comprehensiveness of information on working conditions, labor legislation, and labor movements.

* J. Dewey, *The Child and the Curriculum* and *The School and Society* (Chicago: U. of Chicago Press, 1956). Bound together, these two Dewey classics have been reissued in inexpensive format.

C. Forcey, *The Crossroads of Liberalism* (New York: Oxford U. Press, 1961). A recent interpretation of the influence of the progressive ideologists Herbert Croly, Walter Weyl, and Walter Lippmann on the course of American liberalism from 1900 to 1925.

W. Harbaugh, *Power and Responsibility: the Life and Times of Theodore Roosevelt* (New York: Farrar, Straus and Cudahy, 1961). A first-rate political biography that is much more favorable to TR than Pringle is (see below).

* R. Hofstadter, *The American Political Tradition and the Men Who Made It* (New York: Knopf, 1948). The essays on Roosevelt and Wilson are perceptive.

C. Hopkins, *The Rise of the Social Gospel in American Protestantism, 1865-1915* (New Haven: Yale U. Press, 1940). The best coverage of this topic.

* R. LaFollette, *LaFollette's Autobiography* (Madison, Wisconsin: The Robert M. LaFollette Company, 1913). Personal narrative of a progressive leader.

R. Leopold, *Elihu Root and the Conservative Tradition* (Boston: Little, Brown, 1954). Chapter 4 portrays a conservative spokesman's reaction to the events of the progressive years.

A. Link, *Wilson: the Road to the White House* (Princeton: Princeton U. Press, 1947) and *The New Freedom* (1956). A superior political biography that carries Wilson's career to the fall of 1914 in these volumes.

* W. Lippmann, *Drift and Mastery* (New York: Mitchell Kennerley, 1914). A remarkably prophetic book by one of the original American minds of this century.

* W. Lord, *The Good Years* (New York: Harper, 1960). A superficial yet entertaining account of the years from 1900 to 1914.

C. Madison, *Leaders and Liberals in 20th Century America* (New York: Frederick Ungar Publishing Company, 1961). Contains perceptive essays on TR, Wilson, LaFollette, Brandeis, and Norris.

H. May, *The End of American Innocence* (New York: Knopf, 1959). Places the transition to the cultural outlook of our times in the years from 1912 to 1917.

A. Nevins, *Ford: The Times, the Man, the Company* (New York: Scribner's, 1954). The opening volume of a comprehensive, interpretive biography of Henry Ford and his times.

H. Pringle, *The Life and Times of William Howard Taft*, 2 volumes (New York: Farrar and Rinehart, 1939). This is the standard biography of Roosevelt's successor.

* ————, *Theodore Roosevelt* (New York: Harcourt, Brace, 1931). A Pulitzer Prize biography of Roosevelt.

M. Pusey, *Charles Evans Hughes*, 2 volumes (New York: Macmillan, 1951). Another Pulitzer winner dealing with the life of this reform governor, presidential nominee, and Supreme Court justice.

J. Rayback, *A History of American Labor* (New York: Macmillan, 1959). A recent general history of the labor movement in America.

C. Regier, *The Era of the Muckrakers* (Chapel Hill: U. of North Carolina Press, 1932). Still the fullest account of the muckraking movement.

* R. Robbins, *Our Landed Heritage* (Princeton: Princeton U. Press, 1942). The concluding section is an excellent summary of conservation issues and progress.

D. Shannon, *The Socialist Party of America* (New York: Macmillan, 1955). A survey of the origins and history of the Socialist Party in this century.

L. Steffens, *Autobiography* (New York: Harcourt, Brace, 1931) and * *The Shame of the Cities* (New York: Peter Smith, 1948). Indispensable sources for understanding the muckraking spirit.

M. Sullivan, *Our Times*, 6 volumes (New York: Scribner's, 1926-1935). Still a mine of information about the years from 1900 to 1925.

* H. Swados (ed.), *Years of Conscience* (New York: World, 1962). An excellent anthology of muckraking journalism.

* M. White, *Social Thought in America* (New York: Viking, 1949). The most stimulating treatment of intellectual progressivism. The paperbound edition (Beacon Press, 1957) has an interesting new preface and epilogue.

M. White, *The Autobiography of William Allen White* (New York: MacMillan, 1946). One of the very best introductions to the progressive temper.

## Fiction

* T. Dreiser, *The Financier* (New York: Harper, 1912). The story of Frank Cowperwood, gaudy and unscrupulous tycoon, whose career is modeled after that of the Chicago magnate Charles T. Yerkes.

D. Phillips, *The Plum Tree* (Indianapolis: Bobbs-Merrill, 1905). A lawyer becomes entangled with machine politics, reforms briefly, then plunges into a career as attorney for a power company which leads ultimately to a seat in the United States Senate and personal heartbreak.

* U. Sinclair, *The Jungle* (New York: Viking, 1946). Originally published in 1906, this was probably the most powerful novel of the progressive years.

## Films and Records

*Auto Biography* (Prudential Insurance Company, 29 minutes, sound, black and white). A documentary from television's "Twentieth Century" series on the origins and growth of the automobile industry.

*Awakening Social Consciousness* (National Educational Television, 29 minutes, sound, black and white). A discussion of the change from laissez faire to government regulation during the Progressive Era.

*The Innocent Years* (National Broadcasting Company, 54 minutes, sound, black and white). A superior documentary from the "Project 20" series on turn-of-the-century life in America down to World War I.

*The Times of Teddy Roosevelt* (Prudential Insurance Company, 29 minutes, sound, black and white). From the Prudential's "Twentieth Century" documentary series.

*Woodrow Wilson* (Prudential Insurance Company, 29 minutes, sound, black and white). Another good program from the "Twentieth Century" series.

1898-1914

# Confronting
# the Outer World

## CHAPTER THREE

Troops Landing at Daiquiri, Cuba, June, 1898.

THE MOOD OF THE TIMES

"If we are to be a really great people, we must strive in good faith to play a great part in the world. We cannot avoid meeting great issues. All that we can determine for ourselves is whether we shall meet them well or ill. In 1898 we could not help being brought face to face with the problem of war with Spain. All we could decide was whether we should shrink like cowards from the contest, or enter into it as beseemed a brave and high-spirited people; and, once in, whether failure or success should crown our banners. So it is now. We cannot avoid the responsibilities that confront us in Hawaii, Cuba, Porto Rico, and the Philippines. . . .

"The timid man, the lazy man, the man who distrusts his country, the over-civilized man, who has lost the great fighting, masterful virtues, the ignorant man, and the man of dull mind, whose soul is incapable of feeling the mighty life that thrills 'stern men with empires in their brains'—all these, of course, shrink from seeing the nation undertake its new duties; shrink from seeing us build a navy and an army adequate to our needs; shrink from seeing us do our share of the world's work, by bringing order out of chaos in the great, fair tropic islands from which the valor of our soldiers and sailors has driven the Spanish flag. These are the men who fear the strenuous life, who fear the only national life which is really worth leading. . . .

"We cannot sit huddled within our own borders and avow ourselves merely an assemblage of well-to-do hucksters who care nothing for what happens beyond. Such a policy would defeat even its own end; for as the nations grow to have ever wider and wider interests, and are brought into closer and closer contact, if we are to hold our own in the struggle for naval and commercial supremacy, we must build up our power without our own borders. We must build the isthmian canal, and we must grasp the points of vantage which will enable us to have our say in deciding the destiny of the oceans of the East and the West."

—THEODORE ROOSEVELT, 1899

# THE ROOTS OF ISOLATION

Theodore Roosevelt himself was a key figure in converting the United States from an "assemblage of well-to-do hucksters" to a world power. In a series of roles as naval enthusiast, volunteer colonel in Cuba, vice president, and president, he preached the gospel of the "strenuous life" to millions of Americans. He was himself one of those "stern men with empires in their brains" who thrilled at the prospects before a powerful and growing United States. In the two decades between the war with Spain and America's entrance into World War I, no voice was raised more consistently than his on behalf of expansion, military preparedness, and the assertion of American rights and responsibilities abroad.

## America: A World Apart

But the fight was hard. A sense of separateness, of isolation from the currents of world affairs, ran deep in the American experience. From the beginning Americans shared the feeling of having escaped from Europe and its eternal broils and wickedness. Here was a new continent with a fresh destiny; here one might begin anew the quest for a worldly utopia; here one could find peace from the antiquated concerns of the Old World.

Isolation from the Old World was psychological as well as geographical, cultural as well as diplomatic. Though derived from Europe, American culture always stressed its separateness, its distinctiveness, its newness and originality. In part this was a natural reaction to English and European criticism of the immaturity and imitativeness of Americans. "In the four quarters of the globe," taunted Sydney Smith in his famous article in the *Edinburgh Review* in 1820, "who reads an American book? or goes to an American play? or looks at an American picture or statue? What does the world yet owe to American physicians or surgeons?" The questions were fair enough but they burned deeply in the American breast. American authors, painters, and sculptors became fiercely defensive about the condescending attitude of Europeans. Even physicians and surgeons became nationalists where America was concerned. One noted surgeon complained in 1856 that after 75 years the United States still possessed no original nor independent medical literature and that the writing of Americans was confined to illustrating and commenting on European texts; another criticized his colleagues for copying European ideas and practices and urged American doctors to develop their own techniques and remedies.

Americans were thus isolated from Europe in spirit and purpose as well as in location. This psychological isolation, this refusal to admit the kinship of American culture with that of the Old World, reinforced the geographical isolation. By contrast, north of the border, Canadians, faced with a geographical isolation as real as that of Americans, never felt so cut off from their Old World roots. The indifference of Americans to events outside the nation's borders increased their ignorance of what was happening in the world. A smug provincialism was noted by nearly every European who traveled to the United States in the nineteenth century. Mark Twain gave it humorous native expression in a conversation between Huck Finn and the runaway slave Jim:

"Why, Huck, doan' de French people talk de same way we does?"

"No, Jim; you couldn't understand a word they said—not a single word."

"Well, now, I be ding-busted! How do dat come?"

"I don't know; but it's so. I got some of their jabber out of a book. S'pose a man was to come to you and say Polly-voo-franzy— what would you think?"

"I wouldn' think nuffn; I'd take en bust him over de head—dat is, if he warn't white. I wouldn't 'low no nigger to call me dat."

"Shucks, it ain't calling you anything. It's only saying, do you know how to talk French?"

"Well, den, why couldn't he say it?"

"Why, he *is* a-saying it. That's a Frenchman's *way* of saying it."

"Well, it's a blame ridiklous way, en I doan' want to hear no mo' 'bout it. Dey ain' no sense in it."

## America's Mission

Millions of Americans saw no more clearly than Jim why the rest of the world did not want to be like them. This certainty of the superiority of American institutions and values helps to explain why, considering their origin, Americans had so little interest in the "old country." Through American history runs the theme of the uniqueness of the United States and its importance as an example to the rest of the world. Not only must we be democratic at home, but we must fulfill our mission to carry the mes-

sage of democracy to the other peoples of the world. "Humanity with all its fears," Longfellow wrote of his country, "is hanging breathless on thy fate!" The historian George Bancroft was certain that God had made it part of his grand design that America become a democratic laboratory for the entire world. Lincoln, too, affirmed that the Declaration of Independence meant happiness and freedom "not alone to the people of this country, but hope for the world for all future time." The United States, in the view of its citizens, was a lamp on the horizon; it invited men from all countries to come and emulate them.

## Freedom of Action

The notion that America must play schoolmaster to the globe lay back of many of her self-conscious appeals to world opinion after 1776. But the idea entailed no commitment to action. Time and time again the nation's spokesmen expressed sympathy for the cause of freedom or self-government abroad but refused any active intervention in other nations' affairs. The embattled Greeks in the 1820's, and later the Hungarians in 1848, won a warm response in American opinion for their struggles against oppression, but they got no aid. "I would offer sympathy and God-speed to all, in every land, who struggle for Human Rights," cried Charles Sumner in 1851, "but, sternly as Washington on another occasion, against every pressure, against all popular appeals, against all solicitations, against all blandishments, I would uphold the peaceful neutrality of the country."

The tradition of diplomatic isolation was built on a foundation of geographical security, a desire for cultural separation, and the prospect of exploiting the strife of Europe for America's benefit. In his famous Farewell Address, Washington counseled his countrymen not to forego the great advantages of the American situation by becoming embroiled in the quarrels of Europe. Build American strength, avoid permanent alliances, stay clear of European rivalry, encourage foreign trade—this was the advice of the first President. His successors, in the main, followed this advice. And by the middle of the nineteenth century the tradition was well established that the United States would make no political commitments in Europe and that it would reserve freedom of action wherever its interests were involved.

This did not mean, however, a hermit-like barring of the doors against intercourse with other nations. On the contrary, trade and travel between the United States and foreign nations grew steadily throughout the century. American isolation, even at its peak, was never of the order that Commodore Perry encountered in Japan. Perry's own mission signified a deep interest in the expansion of American trade in the Orient. For the rest of the century Americans were less fearful of playing a strong hand in Asia than in Europe with all its great powers. The isolation of the United States was primarily political and ideological and almost never economic. And the rules were simple: Entanglements in Europe were to be avoided at all costs while those areas still under European control in the New World were to be closely watched and never allowed to expand. Beyond this, American statesmen were free to improvise.

Though aloof from Europe, Americans were from the beginning quick to exploit the opportunities opened up by its quar-

rels. French aid during the Revolution came after a half-century of conflict between the French and English for North America. Then the wars of Napoleon cleared the way for American annexation of Louisiana and shook loose the grip of imperial Spain on Florida. Throughout the nineteenth century the United States was able to play an even larger role in New World affairs because of the divisions and discords of Europe and because of our growing strength. As the century closed, Europe was preparing for a major showdown that would eventually bring Americans a major role in world politics.

These, then, were the great themes of American foreign policy in the nineteenth century: independence of action; the uniqueness and mission of the United States; the refusal to enter permanent alliances; the regulation of European behavior in the New World; and the encouragement of international trade. Long after the nineteenth century closed they continued to exert a strong influence on the policies and imagination of Americans. Gradually, they were superseded or altered in the changed world conditions of the twentieth century. The beginnings of change came during those progressive years described in the last chapter. What were the forces operating then to change the historic orientation of this country toward events outside its borders? How far did Americans go by 1914 in abandoning their old principles? How complete was the emergence of the United States from isolation by the time of the First World War? To these provocative questions we must now turn.

## THE WINDS OF CHANGE

"The number of men and officials in this country who are now mad to fight somebody is appalling," wrote E. L. Godkin,

editor of *The Nation*, in 1894. "Navy officers dream of war and talk and lecture about it incessantly. . . . jingo editors keep up a din day after day about the way we could cripple one country's fleet and destroy another's commerce, and fill the heads of boys and silly men with the idea that war is the normal state of a civilized country." This aggressive, expansionist urge in Americans was hard for many observers to understand. And historians have not found it easy to identify with certainty the men and forces that pushed the United States into its imperialistic phase.

## Underlying Currents

One undeniably potent impulse was the growing strength of the United States. The industrial might of the nation, which by the mid-nineties had thrust her into world leadership in manufacturing output, made her for better or worse a player in the international struggle for power. That struggle had entered a critical stage by the close of the nineteenth century. The world of 1900 was fearful and divided; nationalism and imperialism were forcing the great powers into a fateful competition for prestige and colonies; Britain and France were beginning to feel the loss of vitality that would steadily reduce their power and influence; advances in arms technology augured ill for any war that might result; and already the forces had begun to gather that would erupt in the totalitarian revolutions of our own time.

A weakening Britain, no longer secure in her imperial might, cast about for future allies. Increasingly, after 1895, she befriended the United States and took her part in a series of minor conflicts. Germany, too, tried to enlist the support and friendship of Americans in the two decades before World War I, but with conspicuously less success.

As foreign nations tried hard to get Americans to turn their eyes outward, they got a good deal of help from the changing economic position of the country. Beginning in 1874, the United States had an export surplus. Increasingly thereafter, American farmers and manufacturers shipped more goods abroad than their countrymen consumed in imports. As their interest in such potential markets as China, India, and South America rose steadily in the last quarter of the century, businessmen tended more and more to support such national aims as building an isthmian canal, modernizing the navy, or laying a Pacific cable. This desire for new markets abroad undoubtedly contributed to the nation's willingness to listen to expansionist preaching at the turn of the century.

There can be no question, either, that the course of domestic events after 1890 affected American thinking about foreign policy. The end of the western frontier, the farmer's acute distress, the flooding of immigrants into eastern cities, and the rising clamor for vigorous action by the government all found some echo in American attitudes toward foreign affairs. For many, the closing of the frontier symbolized the end of American opportunity; some accordingly counseling a search for new frontiers outside the continental domain. Then the farm depression of the nineties deepened the sense of crisis and dwindling opportunity.

The new progressive outlook after 1900 sometimes went hand-in-hand with expansionist attitudes. Both the progressive and the expansionist called for a much stronger national government; both tended to glorify action for action's sake; and both shared a faith in the mission of America to bring democracy to the world. It was often the same men who fought the progressives' political battles—Roosevelt, Albert Beveridge, William Allen White, Herbert Croly—who urged the nation to adopt a "large policy" in its foreign relations. Many progressives, spurred by liberal, humanitarian motives, found no contradiction between fighting Spaniards in Cuba and battling business tycoons in Wall Street on behalf of freedom and popular rights.

### The Role of Ideas

The new mood of the nineties owed something, too, to the changing intellectual attitudes of the *fin de siècle*. Such Darwinian slogans as "survival of the fittest," "elimination of the unfit," and "organisms must grow or perish" were bound to be applied to nations as well as to biological organisms. Darwin himself encouraged the self-esteem of Americans when he wrote that "There is apparently much truth in the belief that the wonderful progress of the United States, as well as the character of the people, are the results of natural selection; the more energetic, restless, and courageous men from all parts of Europe having emigrated during the last ten or twelve generations to that great country. . . ."

In that great country itself, a philosopher, John Fiske, and a clergyman, Josiah Strong, gave wide currency to the concept that the Anglo-Saxon "race," which embraced America's English forebears, was especially favored in the struggle for life and was destined to command the destinies of the globe. In his influential book, *Our Country* (1885), Strong argued that the United States must play the role of leader to the whole English-speaking world. "This race," he said of the Anglo-Saxons, "having developed peculiarly aggressive traits calculated to impress its institutions upon mankind, will spread itself over the earth. If I read not amiss, this powerful race will move down upon Mexico, down upon Central and South America, out upon the islands of the sea, over upon Africa and beyond." In the great struggle among races and nations, he wrote thirteen years before the war with Spain, the fitter Anglo-Saxons were certain to survive. That such teaching, avidly

received by the leaders of evangelical Protestantism, had an impact on the American mind seems as certain as any assumption of intellectual influences can be.

Traces of this idea of American racial supremacy can be found in the work of numerous writers, scholars, clergymen, and politicians of the closing years of the nineteenth century. This racialism, it should be said, was of a different character from that used later by Dr. Goebbels and other hate-mongers. Although its adherents used it to justify imperialism, they rarely taught that the differences between races were permanent and ineradicable; and they never called for that savage annihilation of "inferior" races which horrified the generation that knew Hitler.

Another influential American who fell under the sway of the idea of Anglo-Saxon superiority was the naval authority Alfred Thayer Mahan. He admired the achievements of the British people tremendously, especially the building of a great overseas empire on the foundation of strong naval power. Repeatedly he urged Americans to profit from Britain's example. "How much poorer would the world have been," he wrote in 1893, "had Englishmen heeded the cautious hesitancy that now bids us reject every advance beyond our own shore-lines!" In his cele-

brated book, *The Influence of Sea Power upon History, 1660-1783* (1890), he advanced a formula for national power that was studied in every chancery of Europe. The fundamental relationship among nations, he asserted in Darwinian fashion, was a struggle for power. In that struggle, control of the ocean highways of the world conferred a notable advantage. Accordingly, the most desirable location for a nation was one surrounded by water. A strong nation, he told his countrymen (though he was more widely read in Europe than at home), was like a fortress, protected by impenetrable waters, garrisoned by a resolute, technologically skilled people, and free to develop its sea power. Real naval power meant dominance of the sea lanes, which entailed, in turn, a naval force capable of defeating any possible enemy force. It required, too, coaling stations, a merchant fleet, forward bases, and possibly the control of friendly territories in time of conflict. Tirelessly, he argued in books, articles, speeches, and personal letters for a strong, prepared navy, the annexation of Hawaii, an isthmian canal under American control, and the extension of American trade interests abroad.

### The Role of Men

The expansionist ideas of Mahan, Strong, Fiske, and others landed on fertile soil in a small but influential circle around President McKinley. At the head of this receptive group was Theodore Roosevelt, whose interests in the nineties were turning more and more to foreign affairs. Among Roosevelt's friends were Henry Cabot Lodge, a powerful leader of the Senate; John Hay, minister to London and soon to be Secretary of State; Henry White, a career diplomat; Senator J. Donald Cameron of Pennsylvania; and Henry and Brooks Adams, the brilliant grandsons of John Quincy Adams. Other frequenters of Roosevelt's group were Elihu Root, another future Secretary of State as well as Secretary of War; William Rockhill, who was to play a decisive role in shaping the Open Door notes; and Captain Mahan himself. The closeness of these men had important political results: Lodge backed Hay for the post of Secretary of State under McKinley and supported Roosevelt for the job of Assistant Secretary of the Navy; since all were close to Mahan, they were influenced by his ideas on naval pol-

Gallery of the times. Elihu Root, public official; Alfred T. Mahan, naval officer; John Hay, public official; Albert J. Beveridge, senator. (All from Brown Brothers.)

icy; and when Roosevelt became President, he made frequent use of the counsel of all these men.

TR's own strident nationalism owed something to the Darwinism and power politics of the Mahan-Fiske-Strong school. No man in American public life showed greater respect for physical power and the role it played in international affairs. "It is only the warlike power of a civilized people," he once said, "that can give peace to the world." But he justified his respect for might in moral terms. He defended the use of power against weak and unruly states as the obligation of a superior state to bring order to the world. He found it inconceivable that the United States would ever act in an unjust fashion. The Spanish-American War he once characterized as "the most absolutely righteous foreign war of the nineteenth century." Like others in his circle, he believed in the destiny of the Anglo-Saxon peoples to spread civilization around the globe. Law and order would diffuse across the world only through the expanding influence and power of nations committed to those values. Men knew peace, he held, only when "some strong and on the whole just power has by armed force, or the threat of armed force, put a stop to disorder."

### Expanding Horizons, 1865-1898

Well before the war with Spain, the new attitudes and forces at work in American thinking about foreign policy had made their mark. Richard Olney, Secretary of State under President Cleveland (1895-1897), predicted that "though historians will probably assign the abandonment of the isolationist policy of the United States to the time when this country and Spain went to war over Cuba . . . the change was inevitable, had been long preparing, and could not have been long delayed."

Olney may have been thinking of the expansionist William H. Seward, who, as Secretary of State, tried to bring the Virgin Islands and Santo Domingo, as well as Alaska, under the wings of the American eagle. Or he may have had in mind the interventionist schemes of the Grant administration in Cuba and Santo Domingo. But most likely he regarded the "spirited diplomacy" of the nineties under Secretary Blaine and himself as the real point of departure from previous policies. During the Harrison administration (1889-1893), Blaine presided over the first Pan-American Conference, symbolizing a new interest in hemispheric problems and opportunities; he stood up strongly to an outraged Italian government that demanded indemnity for the lives of eleven Italians taken by a New Orleans mob; and he virtually threatened Chile with war if that nation did not apologize for an attack on some American sailors in a Valparaiso saloon. More important, the United States entered into an arrangement with Germany and Great Britain in 1889 for three-power control over distant Samoa and was faced in 1893 with the demand from Americans in Hawaii that the United States recognize their revolt against native rule and annex the islands. The incoming Cleveland administration refused to act, however, and Hawaii was forced to wait another five years outside the gate before being let in as a territory of the United States.

Olney's own tenure as Secretary of State coincided with the last great burst of anglophobia in the United States. War against England, cried one anglophobe, would be the most "just war ever waged by man." The particular occasion for this war sentiment was Britain's refusal to accept an offer of American arbitration in a boundary dispute between British Guiana and Venezuela. On July 20, 1895, Olney sent off a note that Cleveland later christened a "twenty-inch gun." In it Olney asserted that the Monroe Doctrine was involved in the dispute, that Britain must arbitrate, and that the United States would take action to protect its interests. "Today the United States is practically sovereign on this continent," wrote Olney in a famous paragraph; "its infinite resources combined with its isolated position render it master of the situation and practically invulnerable as against any or all other powers." Republicans joined with Democrats in applauding this bellicose dispatch. Cleveland later threatened to run the boundary line himself if Britain continued adamant. At this critical juncture the German Kaiser diverted British attention from Venezuela with a message of congratulation to the Dutch Boers who had just repulsed the Jameson raiders. The war fever died down, Britain cooperated with the American boundary commission, and arbitration was eventually agreed upon.

The Venezuela imbroglio marked a turn in the path of Anglo-American relations. In the midst of the crisis the British colonial secretary, Joseph Chamberlain, declared in a public speech that "War between the two nations, England and the United States, would be an absurdity as well as a crime. . . . The two nations are allied, and more closely allied in sentiment and in interests than any other nations on the face of the earth. . . . I should look forward with pleasure to the possibility of the Stars and Stripes and the Union Jack floating together in defence of a common cause sanctioned by humanity and justice." The sentiment was echoed by many on this side of the Atlantic. In 1897 the passionately pro-British John Hay became ambassador to the Court of St. James's and the next year he was made Secretary of State. The events of the Spanish-American War, especially Britain's lone support in Europe of the American cause, added to the growing friendship between the two countries. In a series of episodes involving Anglo-American conflicts of interests the British showed moderation, restraint, and a conciliatory spirit toward the Americans. Meanwhile, during the nineties and the first decade of the twentieth century, American suspicion of Germany was deepening. Almost consistently the Germans seemed to strike a heavy, clumsy, or belligerent note in their dealings with the United States. This impression may have been due in part to the misrepresentations of British diplomats and journalists, who were closer to American officials than were the Germans, and to the undoubted pro-British sympathies of the Roosevelt-Hay-Lodge circle, but there was no doubt as the tensions built up before World War I where the initial bias of most Americans lay.

One more development in the years before 1898 that showed an American change of heart about making commitments abroad was the building of a strong navy. The naval strength of the country had deteriorated badly in the fifteen years following the Civil War. Many innovations in armor, propulsion, and guns had been passed by in the overriding concern for economy and the maintenance of merely a "defensive" navy. Captains were forbidden to get up steam unless it were absolutely necessary. Even the Chilean navy seemed a formidable threat following the rejection by Chile in the early 1880's of American protests at her territorial demands on Peru. Finally, in 1883, the first steps were taken to rebuild the antiquated American fleet. In the course of the eighties and nineties, stimulated by the new spirit that was causing many Americans to look outward from their continental bastion, Congress steadily raised naval appropriations. The appropriations act of 1890, in particular, was aimed at building a fleet capable of engaging the world's greatest warships. These new ships, Roosevelt wrote later in his *Autobiography*, were sometimes designated as "seagoing coastline battleships" in order to avoid any appearance of expansionist aims. By the time of the Spanish-American War, the new militant spirit affecting American leaders, the influence of Mahan and his views, and the machinations of Theodore Roosevelt as Assistant Secretary of the Navy had combined to create a navy that ranked near the top of the world's fighting fleets.

## THE WAR WITH SPAIN

Olney's prediction that the war with Spain would seem the great turning point in American policy has proved to be true. Seen in retrospect, this spectacular conflict with a European power leading to the seizure of an overseas empire looms as a conspicuous landmark on the field of history. That it did not represent a sharp break with the immediate past we have just demonstrated, but its significance for the future was far greater than the earlier Pan-American conference or the bumptious thrusts against Chile. The humbling of Spain revealed not only the formidable military power that America was building, and her willingness to use it, but, more significantly, her growing desire to play a role in the world race for empire.

### "A Spendid Little War"

The steps that led to empire were taken without deliberation and were never debated by the American people. The immediate background of the Spanish War was an uprising against Spanish rule on the island of Cuba in 1895. The rebels and their oppressors fought savagely, and atrocities were claimed on both sides. A year after the outbreak of hostilities the Spanish commander, General Weyler (called "Butcher" in the yellow press), began herding the Cuban population into hastily constructed concentration camps to simplify the job of hunting down the insurgents. Famine and disease swept through the camps. American opinion, warmly sympathetic to the Cubans from the first, rose to fever heat at the news of these inhumane policies of the Spaniards. Vivid reports of Spanish atrocities appeared in the American press, embellished in the case of the Hearst and Pulitzer papers with sketches, banner headlines, and one-sided accounts of the uprising.

As the war dragged on, the demand for American intervention grew louder. Business spokesmen, in general, sought to suppress interventionist sentiment but were drowned out in a roar of humanitarian zeal to do something about this nuisance so close to our shores. The *Journal of Commerce* called intervention "military insanity" and blamed naval officers and "artificial patriotism" for stirring up the furor. For a while, in 1897, hopes for peace in Cuba brightened with the coming to power of a more liberal regime in Madrid. But the following February two events occurred that were instrumental in precipitating the United States into war. First came the revelation of a private letter of Dupuy de Lôme, Spanish minister in Washington, to a correspondent in Cuba, in which he called McKinley "weak and a bidder for the admiration of the crowd." The letter was stolen and turned over to the New York *Journal*, which bannered the sensational insult before its readers. The second event was the destruction of the battleship *Maine* (which had been sent to Havana a few weeks before to protect

American lives and property) by a mysterious explosion on the 15th of February, 1898. More than two hundred and fifty American lives were lost. The sensational press and many Americans leaped to the conclusion—never proven—that the Spanish had committed the outrage. "The *Maine* was sunk by an act of dirty treachery on the part of the Spaniards," wrote Theodore Roosevelt, then Assistant Secretary of the Navy.

The flood of war sentiment was too much for McKinley. Though the Spanish made important last-minute concessions to the American view, including a halt to the concentration-camp policy, McKinley capitulated to the jingoist fervor sweeping the country and his party counsels. He turned the question of war or peace over to an eager Congress, which now directed the President to use the armed forces to win Cuban independence. Any American intention to annex the island was disclaimed in the Teller Amendment to the war resolution.

The navy was ready. Roosevelt had used his influence to have George Dewey put in charge of the Asiatic squadron and ordered him, one afternoon when the Secretary of the Navy was away, to be ready to strike at the Philippines. "I knew that in the event of war," TR wrote later, "Dewey could be slipped like a wolfhound from a leash." From the time Dewey was unleashed, the war lasted slightly more than one hundred days. Dewey sailed into Manila harbor and blew up ten antiquated Spanish ships in leisurely fashion. Two months later a small Spanish force was sunk off the coast of Santiago in Cuba. Despite bad blundering, a land force under General William Shafter succeeded in smothering the Spanish defenders of Cuba. In the last days of the war General Nelson Miles led a small force into the island of Puerto Rico. Practically unopposed, the expedition was dubbed by the inimitable Mr. Dooley, "Gin'ral Miles' gran' picnic an' moonlight excursion." John Hay expressed the attitude of many delighted Americans when he called it "a splendid little war."

## Democracy and Battleships

But what to do with the Philippines? We were committed to giv-

"Rough Riders' Charge" by Frederick Remington. The advance of the volunteer Rough Riders lacked military form and was called "the school-boy charge" by officers of the regular army. But the reckless attack of the dismounted cavalry, led by Roosevelt, contributed notably to breaking the Spanish spirit. (United Press.)

ing the Cubans their independence, and little Puerto Rico, lying so close to the American coast, seemed destined for annexation. But what of those far-away islands? They would be the real test of American imperialistic intentions. During the summer and fall of 1898 sentiment for retaining the islands soared throughout the country. The business community, largely opposed to war over Cuba, now swung over to the expansionist side. A number of missionary organizations, some of them inspired no doubt by Strong's arguments in *Our Country*, backed the taking of the Philippines. A whole brood of expansionist arguments, hatched during the intellectual ferment of the preceding fifteen years, were now let loose on the side of retaining the far-away islands. Lodge, Roosevelt, Beveridge, Hay, and others in the Roosevelt circle moved into the thick of the fight for imperialism.

The final annexation of Hawaii in the summer of 1898 set a precedent for acquiring an overseas empire. Hawaii, despite its isolation from the continent, gave some promise of becoming an American state because of the large number of Americans there. Would the Philippines? The differences in tradition and culture were tremendous, and six thousand miles of water separated the islanders from the West Coast of the United States. The basic question, said Beveridge in a speech echoing Strong and Fiske, was racial. "God has not prepared the English-speaking and Teutonic peoples for a thousand years," he told the Senate, "for nothing but vain and idle self-contemplation and self-admiration. No! He has made us the master organizers of the world to establish system where chaos reigns. . . . He has made us adepts in government that we may administer government among savage and senile peoples." What of the argument that the Philippines were not contiguous territory? "Our navy will make

them contiguous," declared Beveridge on another occasion. What of the complaint that annexation would violate American ideals of self-government? "The rule . . . that all just government derives its authority from the consent of the governed," Beveridge replied, "applies only to those who are capable of self-government." Filipinos, like Indians and children, were clearly not ready to govern themselves. It was the burden of the white man, wrote Rudyard Kipling in a famous poem addressed to the American people, to uplift and civilize its "new-caught, sullen peoples."

Opposition was strong. Of the imperialists' talk of "duty" and the "destiny" of the United States, one newspaper queried, "What does it mean? Nobody knows. What does Mr. McKinley think it means? Nobody knows, Mr. McKinley probably least of all." The anti-imperialist ranks included a number of prominent Democrats, Cleveland and Bryan among them; such Republican stalwarts as "Czar" Reed, Speaker of the House of Representatives; and a sprinkling of intellectuals (William James, for example), reformers (Jane Addams), and business leaders (Andrew Carnegie). As they saw it, the taking of the Philippines meant a sharp break with American tradition, a violation of American ideals, the imperiling of American security by dangerous commitments abroad, and the creation of two classes of citizenship. Under the Constitution, argued Democratic leaders, there was no place for a colonial system with its denial of the fundamental rights of subject peoples. It was against such a system that Americans themselves had revolted in 1776.

Politics played a part in the debate. Democratic opposition to the annexationist policy of the Republican administration was in part simply politically inspired. At one point it seemed the treaty with Spain

The Dewey Triumphal Arch, lower Fifth Avenue, New York, September 30, 1899. After his victory over the Spanish fleet in Manila Bay, Commodore Dewey was acclaimed a national hero. He was promoted to rear-admiral (and later to admiral), and Congress—in a joint resolution—tendered him its thanks. (New-York Historical Society.)

would go down to defeat in the Senate had not Bryan, still the leader of his party, intervened to urge his followers to approve it. He held out the prospect of making the election of 1900 a mandate on imperialism and setting the Filipinos free if the Democrats were elected. But no election in American politics is likely to hinge on a single question and the election of 1900 was no exception. While Bryan fought to convince the American people that imperialism was the great issue in the campaign, McKinley's followers pointed to the free silver plank that Bryan had forced on the Democratic convention. McKinley's re-election probably owed as much to fear of Bryanism as to support for his stand in taking the Philippines.

### Uncle Sam: Imperialist

Perhaps the most telling argument of the imperialists in 1898 was that America had no practicable alternative to the annexation of the Philippines. If left alone, the Germans or the Japanese might seize them; returning them to Spain seemed unthinkable; and most observers declared the Filipinos themselves unready for self-government. Many Filipinos felt otherwise, however, and followed the leadership of Emilio Aguinaldo in working for independence. When it became clear that America did not intend to give them their freedom, revolt flared and warfare broke out between the Filipinos and the American troops. "Are these our protectors?" wrote Aguinaldo in a proclamation to his followers; "Better death than be related to a people whose evil is inborn! Away with the wretches! Destruction to the Americans!" Two years of exasperating guerrilla warfare cost the United States more casualties than the entire war against Spain. "Destiny is not as manifest as it was a few weeks ago," chided Bryan after the outbreak of Aguinaldo's insurrection.

For better or worse, the United States was now committed to an imperialist policy in the Philippines. But a troubled national conscience made American rule less autocratic and more beneficial than it might otherwise have been. Imperialism was toned down as the Democrats repeatedly took a strong stand against holding the islanders in subservience, while Republicans aimed at preparing them for self-government. Both parties favored efforts to raise the economic, public health, and educational levels of the Filipinos.

William Howard Taft headed a commission sent to the Philippines in 1900 to organize a system of government; subsequently, as civil governor of the islands, Taft helped to carry out the recommendations of the commission. In keeping with its suggestions, most of the rights under the American Constitution were extended to the Filipinos, who were to be regarded as citizens of the Philippines rather than the United States. Training in local government began quickly and in 1907 the Filipinos elected their own national assembly. Later, in the Wilson administration, the islands were made almost self-governing in domestic affairs under the Jones Act (1916). In 1934 Congress declared

for complete independence within a ten-year period, and in 1946, despite the devastating changes wrought by World War II, a Philippine Republic was in fact established.

Dealing with Cuba and Puerto Rico, although troublesome, involved less controversy than determining the future of the Philippines. American troops were withdrawn from Cuba after that liberated island held its first election under a new constitution in 1902. But incorporated into that constitution, at American insistence, was the so-called Platt Amendment (named for Senator Orville H. Platt of Connecticut), which conceded to the United States both the right of intervention to preserve order and a veto over Cuban foreign and domestic policies. On four occasions the United States exercised the right of intervention before the Platt Amendment was formally abrogated in 1934. In Puerto Rico, civil administration was substituted for military government by the Foraker Act in 1900. Gradually, over the years, home rule was extended to the Puerto Ricans: an elected legislature in 1917, a governor of their own choosing in 1948, and a constitution of their own making in 1952. In both Puerto Rico and Cuba, as well as in the Philippines, American occupation brought a general rise in the educational, sanitary, and economic levels of the population.

In the so-called insular cases, decided in 1901, the Supreme Court worried the delicate constitutional question of whether the Constitution followed the flag. At stake was the status of the peoples in the newly acquired territories. Were they citizens? What rights of American citizens could they lay claim to? Did American tariff laws apply to them? The Court held somewhat ambiguously that the new possessions were "unincorporated territories whose residents were entitled to many of the rights of American citizens, such as free speech and freedom of conscience, but not to all such rights; their trade, for instance, was subject to special duties imposed by Congress. Thus the Court's answer to the question of whether the Constitution was in force in the overseas territories seemed to be: yes and no. Said Mr. Dooley, "Some say it laves the flag up in th' air an' some say that's where it laves the constitution."

## A MINOR ROLE ON THE WORLD'S STAGE

"I sigh f'r th' good old days befur we became what Hogan calls a wurruld power," said Mr. Dooley of America's new status in the world. Many Americans felt the same way. The glory of empire seemed less dazzling amid the dangers and obligations that now confronted the nation. The war left us with commitments in the Caribbean, a stake in the power struggles of Eastern Asia, and a growing interest in the alignments and crises of Europe. A strong navy and an isthmian canal now seemed more vital than ever. "In thim days," sighed Mr. Dooley, "we didn't care f'r th' big game goin' on in th' corner. . . . But we cudden't stand it anny longer. We had to give up our simple little game iv patience an' cut into th' other deal. An' now, be Hivens, we have no peace iv mind. . . ."

### Keeping the Door Open in China

In the Far East the diplomatic stake of the United States was raised by our taking the Philippines and by the expectation of an expanded trade with China. That country was desperately weak. Overwhelmed by the Japanese in the Sino-Japanese War of 1894-95, she was even more helpless than before to resist the European and Japanese imperialists who demanded concessions and "spheres of influence" around the great East China ports. For more than half a century the United States had tried to protect its own trading interests in China.

What should she do now? In 1899, John Hay, Secretary of State, dispatched a series of notes to all of the powers with interests in China asking them to agree to preserve equal trading rights for all nations in their respective areas of influence. His move was prompted by American business concern at the carving up of China, British pressure for some kind of joint stand in favor of the Open Door, and the feverish activity of two remarkable individuals, Alfred E. Hippisley and William W. Rockhill, who drew up the actual text of the notes. Hippisley, a British subject, had spent long years in China and was a persistent supporter of the Open Door; Rockhill, whom we noticed earlier in the circle around Roosevelt, was a confidant and special adviser of John Hay. The powers to whom the notes were addressed responded for the most part ambiguously, but the Secretary announced publicly that the replies were "final and definitive." Though hailed as a great diplomatic achievement, in truth the Open Door notes did not announce a policy that was new or that this country would back with force in the future.

Almost immediately, in fact, in 1900 an uprising by violently antiforeign Chinese, called "Boxers" by Westerners, threatened the Open Door and tested our intentions. American troops participated then in the international expedition sent to rescue European and American nationals besieged in Peking. But Hay was apprehensive lest the Boxer intervention be the pretext for slicing up the rest of China among the great powers. In a circular note, he declared American policy to be the preservation of "Chinese territorial and administrative entity." This was a significant addendum to the first Open Door notes, which had said nothing of Chinese independence. Though Hay's warning was probably less important than great-power rivalries in stopping the dismemberment of China, it did represent a new willingness to employ American influence in a distant part of the globe.

### TR and the Orient

John Hay remained as Secretary of State when his friend Theodore

In this cartoon, Uncle Sam forcibly keeps the door open—for himself. (New York Public Library.)

DEAN C. WORCESTER ON THE PHILIPPINES

# HARPER'S WEEKLY
## JOURNAL OF CIVILIZATION

NEW YORK, SATURDAY, NOVEMBER 18, 1899

A FAIR FIELD AND NO FAVOR!
UNCLE SAM "I'M OUT FOR COMMERCE, NOT CONQUEST"

Roosevelt entered the White House in 1901. For the next four years, these two men, remarkably alike in their view of world events, collaborated closely on the forging of an American foreign policy for the twentieth century. Roosevelt, of course, left the stamp of his own vigorous and impatient personality on the conduct of foreign as on domestic affairs. He brought to the presidency a knowledge of the world and its peoples equalled by no predecessor since John Quincy Adams. Seeing the role that power played in international relations, he was determined that America should never again be weak. Two new battleships a year was his aim for the navy, and this goal was largely achieved. "It has been well said," he once remarked, "that there is no surer way of courting national disaster than to be 'opulent, aggressive, and unarmed.'"

His China policy, influenced by Hay and Rockhill, was aimed at keeping the door open in China and preventing the European and Japanese imperialists from finishing off this "sick man of Asia." Yet he largely ignored or underestimated the rising Chinese nationalism which was also dedicated to clearing the country of foreigners. Thus, when the Chinese began a boycott against American goods in 1905, in retaliation for Congress's action in excluding Chinese immigration, Roosevelt replied with a show of force and actually laid plans to invade China.

Of the nations interested in China, Roosevelt came to fear Russia most. Like Mahan and Brooks Adams, TR thought that the Russians represented the greatest threat to the balance of power in Asia. Accordingly, he welcomed the growing strength of Japan as an effective counterweight to Russian ambitions in Manchuria. At the same time he was concerned lest Japan herself become too potent and hence a threat to the power equilibrium. When war broke out between these two competitors in 1904, American sympathy for the Japanese was strong, for, to many, Japan seemed to be protecting the Open Door in resisting the Russian advance in Manchuria. Roosevelt felt a strong sense of responsibility to restore peace and offered the "good offices" of the United States, which were eventually accepted, as a mediator in the war. American policy-makers were apparently ready to accept the substitution of Japanese for Russian development of Manchuria and to acquiesce in the Japanese annexation of Korea; but the Japanese, encouraged by their spectacular victories over the Russians, extended their territorial demands and asked for a large money indemnity from the Russians. At Portsmouth, New Hampshire, where the peace negotiations were carried on in 1905, the indemnity demand became the focus of attention. Finally, as the conference was about to fail, Roosevelt intervened firmly against the Japanese and under tremendous pressure they yielded. In Japan, TR was made the scapegoat for what proved to be an unpopular treaty.

As an aftermath of the Portsmouth agreement, the Japanese took Korea with American approval. In Roosevelt's eyes, this was part of an over-all settlement that would leave the Japanese in control of Korea and with major influence in Manchuria, while British and American power would counterbalance any Russian aggressive intentions to the south. All would stand behind the Open Door.

The hostile feelings of the Japanese toward the United States, allayed somewhat by the Korean agreement, burst out again in 1906. The occasion this time was the action of the San Francisco Board of Education in ordering Oriental children into a special school. "Stand up, Japanese nation!" demanded one Japanese paper. "Our poor boys and girls have been expelled from the public schools by the rascals of the United States. . . . Why do we not insist on sending ships?" Wounded

Japanese pride was salved somewhat by Roosevelt's action in sending two cabinet members to investigate, but the situation was critical. Ultimately the President arranged a compromise known as the "Gentlemen's Agreement" that allowed the Japanese children to return to their schools in return for an end to Japanese coolie immigration to the United States.

Roosevelt then did a characteristic thing. After satisfying the Japanese of his good intentions, he now wanted them to know that he was not afraid of them. Without consulting Congress or the Cabinet, he determined to send the American fleet around the world in a show of preparedness. He wanted also to impress the American people with the might of their new navy, hurry the building of the Panama Canal, and give the navy some much-needed practice in sea manuevers. The "Great White Fleet" made a great impression abroad and was received enthusiastically even in Japan. Japanese school children, carefully coached, sang the "Star Spangled Banner" on the Americans' arrival. Though the sending of the fleet to Japan undoubtedly contributed to a growing friendliness, there were those in Japan who did not miss the significance of this display of force and were determined to build up Japanese military strength.

At the end of the Roosevelt administration a formal agreement on Asian policy was concluded between these two nations whose rise to world power had coincided in time. The Japanese ambassador to the United States, Kogoro Takahira, and Hay's successor as Secretary of State, Elihu Root, agreed to (1) uphold the Open Door, (2) work to maintain the status quo in the Pacific, (3) respect each other's possessions in that region, and (4) support the "independence and integrity of China. . . ." Did this mean that the United States was formally recognizing the Japanese position in Manchuria? On

President Roosevelt meets with plenipotentiaries of Russia and Japan at Portsmouth, New Hampshire, August, 1905. Roosevelt's successful mediation of the Russo-Japanese War greatly increased his prestige at home and abroad, and won for him, in 1906, the Nobel Peace Prize. (New-York Historical Society.)

this question historians have disagreed though there is little question that the Japanese so interpreted it. In other respects, the Root-Takahira Agreement (1908) provides a good summary of Roosevelt's aims and achievements in the Far East.

### Europe: First Involvement

Roosevelt's experience with Far Eastern problems encouraged him to widen his view of world affairs. He soon saw that what was happening in the power struggle in Eastern Asia was related to the shifting pressures in the cockpit of Europe. If America was to play a great role in the world, as he wished, she could not remove herself completely from the game of power politics played in the chanceries of European capitals. Increasingly, especially in his second term,

Roosevelt interested himself in the complex rivalries of the European states.

The old balance of power had been seriously upset by the rise to prominence of an expansionistic, militaristic Germany in the late nineteenth century. Britain, for a century the strongest nation in Europe, began to fear the growing might of Germany more than she did her traditional enemies, France·and Russia. In the scramble to redress the shift in power, Britain allied herself with her former foes against a Germany that claimed Austria-Hungary and Italy as allies. The Balkan peninsula and North Africa provided the scenes for a series of tests of the power and intentions of the two armed camps. One of these involved the United States. In 1905 the Germans became strongly alarmed at French efforts to bring all of Morocco under their control. The German Kaiser went to Tangiers, where he vigorously asserted German intentions not to be squeezed out of commercial and other rights guaranteed by earlier agreement. A full-blown crisis quickly ensued.

Just the year before these events, TR had blusteringly intervened in Moroccan affairs to effect the release of a supposed American citizen, Ion Perdicaris, who was being held by a Moroccan chieftain named Raisuli. On the eve of the Republican convention of 1904 he had authorized Hay to send a telegram to the American consul demanding "Perdicaris alive or Raisuli dead." In truth, the arrangements had already been made for releasing the prisoner and Roosevelt knew that Perdicaris was not an American citizen as claimed, but the political advantage of the telegram proved irresistible.

Now he was asked by Kaiser Wilhelm, with whom he had been carrying on a lively correspondence, to use his influence to arrange a conference to settle the Moroccan question and avert war. Though reluctant, TR consented to seek British and French agreement. He urged the French to attend the conference, privately assuring them that the United States would oppose any unreasonable German demands. After considerable diplomatic work behind the scenes, the conference finally convened in June, 1905, at Algeciras, Spain. Two Americans, one of them Henry White, represented the President and played a conciliatory role. The conference gave France, with the United States backing her at most points, much of what she wanted, but the Germans won a number of minor concessions and the propagandistic victory of seeming to have forced the French into arbitrating their demands. The American role was limited, but it was enough to scare the Senate into announcing that it was "without purpose to depart from the traditional American foreign policy. . . ."

## The New Role in the Americas

In still other parts of the world, American policy thrust out in new directions during the Roosevelt years. Nowhere did the new approach have more immediate consequences than in the lands surrounding the Caribbean Sea. The war with Spain highlighted the importance of this area to the United States and accentuated the demand for an interoceanic canal. After the war, the retention of Puerto Rico and the insistence on the Platt Amendment to the Cuban constitution made it clear that the United States did not intend to withdraw from this strategic area.

Before Roosevelt took office, a way had been cleared through the diplomatic underbrush for the building of an American canal across Central America. He became President just in time to see the Senate ratify the Hay-Pauncefote Treaty (1901), by which Britain conceded to the United States the right to build, control, and fortify a canal and surrendered her rights under an earlier treaty to share in the construction and control of such a canal. But there were other obstacles. A route had not been decided upon. The rights to the Panama route across Colombian territory (Panama belonged to Colombia) were held by a French company that had failed in its attempt to build a canal in the 1880's. Represented in the United States by an American lawyer, William N. Cromwell, and a remarkable Frenchman, Philippe Bunau-Varilla, the company sought to sell its interests in Panama to the United States. Just as American sentiment was swinging sharply in favor of a route across Nicaragua, primarily because of the lesser expense, Bunau-Varilla, the former chief engineer of the French canal project, arrived on the scene. His lobbying instincts were superb. He crowned a series of timely moves with a master stroke in May, 1902, when, just before the critical Senate vote on the treaty, he placed a postage stamp depicting the eruption of a Nicaraguan volcano on the desk of every Senator. In June, 1902, the Spooner Act was passed naming Panama as the site for the isthmian canal providing arrangements could be made with Colombia within "a reasonable time."

The spotlight now turned on Colombia. The French company, whose rights ran out in 1904, was eager to sell; but would Colombia grant long-term rights to its Panamanian territory? Under tremendous pressure the Colombian representative in Washington, Tomás Herrán, signed an agreement with John Hay calling for a canal zone six miles wide to be turned over to the United States for $10 million and an annual payment of $250,000. But the Colombian government balked at these arrangements. Incensed at the prospect of infringement on her sovereignty in Panama and influenced, too, by the prospect of getting the $40 million to be paid the French company if a year's delay could be arranged, the Colombian Senate refused to ratify the Hay-Herrán Treaty.

Roosevelt was in a towering rage. The Colombians were "homicidal corruptionists" and "contemptible little creatures," he declared on various occasions. Events now moved swiftly. Panamanians ripe for revolt, fearful that the canal might go to Nicaragua, worked closely with conspirators representing the French company. The attitude of the United States government was crucial. Would it cooperate? Would it prevent Colombian troops from crushing a revolution in Panama? The conspirators became satisfied that the United States would interpret an old treaty of 1846 with Colombia (then New Granada) that bound both powers to maintain "free transit" across Panama to mean that Colombian troops would not be allowed to land.

On November 3, 1903, the day following the arrival of the U.S.S. *Nashville,* the uprising on Panama began. The American navy stopped Colombia from landing troops. Three days later the United States recognized the Republic of Panama, and in two weeks a pact had been concluded with Panama conveying a ten-mile zone to the United States.

How guilty was the United States? How much responsibility should she assume for the course of events? Though historians have disagreed, there is seemingly conclusive evidence that the United States government did not foment the Panamanian revolution. Whatever credit or discredit is attached to the engineering of the revolt should probably go to Bunau-Varilla. It cannot be denied, however, that the presence of the American naval force made the uprising successful and that the American interpretation of the 1846 treaty was at best questionable, at worst dishonest. Roosevelt and others pointed to the undeniable fact that the Panamanians themselves were anxious to see the canal built across their land and that an isthmian canal would serve the interests of most of the civilized world. But many Americans felt a sense of guilt about the treatment of Colombia. To salve that feeling, during the Wilson administration a treaty was negotiated with Colombia in which the United States expressed "sincere regret" over Panama and promised to pay $25 million as an indemnity. This agreement was blocked by Roosevelt and his friends, but, ultimately, a Republican administration did pay Colombia that sum though it withheld the written apology.

The strong hand that TR showed in dealing with Colombia was symbolic of an important shift in policy toward Latin America. The power of the United States was now felt everywhere in the Caribbean and throughout South America. Even the great powers of Europe deferred to American opinion on matters affecting the Western Hemisphere. When Germany and Great Britain proposed to blockade Venezuela in 1902 to force her to make good her debts, for example, they informed the United States first of their intentions. Even so, American opinion was aroused when the Germans bombarded and destroyed a coastal village. "Worse international manners," fumed an editorial writer in the New York *Times*, "have rarely come under the observation of civilized men." Both Germany and Britain were anxious to arbitrate the dispute and to end the impasse quickly. In February, 1903, the blockading powers signed an arbitration agreement with Venezuela.

What *should* the United States do when a foreign power intervened in Latin America to collect a debt? The question arose again in 1904 when a bankrupt Dominican Republic faced the prospect of European intervention. The hapless Dominican President turned to the United States for help. With misgivings, Roosevelt laid down a new policy in a message to Congress in December, 1904. "Chronic wrongdoing," he told the congressmen, "may . . . ultimately require intervention by some civilized nation, and in the Western Hemisphere the adherence of the United States to the Monroe Doctrine may force the United States, however reluctantly, in flagrant cases of wrongdoing or impotence, to the exercise of an international police power." Thus did Roosevelt add an important corollary to the Monroe Doctrine: The United States would act as policeman in this hemisphere and thereby obviate the necessity of European meddling. To keep the Europeans out of Latin America, we would go in.

In the case of the Dominican Republic, the new policy meant the taking over of customs collection in that country. After that first step, there followed periods of protracted American intervention in Nica-

"Building the Pedro Miguel Lock," Panama Canal, by Joseph Pennell. The Isthmian Canal Commission considered making the canal at sea-level, without locks or building it about 85 feet above sea-level, with locks. The latter plan was adopted as being cheaper, faster to build, and easier to navigate. Actual construction took about 7 years, and cost 366 million dollars. (Library of Congress.)

ragua, Haiti, and Cuba. By World War I, American marines had become familiar with the terrain of all four of these lands. In each, Americans did a great deal to restore financial order, to build schools, hospitals, and roads, and to create a constabulary to prevent future revolutionary disturbances. But a backlog of ill will against "Yankee imperialism" was also built up, especially when the new constabularies were used to support military dictatorships. The last American troops were not withdrawn from the Dominican Republic until 1924, from Nicaragua until 1925, and from Haiti until 1934. Since then, despite serious provocations, no

American marine has seen this kind of duty in Latin America.

North of the border, relations with our Canadian neighbors were generally much better than with the states to the south. Only one serious contretemps disturbed American-Canadian relations in the first decade of the century. The dispute was over the boundary line between Alaska and Canada. With the discovery of gold in northwestern Canada, the exact location of the line became important. At issue was the question whether the boundary in the Alaskan panhandle should follow the heads of the inlets along the coast or the headlands of the peninsulas. The Canadians, who claimed the former, desperately wanted an outlet to the sea. Most of the historical and legal evidence, however, supported the American position and Roosevelt adamantly refused to submit the issue to arbitration. He agreed finally only when convinced that the decision could not go against the United States. Three of the six "impartial jurists of repute," who were to constitute the arbitral commission would be appointed by Roosevelt. To the consternation of Canadians, he appointed Senator Lodge, Secretary of War Root, and Senator George Turner. The commission's decisions, since two of the remaining three commissioners were Canadian, hinged on the lone Britisher, Lord Alverstone. In the background Roosevelt threatened to use troops to take the disputed territory if the tribunal failed to reach agreement. But this proved not to be necessary. Under great pressure from his own countrymen, who were anxious for good relations with the United States, Lord Alverstone held for the Americans. Except for minor concessions to the Canadians, the commission decided all the major issues 4-2 in favor of the Americans' contentions. Roosevelt had not only gained satisfaction of the Americans' claims but had won a notable diplomatic triumph.

## TR's Legacy

When Roosevelt quitted the White House in 1909, he left behind a record of commitments and actions that betokened a revolution in America's position in the world. In the Far East, in Latin America, and even in Europe, the United States was playing a far more vigorous part in world affairs than it was when he succeeded McKinley eight years before. The office of the presidency itself had begun to take on some of the characteristics of world leadership that were to mark it later in the century. To the historian George Trevelyan, TR wrote in 1908 a fitting epitaph for his own conduct of foreign relations: "While President I have *been* President, emphatically. I have used every ounce of power there was in the office . . . and whenever I could establish a precedent for strength in the executive, as I did for instance in regards external affairs in the case of sending the fleet around the world, taking Panama, settling affairs of Santo Domingo and Cuba . . . I have felt not merely that my action was right in itself, but that in showing the strength of, or in giving strength to, the executive, I was establishing a precedent of value."

## Dollars for Diplomacy

TR's successor in the presidency, though he shared many of TR's broad objectives, lacked his aggressive and vigorous spirit. Taft was especially concerned with foreign trade and investment and sought to encourage and promote the interests of American businessmen abroad. Much more than Roosevelt, he was influenced by the desires and interests of the business community. It was far wiser, he felt, to build American influence abroad by sending dollars instead of bullets. In China and Latin America, in particular, he sought to encourage American bankers and merchants to invest abroad. With his Secretary of State, Philander C. Knox, he worked out a complicated plan to force American and other foreign capital into Manchuria as a means of counterbalancing Japanese and Russian interests there. But he succeeded only in arousing suspicion and annoying American bankers who were never enthusiastic about the scheme. Roosevelt wrote skeptically to his old friend: "Never draw unless you mean to shoot . . . as regards Manchuria, if the Japanese choose to follow a course of conduct to which we are adverse, we cannot stop it unless we are prepared to go to war. . . ."

To protect the Panama Canal, Taft encouraged American investors to send capital into the Caribbean. This move would tend, he hoped, to promote financial stability, force European capital out of the area, and give the United States a larger voice in Caribbean affairs. In Honduras, Haiti, and especially Nicaragua, Taft used a combination of dollars and military force to achieve his objectives. To the Latin Americans this was economic imperialism pure and simple, and the hostility aroused by Roosevelt's rough-shod tactics in Panama was magnified many-fold during the Taft years. The germs of the anti-American feeling in Latin America that plagued the United States for half a century afterwards were spawned in the Roosevelt-Taft era.

### Wilson and Moral Diplomacy

The moral note that Roosevelt struck from time to time in his conduct of foreign affairs grew louder during the Wilson administration. No president of this century has thought more consistently than Wilson in terms of eternal values and ideals as the roots of public action. While TR cloaked his reliance on military strength in the language of righteousness, Wilson thought of power as a means of implementing ideals. America, he felt, should use her great moral influence to promote democratic aims in all parts of the world; the American mission had not yet been fulfilled. To his sensitive mind the militarism of Roosevelt and the dollar diplomacy of Taft were equally repugnant. "It is a very perilous thing," he said at Mobile, Alabama, soon after taking office, "to determine the foreign policy of a nation in terms of material interest. . . . We dare not turn from the principle that morality and not expediency is the thing that must guide us and that we will never condone iniquity because it is most convenient to do so."

Yet, for all his insistence on righteousness as the rule of nations, Wilson's policies in Latin America differed little from those of Taft and Roosevelt. Indeed, during the eight years he spent in the White House, the United States intervened in the affairs of Latin America on a scale undreamed of by his predecessors. Nicaragua was made virtually an American protectorate; the Dominican Republic was occupied by American forces; and Haiti became little more than a puppet of the American State Department. The severest test for what Arthur Link has called Wilson's "missionary diplomacy" came in Mexico. Here he confronted a revolutionary regime led by General Victoriano Huerta, who had just accomplished a *coup d'etat* and murdered his democratically minded predecessor. What should American policy be?

Most of the great powers recognized the Huerta regime, as was customary in diplomatic practice, but Wilson was adamant. He refused to recognize a government headed by an assassin. Instead, he announced a policy of "watchful waiting" to see what would happen in Mexico as opposition to Huerta gathered under the banner of Venustiano Carranza. Asked the basis of his Latin American policy, the

President replied: to "teach the South American republics to elect good men!" He won British support for his Mexican position by promising to protect British property should Carranza win and also by his leadership in getting Congress to repeal a law exempting American coastal vessels from Panama Canal tolls—a law the British held to be a violation of previous agreements. Then Wilson hatched a daring scheme. He offered American aid to Carranza against Huerta, providing the former would guarantee an orderly, constitutional regime in Mexico. Carranza, who resented American interference in Mexican affairs, refused, though he did promise to respect the rights of property. Deep in a quandary, Wilson finally took

Pancho Villa (1877–1923), Mexican revolutionary general. Villa began his career as a cattle rustler. His hatred for the "gringos" led to his outrages along the United States-Mexican border. In 1923, Villa and three companions were assassinated. (Brown Brothers.)

Carranza's reply as sufficient token to raise the embargo that had hitherto kept American arms from reaching Carranza's rebels.

Then an incident in April, 1914, drew the United States deeper into the Mexican maelstrom. A number of American sailors were arrested in Tampico by a Mexican detachment, marched through the streets, and finally released. The commanding Mexican colonel expressed regrets but the ranking American officer delivered an ultimatum asking for a formal apology and a twenty-one gun salute to the American flag. Wilson now asked Congress for authority to use force in Mexico. But even before the Senate had a chance to act, Wilson ordered the bombardment and occupation of Vera Cruz, where a German merchant ship was about to land arms for the Huerta regime.

War seemed imminent. Carranza joined Huerta in protesting the American action, and diplomatic relations between the United States and Mexico were cut off. Wilson's diplomacy had brought the nation to a formidable impasse: Either the United States must retreat from its belligerent stand and suffer humiliation, or else she must wage an unpopular war with Mexico. Fortunately, a way out presented itself when the so-called ABC powers (Argentina, Brazil, and Chile) offered to mediate. Though the ensuing conference solved nothing, war was averted and Huerta went into exile in July, 1914.

Carranza was now in power, but still Mexico knew no peace. One of Carranza's lieutenants, Pancho Villa, at this point turned against his chief. The revolution grew even more bloody and anarchic. Foreign property was seized or destroyed by both sides, clergymen were savagely attacked, and anti-American sentiment leaped with the suspicion that Wilson was preparing to back Villa. Ultimately, in October, 1915, Wilson gave de facto recognition to the Carranza government. An enraged Villa now took vengeance upon the United States. In January, 1916, eighteen Americans with safe-conduct passes from Carranza were taken from a train at Santa Ysabel and shot by Villa's men. Two months later, Villa crossed the border at Columbus, New Mexico, and killed seventeen Americans in cold blood.

Wilson now ordered General Pershing south of the border with the command to capture Villa dead or alive. Though Carranza had given ambiguous consent to the expedition, his supporters grew increasingly apprehensive as Pershing moved southward. Noncooperation turned to hostility. When a Mexican general ordered Pershing to stop, Wilson sent 150,000 men to the border. War again seemed imminent. And once more it was averted only by sober second thoughts on both sides and by the growing tension in American relations with Germany, which added to the pressure on Wilson for conciliation. The American troops were finally withdrawn from Mexico in February, 1917, *sans* war, *sans* victory, and *sans* Villa.

Wilson's policy in Mexico, while often blundering and inconclusive, did show a great deal of restraint and patience. To his credit, he turned a deaf ear during these critical years to pleas for more vigorous intervention in the Mexican Revolution. Had he followed the advice of TR and those who counseled forcing our way in Mexico, there would probably have been no social revolution there at all, because the United States would have suppressed it. And few would now deny that the Mexicans had the right to work out their own destiny and attempt the establishment of a democratic regime in their own way. "We can afford," Wilson told

Congress in 1913, "to exercise the self-restraint of a really great nation which realizes its own strength and scorns to misuse it."

The termination of Wilson's intervention in Mexico marked the end of twenty years of revolutionary change in American relations with the outer world. From timid and desultory probing into other parts of the world, American leaders had turned to a vigorous if not always consistent assertion of American rights and interests abroad. In the Far East, the United States had occupied the Philippines, sanctioned the Open Door in China, mediated in the Russo-Japanese War, and reached a somewhat uncertain understanding with Japan. In Europe, we had played a minor role at Algeciras, drawn closer to Britain, and become increasingly suspicious of Germany. In the Western Hemisphere, we had gone farthest of all in sanctioning the use of American military and economic strength to reach our objectives. By the beginning of World War I, the United States had acquired territory in the West Indies, begun the construction of an isthmian canal, built American protectorates in the surrounding lands of the Caribbean, and extended the meaning of the Monroe Doctrine to cover a number of new situations. The policies of the United States, it seems fair to say, had become worldwide in scope during those twenty eventful years. And the commitments, both actual and implied, of the American government during this crucial interval sounded for the first time the themes of involvements and actions whose echoes are still reverberating in the second half of the twentieth century.

## DID AMERICA EMERGE FROM ISOLATION?

Early in this chapter we asked several questions. What forces changed American attitudes toward foreign affairs? How far did we go? In these pages we have been tracing out the answers. But one final question needs to be answered. How complete was the American emergence from isolation? It has become commonplace for historians to point to the years immediately after 1898 as marking a dramatic reversal in historic American attitudes toward world responsibility. In one sense, this is true. Americans did fight a foreign war, dabble in the politics of Europe and Asia, build a strong navy, and enlarge greatly their commitments in Latin America. But in another sense the policies followed between 1898 and 1914 marked no sharp break with the past. The United States still refused to make any foreign commitment limiting American independence of action; no alliances with foreign powers were contracted during these years; the idea of America's peculiar mission in the world was not new; and American intervention south of the Rio Grande was still based on the Monroe Doctrine proclaimed in the previous century. The great themes of American foreign policy before 1898, it might well be argued, survived almost intact to 1914.

Nor did the average American's views of the larger world outside his boundaries undergo great change during these years. It would be hard to show that his cultural nationalism, which had caused him to stress American separateness and exclusiveness in the nineteenth century, had slackened appreciably by 1914. Most Americans still found domestic concerns far more arresting than European quarrels. Walter Lippmann, writing many years later, could recall no personal interest in foreign affairs until after the outbreak of World War I. Like many young reformers, he thought TR quite eccentric for harping about the need for a canal and a larger navy. War was something only "militarists" talked about. "I remained quite innocent," he recalled, "of any understanding of the revolutionary consequences of the Spanish-American War."

Most Americans took no more interest than Lippmann in the events that seem in retrospect so important to our diplomatic history. They frequently seemed to look upon themselves only as casual observers of foreign events who occasionally played a bit role when a full cast was lacking. While their leaders embarked on programs of political and economic imperialism abroad, they tended to remain psychologically and culturally isolated in their thinking. An alarming discrepancy was growing between Americans' commitments outside their boundaries and their willingness to accept full responsibility for their actions. Even their military readiness was periodically endangered by skeptics who felt the United States should disarm and thereby escape involvement in future wars. Most Americans placed great faith in moral preachments against war and in treaties of arbitration or conciliation with foreign countries. It was natural that Bryan, a long-time leader of the peace movement, should negotiate some thirty conciliation treaties with Wilson's full approval during his tenure as Secretary of State.

Significantly, Germany refused to conclude one of Bryan's treaties. The first real test of American isolation came not in 1898 but in 1914 when Germany's drive on the Western front endangered the Western democracies and posed questions that neither Wilson nor the American people had yet squarely faced.

# FOR FURTHER STUDY

*The books by Harbaugh, Hofstadter, Leopold, Link, Mowry, and Pringle cited at the end of Chapter II continue to be especially useful for the topics dealt with in this chapter.*

## General Accounts

T. Bailey, A *Diplomatic History of the American People*, 6th edition (New York: Appleton-Century-Crofts, 1958). This has long been a popular general history of American foreign relations.

* O. Barck, Jr. (ed.), *America in the World* (New York: World, 1961). A useful paperbound collection of documents.

R. Bartlett (ed.), *The Record of American Diplomacy* (New York: Knopf, 1947). An excellent collection of documents and materials bearing on our diplomatic history.

F. Dulles, *America's Rise to World Power 1898-1954* (New York: Harper, 1954). A good account centering on the contest between internationalism and isolationism.

D. Perkins, *The Evolution of American Foreign Policy* (New York: Oxford U. Press, 1948). A delightful little book tracing the main themes of American policy toward other nations.

J. Pratt, A *History of United States Foreign Policy* (Englewood Cliffs, N.J.: Prentice-Hall, Inc., 1955). Another good text.

## Special Studies

H. Beale, *Theodore Roosevelt and the Rise of America to World Power* (Baltimore: The Johns Hopkins Press, 1956). An important reinterpretation of the Roosevelt years which is more sympathetic to the Rough Rider than earlier accounts.

S. Bemis, *The Latin American Policy of the United States* (New York: Harcourt, Brace, 1943). A standard work that stoutly defends American policy.

C. Bowers, *Beveridge and the*

* Starred books are available in paperbound editions.

*Progressive Era* (Boston: Houghton Mifflin, 1932). A very good biography of this Indiana champion of imperialism.

E. Burns, *The American Idea of Mission* (New Brunswick: Rutgers U. Press, 1957). An important recent book exploring the concepts of national purpose and destiny.

T. Dennett, *John Hay* (New York: Dodd, Mead, 1933). The most complete biography of this key figure in American diplomacy.

A. Dennis, *Adventures in American Diplomacy, 1896-1906* (New York: Dutton, 1928). Though a bit dated in some respects, this book is still a valuable summary of these turn-of-the-century years.

F. Dulles, *The Imperial Years* (New York: Crowell, 1956). Covers much the same ground as Dennis but with more recent viewpoints and scholarship.

F. Freidel, *The Splendid Little War* (Boston: Little, Brown, 1958). A pictures-and-text coverage of the Spanish War.

* T. Greene (ed.), *American Imperialism in 1898* (Boston: D. C. Heath, 1955). The pros and cons on the taking of the Philippines from contemporary and historical writings.

* G. Kennan, *American Diplomacy 1900-1950* (Chicago: U. of Chicago Press, 1951). An interpretation by a practicing diplomat that stresses power realities in the making of foreign policy.

A. Link, *Wilson the Diplomatist* (Baltimore: The Johns Hopkins Press, 1957). A valuable analysis and interpretation of Wilson's assumptions, techniques, and achievements in foreign affairs.

W. Millis, *The Martial Spirit* (Boston: Houghton Mifflin, 1931). Perhaps the best general

history of the American war with Spain.

S. Nearing and J. Freeman, *Dollar Diplomacy* (New York: B. W. Huebach and the Viking Press, 1926). A very critical study of American imperialism.

H. Notter, *The Origins of the Foreign Policy of Woodrow Wilson* (Baltimore: The Johns Hopkins Press, 1937). A massive study of the background of Wilson's thought in foreign affairs.

J. Pratt, *America's Colonial Experiment* (Englewood Cliffs, N.J.: Prentice-Hall, 1950). The subtitle indicates the theme: "How the United States Gained, Governed, and in Part Gave Away a Colonial Empire."

———, *Expansionists of 1898* (Baltimore: The Johns Hopkins Press, 1936). Among its themes is the argument that businessmen generally did not clamor for intervention in Cuba.

J. Rippy, *America and the Strife of Europe* (Chicago: U. of Chicago Press, 1938). Argues convincingly that European conflicts have had an enduring effect on the ideology and programs of American diplomacy.

A. Weinberg, *Manifest Destiny* (Baltimore: The Johns Hopkins Press, 1935). A unique and valuable study of the role of ideas and attitudes in American national expansion.

## Fiction and Poetry

E. Howe, *The Story of a Country Town* (New York: Albert and Charles Boni, 1926). First published in 1883, this book is a poignant account of the cultural isolation and narrowness of small-town life in nineteenth-century America.

* H. James, *The Ambassadors* (New York: Harper, 1902). Like many of James' novels, the plot of this one concerns a group of

Americans caught up in the charm and allure of a ripe European culture.

R. Kipling, *A Choice of Kipling's Verse* (New York: Scribner's, 1943). Includes among other selections "The White Man's Burden," which was first addressed to Americans in 1899.

* M. Twain, *The Adventures of Huckleberry Finn* (New York: Harper, 1899). A classic of nineteenth-century literature containing many shrewd insights into the American's outlook on his world.

## Films and Records

*Building the Panama Canal* (Knowledge Builders, 11 minutes, sound, black and white). Begins with some historical scenes of the actual construction of the canal.

*Freedom for the Philippines* (Prudential Insurance Company, 29 minutes, sound, black and white). Though focussed on a later period in Filipino history, this film contains material relevant to this chapter.

*United States Expansion Overseas, 1893-1917* (Coronet Films, 14 minutes, sound, color). Reviews the expansion of the United States in Hawaii, the Philippines, and Central America.

*U.S.A., A World Power* (National Educational Television, 29 minutes, sound, black and white). A televised discussion of late-nineteenth-century imperialism and the expansion of the United States beyond its continental boundaries.

1914-1920

# Armageddon I

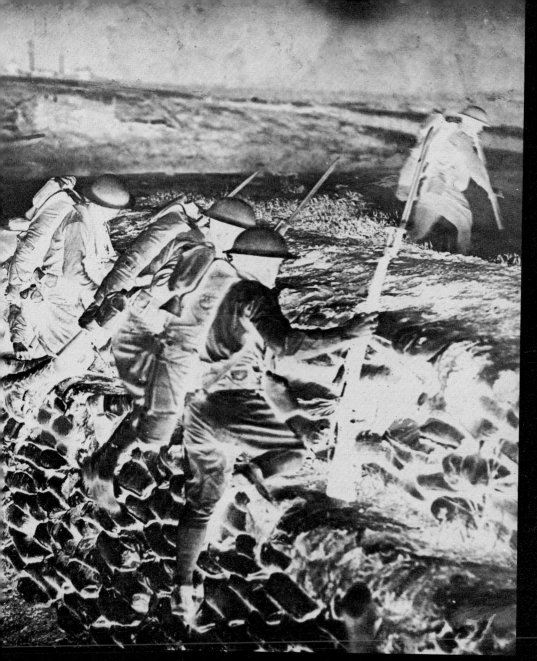

## CHAPTER FOUR

Doughboys charging from a trench, 1918.

THE MOOD OF THE TIMES

"When you know . . . that the sky is full of floating sparks from a great conflagration, are you going to sit down and say it will be time when the fire begins to do something about it? I do not believe that the fire is going to begin, but I would be surer of it if we were ready for the fire. And I want to come as your responsible servant and tell you this, that we do not control the fire. We are under the influence of it, but we are not at the sources of it. We are where it any time may affect us, and yet we can not govern its spread and progress.

"If it once touches us, it may touch the very sources of our life, for it may touch the very things we stand for, and we might for a little while be unable successfully to vindicate and defend them. . . .

"There are two things which practically everybody who comes to the Executive Office in Washington tells me. They tell me, 'The people are counting upon you to keep us out of this war.' And in the next breath what do they tell, 'The people are equally counting upon you to maintain the honor of the United States.' Have you reflected that a time might come when I could not do both? And have you made yourselves ready to stand behind your Government for the maintenance of the honor of your country, as well as for the maintenance of the peace of the country? If I am to maintain the honor of the United States and it should be necessary to exert the force of the United States in order to do it, have you made the force ready? You know that you have not, and the very fact that the force is not ready may make the task you have set for me all the more delicate and all the more difficult."

—WOODROW WILSON, 1916

# THE TROUBLED NEUTRAL, 1914–1917

Wilson's words fell on the ears of an audience grown used to danger and crisis. Two years earlier, in 1914, the American people had watched with fascination and horror the deadly movements that sent Europe reeling into war. First, the heir to the Austrian throne had been slain. Then came the threats, accusations, and warnings that burst like shrapnel in an ominous war of words. These were followed by the dreaded mobilization of the armies and the frantic last-minute moves to avert catastrophe. Finally, the guns sounded. By 1916, the world had grown accustomed, after grim months of carnage and stalemate, to the awful inhumanity that is war.

The First World War runs like a dividing line across the map of modern history. On one side lies a century of relative peace, an optimistic age of economic progress and scientific faith, the confident world of the Victorians; on the other falls an era of violence, a time of insecurity and anxiety, a century of totalitarians. Old power relations were changed at this watershed: Germany, Japan, Russia, China, and the United States were now clearly on the rise, while England and France were definitely on the wane. The economic center of the world shifted from London to Wall Street, and the United States became a creditor nation for the first time. Manners and

morals underwent a revolution during and after the war. The old order of values was seriously shaken: doubt and skepticism, even nihilism, pushed farther to the fore, while traditional Christian values were forced on the defensive. No matter what his station or fortune, the perceptive Englishman, Frenchman, or American found the texture of life somehow different in 1920 from what it had been in 1914.

In the United States the impact of the war was far greater in many more directions than most Americans realized at the time. It marked not only the arrest of the reform impulse but it scattered and demoralized the reformers themselves. Progressivism never fully recovered from the blows dealt it during the war years, and the progressive spirit was overtaken by the cautious, illiberal, and suspicious temper of the early nineteen-twenties. Within the ranks of the progressive intellectuals, split by divisions growing out of the war, Dewey's humane and optimistic liberalism never regained the full-throated assent it had commanded in the prewar years. In literature the war opened a breach between the generation of Hamlin Garland and that of Ernest Hemingway and John Dos Passos. Among radicals the war cast up issues that kept the socialists, Wobblies, and others in constant civil war. As in western Europe, old attitudes and values seemed to disintegrate while new and unfamiliar ones rose to take their place. The war was fought on a highly moralistic plane, but the very frenzy of the idealism made certain that the ultimate reaction would be more intense. Thus, after 1920, few Americans were able to recover the spirit of idealism that had led them to crusade for democracy both at home and abroad.

### First Reactions

The average American of 1920, indeed, had difficulty remembering the sense of shock he had felt at the outbreak of war in 1914. His senses were dulled by six years of crisis and bloodshed. Many had felt in 1914 that war was no longer possible. They thought the whole trend of modern civilization was away from brutality and force. "The friends of peace," wrote an editor of the New York *Times*, "have counted upon the highly civilized nations like England, France, with the United States, to discountenance war, to make wars impossible." War was a reversion to savagery, a backsliding "to the condition of savage tribes roaming the forests and falling upon each other in a fury of blood and carnage to achieve the ambitious designs of chieftains clad in skins and drunk with mead." But when the impossible reversion actually happened, all of man's hopes for peaceful progress and the intelligent solution of social conflicts seemed momentarily dashed. "I had a feeling that the end of things had come," wrote the Secretary of Agriculture, David Houston; "I stopped in my tracks, dazed and horror-stricken."

For more than a quarter-century, the nations of Europe, in Lloyd George's picturesque phrase, had "staggered and stumbled" toward war. The rise of German power, accompanied by a system of military agreements with Austria and Italy, had frightened England, France, and Russia, who were traditional enemies, into an opposing military alliance. Imperial rivalry and nationalistic aspirations in the Balkans had added heavily to the growing danger of war. Then had come the blow-up in the Balkans, when the Austrians moved to punish Serbia for its alleged role in the assassination of the Hapsburg Archduke. First Russia, then Germany, and finally France and Britain were quickly drawn into the vortex of conflict.

To most Americans the war seemed sheer madness. Neither the President nor the public showed any great interest in understanding the power politics, the nationalistic ambitions, or the fears and emotions that underlay the conflict. Scarcely anyone argued that the country had a stake in the war. The effect of the war on the United States, said Wilson, would depend on what American citizens said and did. "Every man who really loves America," he warned, "will act and speak in the true spirit of neutrality, which is the spirit of impartiality and fairness and friendliness to all concerned." Wilson well knew the danger of exciting the passions of a people drawn from many European nations. A strong division of opinion might even be fatal to the internal peace of the United States. The nation must therefore "be neutral in fact as well as in name. . . . We must be impartial in thought as well as in action. . . ."

Wilson was asking the impossible. One of every seven Americans in 1914 was foreign-born, and with their children they accounted for perhaps a third of the American population. They could not easily forget the lands of their birth and culture. Unavoidably, throughout the war years, German-Americans, Irish-Americans, Anglo-Americans, and other

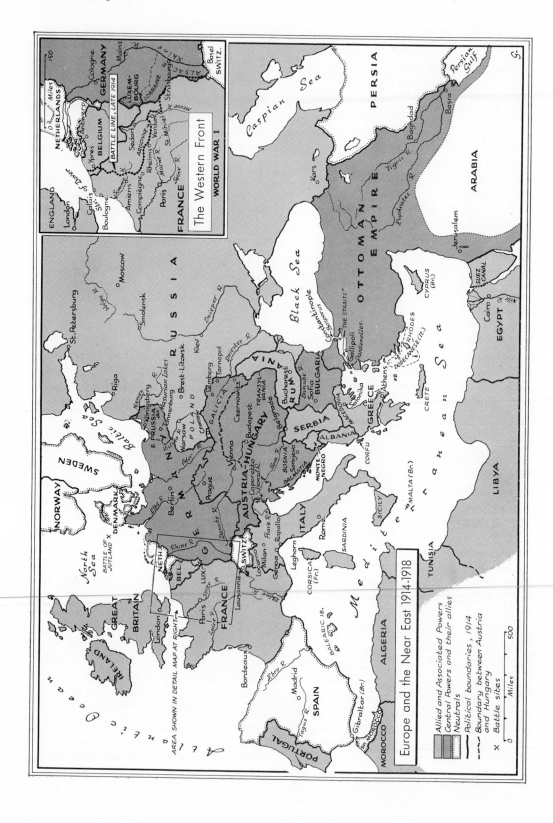

The Western Front
**WORLD WAR I**

BATTLE LINE, LATE 1914

Europe and the Near East 1914-1918

Allied and Associated Powers
Central Powers and their allies
Neutrals
Political boundaries, 1914
Boundary between Austria
and Hungary
Battle sites

Miles
0        500

"hyphenated Americans" were subject to conflicting tugs on their emotions and their politics. Partisanship was inevitable. In the case of Britain, a thousand ties of history, language, law, literature, and tradition strengthened the emotional appeal of her cause. Nor could the sentimental forget the debt America owed to France for her help in the winning of American independence. All in all, the scales of partiality weighed heavily toward the Allies, notably Britain and France.

Events of recent memory, too, sharpened Britain's advantage over Germany in the contest for American favor. For two decades Britain and America had been moving steadily toward one another in recognition of their common interests. In the same interval Germany had suffered from increasing suspicion and doubt about her intentions. The circumstances surrounding the outbreak of war only intensified the suspicion. For Germany's close ally, Austria-Hungary, by refusing to submit the Serbian crisis to arbitration, had set off the train of events that led to general war. Then, once war came, the German armies moved swiftly through neutral Belgium, and the German chancellor shocked world opinion by denouncing the treaty guaranteeing Belgian neutrality as "a scrap of paper." Early reports of German atrocities, now known to be exaggerated, seemed at the time to confirm the picture of Imperial Germany already formed in America.

Even the President and his closest advisors, with one important exception, were not neutral in their private thoughts. There can be no question that Wilson, with his fondness for British institutions and culture, hoped ardently for an Allied victory. Time after time, when Allied fortunes ebbed, the President confided his deepest fears to those around him. His private secretary recalled after the war that Wilson once remarked, "England is fighting our fight and . . . I shall not

. . . place obstacles in her way." Among his near advisors only his Secretary of State, William Jennings Bryan, approached the absolute impartiality that Wilson demanded at the outset of the war. But Bryan's conscience forced him to leave the Cabinet in the first year of war when he felt that Wilson's policies were leading this nation toward involvement. His successor, Robert Lansing, was, by contrast, persuaded early that American security would be endangered by a German victory and looked to the day "when the mass of our people are convinced of the real character of the German government and are awake to its sinister designs. . . ." Of Wilson's other advisors, his personal confidant and emissary, Colonel Edward House, and his ambassador to Britain, Walter Hines Page, made little effort to disguise their strong pro-Allied feelings. In August, 1915, House wrote Page that "Our hopes, our aspirations and our sympathies are closely woven with the democracies of France and England, and it is this that causes our hearts and potential economic help to go out to them. . . ."

## Problems of a Neutral

Nevertheless, for all their private sympathies, Wilson and his administration tried hard to follow a genuinely neutral policy toward the European belligerents, though it was not easy. Basically, they aimed at defending American neutral rights as defined under international law and at staying out of the war. Actually, so long as no vital American interest was threatened, it was inconceivable to most Americans that they could be drawn into the orgy of violence. But the time might come, as Wilson warned in the statement quoted at the opening of the chapter, when the defense of neutral rights and the avoidance of war might become incompatible.

What were neutral rights? There was the rub. Since the last great war a century before, war itself had been undergoing drastic changes. The Napoleonic Wars had introduced the concept of "the nation in arms"—the idea that wars are fought by whole nations and their peoples, not just by professional soldiers —and the Civil War in the United States had provided a foretaste of what modern war would be like. Then, in 1914, came the first real experience of "total war" on a grand scale. Since Napoleon's time, vast technological and industrial advances had taken place that made warfare more ruthlessly efficient. The result was a blurring of the historic distinctions between soldiers and civilians, contraband and noncontraband goods, neutrals and belligerents. What were the "rights" of a neutral in the time of total war? In pragmatic truth, they were only those rights that the belligerents, for whatever reason, chose to respect.

In basing American policy on legalistic and historical grounds, Wilson set his face against the lawlessness and terrorism of the new century. The course he chose would seem archaic and unrealistic to a later generation. At the time, the belligerents, fighting for their very existence, were exasperated by Wilson's legalism and his old-fashioned notions of national honor. So were many of his countrymen. Some of them favored a more outspokenly pro-Allied policy that would look to the eventual commitment of American power in the war; others favored a more strictly impartial position regardless of America's legal "rights." Wilson warned the latter group against accepting "any abridgement of the rights of American citizens in any respect. . . . Once accept a single abatement of right, and many other humiliations would certainly follow, and the whole fine fabric of international law might crumble under our hands piece by piece."

From the beginning, both Britain and Germany followed a strategy of realism aimed at survival. When Wilson proposed that all belligerents accept the unratified Declaration of London (1909), which imposed severe limitations on the use of sea power against neutral trade, Germany, a land power, made haste to agree while Britain, mistress of the seas, politely refused. Britain proceeded to ignore the Declaration's distinctions between contraband and noncontraband goods as she sought to halt every possible shipment of neutral goods destined for the adversary. She took the not unreasonable position that in modern war virtually every item brought into an enemy country, including food, helps the antagonist's forces and prolongs the war. The British took further liberties with the traditional maritime right of visit and search on the open sea, arguing that the bulkiness of modern vessels and the constant submarine danger required them to bring intercepted merchant ships into port before searching them. American shippers were further upset when the British abandoned the stationary blockades used in past wars and dispatched their ships on the high seas to intercept neutral vessels enroute to Germany. They were disturbed, too, when, in early November, 1914, the British sowed mines throughout the entire North Sea so that no neutral ship dared enter the area without stopping first at a British port.

Each of these British moves brought a strong protest from Washington, for the shutting off of German trade hurt American industries besides contravening American interpretations of maritime law. But the British played the game of diplomacy with consummate skill. They delayed; they made minor concessions; they asked for "clarifications"; they promised compensation for any losses. And they succeeded admirably in securing their objective of realizing, as Sir Edward

Grey put it some years later, "the maximum of blockade that could be enforced without a rupture with the United States."

Some Americans, then and later, argued that Wilson should have taken a stronger stand against the British actions. Yet so adroitly did the British dance to the American legalistic tune that at no time during the negotiations did Wilson have any real opportunity to gain the substance of his objectives. Maritime rules, after all, had been rewritten in every war, not least in the American Civil War, and the British legal case was a respectable one. Furthermore, the British controls were applied bit by bit so that American businessmen felt the pressure only gradually and unevenly. Besides, by the time the British blockade of Germany was complete, the war trade between America and Britain had reached boom proportions. And whenever the British *were* caught in some heavy-handed confiscation of a doubtful cargo, they paid so handsomely that the American shipper often profited from the blunder. Finally, in view of the legal character of Wilson's

objections, how could he have moved more decisively in an area of international law so full of contention and uncertainty? As Professor Link concludes, "it would have been more unneutral than neutral for Wilson to have broken the British maritime system by enforcing highly doubtful technical rights under international law." *

The Germans, of course, vehemently protested American acquiescence to the British maritime system. American industry, they charged, was simply delivering munitions into the enemy's hands. America's theoretical willingness to supply Germany on the same basis was little solace. "If it is the will of the American people that there should be a true neutrality," read one German note, "the United States will find some means of preventing this one-sided supply of arms or at least of utilizing it to protect legitimate trade with Germany, especially that in foodstuffs." Even Bryan realized, however, that an embargo on arms would

* A. Link, *Wilson the Diplomatist* (Baltimore: The Johns Hopkins Press, 1957), p. 43.

Bapaume, France. Devastation left in the wake of Allied advance. (New-York Historical Society.)

be a departure from strict neutrality. On January 24, 1915, he told an inquiring senator:

Those in this country who sympathize with Germany and Austria-Hungary appear to assume that some obligation rests upon this Government, in the performance of its neutral duty, to prevent all trade in contraband, and thus to equalize the difference due to the relative naval strength of the belligerents. No such obligation exists; it would be an unneutral act, an act of partiality on the part of the Government to adopt such a policy if the Executive had the power to do so. If Germany and Austria-Hungary cannot import contraband from this country it is not, because of that fact, the duty of the United States to close its markets to the Allies.

Bryan did convince the President that loans by American bankers to finance the war trade were unneutral. With his progressive suspicions of Wall Street, Bryan was certain that money was the worst of all contrabands because it controlled everything else. Therefore, in August, 1914, with Wilson's approval he informed the firm of J. P. Morgan that loans by private bankers to the belligerent governments were "inconsistent with the true spirit of neutrality." In actual fact, this policy was a radical departure from long-standing international practice. During the Civil War, the United States itself had borrowed heavily from European bankers. Gradually, though, as Allied funds became exhausted, the administration retreated from Bryan's position, initially through an ambiguous distinction between "loans" and "credits," finally by abandoning the prohibition altogether. By the time of the latter step (October, 1915), the country faced the prospect of seeing the war boom turn to depression if the Allies were not permitted to borrow heavily to pay for their needs. Even labor and farm organizations, which were strongly opposed to military intervention, favored supplying the Allies because of the obvious economic advantages to the United States.

### Submarines and Modern War

The perils of neutrality mounted as the belligerents grappled to a bloody standstill. Total victory was now the goal of all participants as they sought justification for the dreadful slaughter already committed. No instrument of terror or oppression was too horrible if it lessened the enemy's resistance. The Germans, in February, 1915, announced the opening of submarine warfare against all enemy vessels in a zone enveloping the British Isles. Neutrals were warned against sending ships into the area because of the difficulty of distinguishing them from belligerent vessels, which often flew neutral flags. With this one lightning stroke, Germany illumined the mortal danger in Wilson's policy of defending historic neutral rights amidst the indiscriminate warfare of the twentieth century. For the submarine was a novel weapon of terror. Although Germany had fewer than a dozen seaworthy U-boats in 1914, of which perhaps four could be engaged at once—far too few for a successful blockade—the submarine could frighten the neutrals and intimidate potential American shippers. And it could be justified as a reaction to the illegal British blockade.

Even with this development, Wilson could, if he wished, still retreat. He could acquiesce under protest in the sham submarine blockade as he had earlier in the British practices. Clearly, the stand he now took would determine the framework of German-American relations for the rest of the war, as his earlier stand had established his policy toward Britain. On February 10th, he made his decision. The German government would be held to "strict accountability" for the loss of any American ship or any American lives by submarine action. "To declare . . . a right to attack and destroy any vessel entering a prescribed area of the high seas without first certainly determining its belligerent nationality and the contraband character of its cargo would be an act so unprecedented in naval warfare that this Government is reluctant to believe . . . it . . . possible."

Wilson thus rejected any parallel between the indiscriminate taking of lives by German submarines and the arbitrary interference with trade by British warships. To a later generation, inured to total war, this distinction may seem blurred or partisan; to Wilson's generation—may it not be said to its credit?—it seemed sharp and real.

One point remained ambiguous. Did Wilson's firm warning apply to the loss of life on American ships only, or did it extend to Americans traveling on Allied vessels? The administration did not at first face this question squarely. For some time, Americans continued to embark on belligerent liners and merchantmen. An American citizen was soon killed aboard a British liner. In these circumstances, the German embassy took the unusual step of publishing a warning in New York newspapers that Americans sailed on Allied ships at their own risk. Then, on May 7, 1915, Lieutenant Commander Schwieger of the submarine U-20 discerned the silhouette of a giant liner in the fog off the Irish coast and unloosed a torpedo. As it sank out of sight, Schwieger made out the letters LUSITANIA through his binoculars. More than 1200 persons went down with the ship, including 128 Americans, many of them women and children. To millions of Americans the meaning of modern war was suddenly brought home with a horrifying shock.

"It is a deed for which a Hun would blush, a Turk be ashamed, and a Barbary pirate apologize," said *The Nation*. The magazine went on to echo a widespread sentiment that in sinking the *Lusitania* Germany had sunk herself in the opinion of mankind. "She has affronted the moral sense of the world and sacrificed her standing among the nations." The President was deeply shocked but determined to move deliberately. He told a Philadelphia audience that "There is such a thing as a man being too proud to fight. There is such a thing as a nation being so right that it does not need to convince others by force that it is right." This remark stirred bitter criticism from Theodore Roosevelt and others who were furious with Wilson for not taking an unequivocal and belligerent stand. But Wilson's protest to Germany, while restrained, was firm. He now made it clear that the American government upheld the right of its citizens to sail on belligerent ships and demanded prompt disavowal and full reparation for the losses on the *Lusitania*. When the Germans replied defensively, Wilson sharpened his tone, causing Bryan to resign in protest that the President's stand might bring war. The controversy dragged on for several more months, but in the interim Berlin ordered its U-boat commanders to spare the large passenger liners.

The order was soon violated. On August 19, 1915, the British passenger ship, *Arabic*, was sunk with two Americans aboard. The new clamor of protest so alarmed the German ambassador that he pressed his government to give the United States the following assurance: "Liners will not be sunk by our submarines without warning and without safety of the lives of noncombatants, provided that the liners do not try to escape or offer resistance." For the moment it seemed that Wilson's patient but firm diplomacy had won a great diplomatic triumph.

For more than six months an uneasy truce was maintained. At home Wilson put down a Congressional move to warn Americans against traveling on armed belligerent ships sailing for war zones. "To forbid our people to exercise their rights for fear we might be called upon to vindicate them," he wrote one senator, "would be a deep humiliation indeed." Then, in March, 1916, the Germans broke their pledge not to sink unresisting passenger ships by attacking the French liner, *Sussex*, as it made its way across the English channel. Several Americans were wounded. Now Wilson threatened to end diplomatic relations if Germany did not put an immediate stop to the submarine war against merchant and passenger vessels. The submarine, his note said, was "utterly incompatible with the principles of humanity, the long-established and incontrovertible rights of neutrals, and the sacred immunities of noncombatants."

Germany backed down once more. Against heated, even violent resistance at home, the German chancellor pledged that no more merchantmen or passenger ships would be sunk without warning and humanitarian precautions. But it was now clear that an embittered Germany would respect neutral rights at sea just so long as she believed that America's entrance into the war might rob her of a chance for victory. Ominously, the chairman of the National Liberal party urged the German Reichstag in March, 1916, to recognize the "strong desire in every German . . . for the rejection of all unjustified American interference, and for no hesitation over the question whether a ruthless, resolute waging of war at sea will offend this or that neutral." *

* E. May, *The World War and American Isolation, 1914-1917* (Cambridge: Harvard University Press, 1959), p. 270.

## The Preparedness Fight

As the danger of American involvement in the war rose, pressures increased to put the army and navy in fighting shape. Before mid-1915 Wilson largely ignored the military consequences of the strong diplomatic war he was waging against Germany. The American army was the smallest among the major nations and the navy failed to inspire the respect it had in TR's day. But all through the early months of the war the forces working for preparedness, goaded by Roosevelt and others, gained in strength and importance. Generally, the advocates of preparedness were eastern Republican, critical of the President, and strongly partial to Britain in the European war. Wilson knew, therefore, that he could not continue indefinitely to oppose the preparedness campaign without supplying the Republicans with a ready-made issue in 1916. So, finally, in November, 1915, he presented a plan calling for a greatly enlarged navy, an increase in the regular army, and the replacement of the National Guard with a volunteer reserve force which he proposed calling the Continental Army.

Opposition was heated, especially from leading midwestern progressives, who were convinced that the President had turned his back on their principles. Rural and left-wing groups, especially, were opposed to the preparedness drive. Many of them believed strongly that all wars sprang from economic causes—primarily from the machinations of bankers and industrialists—and they resented the draining away of public funds from reform toward armaments. Within the President's own party, Bryan led a strong antipreparedness crusade that succeeded in blocking the administration program in Congress. In response, in early 1916, Wilson carried his fight to the people with a tour of the

Middle West, but the move accomplished little. Under the pressure of the *Sussex* crisis, though, Wilson did finally gain approval for an increase in the size of the army to about 200,000 men, but he was forced to abandon his Continental Army plan. He had greater success with the naval-building program, which aimed at bringing the American navy abreast of the belligerent fleets in size. In addition, Congress approved bills bringing the state militias under federal control, strengthening merchant shipping, and inaugurating volunteer summer training-camps.

About the whole preparedness fight there hung an aura of unreality, because the United States was preparing to defend itself against dangers that could not be publicly named. Germany was the obvious enemy yet no one could admit this openly for fear of its effect on diplomacy and on German-Americans. The controversy was further clouded by TR's vituperative personal attacks on Wilson. The defenders and enemies of preparedness, according to Preston Slosson, "resembled two little children quarreling in a cage containing a sleeping tiger, but scolding in an undertone so as not to wake the sleeper." * Yet, whatever the contemporary sense of unreality, the attitudes of the two camps toward preparedness, their conflicting views of the role of force in world affairs, their differing assessments of the moral character of the war, and their strongly contrasting leaders adumbrated the fateful showdown of 1919 over America's proper role in the world.

## Wilson versus Hughes: 1916

Following the Sussex pledge, American relations with Germany took a favorable turn. With the submarine issue

* P. Slosson, *The Great Crusade and After, 1914-1928* (New York: The Macmillan Company, 1930), p. 23.

out of the way for the moment, American attention turned away from Germany back to the British maritime system. All through 1916, as the belligerents tried desperately to break the lethal deadlock, American irritation with Great Britain rose. There were many causes. The growing frustration with stalemate stimulated the British to deal more cavalierly with American rights; in searching for contraband they opened American mail; they blacklisted American firms suspected of doing business with Germany; and they stepped up their economic warfare against cargoes bound for Germany. Many Americans were further offended

President Wilson with his secretary, Joseph Tumulty. After the outbreak of World War I, Wilson sought to maintain United States neutrality despite the infringement of American rights. He was doubtful of America's ability to stay out of the war if it continued, and thus made several attempts to mediate. (New-York Historical Society.)

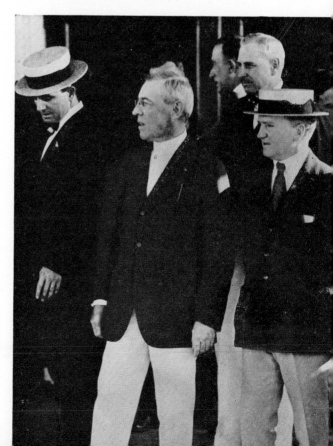

by the brutal harshness of the British suppression of the Irish Rebellion of 1916. By the time of the election of 1916, American relations with Britain had become quite bitter, even dangerous, while tensions with Germany were momentarily forgotten.

During the campaign that year Wilson was caught in a crossfire of criticism from partisans of both sides of the preparedness issue. Republican internationalists, particularly in the East, attacked him for his neutralism and lukewarm attitude toward preparedness. Midwestern progressives, on the other hand, lambasted him for his surrender to the preparedness advocates. To oppose him, the Republicans nominated the only man capable of healing the rift in their party—Charles Evans Hughes. As a Justice of the Supreme Court, Hughes escaped the bitter partisanship of the 1912 campaign. Now Taft told him that it was his duty to "save the party from Roosevelt and the country from Wilson." TR made the endorsement complete by leading a remnant of unenthusiastic Progressives into the Hughes camp. A man of integrity and powerful intellect, the son of a clergyman, a former progressive governor of New York, Hughes was similar to the President in many ways. Roosevelt indeed called him "the whiskered Wilson."

A surprising development at the Democratic convention set the tone for the 1916 campaign. The keynote speaker, Martin Glynn of New York, found his audience warming unexpectedly to his review of historical parallels to Wilson's policy. As he cited each instance where a previous president had sent a diplomatic note instead of urging war, the convention shouted, "What did we do? What did we do?" To which Glynn would roar back, "We didn't go to war! We didn't go to war!" The strong peace sentiment among the delegates was clear to every-

one. The permanent chairman, Senator Ollie M. James of Kentucky, exploited it the following day in his ringing praise for Wilson: "Without orphaning a single American child, without widowing a single American mother, without firing a single gun or shedding a drop of blood, he wrung from the most militant spirit that ever brooded over a battlefield the concession of American demands and American rights."

The campaign was muddled but hard-fought. The mood of the people puzzled both candidates. Wilson knew that he needed strong progressive support if he

Charles Evans Hughes, Republican candidate, campaigning at Red Wing, Minnesota, 1916. Hughes' narrow defeat by Wilson was attributed in large part to tactical errors he made while electioneering in California. (Underwood & Underwood.)

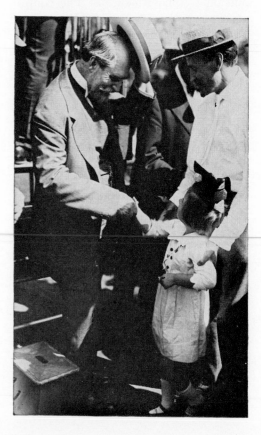

was to win the election. So he allowed himself to be carried along with the peace sentiment, though he knew that the decision for peace or war would be made in Berlin, not Washington. To the appeal of the peace issue he joined a vigorous defense of progressive principles and pointed to the strong reform measures of the previous spring and summer. His strategy succeeded. He was aided by Hughes's straddling stance on progressivism and by Republican attempts to stretch their appeal to such disparate groups as the German-Americans and the Roosevelt nationalists. Still, the outcome was exceedingly close. Hughes swept the populous Northeast, winning 254 electoral and eight-and-a-half million popular votes. But Wilson held the South and West, capturing 277 electoral and over nine million popular votes. The winning combination for Wilson, many observers felt, was made up of peace, prosperity, and progressivism.

## Last Peace Overtures

The popularity of the peace issue and the growing antagonism toward Britain strengthened Wilson's resolve to follow a truly neutral course. Throughout the years of neutrality, as the tragedy deepened in Europe, Wilson had come more and more to regard his nation as the moral trustee of the world. "My interest in the neutrality of the United States," he said in 1915, "is not the petty desire to keep out of trouble . . . I am interested in neutrality because there is something so much greater to do than fight." Early in 1916 he sent Colonel House to Europe to urge an end to the bloody and indecisive war on the Western front. He informed the British through House that he was ready to propose a conference to end the war. To safeguard the Allies, should they endanger their position in

accepting Wilson's offer, House held out the hope that the United States would "probably" join the Allies in the event of a German refusal to parley. Likewise, if the conference failed, this country would "probably" leave the conference as a belligerent on the Allied side. But this was scarcely a firm pledge, and the British and French feared any display of weakness while Germany controlled much of northern France. Furthermore, they, like the Germans, longed for the fruits of military victory to justify the blood and treasure already spent. So House's mission failed.

Now, following the election, Wilson made a final bid for a negotiated peace. He appealed to all belligerents to state their war aims and the terms on which they would end the slaughter on the battlefield. Both sides, but particularly the Allies, were stung by Wilson's statement that "the objects which the statesmen of the belligerents on both sides have in mind in this war are virtually the same. . . ." He received no encouraging replies. Nevertheless, on January 22, 1917, he went before the Senate to warn prophetically that only a "peace between equals," a "peace without victory" could last. "Victory," he told the Senate and the world, "would mean peace forced upon the loser, a victor's terms imposed upon the vanquished. It would . . . leave a sting, a resentment, a bitter memory upon which terms of peace would rest, not permanently, but only as upon quicksand." Wilson's program called for a just peace, based on high principles, and enforced by the common strength of the nations of the world. His daring proposals came to naught but they strengthened the image of Wilson as the moral leader of a war-tired world. "Perhaps I am the only person in high authority amongst all the people of the world," he said, "who is at liberty to speak and hold nothing back."

## THE UNITED STATES AND WORLD WAR I, 1917–1918

### Decision for War

Unknown to Wilson, Germany had already made the decision that would bring American neutrality to an end. Before the imperial throne, on the evening of January 9, 1917, the leaders of the Second Reich determined on a final supreme effort to crush Britain and France at the risk of probable war with the United States. An eyewitness has left us an account of the scene:

Everyone stood around a large table, on which the Kaiser, pale and excited, leaned his hand. [Admiral] Holtzendorff spoke first, and, from the standpoint of the navy, . . . in confidence of victory. England will lie on the ground in at most six months, before a single American has set foot on the continent. . . . [Field Marshal] Hindenburg spoke very briefly, observing only that from the measure [under consideration] a reduction in American munitions exports had to be expected. [Chancellor] Bethmann finally, with a visible inner excitement, set forth again the reasons that had led him in the past to cast an opposing vote against a U-boat war beyond the limits of cruiser warfare, namely concern about the prompt entry of America into the ranks of our enemies. . . . The Kaiser followed his statements with every sign of impatience and opposition and declared in closing that the unrestricted U-boat war was therefore decided.*

The German admirals had won their fight. Henceforth, all vessels entering the war zone, neutral or belligerent, passenger or merchant, would be sunk without warning. No retreat with honor was possible from the position already taken by the United States. Accordingly, Wilson broke diplomatic relations on

* B. Schwertfeger (ed.), *Kaiser und Kabinett-schef* (Oldenburg, 1931), pp. 147-149, quoted in E. May, *op. cit.*, pp. 414-415.

February 3 and preparations for war began. The President clung to the wishful hope that the Germans might be bluffing, that they might avoid any "overt acts" against American shipping. But events marched along quickly now. On February 25 the Cunard liner *Laconia* was sunk with the loss of three American lives. Was this the overt act for which Wilson was waiting? On March 1st came the sensational news of the intercepted telegram from the German Foreign Secretary, Zimmermann, in which he proposed a German-Mexican alliance in the event of war, with Mexico to recover her lost territories of Texas, New Mexico, and Arizona. On March 12, over the opposition of a small group of senators who had blocked Congressional authorization for the move, Wilson ordered armed protection for all American ships sailing for the war zone. An undeclared naval war now opened in the North Atlantic, and in breathless succession four American merchantmen were sunk by the Germans in mid-March.

Wilson made his decision. On April 2, 1917, he asked a joint session of Congress to recognize the belligerent status that Germany had thrust upon the United States. Armed neutrality was impracticable against the submarine, he declared, making a careful distinction between the loss of property caused by the submarine war, which had a parallel in British maritime acts, and the loss of human life. "Property," he insisted, "can be paid for; the lives of peaceful and innocent people cannot be." The war about to begin would be a fight for principle, for ancient standards of justice, for a world "safe for democracy." Not the German people, but German principles were the enemy of the United States. "We have no selfish ends to serve," the President asserted. "We desire no conquest, no dominion. We seek no indemnities for ourselves, no material compensation for the sacrifices we shall freely make." Wilson's opponents, then and later, charged him with being naive or misguided. But none of them could challenge the nobility or idealism of his motives. Not since Lincoln had the nation heard the challenge of such high ideals from their Chief Executive. Thus, it was in a crusading spirit that the United States went to war in 1917.

### Contributing to Victory

American intervention came none too soon for the exhausted Allies. The French offensive on the Aisne had faltered and a wave of defeatism was spreading through the Allied armies. "Let the American soldier come now," demanded Marshal Joffre, the French commander. The gloom deepened with the great Italian defeat at Caporetto and the Russian collapse later in the year. At sea the Germans had begun their critical all-out attack on ships bound for the British Isles. Only the promise of American men, food, munitions, and ships raised the morale of the Allies during this crucial year of 1917.

The first American soldiers landed in France in the summer of 1917, but they did not see much action until October. Division after division followed until more than 300,000 men were training or fighting in France by March, 1918. This number swelled by the end of the war to over two million, nearly three-fourths of whom got into battle. At the head of the American Expeditionary Force (AEF) was General John J. Pershing, who had headed the punitive expedition into Mex-

ico. Both Pershing and the United States government insisted that the AEF not be broken up to supply reinforcements merely, but that it constitute a separate force under American command. In April, 1918, French General Ferdinand Foch was named commander-in-chief over all Allied forces, including the American troops.

Pershing's men helped to repel the German offensive in the spring of 1918. The attack began along a 50-mile front from Arras to La Fère and, as the German divisions advanced, the British Fifth Army was annihilated. In the desperate situation, Pershing offered American troops to plug the gap. These men helped force the Germans back across the Marne at Château-Thierry in June and were then directed to clear the Belleau Wood of enemy troops. After three weeks of bloody trench fighting, American marines on June 25 claimed victory throughout the area.

At the Second Battle of the Marne in July, as the Germans staged their last drive toward Paris, American troops played a decisive role in halting them. Nearly 100,000 Americans were in the line of battle. The German thrust east of Rheims was blunted by mid-July and the threat to Paris was ended. By the end of the summer twenty-one American divisions were in France and the great rollback of the German armies had begun. On July 24, Foch assented to the establishment of a separate United States army in the St. Mihiel salient. In the fall, Americans were involved in the reduction of this salient, in the bitter fighting in the Meuse-Argonne, and finally in the great advance through the Argonne Forest. More Americans lost their lives in that campaign than in the rest of the war. At war's end American casualties totaled nearly 50,000 men killed in action, and a like number dead of disease.

The American military contribution to victory, although minor when laid against the British and French effort, was important, perhaps decisive, in turning the preponderance of strength toward the Allies. The nation had performed a miracle in training two million men and moving them across the Atlantic in only a year and a half. And the boost it gave to Allied morale, with fresh troops and mountains of supplies, was incalculable. Nor should the contribution of the navy be underestimated: It did heroic work in strengthening the Allied blockade, reducing the danger from German submarines, and delivering troops to France. Not a single troop transport bound for France was lost to the enemy.

## A "People's War"

The effect of the fighting in Europe on people at home was sometimes as strong as on the doughboys themselves. Nearly every family had a son or relative of draft age; and many came to know the anxiety of those left behind in wartime. In all, about twenty-six million men registered for the draft, of whom about four million were brought into service. Everyday life was affected by the war in myriad ways: industries, businesses, households, travel, entertainment, books, and even songs and plays were influenced by what was happening overseas. Rare talents found employment in new ways, as Preston Slosson reminds us. "Many expert

"Longshoregirls" loading rattan on freight cars at Bush Terminal Docks, Brooklyn, July, 1917. Girls learned to drive trolley cars, locomotives, cranes, and other equipment used on the dock in loading vessels. (Underwood & Underwood.)

dentists," he writes, "were called into service to perform operations on jawbones broken by shrapnel. Several artists devoted themselves to designing liberty-loan posters. The linguist could work for the censor and examine letters from Persia or Finland. Some college professors developed a latent talent for deciphering the codes of enemy agents. Literary folk who sympathized in any degree with the national effort could find endless opportunities for propaganda, one of the major weapons of modern warfare. [And] actresses and other entertainers were in demand to keep up the morale of soldiers in cantonments or at the front." *

Wilson bent every effort to galvanizing the public's energies for war. In fighting this modern war, vast numbers of men, munitions, ships, and supplies had to be moved. Organization proved to be the key to victory. Railroads, farms, mills, and factories had to be regimented into the rhythm of war. New federal agencies moved into dozens of areas of the economy. A kind of "war socialism" gave the American people their first taste of large-scale planning and government controls over their lives. A newly created War Industries Board, headed by financier Bernard Baruch, had almost dictatorial authority over the allocation of scarce resources, the assignment of production priorities, and the mobilization of American industry for war. When the railroads neared collapse at the end of 1917, a Railroad Administration took over their operation for the remainder of the war. Other segments of the economy were regimented by the War Labor Board, the Fuel Administration, and the Emergency Fleet Corporation.

To conserve food and encourage farm production, a Food Administration was established under the able Herbert Hoover. Farmers, prodded by this agency to produce all they could at prices inflated by scarcity and government demands, more than doubled the value of farm output during the war years. With the slogan, "Food Will Win the War," citizens were urged to conserve food, eat left-overs, plant gardens, and forego meat on Tuesdays and wheat on Mondays and Wednesdays. By such devices, Hoover miraculously tripled the amount of food exported to the Allies over the level in the prewar years.

All these war measures pushed Wilson far beyond the New Freedom or even the New Nationalism in his use of governmental powers. For they conclusively demonstrated the vital role that centralized direction must play in combating a great national emergency. Only a total mobilization of effort could hope to achieve victory in modern war. "The great fact that stands out above all the rest," said Wilson on Flag Day, 1917, "is that this is a People's War." He later expressed his conviction that "The whole Nation must be a team in which each man shall play the part for which he is best fitted." Many of the men around Wilson—Baruch, Josephus Daniels, Hugh Johnson, Franklin D. Roosevelt—recalled their war experience later when the depression of the thirties created an emergency that many regarded as serious as war itself.

In pressing for national unity, Wilson used modern techniques in influencing public opinion about the war. He created a special Committee on Public Information under journalist George Creel to "fight for the minds of men," as a Cabinet member described it. From the very beginning, Creel advocated a new approach to the problems of information and censorship in wartime. Instead of rigid censorship and strict limitations on news, he asked, why not create a positive

* P. Slosson, *The Great Crusade and After, 1914-1928* (New York: The Macmillan Company, 1930), p. 32.

emotion toward the war and its objectives? In answer, he and his agency loosed over the nation a torrent of posters, motion pictures, photographs, speeches, and pamphlets aimed at making America war-conscious. Wilson's speeches were scattered broadcast across the country and dropped by air behind the enemy's lines. Opposition to the war was combated by patriotic and nationalistic appeals. The Draft Act was explained and defended by Creel's Four-Minute Men, a flying corps of speakers who briefly addressed motion picture audiences, schools, churches, and lodge meetings. Unity, patriotism, and victory were the themes hammered home at every opportunity. By the end of the war Creel's propaganda machine was operating with unbelievable efficiency, drowning out criticism of the war, stirring up patriotic sentiment, and weakening the German will to resist. Even in World War II, with its vast apparatus for "psychological warfare," no match for Creel in energy, imagination, and sheer audacity appeared.

Still, he did not succeed in silencing all criticism. Opposition to the war flared up from time to time, notably in the progressive Midwest. Rather exaggerated anti-draft literature, ultimately outlawed, was circulated by socialist and other groups. One lurid pamphlet contained such passages as this: ". . . the recruiting officers are coming. They will take your sons of military age and impress them into the army. . . . They will be shipped . . . to the bloody quagmire of Europe. Into that seething, heaving swamp of torn flesh and floating entrails they will be plunged, in regiments, divisions, and armies, screaming as they go." The drive to stifle such criticism mounted as the war spirit warmed. Persecution and dissension split the ranks of the socialists, who persisted in their antiwar stand. The Socialist leader Eugene Debs was sentenced to a

ten-year prison term for pacifist remarks in 1918. The government used the Espionage Act of 1917 and the Sedition Act of 1918 to strike down opposition to the war effort, especially criticism of the draft. Outside the law, mobs took action

**Sow the seeds of Victory!**
plant &
raise
your own
vegetables

WRITE TO THE
NATIONAL
WAR GARDEN
COMMISSION —
WASHINGTON, D.C.
for free books on
gardening, canning
& drying

"Every Garden a Munition Plant"
Charles Lathrop Pack, President

(Brown Brothers.)

in a number of instances of suspected disloyalty. In southern Illinois, for instance, a young German immigrant was lynched because he reportedly expressed socialist ideas about the war. Elsewhere there were reports of yellow cards being forcibly hung in the windows of German-Americans, of farmers being compelled to buy Liberty Bonds, and of bodily attacks on those thought to be disloyal.

War seemed to heighten the already intense American spirit of nationalism. Demands for the Americanization of the immigrant grew louder, foreign language newspapers declined, and instruction in foreign language, especially German, suffered a sharp reduction. The strains and bitterness of war permitted Congress to enact the first literacy test for immigrants, though immigration had virtually stopped. Over Wilson's veto—he pointed out that the literacy test discriminated in favor of the better-educated Northwest Europeans at the expense of those denied educational opportunity—a measure was passed requiring an immigrant to prove his reading ability before being admitted to the United States.

The war also tightened our cultural ties with Britain. Most men of letters, educators, and editors, who had favored Britain during the neutral years, ardently supported the American intervention in 1917. Many of them interpreted the war in wholly moral terms: Britain and France were fighting for decency, justice, and democracy, while Germany sought only to extend her philosophy of force and militarism. The young English poet, Rupert Brooke, killed in the war, became a hero in American literary circles. Handsome and cynical, Brooke was converted to idealism by war and thanked God "Who has matched us with His Hour, And caught our youth, and wakened us from sleeping. . . . "

To progressive believers in science, intelligence, and progress the war seemed at first a complete reversal of history. Many of them looked to John Dewey for guidance as the cataclysm shook their hopes and ideals. How, they pleaded, could naked force be justified in an era of creative intelligence and social planning? Dewey answered, but his answer did not satisfy all the progressive intellectuals, notably Randolph Bourne. War, said Dewey, was not necessarily incompatible with progress. Force, after all, was morally neutral; it became immoral only when put to wasteful or unintelligent use. Rightly used, it was energy; wrongly directed, it became violence. It was simply a question of means and ends. Force might, then, be employed to good ends, as in resisting conquest or injustice. Dewey came to believe that this was what the British and French were doing in fighting Prussian militarism. British ethics were those of the merchant, Germany's those of the drill sergeant. So when America entered the struggle, Dewey supported Wilson and urged that American force be used for good ends. On this account, he was attacked by the strongly pacifist Bourne for merely rationalizing a surrender to emotion, for seeking to make a holy crusade of an ugly war. Particularly did Bourne denounce the resort to the compulsive powers of the state in wartime. He could see no reason for abandoning sense and suppressing civil freedoms, especially the right to oppose governmental policies, in the name of liberty and justice.

## PEACEMAKING, 1919–1920

Dewey rather than Bourne, however, typified Americans in their attitude toward war. They would fight a brutal war for noble ends. The conflict over neutral rights was transfigured by Wilson's moving prose into a titanic world struggle for peace, self-government, and democracy.

Young Fiorello LaGuardia, then a congressman from New York, expressed the mood simply when he said, "I am against war, and because I am against war I went to war to fight against war." Sadly enough, this crusading spirit in which the war was conducted made the ultimate dis-

Armistice Day, November 11, 1918, New York City. (Brown Brothers.)

illusionment more severe. For terrible problems, worse than those that precipitated the war, showed up starkly in the cold dawn of peace. Their solution required hard, practical decisions that Americans were unprepared to make, and a willingness to compromise and come to terms with a world dislocated by war.

### Wilson's Formula for Peace

Early in 1918 Wilson laid down his idealistic program for peace. In a speech before Congress he summarized in Fourteen Points the goals for which the United States was fighting. He hoped that by enunciating them he could not only nerve the Allied nations, particularly war-torn Russia, to fight on to victory, but also weaken the fighting power of America's enemies by promising a just peace. Briefly, he called for (1) an end to secret treaties, (2) protection of neutral rights at sea, (3) removal of economic barriers between nations, (4) universal reduction of armaments, (5) a just handling of co-

lonial problems at the peace conference, (6) evacuation of all Russian territory, (7) restoration of Belgium, (8) return of Alsace-Lorraine to France, (9) a redrawing of Italian frontiers "along clearly recognizable lines of nationality," (10) autonomous development of the peoples of Austria-Hungary, (11) guarantees of independence and territorial integrity to the Balkan states, (12) protection of minorities in Turkey, (13) an independent Poland, and (14) a League of Nations.

In October, 1918, an exhausted Germany, reeling from new Allied blows, sued for peace on the basis of the Fourteen Points. Wilson showed unusual skill in the armistice negotiations. He held to the distinction between the rulers and the people of Germany and forced the Kaiser to abdicate on November 9th. He secured Allied acceptance of the Fourteen Points as the basis for peace, though the British expressed reservations on Point 2, and the French made it clear they would seek compensation for civilian damages. On

November 11, 1918, over four long years after the opening of hostilities, the Armistice was signed.

As the end of the war came, Wilson made three fateful decisions in quick succession. First, on October 25, 1918, he appealed to the voters to return a Democratic Congress in November to support his leadership in international affairs. The public failed to heed this appeal, however, for the Republicans captured both houses of Congress, thereby dealing Wilson's prestige a severe blow on the eve of peace negotiations. Second, a few weeks later, Wilson announced the members of the American peace delegation. To widespread consternation, Wilson named not one important Republican and not one member of the Senate. Finally, Wilson revealed that he would personally take command of the American delegation to Paris. This step he felt was necessary in order to give the greatest possible force to the American bargaining position. But the move only further strengthened Wilson's personal identification with the peace treaty and made partisanship at home virtually inevitable.

### Wilson at Versailles

Wilson's task was Herculean. Actually, no statesman could have forged an instrument that would satisfy both Wilson's instinct for justice and the Allied demand for revenge. To many Allied leaders, indeed, justice and revenge were one and the same: Germany must be made to pay for her heinous crimes. Yet to his experts Wilson said, "Tell me what is right and I'll fight for it." But what was right? Lines of nationality were hopelessly mixed in eastern Europe and the Balkans; self-determination often conflicted with sensible economic arrangements; and the peoples of Austria-Hungary confronted the peacemakers with an accomplished settlement in Central Europe. The Allies demanded reparations on the basis of Germany's war guilt—but was Germany actually more guilty than other nations in precipitating the war? Everywhere there were hard problems; everywhere practical considerations were at odds with the instinct for justice.

After the greatest welcome ever given an American in Europe, Wilson settled down with the chief allied leaders to work on the treaty. He knew that compromises and concessions were inevitable, but he was determined to create an effective League of Nations to review the work of the conference. At Wilson's insistence, the League was made an integral part of the treaty and Wilson himself was made chairman of the commission that drafted the League's covenant. When word of this reached Washington, ominous rumblings of revolt stirred. The Senate, in a resolution introduced by Henry Cabot Lodge and signed by more than a third of its members, warned that the covenant was unacceptable to them and asked that the establishment of the League be separated from the peace settlement.

After a short visit home to attend to pressing business, Wilson returned to Paris to do battle for his principles. His chief adversary was the grizzled and hard-bitten "Tiger of France," Georges Clemenceau. Cynical about the League and Wilson's approach to peace, Clemenceau once remarked, that "God gave us his Ten Commandments and we broke them. Wilson gave us his Fourteen Points—we shall see." The heart of the conflict was this: Clemenceau made two important demands that violated Wilson's principles. He asked first for heavy German reparations, including the payment of Allied pensions, and then for the detachment of the left bank of the Rhine from Germany. Wilson yielded under heavy pressure on the first but held firm on the second. Clemenceau in turn finally con-

President Wilson and Mme. Poincaré leaving Paris Railway Station on his arrival for Paris Peace Conference, December, 1918. Just behind Wilson is President Poincaré of France, with Mrs. Wilson. (United Press.)

sented to a fifteen-year period of occupation of the Rhineland, administration of the rich Saar basin by the League of Nations for a like period, and a security treaty with Britain and the United States against a German attack. This last surety was subsequently ignored by the United States Senate.

For much of the rest of his time Wilson was occupied by serious conflicts with Italy and Japan. When Premier Orlando persisted in demanding the Adriatic port of Fiume for Italy, despite its being surrounded by the new state of Yugoslavia, Wilson appealed over his head to the Italian people. This maneuver brought denunciation on Wilson not only from Italian leaders but from Italian nationalists of all shades of opinion. Not until after the peace conference was a compromise reached between Italy and Yugoslavia, by which Fiume proper went to Italy and the adjacent Port Baros to Yugoslavia.

The Japanese exploited the Italian crisis to put forward their demand for the economic rights previously exercised by Germany in the Chinese province of Shantung. Again Wilson resisted. More than 30 million Chinese lived in Shantung and he feared the Japanese might occupy the area permanently. Self-determination was once more in danger. Beyond that, there was the persistent problem of Japanese-American tensions. They had reappeared early in Wilson's administration, first over legislation barring Japanese from owning land in California, then over Japan's threats to the Open Door in her so-called Twenty-One Demands on China in 1915. An ambiguous agreement between Secretary of State Lansing and Viscount Ishii in 1917 had reaffirmed the Open Door while recognizing Japan's "special interests" in China. Now, at Versailles, with the Italians already driven from the conference table, Wilson made important concessions to Japan for fear the conference might collapse altogether. The German economic holdings in Shantung went to Japan with the proviso that she would eventually return the province to China. No other action of Wilson's at Versailles so disillusioned his idealistic followers as this "crime of Shantung."

Wilson had to endure further compromises with the disordered and revolutionary world of 1919, a world that seemingly would not stand still long enough for Wilson to impose his ideals upon it. In cen-

130

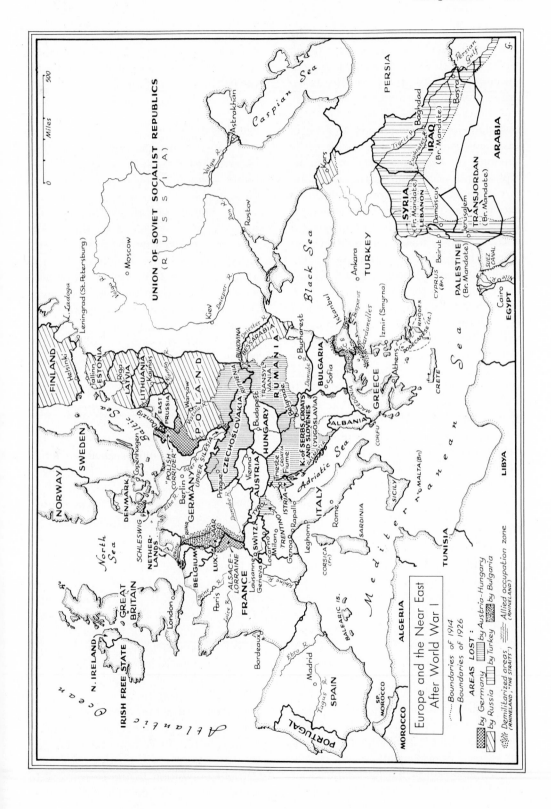

Europe and the Near East
After World War I

Boundaries of 1914
Boundaries of 1926

AREAS LOST:

by Germany   by Austria-Hungary
by Russia     by Turkey     by Bulgaria
Demilitarized areas     Allied occupation zone
(RHINELAND, THE STRAITS)     (RHINELAND)

tral and eastern Europe, for instance, he confronted a series of "succession states" carved out of the decayed Austria-Hungarian empire. Almost spontaneously, as native nationalist movements seized the opportunities left by the postwar chaos, the new states of Czechoslovakia and Yugoslavia emerged from the breakup. Little remained for the peacemakers but to accept the *fait accompli*. Austria and Hungary themselves, now much reduced in size, were separated from each other. As to his promise to recreate an independent Poland, Wilson found he could keep it only at the price of new resentments that would haunt the future: To give Poland a needed outlet to the sea the hapless Germans were forced to surrender a corridor of land dividing East Prussia from the rest of Germany. Germany's former colonies, moreover, were divided among the victors under a new system of mandates administered by the League of Nations. It was not an outright division of the booty of war; but neither did it accord wholly with Wilson's promise of "absolutely impartial adjustment of all colonial claims, based upon a strict observance of . . . the interests of the populations concerned. . . ."

"How splendid it would have been," House wrote in his diary the day after the signing of the treaty, "had we blazed a new and better trail!" The treaty indeed fell short of Wilson's ideals. Yet could it have been otherwise? It is naive to suppose that any single program for peace could have satisfied both the victorious Allies and the beaten Germans, the big nations and the small, the liberals and the advocates of a Carthaginian peace. Selfishness, partisan politics, popular pressures, and vindictive feelings blocked a purely idealistic treaty. Many honestly doubted the realism and practicability of a Wilsonian peace. The settlement became, therefore, an amalgam of harshness and idealism, of stubborn principle and grudging compromise, of long-range wisdom and necessary concessions. It was a peace, as one French historian put it, too mild for the harshness it contained.

## The Great Debate

The exhausted Wilson found his greatest fight still before him. Though public opinion strongly favored the League, opponents of ratification in the United States had gathered their forces in his absence. Now added to the opposition of nationalistic Republicans like Roosevelt and Lodge were many hyphenated Americans and others dissatisfied with the Versailles settlement. German-Americans were convinced the treaty was far too harsh; Italian-Americans remembered Wilson's blocking of Orlando's ambitions; Irish-Americans were distressed by the role Britain and her empire would play in the new League. Many liberals felt that Wilson had compromised too many of his Fourteen Points. Still others were troubled by the seeming surrender of America's historic independence of action to an untried League. "If I have had a conviction throughout my life with which it has been possible for me to be consistent," cried Senator Borah of Idaho, "it has been the conviction that we should stay out of European and Asiatic affairs."

The great fight centered in the Senate where the treaty had to be approved. At the head of the Republican opposition, now in control of the Senate, stood Henry Cabot Lodge, friend of Roosevelt, enemy of Wilson, and chairman of the Committee on Foreign Relations. All his life he had been a strong nationalist and upholder of the traditional principle of independence of action in the conduct of American foreign policy. With opinion running heavily in Wilson's favor, Lodge's strategy was to move for delay, to avoid outright opposition to the treaty, and to "Americanize" the document by adding amendments or reservations. When the debate opened in May, 1919, the Senate lineup was 49 Republicans versus 47 Democrats, with a two-thirds vote necessary for ratification. Since more than a dozen senators, chiefly Republican, were irreconcilably opposed to the treaty and the League, Wilson's only hope lay in lining up a coalition of Democrats with those Republicans who favored mild reservations. But Wilson, worn by the trying months in Paris and tired of making compromises, chose another course. He would go to the country. He would arouse the American people in one last mighty effort on behalf of his ideals.

Against the advice of physicians and friends, Wilson started west on September 3, 1919. At Columbus, Indianapolis, and St. Louis the crowds were enthusiastic but small. His speeches grew more impassioned and poignant. At Omaha he told his hearers, "I can predict with absolute certainty that within another generation there will be another world war if the nations of the world do not concert the method by which to prevent it." At Cheyenne he pleaded for his League so that "the children that crowd about our car as we move from station to station will [not] be sacrificed upon the altar of . . . war." In the Northwest and in California, the enthusiasm for Wilson soared to tumultuous proportions. It reached a peak in Pueblo, Colorado, on September 25, 1919. The crowd roared for a full ten minutes when Wilson appeared and it cheered his every utterance. With tears in his eyes, Wilson poured out his heart to his sympathizers:

Again and again, my fellow citizens, mothers who lost their sons in France have come to me and, taking my hand, have shed tears upon it not only, but they have added, "God bless you, Mr. President!" Why, my fellow citizens, should they pray God to bless me? . . . Because they believe that their boys died for something that vastly transcends any of the immediate and palpable objects of the war. They believe, and they rightly believe, that their sons saved the liberty of the world. They believe that wrapped up with the liberty of the world is the continuous protection of that liberty by the concerted power of all civilized people. . . . These men were crusaders. They were not going forth to prove the might of the United States. They were going forth to prove the might of justice and right. . . . There seems to me to stand between us and the rejection or qualification of this treaty the serried ranks of those boys in khaki, not only these boys who came home, but those dear ghosts that still deploy upon the fields of France.

That night saw the end of Wilson's crusade. His strong spirit failed him; he could go on no longer. He was hurried back to Washington where a severe stroke left him prostrate. For the next seven months the President did not meet his Cabinet, though his mind remained clear. On November 19, 1919, the Senate voted on the treaty with the so-called "Lodge reservations." The most important reservation declared that the United States

"Triumphal entry into normalcy." (New York Public Library.)

assumed no obligation under Article X of the League covenant to help other nations against aggression unless Congress specifically stated so in each instance. Wilson, considering this "a knife thrust at the heart of the treaty," ordered the Democrats to vote against the treaty with the reservations. So the Democrats joined with the "Irreconcilables" to kill the Lodge version; still, they could muster merely 38 votes for Wilson's.

Only a compromise could save the treaty now. But Wilson, enfeebled and embittered, was adamant. On March 19, 1920, the last vote was taken. Twenty-one Democrats deserted Wilson to vote for the Lodge version, making a total of 49 for and 35 against. Seven votes were still needed to reach the required two-thirds majority, but the remaining 23 Democrats remained loyal to Wilson. In desperation, Wilson called for a "great and solemn referendum" on the League question in the forthcoming election of 1920. But the League was buried in the avalanche of votes for Warren Harding. On July 2, 1921, Congress passed a joint resolution declaring the war at an end and a month later approved separate peace treaties with Germany, Austria, and Hungary.

### The World Saved for—What?

That Wilson failed in his grand design for peace is clear. Two decades after the Versailles conference the world was again at war. As Wilson predicted, the children who crowded around his railroad car learned themselves of the horrors and misery of war. Was Wilson responsible? Some have ascribed the evils that fell upon the world after 1919 to his impractical vision, his stubborn idealism, and his failure to compromise. But was it a surfeit of idealism from which the world suffered in 1919? Would a settlement based upon *Realpolitik* have served mankind better? Perhaps, but even a realistic peace could not have survived unless defended; and ultimately Wilson's design failed, not because it was imperfect, nor because the United States rejected the League, but because the victorious states evaded their pledges to uphold it in the crises of the thirties.

Wilson's failure, even his enemies conceded, was a noble one. It was more than a personal tragedy. More than anyone in all human history, he advanced mankind along the road to an international association of peoples. He knew that America's isolation from world politics was over and that his nation had an opportunity unique in history to play a grand role on the world's stage. But his proud spirit could brook no compromise with a vision that promised so much to the future. So a generation would pass before Americans returned to the trail Wilson blazed for them, and they would seek it out only after suffering a second and even more tragic, because foreseen, world conflict.

## FOR FURTHER STUDY

*The books by Borden, Dulles, Kennan, Link, and Notter cited at the end of Chapters Two and Three continue to be especially useful for the topics dealt with in this chapter.*

### General Accounts

S. Bemis, A *Diplomatic History of the United States*, 4th edition (New York: Henry Holt and Company, 1955). Another first-rate textbook in American diplomatic history.

J. Daniels, *The Wilson Era*, two volumes (Chapel Hill: U. of North Carolina Press, 1944-1946). Informative, personalized history by a member of Wilson's cabinet.

* W. Leuchtenberg, *The Per-

* Starred books are available in paperbound editions.

ils of Prosperity, 1914-1932 (Chicago: U. of Chicago Press, 1958). A brief, suggestive, and well-written interpretation of these troubled years.

F. Paxson, American Democracy and the World War, three volumes (Boston: Houghton Mifflin Company, 1936-1948). Useful, detailed account of all phases of the period.

D. Perkins, America and Two Wars (Boston: Little, Brown, 1944). A brief but insightful little volume.

P. Slosson, The Great Crusade and After, 1914-1928 (New York: Macmillan, 1930). Social developments are stressed in this volume in the "History of American Life" series.

## Special Studies

T. Bailey, Wilson and the Peacemakers (New York: Macmillan, 1947). This edition combines Bailey's valuable accounts of the Versailles conference, Woodrow Wilson and the Lost Peace (1944), and the League fight, Woodrow Wilson and the Great Betrayal (1945).

H. Bell, Woodrow Wilson and the People (Garden City, New York: Doubleday, Doran, 1945). An excellent, one-volume study of Wilson, centering on the war years.

E. Buehrig, Woodrow Wilson and the Balance of Power (Bloomington: Indiana U. Press, 1955). Takes the view that the submarine was the "instrument which laid bare the political connection with Europe which most Americans had ceased to believe existed. . . ."

A. Dudden (ed.), Woodrow Wilson and the World of Today (Philadelphia: U. of Pennsylvania Press, 1957). Admirable essays on Wilson's methods and philosophy (Link), neutral policies (Langer), war leadership (Goldman), and peace efforts (Langer).

D. Fleming, The United States and the League of Nations 1918-1920 (New York: Putnam's, 1932). Strongly anti-Lodge in its tone, this volume is a detailed study of the whole League fight.

J. Garraty, Henry Cabot Lodge (New York: Knopf, 1953). The best biography of the controversial Senator.

* T. Greene (ed.), Wilson at Versailles (Boston: Heath, 1957). An excellent selection from conflicting viewpoints of accounts of Wilson's work at the peace conference.

W. Holt, Treaties Defeated by the Senate (Baltimore: The Johns Hopkins Press, 1933). Puts the constitutional phases of Wilson's struggle with the Senate in historical perspective.

* H. Hoover, The Ordeal of Woodrow Wilson (New York: McGraw-Hill, 1958). Interesting view of Wilson's tragedy by a close associate, who later became a Republican president.

R. Lansing, War Memoirs of Robert Lansing (Indianapolis: Bobbs-Merrill, 1935). The recollections of Wilson's Secretary of State.

A. Link, Wilson: The Struggle for Neutrality, 1914-1915 (Princeton: Princeton U. Press, 1960). The third volume, covering the formative years of Wilson's European diplomacy, of an outstanding political biography.

* E. May, American Intervention: 1917 and 1941 (Washington, D.C.: American Historical Association, 1960). Brief survey, for the Service Center for Teachers, of the literature and interpretations of American entrance into the two world wars.

———, The World War and American Isolation 1914-1917 (Cambridge: Harvard U. Press, 1959). An important re-evaluation of the neutrality period based upon much new German material.

W. Millis, Road to War (Boston: Houghton Mifflin, 1935). Reflects the isolationist spirit of the mid-thirties in America, but is still good reading.

H. Peterson and G. Fite, Opponents of War, 1917-1918 (Madison: U. of Wisconsin Press, 1957). The fullest study of this subject.

M. Pusey, Charles Evans Hughes, two volumes (New York: Macmillan, 1951). The 1916 campaign from Hughes' point of view is covered in chapters 31-34.

C. Seymour, American Diplomacy during the World War (Baltimore: The Johns Hopkins Press, 1934). Still indispensable for the whole tangled story of America's foreign relations from 1914 to 1918.

———, American Neutrality, 1914-1917 (New Haven: Yale U. Press, 1935). The best answer to those who charged in the thirties that munitions makers, bankers, or propaganda got us into World War I.

C. Tansill, America Goes to War (Boston: Little, Brown, 1938). Though affected by the "revisionism" of the thirties, this is a very full and valuable treatment of the neutrality years.

A. Walworth, Woodrow Wilson, two volumes (New York: Longmans, Green and Company, 1958). The second volume of this biography describes the war period.

* T. Williams, Americans at War (New York: Collier Books, 1962). Brief but rewarding study of the development of the American military system.

## Fiction

E. E. Cummings, The Enormous Room (New York: Boni and Liveright, 1922). The "enormous room" is a French prison during World War I, where the narrator, an American ambulance driver, studies the strange and amazing ways of his fellow prisoners.

J. Dos Passos, Three Soldiers (New York: George H. Doran Company, 1921). A vivid glimpse of the dehumanizing regimentation and physical horrors of war through the lives of three soldiers.

* W. Faulkner, Soldier's Pay (New York: Boni and Liveright, 1926). A poignant novel of a wounded aviator and the effect of his homecoming on the lives of a number of persons.

E. Hemingway, A Farewell to Arms (New York: Scribner's, 1929). The best-known novel of World War I by an American writer.

## Films and Records

America Comes of Age (Film Classic Exchange, 57 minutes,

sound, black and white). Priceless newsreel clips from the period 1917 to 1919.

*America Goes Back to Europe* (National Educational Television, 29 minutes, sound, black and white). A televised discussion of the coming of the war, American efforts to stay neutral, and how we were drawn into the war.

*Causes and Immediate Effects of the First World War* (International Geographic Pictures, 23 minutes, sound, black and white).

A film covering events from Bismarck's Triple Alliance in 1882 through the treaty of Versailles.

*The Early Days* (McGraw-Hill Company, 28 minutes, sound, black and white). The emergence of the airplane as a military weapon in World War I.

*The Great War* (McGraw-Hill, 54 minutes, sound, black and white). A fine TV documentary film on the First World War from the "Project 20" series.

*Woodrow Wilson: Spokesman for Tomorrow* (McGraw-Hill Company, 27 minutes, sound, black and white). Through newsreel clips and reproductions of documents and cartoons, Wilson's life from 1910 to his death in 1924 is tastefully presented.

*World War I* (Encyclopedia Britannica Films, 28 minutes, sound, black and white). An excellent film depicting the events that led to war, the course of the conflict, and Wilson's role at the peace conference.

# Those
# Golden Twenties

## CHAPTER FIVE

Lindbergh's reception, New York, June, 1927.

THE MOOD OF THE TIMES

"Our Ideal Citizen—I picture him first and foremost as being busier than a bird-dog, not wasting a lot of good time in daydreaming or going to sassiety teas or kicking about things that are none of his business, but putting the zip into some store or profession or art. . . .

"In politics and religion this Sane Citizen is the canniest man on earth; and in the arts he invariably has natural taste which makes him pick out the best, every time. . . . In other countries, art and literature are left to a lot of shabby bums living in attics and feeding on booze and spaghetti, but in America the successful writer or picture-painter is indistinguishable from any other decent business man. . . .

"Some time I hope folks will quit handing all the credit to a lot of moth-eaten, mildewed, out-of-date, old, European dumps, and give proper credit to the famous Zenith spirit. . . . I tell you, Zenith and her sister-cities are producing a new type of civilization. . . .

"The worst menace to sound government is not the avowed socialists but a lot of cowards who work under cover—the long-haired gentry who call themselves 'liberals' and 'radicals' and 'nonpartisan' and 'intelligentsia' and God only knows how many other trick names! . . .

"The ideal of American manhood and culture isn't a lot of cranks sitting around chewing the rag about their Rights and their Wrongs, but a God-fearing, hustling, successful, two-fisted Regular Guy, who belongs to some church with pep and piety to it, who belongs to the Boosters or the Rotarians or the Kiwanis, to the Elks or Moose or Red Men or Knights of Columbus or any one of a score of organizations of good, jolly, kidding, laughing, sweating, upstanding, lend-a-handing Royal Good Fellows, who plays hard and works hard, and whose answer to his critics is a square-toed boot that'll teach the grouches and smart alecks to respect the He-man and get out and root for Uncle Samuel, U.S.A.!"

—SINCLAIR LEWIS, "BABBITT," 1922

# DAWN OF THE "NEW ERA"

The plunge from Wilson's ideals to those of George F. Babbitt, the businessman subject of Sinclair Lewis's novel of the twenties, was steep and unexpected. Ever since the nineties the course of American civilization had been marked by increasing self-criticism, a rising discontent with things as they were, a growing feeling of new responsibilities at home and abroad. Spurred on by what Will White called "crusaders' ardor," the nation had strained for twenty years to adjust its historic ideals to the changed conditions of twentieth-century life. Now, in the decade after Wilson's defeat, the reformers' passion cooled; idealism gave way to cynicism among the young; and Wilson's dream of an international community was quickly forgotten in the sullen nationalism of the age. "What a God-damned world this is!" White wrote a friend just before Christmas in 1920. "If anyone had told me ten years ago that our country would be what it is today . . . I should have questioned his reason."

What a world indeed! No decade of the century, save possibly the thirties, has etched so sharp an image on the nation's memory as these roaring years of negation and prosperity after 1919. Even those whose personal recollections do not extend back to the twenties can call up a mental picture of flappers, speakeasies, scandals, sports spectacles, vintage automobiles, coonskin coats, and ticker-tape

parades. The abiding image is one of release from restraints, of indulgent concern for the individual, of rebellion against authority and outmoded moral codes, of revulsion at the idealism and moral concerns of the prewar generation. "If I am convinced of anything," said H. L. Mencken, High Priest of the Jazz Age, "it is that Doing Good is in bad taste." "It was characteristic of the Jazz Age," wrote F. Scott Fitzgerald, its favorite author, "that it had no interest in politics at all."

## The War and the Twenties

In part, this attitude grew out of the war and the way it was fought. Wilson sought to make a moral crusade out of the sordid business of war. In the grandeur of his vision he ignored everything that contradicted his idealized conception of the struggle. Inevitably, to many who experienced the tragic confusion, the anxious waiting, the random suffering of war, Wilson's lofty words seemed hollow and meaningless. "I was always embarrassed," said Ernest Hemingway's hero in A Farewell to Arms (1929), "by the words sacred, glorious, and sacrifice and the expression in vain. We had heard them, sometimes standing in the rain almost out of earshot, so that only the shouted words came through . . . [but] the things that were glorious had no glory and the sacrifices were like the stockyards at Chicago if nothing was done with the meat except to bury it."

Hemingway along with vast numbers of his countrymen rejected more than the idealism of war, however. By 1929 all moral idealism was under withering attack. The old moral cement, loosened by the Darwinian attacks of the nineties and badly fractured by intellectual progressivism, seemed to disintegrate completely in the twenties. Even the traditional conception of man as a rational creature, guided by ideals and living in a world that supported his purposes, seemed to many thoughtful men to be damaged beyond repair. What was left? Animal faith, said some. Nothing, said others, counseling an "eat, drink, and be merry" philosophy. Still others turned to a stoic code of primitive virtues or to the satisfaction of aesthetic sensibilities as the only way out. Almost none of the leading literary figures of the twenties found much to commend in a commercial America run by George Babbitts. "The whole thing," said Sherwood Anderson of the American scene, "is as ugly as modern war."

The war helped set the stage for the twenties in other ways. The years of struggle accustomed the American people to violence and bloodshed and to the suppression of dissent, preparing them for the gangsterism and the pressures to conform of the decade ahead. The war years also brought a limited prohibition of alcoholic beverages, a prohibition that became universal with the adoption of the Eighteenth Amendment in 1919. The war encouraged, too, a relaxation of morals that may have hastened the general breakdown of traditional moral behavior in the twenties. Finally, the war gave a strong boost to the American economy. Both manufacturers and farmers felt the spur of wartime demands; both were deeply affected for the next decade by the changes wrought by the conflict. In particular, the dye, chemical, and drug industries bene-

fited greatly by the shutting off of German exports and the confiscation of German patents in this country. Notable changes occurred, too, in business organization. Antitrust actions were halted during the war and the trend toward larger and larger organizations went on apace. In many businesses trade associations were formed for the first time during the war or right after it. By the early twenties the trustbusting fervor of the progressive years was almost completely forgotten. A New Era (as businessmen proudly described it) of economic expansion and opportunity seemed at hand.

Not everything that happened in the nineteen-twenties can be blamed on the war, of course. Many of the new attitudes toward sex, prohibition, literature, and manners had their beginning in the pre-war years. Even the sense of moral rootlessness that plagued sensitive souls in the twenties probably owed more to the social and intellectual upheaval of the late nineteenth century than to the war. This was true, too, of the growing doubts about the meaning of such traditional ideals as majority rule, individual freedom, and America's mission to democratize the world. Yet we might properly say that the war, by highlighting in its glare the contradictions and tensions in the American heritage, did serve to expedite these several changes in attitudes.

### Postwar America

The change-over from war to peace was sudden and violent. Wilson and his advisors, having made few plans for peace, were caught unprepared by Germany's abrupt collapse. Demobilization was hurried along a rapid and uncharted course. More than four million men returned to civilian life in the year after the Armistice; wartime controls over business and industry were swiftly abandoned; munitions plants closed and their workers dispersed; and the emergency programs for conserving food, rationing scarce materials, regulating imports and exports, and otherwise regimenting civilian life were quickly brought to an end.

The railroads were a special problem. Their near-collapse in 1917 and their efficient operation by the government pointed to the folly of allowing destructive competition in a vital national service. Most railroad leaders, while demanding return of the roads to private hands, were sympathetic to the idea of a larger governmental role in setting rates and encouraging consolidation of existing lines. The heads of the railroad unions, happy in their wartime prosperity, were even more ardent in supporting government intervention in the industry. Ultimately, they endorsed the plan suggested by Glenn E. Plumb, a lawyer for the unions, which envisioned the purchase and control of all American railroads by a federal corporation run by spokesmen for labor, capital, and the government.

Congress was in no mood, however, for so radical a solution to the railroad problem. The Transportation Act of 1920 (Esch-Cummins Act) turned the lines back to private control but greatly enhanced the power of the Interstate Commerce Commission over them. The Commission now gained the right to overrule state regulations affecting interstate lines, thereby becoming virtually supreme in railroad matters; and it also got authority over new securities issued by the roads. More importantly, under the new law railroad consolidation was no longer forbidden. On the contrary, the Commission was instructed to prepare a plan for merging railroad properties into a limited number of systems. Though this plan largely failed, a considerable number of mergers did take place in the next decade, chiefly through the efforts of private promoters. Another significant feature of the Act was the granting to the Commission of the

power to fix minimum and maximum rates based on the physical value of the railroads. The Supreme Court later emasculated this section, however, when it ruled that physical value should be based on current reproduction costs (which were high), rather than the original cost of construction. Other unsuccessful sections of the law included a railroad labor board to settle labor disputes, which failed to halt a serious shopmen's strike in 1922, and the famous "recapture" clause, later repealed, which was designed to strengthen the weaker roads by forcing the stronger ones to pay half their excess profits (those over 6 per cent) into a contingent fund for loan purposes. All in all, the results of the Act were quite unimpressive in view of the hopes felt for it.

Equally vexing was the problem of merchant shipping. During the war the government had constructed hundreds of vessels to move supplies to Europe. Unlike the rolling stock of the railroads, these ships had no previous owners. They would be needed in a national emergency, yet the temper of the country was opposed to governmental ownership of so vast a commercial treasure. Congress invented a solution in the Merchant Marine Act of 1920, which authorized the government to operate the vessels until private purchasers could be found. Generous terms were offered to buyers, including tax exemptions and liberal loans. A considerable number of ships were sold under the terms of the Act, but the size of the merchant marine did not reach the levels hoped for in 1920.

The hasty conversion from war to peace had its price. Many discharged soldiers found no jobs waiting for them when they reached their home towns. Worse, the Congress reduced by 80 per cent its appropriation to the United States Employment Service, which was seeking jobs for them. A large number of businesses, suffering from the sudden cancellation of war contracts, cut employment just as the soldiers and sailors streamed back to civilian life. Everywhere, in the early months of 1919, there was apprehension about the economic future.

But business swung upwards during the spring and summer. Pent-up civilian demand, part of it European, took the place of the canceled war orders in American factories. The New York Stock Exchange boomed under the impact of new orders from merchants, contractors, and manufacturers. Farm prices remained high as the underfed populations of Europe competed with Americans for the output of America's farms. A sharp inflation, stimulated by the rising demand for goods, their relative scarcity, and easy credit conditions, sent prices soaring.

Then panic struck. In the spring of 1920, prices collapsed. The inflationary spiral reached its upper limit as banks exhausted their credit facilities and the government stopped its heavy war loans to the nations of Europe. Foreign consumers of American food and cotton were no longer able to buy. Many American businessmen, now caught with full inventories, tried to convert their commodities to cash, thereby adding to the deflationary pressures. Thousands of industrial orders were canceled and unemployment rose. At the peak of the recession in 1921, nearly five million men were jobless. Farmers, their crops already planted in many cases, felt the sharpest price drops of all. Wheat that sold for $2.94 a bushel in Minnesota in early July, 1920, brought $1.72 on the same market in December and less than a dollar a year later. Cotton dropped from 37 cents in July to 13 cents in December. The farmers never recovered from the hammer blows dealt them in this 1920-21 recession. Although business began a triumphant recovery in 1922, farming remained a sick industry throughout the twenties.

## Labor Troubles

The workingman, too, suffered in these boom-and-bust years after the war. The inflation of 1919 pushed up his cost of living and the collapse of 1920 threatened his job. Many workers grown used to long hours of overtime during the war were now forced to make a smaller paycheck stretch farther and farther. Nor were the unions able to be of much help to them in the immediate postwar years. For hostile employers, backed by conservative courts and a sympathetic public, unleashed a vigorous counterattack on unionism during this period.

A wave of strikes in 1919 tested the strength of the competing camps. Most spectacular of all was the steel strike organized by William Z. Foster, a radical trade union leader who was later to become a Communist. Conditions in the steel industry were unquestionably bad. Nearly half of all workers still worked a twelve-hour day; half of these the seven-day week. Pay was low, averaging $28 a week for an unskilled laborer. Living conditions were frequently deplorable as many families lived in crowded dwellings without running water or plumbing. Any union organizer was *persona non grata* in this open-shop industry, Foster himself having been run out of a number of steel towns. By the summer of 1919, after a year of organizational effort, the steelworkers' union claimed 100,000 members throughout the industry. In August, the union demands—recognition of the union, a "living wage," and the eight-hour day—were laid before Judge Elbert Gary, chairman of the Board of Directors of the United States Steel Company. But Gary refused to confer with the union leaders, insisting that the only issues were communism and confiscation of property. The strike began at United States Steel on September 22, 1919, and soon spread to other companies. More than 350,000 men left their jobs at U. S. Steel alone. The companies fought back with full-page newspaper advertisements, imported strike-breakers, and a concerted attempt to make "Bolshevism" the central issue. They also planted spies in the local unions and exploited ethnic hatreds among the strikers, especially between Serbs and Italians. The strikers' cause was seriously damaged when rioting and bloodshed at Gary, Indiana, led to the intervention of federal troops. Radical pamphlets seized there were cited as evidence that revolution was the real aim of the strike leaders. Public opinion, previously indifferent, turned strongly against Foster and his strikers. When the strike ended on January 8, 1920, not a single concession had been won. Thanks to the stubborn strength of the steel leaders and the AFL's error in choosing the vulnerable Foster to lead the strike, collective bargaining in steel was indefinitely postponed.

Actually, none of the great 1919 strikes met with much success. In Boston, the policemen went on strike after nineteen of their leaders were dismissed for organizing a union and seeking affiliation with the AFL. A rain of criticism fell on the heads of the striking officers as hoodlums and rowdies took advantage of the unaccustomed freedom. When volunteers failed to maintain order, Governor Calvin Coolidge called out state troops, and the strike was broken. Then President Gompers of the AFL appealed to Coolidge to reinstate the striking policemen, but the Governor replied in a laconic telegram that "There is no right to strike against the public safety by anybody, anywhere, any time." Less disastrous, but still a failure, was the strike of the soft-coal miners. Their leader, John L. Lewis, complained of inflation, low wages, and the seasonal unemployment that plagued the coal industry. To the miners' consternation, however,

the Attorney General of the United States, A. Mitchell Palmer, warned them that the nation was still legally at war and that a coal strike interfering with aid to the Allies would be suppressed. Not unreasonably, the miners condemned the government's position as grossly unfair since the coal operators had been allowed to raise prices sharply after the war. How could the war be over for the operators but not for them? The embittered miners struck anyway. When a federal court ordered the strike order revoked, Lewis complied, but the strike lingered on until the government agreed to a 14 per cent increase in wages and adjudication of other demands.

### The Red Scare

The hue and cry over Bolshevism resounded time and time again in 1919. The steel strike, for example, was "aimed at the overthrow of American institutions," according to the *Literary Digest*. Boston newspapers blamed Bolshevists for the policemen's strike, and one warned that "behind Boston in this skirmish with Bolshevism stands Massachusetts, and behind Massachusetts stands America." Almost every strike of that troubled and violent year was blamed on communist radicals and agitators.

To understand the near-hysteria over Bolshevism, we must recreate the contemporary impression of events. The Bolshevik party under Lenin had seized power in Russia in October, 1917. The following spring, when Russia withdrew from the war amid Allied charges of betrayal and German collusion, Allied troops, including Americans, were sent to Russia to protect Allied supplies and give limited aid to Lenin's enemies. Bolshevism became synonomous with treason during the remaining months of war. Then during 1919 the Reds drove back their enemies inside Russia, won a sympathetic following in Poland, and saw their comrades

Captured strikers being led through the streets of McKee's Rocks by state constables after strike riot in Pittsburgh in 1919. (Brown Brothers.)

establish short-lived soviet regimes in Hungary and Bavaria. The Third International, or Comintern, was organized in the spring of that year to crusade for universal overthrow of the capitalist states. Everywhere the momentum seemed to be gathering for a world-wide revolution. Here in the United States the Bolshevik achievement was hailed with delirious enthusiasm by left-wing socialists, anarchists, and Wobblies, the first group even going so far as to adopt the Bolshevik slogan, "All Power to the Soviets." In the fall of 1919 two new communist parties emerged from the realignment of American radicalism inspired by Lenin's success. One of them, the Communist Labor Party, which was led by such native American radicals as John Reed and Benjamin Gitlow, numbered at least 10,000 members that first year. The other group was called the Communist Party of America, and drew most of its strength of between 30,000 and 60,000 from the foreign-language labor federations.

In retrospect, the danger to American security from this tiny band of unpopular radicals and aliens, as yet unorganized and linked tenuously to a weak and divided Russia, seems miniscule. But in the uncertain atmosphere of 1919 the threat seemed real enough. After all, American troops were in Siberia on an ambiguous mission; wartime hatreds and suppressions of civil liberties had not yet abated; alien workers figured prominently in the great steel and textile strikes of that year; mysterious bomb explosions, probably the work of anarchists, were set off in various parts of the country, including the Washington home of Attorney General A. Mitchell Palmer and, the following year, the Wall Street offices of J. P. Morgan and Company; and scare headlines magnified the significance of these developments out of all proportion. Particularly sensational was the discovery in the New York Post Office in April, 1919, of sixteen bomb packages addressed to such public figures as Justice Oliver Wendell

145

Holmes, J. P. Morgan, and John D. Rockefeller. Fortunately, none of the packages reached their intended victims. Rumors of even worse outrages spread throughout the nation.

"No one who was in the United States as I chanced to be, in the autumn of 1919," wrote an English journalist, "will forget the feverish condition of the public mind at the time. It was hag-ridden by the spectre of Bolshevism." A hundred patriotic groups were active in ferreting out alleged radicals in labor unions, schools, churches, and universities. The recently formed American Legion, especially, was in the thick of the fight "to foster and perpetuate a one hundred per cent Americanism." Instances of mob violence against suspected radicals cropped up frequently throughout the year. In Centralia, Washington, for one, three Legionnaires were shot as they marched on an IWW hall defended by its members. One of the defending Wobblies, who escaped briefly, shot a fourth Legionnaire as the posse closed in on him. That night he was dragged from jail, beaten, emasculated, hung from a bridge, and riddled with bullets.

No one was more certain that the Red danger was real than the stricken President's Attorney General, A. Mitchell Palmer. Soon after the bomb explosion at his house, he asked Congress for a half million dollars to fight America's domestic enemies. He organized a special division of the Justice Department, with J. Edgar Hoover in charge, to compile case histories of all known radicals. On November 7, 1919, he staged raids on the headquarters of the Union of Russian Workers in twelve cities. Truck-loads of propaganda were seized. This federal action led to similar raids on radical organizations by state and local officials in all parts of the country. In New York, for instance, a committee of the New York legislature, headed by Clayton R. Lusk,

staged a number of spectacular raids on radical headquarters, published sensational reports of hidden Bolshevik arms, framed new laws requiring loyalty oaths for teachers and establishing a new state office to investigate and prosecute disloyalty, and succeeded in barring five properly elected Socialists from the New York Assembly.

The peak of the Red Scare was reached in the winter months of 1919-20. In December, 249 radicals, the vast majority of them anarchists without criminal records, were deported by federal authorities on an army transport, the *Buford*, to the Soviet Union. Next came the gigantic raids of January, 1920, when Palmer rounded up thousands of members of the new Communist parties, and put behind bars virtually every Communist leader of consequence in the country. Many of the arrests were made without warrants; families were separated; and prisoners were sometimes held *incommunicado* and denied legal counsel. Palmer even approved the action of the authorities in Hartford, Connecticut, in locking up visitors who came to see the Communists on the ground that their coming was *prima facie* evidence of communism.

Palmer was momentarily hailed as the savior of the nation, even being rated a strong contender for the Democratic nomination to succeed Wilson. But the antiradical drive began to lose momentum after the Palmer raids, and the extreme fear of subversion subsided almost as quickly as it had risen. Most of the Communists were released in time for want of evidence. Since by 1920 communism seemed to have been stopped everywhere outside the boundaries of Russia, the internal danger to the United States seemed correspondingly diminished. Then, too, some Americans were troubled by the disregard for traditional constitutional rights shown by Palmer and the patriotic organizations in their attacks on the radicals. A number of individuals and organizations spoke out in defense of constitutional rights to freedom of speech and conscience. Justice Oliver Wendell Holmes, in his dissenting opinion in the *Abrams* case (1919), warned that "we should be eternally vigilant against attempts to check the expression of opinions that we loathe and believe to be fraught with death, unless they so imminently threaten immediate interference with the lawful and pressing purposes of the law that an immediate check is required to save the country."

But Holmes' warning went unheeded in the most sensational radical case of the nineteen-twenties. A payroll robbery and murder in Massachusetts in April, 1920, led to the conviction of two anarchists, Nicola Sacco and Bartolomeo Vanzetti, on evidence that many authorities regarded as questionable. Both had been active in fomenting strikes and in protesting the Palmer raids. The presiding judge, Webster Thayer, abhorring their radical ideas, seriously prejudiced the jury against the two men. Many persons believed them innocent victims of the hysteria over Bol-

shevism sweeping the United States. Though sentenced to death in 1921, their execution was repeatedly postponed because of the strong protests of liberal and labor groups and the legal actions they supported. Important public figures, including President A. Lawrence Lowell of Harvard and the legal scholar Felix Frankfurter, were drawn into the case. Throughout the country, and even abroad, thousands of sympathizers staged demonstrations and demanded their release. But it was not to be. On August 22, 1927, Sacco and Vanzetti were finally executed. Before he died, Vanzetti gave memorable expression to the meaning of their ordeal:

If it had not been for this thing, I might have lived out my life among scorning men. I might have died, unmarked, unknown, a failure. Now we are not a failure. This is our career and our triumph. Never in our full life can we hope to do such work for tolerance, for justice, for man's understanding of man, as now we do by an accident.

Our words—our lives—our pains—nothing! The taking of our lives—lives of a good shoemaker and a poor fish peddler—all!

The moment that you think of belongs to us—that last agony is our triumph!

## THE SURGE OF NATIONALISM

The Bolshevik scare heightened the antiforeign reaction after the war. Europe now seemed not only the seat of militarism and devious diplomacy but also the home of radicalism, atheism, and other unsavory ideas. Many Americans drew back into a cloak of self-righteousness. Like Babbitt, they praised the superiority of the United States and lamented the backwardness of the rest of the world. "There is only one first-class civilization in the world," said the *Ladies Home Journal.* "It is right here in the United States." They gave thanks for their material wealth and argued that their prosperity

came to them, as one Harvard economist put it, "because we are seeking the Kingdom of God and His righteousness." The nation was returning not only to its diplomatic isolation from Europe but to its cultural aversion as well. Patriotism and Americanism were extolled in every corner of the country. No wonder a visiting Frenchman, André Siegfried, repeated, as a perfect capturing of the American's view of himself in the New Era, the following description that he had heard:

We are the greatest people on earth. Our government is the best. In religious belief and practice we (the Protestants) are exactly right, and we are also the best fighters in the world. As a people we are the wisest, politically the most free, and socially the most developed. Other nations may fail and fall; we are safe. Our history is a narrative of the triumph of righteousness among the people. . . . Our future growth and success are as certain as the rules of mathematics. Providence is always on our side. . . . If other nations will only accept our religious and political principles, and our general attitude toward life, they soon will be, no doubt, as happy and prosperous as we.

## Closing the Golden Door

Fear of Bolsheviks, the renewed nationalism, and the arrival of the first postwar immigrants converged to focus attention on the whole problem of immigration. To the longstanding economic case for limiting immigration, opponents added a cargo of racist arguments stressing the radicalism, unassimilability, and general inferiority of the immigrants from southern and eastern Europe. The foreign-born, according to the influential Henry Pratt Fairchild, a New York University sociologist, were responsible for boss-rule in the cities, the decline in standards of American citizenship, and the mongrelization of our big cities. Other writers, notably Madison Grant and Lothrop Stoddard, gave their racialism a broader application. In *The Passing of the Great Race* (1916), Grant pleaded for racial purity and the exclusion of the "inferior" races of southern and central Europe from the United States. Unless this were done, he warned, the "great race" that had produced the leaders of the past would succumb to "the weak, the broken and the mentally crippled. . . ."

Fear of a great influx of starving East Europeans brought swift congressional action. An emergency measure, passed in May, 1921, limited the number of immigrants from any country to 3 per cent of the persons from that country who were resident in the United States in 1910. The basic law that would control American immigration for the next quarter-century, however, was passed in 1924. This "national origins" act, which became effective in 1929, had as its avowed purpose the maintenance of the "racial preponderance [of] the basic strain of our people." Total immigration was to be reduced to 150,000 persons a year, and each nationality was assigned a quota in proportion to its part in the existing American population. The base year for computing proportions was to be 1920, though until the actual quotas could be figured (an extremely complicated process), the numbers of foreign-born in this country in 1890 were used. Needless to say, this formula discriminated sharply against the new immigrants. Those eligible for immigration from northwestern Europe numbered five times the figure for southeastern Europe. Great Britain alone was able to send 65,000 immigrants a year, while Italy was limited to less than 6,000. The Japanese were barred completely, setting off a wave of protest in Japan. At home, the law encountered little opposition, most of that from the foreign-born themselves, from liberal spokesmen, and from employers who regretted the end of cheap European workers. But during the 1920's the latter found new sources of imported labor in the Philippines, French Canada, and especially Mexico—all excluded from the quota system.

## Nightriders of Bigotry

In one section of the United States the racialism of Grant and Stoddard found an immediate echo. Southerners had long regarded Negroes as being an inferior race that had been degraded by slavery and could not be educated. Only at the bottom of the social ladder, therefore, were Negroes useful to others and to themselves. So long as they stayed there, the white Southerners felt no malice or dislike toward them. Indeed, Southerners felt, only they truly understood the Negroes in all their childishness and tried to protect them from harm. But the war, it was feared, might have given the Negroes false ideas about their "rights" and their place in the community. After all, militant organizations such as the National Association for the Advancement of Colored People had prophesied that things would be different on the Negro soldier's return. "We return from the slavery of uniform," read an editorial in the NAACP organ, *The Crisis*, "to the freedom of civil garb. . . . This country of ours, despite all its better souls have done and dreamed, is yet a shameful land. It lynches. . . . It disfranchises its own citizens. . . . It encourages ignorance. . . . It steals from us. . . . It insults us. . . . We return. We return from fighting. We return fighting."

But they returned to communities where the whites were determined that things must stay as they were. The Ku Klux Klan, revived in 1915 by a Georgia colonel named William Simmons, grew swiftly after the war. After a shrewd promoter, Edward Y. Clarke, was given the job of reorganizing the Klan in 1920, membership leaped apace. Simmons and Clarke catered to all the racial and religious prejudices of the day: xenophobia, anti-Catholicism, anti-Semitism, and anti-Negro sentiment. To these appeals they joined the lure of secret rituals, burning crosses, and bizarre costumes. "Here was a chance," observed Frederick Lewis Allen, "to dress up the village bigot and let him be a Knight of the Invisible Empire."*

* F. Allen, *Only Yesterday* (New York: Harper and Brothers, 1931), p. 65.

A Ku Klux Klan parade down Pennsylvania Avenue in Washington, August, 1925. (Culver Pictures.)

To the surprise of many, the Klan found fertile soil across the Mason-Dixon line, and mushroomed in many parts of the North. Indeed, its greatest significance in the 1920's was the influence it came to wield among nationalistic and anti-Catholic elements there. Its power became decisive, even dominant at times, in a half-dozen statehouses from Ohio to California. In Oklahoma and Indiana, the Klan's influence reached astonishing proportions. By 1924, its year of apogee, membership had skyrocketed to four-and-a-half million.

White supremacy continued to be a prime objective. The Klan joined with other lawless groups in a campaign of violence and terror against Negroes suspected of haughtiness or disrespect. In the first year after the war, more than seventy Negroes were lynched, including ten Negro soldiers, some of them still in uniform. Fourteen Negroes were burned publicly, eleven of them while still alive. Across the country an epidemic of race riots broke out in the tense summer of 1919. Even in the North, where the Klan had not yet gathered strength, racial tensions were high. Worst of all was the battle between Negroes and whites in Chicago, which began on July 27, 1919, with a fight on a Lake Michigan beach. Despite the presence of state militia, the city was subjected to a thirteen-day orgy of stabbings, pillaging, stonings, and pitched battles, in which 38 persons were killed and 537 injured. More than a thousand families, largely Negroes, were homeless at the end of the fray. In Omaha, Tulsa, Knoxville, and other cities, there were similar though less violent outbreaks. One interesting result of the onslaught against Negroes was a short-lived Negro nationalist movement led by a Jamaican, Marcus Garvey. Urging Negroes to be proud of their race and heritage, Garvey argued that their only hope was to flee America and return to Africa to build a country

of their own. Hailed by thousands as the savior of the Negro race, he collected millions of dollars from gullible followers before being convicted of swindle by a federal court.

In the Midwest and Far West, the Klan exploited antiforeign and anti-Catholic feeling far more than the white-supremacy issue. It vented its spleen on immigrants, parochial schools, city bosses, foreign-language newspapers, wealthy Jews, and "wet" politicians. Its greatest strength came from the rural areas and small towns, especially from persons in the lower-middle class. It was weakest where immigrant, labor, and liberal influences were strongest. By the middle twenties its strength was clearly on the wane, thanks to the distractions of prosperity, the pitiless glare of publicity, and the resistance of courageous leaders such as William Allen White, who ran for governor of Kansas on an anti-Klan platform in 1924. Corruption and scandal in the ranks of the Klan also played a part. In Indiana, for instance, the leading Klansman, David C. Stephenson, was disgraced by his sordid attack and murder of an attractive secretary. By the end of the decade, the Klan had slunk back, much reduced in strength, to its original home in the South.

The Klan's stand against foreigners and Catholics, like the earlier drives against radicals and immigrants, was deeply rooted in the desire to preserve an older America against the winds of change. For two-and-a-half centuries America had been a white, rural, Protestant nation. Now, to the rural conservative, the new currents that were revitalizing the country—immigration, science, urban industrialism—seemed like acids corroding away the very structure of society. Prodded by vague dissatisfactions, feeling secure in a mob or behind a Klansman's mask, he struck back blindly, emotionally, and often with savage fury.

### Purging the Textbooks

To the Klan-minded American, the nation's heritage was inviolable. He must preserve the values and traditions of the past by warring against radical, foreign, Catholic, and other "un-American" influences. No area of American life was more sensitive than the training of the young in the history and traditions of the republic. A veritable gale of belligerent feeling swept across the country during the nineteen-twenties against schoolteachers and textbooks that were alleged to be adulterating or questioning the patriotic lessons of history. Nationalistic groups pressured almost every state legislature to pass laws banning the use of textbooks held to be disrespectful of the American tradition. Typical was the New Jersey law forbidding the use in the public schools of any book that "belittles, falsifies, misrepresents, distorts, doubts, or denies the events leading up to the Declaration of American Independence or any other war in which this country has been engaged. . . ." The American Legion undertook a program to encourage the writing of a truly patriotic text in United States history. In Chicago, Mayor William Hale Thompson denounced the superintendent of schools for his lack of vigilance in policing textbooks and promised to "punch King George in the snoot" if he tried to interfere in American affairs. Everywhere during the twenties, history teachers were harassed by parents and organizations complaining that children's school books were not sufficiently patriotic. Scarcely anyone argued that the historian should seek the truth about the past.

## THE HARDING DEBACLE

The country's mood did not escape the notice of politicians in 1920. Time and again in that presidential season, political hopefuls struck notes of negation, fear, withdrawal, caution, and fervid patriotism. "Stabilize America first," shouted Senator Warren Harding of Ohio, "prosper America first, think of America first, exalt America first!" An elder statesman at the Republican convention that year told a reporter that "Moral issues and idealism are going to wait awhile. The country has had its fill of them. Just now it doesn't care a rap about these things. . . ."

### 1920: End of an Era

For the first time since 1892 neither Bryan, nor TR, nor Wilson was in the running for the presidency. The era of the giants was over; the reign of the pygmies about to begin. The Republican party, sensing victory, was determined to erase every trace of Wilsonism from the national scene. Henry Cabot Lodge, the keynote speaker and permanent chairman of the Republican convention, sounded the theme: "Mr. Wilson and his dynasty, his heirs and assigns, or anybody that is his, anybody who with bent knee has served his purposes, must be driven from control." In the party platform, the League plank was masterfully ambiguous, assailing Wilson's treaty, praising the Senate for doing its duty, but holding out a hope for some kind of "international association." The leading contenders for the presidential nomination were General Leonard Wood, Roosevelt's old commanding officer and later governor-general of Cuba, and Governor Frank Lowden of Illinois, who had sturdy farm support. Also in the running was the headstrong Hiram Johnson of California, one of TR's followers in the Progressive bolt of 1912. Behind the scenes, however, the party regulars, feeling certain that the political tides were running strongly in their favor, were determined to have a candidate from within the party organization.

The chances of both Wood and Lowden were seriously damaged by a Senate committee's revelations of unusually heavy and irregular campaign contributions given them. After four close ballots in Chicago, Lodge forced an adjournment. That night a small group of senators met in the suite occupied by Colonel George Harvey at the Blackstone Hotel and reviewed the qualifications of the other candidates. They were looking for a man who had opposed Wilson's League yet could back a league with reservations, who had not left the party in 1912, and who would be amenable to senatorial influence or control. One by one the parade of candidates was cut down until only one, Senator Warren Harding, remained. Popular with the delegates, the antithesis of the idealistic Wilson, Harding appealed to many elements in the convention that were not represented in the famous "smoke-filled room." Harding was nominated, said Harvey later, "because there was nothing against him, and because the delegates wanted to go home." His manager, Harry Daugherty, had four months earlier made the uncannily accurate prediction that Harding would be chosen "about eleven minutes after 2, Friday morning of the convention, when fifteen or twenty men, somewhat weary, are sitting around a table. . . ." It was shortly after 2 A.M. on Friday when Harding entered the Blackstone suite and was told that he was likely to be nominated. Still, before receiving the convention's endorsement, Harding had to overcome the following day a move by the leading candidates to force a weekend postponement, as well as

a last-minute surge of regular interest in Will Hays, the national chairman.

To oppose Harding the Democrats backed his fellow Ohioan, Governor James Cox. He defeated his opponents, Attorney General Palmer, and William G. McAdoo, Wilson's son-in-law and Secretary of the Treasury, on the forty-sixth ballot. Wilson's own intentions in 1920 remain obscure. He refused to rule out a bid for a third term but neither did he seek it. Yet he clearly lacked the vigor to stage a come-back; so the convention ignored him. His party did endorse the League, but left the door open to explanatory reservations about the exact obligations of the United States. Before beginning their campaign, Governor Cox and his running mate, Franklin D. Roosevelt, then Assistant Secretary of the Navy, paid a call on the broken President to pledge their support to the international organization.

The election of 1920 was not the "solemn mandate" on the League that Wilson demanded. It was evidently impossible for Cox and Roosevelt to fight a whole campaign on this single issue, especially when the Republicans were exploiting a whole range of wartime and postwar discontents. Besides, what *was* Harding's position on the League? No one really knew; perhaps Harding himself did not know. Time and time again he said that if elected he would consult the "best minds" to help him determine the most practicable method to join "an association of nations for the promotion of international peace." But while some of the "best minds" in the Republican Party, notably Hughes, Root, and Hoover, were insisting that Harding would lead the nation into a modified league, Harding himself seemed to be telling Republican isolationists that the United States would stay out of any such association.

The returns were overwhelmingly Republican, sixteen million votes to nine million. What did they mean? That Americans were almost two to one against the League? Hardly. More likely, Harding's landslide in 1920 was an expression of exhaustion, of caution and uncertainty, of disgust with the postwar climate in America. It was a vote against Wilsonism and further social upheaval and a vote for what the President-elect had called "normalcy." "When the inauguration was over," wrote Harding's vice president, Calvin Coolidge, "I realized that the . . . radicalism which had tinged our whole political and economic life from soon after 1900 to the World War period had passed."

## "Main Street in the White House"

A friendlier man than Warren Gamaliel Harding never smoked, drank, or played poker in the White House. He was affable, easygoing, tolerant, generous, and kind. Those who had known him as a successful newspaper publisher in Marion, Ohio, told stories of his kindness to animals—how he had paid a boy ten cents to find a home for a stray kitten, or asked a friend not to step on some ants on his front porch. He was impressively handsome and distinguished in appearance; Daugherty thought from the first that he "looked like a President." Driven by an ambitious wife and the irrepressible Daugherty, he had risen swiftly in Ohio politics. He had a direct, open way of speaking, though the content of his speeches was frequently stilted or pretentious. McAdoo once described Harding's addresses as "an army of pompous phrases moving over the landscape in search of an idea." He was touchingly—if disastrously—loyal to his friends, tolerant of their shortcomings, and anxious to accommodate them whenever possible. A Marion friend once asked

him, "Do you know the difference between you and George Washington? George Washington couldn't tell a lie and you can't tell a liar." The quip touched directly on the defect in Harding's character that proved his undoing.

Harding's "Ohio Gang" followed him to Washington. The President put his brother-in-law in charge of federal prisons, made a Marion lawyer Comptroller of the Currency, appointed a friendly rogue named Charles Forbes as head of the Veterans' Bureau, and assigned one of his American Legion comrades to the new post of Alien Property Custodian. Certain Cabinet appointments were scarcely less shocking. He named Daugherty, also of the Ohio gang, Attorney General. An old Senate crony, Albert B. Fall of New Mexico, a known opponent of conservation, was installed as Secretary of the Interior. A man wholly ignorant of naval affairs, Edwin Denby, became Secretary of the Navy. With Daugherty at their head, these men became the President's intimates.

Some of Harding's Cabinet appointments, however, were of a higher caliber. For the post of Secretary of State he got the distinguished Charles Evans Hughes, for Agriculture Henry C. Wallace of Iowa, and for Commerce the energetic Herbert Hoover. Other of Harding's early actions helped to brighten a presidential record that became almost wholly dark. In 1921, for example, he asked Congress to create the Bureau of the Budget to audit federal expenditures and prepare annual budgets for the United States government. And he showed unexpected courage in releasing Eugene Debs from prison (where he had polled some 900,000 votes as the Socialist candidate for President in 1920), in vetoing a soldiers' bonus bill backed by the powerful American Legion lobby, and in persuading the leaders of the steel industry finally to institute an eight-hour day.

## The End of Harding

Almost from the beginning, Harding felt his unfitness for the high office he held. To Will White he cried, "I can take care of my enemies all right. But damn my friends—God damn my friends, White, they're the ones that keep me walking the floor nights." A little later he complained that "This White House is a prison. I can't get away from the men who dog my footsteps. I am in jail." Early in 1923 came the first public hints of the cesspool of corruption that Daugherty and his gang were digging in the capital. Reports reached Harding's office of crooked business in the Veterans' Bureau. Forbes resigned, and before a Senate investigation got under way, the Bureau's legal counsel committed suicide. Forbes was eventually convicted of defrauding the government of fantastic sums, perhaps a quarter-billion dollars in all.

Meanwhile, an old friend of Daugherty's, Jess Smith, had plunged the President into deeper gloom. Smith had come to Washington with Daugherty, occupied a desk in the Justice Department though he held no governmental appointment, and was selling his services as fixer and lobbyist to the highest bidder. Among other deals, he arranged for the illegal transfer to German interests of some bonds from the Alien Property office, a maneuver that brought him $200,000. Smith was hustled back to Ohio, but he returned to Daugherty's apartment in May, 1923, to shoot himself.

Harding apparently never knew about the most sensational scandal of his administration. His old Senate companion, Fall, soon after taking office as Secretary of the Interior, had urged the transfer

Shortly after the Teapot Dome scandal broke, this cartoon was printed in "Life" (March 6, 1924), with the title, "Bargain Day in Washington: If the craze for Government property continues." Being hauled away, along with the White House and Washington Monument, is the "Navy—Slightly S-oiled."

to his Department of naval oil reserves in California and Wyoming. Harding and his fumbling Secretary of the Navy, Edwin Denby, acquiesced. Fall then leased the Elk Hills reserve in California to Edward L. Doheny and the Teapot Dome reserve in Wyoming to Harry F. Sinclair; the two recipients were well-known and heavy contributors to Harding's campaign. These properties were worth at least $100 million in profits. Doheny now made Fall a "loan" of $100,000, which was delivered in cash in a little black bag. From Sinclair came bonds, cash, and cattle worth perhaps $300,000. On October 25, 1923, Senator Thomas J. Walsh of Montana demanded a full-fledged investigation of the circumstances surrounding the two leases. The salient facts were gradually uncovered. Fall was fined $100,000 and sent to jail for one year, while Doheny and

Sinclair were acquitted for lack of sufficient evidence, though Sinclair was sentenced to short jail terms for contempt of the Senate and for tampering with a jury.

Before the full extent of the corruption in his administration was known, however, Harding was dead. He had set off in the summer of 1923 on a long speaking tour that took him across the continent and to Alaska. He seemed nervous, played bridge incessantly, and could not relax. Instead of helping him, the long journey further exhausted his failing energies. In San Francisco, apparently after suffering a heart attack and the onset of pneumonia, the President finally succumbed to an apoplectic stroke. Warren G. Harding was mercifully spared the realization of the full measure of difference that separated him from George Washington.

## NEW ERA: HIGH NOON

### Coolidge: Man and President

Harding's death made Calvin Coolidge President. The party bosses had not wanted him for the second place in 1920, but the hard-driven delegates, having accepted Harding, revolted against further dictation. A native of Vermont, a lawyer and veteran of Massachusetts politics, Coolidge was catapulted to fame by his minor role in the Boston police strike. He was a dour, quiet, unassuming little man with a pinched face and a high nasal voice. TR's daughter thought he looked as if he had been "weaned on a pickle." He was painfully shy: "I do not think you have any comprehension," he once said, "of what people do to me." He believed firmly in the New England virtues of frugality, moderation, and rugged individualism,

and he distrusted government, especially on the national level. "If the Federal government should go out of existence," he once said, "the common run of people would not detect the difference . . . for a considerable length of time." Not government, but commerce and industry were, in his view, the paramount concerns of the nation. "The chief business of the American people," he remarked in an oft-quoted aphorism, "is business."

Economy was the keynote of his administration. He sought to reduce governmental expenses, bring tax rates down, and cut the size of the national debt. The function of government, he argued, was to make itself increasingly less necessary. He rejected completely the Wilson-Roosevelt view of the presidency. The presidency is strictly an executive office,

President Coolidge accepting an ear of corn from a 4-H delegation from Indiana. (Library of Congress.)

he said, a "place of last resort to which all questions are brought that others have not been able to answer." So the chief executive has no business coercing the people's representatives on Capitol Hill as Wilson had done. The President should administer, not lead.

His policies varied little from those of his predecessor. He agreed with Harding that the League question was dead and followed him in advocating American adherence to the World Court, opposing the cancelation of the Allied war debts, and vetoing another soldiers' bonus bill. This time, however, the bonus bill, calling for paid-up annuity policies to fall due in twenty years, was passed over the presidential veto.

Coolidge paid little attention to what he called the "errors in judgment" of the Harding era. He retained the Harding Cabinet, including Daugherty, until the pressure for Daugherty's dismissal grew

too intense to ignore. For most people, though, the President's own rugged integrity was assurance enough that all traces of the "Ohio Gang" would be wiped out.

## The Economics of Prosperity

One member of Harding's Cabinet whom Coolidge retained became a symbol and hero of the New Era. He was Andrew Mellon, a Pittsburgh multimillionaire, who had made a fortune as head of the aluminum monopoly and as a financial tycoon, and served as Secretary of the Treasury under the three Republican presidents in the twenties. Mellon was convinced that government should be run on business principles. This meant a balanced budget, efficient but reduced services, a dwindling national debt, and lowered taxes, especially in the higher-income brackets. He was strongly opposed to heavy taxes on what he called "wealth in the making." Only through the creation of new jobs by energetic entrepreneurs was the sum total of wealth ever increased. Everyone knew, he said, of businesses abandoned or never started because of incentive-destroying taxes.

In 1921 he got Congress to cut the maximum surtax rate to 50 per cent from its wartime high of 65 per cent. The excess-profits tax of the Wilson years was abandoned, and, as a concession to lower-income citizens, exemptions for dependents and heads of families were raised. Mellon's program was not fully realized until 1926, however, when the surtax was cut to 20 per cent, gift taxes were repealed, and estate taxes sharply reduced. A man earning a million dollars would now pay less than $200,000 in federal taxes, compared with more than $600,000 in Wilson's day. Few concessions were made this time to the small taxpayer.

The government's business program of the twenties also called for a high tariff, friendly administrators in such regulatory agencies as the Federal Trade Commission, and the liquidation of wartime projects that competed with private enterprise. Government must once more be a partner to business rather than its scourge as in the Wilson and TR years. In 1922, under President Harding, the Fordney-McCumber Act pushed tariff duties to their highest level in American history. Though some farm duties were increased, the bill was designed primarily to satisfy manufacturers' demands for added protection. It even shielded the war-born chemical and dye industries from competition. Lip service was paid by its Republican sponsors to the principle of equalizing production costs at home and abroad, and the tariff commission was empowered to recommend further increases or decreases up to 50 per cent, but few changes were made in practice.

The regulatory agencies also fell subject to the new philosophy of giving business what it wanted. Coolidge, for instance, appointed to the Federal Trade Commission a man who believed the Commission had been "a publicity bureau to spread socialist propaganda." Originally established to curb monopoly, the Commission now encouraged the formation of trade associations that in fact limited competition.

Business itself was undergoing important changes in the twenties. The trend toward consolidation in business enterprise, checked during the progressive years, picked up again with new vigor. The favorable attitude of the government, the easy availability of money and credit, and the rise of vast new industries encouraged the trend. In electrical equipment, iron and steel, automobile, and telephone and telegraph industries, a high degree of concentration and control was reached. And this concentration of industry gave a strong boost to scientific management. Frederick Taylor, a pioneer in this field, sounded the death knell of the old system of personal control when he wrote, "No great man can hope to compete with a number of ordinary men who have been properly organized so as efficiently to cooperate." And so the management of the great American corporations during the twenties became a highly specialized affair, with vice presidents assigned to manufacturing, research, advertising, purchasing, and other lines of activity. The gulf between the owners of industry and the managers grew wider. Corporations were becoming little worlds of their own with tightly knit bureaucracies, internal politics, and ladders of organization.

### The Businessman's Outlook

The businessman's view of his world in this decade of change, if we are to believe his spokesmen, was strongly materialistic. Progress and achievement were measured in increasingly quantitative terms, and the fundamental and permanent human motives were held to be selfish in nature and economic in content. "The 100 per cent American," wrote William Feather, a publishing executive, "believes in the doctrine of selfishness, although he is often ashamed to admit it. . . . The American idea is that every man is out to promote his own interest, and he has discovered that the best way to do this is to make himself useful to others." * Altruism as a motive in life clearly belonged only to the mentally disturbed. "It is inconceivable," Feather continued, "that anyone except a nut should give something for nothing." Even artists and authors had bills to pay and were "moved by the identical economic urge that prompts a businessman to get out of bed in the morning however cold his room may be." James Truslow Adams, in *Our Business Civilization* (1929), agreed with this diagnosis so far as it applied to America, but he queried, "Can a great civilization be built up or maintained upon the philosophy of the counting-house and the sole basic idea of a profit?"

Adams's question did not bother those who believed that business is the basic institution of society. No more than Babbitt did the average businessman lament the lack in America of artists "feeding on booze and spaghetti." Indeed, they considered an attack on the pre-eminence of business as an attack on society itself. All other activities—art, literature, education, journalism, government—took their importance from their relation to the commercial spirit. "In making the business men the dominant and sole class in America," Adams warned, "the country

is making the experiment of resting her civilization on the ideas of businessmen. The other classes, dominated by the business one, are rapidly conforming in their philosophy of life to it." And so, much of the life of the twenties came to rest on the ideas of businessmen. The gospel of success, prosperity, optimism, and individual opportunity that Babbitt preached was dinned into the ears of a whole generation. Typical of this campaign were the themes of such popular magazine articles of the day as "How Charlie Taught Me to Laugh at Failure," "A Man's Debts are Sometimes the Measure of His Courage," and "How an 'Ordinarily Stupid Boy' Became a Great Merchant."

### The Seven Fat Years

There was good cause for this optimism in the prosperous twenties. From the business recovery in 1922 to the stock market collapse in 1929 the cycle of American prosperity spun higher and higher. Living standards for the majority of citizens rose steadily, the flow of consumer goods broadened to a torrent, the economic opportunities open to talent and imagination exploded in all directions. At the beginning of the decade only one city family in five had a telephone, one in three had an automobile, and perhaps one in ten thousand had a radio. Electricity had been brought to only one city home in ten and to virtually no farm homes; most homes therefore necessarily lacked vacuum cleaners, refrigerators, washing machines, and other electrical appliances. Plainly, stupendous business opportunities lay just ahead. And to realize those opportunities, businessmen conducted a great advertising campaign throughout the twenties, put a new stress on "service" to customers, and introduced installment buying on a large scale for the first time. Public relations became a profession as Edward Bernays,

---

* I am indebted for this quotation and a number of the ideas in this section to J. Prothro, *The Dollar Decade* (Baton Rouge: Louisiana State University Press, 1954).

a veteran of the Creel Committee, showed his generation how psychology could be applied to the sale of goods and services.

The central economic fact of the twenties was a tremendous increase in the technical efficiency and productivity of American industry. Output per man-hour leaped perhaps 40 per cent during the decade. Yet to maintain prosperity and full employment, these remarkable technological gains had to be translated into increased purchasing power for potential customers. This translation, unfortunately, was not achieved. Wages rose, but not as fast as production, and prices failed to fall because of the suppression of competition in the big industries. Real wages (wages matched against what they will buy) went up about 26 per cent, while manufacturing output shot up 64 per cent during the twenties. Where, then, did the gains go? Mainly into profits, which soared about 80 per cent during the boom years. Yet these profits were denied an outlet in plant expansion because the lagging consumer demand could not absorb added production. Instead they were pushed, especially in the late twenties, into the securities market. Mellon's tax policies made things worse by freeing still more profits for stock market speculation. Thus by 1929 stock values were out of all proportion to the real wealth they represented.

Greatest of the new manufacturing giants of the twenties was the automobile industry. A hundred new lines of economic activity—tires, road-building, filling stations, repair shops—revolved around this booming business. Its effect on American life in broadening horizons, ending the isolation of the farmer, developing the motorized suburb, promoting the relocation of industry, and bringing sudden death to thousands of Americans (32,000 in 1930) can scarcely be exaggerated. The growth of the use of the automobile was phenomenal: Only eight million passenger cars were registered in the United States in 1920, compared with twenty-three million in 1929.

The mass production of automobiles was largely the achievement of one man, Henry Ford, who became the industrial hero of the New Era. Born on a farm near Detroit in 1863, Ford was a mechanical genius who tested his first internal combustion engine in 1893. At age 40 he sold his first automobile. His fame came still later with the introduction of the famous "Model T," the expansion of his factories, and the decision in 1914 to pay his workers five dollars a day. There was something prophetic in his vision of

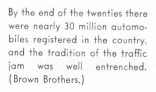

By the end of the twenties there were nearly 30 million automobiles registered in the country, and the tradition of the traffic jam was well entrenched. (Brown Brothers.)

the role that the automobile would play in modern life. He was determined to build a "low-cost car" within the reach of every pocketbook by cutting prices, reducing the profit of each unit, and paying decent wages. "There is no doubt," he had said in 1912, "that the man who can produce a car that will be entirely sufficient mechanically, and whose price will be within the reach of the millions who cannot yet afford automobiles, will not only grow rich but be considered a public benefactor as well." Ten years later there was no doubt that this man was Ford himself, whose Model T had ended the luxury era in automobiling. Despite some disagreeable streaks in his character, notably his anti-Semitism and his paternalistic views on labor, Ford became the most extravagantly admired industrialist of the New Era, not only in the United States but all over the Western world.

Other new industries, too, were booming. Radio became a big business during the 1920's as the mass production of receiver sets began and radio broadcasting reached nation-wide proportions. By 1927 both the National Broadcasting Company and the Columbia Broadcasting Company had been organized, and three years later the Census Bureau reported that 40 per cent of all American families owned radios. Commercial aviation, too, became a reality with the swift expansion of regularly scheduled air service, beginning in 1926, and the inauguration of air mail service by private carriers in the mid-twenties. By 1930, more than a hundred airlines were providing some kind of freight, mail, or passenger service. Another industry that finally reached major proportions in the decade was motion pictures. With a capital investment of over $2 billion in 1930, this booming industry was employing 325,000 persons and bringing recreation to an estimated 115 million Americans each

week. In these and other industries, as well as among Ford's competitors in the automobile industry, the 1920's were years of mushrooming growth, of swift expansion of markets, and of proliferation of new companies.

## The Fortunes of Labor

Labor, too, made significant gains. By 1924, ten years after Ford's dramatic announcement of the five-dollar day, the average daily wage for eight hours work in all American factories had slightly surpassed this mark. The median work week was cut during the same period from fifty-five to fifty hours. After spectacular advances during the war years, labor's progress was gradually slowed in the twenties by increasing employer resistance and a less favorable public opinion. Largely because of such opposition, most of the big postwar strikes had failed, as we have seen, and new strikes in the coal and textile industries in the early twenties met with little success. Union membership actually fell off during the postwar decade under the leadership of the aging Gompers and his conservative successor, William Green. In these years, employers conducted a successful campaign, which they called the "American Plan," to destroy the power of unions and make the open shop universal. The federal courts cooperated by approving "yellow dog" contracts that forbade workers, as a condition of employment, to join unions; by issuing injunctions freely against strikers; and by setting new limits on boycotts and picketing. To appease the frustrated workers, employers did introduce "welfare capitalism" schemes, such as profit-sharing, pension, and insurance plans, and company unions. Yet such sops to labor were not really characteristic. The authentic aggressive mood of the business community in the twenties was well if perfervidly expressed in a 1925 speech by John E.

Edgerton, president of the National Association of Manufacturers:

The palatial temples of labor whose golden domes rise in exultant splendor throughout the nation, the millions of dollars extracted annually by the jewelled hand of greed from the pockets of wage-earners and paid out in lucrative salaries to a ravenous band of pretenders, tell the pitiful story of a slavery such as this country never knew before. . . . It is your duty to break the shackles that have been forged upon the wrists of those who labor with you by showing them in your daily contact and attitudes that you are their best friends and that it is not necessary for them to follow the false leadership of designing pirates who parade in the guise of the workingman's friend.

The closing of the gates to cheap European labor helped raise the workers' standard of living in the twenties. In all, the real earnings of American workers, as we have seen, rose by more than a fourth during the decade. Unemployment was low after 1921, except for a brief recession in 1924, when the total number of jobless reached two million. To realize more than the bare essentials of life, however, many families found it necessary to depend on more than one breadwinner. Women who had gone to work for the first time during the war found it impossible to quit as long as their labor was in demand. The share the wage-earning family enjoyed of the national income, even at the height of prosperity, was nevertheless modest. In 1929 families living on less than $2000 a year made up 60 per cent of the nation's population but got only 24 percent of its income, while families receiving more than $5000 a year constituted only 8 percent of the population, yet took in 42 percent of the income.

## The Woes of the Farmer

Next to industrial laborers, farmers made up the largest single group of low-income families in the twenties. Farming never recovered from the price collapse of 1920-21 and the farmers' woes multiplied as the decade wore on. "I have farmed or hired farming done west of the Missouri for fifty-five years," wrote a Colorado farmer in 1921, "but never seen as discouraging times for the farmer as at present." * Farm income fell from its artificial high of $14 billion in 1919 to $12 in 1920, then to $8 billion in 1922, and finally hovered around $9 to $10 billion for the rest of the decade. Yet the prices farmers paid for the things they needed rose steadily; both the wages demanded for hired labor and, especially, their taxes increased spectacularly; and their indebtedness grew heavier as the years of decline wore on. Bankruptcy, foreclosure, and ruin marked the history of many farm families, particularly those that were producing staple crops, during these anguished years. In all, approximately four million persons joined the flight from the farm between 1919 and 1929.

The heart of the farmers' problem was their inability, even when organized, to exert much control over the market. While industrialists and merchants cooperated to control prices, wages, and output, farmers continued to compete in a free and unregulated market. When recession threatened, manufacturers reduced production, laid men off, and closed plants if necessary. But the farmers, goaded by low prices, continued to produce at the same or a higher level in a vain attempt to maintain their income. The vital difference between the "managed" prices of the industrialist and the competitive prices forced on the farmer was soon made starkly clear in the great depression of the thirties. As the depression began, motor-vehicle output dropped 80 per cent in just a few brief years, yet automobile prices fell only 16 per cent;

* G. Fite, *George N. Peek and the Fight for Farm Parity* (Norman: University of Oklahoma Press, 1954), p. 3.

on the farms, in contrast, prices declined 63 per cent in the same period, while farm production slipped only 6 per cent.

From the grim perspective of the postwar years farmers looked back with nostalgia to the war period and some wondered why government could not aid them in peace as it had in war. As early as 1921 two Moline farm implement executives, George Peek and Hugh Johnson, had worked out a plan to use the power of government to get farmers to work together. "You can't sell a plow to a busted customer," Peek is reputed to have remarked. The farmer's problem, Peek believed, was that he bought in a protected market but sold in a competitive one. Tariffs would not help him, because his surpluses forced prices on the home market down to world market levels. Peek's solution was to dump the surpluses abroad at whatever price they would bring, while artificially preserving higher prices at home. Domestic prices would be pegged at a level commensurate with a fair exchange value in industrial goods. To determine a fair level of exchange, the years just before World War I would be considered fair, or "parity," years. A sliding tariff would protect prices on the domestic market. As a result, Peek argued, farm prices would rise and fall with the general price levels and assure farmers a fair and stable income. Like the tariff-protected industries the farmers would also be "up on stilts."

Peek convinced a majority of farm leaders that his complicated plan was sound. Spokesmen for the embattled farmers put heavy pressure on Congress and Secretary of Agriculture Wallace, who was sympathetic to the program. Finally, in 1924, the plan was introduced into Congress by Senator McNary of Oregon and Representative Haugen of Iowa. Under it, a government corporation would purchase surpluses of major crops and sell them abroad at world prices; losses in foreign sales would be paid by the farmers through a tax or equalization fee on the commodities they sold. Defeated then in the House amid a chorus of denunciation from business leaders, newspapers, and the Coolidge administration, the bill gained strength as the farm depression deepened. At length, on February 17, 1927, after three years of constant fighting by farm spokesmen, it passed the gauntlet of Congress. But Coolidge rejected it with a stinging veto, charging that it was unconstitutional, economically unsound, and contrary "to our traditions, the philosophy of our government, the spirit of our institutions, and all principles of equality." The following year he vetoed it again.

Meanwhile, the disgruntled farmers tried other remedies to improve their lot. Many flocked into farm organizations. The American Farm Bureau Federation, made up of representatives of the farm bureaus authorized by the Smith-Lever Act, was organized in 1919 and grew rapidly during the twenties. The older Grange and the liberal Farmers' Union, established in 1902, also expanded their membership. In the Midwest, the Non-Partisan League, founded in 1915, was active in the fight for state ownership of elevators, mills, and packing houses in North Dakota, Minnesota, and other states. All these organizations agitated for tax relief, improved farm credit, and cooperative marketing.

Many of these same objectives were pursued nationally by the "Farm Bloc," a bipartisan group of congressmen from the West and South. Probably the two most important of the Farm Bloc's achievements were the Capper-Volstead Act (1922), which exempted farm cooperatives from antitrust suits, and the Intermediate Credits Act (1923), which established twelve new credit banks empowered to grant credit to farmers for periods of six months to three years.

## Progressives at Bay

A number of the Farm Bloc leaders were old progressives who felt uncomfortable in the conservative atmosphere of the twenties. "At no period in my public life," said George Norris later, "did I feel greater discouragement than during those years." Norris himself led a valiant fight to prevent the government nitrate plants and dam at Muscle Shoals, Alabama, from being turned over to private enterprise. Henry Ford offered to buy the whole development for a small fraction of its cost, but Norris, chairman of the Senate Committee on Agriculture, blocked the sale. The Nebraska Senator saw the tremendous power potential of the Tennessee River and proposed that the government itself develop Muscle Shoals for the people of the region. But this scheme seemed far too socialistic for the mood of the twenties. Both Coolidge and Hoover vetoed it after Norris miraculously steered a bill twice through the Congress.

That Norris got his measure through Congress at all shows that there was still fire in the ashes of progressivism. Throughout the twenties progressives showed surprising strength in Congress, though they were never able to capture the White House. Time and time again, they rallied behind a measure like the Norris bill or the McNary-Haugen plan only to be defeated by a presidential veto. They did succeed, nevertheless, in passing the Capper-Volstead law, modifying Mellon's drastic tax proposals, adding agricultural goods to the Fordney-McCumber tariff, and shutting the door on immigration, restriction of which had long been advocated by a number of progressive spokesmen. What the progressives needed, if they were to regain their earlier momentum, was a united program and a leader. But the rural and urban strands of the old progressive alliance

were being pulled in opposite directions during much of the twenties. Wilson's party, in particular, was being torn apart by the struggle between the Northern city machines, identified with immigrants, Catholics, and antiprohibitionists, and the rural cliques backing nativism, religious fundamentalism, and the Klan; while the Republican party, on the other hand, seemed securely locked in the grip of standpat conservatives.

The split in the Democratic party emerged into the open in 1924, when the Klan and prohibition became the central issues at the Democratic convention in New York. The Northern machines backed Al Smith, progressive governor of New York, while the rural faithful stood behind William McAdoo, who had the support of the Klan and the prohibition forces. Smith was a Catholic, a "wet" on the liquor question, and a Tammany regular who had pushed through a program of social reform during his two terms as governor. The two camps fought to a desperate standstill. After 103 weary ballotings, the nod went to a dark horse, John W. Davis of New York, an able lawyer with Wall Street connections. By a single vote, 543 to 542, the convention refused to condemn the Klan in its platform, but no agreement could be reached on prohibition. The convention simply condemned the Republicans for their failure to enforce the prohibition act. Even the League of Nations could no longer unite the Democrats, though Newton Baker, Wilson's Secretary of War, pleaded eloquently that the 1917-18 sacrifices be "really perfected." The Democrats responded by recommending that the question of America's joining the League be submitted to a popular referendum.

A third candidate faced Davis and Coolidge in 1924. Progressive hearts beat faster in the knowledge that they had at last the opportunity to vote for "Fighting

Bob" La Follette, now almost seventy years old. His candidacy had grown out of a Conference for Progressive Political Action called in 1922 by the heads of the railroad brotherhoods and attended by a number of other union leaders, several old progressives, and members of the fading Socialist Party. The Democratic disruption in 1924 made the time seem ripe for another third party on the national level. La Follette chose Burton K. Wheeler as his running mate and wrote the new party's platform, which differed little from TR's program of 1912. He asked for the nationalization of railroads and certain national resources, a reduction of taxes on lower incomes and an increase for the rich, a constitutional amendment to enable Congress to override judicial vetoes, abolition of the injunction in labor disputes, and a number of relief measures for farmers.

Although he accepted the endorsement of the AFL and the Socialists, La Follette rejected Communist support, because he said, "[they] are antagonistic to the progressive cause and their only purpose in joining such a movement is to disrupt it."

The outcome of the three-way race revealed the weakness of progressivism in the New Era. Coolidge swamped both his rivals with nearly fifteen million votes to the eight million for Davis and almost five million for La Follette. All the Davis electoral votes (136 out of 531) came from the South, while La Follette carried only his own state of Wisconsin (13 votes). Franklin D. Roosevelt, who had hobbled on crutches to the rostrum to nominate Smith at Madison Square Garden, wrote prophetically to a friend, "In 1920 . . . I remarked to a number of my friends that I did not think the nation would elect a Democrat again until the Republicans had led us into a serious period of depression and unemployment. I still [think] that forecast holds true, for much as we Democrats may be the party of honesty and progress the people will not turn out the Republicans while wages are good and the markets are booming. Every war brings after it a period of materialism and conservatism; people tire quickly of ideals. . . ." *

## "THE GAUDIEST SPREE IN HISTORY"

The generation of the twenties may have been tired of ideals and politics but it seemed to be having a good time. With exuberance and vitality Americans revolted against the manners and morals, dress and customs, taboos and restraints of the past. A whirlwind of social and moral change swept through these seemingly happy and carefree years. Scott Fitzgerald, who most accurately caught their spirit in literature, called the twenties "the gaudiest spree in history." Those who joined in it were the first generation that would seem modern to their successors at mid-century. Their enthusiasms, their heroes, their books, and their recreations would strike a familiar note four decades later. And their attitudes toward manners, sex, and alcohol had more in common with the generation of 1960 than with that of 1910. Modern public relations, ballyhoo advertising, and journalistic scandalmongering were born in this eventful decade. And these were the years, too, when automobiles, radios, movies, and other familiar features of contemporary life first came into general use. Even the songs of the twenties,

* F. Freidel, *Franklin D. Roosevelt: The Ordeal* (Boston: Little, Brown and Company, 1954), p. 183.

especially the jazz, found a permanent place in the nation's memory.

## The Prohibition Fiasco

One phenomenon of the era that symbolized to the young the hypocrisy and moral meddling of their elders was prohibition. The attempt to outlaw intoxication by federal mandate became a kind of *leitmotiv* of the age, inseparable from the moral letdown, flouting of authority, and revolt against idealism that accompanied it. Bootlegging and gangsterism were only the outward extreme manifestations of an inner change in traditional American attitudes toward law and order. Whole sections of the nation suddenly seemed bent on flouting or ignoring a federal statute. Illegal drinking came to be taken for granted in millions of American homes, including, in Harding's day, the White House itself.

To implement the Eighteenth Amendment, which went into effect on January 17, 1920, the Volstead Act provided for federal enforcement of prohibition. The Act prohibited the manufacture or sale of intoxicating liquors, which were defined as those containing an alcoholic content of one-half of one per cent. The militant Anti-Saloon League, far from satisfied with its legislative successes, now launched a campaign for strict enforcement. In state after state the League forced often reluctant legislators to pass enforcement codes to supplement those of the federal government. Its policies were shrewdly realistic and hard-driving, offering its considerable political support to all those who promised to tighten the stranglehold on Demon Rum, regardless of their personal attitudes toward alcohol. H. L. Mencken, in a savage parody of League activities, wrote, "If Beelzebub, running on one ticket, agreed to support prohibition, and the Archangel Gabriel, running on another, found himself entertaining conscientious doubts, they were instantly and solidly for Beelzebub, and they not only gave him the votes that they directly controlled, but they also gave him the benefit of a campaign support that was ruthless, pertinacious, extraordinarily ingenious, and overwhelmingly effective."

In the dangerous no-man's-land between private desire and public suppression, enormous prizes lay waiting for the successful bootlegger. And the channels to success followed many courses. Liquor might be smuggled in from Canada, Mexico, or the West Indies; industrial alcohol could be redistilled; trucks carrying alcohol seemed to invite hijacking. Violence and gang warfare exploded as underworld leaders reached for the forbidden fruit. In Chicago, the infamous Al Capone, bullet-headed, scar-faced, and syphilitic, built a formidable empire on bootlegging and a force of 700 hired killers. Capone's men, who became experts in the use of sawed-off shotguns and Thompson submachine guns, mowed down rival gangs. They assassinated the O'Banion gang, for example, by posing as policemen; after disarming the seven O'Banions and standing them against the wall, they calmly cut them down with submachine-gun fire. By the end of the decade, Capone and his mobsters, lords of the Chicago underworld, with policemen, politicians, and at least one local mayor in their pay, had an annual income of $100 million. Ironically, it was an income tax charge that finally sent Capone to a federal prison in 1931. By this time as we shall see, the mood of the country, stimulated by the failure of enforcement, the spread of gangsterism, and the overriding concern with the depression, had turned sharply against prohibition.

## Women and Morals

According to Walter Lippmann, the principal achievement of the gangster-ridden twenties was that they "brought about the dissolution of the ancestral order." Life had a different flavor from what it had before the war. Manners and morals were changed. The authority of the past was broken. The old structure of values dissolved. Youth seemed restless, uneasy, disaffected. Perhaps the greatest visible change was in the appearance and conduct of women. To those who had grown up before the war the young woman of the twenties seemed to delight in flaunting her unconventional behavior. She hiked her skirts above her knees, bobbed her hair, smeared cosmetics across her face. She drank openly with men, smoked cigarettes, and talked about subjects long taboo in polite society. Her manner was breezy, slangy, and informal; her silhouette slim and boyish; her outlook gay and confident.

Women won the right to vote in 1920 by Constitutional amendment, though they had already achieved it in nearly half the states before the adoption of the Nineteenth Amendment. The victory was part of the general movement toward sex equality. Already the American woman was beginning to enjoy some of the mechanical aids that were to cut the burden and drudgery of household work. She was winning, too, a measure of educational and business equality with men, though discrimination was still strong.

What was hardest for the old generation to understand was the breakdown of formality in relations between the sexes. According to the Victorian code of the prewar years a young woman's innocence had to be shielded from the crudities and temptations of the world. The essence of romance was mystery; courtship must therefore be conducted with great indirection and subtlety; it was all rather an exciting game played for a serious purpose. To the youngsters of the twenties, however, the game seemed hypocritical and one-sided, the double standard a lingering reminder of male domination. And so they kicked over the traces. Dating without chaperones became common; automobiles carried young couples beyond the reach of prying relatives; roadhouses or speakeasies became rendezvous for youth out on a spree; and darkened movie houses afforded an unaccustomed freedom. Sex was talked and written about much more freely than in any previous age. The writings of the Austrian psychoanalyst Sigmund Freud became popular, the tabloid press grew increasingly sensational, and Hollywood sirens staged amorous escapades for their box-office value. Whether sexual promiscuity increased in the twenties cannot be proved, though youth was certainly subject to temptations undreamed of by the fearful Victorians.

Still, the emancipated woman of the twenties was not necessarily happier than her Victorian forebears. Greater freedom often brought insecurity and disillusionment. Elmer Davis called attention to a heroine of a novel he had read who "indulged in 259 amours, if I remember correctly, without getting the emotional wallop out of any of them, or out of all of them together, that the lady of Vic-

torian literature would have derived from a single competently conducted seduction." Once married, a woman of the twenties was far more likely to end her marriage by divorce than her mother had been. In the years between 1914 and 1928 the ratio of divorces to marriages rose from one in ten to one in six. The modern woman also had fewer children. Family size, especially among the well-to-do, declined in deference to urban conditions, educational costs, and rising standards of comfort.

### The Hero

The collapse of familiar ideas and patterns of conduct disturbed more persons than the emancipated women of the Jazz Age. Despite the rejection of all idealism at the surface of American life, the hunger for authentic ideals remained. From time to time this hunger found outlet in the achievements of some individual who seemed to scorn the cynicism and grossness of the age. No period in modern history has been so hero-mad, so anxious to lionize the solitary man who stood out from the crowd, who grappled with nature, or simply refused to obey the herd-instinct. In a time of large organizations, when the individual seemed to count for less, the man who believed in himself, who kept his faith and courage, seemed all the more remarkable. And so the twenties saw the most astonishing procession of heroes of any decade in the century: aviators, explorers, adventurers, and a hundred varieties of sports figures. So impressive were the giants of this "Golden Age of Sports"—Bobby Jones, Bill Tilden, Babe Ruth, Jack Dempsey, Gene Tunney, Red Grange, the Four Horsemen, Gertrude Ederle—that their names were still household words a third of a century later.

But the greatest of the heroes of the twenties was Lindbergh. More than the others, he seemed to stand for something that the Jazz Age had forgotten. Born in Minnesota, the son of a hard-bitten Congressman who had opposed American entry into war in 1917, Charles A. Lindbergh, Jr., was a boy mechanic, a daredevil motorcyclist, a barnstorming stunt man, and an Army mail pilot before fame came to him in 1927. In his daring plan to fly the Atlantic from New

Gallery of the twenties: A. Mitchell Palmer, Attorney-General; H. L. Mencken, journalist; Al Capone, gangster; Babe Ruth, baseball player. (First three, Brown Brothers; Ruth, Culver Pictures.)

York to Paris alone in a single-engine plane, to compete for the Orteig Prize of $25,000 against well-financed veteran pilots, he personified all that the twenties wanted to admire—courage in a time of cynicism, simplicity in a time of big organization, idealism in a time of commercialism. As his plane headed north to Newfoundland and then out over the Atlantic, a hundred million Americans seemed suddenly to focus their minds and hearts with one accord on this solitary boy facing death and loneliness in a tiny machine throbbing its way toward Europe. People climbed on rooftops to catch a glimpse of his plane; they huddled around radio loudspeakers for the latest word of his progress; a crowd of 40,000 at Yankee Stadium rose for a moment of silent prayer; and the humorist Will Rogers started his nightly column, "No attempt at jokes today. A slim, tall, bashful, smiling American boy is somewhere over the middle of the Atlantic ocean, where no lone human being has ever ventured before. . . ."

At Le Bourget airfield in Paris, the next evening, several hundred thousand Frenchmen deliriously hailed the American's achievement. He was brought back from Europe on a cruiser dispatched by President Coolidge. His welcome home was stupendous; probably no American has ever heard such a tumult as that surrounding his trip down Broadway. "He has displaced everything that is petty, that is sordid, that is vulgar," said Charles Evans Hughes, by now Chief Justice of the United States. "What is money in the presence of Charles A. Lindbergh? . . . America is picturing to herself youth with the highest aims, with courage unsurpassed; science victorious. . . . We are all better men and women because of this exhibition in this flight of our young friend. Our boys and girls have before them a stirring, inspiring vision of real manhood." The twenties at last had its authentic hero. Significantly, he was a man whose values seemed to have little in common with those of the New Era. Though the flight was a triumph of careful planning and engineering genius, it was celebrated largely as a victory for in-

Emancipated women of the era. Bathing beauties of 1922, Washington, D.C. (Library of Congress.)

dividualism and pioneer virtues. He, as John W. Ward expressed it, "gave the American people a glimpse of what they liked to think themselves to be at a time when they feared they had deserted their own vision of themselves." *

## THE BATTLE AGAINST CONFORMITY

Others besides Lindbergh, whether consciously or unconsciously, found the values of the New Era hollow and mean. To many sensitive and intelligent souls the crucial task of the nineteen twenties seemed to be to find breathing space for the expression of independent ideas and unconventional behavior. They hated the hypocrisy, materialism, Babbittry, social conformity, and "catchpenny opportunism," as Van Wyck Brooks called it, of the life they saw about them. And they sensed, too, the growing cleavage between preaching and practice, between traditional ideals and reality, in almost every branch of their experience. Freedom seemed to have turned into conformity, individualism into organization, and popular rule into the tyranny of the majority. The American Dream, in short, had become the American Success Story. Moral behavior now being governed by little more than a fear of what people might say, the past seemed useless as a guide to the present. "Here was a new generation," said Fitzgerald, "grown up to find all Gods dead, all wars fought, all faiths in man shaken."

The past had closed in. For half a century the onward rush of science, industry, and urban life had been narrowing the choices, transforming the outlook of the settled agricultural nation of Lincoln's day. The new intellectuals scoffed at Puritans, fixed ideals, social reforms (especially prohibition), bourgeois habits, and religious fundamentalism. Some had lost all faith. "Our nada who are in nada," wrote Hemingway in a boldly nihilistic parody, "nada be thy name thy kingdom nada thy will be nada in nada as it is in nada." Conformity and lack of imagination became the deadly sins in the catechism of the liberal intellectual. Some took flight from Babbitt's America; others mercilessly lampooned its intellectual vacuity; all lamented what had happened to their country. "Lovers of beauty,/starved,/Thwarted with systems,/Helpless against the controls," wrote the embittered Ezra Pound.† "We have no heritages or traditions to which to cling," said Harold Stearns in introducing a book on American civilization, "except those that have already withered in our hands and turned to dust." **

### Monkey Trial

Only the right to speak one's mind seemed at all important among America's traditions. But even this was threatened by the Red Scare and a half-million Babbitts anxious to ferret out "the long-haired gentry who call themselves 'liberals' and 'radicals' and 'nonpartisan' and 'intelligentsia' and God only knows how many other trick names!" Worst of all the threats, in the view of many concerned citizens, were the efforts of zealous fundamentalist religious sects to ban the teaching of evolution in the public schools. The fundamentalists were

* J. Ward, "The Meaning of Lindbergh's Flight," *American Quarterly*, X (Spring, 1958), p. 6.

† From *Personae: The Collected Poems of Ezra Pound.* Copyright 1926, 1954 by Ezra Pound. Reprinted by permission of New Directions.

** H. Stearns (ed.), *Civilization in the United States* (New York: Harcourt, Brace and Company, 1922), p. vii.

William Jennings Bryan, in pith helmet, arriving at Dayton, Tennessee, for the Scopes trial. (Underwood & Underwood.)

religious conservatives, disturbed by the momentous changes in science and modern life, who viewed science as a demonic force tempting God-fearing Christians away from their time-proven beliefs. During the early twenties they organized as Bible Crusaders or joined the Anti-Evolution League and, under one name or another, induced legislatures in Tennessee, North Carolina, Florida, and Texas to pass laws limiting the use in schools of material supporting evolution.

When the American Civil Liberties Union offered to defend any teacher who would test these laws, in Dayton, Tennessee, a popular football coach and science teacher named John Scopes was persuaded to make the attempt. He was brought to trial in July, 1925. In what became a carnival-like atmosphere, Scopes was thrust into the background as journalists, ministers, fundamentalists, and the curious flocked into town. To defend him a brilliant corps of lawyers was assembled under Clarence Darrow, the most famous criminal lawyer in America and a well-known agnostic. Leading the prosecution was the aging William Jennings Bryan, fresh from a personal crusade against evolutionist teachings in the South and West,

who was making his last public appearance before death took him shortly after the trial. When the judge refused to admit expert testimony from scientists, the outcome of the trial was decided, but Darrow was more interested in the larger court of public opinion than in the local ruling. His chance to ridicule fundamentalism came when Bryan took the stand as a Bible authority.

Q—Now, you say, the big fish swallowed Jonah, and he there remained how long? three days? and then he spewed him upon the land? You believe that the big fish was made to swallow Jonah?
A—I am not prepared to say that; the Bible merely says it was done.
Q—You don't know whether it was the ordinary run of fish, or made for that purpose?
A—You may guess; you evolutionists guess.

Since the lone legal issue was whether Scopes had actually violated the law, the case was ended quickly. His fine was later rescinded by the state supreme court but his conviction and the anti-evolution law were upheld. The fundamentalists won the battle but their opponents won the war. For thanks to Darrow and the Civil Liberties Union, the case dramatized the danger to academic freedom and civil liberties from a zealous minority determined to impose its views on the coming generation. The fundamentalists suffered defeat after defeat in the latter half of the twenties until at the end of the decade the anti-evolution crusade was virtually dead.

## The "Lost Generation"

One of the reporters at the Dayton trial was H. L. Mencken, already famous as the sharp-tongued spokesman for American intellectuals. He lived up to his reputation. He berated the "gaping primates" and "homo boobiens" of the "Bible belt." Caustically he described the "theological mountebanks" behind the Tennessee law. He found Dayton, like the rest of America, a desert of philistine vulgarity. Mencken was founder and editor, along with George Jean Nathan, of the *American Mercury*, an interpreter of Nietzsche, a student of American language, and a friend and critic of a number of rising authors. Mercilessly, throughout the twenties, he mocked the stupidities, manners, herd instinct, and hypocrisy of the *Genus Americanus*. Invariably he supported every semblance of individualism, no matter how wrong-headed. Democracy, he came to suspect, was a system that destroyed liberty, ignored the exceptional man, and catered to the weaknesses of the lumpish average. The fear of Bolshevism was "a popular mania that has had no equal in America since the early Puritans . . . saw a torturable witch in every old woman who had lost her teeth." But Mencken offered no way out for the "peasant civilization" that he so savagely attacked. He was not interested in reform. Indeed, only a small elite was even capable of enjoying the zoo that was America. Not a ray of humility or tenderness lightened his theatrical assaults. His attraction was greatest for the young intellectuals of the twenties, who extravagantly admired his daringly humorous assaults on the conventions and foibles of the time. Badly needed as Mencken's stabbing pen was in the twenties, however, he was essentially irresponsible and, except for his language studies, has declined sharply in his appeal to successive generations of readers.

These strange, rebellious years of the twenties did produce, however, a half-dozen of the best-known American writers of the century. Uprooted by war and social upheaval, they sought for meaning in the blur of unstable impressions that crowded on their attention. "You are all a lost generation," said Gertrude Stein to Hemingway and the phrase stuck. The literary revolt that began thirty years before now reached its fulfillment; the genteel tradition being all but dead, the younger writers experienced none of the opposition met by Crane and Dreiser. Indeed, the public of the twenties came to expect in its literature the same loose manners, skepticism about ideals, and obsession with sex that it saw in real life. Freud had given the young writers their clue to man's personality. "If there is anything you do not understand in human life," wrote Sherwood Anderson in *Dark Laughter*, "consult the works of Dr. Freud." Hemingway added a philosophy. "I was not made for thinking," said Lieutenant Henry in *A Farewell to Arms*, "I was made to eat. My God, yes. Eat and drink and sleep with Catherine."

Both Anderson and Hemingway shared in the revolt against reason that seemed the dominant literary theme of the age. Man was the creature of uncontrollable forces, the naturalists of the nineties had taught, but the new writers found these forces within rather than outside man. The men and women of Anderson's tales in *Winesburg, Ohio* (1919) were twisted and thwarted by neurotic impulses, sexual repressions, and subconscious anxieties. Like many writers of the period, Anderson was fascinated by the abnormal, the clinical, the decadent. For Hemingway, too, truth seemed always to be mean, violent, lonely, or sordid. Ideals were meaningless. Morals had lost their anchor in religion. "So far, about morals," he wrote "I know only that what is moral is what you feel good after and what is immoral is what you feel bad after." Only such primitive virtues as strength, courage, and loyalty made one man more worthy of note than another.

Writers were sensitive, of course, to the climate of postwar America. Most, however, lacked the experience or perspective to give it meaning. Sinclair Lewis, with his explorations of *Main Street* (1920) and the life of *Babbitt* (1922), and F. Scott Fitzgerald, in his profiles of the Jazz Age in *This Side of Paradise* (1920) and *The Great Gatsby* (1925), penned the most enduring portraits. Lewis was driven by a vision of what America might be and the realization of how far she had fallen. Ill at ease in the America of Henry Ford and Al Capone, he was sickened by the standardization, the hustling for hustling's sake, and the pale conformity of everyday life. He set out to analyze the small town and the bustling city of his native Midwest in stinging if sympathetic terms. Fitzgerald took for his special province the manners and morals of the leisure class, especially those of its members who were young enough to appreciate the parties, jazz, and loosened moral restraints of the era. In *This Side of Paradise* he gave voice to the revolt of "flaming youth," with its jaunty insolence, its flippant speech, and its casual attitude toward sex. The war, said his hero, "sort of killed individualism out of our whole generation." His greatest achievement was his portrait of Jay Gatsby, a bootlegging romantic who tries to recapture the love of an upper-class beauty by extravagant and ostentatious parties attended by all the society types of the day. In the end he is ignored in his agony and death by all his former friends, the parties come to a halt, and the lights of the great Gatsby rented mansion go out for good. Out with them, Fitzgerald seemed to be saying, went the flickering lights of the whole tinsel epoch of which Gatsby was the symbol.

Poetry and drama were spurred by many of the same themes that dominated the novels of the twenties. Greatest of the playwrights of the decade was Eugene O'Neill, who used Freudian themes to portray the tensions and contradictions of modern life. Brilliant, moody, often angry at the civilization he saw about him, O'Neill wrote some of the most powerful and original plays in all American history. In *The Emperor Jones* (1920) he described the psychological collapse of a Negro dictator who is haunted by inner torment while being pursued by his own subjects; *Desire under the Elms* (1925) unfolds the story of a greedy and sensual woman who marries a widower and then seduces his son in order to have a child to inherit the older man's property; and *The Great God Brown* (1926) makes use of masks to highlight the spiritual emptiness of the central character, who is a successful business executive. By the end of the twenties, O'Neill had gained recognition as the first American playwright to rank with the leading dramatists of Europe.

The poets were likewise uncomfortable in a world of businessmen and engineers. Expatriate writers like T. S. Eliot and Ezra Pound made clear their revulsion at the emptiness of American life. In *The Waste Land* (1922), Eliot penned perhaps the most powerful indictment of the spiritual aridity of modern civilization ever written. Vachel Lindsay evidenced a similar disgust, along with Lewis, Hemingway, and Sherwood Anderson, with the values of the contemporary businessmen when he wrote:

> I hope all men
> Who think like this
> Will soon lie
> Underground.

The poems of Robinson Jeffers, like the plays of Eugene O'Neill, were full of violence and sexual perversion, and Edwin Arlington Robinson's work showed the strong influence of the postwar literary mood of disillusion.

In the arts, as well as in literature, the nineteen-twenties was a season of probative, effervescent activity. American musicians were now playing the works of such promising young composers as Aaron Copland and Roy Harris, as well as the tunes and, later, opera of George Gershwin, who made the first serious use of jazz rhythms. Jazz itself was widely hailed in the twenties as the most significant contribution yet made by Americans to the field of music, and the names of leading jazz musicians, notably Louis Armstrong, "Jelly Roll" Morton, and "King" Oliver, became household words. In painting, John Marin was producing some of the most forceful expressionist water colors yet seen in America, while Georgia O'Keeffe and others were experimenting with colorful, abstract designs. On the stage, the leading actors of the decade—Walter Hampden, Katharine Cornell, Alfred Lunt, Lynn Fontanne, Eva Le Gallienne—were bringing new life to the theatre and making Broadway one of the world's dramatic centers. And, far from least, American movie directors were making important contributions to the art and technique of film production. Many of the films produced during the twenties, even before sound was added, reached a high level of excellence, while some of the others, notably those that deliberately exploited sexual and sensational themes, had an unfortunate impact on America's view of itself and its image abroad.

## Intellectual Pessimism

By the end of the twenties, doubt and skepticism had eaten deeply into the positive assurance with which the nineteenth-century American looked at his universe and his society. Cultural and ethical relativism had become steadily more fashionable during the decade. What support remained for fundamental values and beliefs in a Darwinian universe of random chance? Anthropologists now looked at the values of each society in its own terms, refusing to make "value judgments" that would condemn any way of life as inferior to their own. The behavioristic school of psychology, which enjoyed a popular vogue in the twenties, agreed with the Freudians that man's behavior could not be explained by willful choice alone. Man was the creature of environmental stimuli as conditioned by experience and culture; man's most complicated acts, according to J. B. Watson, were "but combinations of . . . simple stimulus-response patterns of behavior." All human reactions that could not be studied in their simplest physical and chemical components were assumed not to exist. Of consciousness the behaviorist had nothing to say. "How can he?" said Watson. "He has neither seen, smelled nor tasted consciousness. . . ."

Everything seemed to conspire to reduce the area of certainty in human affairs. Darwin had put man squarely in the animal kingdom; the new doctrines in psychology and anthropology seemed to rob him of moral choice and make him a slave to blind impulse and tribal custom. Life in the great cities appeared to dehumanize man. Man seemed less the master of his fate in the concrete jungles of Metropolis, where decisions affecting his future were made remotely, impersonally, and often anonymously, than in his rural habitat. "Beneath the organized vivacity of our American communities," wrote Lewis Mumford in 1926, "who is not aware of a blankness, a sterility, a boredom, a despair?" All behavior appeared relative—to environment, to opportunity, to psychological impulse, to property relations, to conditioning, or to some other factor beyond individual control. Suddenly, the great victories won by Dewey and the intellectual progressives two decades earlier seemed, to some intellectuals at least, to turn to ashes. Freedom from tradition and conventional values now appeared to mean only uncertainty, relativity, and chaos. "By the dissolution of their ancestral ways," wrote Walter Lippmann in *A Preface to Morals* (1929), "men have been deprived of their sense of certainty as to why they were born, why they must work, whom they must love, what they must honor, where they may turn in sorrow and defeat. They have left to them the ancient codes and the modern criticism of these codes, guesses, intuitions, inconclusive experiments, possibilities, probabilities, hypotheses. . . . There is gone that ineffable certainty which once made God and His plan seem as real as the lamp-post."

The acids of modernity, as Lippmann called them, ate deeply into the foundations of the value structure of Western civilization. Through the world of philosophy, art, and letters ran the anguished realization that doubt and anxiety were the fate of modern man. Henry Adams, historian, esthete, and grandson of a president, had seen it coming and died in despair and disillusionment in 1918. The year of Adams's death the British philosopher Bertrand Russell warned that modern faith could be built only on unyielding despair. In Vienna, Sigmund Freud wrote in 1930 that modern man, for all his technical feats, was no happier than his ancestors. "What do we gain by a long life," he queried, "when it is full of hardship and starved of joys and so wretched that we can only welcome death as our deliverer?" In Germany, the philosopher Karl Jaspers noted the "despiritualization of the world . . . the unprecedented vacancy of existence, a sense of vacancy against which even the keenest skepticism of classical times was safeguarded. . . ." In the United States, Reinhold Niebuhr was becoming a convert to the "theology of crisis," rejecting the easy optimism of the religious modernists for a pessimistic realism about man's comprehending God's purposes.

The shock of these intellectual blows on the minds of sensitive critics and observers was profound. Aside from Lippmann, the drama critic Joseph Wood Krutch portrayed most acutely the feeling of emptiness that came over the intellectuals' world. In *The Modern Temper* (1929) Krutch described the destruction of the humane, moralistic, man-centered world of the nineteenth century by the relentless pressures of a materialistic science. The world revealed by science, especially the sciences of biology and psychology, was no longer one in which the human spirit could breathe free. Yet, he said, deep in the human psyche is the need to believe that right and wrong can be separated, that love is more than Robinson Jeffers' "furious longing to join the sewers of two bodies," and that man has meaningful choices to make in his actions and beliefs. But each of these beliefs is an illusion according to modern science. What, then, can man do? He has no real choice, Krutch argued. He cannot pretend that the old values still live because, once known to be fiction, they lose their power to make life meaningful. Deliberate efforts to find a rational justification for life must fail since they are in themselves a confession of weakness; life at its strongest needs no justification. Perhaps Western civilization was doomed to fall to the new barbarians in Moscow whose simple optimism, said Krutch in 1929, was reminiscent of the founders of Western culture. Whatever the success of the Communists, we would not be rejuvenated: "Skepticism has entered too deeply into our souls ever to be replaced by faith, and we can never forget the things which the new barbarians will never need to have known." At least we were not dupes; we had discovered the trick that fate had played on us. If we were to perish, Krutch declared, we should do so with courage. "We should rather die as men," reads his final sentence, "than live as animals."

## TWILIGHT OF THE NEW ERA

The pessimism of Krutch, curiously enough, would seem unreal in just a few short years. So, too, the artistic luminescence of the twenties would seem frivolous and decadent from the perspective of the depression-ridden thirties. Devastating new problems, undreamed of in the smug climate of the twenties, were just over the horizon. From the vantage point of the depression, the intellectual life of the twenties, for all its vigor and creative imagination, would seem reactionary and blind to the things that by then concerned Americans most. Its thought would come to seem sterile and unimaginative—descriptions its spokesmen applied to the business civilization around them. Particularly did the succeeding generation score their lack of ideals, their whining self-indulgence, and their arrogant distrust of democracy. With the return of idealism in the dark depression years, politics and reform, both taboo subjects in the twenties, would return to the center of the stage, as Franklin Roosevelt had said they would.

### The Election of 1928

The presidential contest of 1928 marked the end of a political era.

Pressures were now building that would find release only in the policies and programs of the New Deal. The zany inflation of securities on the stock exchange was already troubling a number of politicians and businessmen. Farmers, deeply concerned over their failure to share in the prosperity of the twenties, were whooping it up for the McNary-Haugen bill, which would serve as a landmark in the history of the welfare-state idea. Some of the political cleavages of the New Era that had paralyzed reform activity were beginning to show signs of healing. And, most significantly, the big-city politicians were marshaling a huge urban vote for the Democratic Party, thus paving the way for the New Deal coalition of the nineteen-thirties.

Roosevelt again nominated Al Smith as the "Happy Warrior" of the Democratic party. This time Smith met no serious opposition. McAdoo was inactive and the Northern machines were determined to take no one else. To balance the ticket the Democrats chose as his running mate a rural Southerner, Senator Joseph T. Robinson of Arkansas. The platform assailed the Harding scandals, promised a fairer tariff, advocated more rights for labor, pledged a stringent enforcement of antitrust laws, and urged independence for the Philippines and noninterference in Latin America. Prohibition was still a problem. The Democrats promised an "honest effort" to enforce the law, but Smith made it clear that he favored ultimate repeal. The farm plank also caused concern. After a lengthy battle the party endorsed the principles of McNary-Haugenism, though Smith's own position was not as clear as most farm leaders would have liked.

The Republicans endorsed the man who seemed best able to translate the business philosophy of the New Era into a living reality. With Coolidge's famous announcement that "I do not choose to run," the favorite for the nomination became Herbert Hoover. A native of West Branch, Iowa, an enormously successful mining engineer, Hoover had been Food Administrator and director of Belgian and European relief during the Wilson era. During the twenties he had done an outstanding job as Secretary of Commerce in both the Harding and Coolidge cabinets. Hoover argued in a book he wrote in 1922 that it was America's task to find a middle way between the reactionary, caste-bound capitalism of Europe and the dangerous road that led to socialism. A cooperative capitalism must provide equality of opportunity so that all Americans could find outlets for their talents. During the campaign he defended the policies of the New Era and warned that the American system of "rugged individualism" was the only alternative to paternalistic European doctrines. The Democrats, he charged, were headed toward socialism with their support of McNary-Haugenism and government power projects. "I have seen," said Hoover, speaking of government in business, "its tyrannies, its injustices, its destructions of self-government, its undermining

of the very instincts which carry our people forward to progress. I have witnessed the lack of advance, the lowered standards of living, the depressed spirits of people working under such a system." The American system, declared Hoover in his last speech of the campaign, was superior: "It has come nearer to the abolition of poverty, to the abolition of fear of want, than humanity has ever reached before."

But for all the talk of philosophies of government, the real issues in 1928 were prosperity, prohibition, and Smith's fitness for the presidency. It was unlikely, as Roosevelt said in 1924, that any Democrat could have captured the White House in the frenzied prosperity of the twenties. The only question then is

Al Smith during the 1928 campaign. (Brown Brothers.)

whether another Democrat, not a Catholic, wet, or a big-city spokesman, might have made a stronger showing than Smith. This seems problematical since he evoked a fervent admiration among big-city workingmen of immigrant origins that no other Democrat could have equaled. He was certainly straightforward on the issues affecting himself. His opposition to prohibition was unequivocal. He met questions about his religion with the declaration that he believed "in the absolute separation of church and state and in the strict enforcement of the provisions of the Constitution that Congress shall make no law respecting an establishment of religion or prohibiting the free exercise thereof." He made no effort to conceal his Bowery accent, Tammany background, or big-city ways.

Smith polled as many votes as Coolidge in 1924 but lost to Hoover, twenty-one million votes to fifteen million. Hoo-

### 1928 Election

| | Popular Vote | Electoral Vote |
|---|---|---|
| Smith (D) | 15,016,443 | 87 |
| Hoover (R) | 21,392,190 | 444 |
| Other | 470,781 | 0 |

ver captured 444 electoral votes and forty states. The outcome helped to harden the political legend for another three decades that a Catholic could not be elected President of the United States. But perhaps the most remarkable fact about Smith's showing was not how poorly he ran in the South (he carried only six Southern states) but how well he ran in the North.

In the nation's twelve largest cities Smith won a plurality of 38,000 votes over Hoover while Coolidge had won these same cities by more than a million votes in 1921. The elements of the later victorious Democratic coalition of 1932 were already beginning to fall into place.

### "Some May Grow Worse"

When the new President took office on March 4, 1929, the prospects for the country had never seemed brighter. The stock market stood at an all-time high; the wheels of industry were turning smoothly; unemployment had dropped to less than a half-million, the lowest figure of the decade. Even farm income seemed to be on the rise. The population of the nation crossed the 120 million mark sometime in the late twenties. All these people would need more food, more houses, more automobiles, more electrical appliances—especially the 68 million persons who lived in cities, or 56 per cent of all Americans. The census of 1920 had marked the first time that those living in towns of 2500 population or more outnumbered those living in rural areas. This shift reflected the growing importance of manufacturing and city employment. For every ten persons engaged in farming in 1929, seventeen were employed in manufacturing, mining, construction, or transportation industries. Increasing numbers of Negroes were leaving the South for the booming industries of the North; of nearly eleven million Negroes born in the South, 1.4 million, or 13 per cent of them, were living in another region in 1930.

There were signs, however, though few saw them, that all was not well in 1929. One who did was Wesley C. Mitchell, a noted economist and student of business cycles. In the spring of 1929 he concluded a massive eight-year-long study of the American economy with these prophetic words: "Even on the face of affairs, all is not well. Americans have seen more uniformly fortunate times. . . . The conditions of agriculture, the volume of unemployment, the textile trades, coal mining, the leather industries, present grave problems not only to the people immediately concerned, but also to their fellow citizens. How rapidly these conditions will mend we do not know. Some may grow worse. . . ."

## FOR FURTHER STUDY

*The books by Commager, Hofstadter, Kazin, Leuchtenberg, Nye, Shannon, Slosson, and Sullivan cited in previous chapters continue to be especially useful for the topics dealt with in this chapter.*

### General Accounts

* F. Allen, *Only Yesterday* (New York: Harper, 1931). A superb, entertaining, and delightfully written history of the twenties.

* J. Hicks, *Normalcy and Reaction* (Washington: American Historical Association, 1960). A pamphlet for teachers describing recent interpretations and books dealing with the years from 1921 to 1933.

————, *Republican Ascendancy, 1921-1933* (New York: Harper, 1960). An admirable summary of recent scholarship, this is a volume in the "New American Nation" series.

*Recent Economic Changes in the United States*, two volumes (New York: McGraw-Hill, 1929). The invaluable report and studies of the Committee on Recent Economic Changes established in 1921 under Herbert Hoover.

*Recent Social Trends*, two volumes (New York: McGraw-Hill, 1933). Another important governmental study compiled under the chairmanship of Wesley C. Mitchell.

A. Schlesinger, Jr., *The Crisis of the Old Order, 1919-1933* (Boston: Houghton Mifflin, 1957). An important general examination of the politics and ideas of the New Era and Hoover

* Starred books are available in paperbound editions.

years from the standpoint of "The Age of Roosevelt."

K. Schriftgiesser, *This Was Normalcy* (Boston: Little, Brown, 1948). A journalistic but stimulating account of the politics of the twenties.

G. Soule, *Prosperity Decade* (New York: Rinehart, 1947). The best general study of the economic developments of the New Era.

### Special Studies

J. Adams, *Our Business Civilization* (New York: Albert and Charles Boni, 1929). Useful for understanding the temper of the New Era.

S. Adams, *Incredible Era* (Boston: Houghton Mifflin, 1939). The life and times of Warren Harding told somewhat sensationally by a newspaperman.

M. Cowley (ed.), *After the Genteel Tradition* (New York: W. W. Norton and Company, 1937). Uneven sketches of some of the more important literary figures of the decade.

*————, *Exile's Return* (New York: Viking, 1951). The literary climate of the nineteen-twenties explained by one who shared it.

K. Davis, *The Hero: Charles A. Lindbergh and the American Dream* (Garden City, New York: Doubleday, 1959). A brilliant biography of Lindbergh which explores the meaning of his life and achievement.

T. Draper, *The Roots of American Communism* (New York: Viking, 1957). An important study, one of a series on communism and American life sponsored by the Fund for the Republic.

G. Fite, *George N. Peek and the Fight for Farm Parity* (Norman: U. of Oklahoma Press, 1954). Probably the best introduction to the farm problem of the twenties.

J. Franklin, *From Slavery to Freedom* (New York: Knopf, rev. ed., 1960). This history of American Negroes contains an excellent chapter on the Negro's trials in the twenties.

F. Freidel, *Franklin D. Roosevelt: the Ordeal* (Boston: Little, Brown, 1954). This second volume of an excellent biography of FDR is very useful in understanding the politics of the Democratic party from 1920 to 1928.

* C. Glasrud (ed.), *The Age of Anxiety* (Boston: Houghton Mifflin, 1960). A wonderful collection of source materials illustrating the development of the anxious temper of the modern age.

* S. Grebstein (ed.), *Monkey Trial* (Boston: Houghton Mifflin, 1960). A good collection of research materials, including most of the transcript of the trial, on the Scopes affair.

O. Handlin, *Al Smith and His America* (Boston: Little, Brown, 1958). A short biography of

Smith stressing the significance of his career in American politics.

F. Hoffman, *The Twenties* (New York: Viking, 1955). This excellent study seeks to look at the 1920's from the perspective of its literature.

H. Hoover, *The Memoirs of Herbert Hoover: the Cabinet and the Presidency* (New York: Macmillan, 1952). An autobiography covering the years from 1920 to 1933 when Hoover was Secretary of Commerce and President.

* M. Jones, *American Immigration* (Chicago: U. of Chicago Press, 1960). A brief study by an Englishman that looks at the newcomer both as an emigrant from Europe and an immigrant to the United States.

* J. Krutch, *The Modern Temper* (New York: Harcourt, Brace, 1929). The best statement of the intellectual pessimism of the late twenties.

* W. Lippmann, *A Preface to Morals* (New York: Macmillan, 1929). An acute analysis of the liberal disillusionment with the results of intellectual progressivism.

* R. and H. Lynd, *Middletown* (New York: Harcourt, Brace, 1929). This study of an average American community of the twenties became the best-known sociological work of the period.

R. Miller, *American Protestantism and Social Issues, 1919-1939* (Chapel Hill: U. of North Carolina Press, 1958). Contains much interesting material on the decline of the Social Gospel and clerical attitudes in the twenties.

E. Moore, *A Catholic Runs for President* (New York: The Ronald Press Company, 1956). The best study of the Catholic issue in the 1928 campaign.

M. Moos, *The Republicans* (New York: Random House, 1956). The only full history of the Republican party.

R. Murray, *Red Scare* (Minneapolis: U. of Minnesota Press, 1955). The best account of the drive against radicals in 1919 and 1920, which the author thinks reflected a "national hysteria."

A. Nevins and F. Hill, *Ford: Expansion and Challenge 1915-1933* (New York: Scribner's, 1957). A massive work of scholarship on the years when Ford became a household name.

* G. Norris, *Fighting Liberal* (New York: Macmillan, 1945). The autobiography of George Norris, progressive leader and champion of the T. V. A. idea.

* H. Pelling, *American Labor* (Chicago: U. of Chicago Press, 1960). Contains a good chapter summarizing labor's fortunes during the twenties.

J. Prothro, *The Dollar Decade* (Baton Rouge: Louisiana State U. Press, 1954). A stimulating and highly valuable analysis of business ideas during the decade of the nineteen-twenties.

E. Roseboom, *A History of Presidential Elections* (New York: Macmillan, 1957). An indispensable survey of all presidential contests through 1956.

A. Siegfried, *America Comes of Age* (New York: Harcourt, Brace, 1927). A famous Frenchman's interpretation of what he saw and learned of the United States.

H. Stearns (ed.), *Civilization in the United States* (New York: Harcourt, Brace, 1922). A critical, often hostile, view of all phases of American life as seen by more than a score of writers.

M. Sullivan, *The Twenties* (New York: Scribner's, 1935). This is Volume VI of Sullivan's delightful potpourri of information on "Our Times" from 1900 to 1925.

J. Ward, "The Meaning of Lindbergh's Flight," *American Quarterly*, X (Spring, 1958). A very thoughtful examination of the significance of Lindbergh's flight to the social and intellectual life of the twenties.

* B. Ziegler (ed.), *Immigration: an American Dilemma* (Boston: Heath, 1953). A valuable collection of arguments by contemporaries and historians on America's immigration policy.

### Fiction and Drama

* J. Dos Passos, *U.S.A.* (New York: The Modern Library, 1930-1937). This famous trilogy of novels—*The 42nd Parallel*, *Nineteen Nineteen*, and *The Big Money*—forms the best literary study yet made of the meaning of the years covered in this chapter.

* F. Fitzgerald, *The Great Gatsby* (New York: Scribner's, 1925). Contains perhaps the best insight into the spirit and attitudes of the twenties to be found in any single book.

J. Hutchens (ed.), *The American Twenties* (Philadelphia: Lippincott, 1952). A good anthology of short stories, poetry, and excerpts from novels of the twenties.

* J. Lawrence and R. Lee, *Inherit the Wind* in L. Kronenberger, ed., *The Best Plays of 1954-1955* (New York: Dodd, Mead, 1955). Dramatic version of the famous "monkey trial" debate between Darrow and Bryan.

* S. Lewis, *Main Street* (New York: Harcourt, Brace, 1920). A trenchant novel exposing the pettiness, dreariness, and dullness of life in the "Gopher Prairies" of America.

* ———, *Babbitt* (New York: Harcourt, Brace, 1922). The classic study of the "God-fearing, hustling, successful, two-fisted" booster and Rotarian.

* D. Schary, *Sunrise at Campobello* in L. Kronenberg, ed., *The Best Plays of 1957-1958* (New York: Dodd, Mead, 1958). A play centering around Franklin D. Roosevelt's fight against polio climaxed by his nominating speech for Al Smith in 1924.

### Films and Records

*The Farm Problem* (McGraw-Hill, 15 minutes, sound, black and white). A film survey of the American farm problem beginning with the 1920's that emphasizes causes and attempted remedies.

*The Golden Twenties* (McGraw-Hill, 68 minutes, sound, black and white). Based on contemporary newsreels and films, this March of Time film helps to recreate the fashions, sports, politics, entertainment, and business spirit of the twenties.

*I Can Hear It Now, 1919-1932* (Columbia Records, edited by Murrow and Friendly). The voices of history from 1919 to FDR's victory in 1932 on records.

*The Movies Learn to Talk* (Prudential Insurance Company, 28 minutes, sound, black and white). Another entertaining and instructive film from the "Twentieth Century" series.

*Sport's Golden Age* (McGraw-Hill, 16 minutes, sound, black and white). Includes many of the sports champions of the twenties.

*Two Decades of History* (Teaching Film Custodians, 23 minutes, sound, black and white). Film highlights of the years 1927 to 1947, beginning with newsreels of Lindbergh's reception after his trans-Atlantic flight.

# Nadir

CHAPTER SIX

Hooverville, Seattle.

THE MOOD OF THE TIMES

"Somewhere in Tin Mountain, the four-acre jungle on the Red Hook waterfront in Brooklyn, Louis Bringmann put down his old sea chest last night and looked about him for a place to sleep. He was 60 years old, penniless, friendless and jobless.

"Up to 9 A.M. yesterday Louis Bringmann had had a home on the top landing of the Atlantic Theatre. . . . Patrolman Richard Palmay of the Bergen Street police station climbed the fire-escape at 8 A.M. with orders to 'remove the fire hazard. . . .' On the cardboard wall was a neat sign, done in old-school flourishes and shading:

NOTICE

Please be kind enough not to destroy or take anything from this resting place. I am out of work and this is all I have. I have no money and can't find a job, so please leave me alone. . . .

" 'You'll have to move, old man.' He hated the job. . . .

"The snow-white head nodded. . . .

"He had known of Tin Mountain before, but he was proud. In Tin Mountain, a sprawling village of tin huts and makeshift dugouts at the foot of Henry Street, are all types of men. . . . One of its streets has the bitter legend on a placard, 'Prosperity Boulevard.'

"Late in the afternoon he was still sitting on the little chest that contains the meager souvenirs of better days—a few faded menus he had made up when he was head chef of one of the big Manhattan hotels. He wouldn't tell which one.

" 'The past,' said Louis Bringmann, 'is a turned-over page. When I read it I read alone. They tell me now that I'm even too old for dishwashing—that's the whole story. I have no friends and my money is gone.' "

—THE NEW YORK TIMES, JULY 9, 1932

# THE ROAD TO DEPRESSION

"I have no friends and my money is gone." How often these melancholy words were heard in the dark days of 1932! Louis Bringmann, if he were like most Americans, felt deep pessimism as he tasted the bitter fruits of economic stagnation and lengthening breadlines. Probably he tried as others did to make some sense out of the catastrophic changes that had come over American life since 1929. How was it possible for a nation that had reached such peaks of prosperity a few short years before to plunge so deeply into economic chaos? How could one understand a system that consigned millions of city-dwellers to hunger while farmers burned corn and stuffed wheat into swollen granaries? What had happened to the New Era confidence that led Herbert Hoover to predict a "chicken in every pot and two cars in every garage"?

## The New President

The New Era was dead. It died within eight months of the day Hoover took the oath of office. The collapse of prosperity cannot be blamed on Hoover—no president could have foreseen or prevented the chain of events that led to disaster—but for years to come Hoover would carry the albatross of depression about his neck. This was a supreme irony. For Hoover had become a national figure as the result of his humanitarian efforts on behalf of suffering and starving Bel-

gians in 1915; after the war he directed relief efforts in Europe; and throughout the twenties he appealed to liberal and generous spirits as a warm-hearted humanitarian who knew how to act swiftly in times of social crisis. Yet many Americans would remember him as the president who refused to feed hungry Americans in 1932; his memory would be reviled quadrennially in every political campaign for a quarter-century; and he would become the butt of cruel jokes aimed at his supposed callousness in the face of human suffering and want. For in his four-year ordeal in the White House, Hoover put to the supreme test the suitability of traditional American ideals to the new urban-industrial age. In the name of the nineteenth century and the American tradition Hoover made a last desperate stand on behalf of individualism, limited government, personal liberty, inevitable progress, and unbounded optimism about the future.

He had many assets in the fight. Himself the product of American opportunity, he had modest beginnings: A blacksmith's son in a little Quaker community in Iowa, he was orphaned at nine, then sent to join an uncle in Oregon. He entered the new Leland Stanford University "on a shoestring of money and a thimbleful of preparatory education." Fascinated by geology, he became a mining engineer, worked briefly as a day laborer, and then got his big chance when he was hired by a London firm to do mine scouting in Australia. From 1897 to 1911 Hoover undertook mining enterprises on four continents, accumulated a personal fortune, and settled down in London to direct his far-flung interests. At the outbreak of World War I, he plunged into the work of helping stranded Americans to get home, then turned his attention to the task of Belgian relief. By 1919, according to a London journal, he was "the biggest man who has emerged on the Allied side during the war." During the twenties, as Secretary of Commerce under two Republican presidents, he was perhaps the most appealing spokesman and representative of the New Era. A born organizer, a man of integrity and personal rectitude, he was a successful executive who inspired loyalty in his followers, and he had the New Era's passion for business and industrial efficiency. His beliefs were those of the New Era, refined of any narrow selfishness or partisanship—unlimited opportunity, private enterprise, "rugged individualism," a bullish optimism about the future, and confidence in a government that would give timely if limited aid to business.

But Hoover had liabilities, too. He had no real stomach for politics. He never enjoyed the give-and-take, the playful exuberance, the game-like quality of political life. He particularly resented the press, which seemed always to distort or misrepresent his intentions and actions. Accustomed to leading men by executive command, he showed little skill in working with a Congress made up of politicians. To his enemies in that body he could seem autocratic, even ruthless, and sometimes he appeared petty or mean of temper. His lack of humor prevented him from releasing pent-up antagonisms or appreciating the ironies of political life. And his shyness made him appear snobbish or standoffish at times. Lacking in political color, he preferred dogged argument to dramatic public appeals. Most surprising of all, the President seemed indecisive and vacillating when confronted by the mammoth decisions that needed to be made after 1929. On the tariff question, prohibition, even public power, his stand was not always clear or straightforward. Nor could he make up his mind on the policies he wished to follow in combating the depression.

President and Mrs. Hoover arriving at Washington with friends. (Library of Congress.)

## Forgotten Achievements

Sometimes it seems looking back as if Hoover spent all his time from 1929 to 1933 fighting the great depression. This is not quite true. Much of his time was taken up with foreign affairs and domestic problems not immediately related to the depression. Throughout his administration, for instance, he was deeply interested in problems of conservation, especially the uses of water power, the improvement of inland waterways, and the establishment of reclamation and irrigation projects. His opposition to federal operation of the Muscle Shoals enterprise has clouded appreciation of his encouragement of other power projects, notably the Hoover Dam on the Colorado River, which private utility interests were anxious to see built. Hoover also began work on a large number of other public works—buildings, bridges, highways—though he remained doubtful of their value in promoting economic recovery. In the fields of housing, child welfare, prison reform, and statistical study of social trends, President Hoover also performed notable services. A National Housing Conference he called in 1931 was responsible for a series of valuable studies and recommendations that were heeded by both his own and the Roosevelt administrations. Hoover was also much interested in the health of children—he had founded the American Child Health Association in 1919—and invited a pioneering national conference in this field to the White House in 1930. And Hoover was responsible, too, for a good deal of reorganization in the executive departments of the government, including the establishment of the Veterans Administration in 1930.

## The Great Crash

The event that did engage most of the President's attention, the economic collapse, when it came, came suddenly. There had been signs for some years, to be sure, that all was not well, but they had gone unheeded. Following the smash of a great real estate boom in Florida in 1926, the New York Stock Exchange had become almost the sole center of financial speculation. Prices of stock shot upwards in 1927 as brokers' loans—meaning loans negotiated by brokers to carry their customers and backed by stock as collateral—increased by an amazing 29 per cent. The Federal Reserve Board, anxious not to discourage the rising market, lowered its discount rate on loans to 3½ per cent. Under the stimulus of easy money, low interest rates, and unlimited confidence, a great bull market developed for all kinds of market securities in 1928 and 1929. President Coolidge announced that he did not consider brokers' loans too high, which seemed to give White House blessing to the rising market. As the buying became feverish after March, 1928, the Federal Reserve banks, becoming increasingly alarmed, raised their rediscount rate to 4 per cent, then 4½ per cent, finally to 5 per cent, but without noticeable effect. Though the market dipped in June, it recovered quickly, then began to soar after Hoover's election in November. The Federal Reserve Board, fearful that further raises in the rediscount rate might handicap legitimate business and bring on a smash-up, ordered its member banks not to use their resources in support of market activities. But several New York banks, led by the National City Bank, intervened to offer money for downpayments on stock at 15 per cent interest. Again the market rallied. By the summer of 1929 stock prices were in the stratosphere, and brokers' loans amounted to nearly a billion dollars. In September stock levels reached their cloud-wreathed peak.

The market slipped late that month.

On September 26, the Bank of England, concerned over the flow of gold to America for investment purposes, raised its interest rate. As a result, stores of English money went back across the Atlantic. A number of alarmed speculators in this country also began to cash in. By early October there was widespread concern, but Professor Irving Fisher of Yale issued a classic assurance that stock prices had reached "what looks like a permanently high plateau." On October 23 a torrent of liquidation brought six million shares onto the Exchange floor. The next day—"Black Thursday"—panic struck. Within a few hours occurred the most disastrous drop in the history of the Exchange as thirteen million shares changed hands. A growing sense of helplessness and bafflement settled over the market. The pall of gloom was lightened briefly by the news that a senior Morgan partner, Thomas W. Lamont, was meeting with representatives of the great New York banks. A quarter-billion dollar pool was raised by the bankers to steady prices. But on Tuesday, October 29, the bottom dropped out. More than sixteen million shares were exchanged as huge amounts of stock were thrown on the Exchange for whatever they would bring. Billions of dollars of paper profits were gobbled up in a day. "The crowds about the ticker tape," said the New York *Times* next day, "reflected in their faces the story the tape was telling. There were no smiles. There were no tears either. Just the camaraderie of fellow-sufferers. Everybody wanted to tell his neighbor how much he had lost. Nobody wanted to listen. It was too repetitious a tale. . . ."

### Why?

No expression of cheery optimism rallied the market this time. The whole business world was shaken by the dismal news from Wall Street. Industrial production and business activity began to falter. Almost at once, it seemed, the economy started down the long valley of liquidation and depression. Adversity ground stock prices down and down and still further down. The index of common stock prices (1926=100) showed a calamitous drop from 190 in 1929 to 150 in 1930, and finally to 49 in 1932. Like a house of cards in a gust of wind, the whole sensitive economic balance between finance and the productive sectors of the economy was upset by the disaster at Broad and Wall streets.

Why did the booming prosperity of the twenties end so abruptly? Why did buoyant optimism yield so swiftly to pessimistic despair? What were the causes of the massive economic depression that began in 1929? Economists and historians have not really answered these questions in full, but with the advantage of lengthening perspective they have come close to agreement on the major forces involved.

It is now clear that the economy of the twenties was by no means as strong as it seemed to those who lived through the boom years. We now see that the weaknesses in farming, textiles, and coal mining were far more important than the economists of the New Era thought. An uneven distribution of the national income was also an abiding source of trouble. The upper 10 per cent of the population had as much income as the lower 70 per cent; and while the top 10 per cent was using a large portion of its surplus income to feed the bull market on Wall Street, the rest of the population was unable to buy enough to create sufficient demand for continued industrial expansion. Measured by the capacity of Americans to consume, the industrial plant of the country was overbuilt in 1929; saturation of demand followed quickly on the heels of the economic turndown. Even before the Great Crash, in fact, the construction and automobile industries were

Depositors swarm around The Bank of United States but the doors are closed. The year was 1933. (Brown Brothers.)

suffering from tell-tale symptoms of a glutted market.

Not only was the spread of income in the twenties too one-sided, but prices also remained dangerously high in many supposedly competitive industries. Thus the vast increases in productivity during the New Era were not reflected in what consumers had to pay. Indeed, price competition almost disappeared in a number of America's major industries as trade associations, holding companies, and semimonopolies were formed in business after business. Chain food-stores, telephone and telegraph monopolies, and utilities empires were becoming familiar features of the American scene. As the most notable example of this development, Samuel Insull, until his bankruptcy and exposure in 1932, reared a giant pyramid of holding companies that made him master of a billion dollars' worth of utilities companies in the United States.

The banking structure was nearly as decrepit as the corporate system. As yet, the basic fact of American banking was still a great host of individual banks of differing merit each going its separate way. Cooperation, even in times of crisis, was difficult. The Federal Reserve System,

188

as the chaotic events of 1929 testified, was powerless to arrest or control an unsound financial boom. Nor was the bankers' task made easier by the rickety structure of international finance reared during the twenties. Throughout the decade the United States had an excess of exports over imports and made up the balance by foreign loans that were often poorly secured. These loans helped make it possible for Germany to meet her reparations payments to the Allies who, in turn, used them as a means of meeting their war debt obligations to the United States. When economic crisis forced a stop in the flow of American dollars abroad after 1929, a wave of disturbances was set in motion that would return to America with tripled impact.

The stock market crash of 1929 hit directly on the weakest spots in the economy of the New Era. It affected most immediately the well-to-do who controlled a disproportionate share of the nation's income. It forced many of the unsound holding companies, such as Insull's, into bankruptcy and ruin. It stopped the flow of American loans to Europe. And it shattered the confidence of the businessmen and financiers who were the strongest and most representative figures of the New Era. In trying to escape the worst ravages of the economic catastrophe that followed, they brought further ruin on themselves and millions of innocent persons dependent on them for their livelihoods. Before the depression had run its course, the businessman-hero of the twenties was driven from the pedestal he had occupied for so long.

## HOOVER AND THE CRISIS

### The Quest for Explanation

The Wall Street smash-up sent tremors of shock through all strata of the nation's life. In the scramble of reassuring statements and public optimism many citizens perceived the deep concern of the business community. Like the crowds huddled around the ticker-tapes on October 29, everyone wanted to talk, to reassure his neighbors, but very few seemed to be listening. Hoover seconded business spokesmen in declaring the market collapse an isolated phenomenon of no great significance to the business world in general. He told Congress in December, 1929, that the crash was the result of "a wave of uncontrolled speculation in securities, resulting in the diversion of capital from business to the stock market." The economy, however, was "fundamentally sound." No one seemed to realize the dimensions of the impending catastrophe. Everywhere, in the first months after the crash, there was talk of "minor readjustments," "temporary unemployment," and "improved prospects."

As industrial orders fell off, jobs became scarce and breadlines appeared for the first time since 1921. A mood of helpless anguish settled over the nation, and the optimism, frivolity, and polite cynicism of the twenties disappeared. Politics became interesting once more as people searched for explanations and tried to give some meaning to the drastic changes in their personal fortunes. A new interest in the social sciences, particularly in economics, was noted in publishing and educational circles. Newspaper columnists, particularly, struggled manfully with the problem of explaining to the public a phenomenon they did not really understand themselves. To the vast majority of that public there seemed no rhyme or reason to the economic landslide. As conditions grew steadily worse, their anguish turned to resignation or desperation, and a gnawing fear that things might become still worse converted many to doctrines they had once considered radical. Everyone asked the question: why? "We got more wheat, more corn, more food, more cotton, more money in the bank, more everything in the world," said the humorist Will Rogers, "yet we are starving to death. We are the first nation in the history of the world to go to the poorhouse in an automobile."

### Tariffs and Farmers

As usual, the farmer suffered the swiftest drop in prices. The depression swept away his remaining foreign markets and slashed the incomes of his city customers. Farm prices fell a brutal 40 per cent between 1929 and 1932 until farmers were receiving only a third of the prices they got during World War I. Net farm income plunged from 6.7 to 2.3 billion dollars in the same period. Yet farmers, no closer to control over their output than in the nineties, continued to produce nearly as much as before. Mortgage indebtedness weighed even heavier than overproduction. The forced sale of farms leaped from twenty per thousand farms in the late twenties to almost fifty per thousand in the early thirties. In the opinion of W. Arthur Lewis, an English economist, the precipitous decline of farm prices was the chief cause of the severity of the Great Depression.

Even before the 1929 debacle, President Hoover had called a special session of Congress to deal with the farm crisis. During the campaign he promised Senator Borah of Idaho that if elected he would move swiftly to raise tariff duties on farm produce. But rebellious congressmen turned the President's special session into an orgy of general tariff revision. The farm increases were approved but so were a host of other increases in almost every category of industrial goods. Despite opposition from such progressives as Norris and Robert La Follette, Jr., the Hawley-Smoot Tariff was rammed through the Congress under the generalship of Senators Reed Smoot of Utah and Joseph Grundy of Pennsylvania. Grundy had been appointed to fill the seat of a man whom the Senate, led by Norris, had refused to recognize because of his excessive campaign expenditures. As a freshman Senator, Grundy won enough Western acquiescence to get the bill passed. The majorities behind the Hawley-Smoot Act, however, came principally from the industrial Northeast. President Hoover, who was unhappy with the measure, waged an indecisive and ineffective counter-campaign but finally signed it in mid-June, 1930. When more than a thousand leading economists urged Hoover to veto it, prophesying that it would bring foreign retaliation and that no one, including the farmer, would benefit, the Republican National Committee implied that they were "communists, socialists, and radicals." As finally passed, the Hawley-Smoot tariff raised import duties to their highest levels in

history, in some cases twice the level reached under the Fordney-McCumber Act.

Hoover had also recommended to the special session that it enact legislation to aid the farmer in marketing his produce effectively. While the McNary-Haugenites watched glumly from the sidelines, Congress enacted the Agricultural Marketing Act (1929), which embodied most of the ideas for which Coolidge and Hoover were contending during the nineteen-twenties. The Act aimed at the stimulation of cooperative marketing in each of the great farm commodities. A half-billion dollars was made available in loans to cooperatives to be used in controlling the flow of farm commodities into the market. If cooperatives were in control of a major part of each crop, it was felt, they could avoid the seasonal glutting of the market that depressed the prices of farm goods. Farmers, like businessmen, could regulate the cut-throat competition that depressed prices and hurt morale. The law also made possible the establishment, should the situation require it, of government-financed stabilization corporations to buy up unusual surpluses.

Early in 1930 the Federal Farm Board, set up to administer the Act, tried to halt the ruinous decline in farm prices set off by the stock market crash by establishing grain- and cotton-stabilization corporations to buy large quantities of wheat and cotton. But prices continued to sink, despite a growing stockpile of surpluses. Clearly, more money was needed if prices were to be kept up by government action. So in 1930 the Board tried to get farmers to cut their wheat acreage, but the move was met with open opposition. By 1931 the Farm Board was an admitted failure and most of the old McNary-Haugen leaders, many of them Republicans, were looking to Hoover's defeat in 1932 as their only salvation.

In the interim before the 1932 election a number of farm leaders were becoming interested in a new farm plan championed by two agricultural specialists, John D. Black of Harvard University and M. L. Wilson of Montana State College. This was the so-called domestic allotment plan, whose central features were acreage restrictions and benefit payments to farmers. Farm output, said Black and Wilson, must be adjusted to consumer demand. Surpluses could not be dumped abroad, as the McNary-Haugenites wanted, because the depression was forcing European governments to protect their own farmers. Instead, they advocated, farmers who adjusted their output to current demand should be rewarded by allotment payments from the government. The government, in turn, might reclaim its losses through a special tax on farm produce to be collected by food processors and other middlemen. By 1932 Franklin D. Roosevelt, now a leading contender for the presidency, was seriously interested in the plan. Later, in fact, from the parity idea of George Peek and the domestic allotment plan of Black and Wilson, Roosevelt would construct his own agricultural program of the thirties. Said George Peek in 1932: "It looks to me as though in the campaign for Roosevelt . . . we are in the last line trenches and if he is not elected that agriculture is doomed to peasantry." *

### Managing the Depression

Hoover meanwhile was taking an increasingly serious view of the depression. Soon after the market collapse, he called a number of the nation's leading business and labor leaders to the White House for conferences. The businessmen he urged to hold wages up and expand construction; the union chiefs he

* G. Fite, *George N. Peek and the Fight for Farm Parity* (Norman: University of Oklahoma Press, 1954), p. 239.

Breadline in New York City during the Depression. (United Press.)

convinced to cancel plans for strikes and wage increases. Voluntary cooperation, he insisted, was the essence of the American Way. "Economic depression," he warned, "cannot be cured by legislative action or executive pronouncement." Nevertheless, he did press for an increase of nearly a half billion dollars in federal expenditures for public works.

At first, his program seemed to be taking effect. An upturn in business in the early months of 1930 caused the President to announce in March that "all the evidences indicate that the worse effects of the crash will have been passed within the next sixty days. . . ." But his hopes were dashed by further increases in unemployment in the summer months and a severe drought that added to the farmers' misery. By the fall of 1930 he had come to regard the depression as international in scope and not just the aftermath of a

Wall Street panic. "This depression is world-wide," he said at Cleveland in October. "Its causes and effects lie only partly in the United States." But this did not mean that America was helpless to solve its problems. As one step toward a solution, he created an emergency Committee for Unemployment Relief under Colonel Arthur Woods to coordinate local relief work and collect information and suggestions for combating unemployment. The Woods Committee, however, proved to be quite ineffective in solving the staggering problems created by mass unemployment.

In 1931 came the backwash from the tumbling of the rotten structure of international trade and finance. The Austrian state bank—the *Kreditanstalt*—collapsed, endangering the great banks of Germany and threatening American investments abroad. When the Darmstaedter bank, the largest in Germany, fell, a banking panic spread over Europe. Hoarding and contracted credit added further gloom to the economic outlook on both sides of the Atlantic. To relieve some of the tremendous pressure on Germany, Hoover proposed a moratorium on war debts and reparations payments, a proposal which was quickly accepted; in actual fact, of course, the Allied nations were preparing to cancel reparations anyway in expectation that the war debts would likewise be wiped out. Britain left the gold standard in 1931 and other nations followed her during the next few years. World trade, restricted by economic depression and the effects of the Hawley-Smoot tariff, fell to a trickle.

By 1931 Hoover was ready to back measures he would have opposed two short years before. But now the banks, insurance companies, and railroads were in mortal danger. The deflationary spiral had begun to slice into the basic financial structure of the nation. If these giants fell, he reasoned, all else would go too.

Voluntary action, he now decided, was not enough. In his message to Congress in December, the President called for a gigantic loan agency, subsequently named the Reconstruction Finance Corporation, to pour government funds into the tottering banks and bigger businesses. Its purpose, he argued, was to stop the murderous deflation and thereby protect jobs and savings. His proposal did not contradict, he insisted, his continued opposition to direct federal relief to the unemployed and to farmers. Sticking to his guns, he vetoed a bill to pay veterans their bonus in advance of the agreed time and another proposal by Senator Norris for government operation of Muscle Shoals. He also blocked a Democratic multi-billion-dollar public works program, though he did ultimately approve a bill calling for the expenditure of a billion-and-a-half dollars on self-liquidating public projects. He approved, too, a plan submitted in July, 1932, for the Reconstruction Finance Corporation to lend $300 million to the states for relief work. The President also signed bills providing additional credit for farmers facing foreclosure and giving Federal Reserve banks greater flexibility in meeting reserve requirements.

These measures were taken hesitantly, reluctantly, as emergency actions merely and not as fixed government policy. The main impulse to recovery, Hoover still felt, must come from business itself rather than government. Hoover did not by any means break out the deck for the New Deal, though some historians, anxious to be fair, have tried to assign him the responsibility. Certainly Hoover himself has declined the credit. He may have anticipated many New Deal measures—doubtless Coolidge under similar pressure would also have done so—but his basic attitudes and beliefs on the proper relationship of government to business remained fixed during and after his years in the White House. In his stand on deficit financing, unbalanced budgets, governmental competition with private industry, and federal controls over business, Hoover was far closer to McKinley than to his first Republican successor after the New Deal. Thus, in vetoing the Muscle Shoals bill, Hoover expressed his deep conviction that it would "break down the initiative and enterprise of the American people," destroy the "equality of opportunity of our people," and negate "the ideals upon which our civilization has been based." Such statements continued to characterize his position on all the measures looking toward the establishment of a "welfare state" in America.

## A CIVILIZATION IN TURMOIL

### Social Impact of the Depression

In all American history no single economic event affected so many people with such lasting consequences as the Great Depression. It cut deeply into the fabric of American life, brought millions of Americans to the brink of personal catastrophe, and raised gnawing doubts about the soundness of the nation's basic institutions. Thanks to the mighty thrust toward industrialism and urbanism since 1865, the nation was more tightly knit together, more sensitive to remote disturbances in the economy, more helpless in the face of crisis than ever before in its history. For almost a century American workers had been drawn in increasing numbers into the great impersonal factories, farmers had grown more and more dependent on a complex international market, and small businessmen had found themselves losing out to larger and better organized aggregations of capital. In the twenties these trends were stepped up so much that by the thirties, the average American was completely dependent for his livelihood and his security on conditions beyond his personal control.

When catastrophe came, it was swift, sudden, and overwhelming. Within three years of the stock market collapse, the total physical output of goods in the United States fell 37 per cent. Steel production, long the barometer of an industrial economy, shrank from 56 million tons in 1929 to 13 million tons in 1932. Construction was almost at a standstill. New residential building fell from $3.8 billion in 1928 to $0.3 billion in 1933, while industrial construction dropped from a peak of $949 million in 1929 to a pitiful $74 million in 1932. The value of stocks listed on the New York Exchange plummeted from $87 billion to $19 billion. New capital issues, to finance new business and industrial developments, went from $10 billion in 1929 to less than $1 billion in 1933. Incomes dropped sharply as wages fell 60 per cent, salaries 40 per cent, and dividends 57 per cent. Bank failures, which had averaged less than 700 per year in the twenties, rose sharply, reaching the calamitous total of 4000 in 1933.

These are cold statistics; they cannot begin to describe the suffering and privation they represent. They stand for the ranks of the jobless that swelled with each downturn in business activity. Unemployment figures, though not completely reliable, probably reached eight million in 1931, twelve million in 1932, and possibly thirteen million in 1933. In New York City alone a million persons were without jobs in 1932; Cleveland counted half its labor force as jobless; and in Donora, Pennsylvania, only 277 of 13,900 persons normally employed were able to continue work on a regular basis. But these, too, are cold statistics. In human terms the meaning of these figures staggers the imagination. Arthur Schlesinger, Jr., has vividly recalled why these days of depression left such a deep mark on the unemployed:

As savings end, borrowing begins. If there is life insurance, borrowing on that, until it lapses; then loans from relatives and from friends; then the life of credit, from the landlord, from the corner grocer, until the lines of friendship and compassion are snapped. Meat vanishes from the table; lard replaces butter; father goes out less often, is terribly quiet; the children begin to lack shoes, their clothes are ragged, their mothers are ashamed to send them to school. Wedding rings are pawned, furniture is sold, the family moves into ever cheaper, damper, dirtier rooms. . . . And every week, every day, more workers joined the procession of despair. The shadows deepened in the dark cold rooms, with the father angry and helpless and ashamed, the distraught children too often hungry or sick, and the mother, so resolute by day, so often, when the room was finally still, lying awake in bed at night, softly crying.*

Actual starvation, while probably infrequent, was not unknown in these dark years. Accounts of starving families, youths roaming the countryside living on berries and apples, and cases of malnutrition in the local hospitals can be found in all the great metropolitan dailies of the period. For eleven days in 1932 the jobless of Philadelphia were totally without aid as private relief funds gave out. Some lived on stale bread and cocoa, others had potatoes or rice to fall back on, still others were lucky enough to borrow a little money. "The hospitals have had definite cases of starvation," reported Karl de Schweinitz, executive secretary of

* A. Schlesinger, Jr., *The Crisis of the Old Order* (Boston: Houghton Mifflin Company, 1957), p. 168.

the Community Council of Philadelphia.

Across the country flew shocking reports of men and women scavenging in garbage dumps, hungry hitchhikers living by their luck and wits, and forest fires started by jobless timber workers and bankrupt farmers anxious to earn a few dollars as fire fighters. Every city had its problems. Typical perhaps was Detroit, with 200,000 persons on public relief, fifteen banks closed, 4000 children lining up with their parents and other adults in breadlines, 7500 eviction proceedings each month, and a jump of 30 per cent in the suicide rate. Of Muncie, Indiana, the sociologists Robert and Helen Lynd said, in their study of *Middletown in Transition* (1935), that "the great knife of the depression has cut down impartially through the entire population cleaving open lives and hopes of rich as well as poor. The experience has been more nearly universal than any prolonged recent emotional experience in the city's history; it has approached in its elemental shock the primary experiences of birth and death."

The social impact of the depression was indeed powerful and universal. It strained families and broke up marriages; it affected the authority of the father in suffering homes; it sent many boys and young men "on the road" to search for opportunity; it postponed marriages and made families smaller; it affected fashions, recreations, manners, and morals in all strata of society. The concerns of the Lost Generation now seemed archaic and unimportant. "I am now definitely ready to announce," said Robert Benchley, dramatic critic for *The New Yorker*, "that Sex, as a theatrical property, is as tiresome as the Old Mortgage. . . . I am sick of rebellious youth and I am sick of Victorian parents and I don't care if all the little girls in all sections of the United States get ruined or want to get ruined or keep from getting ruined." Many other battles that seemed important in the twenties were forgotten. Those old enemies, the fundamentalists and modernists, buried the hatchet in favor or more immediate concerns. Freudianism now seemed less important and interesting than economics and history, and politics became exciting again as many who had snubbed it in the twenties turned to it with zest. A note of seriousness was creeping back into the thought and behavior of the intellectuals. Everywhere, in the early thirties, ran a sense of deep social change, of being a part of sweeping events that were only dimly understood.

### Bonus Marchers

There was fear, too: fear of unemployment, of the unknown future, of violence or even revolution. "I'm afraid, every man is afraid," said Charles M. Schwab of United States Steel; "I don't know, we don't know, whether the values we have are going to be real next month or not." When Congress voted in 1932 to cut governmental salaries 10 per cent, Hoover secretly urged the lawmakers to exempt soldiers and sailors from the cut so that they would not be disgruntled in the event of domestic upheaval.

Hoover was thinking perhaps of the bold but tragic gathering of the Bonus Army in Washington in the summer of 1932. The march of unemployed veterans on the capital began in Portland, Oregon, among a group of restless men who demanded that Congress pay immediately the bonus due them in 1945. Driven to desperation, jobless veterans across the country began to view the bonus as a just debt owed them by the nation for their wartime sacrifices. And now was the time they needed the money, not some remote date in the future. As hope for bonus legislation faded in the spring of 1932, veterans began organizing for the trip to

Washington. The Portland marchers were joined by others from every part of the country. By the end of May, more than 8000 were living in ramshackle shacks, tents, and deserted buildings in the capital. Organized in military fashion, they were commanded by Walter W. Waters of Portland. Communists sought to infiltrate the movement and managed to gain a foothold in several contingents, but they did not at any time dominate the so-called Bonus Expeditionary Force.

Washington police, led by a retired brigadier-general named Pelham Glassford, cooperated with the veterans, helped them find billets, and soothed ruffled tempers. On June 17, 1932, the B. E. F. heard the news that the Senate had again killed the bonus bill. Fearing unrest, Waters called on the perhaps 20,000 marchers assembled on Capitol Hill to demonstrate their patriotism. He led them in the singing of "America," then marched them back to their billets. Several thousand now left Washington, some taking advantage of Hoover's offer to lend them the return fare to their homes. But nearly 15,000 men remained in the capital under a close military discipline as conditions in their jerry-built quarters on Anacostia Flats deteriorated.

Tempers rose to fever pitch as Congress prepared to adjourn in mid-July. The President, who had ignored the bonus marchers, now grew increasingly concerned as the veterans lingered beyond the day of adjournment. And he committed a colossal blunder. He gave orders to Washington police on July 28 to evacuate a number of empty buildings on Pennsylvania Avenue in which veterans were living; this was apparently part of a plan to drive the B. E. F. out of Washington. But the veterans refused to move, a small group of Communists charged the police, and in the resulting melee several policemen and veterans were injured. Several hours later, when a jittery policeman fired into a crowd of veterans, two members of the B. E. F. were killed and several were wounded before Glassford could stop the shooting. "The trouble began," Glassford told reporters, "when I was compelled to enforce an order which I considered unnecessary."

Glassford held out against any call for federal troops. But the Commissioners of the District of Columbia called on the White House for help. Orders went out to General Douglas MacArthur to disperse the bonus marchers. With tear gas and cavalry charges troops drove the embattled veterans out of their billets on Pennsylvania Avenue, then moved on to Anacostia with tanks and fixed bayonets. The only reported casualty was a three-month-old baby who died from inhaling tear gas from a bomb thrown at his father. Fires were lighted in the veterans' billets; soon the bonus marchers themselves were igniting their dwellings. They offered no resistance. By morning some 7000 men, women, and children had straggled out of the capital.

Hoover defended his action as necessary to public order. The mob of veterans, he charged, was dominated by Communists. MacArthur argued that the veterans were animated by "the essence of revolution." Both said that the bonus marchers hoped to seize control of the government. Many Americans, who disliked the tactics of the B. E. F., applauded Hoover's action. But others, probably more numerous, liked Hoover's tactics even less. However misguided their leaders, however mistaken their objectives, the bonus marchers were after all unemployed Americans who had served their country in war. So reasoned many sympathetic veterans who had not joined the march and other jobless citizens who knew what unemployment meant. No action of Hoover's in 1932 dramatized so clearly the growing gulf between the administration and the people. "What a

pitiful spectacle," wrote an editor in the Washington *News*, "is that of the great American Government, mightiest in the world, chasing unarmed men, women, and children with Army tanks."

## Rural Violence

Farmers, too, were sunk in despair in 1932. Their condition was worse than at any time within the memory of living men. Fits of sporadic violence and ugly defiance of law ran through a number of farm communities. "They are just ready to do anything to get even with the situation," the president of the Farmers' Union told a Senate Committee. "I almost hate to express it, but I honestly believe that if some of them could buy airplanes they would come down here to Washington to blow you fellows all up. . . . The farmer is naturally a conservative individual, but you cannot find a conservative farmer today. . . . I am as conservative as any man could be, but any economic system that has it in its power to set me and my wife in the streets, at my age—what can I see but red?"

The region of greatest unrest was Minnesota, Iowa, and the Dakotas. Instances of violence in these states were reported with increasing regularity in 1932. A farm holiday was called by Milo Reno, a militant leader of the Farmers' Union, to keep food off the market until prices rose. Pickets paraded across highways leading into Sioux City, Des Moines, Council Bluffs, and other Midwestern market towns. Farmers trying to carry their goods to market had their windshields smashed, their milk spilled, or their vegetables scattered across the highway. The farm holiday movement, while it had its brief moments of success, failed because of inadequate organization and poor cooperation from many farmers. And because, too, of state troopers who broke the cordons around many of the blockaded cities. More successful were the efforts of agrarian radicals to block mortgage sales of land confiscated from bankrupt farmers. Sheriffs were intimidated, bidders at auction sales of confiscated property threatened, and one judge, in Le Mars, Iowa, was dragged from the bench and beaten into unconsciousness. The seriousness of the farm crisis was apparent to every observer by the end of 1932.

### Fissures of Doubt

Farm violence and the B. E. F. were something new in the American experience. Mass protests, marching men, and threats of violence were reminiscent of Europe's disturbed social order rather than of the United States. By the summer of 1932, some of America's basic institutions and beliefs seemed to be crumbling. For in this enormous crisis conventional values appeared to give little comfort. Optimism had all but disappeared; faith in the ability of the economic system to weather the crisis was weakening; belief in progress seemed hollow to some; even liberty no longer seemed a supreme value. The historian Carl Becker asked a Cornell student in 1932 what he thought of liberty and the student, thinking of the nearby town of Liberty, replied, "I've never been through it; I don't drive a car." Perhaps liberty was no more, Becker suggested, than a way station on the main traveled road of human history—"a place which humanity passes rapidly through." Those who defended traditional values—liberty, individualism, progress, opportunity, limited government—seemed in 1932 to be defending a social order that had brought them to desperation and ruin.

Doubts about traditional values rose up in even normally conservative circles. In 1932 the Federal Council of Churches repudiated the business spirit of the twenties and called for "subordination of spec-ulation and the profit motive to the creative and cooperative spirit." The General Conference of the Methodist Church went even further in demanding the replacement of "unplanned competitive industrialism" by "a planned industrial economy." And how shocking it must have seemed to some churchgoers when the National Council of Methodist Youth stated flatly in 1934 that "We endorse socialism, as being, at present, the most workable political expression of Christian social ideals." Praise for the Soviet Union was not uncommon in the church magazines and the pronouncements of some denominations in the early nineteen-thirties.

The attraction of communism, weak though it was, was immeasurably enhanced by the economic collapse in the United States. To some who were drawn into the communist orbit, the Soviet system seemed to hold out at least the promise of jobs and security—when a Russian agency advertised in 1931 for 6000 skilled workers to come to the Soviet Union, more than 100,000 Americans made application. Others saw in commu-

Farmers dump milk cans during Wisconsin milk strike, 1933. (Brown Brothers.)

nism an answer to the economic riddle of why capitalism had collapsed; still others were driven by desperation, loneliness, or guilt. The appeal of communism was greatest among the haunted intellectuals who were looking for answers and assurances. "I was on the side of history," recalled J. B. Matthews, a writer who later became research director of the House Un-American Activities Committee, "where I could look across and view with sincere pity the floundering liberals and the obstructing capitalists." But the number drawn into the web of communism was small: At most 12,000 Americans were in the Communist Party at the peak of popular distress in 1932. Significantly, few of these were from the working class that suffered most from the trials of the era.

Sensitive observers in all fields of endeavor felt the growing crisis of values in American life. The effect of the depression on writers was as obvious, wrote the noted critic Alfred Kazin, as an earth-quake. Writers became obsessed with society; instead of rebelling against it they now tried to understand and reform it. A violent naturalism was the literary equivalent of bonus marching and rural upheaval. Every writer seemed to want to expose the "truth," to protest what was happening, to shock his fellow Americans into awareness and action. Educators, too, were frequently sensitive to the contradiction between the promise of America and the realities around them. "Dire poverty walks hand in hand with the most extravagant living," wrote George S. Counts, a disciple of John Dewey; "breakfastless children march to school past bankrupt shops laden with rich foods gathered from the ends of the earth; strong men by the million walk the streets in a futile search for employment and with exhaustion of hope enter the ranks of the damned. . . . " Would the schools dare to build a new social order?—this was Counts's challenge to educators and parents in 1932.*

## POLITICAL STALEMATE

By 1932 pessimism seemed the dominant mood of the nation. Basic American beliefs in human liberty and democratic self-government were shaken by the dual impact of economic upheaval and the intellectual doubt we noted in the last chapter. Democracy, which had grown up in an intellectual climate of freedom and belief in man's rationality, was under attack in all parts of the Western world. "We have fallen so low," wrote the literary historian Vernon Parrington in one of his last essays, "that our faith in . . . the excellence of democracy is stricken with pernicious anemia." A paralyzing failure of will seemed to have afflicted those particular men who might have been expected to provide leadership and ideas that would aid in the fight against catastrophe.

### The Relief Problem

The political leaders were of little help. For public confidence in politicians, as in businessmen, had collapsed with the New Era. Hoover had raised false hopes of a return to prosperity so often that few believed him when he announced in the summer of 1932 that the bottom of the depression had been reached. Further, the President and Congress were locked in hopeless stalemate, having been at loggerheads ever

* G. Counts, *Dare the School Build a New Social Order?* (New York: The John Day Company, 1932), pp. 32-34.

since the Democratic sweep of Congress in 1930. Hoover continued to argue that relief was not a national responsibility, while Democratic leaders clamored for federal intervention. The issue was clear. Federal intervention, Hoover charged, would destroy private initiative and local responsibility; failure to act, replied the Democrats, meant hunger and misery for millions.

But what were private initiative and local responsibility doing to relieve the awful plight of millions? Private philanthropy was largely exhausted by 1931. So the growing numbers of unemployed imposed a gargantuan responsibility upon municipal leaders, many of whom lacked the authority or funds to move decisively. Some city governments refused at first to be held accountable for the relief of the unemployed, preferring to work through private charities. Eventually, though, most cities were compelled by the urgency of the crisis to act, but their funds ran out quickly. The states were equally reluctant to assume the burden. New York State, under Governor Franklin D. Roosevelt, was the first to take full responsibility for the jobless in 1931. Again, however, other states were forced to follow. By the summer of 1932 many of the states, too, were in deep financial trouble with expenditures mounting and revenues declining.

Hoover's critics saw a serious contradiction in his willingness to help big businesses through the R. F. C. while refusing to aid unemployed Americans. "We shall help the railroad; we shall help the financial institutions; and I agree that we should," said Senator Wagner of New York. "But is there any reason why we should not likewise extend a helping hand to that forlorn American, in every village and every city of the United States, who has been without wages since 1929? Must he alone carry the cross of individual responsibility?" More than any

other single issue, Hoover's attitude toward federal relief prepared the way for his political demise in November, 1932.

### The Noble Experiment

Another issue aggravated by hard times was the fight over prohibition. During the prosperous twenties the "experiment noble in purpose," as Hoover called it in his first campaign, had been hooted at, ridiculed, and systematically evaded by large segments of the population. But in the depression years prohibition became a symbol of other failures of the New Era. Critics charged that it robbed thousands of men of legitimate employment and deprived the states of needed revenues. Worse of all, it had failed to achieve the idealistic ends promised by its champions. By the early thirties the nation's mood seemed clearly to be swinging toward repeal of the Eighteenth Amendment.

President Hoover found it difficult to make up his mind on the issue. He appointed a special commission headed by former Attorney General George W. Wickersham to investigate the whole enforcement problem. The Commission reported in 1931 that enforcement had failed, corruption was on the increase, and respect for the law was declining as a result. But the Commission was divided and ambiguous in its recommendations for the future; most of its members seemed to favor some kind of revision of the Volstead Act and a strengthening of law enforcement agencies. Hoover tried manfully to enforce the law but where local sentiment was opposed he was no more successful than Harding or Coolidge. Not until August, 1932, did the President finally come to feel that the Eighteenth Amendment should be repealed. In the meantime, he had encouraged his party to frame a wonderfully ambiguous plank on prohibition at the Republican convention in June. "The

During Prohibition, federal agents resorted to astounding disguises. Here are two in street and working clothes. (Underwood & Underwood.)

people," said the assembled Republicans, "should have an opportunity to pass upon a proposed amendment, the provisions of which, while retaining in the Federal Government power to preserve the gains already made in dealing with the evils inherent in the liquor traffic, shall allow the States to deal with the problem as their citizens may determine, but subject always to the power of the Federal Government to protect those States where prohibition may exist and safeguard our citizens everywhere from the return of the saloon and attendant abuses."

### Hoover versus Roosevelt

Hoover's popularity reached its nadir in that summer of 1932. He was renominated by the Republicans without

enthusiasm and without much hope. His policies were praised unstintingly; his platform, aside from prohibition, occasioned little debate. The permanent chairman, Congressman Bertrand H. Snell of New York, competently summarized the case for Hoover in 1932: "He solidified labor and capital against the enemy. He avoided the deadly pit of the dole. . . . He beat off the attacks upon railroads, agriculture, banks, and public securities. He warded off the stealthy approach of panic by the way of Germany. He preserved the integrity of the gold standard."

The Democratic convention in 1932 promised to be a horse race. Although Governor Franklin D. Roosevelt of New York appeared to have a majority of the delegates behind him, he faced fierce resistance from the lieutenants of Al Smith, who had cooled noticeably toward Roosevelt since 1928. Smith worked strenuously to build a block of anti-Roosevelt strength large enough to keep FDR from getting the two-thirds vote he needed. His apparent strategy was to encourage the other candidates, notably John Nance Garner of Texas, who was speaker of the House of Representatives, and the favorite-son candidates, to stay in the race long enough to stop Roosevelt and force a compromise. Of the dark horse possibilities discussed in 1932, the name of Newton D. Baker, a disciple of Wilson and a conservative corporation lawyer, came up more often than any other.

Ever since 1928 Franklin D. Roosevelt had been mentioned with increasing frequency as the Democratic hope for 1932. He won the governorship in New York by a narrow margin in 1928, while Smith was going down to defeat. Two years later he inflicted a crushing defeat on New York Republicans when he was re-elected Governor by three-quarters of a million votes. As the depression deepened, his moves in New York State to relieve want and stimulate recovery were widely reported throughout the country. Roosevelt's lieutenants, notably James Farley and Louis Howe, worked feverishly to build up his support among Democrats of the South and West to counteract Smith's popularity in the Northeast. They stressed his social background, the importance of his name, his Protestantism, his progressive record as Governor, his battles with Tammany, and his "reasonableness" on prohibition as compared with Smith's forthright stand for repeal.

So successful were Farley and Howe in constructing an image of Roosevelt as an amiable, open-minded, and mildly progressive man who could unite the Democratic Party that many eastern leaders of opinion doubted his capacity for strong leadership. Roosevelt, charged many of these critics, was trying to straddle the whole country. He was too cautious, too anxious to please, too lacking in ideas or plans of his own. He was no crusader, said the columnist Walter Lippmann: "He is a pleasant man who, without any important qualifications for the office, would very much like to be President." In Lippmann's judgment, FDR, for all his generous sympathies and good intentions, "simply does not measure up to the tremendous demands of the office of President."

The crucial point in the convention came at the close of the third ballot. Roosevelt's strength, thanks to Farley's holding back a few votes on the early ballots, had inched up to 682, still 87 short of two-thirds, and many delegates thought he had been stopped. At this critical juncture, William Randolph Hearst, who was skeptical of Roosevelt but feared that a deadlocked convention might back the internationalist Newton Baker, advised Garner to release his delegates to Roosevelt. Garner was already

leaning in that direction, fearing a repetition of the 1924 disaster. California and Texas now swung to FDR, though not without a pledge that Garner must be the vice-presidential nominee, and the die was cast. There was drama in the announcement of the decision by William Gibbs McAdoo, victim of the two-thirds rule in 1924, who declared from the rostrum that California "did not come here to deadlock this convention or to engage in another disastrous contest like that of 1924." Only Smith held out, refusing to make the nomination of his old friend unanimous.

The Democratic platform, though it had wide appeal, was vague and contradictory. It embraced such conservative planks as a balanced budget, reduction of governmental expenditures, a sound currency, and removal of government from all fields of private enterprise. But it called also for federal aid in unemployment relief, expanded public works, both unemployment and old age insurance, and "effective control of crop surpluses." The causes of the depression were declared to be "the disastrous policies pursued by our government since the World War, of economic isolation, fostering the merger of competitive businesses into monopolies and encouraging the indefensible expansion and contraction of credit for private profit at the expense of the public."

The platform reflected Roosevelt's own flexible ideology in 1932. Where Hoover was uncompromising in his condemnation of unbalanced budgets, currency tinkering, and large-scale governmental intervention, Roosevelt seemed to be of two minds on these issues. He attacked Hoover for unbalancing the budget and engaging in "reckless and extravagant" expenditures, yet promised programs that would lead inevitably to deficit spending. He talked often of sound money, yet

seemed willing to consider radical monetary measures. All that seemed clear to
many neutral observers in 1932 was that
Roosevelt was willing to experiment, that
he felt deep sympathy for the unemployed, that he believed in conservation,
low tariffs, and public power, and that he
had championed many welfare measures
during his tenure as Governor of New
York. On fiscal and monetary policies he
seemed torn between his personal conservatism and his sense of obligation to
those in need. The differences between
Hoover and Roosevelt seemed to many
sensitive citizens in 1932 to lie less in
fundamental philosophy than in temperament and personality. While the President was beaten, tired, and discouraged,
Roosevelt appeared confident and serene,
sure of himself and of what he wanted.

That ideological differences did exist
between Hoover and Roosevelt became
clear in the aftermath of the election.
Even in 1932, the candidates seemed at
times to be sharply aware of the growing
gulf between them. At the Commonwealth Club in San Francisco, Roosevelt
made his clearest statement of the need
to revive and expand the principles of
progressivism. Democracy, he said, was a
quest, a never-ending search for a better
life; the only real issue in government was
"whether individual men and women will
have to serve some system of Government
or economics, or whether a system of
Government and economics exists to
serve individual men and women." An
examination of American history would
show how the coming of industry and
great cities had imposed a strain on traditional American political and economic
ideas. Individualism and opportunity in
the old sense, he warned, no longer existed. The last frontier had been reached
and "we are now producing a drab living
for our own people." Workers, farmers,
and small businessmen—all were running
a losing race against economic oligarchy.

Therefore, government must see to it that
economic power was used in the public
interest and that the individual had some
shelter from such economic storms as the
one that began in 1929.

Hoover, in answering Roosevelt, said
that the 1932 campaign was more than a
contest between two men or two parties;
it was "a contest between two philosophies of government." His opponent, he
charged, was exploiting human misery in
"proposing changes and so-called new
deals which would destroy the very foundations of our American system of life."
He attacked Democratic demands for
currency inflation, governmental intervention in the power and banking businesses,
and tariff reduction. If the Hawley-Smoot
duties were appreciably lowered, warned
Hoover, "The grass will grow in streets
of a hundred cities, a thousand towns;
the weeds will overrun the fields of
millions of farms if that protection be
taken away." He particularly condemned
Roosevelt's idea, expressed in the Commonwealth Club speech, that America
had reached the zenith of its economic
development. This was a counsel of despair, said Hoover, not the spirit that had
built the United States. In his opponent's
speeches he foresaw a vast expansion of
the federal government, the growth of a
huge bureaucracy, and a gigantic increase

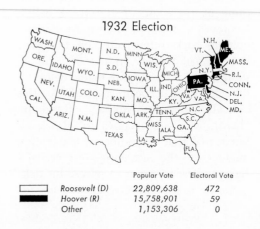

1932 Election

| | | Popular Vote | Electoral Vote |
|---|---|---|---|
| ☐ | Roosevelt (D) | 22,809,638 | 472 |
| ■ | Hoover (R) | 15,758,901 | 59 |
| | Other | 1,153,306 | 0 |

of expenditures. "The spirit of liberalism," Hoover said grimly, "is to create free men; it is not the regimentation of man under government."

On Election Day, 1932, nearly forty million Americans went to the polls. When the day was done, Hoover had been swept out of office in a landslide as great as the one that had brought him to power. Roosevelt received almost 23 million popular votes, and carried all but six states (four of them in New England). Hoover garnered fewer than 16 million votes, while the Socialist Norman Thomas won almost 900,000 votes and the Communist William Z. Foster received 100,000. This was the most drastic reversal in party fortunes in the political history of the United States.

With Hoover's defeat came the end of a long tradition. He was the last presidential candidate to espouse squarely the political doctrines of nineteenth-century liberalism. All the things that Hoover believed in—limited government, economic liberty, inevitable progress, and a bullish optimism about America's future—had been put into eclipse by the black fears inspired by the Great Depression. For half a century the onrush of the great forces shaping modern America had steadily reduced the role and significance of the individual in economic and social life. The tensions and pressures unleashed by industrialism, urbanism, and the decline of absolute values in the intellectual world had created a host of personal anxieties and insecurities that were magnified by the events after 1929. For the first time in the experience of the United States many Americans were seized by doubts: about capitalism, individualism, political liberty, and the American mission to carry democracy to the world. Could American faith in these values be rekindled at a time when Hitler and others were turning their backs on them? Could American confidence and morale

be restored in sufficient measure to meet the threat of the self-confident totalitarians about whom Joseph Wood Krutch had warned? Much would depend on the ability of the new administration to dispel the prevailing pessimism and find a *via media* between nineteenth-century liberalism and twentieth-century totalitarianism.

### The Nation Waits

Four long months separated Roosevelt's victory at the polls and his assumption of power on March 4, 1933. Senator Norris had introduced the Twentieth Amendment to begin the terms of office of the new President and Congress in January but it was not ratified in time to affect the election of 1932. In Febru-

This 1933 cover of the magazine "Vanity Fair" graphically and succinctly contrasts that year with 1929. (New York Public Library Picture Collection.)

ary, 1933, the last lame-duck Congress submitted the Twenty-First Amendment ending prohibition, and it was approved by the end of the year.

President Hoover, alarmed at the banking crisis developing during the winter of 1932-33, sought Roosevelt's cooperation in meeting the emergency. Bank after bank closed its doors as panicky depositors lined up to claim their savings. Hoover made it clear that he believed the banking collapse was due to fear of the new Administration in banking and business circles. He called on Roosevelt to assure the public that he would not tinker with the monetary system, engage in deficit financing, or unbalance the budget. To other correspondents Hoover explained that Roosevelt must disavow the Tennessee Valley proposals and any heavy expenditure for public works. "I realize that if these declarations be made by the President-elect," Hoover wrote a friend, "he will have ratified the whole major program of the Republican Administration; that is, it means the abandonment of 90 per cent of the so-called new deal." Roosevelt at first ignored Hoover's entreaties, then politely declined to cooperate in Hoover's program. The President-elect not only disagreed with Hoover's political philosophy in combating the Depression but was most anxious to avoid any close identification with a repudiated administration. The success of his own program, he felt, would largely depend on his ability to inspire confidence and give the nation a sense of moving in a new direction. He believed, furthermore, that the long lines of anxious depositors before the nation's banks were not as concerned about his forthcoming policies as they were about the soundness of the banks that held their money.

As Roosevelt prepared to take office in early March, 1933, he wrote an introduction to a collection of his campaign speeches that was about to be published. In one of these speeches at Oglethorpe University, he had sounded the note that would characterize the frenzied early days of the New Deal. "The country needs and, unless I mistake its temper, the country demands bold, persistent experimentation," FDR had said. "It is common sense to take a method and try it; if it fails, admit it frankly and try another. But above all, try something."

The New Deal years of trial and experimentation were about to begin.

# FOR FURTHER STUDY

*The books by Allen, Hicks, and Schlesinger cited at the end of Chapter V continue to be especially useful for the topics dealt with in this chapter.*

## General Accounts

H. Hoover, *Memoirs: The Great Depression, 1929-1941* (New York: Macmillan, 1952). Hoover's apologia and explanation of events following his presidency.

B. Mitchell, *Depression Decade* (New York: Rinehart, 1947). An excellent volume in *The Economic History of the United States* series covering the years from 1929 to 1941.

H. Warren, *Herbert Hoover and the Great Depression* (New York: Oxford University Press, 1959). Sympathetic yet fair, this is the best single volume on the subject.

D. Wecter, *The Age of the Great Depression, 1929-1941* (New York: Macmillan, 1948). Good on the social impact of the Depression years.

R. Wilbur and A. Hyde, *The Hoover Policies* (New York: Scribner's, 1937). A defense of Hoover's program by his former secretaries of Interior and Agriculture.

## Special Studies

A. Berle and G. Means, *The Modern Corporation and Private Property* (New York: Macmillan, 1932). A classic account of the divorce of ownership from control in modern business life.

I. Bernstein, *The Lean Years* (Boston: Houghton Mifflin, 1960). A penetrating economic analysis of the American worker from 1920 to 1933.

M. Curti, *The Growth of American Thought* (New York: Harper, second edition, 1951). An excellent intellectual history, this book contains some good insights into the impact of the Depression on the world of ideas.

F. Freidel, *Franklin D. Roose-velt: The Triumph* (Boston: Little, Brown, 1956). The most detailed and reliable account of Roosevelt's political career from 1928 to 1932.

* J. Galbraith, *The Great Crash, 1929* (Boston: Houghton Mifflin, 1954). A delightfully written interpretation of the stock market collapse, its causes and consequences.

H. Hoover, *The Challenge to Liberty* (New York: Scribner's, 1934). Indispensable for understanding Hoover's ideological orientation.

W. Johnson, *1600 Pennsylvania Avenue* (Boston: Little, Brown, 1960). A study of "presidents and the people, 1929-1959", the opening section deals ably with Hoover's failure to lead effectively.

W. Lippmann, *Interpretations, 1931-1932* (New York: Macmillan, 1932). Useful for recapturing contemporary feeling about events and personalities in the early thirties.

D. Pearson, *Washington Merry-Go-Round* (New York: Horace Liveright, 1931). Another useful contemporary impression of men and events during the Depression years.

R. Peel and T. Donnelly, *The 1932 Campaign* (New York: Farrar and Rinehart, 1935). Still a useful book despite having been written so soon after the campaign.

F. Roosevelt, *Looking Forward* (New York: The John Day Company, 1933). A collection of Roosevelt's speeches and articles written prior to 1933.

* D. Shannon (ed.), *The Great Depression* (Englewood Cliffs: Prentice-Hall, 1960). This is a first-rate collection of con-

* Starred books are available in paperbound editions.

temporary documents dealing with the Depression.

G. Soule, *The Coming American Revolution* (New York: Macmillan, 1935). Illustrates the pessimism of the scholarly community, in this case of an economist, concerning the possibility of reform and orderly change.

H. Wish, *Society and Thought in Modern America* (New York: Longmans, Green, 1952). Another good social and intellectual history dealing topically with the years since 1865.

## Fiction and Drama

C. Brody, *Nobody Starves* (New York: Longmans, Green, 1932). A realistic novel of the effects of the Depression on the economic life and morale of factory workers in an industrial town near Detroit.

* E. Caldwell, *Tobacco Road* (New York: Duell, Sloan and Pearce, 1932). The plight of the rural South is reflected in the destitute sharecropper, Jeeter Lester, whose futile hopefulness in the face of incredible hardship seems both tragic and comic.

* J. Farrell, *Studs Lonigan* (New York: Modern Library, 1938). A powerful novel of the gradual hardening and disintegration of a young Irish lad amid the slums and spiritual poverty of South Side Chicago.

## Films and Records

*The Bank Holiday Crisis of 1933* (McGraw-Hill, 27 minutes, sound, black and white). A kaleidoscopic treatment of America during the week when all banks were closed, through the "You Are There" technique; includes films of FDR's inauguration and his first "Fireside Chat."

*The Boom and the Bust* (National Educational Television, 29 minutes, sound, black and white). A televised discussion of conditions and business attitudes during the 1920's and the coming of the Great Depression.

*Headlines of the Century, Part V, 1928 to 1932* (Teaching Film Custodians, 10 minutes, sound, black and white). Contains some interesting newsreel clips.

*The '29 Boom and '30's Depression* (McGraw-Hill, 15 minutes, sound, black and white). An attempt to recreate by film and dialogue the prosperity of the twenties and the economic crisis of the thirties.

1933-1938

# Rekindling
# the Democratic Faith

## CHAPTER SEVEN

Franklin D. Roosevelt.

THE MOOD OF THE TIMES

"This is a day of national consecration. . . . This is pre-eminently the time to speak the truth, the whole truth, frankly and boldly. . . . The only thing we have to fear is fear itself—nameless, unreasoning, unjustified terror which paralyzes needed efforts to convey retreat into advance. . . .

"Only a foolish optimist can deny the dark realities of the moment. Yet our distress comes from no failure of substance. We are stricken by no plague of locusts. . . . Plenty is at our doorstep, but a generous use of it languishes in the very sight of the supply. Primarily, this is because the rulers of the exchange of mankind's goods have failed through their own stubbornness and their own incompetence, have admitted their failure and abdicated. Practices of the unscrupulous money changers stand indicted in the court of public opinion, rejected by the hearts and minds of men. . . . They have no vision, and when there is no vision the people perish. The money changers have fled from their high seats in the temple of our civilization. We may now restore that temple to the ancient truths. The measure of the restoration lies in the extent to which we apply social values more noble than mere monetary profit. . . .

"We face the arduous days that lie before us in the warm courage of national unity; with the clear consciousness of seeking old and precious moral values; with the clear satisfaction that comes from the stern performance of duty by old and young alike. We aim at the assurance of a rounded and permanent national life. . . . In this dedication of a nation we humbly ask the blessing of God. May He protect each and every one of us! May He guide me in the days to come!"

—FRANKLIN D. ROOSEVELT, 1933

# THE SECOND ROOSEVELT

These words from Franklin Roosevelt's first inaugural address fell on a nation paralyzed by fear and anxiety. The winter of 1932-33 had been desperate for millions of American families, as the business recovery hoped for during the preceding summer failed to materialize. With close to thirteen million men out of work, relief had become a staggering burden for the impoverished states and communities. With bankers facing their worst crisis in the nation's history, panic seized large segments of the population as bank after bank closed its doors in the early months of 1933. To halt the panic and enable the bankers to regroup their forces, a number of governors had declared "banking holidays." In the early morning hours of March 4, 1933, the new Governor of New York, Herbert H. Lehman, succumbing to tremendous pressure, closed the great banks of his state. The economic heart of the nation seemed virtually to stop as the new President took the oath of office and began his inaugural address.

"The only thing we have to fear is fear itself," said Franklin Roosevelt in words used before by Hoover and members of his Administration. Could the new President inspire confidence where Hoover had failed? What ideas did he have for combating the depression? What was his social outlook? How did he view the office of the Presidency? What manner of man was Roosevelt? Few people out-
210

side New York knew much about him in 1933 and even old friends were unsure of his capacity to lead in such a crisis. But all were heartened by the cheerful confidence he displayed as he took on the greatest burden of any president since the Civil War.

## The Making of a President

All his life Franklin Roosevelt had known comfort and security. The only child of wealthy Hyde Park (N.Y.) parents, he had grown up in an atmosphere of lavish affection and aristocratic ease. He studied under tutors, spent quiet summers in Europe, and enrolled in his fourteenth year at the exclusive preparatory school in Groton, Massachusetts, where he was remembered as friendly, open, and unaggressive. He fit easily into the Groton pattern. The headmaster recalled that he was "a quiet satisfactory boy of more than ordinary intelligence, taking a good position in his Form but not brilliant. . . . We all liked him." In 1900, now eighteen years old, the young FDR entered Harvard University. Here, once more, he performed adequately but did not excel in his studies. His real interests ran to extracurricular activities, especially journalism, and in his last year he was made editor-in-chief of *The Crimson*. He was, according to all accounts, handsome, affable, and friendly. He liked people. Some detected a trace of snobbishness, while others thought him a bit priggish and shallow; certainly few marked him as destined for greatness in any field.

After Harvard he enrolled in the Columbia Law School, where he studied law without enthusiasm until he passed the bar examinations in 1907. In the meantime he married Eleanor Roosevelt, a distant cousin of his and niece of Theodore Roosevelt, who, then President, came to New York to give the bride away. The example of the energetic TR burned brightly before the young man. The elder Roosevelt was living proof of the joys and satisfactions derived from a life devoted to public service, an embodiment of the Groton ideal of service to the nation and to the unfortunate. His titanic enthusiasms seemed to bear everything before him. Young FDR was greatly impressed by "Uncle Ted" and would later model his own political career on that of his distinguished relative.

The Roosevelt name was always an asset to FDR. Though his branch of the family had long been Democratic, he benefited from the fame of his Republican kin. In his first campaign—for the New York State Senate—he frequently opened his speeches with a smile and the remark: "I'm not Teddy." The year was 1910. In an open, red Maxwell he toured the normally Republican countryside of his native Dutchess County, talking, joking, and flashing a broad friendly smile. After his election, he immediately threw himself into a much-publicized crusade to prevent Tammany Hall from sending its candidate, "Blue-eyed Billy" Sheehan, to the United States Senate. The selection lay, in these years prior to the adoption of the Seventeenth Amendment, with the state legislature. Though he won only a Pyrrhic victory—he was forced to accept a man even more closely tied to Tammany than Sheehan—Roosevelt gained valuable publicity and experience. And

he won a host of new political friends, the most important of whom was the Albany reporter, Louis Howe, who attached himself with a fierce and unshakeable loyalty to Roosevelt's political bandwagon. "Almost at the very first meeting," Howe recalled later, "I made up my mind that . . . nothing but an accident could keep him from becoming President of the United States."

Strongly attracted by Wilson's idealism and progressive principles, Roosevelt was quick to support his cause among New York Democrats in 1912. This brought him an appointment to TR's old post of Assistant Secretary of the Navy, and for seven years FDR served in the Wilson Administration, showing unexpected executive abilities and gaining invaluable political experience. In 1920 he resigned to run as Cox's partner in the ill-fated campaign against Warren Harding. After his defeat, he returned to private life for the first time in a decade.

Disaster struck in August, 1921. Following a swim in the cold waters off Campobello Island, Roosevelt's summer home in the Bay of Fundy, he suffered a severe attack of poliomyelitis, which paralyzed his legs. For long months he battled to regain his health, imposing a fierce discipline upon himself and trying every exercise and treatment known. Gradually he learned to stand again with the aid of crutches and heavy iron braces. Encouraged by his wife and the irrepressible Howe, he resumed his political and business activity, dabbling in banking and construction projects, and was sufficiently recovered by 1924 to nominate Al Smith at the Democratic convention. During the next few years he spent a large part of his time at Warm Springs, Georgia, where the mineral springs seemed to exert a healing effect on his shattered legs. Then, against his personal wishes, he was persuaded to run for Governor of New York in 1928, in order to strengthen the Democratic ticket in the Smith-Hoover race. Surprisingly, as we have seen, he was elected by a few thousand votes while Smith was losing to Hoover. His resounding triumph two years later made him the outstanding candidate to oppose Hoover in 1932.

What the ordeal of polio meant to Roosevelt has long been debated by those familiar with his career. His Secretary of Labor, Frances Perkins, argued that he underwent a spiritual transformation during his years of illness which "purged the slightly arrogant attitude he had displayed on occasion before he was stricken." His ordeal, she felt, made him more sympathetic, patient, and understanding of other people's troubles. Others are not sure. Perhaps, it has been said, his illness only brought out latent tendencies in his personality that might have developed anyway. No one would argue that a personal crisis so serious as the bout with polio left no marks at all on Roosevelt. When asked once how he could be so serene amid so much tension and trouble, he replied, in one of his few references to his affliction, "If you had spent two years in bed trying to wiggle your big toe, after that anything else would seem easy!"

## The Man and the Personality

Courage was one quality that nearly everyone close to FDR usually saw in him. To those who were with him in the crisis of 1933, Roosevelt seemed confident, serene, buoyant, and full of the enjoyment of life. He loved power. No one since TR had enjoyed being President as much as the second Roosevelt did. He seemed never to worry, never to doubt his decisions, never to be unsure of himself. His resiliency and capacity to withstand rebuffs were a phenomenal source of strength, and his personal charm exerted a powerful magnetism on friend and foe alike. In public and private discussion, his control over his feelings gave

him a strong advantage. Even those who distrusted his judgment admired his temperament. The aging Oliver Wendell Holmes spoke for many such skeptics when he described Roosevelt as "a second-class intellect—but a first-class temperament!"

No two persons found the same things in Roosevelt. "He was the most complicated human being I ever knew," said Frances Perkins. Others agreed. He seemed never to reveal his innermost feelings, always to be trying to adjust his private behavior to the public image he was creating. Kind, gracious, invariably thoughtful, he surely was, yet he could occasionally tease those closest to him almost without mercy. No man of his generation was more at home amid new ideas, new friends, or new projects, yet he felt a deep conservative regard for the values and way of life he had known in Hyde Park. He could be hard and unyielding at times and unbelievably flexible at others. Indeed, he could be courageous and devious at almost the same time. He loved to play a variety of roles, taking pride in his versatility, his skill at party politics, his knowledge of business and national affairs. Intelligent, quick to grasp new ideas, and possessed of a phenomenal memory, he learned more from people than from the printed page. And all his life, especially after becoming a cripple, he was deeply sensitive to other people and was inclined to cast social problems in strongly personal terms.

His superb political skill derived in large part from this genuine interest in people. Not abstractions, but the plight of individual human beings seemed always to be the focus of his attention. He framed ideas in simple, homely terms, using examples his hearers would know and understand. He created a sense of intimacy, a personal bond with his followers that a later generation would find hard to understand. No one who heard his radio addresses, especially his "Fireside Chats," however, will fail to understand the basis of his enormous popularity. He succeeded as no president had since Jackson in identifying himself with the broad aspirations of the common man. "He did not seem to be someone far removed, fighting their battles in a rarefied atmosphere," wrote Judge Samuel Rosenman, his speech writer. "He was right down in the sweaty arena with them, side by side, expressing what they were thinking, doing what they wanted done, taking his strength and his boldness from their strength and their support—making them feel that he and they were all doing it together." *

## The Leader and His Program

Under FDR the nation once more had a sense of being led. From the hour of his inauguration through the dramatic first hundred days of hurried action and on through the years to his death in 1945, Americans were conscious, in some cases uncomfortably so, of determined leadership at the head of the nation. No president has ever made fuller use of the power of the press and the radio in rallying public support for his program. Congress was under almost constant pressure, as FDR rallied opinion, cajoled leaders, brandished patronage, drafted key measures in the executive branch, and wielded his veto power. Of 631 bills rejected by the President between 1933 and 1945, only nine passed over his veto. His own view of the presidency, like that of TR and Wilson, was that of "a place of moral leadership." Years before, during his vice-presidential campaign in 1920, FDR explained his theory of the office: "As I recall history, most of our great deeds have been brought about by Executive Leaders, by

the Presidents who were not tools of Congress but were true leaders of the Nation, who so truly interpreted the needs and wishes of the people that they were supported in their great tasks." It was clearly Roosevelt's determination to be one of those "true leaders of the Nation."

But where would he lead it? What was his program? That he was no radical seems clear enough. He took capitalism for granted, but thought it should be made responsible and humane. He believed business could be run in a fair and honest way so that all concerned— workers, managers, and stockholders— would benefit. His own standards of fairness and honesty being derived from the secure Victorian world he had known at Hyde Park and Groton, his approach to social questions, like that of TR, was basically moral: Trust in human decency, believe in democracy, resist evil, and have faith in God and His purposes in the world. Always the pragmatist, he plainly distrusted radical solutions and doctrinaire philosophies. When a young reporter asked him his social philosophy, Roosevelt replied simply, "Philosophy? I am a Christian and a Democrat—that's all."

Roosevelt became president at a time when democratic values were undergoing a supreme test. Individualism, democracy, and freedom were under attack not only from skeptics and doubters at home but from the growing army of totalitarians abroad. Could a bridge be built between the old values and a modern urban-industrial society? Could faith in democratic values be rekindled in a time of catastrophic change? Was there a middle way between a rugged individualism that ignored the crisis of modern capitalism and a totalitarianism that sacrificed personal freedom for material security?

Roosevelt believed strongly in the middle way. He never doubted for a moment the capacity of American society to with-

* S. Rosenman, *Working with Roosevelt* (New York: Harper, 1952), p. 549.

stand the onslaught of economic depression at home and totalitarianism abroad. But neither did he question the need to readjust social institutions to the facts of modern life. Roosevelt often described himself as a bridge between an old and a new America. He spoke of the old order as a "horse-and-buggy world," while the new America was made up of machines, large-scale enterprise, and great aggregates of power. More than any man of his time, in the opinion of Rexford Tugwell, a member of his "Brain Trust," Roosevelt eased the transition of America from the old individualism to the new collectivism. This meant, in economic terms, a shift "from unlimited to regulated competition with some direction and some weighting in favor of those with the least power to bargain; and from individual responsibility for all the risks of life to security for all in sickness, unemployment, and old age." *

Roosevelt never framed his goals as clearly as Tugwell and others would have liked. Historians and political scientists have since criticized him for his lack of a comprehensive program. But it was Roosevelt's strength, as well as his weakness, that he was willing to experiment without an over-all plan, to apply the pragmatic test of how well his programs worked, and to keep his mind open about the future. He likened himself to a quarterback calling signals on a constantly shifting field. Each new move was judged by its political and moral (and to FDR, as to the progressives, these words meant nearly the same thing) consequences. Certainly this preference for action, experiment, and new ideas perfectly fitted the mood of the nineteen-thirties. If, as Professor Mario Einaudi has written, the democratic leader is the man best able to express the urge of his society to achieve common and deeply felt needs, democracy faltering when the leader fails to identify these needs and realize them, then, by this test, FDR was "the supreme democratic leader of our time." †

* R. Tugwell, *The Democratic Roosevelt* (Garden City, N.Y.: Doubleday and Company, 1957), p. 9.

† M. Einaudi, *The Roosevelt Revolution* (New York: Harcourt, Brace and Company, 1959), p. 59.

Gallery of New Dealers: Harry Hopkins, relief administrator; Harold L. Ickes, Secretary of the Interior; James Farley, Democratic party leader and Postmaster-General; Henry A. Wallace, Secretary of Agriculture. (All from Brown Brothers.)

# THE COMING OF THE NEW DEAL

## The Men Around Roosevelt

The New Dealers, many of them if not all, shared Roosevelt's distrust of theories and comprehensive solutions. The President surrounded himself with men and women who were hungry for action, anxious to try new approaches, and dedicated to his concept of public service. Political matters fell to the master strategists Farley and Howe, who interested themselves but little in the details of the New Deal program. For economic ideas he turned in the winter of 1932-33 to a small circle of college professors: Raymond Moley, a political scientist and organizer of the "Brain Trust," Rexford Tugwell, a close student of agricultural economics, and Adolf Berle, a brilliant law professor with a strong interest in credit problems.

Others joined the circle from time to time. To his Cabinet he appointed a wide range of persons: the old Progressive, Harold Ickes, to Interior; the dignified Tennessean and low-tariff advocate, Cordell Hull, to State; an amiable Republican banker, William Woodin, to Treasury; the serious, idealistic Henry A. Wallace, son of a former Cabinet member, to Agriculture; an old Wilsonian, Homer Cummings, to be Attorney General (following the premature death of Thomas J. Walsh, the Teapot Dome investigator, before he could take office); the first woman Cabinet member, Frances Perkins, to Labor; and Farley to the traditional campaign manager's job, Postmaster General. There were other less notable appointments and a number of early changes. Woodin, for one, was replaced by FDR's Dutchess County neighbor, Henry L. Morgenthau, Jr., in the second year of the first term. To fill the lesser posts in the government, thousands of young men and women flocked to Washington to participate in the wide array of exciting new programs. For many of them these early days under the New Deal would remain the high point of their lives. Morgenthau called them "unforgettably thrilling."

## The First New Deal

No one could quite recreate the excitement of these first weeks under Roosevelt. The depression had reached its nadir; a mood of helpless resignation had settled over the business community; the banking crisis climaxed on Inauguration Day itself; and millions of unemployed Americans were looking eagerly to the new administration for relief and assistance. Action was the keynote of Roosevelt's response. Congress was in a frenzy of activity in the one hundred days from March 9 to June 16, 1933, as the President pressed for more and

more laws to combat the depression. Measure after measure was passed, many of them of supreme importance to the nation, with only a few hours or days of debate. The basic New Deal programs for ending the banking crisis, stimulating business recovery, restoring agriculture, providing relief, regulating the stock market, and realizing the dream of a Tennessee Valley Authority were approved by Congress in this brief period. Never in the history of the nation has so much important legislation been passed in so short a time.

The most urgent crisis facing the nation in March, 1933, was the banking collapse. Here the new administration acted swiftly, confidently, and on the whole successfully. Roosevelt and his advisers sensed that the banking panic arose out of a failure of confidence. When he took office most of the nation's banks were already closed. He now declared a national "banking holiday" and demanded emergency powers over banking and currency from a Congress that swiftly granted them. He stopped the flow of gold from the Treasury by forbidding its hoarding or export, except under license. As he prepared to order the reopening of the banks following inspection by Treasury officials, the President took to the air to assure the American people that the crisis had passed. "I can assure you," he said in his first Fireside Chat, "that it is safer to keep your money in a reopened bank than under the mattress." Would the people believe him? The next day the banks began to reopen their doors. No panic occurred. Within the first month a billion dollars in currency and gold flowed back into the nation's banks. The great majority of the institutions, found to be sound, reopened under license from the Treasury Department or state banking authorities. The crisis seemed gradually to pass away. On June 16, Congress completed the cycle of banking

reform by passing the Glass-Steagall Act, which separated commercial banks from their investment affiliates, in order to keep them from becoming involved in stock market speculation as in the twenties. The bill also established a federal system of insurance on bank deposits.

In order to protect investors further, Congress hurried through a "Truth in Securities" Act, which required companies issuing new securities to register them with the Federal Trade Commission, and disclose full and accurate information about them. Enforcement of the law was transferred the following year to a Securities and Exchange Commission, whose responsibility it became to police the security exchanges of the nation. All trading in securities now came under the regulations of the SEC, price manipulation was forbidden, and the Federal Reserve Board was empowered to control the use of credit in financing the purchase of stocks.

Would Roosevelt go beyond these conservative reforms in banking and securities and interfere with the currency? Would he devalue the dollar? Inflationary pressures were heavy by the spring of 1933. Since, some held, the depression was the result of a collapse in prices, certain influential economists believed that a reduction in the gold value of the dollar would raise the general price level and promote American trade. Congress tried to force Roosevelt's hand by passing the Thomas Amendment to the farm bill, which empowered the President to issue paper money, reduce the gold content of the dollar, or coin silver at the old ratio of sixteen to one. On April 19, Roosevelt did abandon the gold standard, ending the attempt to hold American currency stable with other world currencies, and a slight increase in prices at home resulted. He refused, however, to use the other powers given him to inflate the currency. In June, he sharply rejected a proposal made at the World Economic Conference in London to stabilize once more the gold value of currencies. The raising of prices in the United States, he decided, must take precedence over international stabilization.

Inflationary pressures mounted rapidly in the fall of 1933. When it became clear that his recovery program would not bring the hoped-for increase in commodity prices, Roosevelt was told that only currency manipulation could bring an increase in prices. He decided to make the experiment. In late October the government began to buy gold at prices set by the President in the expectation that this would force up the price of gold and with it the price of other commodities. "The definite policy of this Government," FDR explained in a Fireside Chat, "has been to restore commodity price levels." Each morning a bedroom conference was held in the White House to set the price of gold for the day. Gradually the price of gold was bid up to $35 an ounce. But the results were disappointing. Some prices went up but others did not. Farm prices actually dropped a bit in November and December. Nevertheless, some gains were realized and the debt burden of the farmers was lightened somewhat by the devaluation policy. In January, 1934, Congress passed the Gold Reserve Act, which set the price of gold at $35 an ounce and reduced the value of the dollar to 59.06 per cent of its former gold content. The gold standard of McKinley's day was gone, probably forever.

Meanwhile, during the first hectic session of Congress under Roosevelt, the New Deal programs for dealing with the business and farm depressions had taken shape. Behind the recovery measures lay the belief that the economy had been overexpanded and production must be curtailed. Prices had to be restored and maintained. To achieve these ends a large measure of national planning was believed necessary. The basic conception of the National Industrial Recovery Act (NRA) was that representative committees from each of the major industries, such as steel, textiles, and bituminous coal, should draw up codes of fair practice for the entire industry. These codes would end cutthroat competition, stabilize prices, and protect the wages and working conditions of the laborer. Many of the codes adopted were modeled on the trade association codes worked out in the nineteen-twenties. In essence, then, NRA was a scheme for self-government in American industry that, it was hoped, would revive business morale and promote recovery. To facilitate the program, antitrust laws were suspended. In exchange for this new freedom to control its own affairs, business was to recognize labor's right to organize and bargain collectively under Section 7A of the law. Once agreed upon, these codes would be given the authority and support of the United States government.

To administer the new law, the colorful and forceful General Hugh Johnson was appointed NRA director. Immediately he began a campaign to get businessmen to agree to ban child labor, hold the work week to forty hours, and keep wages above the $12 to $15 mark. Cooperating businesses displayed a "Blue Eagle" emblem in their windows. Parades were held in many cities to dramatize the program. In all, more than 500 codes affecting twenty-two million workers were drawn up in the first six months after the passage of the law.

But the NRA never fully satisfied the hopes felt for it. A sharp rise in prices and industrial output did take place in 1933 but the buying power of the consumer failed to keep pace. As part of the effort to promote recovery, a public works spending program (PWA) under

Harold Ickes was set up to pump new money into the economy. Authorized to lend money for projects built by public authority, the PWA made possible over a period of years the erection of a considerable number of bridges, highways, and public buildings, but Ickes' slow and cautious administration of the fund prevented it from having any immediate effect on the crisis of 1933. Then, too, the NRA codes often proved unenforceable; some operated to the advantage of the large firms that had drawn them up. A number of industries, moreover, had speeded production in anticipation of the NRA restrictions, which further glutted the industrial markets. Many small businessmen protested the dominant role played by big business in the code authorities, while others resented the protection given labor in its organizational efforts. Labor, for its part, felt excluded altogether from the vital decisions reached by the code-makers. After a spurt upward in the summer, industrial production began to plummet again in the fall of 1933. Though the NRA dragged on for another two years, until the Supreme Court ruled it unconstitutional in the *Schechter* case, its basic formula for solving the depression by using the power of government to adjust production to demand had clearly failed.

The New Deal's approach to the farm crisis was similar but more successful. Farm output, it was argued, must be curtailed in order to raise prices. Under the Agricultural Adjustment Act (AAA) of 1933, to get the growers of basic crops to restrict their plantings, benefit payments were to be given cooperating farmers. A processing tax was to be collected from millers, meatpackers, and other middlemen to finance the program. Later, when the Supreme Court found the tax illegal in the *Butler* case, the basis for the payments to farmers was shifted

to soil improvement and conservation. Quotas for basic crops were set by agreement between AAA officials and individual farmers. To meet the emergency of 1933, when bumper cotton and hog production threatened to overwhelm the market, Secretary Wallace ordered the ploughing up of ten million acres of cotton and the destruction of millions of young pigs. Though momentarily unpopular with the public, the New Deal program, which incorporated the principles of domestic allotment and parity income from the pre-Roosevelt years, did help to raise farm prices. Just as important in raising prices, however, and perhaps more so, were the effects of the terrible drought and dust bowl conditions of 1934, which sharply cut farm output. Whatever the cause, by 1937 net farm income had doubled over 1933 and the ratio of prices received by farmers to those they paid out rose from 60 to 92. Part of the increase was due, of course, to the government payments given farmers. For the majority of farmers, in any case, the farm crisis was eased by the end of the thirties.

In some sections of the country, despite the AAA, want and misery continued to be the lot of the rural population. Notably, the destitute sharecroppers and tenant farmers of the South did not partake fully of the benefits of the program. Some, to be sure, were beneficiaries of special relief programs or were able eventually to buy or lease farms with funds provided in the Bankhead-Jones Act (1937). But their problem was never fully solved. And in the Southwest, victims of the dust bowl left the sandy soil of Oklahoma and its neighboring states to seek employment on the great farms of Southern California. Hundreds of thousands of these Americans took to the road in ancient jalopies piled high with mattresses, furniture, and children to seek their fortunes, often vainly, in the

NRA parade in New York City. (Brown Brothers.)

Far West. The drift of the population to the cities was halted in the thirties by the lack of industrial opportunity and was not resumed until the war years. By that time, the great demands stimulated by war had created a plentiful supply of jobs in both industry and agriculture.

There were still other measures that were pushed through Congress in that first frenzied session in 1933. Before going home, Congress passed more than a dozen major new laws. In addition to NRA, AAA, and the new banking and security laws, the following legislation was added to the statute books in the first flurry of activity:

1. The Economy Act, giving the President broad powers to cut federal salaries as much as 15 per cent and reduce veterans' pensions and allowances.

2. The Civilian Conservations Corps Act, to give temporary work on conservation projects to unemployed young men. Between 1933 and 1941 over two million youths spent time in the CCC camps, working at road construction, reforestation, prevention of soil erosion, and national park and flood control projects.

3. The Federal Emergency Relief Act, setting up a national program to administer federal relief funds. Under Harry L. Hopkins, a dedicated, hard-driving social worker, relief funds were disbursed to the states, half of them in direct grants, the balance on the basis of $1 of federal help for every $3 expended by state and local sources.

4. The Emergency Farm Mortgage Act, enabling farmers to refinance their mortgages through the federal land banks.

5. The Home Owners Loan Act, to rescue home owners faced with foreclosure on their mortgages.

6. The Farm Credit Act, enabling farmers to get credit on easier terms.

7. The Railroad Coordination Act, appointing a Federal Coordinator of Transportation to make recommendations to ease the plight of the railroads.

8. The Tennessee Valley Authority Act, realizing Norris's old dream of a unified program of federal development for the Tennessee Valley.

Of all the laws passed during the Hundred Days none had more enduring significance or excited more lasting controversy than the one creating the Tennessee Valley Authority. Its passage, according to Senator Norris, was "emblematic of the dawn of that day when every rippling stream that flows down the mountainside and winds its way through meadows to the sea, should be harnessed and made to work for the welfare and comfort of man." But others believed with Hoover and Coolidge that the plan involved a fundamental departure from basic American traditions. These critics challenged the TVA's constitutionality, its large-scale planning, and its competition with private utilities industries. The powers of the board of directors, appointed by the President, were vast: building dams, controlling floods, providing a navigable channel in the river, constructing power plants and transmission lines, reforesting the land, planning new industries, manufacturing fertilizers, and a score of other responsibilities. The electricity generated by the great dams foreseen in the Act was to be sold to meet the costs of the Authority. In selling electricity, preference was to be given to publicly owned corporations or cooperatives.

All through the thirties the TVA fought suspicious state governments and hostile private power companies. Not until 1939 did the courts finally uphold its right to produce and sell electricity as authorized by the Act. So progress was understandably slow in face of the constant litigation and business opposition. In all, the agency built thirty dams to control the heavy rains that fell in the Valley. And gradually the dams brought under control the once-destructive floods that struck at hundreds of communities. Thanks to an eleven-foot channel that made navigation possible over 630 miles of inland waterway, river traffic increased sixty times between 1933 and 1956. Reforestation was begun over 300,000 acres of the Valley and a series of recreational, forest, and fish-and-wildlife preserves were set aside. Notable work was done, too, in soil conservation.

Most controversial of all the Authority's activities was the generation of electricity. The average family in the Valley may have consumed less power than the national median in 1933, but it consumed twice as much in the 1950's. And the cost of electricity to the TVA consumer in 1955 was less than half the national average. Nineteen of every twenty farms were electrified in 1955 as compared with less than one in twenty in

1933. Hundreds of new industries, too, made use of the cheap power. The producers of private power charged that the advantages of TVA were a result of faulty cost accounting or of the great resources of the United States government, which private industry felt enabled the agency to underwrite losses; nevertheless, the achievement was indeed a magnificent one.

Perhaps the most revolutionary aspect of the TVA was the concept of a unified approach to the water problems of a region. Heretofore, irrigation was the exclusive concern of the Department of Agriculture, flood control and navigation of the Army Corps of Engineers, and reclamation and power of the Department of the Interior. In the Tennessee Valley great multipurpose dams to check floods, facilitate navigation, and generate power reflected a unified direction. And with control lodged in a single authority, bureaucratic waste and conflict were largely avoided. Looking back at the first twenty years of TVA in 1953, the chairman of its board of directors, Gordon R. Clapp, regarded comprehensive planning as its greatest achievement. "For the first time," he wrote, "a single agency was given responsibility for a unified approach to the development and wise use of natural resources in a specified region. The eternal cycle of the raindrops was to be harnessed—in the forests, on the cultivated land, and in the streams. . . . None of these activities was new to the Federal Government, nor was TVA endowed with any powers new to government. The uniqueness of TVA lay in the range of functions combined for administration in one agency in one area— a river valley."

Aside from espousing TVA, Roosevelt and the early New Dealers were more conservative than radical. The revolutionary features of their program lay in the decisiveness of their action and the flexibility of their approach rather than in their doctrines. The banks were closed but they were reopened without fundamental change. Business recovery was to be stimulated through suspending antitrust laws and encouraging industrial self-government—the NRA was welcomed, avidly at first, by the greater part of the business community. At first Roosevelt meant to keep even his campaign promises of cutting governmental expense and balancing the budget. And many of the early New Deal programs, notably the AAA, were intended to pay for themselves. Nor were the men around Roosevelt in these early years regarded as radicals by their contemporaries. The Cabinet members ranged from conservatives to mild liberals, and some of the men closest to FDR were strongly conservative in their financial views, notably Lewis Douglas, Director of the Budget, and his two Secretaries of the Treasury, William Woodin and Henry Morgenthau, Jr. It seems clear, as Frank Freidel has pointed out, that Roosevelt intended during much of his first term to be President of all the people, to avoid extreme partisanship, and find a middle way among the dogmatic solutions being offered at every hand. And he seemed to be succeeding. "Never in the history of this nation," said the president of the United States Chamber of Commerce in 1933, "has any government more courageously and fully attempted to deal with so many and such far-reaching problems."

## REACHING FOR JACKSON'S MANTLE

But every honeymoon, however protracted, must come to an end. By 1934 partisans of both the extreme left and the extreme right had taken the measure of the New Deal and begun their campaigns against it. Many businessmen were restive under NRA restrictions and complained of the favoritism shown organized labor. Others protested at the growing imbalance in the budget, the increase in government spending, or the devaluation of the dollar. Those with a score to settle with FDR, notably Herbert Hoover and Al Smith, attacked the New Deal as the abandonment of liberty and all that was sacred in the American tradition. From the left came criticisms of Roosevelt's conservatism, his opportunism, and his willingness to work with Wall Street and big business. As the pressures mounted, FDR was urged to take a clearer stand on a host of issues that he had thus far safely ignored.

**Thunder from Right and Left**

In the summer of 1934 a coalition of conservative Democrats and wealthy businessmen joined forces to form the American Liberty League. The League's objectives, according to Jouett Shouse, former campaign manager for Al Smith, were to teach respect for the rights of persons and property, and to safeguard private enterprise in America. The League appealed to the Constitution as the basis of American liberties and philosophy of government. Financial support for the League's program came from wealthy bankers, manufacturers, and commercial interests. Unmoved, Roosevelt asked his hearers in a Fireside Chat in June, 1934, to ask themselves whether in fact they felt any loss of their constitutional liberties under the New Deal. Read the Bill of Rights, he told his audience, "and ask yourself whether you personally have suffered the impairment of a single jot of those great assurances."

Most citizens would have answered that they had not. Yet the middle thirties was the season for demagogues at both ends of the political spectrum. The craving for easy formulas of recovery induced millions to listen to men they would have dismissed as fanatics a few years before. The loudest and most dangerous was Huey Long, the master of a dictatorial, quasi-fascist regime in Louisiana, who now used the forum of the United States Senate to advocate a national share-the-wealth program. Ambitious, unprincipled, with an eye on the

Father Coughlin was known as the radio priest because of his weekly broadcasts. At one time he had supported Roosevelt, but by the time the publication pictured here was issued, he was bitterly denouncing the government.

Presidency itself, he promised every family "the comforts of life up to a value of from $5000 to $6000." He claimed three million members for his Every-Man-a-King clubs. On September 8, 1935, before his plans were fully made, Long was shot by a young doctor, whose father had been a victim of Long's perfidy. In Detroit, a radio priest named Charles E. Coughlin, like Long a defector from the New Deal, broadcast each Sunday afternoon a weird mixture of socialism, Populism, and antisemitism. Millions of listeners sent him money; thousands enlisted in his National Union for Social Justice; even FDR became concerned at his growing popularity. Though his program was vague and contradictory, he seemed to strike a responsive chord in the homes of millions of frustrated victims of the depression. In California, a retired doctor, Francis E. Townsend, concocted a scheme for solving the depression by paying every person over sixty years of age $200 a month on the condition he spend it in thirty days. His crusade grew out of the indignation he felt when he saw three elderly women foraging in a garbage can outside his home. The scheme was avidly praised by millions of destitute citizens. In all, more than twenty-five million people signed their names to petitions asking Congress to enact the Townsend Plan. Both the Coughlin and Townsend movements, however, were submerged in the second great wave of New Deal legislation after 1935.

Radical movements of all kinds found sympathetic support. Upton Sinclair, for instance, nearly won the governorship of California by the slogan, End Poverty in California. Domestic Marxists found their version of history and social struggle more popular than at any other time in the twentieth century. The Communists lashed Roosevelt and the New Deal as the precursors of American fascism.

Roosevelt's program, according to the 1934 convention of the Communist Party, was "serving the interests of finance capital and moving toward the fascist suppression of the workers' movement." Yet, even in the depths of misery and depression, the Communists failed to attract a mass following for their doctrines. Except for a fringe of intellectuals and young students they made no impression at all on thoughtful Americans. A trace of Communist infiltration did take place in New Deal agencies and in labor unions, particularly the CIO, but its effect on American government and society was minimal. Even less forceful than the lure of Communism in the mid-thirties was that of fascism, which enjoyed only a brief vogue among a few intellectuals and demagogues.

### The Second New Deal

The pressure of radicals and extremists rose with the failure of the New Deal to restore full prosperity. Though a measure of recovery had taken place, the mood of the nation was still cautious in 1934 and 1935. Investment was slow, businessmen were reluctant to expand their operations, and unemployment remained high. To stimulate housing, Congress created in 1934 the Federal Housing Administration, which was charged with insuring loans for new construction and home improvements, but the housing industry still lagged. More than nine million men were still jobless, some having been unemployed for four years or more. A wave of serious strikes in 1934 added to the mood of crisis. Though many people felt confidence in Roosevelt, others grew skeptical of his ability to end the economic crisis. How did he stand on proposals of more drastic reform? Would he act to end the gnawing insecurity of the aged, the jobless, and others who swelled the following of the demagogues? Would he side with labor

or management in the bitter struggle over labor's right to organize and bargain? Was the New Deal over, or had it just begun?

During 1934, the nation's mood alternated between hope and despair. In the Congressional elections in November, recovery was the key issue. While the Liberty League assailed the New Deal for the boldness of its programs, radical groups demanded even more revolutionary steps. Republicans generally campaigned against the New Deal, charging Roosevelt with subverting the Constitution and spending the nation into ruin, while Democrats flocked to the President's banner. To the surprise of many, the Democrats not only held their majority, unusual enough in a mid-term election, but actually gained ten seats each in the House and Senate.

The turning point in the New Deal came in 1935. In the spring the Administration suffered a series of setbacks in the courts, climaxed by the Supreme Court's decision against the constitutionality of NRA. Criticism of the New Deal mounted in all directions. On the one hand, the United States Chamber of Commerce sharply attacked the President in April, warning him against further reforms, particularly labor and social security laws. On the other, unions were clamoring for new protections now that NRA was dead. Roosevelt felt driven not only by the pressures from the left but what he regarded as betrayal by the business interests on the right. The Chamber of Commerce, he wrote a business friend, "has a one hundred per cent record of opposition to things like factory inspection, excessive hours, elimination of child labor, old age pensions, unemployment insurance—year after year the same old story." Why, he asked, had the Chamber never initiated or pressed a single item of social betterment? In his judgment, the New Deal had cooperated with business, solicited its advice, and given it a free hand under the NRA. Now business had turned against him and Roosevelt was angry.

More and more, in 1935 and 1936, Roosevelt aligned himself with the reform-minded, antibusiness coalition that arose out of the ashes of the first New Deal. Increasingly, he turned to his more liberally-minded advisers, notably Hopkins, Wallace, and Ickes, for direction and counsel. His greatest political strength, he came to realize, lay with farmers, city workers, and the underprivileged. Where he had earlier avoided extreme partisanship, even to the extent of advising against a Jefferson-Jackson Day dinner, he now stressed his kinship with Jackson and the party of the common man. A raft of new legislation was passed in 1935 that reflected in part this new orientation of the President.

During this second flurry of New Deal legislation from April to August, 1935,

Roosevelt once more threw himself into the Congressional fray. His lieutenants forced measure after measure through a mildly resisting Congress. The Wagner Labor Relations Act, which Roosevelt had previously regarded with indifference, now went through with a rush. Congressional leaders marshaled heavy support for the Social Security Act. The holding company bill, aimed at splitting the giant utility aggregates, was now approved with its famous "death sentence" clause, which set a term of five years for the dissolution of any holding company that could not demonstrate its localized, efficient, and useful character. A new tax bill, sharply raising the levies in the upper-income brackets, was added to the statute books. To alleviate the condition of impoverished farm families, a Resettlement Administration was created to help relocate destitute or low-income families, establish subsistence homesteads, and build suburban developments

A PWA project, building a road at Arlington National Cemetery, 1936. (New York Public Library Picture Collection.)

for low-income city workers. Farm families benefited, too, from the Rural Electrification Administration Act, which gave the REA responsibility for bringing electricity to rural areas not served by private companies. And also in 1935, Congress passed a Banking Act, which greatly increased the powers of the Federal Reserve Board over the rediscount rates, reserves, and open-market operations of member banks. The effect of these banking changes was to centralize credit control in the federal government, whose bonds the Federal Reserve System was now committed to maintain at stable price levels.

Roosevelt moved quickly, too, to create the Works Progress Administration authorized by Congress in April. Under Harry Hopkins' directions, the WPA program was aimed at putting to work not only blue-collar workers but musicians, teachers, writers, and other unemployed persons at public jobs that would salvage their self-respect. Almost nine-tenths of all the funds spent on WPA projects went directly into wages and salaries. By 1936, over three million persons were on WPA rolls and by the time of its dissolution in 1943, eight and a half million people had been employed at various times. During its eight years of life WPA built 650,000 miles of highways and streets, erected or repaired 250,000 bridges and public buildings, and operated hundreds of community recreation and educational centers. In addition, WPA employees wrote more than a score of guidebooks, played hundreds of concerts, and staged numerous plays. Though condemned by critics for its inefficiency and waste, WPA contributed appreciably to the rise in purchasing power and in national morale during the latter nineteen-thirties.

Though too late to be of much help in the thirties, the Social Security Act proved to be the most fundamental and significant of the New Deal programs.

Providing for old-age pensions and unemployment insurance, as well as aid to certain classes of handicapped and dependent persons, the Social Security program was to be financed through a series of payroll taxes. The pension plan was to be administered by the federal government through contributions by employers and employees alike. The tax rate was to rise gradually from 1 per cent of the wage of each worker to 3 per cent in 1949. Benefits would begin in 1942 in accordance with the wage and length of contributions of individual workers. Unemployment insurance, on the other hand, was to be administered through the states by funds collected from a federal unemployment tax on payrolls. The Social Security program was not without its opposition, particularly from Republicans who strongly attacked it in 1936 and occasionally thereafter, but it became in time a fixed part of the American scene.

### The Election of 1936

By 1936, Roosevelt had moved sharply to the left of center. His legislative program of the preceding year had taken the wind out of the radicals' sails. His opposition to the conservative forces aligned against him was now unmistakable. At Franklin Field in Philadelphia, in accepting his party's second nomination, he made his position clear: ".The economic royalists complain that we seek to overthrow the institutions of America. What they really complain of is that we seek to take away their power. . . . In vain they seek to hide behind the flag and the Constitution. In their blindness they forget what the flag and the Constitution stand for. . . . Better the occasional faults of a government that lives in a spirit of charity than the consistent omissions of a government frozen in the ice of its own indifference."

At Cleveland the Republicans passed

over two Senators, William Borah of Idaho and Arthur Vandenberg of Michigan, both of whom had been mentioned for the nomination, and chose Governor Alf Landon of Kansas. Landon was a middle-of-the-roader, an old follower of TR's, whose political record included being re-elected in 1934 and balancing the Kansas state budget. Earnest, quiet, unimpressive in appearance, Landon seemed the perfect contrast to the irrepressible showman in the White House.

He began his campaign by mildly disagreeing with the Republican platform, which had blasted the New Deal for violating American liberties, contravening the Constitution, flouting the Supreme Court, and destroying the morale of the American people. Social security, the platform declared, was unworkable; relief should be returned to local administration; tariffs were too low; and the nation must return to a balanced budget. Landon did not go quite so far. He even seemed at first to promise that most New Deal benefits would be retained but at lesser cost and under better administration. He avoided close identification with the Republican leaders of the twenties; even Hoover was given a chill welcome at

Landon headquarters. But as the campaign wore on he became more strident. He attacked social security and denounced the reciprocal trade policy. In October he charged that Roosevelt was leading the nation down the road to dictatorship. "No nation," he warned ominously, "can continue half regimented and half free." From the Republican National Committee came the sober pronouncement that Roosevelt was "the Kerensky of the American revolutionary movement." Disaffected Democrats joined the Republicans in lambasting the President. Even Bainbridge Colby, an old Wilsonian, charged in the heat of the campaign that FDR had "gone over hook, line, and sinker to the Communists and Socialists, by whom he is surrounded." Most painful of all to the President were the blistering attacks of his old friend, Al Smith, whose resentment of Roosevelt's success, coupled to his conservative reaction to the New Deal, had turned him to bitterness.

Roosevelt warmed to the fight in late September, and aimed his campaign as much at the American Liberty League as at the Republicans. Actually, the bitter

FDR chats with a farmer in Mandan, North Dakota, during the election year, 1936. (Resettlement Administration Photograph by Rothstein; New York Public Library Picture Collection.)

criticism of his opponents made his task easier. In one month on the stump— "the greatest piece of personal campaigning in American history," said Farley—he turned the campaign into one long victory parade. Everywhere he found mammoth crowds, tremendous enthusiasm, and a pathetic eagerness to demonstrate approval of New Deal programs. His last major speech was at Madison Square Garden on October 31. The mood of the crowd was revivalist, the applause thunderous. Time and time again they leaped to their feet to cheer. "Never before in all our history," said Roosevelt of the powerful mass of business interests, wealth, and newspapers opposing him, "have these forces been so united against one candidate as they stand today. They are unanimous in their hate for me—and I welcome their hatred. I should like to have it said of my first Administration that in it the forces of selfishness and of lust for power met their match. I should like to have it said of my second Administration that in it these forces met their master."

The outcome surprised even Farley. He had predicted that FDR would carry every state except Maine and Vermont. He did, but more. He carried with him the largest House majority since 1855 and the largest Senate majority since 1869. In the popular ballot he won 27,751,597 votes to Landon's 16,679,583. William Lemke, the aspirant supported by Coughlin, Townsend, Gerald L. K. Smith, and other demagogues took fewer than 900,000 votes, the Socialist candidate, Norman Thomas, got 187,720, while Earl Browder, the Communist nominee, received only 80,159. The Communist and Socialist totals were sharply down from 1932. Even Roosevelt's enemies were astonished. William Randolph Hearst, whose papers had lambasted FDR in the campaign, sent his employees a telegram in which he said, "When I was a great admirer and supporter of Mr. Roosevelt . . . I gave him a picture of Andrew Jackson and a letter of that great Democrat. I thought then that Mr. Roosevelt resembled Jackson. Perhaps I was more nearly right then than later. Perhaps Roosevelt, like Jackson, has given essential democracy a new lease of life and will establish it in power for a generation."

## The Roosevelt Coalition

FDR's great victory in 1936 betokened a political revolution. The Civil War had left the nation Republican; now the depression and the New Deal had converted it to the Democratic faith. In the Democratic coalition that elected Roosevelt in 1936 were all the elements that made it the majority party for the next quarter-century. The formula comprised organized labor, Midwestern farmers (to 1952), Negroes, big-city immigrants, and middle-class independents and intellectuals.

Many Roosevelt voters were children of the thirteen million immigrants who came to the United States between 1900 and 1914. Having come to maturity in an insecure and critical time, many of them benefited from the New Deal programs and they repaid in political coin the benefits they had received. From the South, too, streams of Negro migrants had poured north since 1914. These Negro voters were won over to the New Deal not by civil rights legislation but by the fight waged against discrimination in administering relief and welfare programs. Hopkins fought hard to end racial discrimination in the relief program, while Ickes ended segregation in the Interior Department and vigorously championed the cause of the Negro. Eleanor Roosevelt was openly sympathetic to Negro rights. More and more, as the thirties wore on, it became apparent to most Negro leaders that the strongest champions of their rights in and out of government were northern Democrats.

Another strong new element in the Democratic coalition was organized labor. Encouraged by NRA and the Wagner Act, both of which guaranteed labor's right to organize and bargain with employers, union membership shot up dramatically in the thirties. "President Roosevelt wants you to join a union" read some of the recruiting posters of the day. From fewer than three million persons in 1933 labor unions increased their membership to almost nine million in 1939. Early in the period, sensing labor's opportunity, John L. Lewis led a group of dissident unionists in the formation of the Committee for Industrial Organization within the AFL. Lewis had long wanted to organize the workers in the mass industries, especially steel, automobiles, and rubber, without regard for the traditional craft lines observed in the AFL. "Organize the unorganized," he cried at the AFL convention of 1935, "and in doing this make the AFL the greatest instrument that has ever been forged to befriend the cause of humanity and champion human rights." Now he had his chance, and the CIO grew swiftly. Unskilled workers, Negroes, recent immigrants, and women came into the labor movement with a rush. In 1938 the CIO broke its remaining ties with the AFL and reorganized as the Congress of Industrial Organizations. What this sensational growth in labor strength meant politically is indicated by union gifts to FDR's 1936 campaign, which reached a total of nearly a million dollars.

Labor's bargaining position against management was immeasurably improved by its rapid growth. Not only was the right to bargain now protected by federal law but unions were also shielded by the Norris-LaGuardia Act (1932) from "yellow dog contracts" and federal court injunctions in labor disputes. Under the

Wagner Act, a National Labor Relations Board was set up to supervise elections for certifying unions as bargaining agents, and to hear complaints against employers for refusing to bargain or to permit organizational attempts. Employers argued that a vast number of "unfair labor practices" were prohibited for them, while nothing was banned for the unions. Moreover, company unions were virtually outlawed by the Wagner Act, and closed shops became the order of the day in many places of employment.

The middle thirties was a season of labor violence, as union leaders pushed hard to organize the nation's big industries. In 1937 alone nearly five thousand strikes, involving close to two million workers, took place. Seven per cent of the entire labor force in the United States was out on strike sometime during that year. The battle to unionize the great steel industry had begun the preceding year under the leadership of Scottish-born Philip Murray. He won a signal victory over United States Steel when the company capitulated in March, 1937, without a major fight. The company leaders found they could not count on help from state governments nor on a sympathetic public opinion. Indeed, the Governor of Pennsylvania held out the promise of relief to the steelworkers should a strike develop. Several of the smaller steel companies did resist, however, notably Republic Steel, under the leadership of the union-hating Tom Girdler. In the late spring of 1937, clashes in Republic plants in South Chicago and Massillon, Ohio, took the lives of several strikers. A Senate committee, headed by Robert LaFollette, Jr., was sent to investigate and reported numerous violations of the Wagner Act on the part of employers. Most of the plants, LaFollette announced, maintained arsenals of firearms and hired corps of labor spies and *agents provocateurs*. The National Labor Relations

Strikers blockade the Ford Motor Company, April, 1937. (Brown Brothers.)

Board also intervened in the steel strike and ultimately forced the companies to bargain in good faith with the steel-workers' union.

Labor leaders encountered much stiffer, if less fatal, resistance in their effort to unionize the automobile industry. In early 1937, a spectacular CIO sit-down strike in General Motors plants was met by determined company efforts to dislodge the strikers. Governor Frank Murphy of Michigan was urged to use the National Guard to clear the plants but Murphy refused. Then the strikers ignored an order from a Circuit Court to leave the property under pain of imprisonment and a $15 million fine. The sheriff, ordered by local officials to arrest the strikers, turned to Governor Murphy, who again refused troops. Behind the scenes, FDR brought tremendous pressure to bear upon officers of the company. Finally, on February 11, 1937, General Motors surrendered. A month later the Chrysler Corporation also recognized the United Automobile Workers union. Only Henry Ford held out; ultimately, he, too, was forced to consent to the unionization of his plants in 1941. Thus, by the outbreak of World War II, labor had come within sight of the goal of organizing all the basic industries of the United States. The victory, as union leaders well knew, was due as much to the new political climate of the New Deal as to their own long struggle.

## STALEMATE

The labor violence of 1937 badly frightened many influential members of the middle class. The feeling was growing among many moderate persons that the balance of power had shifted too quickly and too far in labor's direction. As a consequence, criticism of the Wagner Act and the National Labor Relations Board mounted in the late thirties. This shift in opinion coincided with a series of other New Deal setbacks that converted FDR's great victory of 1936 into a paralyzing stalemate: the Supreme Court fight, the recession of 1937-38, and the attempted purge of disloyal Democrats. By the end of 1938, two years after FDR's epochal triumph, the journalist Walter Millis could say of the New Deal that it "has been reduced to a movement with no program, with no effective political

229

organization, with no vast popular party strength behind it, and with no candidate."

What had happened? In part, the shift was due to Roosevelt's own cockiness as he surveyed his smashing electoral triumph. His confidence leaped with the size of his victory; he tended more and more to keep his own counsel; he threw caution to the winds; and he committed a series of grave tactical errors. But there were deeper causes as well. By 1937 the major reforms of the New Deal had been completed. The goals of historic American progressivism were now largely achieved. There were few new directions in which the New Deal could go. As economic conditions improved, the zeal for change and experiment began to fade. A sharp middle-class reaction against further upheaval grew increasingly more apparent. Amid this atmosphere of exhaustion and accumulated irritations, only a strong, united, and determined group of leaders in Congress could push ahead with new programs.

## The Supreme Court Struggle

But Roosevelt never informed his Congressional lieutenants of the staggering new measure he proposed in February, 1937. The Supreme Court, he told the Congress and the nation, had obstructed vital legislation. It had grown old and conservative; it was out of touch with the times; it could not keep up with the flood of cases before it; it needed new blood. Furthermore, the President argued, the framers of the Constitution had deliberately left the number of judges on the Court flexible because they knew that changing times would require changes in the makeup of the Court. For every Supreme Court justice who failed to leave the bench at seventy, Roosevelt now proposed, the President would be empowered to appoint an additional justice. Under the legislation sent to Congress,

he would be authorized to add as many as six new justices to the Court.

A large part of FDR's argument seemed clearly disingenuous. Not the efficiency of the Court but its conservatism was the real issue. In a long series of cases a great deal of the basic legislation of the early New Deal—NRA, AAA, the Railroad Retirement Act, the Farm Mortgage Act— had been declared unconstitutional by the Supreme Court. In reaching decisions, the Court, particularly the conservative justices—George Sutherland, James C. McReynolds, Pierce Butler, and Willis Van Devanter—seemed to view any intervention by government in economic affairs with extreme suspicion. They were usually joined in their decisions by Chief Justice Charles Evans Hughes and Owen J. Roberts, while the progressive jurists—Louis D. Brandeis, Benjamin N. Cardozo, and Harlan F. Stone—often found themselves dissenting from the Court's opinion. By the majority's decisions, both state and federal governments were barred from interfering in a number of areas of economic life. Particularly, they seemed to interpret the interstate commerce clause as applying only to goods in transit across state lines, a view that infuriated Roosevelt. In *Butler* v. *United States*, for instance, the Court held the AAA unconstitutional because farm commodities were not interstate commerce and Congress could not therefore use the taxing power to regulate agriculture. No wonder that New Deal administrators lived in constant dread of judicial intervention. Even programs upheld by the Supreme Court, such as TVA, were harassed by injunctions granted by conservative judges in lower courts. Roosevelt, in basing his case against the judiciary on grounds of age and inefficiency, blundered seriously. "I made one major mistake," he admitted later, "when I first presented the plan. I did not place enough emphasis upon the real mischief—the kind of decisions which, as a studied and continued policy, had been coming down from the Supreme Court."

Opposition was widespread, not only from Republicans and conservative Democrats, but a number of Roosevelt's closest supporters in Congress now deserted him. A torrent of protest flooded in from journalists, lawyers, and the general public. Chief Justice Hughes threw a bombshell into the Senate hearings on the matter with a letter stating that the Court was abreast of its work and that increasing the Court's size would only reduce its efficiency. As witness after witness aired his opposition before the committee and the press, support for the plan faded. Roosevelt fought back hard but without his usual effectiveness. The

A cartoonist's comment on the court-packing plan, 1937. (Russell in the Los Angeles "Times"; New York Public Library Picture Collection.)

Court itself struck another strong defensive blow by upholding the Wagner Act and the Social Security law. Roosevelt still refused to abandon his scheme,

threatening privately to give open opposition to any Democrat who fought the Court plan. Once more the Court countered with a killing blow, timing the resignation of Justice Van Devanter with the crucial committee vote on the bill. Defeated, Roosevelt now tried for a compromise. Again he was thwarted, when his Senate Majority Leader, Joseph T. Robinson, died at the peak of the compromise effort. When Vice President Garner returned from Robinson's funeral he told Roosevelt what the President already suspected: "You are beat. You haven't got the votes."

Roosevelt accepted defeat with good grace. The shift of the Court toward liberalism in interpreting New Deal laws, he said, meant that he had won the war and lost only a campaign. As justice after justice retired, to be replaced by more liberal men, notably Hugo Black, William O. Douglas, and Felix Frankfurter, Roosevelt found the Court viewing his program with steadily increasing sympathy. After 1937, in fact, both federal and state governments were free to engage in extensive regulation of the nation's economic life. But the Court fight, nevertheless, left deep scars. It frightened still further the moderate middle-class voters who had supported FDR in his first term. It demonstrated, too, that the President was not invulnerable and that he could blunder badly when he failed to consult the skilled political leaders around him.

### The Roosevelt Recession

He barely recovered from the Court defeat when another crisis burst upon his Administration. In the fall of 1937 business activity went into a frightening nosedive. Stocks began once more to fall in value; production dropped; and ominous signs of rising unemployment appeared. The gains in employment and production since 1933 seemed about to be wiped out. For four years a slow revival of prosperity had been underway: The manufacturing index (1899 = 100) had risen from 197 in 1932 to 376 in 1937; industrial and residential construction had tripled in the same period; steel production had quadrupled since 1932; and personal income had risen about 50 per cent. But there were dark shadows in the picture. National income had still not reached its 1929 level, nearly seven million men were unemployed, and businessmen still feared to take risks. Only the deficit financing of the New Deal appeared to be keeping the recovery boom alive.

So optimistic was Roosevelt in early 1937, however, that he cut spending, shaved WPA rolls, and encouraged Morgenthau to begin planning for a balanced budget. By September the government deficit for 1937 was running at least two billion dollars lower than in preceding years. But now, as the economy dipped, he faced a cruel decision. Should he continue with his conservative budget policy, aimed at inspiring business confidence, or must he return to deficit spending? Even after stock market sales reached panicky proportions in October, Morgenthau continued to argue for a conservative policy, telling the Academy of Political Science in November that the government would make "a determined movement toward a balanced budget." The crisis worsened through the winter and early spring, however. Two million new jobless men applied for relief or WPA employment. On February 1, 1938, the British economist, John Maynard Keynes, wrote Roosevelt that government spending was the only recourse now. But still Roosevelt held out against a resumption of large-scale spending, hoping against hope that the economy would rally.

Finally, in April, 1938, reluctantly abandoning his hopes for a balanced budget, the President acted, announcing a new program of heavy spending for public works, conservation, slum clearance, farm relief, and other projects. Congress quickly supplied the new funds, business responded promptly, and the worst of the "Roosevelt Recession" was soon over. But it left the helpless feeling that the New Deal had become the prisoner of its own spending policies. In the Administration, Morgenthau, overruled, threatened to resign, but Roosevelt persuaded him to stay on. Outside it, former President Hoover and others were now more certain than ever that the New Deal was bankrupt and had brought ruin rather than recovery to the American people. But later, after the huge outlays for war had brought levels of production and employment undreamed of in 1938, many economists thought that Roosevelt's error in combating the depression had been not too much but too little spending. The war experience seemed to suggest, at any rate, that an unbalanced budget did not necessarily mean economic catastrophe.

Meanwhile, in 1937 and 1938, came the last flowering of New Deal reform measures. A United States Housing Authority was created in 1937 to wage war on the slums that disfigured America's large cities. Through it the government offered loans to state or local agencies undertaking to replace slum dwellings with low-rent public housing. By 1941 over five hundred such projects, containing 161,000 dwelling units, were under construction. To remedy complaints against the operation of the Securities and Exchange Commission, set up in 1934 to police the stock market, a thorough reorganization was effected. To meet some of the continuing problems of farmers, a Farm Security Administration was created to give aid to tenant farmers, share-croppers, and farm laborers; and a new AAA bill was approved in

1938 to permit a variety of approaches to marketing control (soil-conservation payments, marketing quotas, export subsidies, and crop loans) and allow the government to store bumper crops against lean years in an "ever-normal granary." Finally, in June, 1938, the Administration pushed through Congress the Fair Labor Standards Act, forbidding child labor and setting a minimum wage (25 cents an hour, to be raised gradually to 40 cents), and maximum hours (44 per week, later lowered to 40) for most workers in interstate industries. Time-and-a-half was to be paid for all overtime work. This law was the last major New Deal measure passed by Congress.

Also in 1938 Roosevelt began a crusade against monopoly, reversing the old NRA policy of suspending the antitrust laws and cooperating with business. "Among us today," the President announced, "a concentration of private power without equal in history is growing." One-tenth of one per cent of American corporations, he said, owned 52 per cent of all corporate assets. During the depression years monopoly had increased "at the expense of smaller competitors who are weakened by financial adversity." The real danger to American liberties, he warned, came not from government but from "that concentrated private economic power which is struggling so hard to master our democratic government." The large business interests, while proclaiming free enterprise, were in actual fact suppressing it, he held. Every major New Deal measure, according to Roosevelt, was under attack from business spokesmen. Like Wilson, FDR had come to regard bigness in industry as a danger to both economic and political democracy.

As a consequence of the President's new conviction, a trust-busting campaign was begun under Thurman Arnold, head of the Antitrust Division of the Depart-

ment of Justice; and the President and Congress jointly appointed a Temporary National Economic Committee to investigate the concentration of economic power in the United States. That Committee's hearings and studies yielded a series of fruitful reports on the state of the nation's economy. The Administration carried out several hundred large-scale investigations of businesses suspected of thwarting competition, and it tried almost a hundred cases in the courts. The antitrust drive proved especially popular with the old progressives, many of whom had been restive under the NRA policy.

## Purging the Disloyal

The exasperated President, discouraged by the turn of events since his re-election, suffered another sharp defeat in the mid-term elections of 1938. Determined to shoot back at the conservative Democrats who were sniping at his program in Congress, Roosevelt announced that he would intervene in several primary elections. This meant placing his own great prestige on the scales beside little-known liberal candidates in an effort to outbalance the weight of well-entrenched Democratic conservatives. Such well-known Democrats as Millard Tydings of Maryland, "Cotton Ed" Smith of South Carolina, and Walter George of Georgia came under the President's attack. With Senator George on the same platform, FDR, after calling him "my personal friend" and "a gentleman and a scholar," assailed him for failing to show "a constant active fighting attitude in favor of the broad objectives of the party and of the Government as they are constituted today." It was a dramatic and courageous performance, but to no avail. George, Smith, Tydings, and most of the men Roosevelt opposed came through the purge with colors flying. The President had intervened with too little and too late. For five years he had failed to reorganize his party around New Deal objectives but had been content to work with all shades of opinion. His personal popularity and political skill, still undiminished, were not transferable to little-known men fighting well-organized machines. The day had passed when Roosevelt could work his magic, almost without opposition, in the halls of Congress.

By the end of 1938, with the New Deal becalmed, Republicans registered their first Congressional gains in ten years. They, with the help of conservative Democrats, could now block further reform measures. Only the President's executive reorganization plan, which they did not strongly oppose, passed the gauntlet of Congress in 1939. Under its provisions, the President was allowed to regroup and simplify the many federal agencies, boards, and other administrative units that had grown up since TR's day. Roosevelt immediately re-grouped some fifty governmental units in the executive departments, principally into three new agencies, the Federal Security Agency, the Federal Works Agency, and the Federal Loan Agency, and reorganized the executive office of the President.

Meanwhile, the growing threat of war in Europe had begun to put domestic affairs in the shade. The entire nation watched in breathless suspense the events leading to the Munich Conference in September, 1938. Four months later, in a message to the new Congress, Roosevelt declared that "We have passed the period of internal conflict in the launching of our program of social reform." The energies frustrated by political stalemate began to find release in the international arena. More and more of the President's valuable time was taken up with the threat of imminent war in Europe. By 1939, the New Deal was over.

## THE ENDURING NEW DEAL

The world crisis of the late thirties was not unrelated to the economic crisis of the early thirties. Everywhere in the Western world the inheritance of democratic values was undergoing testing and redefinition in this crucial decade. Could individualism be reconciled with the new social demands of an industrial society? Could the Western democracies, torn by serious economic disorders at home, meet the menacing challenge of the self-confident totalitarians? Was freedom, as Carl Becker had suggested, only a way station on the road of human history?

### Changing Values

The central meaning of the New Deal, according to the Italian-American scholar, Mario Einaudi, was the boost it gave to the American democratic faith. Out of the experience of combating the depression grew a new sense of mutual dependence and an important extension of human rights and dignity. "Essentially," Professor Einaudi writes, the New Deal was "an effort to reestablish the sense of community in a free industrial society and to come to terms with its requirements," and it was also "the most important attempt in the twentieth century to affirm the validity and the central role of the political instruments of democracy in facing the crisis of our times. While democracy was being routed all over the world by the totalitarians and the technicians, it triumphed in the United States." *

* M. Einaudi, *The Roosevelt Revolution* (New York: Harcourt, Brace and Company, 1959), p. vii.

What was this new sense of community? It was the feeling, induced by prolonged crisis, of being responsible for one another's welfare. All were in the same boat; all had suffered together; now all were working to build a better life. "The spirit of the frontier husking bee," said Roosevelt in 1938, "is found today in carefully drafted statutes. . . ." The old adherents of individual freedom had stressed the rights which the individual enjoyed against the community; now people were stressing rights within the community, because everyone had a responsibility for the general welfare. The economic system, Americans came to see, existed to serve the whole community and not just a few; when it faltered, the government need not sit idly by and watch the whole community pay the price for the mistakes of a few. A democratic society could solve its own problems, master its own fate, and need not be hamstrung by economic dogma.

Democracy itself underwent a sharp redefinition. The word was used less and less to describe a form of government, more and more to characterize a way of life in which economic opportunity and social justice were as important as political rights. Political processes, said John Dewey, were a means of reaching vital social ends: the general welfare of the whole society and the full development of human beings as individuals. Democracy had fallen in other lands because it had been interpreted too narrowly. "It had not become part of the bone and blood of the people," he warned in 1937; "unless democratic habits of thought and action are part of the fiber of a people, political democracy is insecure. It cannot stand in isolation. It must be buttressed by the presence of democratic methods in all social relationships."

Strong government, the nineteenth century had believed, meant weak liberties. Hoover, too, had insisted that there was no middle way between the tyranny of strong government and the chaos of economic individualism. Every New Deal measure that strengthened governmental authority, the conservatives felt, threatened the old values of private freedom and limited government. In the growing bureaucracy of the federal government they saw the end of republican government in America. Many of them sincerely believed that democracy was already dead or dying, that it could not weather the crisis of the thirties. "Why is it," wrote Will Durant in 1934, "that democracy has fallen so rapidly from the high prestige which it had at the Armistice? . . . Why is it that in America itself —in the very temple and citadel of democracy—self-government has been held up to every ridicule, and many observers count it already dead?"

Against extremists on both sides, Roosevelt insisted there was a middle way. Between the do-nothing philosophy of Hoover and the do-all philosophy of Stalin lay a vast field for limited, pragmatic governmental intervention. Not strong government, but weak government, had produced the terrible regimes in Russia, Germany, and Italy. "Democracy has disappeared in several other great nations," said the President in 1938, "not because the people of those nations disliked democracy, but because they had grown tired of unemployment and insecurity, of seeing their children hungry while they sat helpless in the face of government confusion and government weakness through lack of leadership in government." It was in desperation that they chose to sacrifice liberty in the hope of "getting something to eat." To make democracy work in America, FDR warned, it must be shown that government is capable of protecting the security of the people.

Two American intellectual traditions met and coalesced in the crisis of the thirties to produce the New Deal. One of them, pragmatism, expressed the American's instinct for action, his distrust of dogma, and his preference for practical, trial-and-error solutions. The other, progressivism, had grown out of his compassion for the underdog, his faith in democracy's ability to preserve and strengthen itself, and his acceptance of the benevolent possibilities of regulatory action by government. The result was a dynamic, many-sided, politically-oriented reform movement, often inconsistent or contradictory, that dominated every area of American life and thought between 1933 and 1939. Concrete economic measures preceded any thought of abstract ideology. "The winter's coal, the plumbing, the interest on the mortgage, a good diet, the baby's milk," said Frances Perkins, "must always precede generalized abstract theory in our own thinking." The pragmatic revolution that began with James and his colleagues in the 1870's seemed thus to have culminated in a clean sweep of the fields of political and social thought.

Individualism in the old sense died in the nineteen-thirties. So did the traditional concept of limited government. Much, however, remained of the attitudes and values of an earlier day. Specifically, public belief in democratic processes was probably stronger at the end of the thirties than at the beginning; attachment to such individual freedoms as free speech and freedom of worship grew more tenacious in face of what was happening in Europe; and the traditional American optimistic faith in the future, while shaken, was still apparent even in the depths of depression. A new consensus of democratic values—less stridently individualistic, less materialistic perhaps, but still stressing individual freedom, self-government, equal opportunity, and confidence in America's future—had arisen in response to the continued impact of technological and social forces. This rekindled democratic faith would now be put to renewed trial and test in the totalitarian crisis that began in the late thirties.

## The Roosevelt Revolution

In assessing the meaning of the New Deal in American history, a few more questions must be answered. We know that the Roosevelt years brought a substantial shift in the economic balance of power among workers, farmers, businessmen, and the underprivileged and that this shift was accompanied, indeed made possible, by a vast increase in the powers and responsibilities of the federal government. But were these changes the natural fulfillment of earlier progressive aims or did they represent a sharp discontinuity with the historic past? Was the New Deal, in short, a revolutionary or an evolutionary break with American traditions? Did it in fact start us down the road to socialism, as some critics have charged? And how much of the New Deal has now become a permanent part of our national heritage? Let us see.

The kinship of the New Deal with the progressive movement is complex. A large part of the New Deal program seemed an extension and fulfillment of earlier progressive programs. The anti-monopoly crusade, parts of the AAA program, stock market controls, currency inflation, even TVA perhaps, would not have seemed strange to some political old-timers. Certainly the New Deal attracted the support of a number of the old progressives such as Ickes, Norris, LaFollette, and others. Roosevelt himself had known the progressive temper at first hand and had held an important office in the Wilson years. Nevertheless, there were significant differences. Roosevelt moved far beyond either Wilson or TR in the use he made of the powers of government. Not only did he use government to regulate economic life, as in Wilson's day, but under him it became a positive force guaranteeing a minimum standard of existence for the whole population. The national government now provided relief, established jobs, helped labor, bought surpluses, guaranteed deposits, democratized corporations, and redistributed income. In 1929, the most affluent 5 per cent of the population got a third of the nation's income; by 1939 it was getting only 27 per cent; and by 1952 its share had fallen to 16 per cent. This change, in large part, was due to tax and welfare policies started by Franklin Roosevelt. .

This revolution in the role of the federal government in American life was in fact the most striking change wrought by the New Deal. Even the cautious New York *Times*, in a kind of obituary of the New Deal in 1938, wrote that "an increasing number of Americans, irrespective of party line, have come to regard, as both necessary and desirable, a larger share of responsibility on the Government's part in the policing of financial markets, in the achievement of essential social reforms and in the attainment of a generally higher standard of living for underprivileged people." For the "quickening of the American conscience" that brought this change the *Times* credited Franklin Roosevelt.

Did the New Deal launch a socialistic program for the United States? Certainly FDR stole the thunder from the Socialists with some of his bolder measures. The New Deal split the Socialist vote, lured a number of the movement's leaders into the Roosevelt camp, and seriously weakened the party's appeal. The Socialist vote for Norman Thomas fell from 881,951 in 1932 to 187,720 in 1936. Ideological divisions further splintered Socialist influence. But most Americans did not think of the New Deal measures as socialistic in nature. Indeed, many argued that

only the energetic efforts of Roosevelt saved the floundering capitalistic system of private ownership and control. Without question he could have socialized both the banking system and the railroads, had he chosen, in 1933. He did not. Repeatedly, he said that he wanted to reform capitalism, not destroy it. And in this he largely succeeded.

Perhaps the most effective reply to the charge of socialism came from the Socialist leader, Norman Thomas. Was the New Deal socialism? Thomas asked over the radio in 1936. Emphatically not. FDR had not carried out the Socialist program —"except on a stretcher." Naming the major New Deal measures, he denied that they were socialistic. The banks? Roosevelt had given them back to the conservative bankers. The Holding Company Act? A real Socialist, said Thomas, would have nationalized the utilities companies, not merely broken them up. Social security? According to Thomas, the New Deal program was weak and inadequate. And so he continued down the list —NRA was state capitalism, AAA a capitalistic scheme to control production, and CCC only a forced-labor plan. None of the New Deal programs, with the possible exception of TVA, ever came close to meeting Thomas's Socialistic test of full public ownership and control of the basic factors of production.

Of the permanence of the Roosevelt Revolution there can now be little question. So long as Roosevelt was alive, it was sometimes argued that his reforms would collapse with the end of the hypnotic influence he exercised on American voters. But polls taken in 1948 revealed that even a majority of Republicans favored such major New Deal reforms as TVA and Social Security. Nor was the New Deal program repudiated by the incoming Republicans in 1953. No less than FDR, President Eisenhower was committed to the protection of prosperity by governmental action. No important New Deal measure was repealed in his administration. A decade after Roosevelt's death, then, the New Deal had become so much a part of American life that no political party or candidate dared to attack it publicly. The Roosevelt Revolu-

tion of 1933 to 1939, it now seems clear, brought a decisive transformation of American thought and attitudes in response to those new forces of industrialism, urbanism, science, and mass immigration unleashed in the closing years of the nineteenth century.

## LIFE AND LITERATURE IN THE THIRTIES

The new stream of values and attitudes in the 1930's flowed into nearly every nook and cranny of American life. A current of social-mindedness and concern for the future surged through the lives of men and women who, a decade earlier, were floundering in hopeless despair at the crassness and materialism of American life. Confronted with the suffering of millions at home and the disappearance of democracy abroad, they now rallied behind the forces of reform and in the process often found their faith in America and its democratic values restored.

Everywhere the depression cut into familiar patterns of thought and action and forced lives into new channels. Family life, morals, recreation, reading habits, even school attendance, were all touched by the economic storms that beat down upon the nation. Important demographic consequences were noticed as the depression deepened and lengthened. The rate of population growth slowed appreciably, the census of 1940 recording a figure of only 132 million as against 123 million in 1930; this was an increase of only 6 per cent, as compared with a 14 per cent rise in the twenties. The declining birth rate, along with advances in medical and health practice, caused the average age of the population to rise. The proportion of Americans over 65 years of age jumped from 5.4 per cent in 1930 to 6.9 in 1940. Census reports showed that Americans were still mobile, though

fewer sought the cities than in any decade of the century. People were now looking westward for opportunity—California's population, for instance, climbed 21 per cent in the thirties. Negroes continued to move north, though at a somewhat slower rate than in the prosperous years of World War I. And the movement of immigrants from overseas ceased almost altogether during the depression years.

### The Literature of Crisis

Amidst the ceaseless movement, biting poverty, and social upheaval of the thirties, American writers struggled to make their writing relevant to the concerns of a nation in crisis. No other group of Americans responded so sharply and sensitively to the change in the national mood as literary men and women. If freedom for the writer and artist was the dominant theme of the literary world of the twenties, concern for one's fellow man unified the writing of the thirties. Even Marxist writers now got a hearing as "proletarian" novelists, using literature as a vehicle of economic and social protest, penned bitter stories of dispossessed Americans fighting capitalistic greed and injustice. Throughout the decade, novelists, poets, and journalists alike were heavily influenced by the social and economic thought of liberals and radicals.

No two adjacent decades in American literary history contrasted so sharply as the twenties and thirties. John Dos Passos, whose career spanned both periods, pleaded with his fellow writers in 1930 to throw off the attitudes of cynicism and escape of the twenties and be concerned with what was happening about them. "It's as if the carnage of the European war and . . . the rapid mechanization of life has entirely dulled the imaginative response," he complained. The critic Bernard De Voto, looking back on the writing of the twenties, was even sharper in his criticism. "There is something intrinsically absurd," he charged, "in the image of a literary man informing a hundred and twenty million people that their ideals are base, their beliefs unworthy, their ideas vulgar, their institutions corrupt, and, in sum, their civilization too trivial to engage that literary man's respect."

It was John Dos Passos and John Steinbeck who in temperamentally different ways were most attuned to the changed social climate of the thirties. In the USA trilogy, Dos Passos wrote a kind of social history of the years of boom and bust before 1929. With passionate concern, he detailed the spiritual and moral collapse of a civilization built on selfishness and waste. After tracing the lives of a handful of representative figures of the New Era, the last volume closes with one of them dead in a drunken brawl, another the victim of an automobile smash-up, another suffering physical and moral disintegration in Hollywood, and still others abandoned, degenerate, or approaching nervous collapse. Their lives had been hollow; their motives purely selfish and materialistic; their end, he seems to say, deserved. In the final scene the homeless Vag stands beside the Lincoln Highway, hoping for a ride, while his

Head swims, belly tightens, wants crawl over his skin like ants: went to school, books said opportunity, ads promised speed, own your home, shine bigger than your neighbor, the

A Dust Bowl farmer raising a fence to keep it from being buried, Cimarron County, Oklahoma, 1936. Such men as this, driven from their farms, became the migrant "Okies" Steinbeck wrote of in "The Grapes of Wrath." (Farm Security Administration Collection, by Arthur Rothstein; Library of Congress.)

radiocrooner whispered girls, ghosts of platinum girls coaxed from the screen, millions in winnings were chalked up on the boards in the offices, paychecks were for hands willing to work, the cleared desk of an executive with three telephones on it;

waits with swimming head, needs knot the belly, idle hands numb, beside the speeding traffic.*

Steinbeck wrote the book that best evoked the atmosphere of crisis of the nineteen-thirties. In *The Grapes of Wrath*, the story of the dispossessed "Okies" who trekked to California in search of a future, he caught the divided spirit of the victims of economic catastrophe, afraid yet courageous, uncertain yet confident, bitter yet hopeful of a brighter future. The flight of the Joad family was symbolic of a civilization's failure to care for its own, an indictment of a way of life that sacrificed the happiness of man to the profit motive. A spirit of passionate indignation runs throughout this account of the nation's children hungry amidst

* J. Dos Passos, *The Big Money* (Boston: Houghton Mifflin, 1936), p. 561.

rotting food—"children dying of pellagra because profit cannot be taken from an orange"—and the great companies that 'did not know that the line between hunger and anger is a thin line."

Full of passion and righteous anger, Steinbeck's book was the *Uncle Tom's Cabin* of the depression years, a bitter yet poignant picture of what the blindness and insensitivity of men in high places had done to other human beings. It harked back to the reforming tradition of Garland, Norris, and London. And it pressed hard on the affirmative note in the midst of catastrophe: "You got to have patience," said Ma Joad to her son. "Why, Tom—us people will go on livin' when all them people is gone. Why, Tom, we're the people that live. They ain't gonna wipe us out. Why, we're the people—we go on."

This affirmative note was largely lacking in the raw, angry novels of James T. Farrell. No writer of the thirties attacked more pitilessly the spiritual poverty produced by an acquisitive, materialistic society. Like Dos Passos and Steinbeck, he wrote in a strongly naturalistic vein and was sharply influenced by the Marxist currents of the decade. Studs Lonigan, his most important literary creation, was a sensual, gregarious product of lower-middle-class Chicago who is brought to ruin by the relentless pressures of a coldly impersonal community. All the institutions that might have saved him—home, church, school—break down in the violent, primitive world of South Chicago. Studs finds his home life boring, strife-ridden, and largely irrelevant to his needs and interests. Church and school are mere rituals, drudgeries, without meaning to his adolescent concerns. Only the poolroom, the streets, the gang, and the burlesque shows can fill his appetite for sex, comradeship, and recognition. With Farrell, the school of literary naturalism that began with Crane and Dreiser had

found a fulfillment and a termination. The techniques of photographic realism, of raw shock, of sociological reporting, could go no further. Life, Farrell seemed to say with the seventeenth-century philosopher Hobbes, was poor, nasty, brutish, and short.

Other writers looked beyond the crisis of the thirties for the roots of the conflict in human existence. The hatreds and miseries of the world of William Faulkner, as depicted in a series of novels, found their origin in part in an older South of slavery and Reconstruction. The years of depression seemed only incidental to the playing out of a drama composed of human frailty, racial tensions, economic pressures, and the decay of the Southern aristocracy. No one has written of the modern South, its violence, its brooding memories, its abiding conflicts, with more power or deeper understanding than this gifted scion of an old Mississippi family. Farther east, the North Carolinian Thomas Wolfe likewise found that the awesome problems of human existence arose out of deeper soil than the depression of the thirties. In *You Can't Go Home Again*, he gave voice to his own deep conviction that mankind's implacable enemy was not born yesterday and did not come to maturity in 1929. Rather, said Wolfe, "the enemy is old as Time and evil as Hell and has been here with us from the beginning." The sinfulness of man, both Wolfe and Faulkner believed, could not be explained in any narrow framework of economic collapse or social determinism. Wolfe, like Faulkner, was strongly drawn to the example and promise of America in a world where freedom and human dignity were under mounting attack. In eloquent words he spoke of his faith that "the true fulfillment of our spirit, of our people, of our mighty and immortal land, is yet to come. I think the true discovery of our own democracy is still before us. And I think that all these things are certain as the morning, as inevitable as noon."

Among poets and dramatists stirred many of the same currents that found expression in novels. A new social consciousness marked much of the writing that appeared in the thirties. Stephen Vincent Benét, for instance, warned of the dangers of Fascism in *Litany for Dictatorship*, while Archibald MacLeash was urging appreciation of the common people in his *Public Speech*. Edna St. Vincent Millay, whose reputation in the twenties had rested on the freshness of her style, now wrote of a "Conversation at Midnight" about the pressing social concerns of the day; and Carl Sandburg, whose thumping verse had attracted much critical attention earlier, now affirmed simply in *The People, Yes** that

> The people will live on.
> The learning and blundering people will live on.
>> They will be tricked and sold and again sold
> And go back to the nourishing earth for rootholds,
>> The people so peculiar in renewal and comeback,
>> You can't laugh off their capacity to take it.

On the stage the social currents of the thirties found outlets in such political satires as *I'd Rather Be Right* by George S. Kaufman and Moss Hart, and in the powerful dramatization of Erskine Caldwell's *Tobacco Road*, a story of degradation among Southern sharecroppers.

### The New Deal and the Arts

Other playwrights, meanwhile, had banded together to form the Theater Union and the Group Theater in New York in order to produce leftist plays. Most of the leaders of the group—Elmer Rice, John Howard Lawson, Lillian Hellman, and especially Clifford Odets—were

\* C. Sandburg, *The People, Yes* (New York: Harcourt, Brace & World, 1936), stanza 107, p. 284.

strongly influenced by Marxism, and their plays sharply condemned the capitalistic system. One of the plays, *Waiting for Lefty*, by Clifford Odets, depicted a union meeting in progress during which a strong conflict develops between the militant membership and the reactionary leaders. As the play closes, a strike vote is put to the audience itself with a ringing challenge to join in the fight against greed and class domination.

The theater, like all the other arts, suffered a loss of financial and public support during the depression years. Enormous numbers of actors, painters, musicians, and writers were without jobs, and newcomers hesitated to enter such unpromising fields. Many artists argued that it was government's duty to support cultural endeavors that private philanthropy had failed to support. In 1935, under the WPA program, a Federal Arts Project was established to provide temporary employment for jobless writers and artists. In all, more than 40,000 persons participated. Artists, good and bad, were put to work at murals, paintings, and statues for public buildings or parks; community art centers were set up to give free instruction in the arts; and traveling exhibits brought works of art to many parts of the country where they were novel or strange. The music project supported symphony orchestras in over a hundred cities, arranged for the performance of new compositions, and brought concerts to many communities that would otherwise have been without them. Writers were put to work compiling guidebooks for the states.

More controversial was the theater project. Aside from forming 158 theatrical companies to stage shows at popular prices, it enabled scores of young writers to produce experimental plays. Many of them pleaded strongly for some kind of collectivist action against the alleged injustices of American life. Some of the plays were denounced as communistic and an explosive controversy developed. Finally, in 1939, Congress, because of the pressure, put an end to the project. In all, more than forty million persons saw the WPA plays, of whom half had never been inside a theater before.

The turmoil of the decade affected all quarters of the artists' world. Not only dramatists but painters, musicians, and other artists were drawn by the impulse to social action and by the desire to glorify America. A school of regional art burgeoned in the thirties that lovingly depicted American scenes and virtues. The Iowan Grant Wood painted the strong faces and lonely countryside of his native Midwest; John Steuart Curry described the struggles of rural Americans against the mighty forces of nature; and Thomas Hart Benton filled his canvases with sympathetic portraits of Southern sharecroppers and Negroes, while upbraiding his countrymen for failing to appreciate American art. "No American art," said the nationalistic Benton in 1932, "can come to those who do not live an American life, who do not have an American psychology, and who cannot find in America justification of their lives."

### The Great Audience

For the vast majority of Americans who rarely visited an art gallery or read the works of Steinbeck or Farrell the private world of imagination was often dominated by radio and motion pictures. Both were in their heyday in the nineteen-thirties. Radio had become commercially successful in the early twenties, beginning with station KDKA in Pittsburgh, and had grown rapidly since. Millions of American families gathered in the living room each evening to hear their favorite weekly drama, comedy show, variety program, or quiz show. As the news from Europe grew more grave in the late thirties, more and more time

was devoted to news broadcasts. Few older Americans will forget the voices of such well-known commentators as Elmer Davis, H. V. Kaltenborn, Lowell Thomas, or Raymond Gram Swing. At election time, every politician of note took to the air waves, reaching millions of voters at once; no one, however, was more successful in exploiting this new medium than the President himself.

For entertainment, radio's only serious competition in the thirties was provided by Hollywood. The motion-picture industry had grown up in the World War I period, became one of America's biggest businesses, and began the conversion to "talkies" in 1927. By 1930 the average weekly attendance at motion pictures

Shirley Temple, the epitome of escapist entertainment in the thirties. (Culver Pictures.)

had reached the incredible figure of one hundred million. The themes of the films produced were almost wholly escapist: light romances, historical spectacles, Western adventures, comedies, and detective stories. In a class by herself was Shirley Temple, the child star of the thirties, whose films were described by one critic as "small miracles of inoffensive sentimentality." Occasionally a film attempted to deal with some of the real problems of the period, as in the film version of *The Grapes of Wrath* or Charles Chaplin's *The Great Dictator*. On the whole, however, the film industry of the thirties contributed little to the understanding of the crisis that Americans were undergoing in their daily lives.

That a film like *The Great Dictator* should be produced at all was evidence of a growing American sensitivity to the totalitarian challenge to democratic values. Increasingly, as the turbulent years of the New Deal came to an end, the nation turned its attention outward once more. Europe again became the center of American concern as it had been in the days of Woodrow Wilson two decades before. America's business in Europe, Wilson had said in 1919, was unfinished. Twenty years later his compatriots realized vividly how right he was. We must now turn to an examination of those melancholy events that separated the Versailles Conference of 1919 from the Munich Pact of 1938.

## FOR FURTHER STUDY

*The books by Johnson, Mitchell, and Wecter cited at the end of Chapter Six continue to be especially useful for the topics dealt with in this chapter.*

**General Accounts**

D. Brogan, *The Era of Franklin D. Roosevelt* (New Haven: Yale University Press, 1950). A useful little summary of the main New Deal programs and conflicts.

D. Congdon (ed.), *The Thirties* (New York: Simon and Schuster, 1962). An outstanding anthology of political, literary, and journalistic writing of the nineteen-thirties.

M. Einaudi, *The Roosevelt Revolution* (New York: Harcourt, Brace, 1959). Aimed at Europeans as well as Americans, this is the most important single volume on the meaning and significance of the New Deal years.

* F. Freidel, *The New Deal in Historical Perspective* (Washington, D.C.: American Histori-

cal Association, 1959). This is a little pamphlet for teachers that summarizes recent scholarship on the New Deal.

* D. Perkins, *The New Age of Franklin Roosevelt, 1932-45* (Chicago: U. of Chicago Press, 1957). Another short, masterly survey of the whole Roosevelt period.

J. Woods, *Roosevelt and Modern America* (New York: Macmillan, 1959). A good little volume in the British "Teach Yourself History" series.

**Special Studies**

* F. Allen, *Since Yesterday* (New York: Harper, 1939). An entertaining, informal history of the 1930's that does not quite come up to his brilliant *Only Yesterday*.

J. Blum, *From the Morgenthau Diaries: Years of Crisis, 1928-1938* (Boston: Houghton

Mifflin, 1959). An invaluable, closely researched account of Morgenthau's public activities based chiefly on the diaries.

J. Burns, *Roosevelt: The Lion and the Fox* (New York: Harcourt, Brace, 1956). A brilliant political biography that focuses sharply on the strengths and weaknesses of Roosevelt's leadership.

* A. Cope and F. Krinsky (eds.), *Franklin D. Roosevelt and the Supreme Court* (Boston: Heath, 1952). A good collection of materials on the controversy over the court-packing plan.

* W. Davies and W. Goetzman (eds.), *The New Deal and Business Recovery* (New York: Holt, 1960). A stimulating pamphlet containing documentary excerpts and editorial commentary on the NRA and AAA programs.

J. Farley, *Behind the Ballots* (New York: Harcourt, Brace,

* Starred books are available in paperbound editions.

1938). Interesting glimpses of the career and thinking of FDR's political strategist.

————, *Jim Farley's Story* (New York: Whittlesey House, 1948). A later, fuller, and much more critical account of Farley's years with Roosevelt.

J. Flynn, *The Roosevelt Myth* (New York: Devin-Adair Company, rev. ed., 1956). The most unsympathetic full-length account of Roosevelt and the New Deal yet written.

D. Fusfield, *The Economic Thought of Franklin D. Roosevelt and the Origins of the New Deal* (New York: Columbia U. Press, 1956). Argues that FDR had a more coherent economic philosophy than other writers have been willing to admit.

H. Ickes, *The Secret Diary of Harold L. Ickes*, 3 volumes (New York: Simon and Schuster, 1953-1954). A mine of "inside" information and personal reactions to the New Deal by one of the most prolific diarists of the Roosevelt administration.

R. Jackson, *The Struggle for Judicial Supremacy* (New York: Knopf, 1941). One of the best treatments of the court fight by one of Roosevelt's Attorney-Generals who subsequently became a member of the Supreme Court himself.

D. Lilienthal, *TVA: Democracy on the March* (New York: Harper, 1944). An eloquent affirmation of faith in the regional approach to economic development by a long-time chairman of the TVA.

R. Lord, *The Wallaces of Iowa* (Boston: Houghton Mifflin, 1947). A warm portrait of several generations of the Wallace family, of which approximately half is devoted to Henry A. Wallace.

* S. Lubell, *The Future of American Politics* (New York: Harper, 1951). An immensely suggestive book centering on the revolution in modern politics occasioned by mass immigration and the rise of the city.

F. Perkins, *The Roosevelt I Knew* (New York: Viking, 1946). Of all the intimate memoirs by those who knew FDR, none has surpassed this one for insight and understanding.

* D. Potter and W. Goetzmann (eds.), *The New Deal and Employment* (New York: Holt, 1960). A useful collection of documentary material and connecting comment on the Wagner Act and WPA in pamphlet form.

E. Robinson, *The Roosevelt Leadership, 1933-1945* (Philadelphia: Lippincott, 1955). A study stressing the weaknesses in Roosevelt's leadership.

* E. Roosevelt, *This I Remember* (New York: Harper, 1949). Indispensable for the personal and family side of Roosevelt's life.

S. Rosenman, *Working with Roosevelt* (New York: Harper, 1952). Excellent for understanding how FDR's speeches were put together.

A. Schlesinger Jr., *The Coming of the New Deal* (Boston: Houghton Mifflin, 1959), and *The Politics of Upheaval* (Boston: Houghton Mifflin, 1960). These are volumes 2 and 3 of Schlesinger's monumental study of "The Age of Roosevelt," by all odds the most important and thorough study yet made of the Roosevelt years.

* R. Sherwood, *Roosevelt and Hopkins* (New York: Harper, 1948). A Pulitzer-Prize winning study of the relations between FDR and the man who became virtually his "assistant President."

R. Tugwell, *The Democratic Roosevelt* (Garden City, N.Y.: Doubleday, 1957). A massive biography by a former "Braintruster" stressing the impact of FDR's early life on his later outlook and policies.

## Fiction and Drama

* J. Dos Passos, *U.S.A.* (New York: The Modern Library, 1937). A three-part narrative of life in the United States from the turn of the century to 1930 portrayed through the lives of several characters interspersed with snatches of biography, newspaper headlines, and popular songs.

* J. Farrell, *Studs Lonigan* (New York: The Modern Library, 1938). Another trilogy of novels depicting the youth and decline of a Chicago youngster.

C. Odets, *Six Plays by Clifford Odets* (New York: The Modern Library, 1939). Contains "Waiting for Lefty," a representative play of the strife-torn thirties.

* J. Steinbeck, *Grapes of Wrath* (New York: The Modern Library, 1939). The novel that best caught the perplexed and angry mood of the thirties.

* T. Wolfe, *You Can't Go Home Again* (New York: Harper and Brothers, 1940). The last novel of one of the most powerful writers of the present century.

## Films and Records

*F.D.R. Speaks* (Washington Records). Six hours of Roosevelt's speeches and fireside chats that provide an unparalleled insight into the atmosphere of the years from 1932 to 1945.

*Franklin Delano Roosevelt* (Official Films, 20 minutes, sound, black and white). Highlights of the public and private life of FDR from the beginning of his political career in 1910 to his death in 1945.

*I Can Hear It Now, 1933-1945* (Columbia Records, edited by Murrow and Friendly). A skillful recreation of the mood and life of these years through brief excerpts from speeches and public statements joined together by commentary from Edward R. Murrow.

*Life in the Thirties* (National Broadcasting Company, 58 minutes, sound, black and white). A wonderful evocation of the sights and sounds of the thirties in a "Project 20" film.

*Rendezvous with Destiny* (N.B.C. Documentary Records, edited by Cesar Saerchinger). Includes excerpts from 24 public speeches by FDR, including the first and second inaugural addresses and the message to Congress of January 4, 1939.

*The Three R's—New Deal Version* (National Educational Television, 29 minutes, sound, black and white). A televised discussion of the legislation and leadership of the period.

# Between Two Wars

Nazis saluting and crying "Heil Hitler", 1938.

THE MOOD OF THE TIMES

"I came out of all these experiences with one absolute conviction, which was: America, with its skill in organization and the valor of its sons, could win great wars. But it could not make lasting peace. I was convinced we must keep out of Old World wars, lend ourselves to measures preventing war, maintaining peace and healing the wounds of war.

"I came to this conclusion because of irreconcilable conflicts in concepts and historic experience between the New World and the Old World. They reached into depths of our international relations, government, social and economic life. They confronted me daily during the war, the Armistice, and in the confusion of making peace. . . .

"European countries had been afflicted for hundreds of years by rivalries and conflicts over their holdings and their expansions. They had relied, and inevitably must continue to rely, upon military strength, military alliances, "balances of power," and power politics for the protection of their possessions. . . .

"In sum, the forces which lay behind the rejection of American ideas at Paris were far deeper than the intrigues of diplomacy or the foibles of European statesmen. Here was the collision of civilizations that had grown three hundred years apart. The idealism of the Western World was in clash with deep forces in Europe with its racial *mores* and . . . grim necessities. . . ."

—HERBERT HOOVER, writing of the period after 1919

# THE RETREAT FROM EUROPE

Hoover's feelings about the war of 1914-1918 and its results mirrored a widespread reaction. Wilson's crusade in Europe, it gradually became clear, had not changed deeply rooted American convictions about foreign policy. No less than in Cleveland's day, Americans in the twenties insisted on the unique mission of the United States, the need to maintain independence of action and avoid permanent alliances, and the right to regulate European behavior in the Western hemisphere. The war, for all its casualties and suffering and high-flown rhetoric, seemed not to have penetrated very deeply into the substratum of American attitudes about foreign relations. "Hate, jealousy, bitterness, distrust, and anger are everywhere," complained the *Nation* in surveying the postwar scene; "the world is much worse off after the holy war to save humanity than it was before . . . the ghastly crime of taking part in any such mass murder punishes direly those who participate. Was this ever clearer than today?"

Disillusionment with the war, the peace treaties, and the League of Nations touched every facet of American thinking. Distrust of foreign developments and vigorous nationalism were the hallmarks of many postwar policies. The Red Scare of 1919, the new tariff levies of 1922, and the Immigration Act of 1924 were all linked in some degree to these attitudes. Harding interpreted his landslide election

to mean that he had a mandate to reject the League, and his successors did not dispute his judgment. Ignoring the manifesto of the thirty-one leading Republicans who had claimed that a vote for him was the best way to get the United States into the League, he announced instead that "the new Administration . . . definitely and decisively put aside all thoughts of entering the League of Nations. It doesn't propose to enter now, by the side door, back door, or cellar door."

## Underlying Assumptions

Beneath the diplomacy of the Harding-Coolidge era ran many strong currents of conviction about America's proper role abroad. The First World War, it was now assumed, had been a mistake, a deviation from the normal course of events that could not happen again. "It is as if the war had never been," wrote the novelist Robert Herrick in 1921. "Three years after the bloodiest conflict known to mankind . . . it is impossible to guess that anything momentous has happened to the world, to life itself since 1914." Europe, most Americans of the twenties seemed to feel, needed no help from the United States. It could solve its own problems; if not, that was no concern of ours. Americans might find it necessary to intervene in minor ways in the Far East, but Asians, too, could largely care for themselves. The real force for peace in the world,

248

many professed to believe, was moral strength rather than military weapons; since militarism led only to conflict and war, only an enlightened world opinion could produce an abiding peace. Hoover expressed this faith in moral force in memorable fashion in 1919:

It grows upon me daily that the United States is the one great moral reserve in the world today. We cannot maintain the independence of action through which this reserve is to be maintained if we allow ourselves to be dragged into European entanglements over a period of years. In my view, if the Allies cannot be brought to adopt peace on the basis of the 14 points, we should retire from Europe, lock, stock, and barrel. We should lend to the whole world our economic and moral strength or the world will swim in a sea of misery and disaster worse than the Dark Ages. If they cannot be brought to accept peace on this basis, our national honor is at stake and we should have to make peace independently and retire.

With minor exceptions, the United States did "retire from Europe, lock, stock, and barrel" in the twenties. Throughout most of the decade the American government maintained a frigid attitude toward the League of Nations and many Americans viewed even the World Court with suspicion and distrust. The victory of the "Irreconcilables" over Wilson now seemed complete. All through the twenties Republican administrations continually deferred to Senate leaders who zealously guarded their Constitutional prerogatives in foreign policy and were constantly wary of infringements of American sovereignty. In no other decade of the nation's history, probably, has the Senate enjoyed so commanding a role in foreign affairs.

But Wilsonism was not completely snuffed out. Among educators, liberal clergymen, and some journalists and politicians, the flame of Wilson's idealism burned on amid the suffocating isolationism of the twenties. Many joined the League of Nations Non-Partisan Association or the Woodrow Wilson Foundation, both of which were established to work for his objectives. From time to time, as in the World Court fight (see pp. 254-5), the old Wilsonians threw themselves again into the fray in the hope of winning at least a minor skirmish against the triumphant isolationists. A few even clung to the belief that the United States might yet enter the League. Though their efforts were largely fruitless, the zeal of the Wilsonians kept the isolationists on notice that their doctrines would not go unchallenged as in the old days before 1914. The isolationist position, though its defenders did not know it, had been undermined by the technological and social forces that were fashioning the modern world. For better or for worse, the United States was now a contestant in the world power struggle, and there could be no permanent turning back. "We cannot avoid meeting great issues," Theodore Roosevelt had said a quarter-century before. "All that we can determine for ourselves is whether we shall meet them well or ill." How right he was is well illustrated by the tragic story of American diplomacy between the wars.

## DIPLOMACY OF THE TWENTIES

### Hughes and the Washington Conference

No abler man sat in Harding's cabinet than his brilliant Secretary of State, Charles Evans Hughes. To him fell the Herculean task of nurturing a viable foreign policy in the rocky soil of the early twenties. Bound by the isolationists in his own party, he could make no move toward cooperating with the League or toward sharing with Europe in the solution of the problems left by the war. Yet he was realistic enough to know that the United States could not escape entirely from the responsibilities of power. What could he do to make American influence felt in the deteriorating world situation without alienating the isolationists? Hughes found the answer in disarmament. Here was ground upon which Republican moderates and isolationists could meet, where even Wilsonians would feel at home. If only the major powers could be induced to limit their armaments, Hughes felt, the pressure for American participation in defense treaties and the League of Nations would end, taxes could be cut, and the whole world would feel more secure.

Hughes worked for disarmament against a background of tension in the Far East and rivalry among the great powers for naval supremacy. By the time Hughes became Secretary in 1921, Americans were seriously concerned about events in the Orient. To begin with, the dispute over Shantung at Versailles had left a residue of bitterness in both America and Japan. This unpleasantness was heightened by the presence of American and Japanese troops in Siberia, where both were ostensibly guarding military supplies following the Soviet capitulation to Germany in 1918. In truth, the Americans were also keeping an eye on the Japanese, whose motives in the Siberian expedition were suspect. After the withdrawal of United States troops in 1920, the Japanese stayed on, thereby adding to American suspicions. Further ill-feeling was aroused by Japanese claims on Yap, a tiny island in the Carolines which formerly belonged to Germany, and which Wilson had wanted to see internationalized because of its strategic importance as a cable station. But the Japanese, with British

approval, had taken the island as a mandate in accordance with a general understanding with Britain that she would receive all German possession in the Northern Pacific. When Hughes took office, he raised a question as to Japan's legal right to the mandated islands.

A serious naval race was also in progress by 1921. Both Japan and the United States, as well as Great Britain, continued their wartime naval-building programs into the postwar era. The Japanese were fearful that the build-up of the American navy begun in 1916 and resumed at war's end was aimed at them. The British, alarmed by the American threat to their traditional supremacy on the seas, were determined to keep pace. The American government, for its part, was apprehensive about the Anglo-Japanese Alliance, which had been concluded originally in 1902 as a check on Russian and German ambitions in the Far East. Would Britain be forced by this Alliance to side with Japan if the Japanese went to war with the United States? The Canadian Prime Minister, Arthur Meighen, shared this apprehension and at a British Imperial Conference in London in 1921 strongly opposed renewal of the Alliance, due to expire that year.

Britain was now under heavy pressure to abandon or alter her treaty with Japan. Already, in December, 1920, Senator Borah had introduced a resolution, which Congress approved the following March, urging the President to invite Britain and Japan to a conference on the naval armaments race. In early July, exploratory messages were exchanged between London and Washington on the desirability of discussions of naval limitation and Far Eastern questions. Hughes could now press forward with his plan for a general conference of naval and Far Eastern powers in Washington. Only Japan proved reluctant. She qualified her final acceptance with the warning that the conference must avoid "problems such as are of sole concern to certain particular powers or such matters that may be regarded as accomplished facts. . . ."

Nine nations were represented at the Washington Conference of 1921-22. Aside from the representatives of Britain, Japan, and the United States, delegates came from France, Italy, Belgium, China, the Netherlands, and Portugal. It was the most important international conference since Versailles. Hughes made it very clear that this was to be an American show and that the initiative lay in his hands. He performed notably as ring-master, for, before the conference adjourned, the assembled dignitaries had negotiated three important treaties.

By far the most significant was the naval-limitation treaty. In his opening address as chairman of the conference, Hughes laid bare a startling proposal. For ten years, said Hughes, no capital ship should be constructed. Beyond this, reductions in current strength should be made by scrapping battleships, cruisers, and other vessels built or abuilding so that the navies of the United States, Britain, and Japan would maintain a ratio of 5-5-3 in all categories. This ratio reflected the existing strength of the three powers in capital ships built or under construction. In all, Hughes offered to scrap fifteen uncompleted American ships under the 1916 program and fifteen old battleships for a total of thirty capital ships with an aggregate tonnage of almost a million tons. The British, too, were to scrap some twenty-three ships, a greater destruction, as one writer put it, than "all the admirals of the world had destroyed in a cycle of centuries." The Japanese were also told that they must sink or abandon plans for a half-million tons of their fighting fleet. "With the acceptance of this plan," Hughes concluded, "the burden of meeting the demands of competition in naval armament will be lifted. Enormous sums will be released to aid the progress of civilization.

Chief participants at the Washington Disarmament Conference, left to right: A. J. Balfour (Britain), Hughes, Aristide Briand (France), Carlo Schanzer (Italy), Baron de Cartier de Marchienne (Belgium), and Prince Tokugawa (Japan). (Underwood & Underwood.)

. . . Preparation for offensive naval war will stop now."

A burst of excited cheering met Hughes' dramatic and unexpected proposals. "It was probably the most wonderful and sensational thing that ever occurred in an international conference," wrote one newspaperman. The meeting now got underway with tremendous momentum. The British were quick to accept the principles laid down by Hughes, and gradually the committees worked out the details of the treaty. But the Japanese, sensitive to the implications of inferiority in the 5-5-3 ratio, were reluctant to accept the Hughes program. Eventually, they too consented, but at the price of a promise from the United States not to fortify its Pacific Islands. This proved to be the critical concession: Both the United States and Britain now agreed to leave some of their Pacific possessions unarmed in order to gain Japanese acquiescence in their naval superiority. Then the French created further obstacles for Hughes by demanding 350,000 tons of capital ships, double the amount to which they were entitled on the basis of existing strength. Yet finally, they too succumbed, though they refused to agree to any limitation on cruisers, destroyers, or submarines. When Italy, like France, accepted the short end of a 5-5-3-1.75-1.75 ratio, the Five-Power Naval Treaty was concluded.

The problem of the Anglo-Japanese Alliance still remained, however. The British offered early in the conference to support a three-way pact with the United States and Japan by which all three powers would respect one another's rights in the Pacific and consult together if these rights were threatened. Hughes suggested that France be added to the pact —in part to salve aching French pride— and that the Anglo-Japanese Alliance be specifically abrogated. What resulted was the Four-Power Treaty, chiefly Hughes's work, which stipulated that in the event of threatening action from another power the signatories would "communicate with one another fully and frankly in order to arrive at an understanding as to the most efficient measures to be taken. . . ." This language proved to be a little strong, however, for some of the suspicious isolationists in the Senate, who forced an explanatory reservation that the treaty involved "no commitment to use armed force, no alliance, no obligation to join any defense." The disgusted Hughes wrote a friend that "I am at a loss to understand how those who have attained the high position of Senator can permit themselves to indulge in reckless characterization of other peoples and to manifest in a manner so injurious to the conduct of our foreign relations their opposition to the work of the conference."

Finally, the delegates of all nine nations turned their attention to the problem of China, and produced the Nine-Power Treaty. The signatories to it agreed to respect the sovereignty and independence of China and to uphold the principle of the Open Door. This was the most important affirmation of Hay's historic doctrine since he first enunciated it in 1899. But whatever force it carried was purely moral; no provision was made to defend the principles of the Open Door by force. Outside the framework of this treaty, the Japanese agreed to restore Chinese sovereignty in Shantung, as they had promised at Versailles, and announced their intention to surrender the special privileges in China they had claimed under the Twenty-One Demands. A further treaty growing out of the Washington Conference assured the United States of free access to the Japanese mandates awarded at Versailles. Japan promised, too, to withdraw from Siberia, an understanding which was accomplished later in 1922.

Despite the ameliorating effects of the

Washington Conference, the fruits of the meeting began to go sour when tension with Japan mounted again only two years later. In the immigration legislation introduced into Congress in 1924 was a provision that aliens ineligible to citizenship—meaning the Japanese—should be excluded altogether. The Japanese were furious. So was the State Department. Since the quota system, if applied to Japan, would have yielded only a trickle of Japanese immigrants each year, was it worthwhile, Hughes asked the chairman of the responsible House committee, "to affront a friendly nation with whom we have established the most cordial relations, and what gain would there be from such action?" Hughes, fearing that Japanese exclusion might undo the work of the Washington Conference, advised the Japanese ambassador to set down his country's position in a letter to the State Department, which he then turned over to Congress. Unfortunately, the letter contained a reference to the "grave consequences" that would follow enactment of the legislation. Congress took affront at this undiplomatic language—Lodge called the ambassador's letter a "veiled threat" to the United States—and rushed the measure through to passage. Resentment was profound in Japan, where the press was full of outraged denunciations of this insult to national pride. Indeed, the day on which the new law was to take effect was declared a day of national humiliation. "It is a sorry business," Hughes wrote a friend. "It has undone the work of the Washington Conference and implanted the seeds of an antagonism which are sure to bear fruit in the future."

Hughes' great achievements at the Washington Conference were further clouded in the years ahead: The limitations on armaments were to be renounced in the years of feverish rearmament of the thirties; in 1931, Japan violated the Nine-Power Treaty with impunity; and America's concessions to the Japanese on fortifications in the Pacific came back to haunt the nation later. Yet the Washington Conference, it should be said, did promote a general relaxation of international tension in the twenties. It did open a way out of the troublesome Anglo-Japanese Alliance that had caused American diplomats so much concern. It did give formal recognition to the American policy of the Open Door. And it did promote agreements on Yap, Shantung, and Japanese penetration in Siberia. Against the background of his time and circumstances, Hughes' achievement was considerable. He surrendered only potential American fortifications and naval superiority—he could never be certain that Congress would make them real—for concessions that seemed reasonable in the light of the times. In an era of narrow nationalism and limited vision, Hughes worked surely and effectively with the diplomatic weapons at his disposal. Historians of American diplomacy have consequently ranked him very high in the performance of his office.

### The Diplomacy of the Dollar

In addition to the arms race, another source of concern to Hughes and his successors was the vexing matter of the Allied war debts. All through the twenties the debtor nations urged the cancellation of the more than $10 billion in wartime loans owed the United States. Had not the money been used in the common fight against Kaiserism? Had it not been spent primarily in the United States itself for purchases that stimulated American prosperity? And how could the money be repaid anyway when gold was scarce in Europe and American tariffs discouraged any repayment in goods? But Americans of the twenties saw the matter differently. The money had unquestionably been *lent* to Europe; it was a valid debt; and to relieve

Europeans of responsibility for it would only throw a greater burden on American taxpayers. At the Versailles Conference, it was now argued, the Allies were the beneficiaries of rich territories and reparation payments taken from Germany, while the United States got nothing but ingratitude. Furthermore, several billion dollars of the outstanding debt had been advanced to the European nations *after* the shooting was over.

Gradually, under heavy American pressure, the debtor nations came to terms. The debts were to be repaid over long periods at an interest rate well below the originally scheduled 5 per cent. France, however, agreed to fund her debt only after settlement of the question of German reparations. Then when the Germans failed to meet their reparation payments in 1923, French troops entered the rich Ruhr Valley. It took a special committee, headed by the American Charles G. Dawes, to finally establish in 1924 a schedule of reparation payments more nearly in line with Germany's capacity to pay. Despite this unofficial cooperation with the Reparations Commission, the United States government continued to insist that the debts owed this country had no connection with reparations. That a number of the European nations were directly dependent on German payments to meet their American obligations was entirely ignored.

The flow of American capital to Europe in the twenties, as we have seen, helped to make this rickety system of international finance work. Thus the whole Western world came to be largely dependent on a high level of American economic activity, and a considerable part of American loans abroad went to pay existing international obligations. Yet the volume of foreign trade, while larger than before the war, failed to keep pace with the prosperity of the times. Though Herbert Hoover worked hard as Secretary of Commerce under two presidents to increase American business abroad, he did little to raise the volume of American imports. American foreign investments rose from $2.5 billion in 1914 to $13.5 billion in 1928, while the value of American imports increased only slightly from $2 billion to $4 billion in the same period. In the long run, European borrowers could pay the interest and principal on their investments and loans only by selling their goods and services to the United States. But the Fordney-McCumber Act of 1922, as we saw in Chapter Five, put new obstacles in the path of foreign trade with the United States. When the depression came, it struck a smashing blow at this wobbly financial structure. At the very time when large movements of American capital abroad might have stabilized European governments, the flow of capital was stopped. The political costs of this dollar diplomacy in governmental insecurity and the temptation to seek nationalistic solutions to economic problems were, according to Professor Herbert Feis, "lamentable." *

### The World Court Fight

Of all the foreign questions of the mid-twenties none had greater appeal for the old Wilsonians than the issue of American membership in the World Court. The idea for an international court of law to settle disputes was first advanced by John Hay through the American delegation to the First Hague Conference in 1899. It was brought up again by Elihu Root in the Second Hague Conference in 1907 and became a plank in the Republican-dominated League to Enforce Peace. Hughes, while a candidate for President, had warmly endorsed the idea in 1916. Now the Court was a reality, having been created by a special

* H. Feis, *The Diplomacy of the Dollar: First Era 1919-1932* (Baltimore: The Johns Hopkins Press, 1950), pp. 61-63.

committee that included Elihu Root and having been approved by the requisite number of states in 1921. Though it was an organ of the League of Nations, membership was open to states not members of the League.

Both Harding and Coolidge, though aloof from the League, urged American adherence to the World Court, and both political parties endorsed the idea in the summer of 1924. In March, 1925, the House of Representatives, by an overwhelming majority, passed a resolution favoring American participation in the Court. But the Senate, still strongly dominated by isolationist leaders, feared that the Court was a Trojan horse put forward by League supporters. Opposition from the isolationist press, especially the Hearst papers, grew intense. After bitter debate, the Senate approved adherence to the Court in 1926 but only with strong reservations concerning advisory opinions and America's right to full consultation in Court affairs. Members of the Court accepted all the reservations excepting the one on advisory opinions, which held that the Court must give no advisory opinion on a question involving the United States without the latter's consent. In 1929, the aging Root was sent to Europe once more to work out a formula under which the United States might join the Court, but before his compromise proposal could be acted on, the great depression had diverted attention away from the issue. New attempts were subsequently made in the Hoover and Roosevelt administrations to get the World Court protocol through the Senate but all efforts failed. The deep nationalism of the period was a stumbling block in the way of even this largely aimless step toward international cooperation.

The American attitude toward the League itself, however, became somewhat less hostile as the nineteen-twenties wore on. The United States withdrew completely at first from any contacts with League agencies; official correspondence from the League lay unanswered in government offices for weeks. Then, gradually, the government took a few cautious steps toward cooperation. Unofficial "observers" were sent to League meetings on such uncontroversial subjects as epidemic control and restriction of white slavery. In 1924 the United States was officially represented at a League conference on opium. By the end of the decade America had taken part in some forty League conferences and had stationed a number of permanent officials in Geneva. As the world crisis deepened in the early thirties, the ties between the United States and the League became even closer.

## Toward a New Latin American Policy

There was gradual change, too, in American policy toward her neighbors to the South. Harding, who had criticized Wilson's intervention in the Caribbean, took steps that led to the withdrawal of American marines from the Dominican Republic in 1924. Secretary Hughes, too, adopted a conciliatory attitude. He denied on several occasions any imperialistic connotations to the Monroe Doctrine. Though he did not renounce America's right of intervention in Latin America, he asserted that the United States had no intention "to superintend the affairs of our sister republics, to assert an overlordship, to consider the spread of our authority beyond our own domain as the aim of our policy, and to make our power the test of right in this hemisphere."

In 1925 Coolidge matched this assertion with action by withdrawing American marines from Nicaragua. Almost immediately, however, civil war broke out. With American property and lives in danger, the marines were returned. But since their presence seemed to many observers to give substantial support to the faction friendly to American interests, a storm of disapproval broke out throughout Latin America. At home there was also loud criticism, particularly from Democratic and anti-imperialist groups. Coolidge, asked if the United States were engaged in open hostilities against Nicaraguans, replied that "We are not making war on Nicaragua any more than a policeman on the street is making war on passers-by." Opposition mounted when the American-backed faction proved unable to suppress its enemies. Coolidge cast about for a way out of the dilemma. Finally, he sent Colonel Henry L. Stimson, who had been Taft's Secretary of War, to seek a solution in Nicaragua. Stimson worked out an agreement between the two leading factions calling for disarmament of both sides and American-supervised elections. The fairness of the subsequent elections is attested to by the triumphs of the anti-American party in the balloting of 1928, 1930, and 1932. Relations with Nicaragua improved steadily and, beginning in 1931, the marines were gradually withdrawn, the last of them in 1933.

Another serious Latin American controversy developed with Mexico. This one concerned mineral rights held there by a number of American corporations.

According to the Mexican Constitution of 1917, all the country's oil and mineral resources belonged to the nation. For a number of years, however, the Mexican government had respected American property titles that antedated the Constitution. Now President Calles, who was elected in 1924, began to carry out land reforms that threatened a number of these titles. In the United States, business and nationalistic groups applied pressure to the Coolidge administration to intervene in Mexico.

Once more, however, strong sentiment developed against forceful measures. As with Nicaragua, the State Department was accused of shaping its policy to favor American business interests. Again Coolidge fell back on the idea of a special mission. In 1927, he sent an old classmate, Dwight W. Morrow, to seek a peaceful solution. From the moment of Morrow's arrival in Mexico City, American-Mexican relations seemed to improve. His friendliness, simplicity, and good will captivated the Mexicans. "He applauded their food," wrote Harold Nicolson, "their climate, their agriculture, their hats, their ancient monuments, the bamboo cages in which they kept their tame parrots, their peasant industries, their patriotism, their volcanoes, even their finances.

Two diplomats who improved our Latin-American relations in the twenties: Henry L. Stimson (left), who went to Nicaragua, and Dwight W. Morrow, who was Ambassador to Mexico. (Both Culver Pictures.)

Here at last was a North American who neither patronized nor sneered." To aid his cause he brought the popular Charles A. Lindbergh, fresh from his conquest of the Atlantic, to Mexico and also imported the humorist Will Rogers for speeches and handshakes.

By the beginning of 1928 Morrow had settled some of the more vexing aspects of the controversy. Most important, he suggested that the Mexican Supreme Court be allowed to rule on the question of American oil rights, pointing out that if that body followed its earlier precedents a settlement would quickly follow. The court decision Morrow wished followed within a fortnight and serious negotiations began. Mexico now recognized the oil titles antedating 1917 and agreed to compensate American owners for expropriated properties acquired after that date. While there were still outstanding difficulties, which would erupt again in the thirties, Morrow succeeded in bringing about a new and friendly rapport between the two nations.

The Morrow Mission marked a turning point in American relations with Latin America. Increasingly, after 1928, the United States grew more conciliatory in its dealings with the states to the south and more reluctant to use force against them. Coolidge opened in person the Pan-American Conference held in Havana in 1928, and that fall President-elect Hoover made a good-will tour of South America. In the State Department, too, a remarkable change of attitude was indicated in a memorandum prepared by Undersecretary J. Reuben Clark. He concluded that the Roosevelt Corollary was "not justified by the terms of the Monroe Doctrine." Intervention in Latin American affairs, while perhaps necessary for self-preservation, said Clark, should not be represented as a corollary of Monroe's warning to Europe to keep hands off America. Two years later, in 1930,

Hoover ordered the publication of this so-called Clark Memorandum and assured the Latin American nations that its principles had now become American policy. Though the right of intervention was not renounced and though Latin Americans were still suspicious of the intentions of the United States, the policies of the Republican administrations of the twenties went far toward laying the foundations for the later Good Neighbor policy. The Stimson and Morrow missions, the withdrawal of some American troops, and the Clark Memorandum were major milestones on the road to better Latin American relations.

### Outlawing War

The year 1928 was also notable for one of the strangest pacts in the history of modern diplomacy. It followed the failure of the Geneva Disarmament Conference the year before to halt the naval race in the construction of cruisers, submarines, and other ships not limited by the Five-Power Treaty. The conviction was growing throughout the world that arms limitation was futile or impracticable. The way to insure peace, many were beginning to argue, was to abolish war altogether. When, in April, 1927, the Foreign Minister of France, Aristide Briand, announced that France was prepared to reach an agreement with the United States outlawing war, a number of American peace organizations advocated the acceptance of Briand's offer. Professor James T. Shotwell, who had helped convince Briand of the feasibility of such a pact, and other well-known Americans, including Senator William E. Borah and President Nicholas Murray Butler of Columbia University, led the fight for American participation. Their endorsement greatly embarrassed the Secretary of State, Frank B. Kellogg, to whom it seemed clear that France was seeking to bind the United States from threatening force if France should again be required to violate neutral rights as in 1914-1917.

As the pressures on Kellogg mounted, he searched diligently for a way out of the box he was in. He could no more refuse to denounce war, when asked publicly to do so, than he could declare himself in favor of sin. Finally, he found a solution. The antiwar pact, he proposed to Briand, should be broadened to include all peace-loving nations. This ploy was in accord with the general diplomatic rule-of-thumb that the effectiveness of a treaty decreases with the number of its signatories. The shoe was now on the other foot, as Briand squirmed to avoid the appearance of being opposed to the idea of all mankind's denouncing war. But finally he had to hop into Kellogg's trap. After lengthy diplomatic maneuvering, the Kellogg-Briand Pact was signed in Paris on August 27, 1928. It was ultimately approved by virtually every nation in the world. A world half-way between wars paused solemnly to assure itself that it opposed "recourse to war for the solution of international controversies, and renounce[d] it as an instrument of national policy. . . ." Only defensive wars —and what nation ever admitted that it was committing aggression?—were permitted under the pact. One American Senator called the pact an "international kiss," while another, Carter Glass of Virginia, told his constituents, "I am not willing that anybody in Virginia shall think that I am simple enough to suppose that it is worth a postage stamp in the direction of accomplishing permanent peace." But there were other Americans, probably more numerous, who believed that this Pact of Paris would usher in a new era of world peace. "Had an agreement of this kind been in existence in 1914," said President Coolidge, "there is every reason to suppose that it would have saved the situation and delivered the world from all the misery which was inflicted by the great war." Later, the pact would be used to bolster the argument for collective security and to provide evidence of Germany's violation of international agreements.

## DEPRESSION AND DIPLOMACY, 1929–1933

When Herbert Hoover took office in 1929, the auspices for peace seemed more hopeful than at any time since the war. "There is the most profound outlook for peace today that we have had at any time in the last half century," Hoover wrote to Henry Stimson, his Secretary of State. The danger of war in the thirties, Hoover believed, was far less than it had been in the twenties.

Then came the depression. The impact of this economic catastrophe on politics and international finance was profound and lasting. Many of the European nations, as well as the United States, sought nationalistic solutions to their problems; the Versailles settlement came under increasing attack from the dissatisfied powers; and the questions of war debts and reparations brewed up a storm of new controversy. Their energies diverted by internal economic concerns, statesmen became increasingly timid in the democracies at the very time they were becoming more aggressive in Germany, Italy, and Japan. Within four years of the onset of the depression, Hitler had come to power in Germany, the Versailles settlement was in serious danger, and the peace of the Far East had been broken. "The old order was slipping sadly by 1933," Robert Ferrell writes, "and the cause of this change was, more than anything else, the sapping of the will of liberal elements in the populations of the Western nations: beset by economic disaster, people lacked courage to stand against aggression, especially when as in the years after 1929 the forces of disorder and immorality were moving in a veiled and not yet clearly recognizable manner."*

## The London Naval Conference of 1930

A final desperate effort at disarmament was mounted during the Hoover years. Hoover, alarmed at the sharp competition in cruisers and other lighter vessels since the Washington Conference, accepted with alacrity an invitation from Great Britain to hold a disarmament conference in London. The enterprise was plagued, however, by technical discussions and the unwillingness of the French to cooperate in further arms reduction without assurances of military support from the United States. The United States, Britain, and Japan finally reached an agreement setting an upper limit in all categories of vessels, but it was weakened by an escalator clause permitting the signatory powers to ignore the limitation if another nation not bound by the treaty should undertake a building program. All in all, the results were too meager to warrant the high hopes felt for the conference. One American newspaper complained that the United States had received "only crumbs, rather poor crumbs, too."

The Hoover Administration did its best to promote the cause at the last major conference on the subject during the interwar years, one held in Geneva in 1932. To this World Disarmament Conference Hoover proposed the abolition of all offensive weapons. When this was ig-

nored, he dramatically suggested that all existing armaments be cut one-third. But despite some enthusiasm for Hoover's plan, most of the nations represented at Geneva were fearful of the deteriorating world situation and reluctant to trust in formulas. After 1932, as the big nations turned one after another toward heavy rearmament, the dream of disarmament began to fade.

## The Hoover Moratorium

The deepening world depression sharply accentuated the problem of intergovernmental debts. Though Germany's burden of reparations had been further cut from the levels set in 1924 by the Young Plan in 1929—the work of a new committee headed by another American, Owen D. Young—she nevertheless found it difficult to meet her obligations in the depression years. The Allies in turn were unable to find the exchange necessary to meet their payments to the United States. The Hawley-Smoot Tariff contributed to the stagnation of trade, leaving few opportunities for international exchange. In 1931 financial panic spread from Austria across Europe, undermining the whole structure of intergovernmental debts, and then reached the United States, as we saw in Chapter 6.

To save the situation, President Hoover proposed a one-year moratorium on all intergovernmental payments. This was hailed in most European capitals as a masterful stroke at a critical moment in Western history. But then the Allies moved beyond Hoover's temporary moratorium to demand the cancellation of all such obligations. At Lausanne in 1932 Germany's creditors reached an agreement that called for the virtual cancellation of German reparations if a satisfactory solution to the war debt question could be reached with the United States. Hoover, however, would not con-

* R. Ferrell, *American Diplomacy in the Great Depression* (New Haven: Yale University Press, 1957), p. 5.

sider cancellation and continued to insist that reparations and war debts were unrelated. In actual fact, neither Germany nor the Allies were able to meet their international payments. At the end of 1932, six of the debtor nations, led by France, defaulted on their debts to the United States. Only Finland, with a tiny debt, kept up her payments during the thirties.

## The Manchurian Crisis

The axis of postwar history turned the world gradually from peace toward war during the depression years of the thirties. Events took place in Europe and the Far East that decisively affected the history of the world for years afterward. Indicative of what was to come was the trend of events in Manchuria, where Japanese and Russian ambitions had been in conflict for more than a quarter-century. First, in 1929, friction between China and Russia over the Chinese Eastern Railway led to an undeclared war. A Soviet army entered Manchuria in November in retaliation for Chinese violations of certain Russian treaty rights. Secretary Stimson sought to rally world opinion on behalf of peace, reminding both nations of their obligations under the Kellogg-Briand Pact. But the Soviet Foreign Minister sharply criticized Stimson for his intervention and expressed amazement that the United States, which did not recognize the Soviet government, should presume to offer it advice. Peace was restored only when the weak Chinese government agreed to respect Soviet treaty rights in Manchuria.

Second, and more serious, was the struggle between Japan and China in Manchuria. The Chinese resented the special position held by Japan in Manchuria, just as they did the special Russian rights. But the Japanese saw in Manchuria's mineral resources and thinly populated territory an ideal area for their own future economic expansion. They were also intensely fearful of the build-up of Soviet strength along the Siberian-Chinese border. A series of minor disputes between Japan and China culminated in a major crisis in 1931, when the Japanese army, following a bomb explosion on the line of the South Manchurian Railroad, moved out of the special railroad zone assigned it by treaty and occupied the city of Mukden.

China appealed for help as Japanese armies began to overrun all of southern Manchuria. Stimson, who had counseled patience at the first news of invasion, now convinced President Hoover that the United States should cooperate closely with the League of Nations. In the face of loud outcries from the isolationist press, an American was appointed to sit with the League Council while it considered the Manchurian crisis. In early 1932, Stimson laid down his Doctrine of Nonrecognition, saying that the United States "does not intend to recognize any situation, treaty, or agreement which may be brought about by means contrary to the covenants and obligations of the Pact of Paris. . . ." He expected Britain and France to follow his lead but was disappointed when Britain professed faith in Japan's intentions to hold to the Open Door policy. It became clear to the Japanese that the United States, its government acting alone and its populace divided in its thinking, would not exert force to stop Japanese aggression in Manchuria. "The American people," asserted the Philadelphia *Record*, "don't give a hoot in a rain barrel who controls North China."

Late in January, 1932, the Japanese moved to occupy Shanghai in order to punish the Chinese for boycott measures they had taken against Japanese trade. American sympathy for China, strong from the first, now increased sharply. Stimson said later that he was reminded

On opposite sides of the world in the thirties there were foretastes of the militarism and violence that were to sweep across the globe at the end of the decade. Left, in a Madrid barracks, Spanish loyalists discover the bodies of rebels who had killed themselves rather than surrender. Right, Japanese troops on their way to fight in Manchuria wave flags emblazoned with the rising sun, the national symbol. (Left, United Press; right, Underwood & Underwood.)

of the revulsion of feeling against Germany in 1914 after she had invaded Belgium. A number of Americans now began to urge some kind of action, many favoring an economic boycott. But others, probably more numerous, were fearful of the consequences. President Hoover, for one, was strongly opposed to economic coercion, believing that it would lead to war.

Stimson made one last effort to get Britain to take cooperative action in the crisis. He urged that a strong protest be made to Japan on the basis of the Nine-Power Treaty. Britain, however, responded coldly, so the project was abandoned. Failing in this, Stimson now presented his views in a public letter to Senator Borah, chairman of the Foreign Relations Committee, in which he referred to the Nine-Power Treaty and America's intention to stand on its treaty rights in the Far East. He urged other nations to follow the American example of not recognizing the Japanese conquest of Manchuria. The League of Nations subsequently adopted a resolution endorsing the Stimson Doctrine. It also approved the report of the Lytton Commission, appointed by the League, which had investigated and generally condemned Japan's action in Manchuria. But no one, including the United States, was willing to take forceful action to halt the Japanese advance.

It was often said in later years that World War II began with the Manchurian invasion of 1931. Indeed, the flood of aggression that surged through the thirties doubtless found one of its sources in the successful Japanese defiance of the League and world opinion. Though Stimson had pushed far beyond the timid isolationism of the twenties, he knew that American opinion would not sustain any use of force in the Far East. "Never in history," another Cabinet member wrote Stimson in 1932, "have the American people been so isolationist as now." So, isolationist America found itself in the anomalous position of condemning Japanese aggression while refusing to use military or economic power to halt it. That this was a dangerous and unrealistic attitude subsequent events were to prove conclusively.

261

## THE APPROACHING STORM, 1933–1938

### Roosevelt and Foreign Affairs

The nationalists of the postwar years, their influence heightened by domestic depression and the trend of events abroad, continued to hold sway during Franklin Roosevelt's first term as president. Though cosmopolitan in background and Wilsonian by conviction, FDR was too preoccupied with the New Deal in his first four years in office to dare any radical departures in foreign policy. His own policies as president scarcely departed from Hoover's on war debts, disarmament, cooperation with the League, and events in the Far East, and he continued Stimson's nonrecognition of Japanese conquests in Manchuria. He was the first Democratic candidate to deny explicitly any intention of getting the United States into the League. And he offered no resistance to Congressional pressures, which were motivated in part by a desire to avoid conflict with the Japanese, to get the United States out of the Philippines. Even his Good Neighbor policy in Latin America did not mark any sharp break with the recent past.

Roosevelt's innovations in foreign policy, such as recognizing Soviet Russia, were motivated as much by domestic events as by international considerations. Trade with the Soviets had fallen off sharply since the onset of the depression. Recognition of the Soviet Union, it was hoped, might open up a great new market for American goods. Ever since 1917 the United States had withheld from entering into diplomatic relations with the Soviet regime on the grounds that it had repudiated international agreements, inspired subversive propaganda, and would not honor claims or debts from the Czar-

ist or revolutionary period. Now, though the Russians said nothing explicit about claims or debts, they did promise to stop spreading revolutionary propaganda in the United States. This promise was not kept, however, and the hoped-for flood of Soviet trade also failed to materialize. As a result, relations between the two countries remained cool throughout the thirties.

Domestic considerations also caused Roosevelt to refuse to cooperate at the London Economic Conference of 1933. The purpose of this conference was to increase world trade and promote currency stabilization. Attention quickly centered on the latter question, especially the desirability for Britain and the United States to return to the gold standard. The gold bloc nations at the conference, notably France, Italy, and Switzerland, insisted that a return to an international monetary standard was essential to economic recovery. When Roosevelt received a currency-stabilization proposal from the conference, however, he vetoed it in a sharp message criticizing the delegates for their concentration on the currency question. Actually, Roosevelt was fearful that currency stabilization might lose for the United States the slight rise in prices that had been achieved since his inauguration, and, like all national leaders at the time, he was giving domestic recovery precedence over international cooperation. In accordance with the advice of his economic counselors, he wanted the dollar to remain flexible, a policy he knew would be difficult to maintain if the dollar were tied to world trade. Though Roosevelt was strongly criticized abroad for his action, he was loudly praised by many at home for setting national above international considerations. The whole episode was a vivid illustration of the way the depression affected the course of American and world diplomacy.

## Reciprocal Trading

Still, the desire for world trade prompted Roosevelt's widest immediate deviation from the policies of his predecessor. President Hoover had approved the notorious Hawley-Smoot Tariff, which had provoked, in Secretary Hull's words, a "vicious spiral of retaliation and counterretaliation." Hull believed that American recovery could be complete and lasting only with vigorous international trade. Such domestic industries as tobacco, cotton, copper, and light machinery, for instance, were heavily dependent on foreign markets. The drying up of trade had also deepened the depression in many European countries. Though President Roosevelt, intent on raising prices, was fearful at first of the effects of competition from cheap foreign goods, he was convinced by the enthusiastic reception given Hull's low-tariff ideas at the Inter-American Conference at Montevideo in December, 1933, that some reciprocal lowering of trade barriers was necessary. So, with the President's support, Hull's program for gradually reducing tariffs through piecemeal agreements with foreign countries was passed by Congress in June, 1934. The President was authorized by this Trade Agreements Act to negotiate pacts by which tariff rates could be reduced as much as 50 per cent in exchange for concessions by America's trade partners. Significantly, Congressional assent was not necessary for the conclusion of individual accords, thus clearing away an obstacle that had hindered earlier reciprocity treaties.

Between 1934 and 1939 Hull arranged trade agreements with twenty-one countries. Of these, the most important was with Canada: The United States removed duties on products that made up almost half the total annual purchases from Canada, while, in return, Canada made direct tariff reductions on almost a third of its dutiable imports from the United States. Significant agreements were also worked out with France, Great Britain, Brazil, and Czechoslovakia. The outbreak of war in 1939, though, put an end to negotiations with the industrial powers.

The Hull program opened up a new chapter in American tariff policy. It avoided both the "free-trade" ideal of the nineteenth century and the legislative logrolling that had plagued every previous attempt at tariff reform. In piecemeal fashion, Hull lowered American tariffs an estimated 29 per cent by the end of the thirties, simultaneously gaining concessions abroad for American exporters of cotton, tobacco, and other commodities. Under these conditions American exports increased more than 40 per cent during the decade. To many international observers the Hull program was one of the few hopeful signs of the time; it was, in Sumner Welles's words, "one spark of sanity in a world outlook that seemed wholly and hopelessly dark."

## Good Neighbor Policy

Another of Roosevelt's policies that gained almost universal approval during his first term was the deliberate cultivation of good relations with Latin America. This policy, which had roots in earlier administrations, was not, as it might at first seem, inconsistent with isolationism. The Monroe Doctrine, after all, was an expression of nationalism for the Western Hemisphere and embodied the idea of a New World separate from the Old. The use of that doctrine to support intervention in Latin America was actually relatively new and had recently been repudiated in the Clark

Memorandum. There was nothing in the foreign outlook of Americans during the interwar years that opposed the improvement of relations with their neighbors.

What was the Good Neighbor policy? In essence, it was simply the principle of nonintervention in the affairs of independent states. At the Montevideo conference in 1933 Secretary Hull gave his support to an inter-American pact which stated flatly that "No state has the right to intervene in the internal or external affairs of another." Roosevelt joined him in declaring from Washington that American policy was definitely opposed to any armed intervention. The reaction from the Latin American states was warm and enthusiastic. "There is in the White House," said the Mexican delegate, "an admirable, noble, and good man—a courageous man who knows the errors of the past but who feels that the errors really belong to the past."

The Good Neighbor policy was first seriously tested in Cuba, where grave disorders broke out in 1933. Hard-hit by depression and governed by a cruelly autocratic regime, the Cubans staged a violent general strike against their government. Roosevelt's special envoy, Sumner Welles, was convinced that the Cuban President, General Gerardo Machado, must step down before order could be restored. Threatening the withdrawal of diplomatic recognition and hinting at the use of troops, he succeeded in convincing Machado that he must resign. Yet Machado's successor, Dr. Carlos Manuel de Céspedes, was closely linked to the old regime and was quickly overthrown by Cuban Army troops led by Sergeant Fulgencio Batista. What should the United States do now? Welles again pressed for vigorous action, including the use of American warships, but FDR and Hull, more cautious, soft-pedaled talk of armed intervention. The Administration's caution was due, in part, to growing concern

throughout Latin America that the United States might intervene forcefully in Cuba. By the time of the Montevideo Conference in December, the situation in Cuba was completely stalemated. Fear was growing in Washington that the Latin American nations, particularly Mexico, might seize the initiative at Montevideo and force renunciation by the United States of its claim to the right to intervene in their affairs. But the crisis was eased by Hull's pledge of nonintervention at Montevideo and by Batista's action in January of putting a conservative into the post of president of Cuba. Later, in May, 1934, the Platt Amendment, which had given the United States the legal right to intervene in Cuba, was specifically abrogated by the American government. Out of the Cuban imbroglio of 1933-34, therefore, came the first concrete application of the Good Neighbor policy; this was followed in August by the withdrawal of the last United States marines from Haiti and, two years later, by a pact with Panama that redressed a number of grievances of that tiny republic.

With the danger of war in Europe becoming more imminent, Roosevelt moved to broaden the Good Neighbor policy into a collective security pact. In 1936, Roosevelt personally told the delegates to a special inter-American conference in Buenos Aires that the whole hemisphere must be "prepared to consult together for our mutual safety and our mutual good." The Monroe Doctrine, the delegates understood him to be saying, must be made multilateral. Two years later, at Lima, the American states declared themselves unanimously opposed to aggression and set up machinery for mutual discussion in times of emergency.

As the decade came to a close, the Good Neighbor policy faced its most severe trial in Mexico. In 1938, the Mexican government expropriated outright all foreign land and oil holdings, many of them owned by Americans. Pressures rose on the Roosevelt administration to take vigorous measures. The British, after seeking a settlement, broke off diplomatic relations with Mexico. But Roosevelt counseled patience and refused to countenance military or economic coercion against the Mexicans. In 1941, as the United States approached war, a settlement of American claims was made. Mexico agreed to pay $40 million to American claimants, exclusive of those holding oil titles, and consented to the establishment of a special Mexican-American commission to evaluate and adjudicate the oil claims. The commission's report, which valued the oil claims at $24 million (exclusive of Standard Oil claims, which were privately settled), was approved by the United States government despite strong protests from the oil companies. By 1949, all American oil properties in Mexico had been liquidated. Without question, the American government sacrificed a strong financial claim on the part of some of its citizens for the good will of the Mexican government. But when the United States entered the war, three weeks after the signing of the Mexican agreement, it began to reap the rewards of its policy in the remarkable unanimity of the American states.

## What Price Neutrality?

The depression of the thirties exacerbated the isolationist mood of the twenties. In trying to save itself, each nation disregarded the interests of its neighbors. Throughout the world the emphasis was on national recovery, manipulation of currencies, and protection against outside competition. Other nations were made scapegoats for the economic catastrophe; Hoover, as we have seen, blamed international causes for the American collapse. Distracted by their own concerns, bedeviled by domestic problems, the people in the Western democracies were extremely reluctant to venture into the international arena to combat the totalitarians. As Japan, then Germany and Italy, sought to break down the Versailles system, a mood of helpless timidity settled over the democratic world. The dangers to peace were underscored by embittered nationalists who counseled the United States and other countries to beware of being trapped again into fighting a needless war. "Keep us out of war" was the isolationist cry of the thirties, just as "Keep us out of the League" had been their slogan in the twenties.

Isolationism fed on the growing disgust at American entry into the First World War. Wilson's idealism was now portrayed as naive; Germany's responsibility for the war was denied; and American policy was condemned for either its unneutrality or its surrender to propagandists and munitions-makers. "If we can but understand how totally and terribly we were 'taken in' between 1914 and 1918," wrote the historian Harry Elmer Barnes, "we shall be the better prepared to be on our guard against the seductive lies and deceptions which will be put forward by similar groups when urging the necessity of another world catastrophe. . . ." * In their search for scapegoats, Barnes and other historical revisionists blamed Wilson, propaganda, unneutrality, European statesmen, or war profiteers for the American entrance into the war. Wilsonian idealism was likewise attacked in such novels as Dos Passos's *Three Soldiers* and Hemingway's *A Farewell to Arms*.

That American intervention in World War I had been a mistake was the conclusion of many citizens who followed the sensational 1934 investigations of the Nye

* H. Barnes, *The Genesis of the World War* (New York: Alfred A. Knopf, 1926), p. 682.

Committee into war-profiteering. Senator Gerald P. Nye of North Dakota, an extreme isolationist, summoned bankers and munitions manufacturers before his Senate group to substantiate his conviction that these "merchants of death" had lured the United States into the war. This conviction became basic isolationist doctrine, reinforcing the determination of many Americans not to get embroiled again in Europe's endless wars. Walter Millis's immensely influential book of 1935, *The Road to War*, pounded on the notes of America's economic ties to the Allies and the influence of British propaganda. On the book jacket appeared the warning of how "a peace-loving democracy, muddled but excited, misinformed and whipped to frenzy, embarked upon its greatest foreign war. . . . Read it and blush! Read it and beware!"

Out of the Nye investigations and the growing danger of war in Europe came the neutrality laws of 1935-1937. A joint resolution by Congress in 1935 prohibited the export of "arms, ammunition, or implements of war" to nations at war, and barred American vessels from carrying such weapons to the port of any belligerent country or to a neutral port for trans-shipment. The President was also authorized to restrict at his discretion the travel of American citizens on belligerent ships in wartime—clearly, the measure was aimed at avoiding a repetition of the problems that had brought the United States into the First World War. The resolution made no distinction in shipping arms between aggressor nations and victims of attack. This lack of flexibility, Roosevelt warned, as he reluctantly signed the measure, "might drag us into war instead of keeping us out."

When Italy invaded Ethiopia in 1935, FDR had no choice but to invoke the neutrality provisions. He did try to supplement the arms embargo with a "moral embargo" on oil and other supplies Italy

needed by asking American exporters to keep their shipments of these commodities at prewar levels. In 1936 the Spanish civil war presented a special problem, since it did not fall within the terms of the neutrality legislation. Roosevelt was determined, however, to follow Europe's lead in adopting a policy of nonintervention, and Congress quickly supported him in a resolution extending the arms embargo to the Spanish war. In actual fact,

Mussolini haranguing a mob. (United Press.)

the nonintervention policy was a farce, because both Hitler and Mussolini were giving active military aid to the rebels led by General Franco, while Stalin was giving some help to the Spanish government. The effect of these neutralist policies of the Western democracies, including the United States, was to deal collective security another hard blow, while playing into the hands of the Fascists by enabling them to establish a friendly government in Spain.

In 1937 Congress put the neutrality laws into so-called permanent form. The arms embargo and ban on shipping weapons were retained, American citizens were now forbidden to travel on belligerent ships instead of merely being warned that such travel was at their own risk, and a temporary "cash and carry" clause empowered the President to require that foodstuffs and other material not banned under the law be paid for in cash and transported in the belligerents' own vessels. This last provision expired in May, 1939, four months before the outbreak of World War II.

The United States was now prepared, or so it seemed, against being drawn into any new European war. Every precaution had been taken against repeating Wilson's supposed mistakes after 1914. The Neutrality Act, commented the New York *Herald Tribune* with heavy irony, ought to have been entitled: "An Act to Preserve the United States from Intervention in the War of 1914-1918." But the political analyst Samuel Lubell was perhaps closer to the truth when he suggested that the law might better have been called "An Act to Prove That Those Who Opposed Our Entry into the War of 1914-18 Were Right." * As some contemporary writers observed, the neutrality laws did a disservice to the cause of peace and democracy, for they gave unmistakable notice to Hitler and his kind that if they attacked the democracies, their victims could expect no aid from the United States. "I see two thugs about to start an assault on my honest neighbor next door," wrote Walter Lippmann. "As he may expect me to hand him a stick to help beat them off, I am signaling the

thugs to go ahead and I'll keep clear. I am neutral."

## The Growth of Fascism

By the time of the neutrality laws, the menace of Fascism to world peace had become starkly clear. In Italy, Germany, and Japan, in varying degree, totalitarian movements based on a complete rejection of the democratic, Christian values of Western civilization had come to power. In all three states, new leaders exalted power, glorified the state, and appealed to the national egos of their peoples. Individualism became a mark of disobedience to the state, democracy was called a sham and a myth, and the dignity of man found no place in their official doctrines. All opposition to the ruling parties was ruthlessly crushed. A grand design was smashed down with varying success on the body politic of all three states in an effort to create a single monolithic social structure. Total subordination, total control, and total loyalty became the hallmarks of a successful "totalitarian" state.

The German version of fascism was undoubtedly the most successful and the most totalitarian. Built on a claim of the biological superiority of Germans and Aryans as a race, Hitler set it as his goal to make them masters of the world. This involved exterminating the most inferior races and dominating the others. It further necessitated rooting out all vestiges of "degenerate" ideas and institutions. It was the task of the *leader* (Fuehrer) to get the job done. He was the self-appointed "savior" who must "redeem" the race, the nation, the *Volk*, from the misery heaped on them by Jews, Bolsheviks, Slavs, and the victorious Allies of World War I.

Playing his role as "redeemer," Hitler imposed his design on German society. He replaced the free-market system with a planned-price system, substituted state

* S. Lubell, *The Future of American Politics* (New York: Harper and Brothers, 1951), p. 141.

regulation for individual initiative, and altered the concept of individual ownership. The government became the total possession of the National Socialist Party. The secret police were given free reign, and the entire country was placed under the severest form of censorship. No institution, no family, no person, was beyond the party's control and surveillance. Jews were humiliated, beaten, robbed, and later slaughtered by the millions, while many other Germans were mustered into the army and trained to die for the fatherland. "War is the origin of all things. Let us go back to the primitive life of savages." This was Hitler's counsel.

In rapid succession, following his coming to power in 1933, Hitler took Germany out of the League, repudiated the Versailles Treaty, and began an intensive rearmament drive. While Mussolini's invasion of Ethiopia was giving alarm to Italy's former allies, England and France, Hitler seized the opportunity to remilitarize the Rhineland and occupy it with German troops in direct violation of the Versailles Treaty. Though Britain and France, along with other League nations, denounced the German action, they made no move to halt the spread of German power. This appeasement of the dictators in the Rhineland and in Ethiopia virtually put an end to hopes for a genuine system of collective security in Europe.

Meanwhile, across the world, the Japanese, too, caused Britain and America much concern by their belligerent talk and their expansionist designs on neighboring territory. Though Roosevelt and Hull stood by the Nonrecognition Doctrine, they did not attempt to open old wounds by challenging the Japanese position in Manchuria. On the surface, at least, relations between the two countries were friendly during much of Roosevelt's first term. But in 1937 the situation changed rapidly. Japanese armies, without a declaration of war, moved rapidly into North China and imposed Japanese rule on the conquered areas. As the American attitude toward this new aggression stiffened, the Japanese became more belligerent toward the United States and its citizens in Japan. Refusing to attend a conference of signers of the Nine-Power Treaty in Brussels in November, the Japanese denounced the treaty and all attempts to intervene in the Sino-Japanese war. Then, in December, 1937, an American gunboat, the *Panay*, was bombarded and sunk by Japanese planes in the Yangtze River in China. Though the flyers claimed the attack was a mistake, the visibility had been good and the American flag was prominently displayed. Many Americans were thoroughly aroused by the assault and only profuse Japanese apologies and offers of indemnity helped to calm them down. As the year 1938 opened, events in the Far East had produced a major crisis for United States policy, just as Hitler's moves in Europe had frightened the American people into the awful realization that war was possible.

## Isolationists and Internationalists

As the danger of war grew stronger, a deep fissure began to open up in American opinion. More and more, as the Germans, Italians, and Japanese hammered away at the Versailles settlement, a growing number of Americans began to speak out against the foolishness of the isolationist policy. The Neutrality Act of 1937, said a New York *Times* editorial writer, signalized the bankruptcy of American leadership. "Treaty-breaking governments and dictators," according to the *Times*, "have become convinced that for no cause short of actual invasion will the United States initiate or join in any effective movement to assure world peace." If the United States was out to save only its own skin, then it must bear a heavy responsibility for whatever should occur. Events were conceivable, the *Times* editor warned, that would "make junk overnight of the so-called Neutrality Act."

Other groups in American society were alarmed at the short-sightedness of American policy. The old Wilsonians rose once more to the challenge; Jews were shaken by Hitler's anti-Semitic programs; large numbers of intellectuals stirred to the danger confronting European democracy; and informed citizens generally began to awake to the threat posed by the revisionist powers. As they witnessed, both in Europe and the Far East, a recrudescence of doctrines of force and might, many Americans saw that more was involved than just economic justice between so-called "have" and "have-not" nations. "There are two irreconcilable systems of government in the world today," Harold Ickes wrote in his diary on December 18, 1937. "On the one side is fascism and on the other is democracy. . . . Pacifist though I am, I am becoming imbued with the idea that sooner or later the democracies of the world, if they are to survive, will have to join issue—armed issue—with the fascist nations. That will mean that America and Japan will be at war."

Two months before Ickes' diary entry, Franklin Roosevelt began the long and difficult fight to bring American opinion and might onto the side of those opposing Hitler and his allies. In a speech in Chicago, he declared that "peace-loving nations" must "make a concerted effort in opposition to those violations of treaties and those ignorings of humane instincts which are today creating a state of international anarchy and instability from which there is no escape through mere isolation or neutrality." War, he went on to say, should be quarantined like a contagious disease. Though the speech was strongly criticized—revealing the power of the isolationist press—it gave new courage

to those who were in the fight against isolationism in these critical years.

By the time of Roosevelt's "quarantine speech," the international situation had grown critical. Mussolini had completed his conquest of Ethiopia, Hitler had remilitarized the Rhineland and was preparing to take even bolder steps, and the Japanese military chiefs had invaded North China. It was in response to the last move that Roosevelt timed his quarantine message, for the invasion of China threatened American interests in the Far East and challenged the Open Door doctrine. Henry L. Stimson, now a private citizen, wrote a public letter to the New York *Times* in which he denounced the "wave of ostrich-like isolationism" that had paralyzed America's will. He urged American cooperation with the League, as in the Manchurian crisis, and praised Roosevelt's Chicago speech. Of the neutrality policy forced on the Administration by the isolationists Stimson said that it attempted "to impose a dead level of neutral conduct on the part of our Government between right and wrong, between an aggressor and its victim. . . . It won't work. Such a policy of amoral drift by such a safe and powerful nation as our own will only set back the hands of progress. It will not save us from entanglement. It will even make entanglement more certain."

Each move by the Administration to bring American power and influence to bear in the critical world situation brought anguished screams from the isolationists. Isolationism was at high tide in 1937 and 1938, and FDR was forced to move with extreme caution. For one thing, his own power and influence were sharply diminished by the Court fight at the very time when he needed public confidence behind his diplomacy. For another, public opinion, strongly affected by fear of war and revisionist interpretations of World War I, was a formidable barrier. In a poll in 1935, two out of every three Americans answered "No" to the question: "If one foreign nation insists upon attacking another, should the United States join with other nations to compel it to stop?" Two years later, another poll revealed that a similar number believed that American participation in World War I had been a mistake. In January, 1938, the isolationists forced a vote on the controversial Ludlow Amendment to the Constitution, which would have required a popular vote, except in case of attack, before Congress could declare war. Both Roosevelt and Hull spoke strongly against it, the former warning that it "would cripple any President in his conduct of our foreign relations, and it would encourage other nations to believe that they could violate American rights with impunity." By a vote of 209 to 188 a motion to consider the Amendment was turned down in the House of Representatives. This might be taken as the bench-mark of interwar isolationist strength.

Nineteen thirty-eight was a year of continual crisis. The battle over the Ludlow Amendment was followed by other critical international moves: Hitler's seizure of Austria; a moral embargo on sending planes to Japan; an American loan to China; and the crisis over Czechoslovakia. After he had incorporated Austria into the Third Reich, Hitler complained that Czechoslovakia was a wedge driven into the heart of the new Germany. Behind the Czech frontiers, in an area called the Sudetenland, lived three million Germans, who had long been a thorn in the side of the Prague government. Hitler carefully nurtured their complaints, while playing on Allied fears that he would make war if the Sudeten Germans were not incorporated into the German Reich. Only force, either from Russia or the Western powers, could have stopped Hitler. But they were suspicious of each other, fearful of war, and loath to believe that Hitler meant what he said. As Hitler prepared to attack Czechoslovakia, Prime Minister Neville Chamberlain of Britain flew to Germany to confer with him. Through Chamberlain's efforts a conference was called in Munich in late September, at which Great Britain and France granted Hitler everything he wanted. Chamberlain told the British people that he had brought back "peace with honor. I believe," he added, "it is peace in our time." But Winston Churchill, leader of the fight against appeasement, called the Munich pact "a total and unmitigated disaster."

Roosevelt tried desperately to use American influence in the crisis without making American commitments. It proved to be an impossibility for when

Der Fuehrer being welcomed in the Sudetenland as Nazi troops occupied the zone. Behind Hitler stands Goering. (United Press.)

it became clear that the United States would play no decisive role, he was largely ignored by both Chamberlain and Hitler. The crack between ideals and practice, between programs and preachments, that had opened several decades earlier in the making of American policy now became a dangerous gulf. Our hopes, our ideals, our values were all intimately involved in the European struggle, as Roosevelt and others keenly felt, but so strong was the isolationist grip on the minds of Americans that no statesman dared say openly what he knew to be true. "My theory is that if the democratic theory of government is fighting for its life," Ickes wrote in his diary in 1938, "we will have to fight for it sooner or later, and if we put it off too long, watching other democratic governments succumb to fascism, we will be forced to fight in the most disadvantageous circumstances."

As 1939 opened, Roosevelt went before Congress to deliver some bold and urgent thoughts on the world crisis. "A war which threatened to envelop the world in flames," he said of the Czech crisis, "has been averted; but it has become increasingly clear that world peace is not assured. . . . There comes a time in the affairs of men when they must prepare to defend, not their homes alone but the tenets of faith and humanity on which their churches, their governments and their very civilization are founded. The defense of religion, of democracy and of good faith among nations is all the same fight. To save one we must now make up our minds to save all."

Something more than mere words, said the President, might be necessary to defend historic American values. As yet he said nothing of force and hinted only at possible changes in the neutrality laws. But he had passed the turning point. For the next two-and-a-half years Roosevelt would fight to convert a nation that had long been swayed by isolationism into a bulwark of defense of democratic liberties. The image of Wilson, which he had done much to blur in his own first term, would now dominate his thoughts more and more. For a score of years, Americans had denied Wilson, berated his principles, scorned his ideals and his League—now they would awaken once more to his call for them to shoulder the responsibilities of power.

## FOR FURTHER STUDY

*The books by Bailey, Ickes, Johnson, and Pusey cited in previous chapters continue to be especially useful for the topics dealt with in this chapter.*

### General Accounts

N. Blake and O. Barck, Jr., *The United States in Its World Relations* (New York: McGraw-Hill, 1960). A recent and well-organized textbook in American diplomatic history.

R. Ferrell, *American Diplomacy* (New York: W. W. Norton, 1959). Another well-regarded text in diplomatic history.

A. Nevins and L. Hacker (eds.), *The United States and Its Place in World Affairs, 1918-1943* (Boston: Heath, 1943). A series of essays of varying merit on European and American diplomacy between the wars.

### Special Studies

* S. Adler, *The Isolationist Impulse* (New York: Abelard-Schuman Limited, 1957). A brilliant interpretation of the

* Starred books are available in paperbound editions.

sources and influence of isolationism on twentieth-century American diplomacy.

S. Bemis, *The Latin American Policy of the United States* (New York: Harcourt, Brace, 1943). This is a standard, though somewhat outdated, account.

T. Bisson, *America's Far Eastern Policy* (New York: Macmillan, 1945). An historical and critical survey with emphasis on the period 1931-1941.

E. Borchard and W. Lage,

*Neutrality for the United States* (New Haven: Yale U. Press, 1937). Argues strongly for the view that America's unneutrality brought us into World War I and that it should not be allowed to happen again.

R. Current, *Secretary Stimson* (New Brunswick, N.J.: Rutgers U. Press, 1954). A somewhat hostile account of Stimson's role in the making of American policy.

A. DeConde, *Herbert Hoover's Latin-American Policy* (Stanford: Stanford U. Press, 1951). A useful summary of Hoover's little-known efforts to improve relations with Latin America.

H. Feis, *The Diplomacy of the Dollar: First Era, 1919-1932* (Baltimore: The Johns Hopkins Press, 1950). A most useful little book on foreign economic policies of the twenties.

R. Ferrell, *American Diplomacy in the Great Depression* (New Haven: Yale U. Press, 1957). By all odds the best book to appear on the Hoover-Stimson foreign policies.

————, *Peace in Their Time* (New Haven: Yale U. Press, 1952). An important interpretation of the Kellogg-Briand Pact and its origins.

D. Fleming, *The United States and World Organization, 1920-1933* (New York: Columbia U. Press, 1938). A critical but very thorough account of America's relations with the League, as well as general American attitudes toward foreign affairs during these years.

A. Griswold, *The Far Eastern Policy of the United States* (New York: Harcourt, Brace, 1938). Still a basic study in a very difficult field.

E. Guerrant, *Roosevelt's Good Neighbor Policy* (Albuquerque: U. of New Mexico Press, 1950). A brief, factual survey of the main features of the Good Neighbor policy from 1933 to 1945.

C. Hull, *The Memoirs of Cordell Hull*, two volumes (New York: Macmillan, 1948). An indispensable source in dealing with Roosevelt's foreign policy.

E. Morison, *Turmoil and Tradition* (Boston: Houghton Mifflin, 1960). An excellent study of the life and times of Henry L. Stimson.

A. Nevins, *The New Deal and World Affairs* (New Haven: Yale U. Press, 1950). A brief but very useful account, covering the years from 1933 to 1945.

————, *The United States in a Chaotic World* (New Haven: Yale U. Press, 1950). From the same Yale Chronicles series as the preceding book, this volume covers the years 1918-1933.

R. Osgood, *Ideals and Self-Interest in America's Foreign Relations* (Chicago: U. of Chicago Press, 1953). A brilliant interpretation of the motives behind American foreign policy in the twentieth century.

D. Perkins, *A History of the Monroe Doctrine* (Boston: Little, Brown, 1955). A summary of the author's detailed studies of the Monroe Doctrine, this book contains some interesting chapters on American policy in Latin America in the interwar years.

H. Stimson and McG. Bundy, *On Active Service in Peace and War* (New York: Harper, 1947). A thoughtful and well-written memoir of one of the key figures in the diplomacy of the interwar period.

J. Vinson, *The Parchment Peace* (Athens: U. of Georgia Press, 1955). An interesting monograph on the role of the United States Senate in the Washington Conference.

————, *William E. Borah and the Outlawry of War* (Athens: U. of Georgia Press, 1957). Another monograph on the role of the Chairman of the Senate Foreign Relations Committee in the framing of the Kellogg-Briand Pact.

S. Welles, *The Time for Decision* (New York: Harper, 1944). Contains some interesting observations on the Good Neighbor policy by one of its principal architects.

## Fiction and Drama

M. Anderson and L. Stallings, "What Price Glory?" in *Three American Plays* (New York: Harcourt, Brace and Company, 1926). A drama that debunks war as glory and inquires into war's true effects.

J. Dos Passos, *Three Soldiers* (New York: Doran, 1921). A bitter invective against the monotony, tyranny, and degradation of life in the American army during World War I.

* E. Hemingway, *For Whom the Bell Tolls* (New York: Charles Scribner's Sons, 1940). A widely read story of love and war in Spain as guerrilla fighters, including an idealistic American, strike blows for freedom behind the front lines.

* E. Remarque, *All Quiet on the Western Front* (Boston: Little, Brown and Company, 1929). A powerful pacifistic novel of the twenties whose matter-of-fact descriptions of the horrors of war exerted a profound influence on the American mind.

## Films and Records

*Crisis at Munich* (Prudential Insurance Company, 28 minutes, sound, black and white). An outstanding documentary of the events surrounding the historic conference at Munich.

*From Kaiser to Fuehrer* (Prudential Insurance Company, 28 minutes, sound, black and white). How the defeat of Germany in World War I, the Allied indecisiveness at Versailles, and the Great Depression made possible the rise of Adolf Hitler.

*The Twisted Cross* (McGraw-Hill, 54 minutes, sound, black and white). The story of Hitler and the Nazi movement, taken largely from German news films.

*War in Spain* (Prudential Insurance Company, 28 minutes, sound, black and white). A good film record of the disastrous civil war that helped pave the way for World War II.

*World War II* (Prologue, USA) (Encyclopedia Britannica, 28 minutes, sound, black and white). The effect of world events on American opinion and policy from the invasion of Manchuria to Pearl Harbor.

1939-1945


# *Armageddon II*

## CHAPTER NINE

Marine patrol on Saipan.

THE MOOD OF THE TIMES

"The stream of human history appears to be rushing toward the brink of a cataract. . . . Events move faster than thought. Tomorrow the world will have been profoundly altered. It may be a world of Hitler triumphant, or of Hitler defeated, or of Hitler checked, with the final issue postponed to a later day. . . .

"What, then, shall we do? It is evidence of adherence to the American creed that so many Americans in these dark hours are asking that question. . . . since 1918 we have descended into a deep trough of skepticism and discouragement. The postwar generation of American youth has grown to manhood in an era of economic depression and conflicting ideologies. The declared enemies of democracy have been winning all the notable victories, and Americans admire success. . . .

"If we are to meet the attack of the formidable adversary who threatens us today, we must exceed him in force. There is not one force for totalitarianism and another for democracy. . . . A family, enjoying the felicities of home, does not, when a burglar is climbing in the window, say: 'Let us sit by the fireside and perfect our domestic life.' Unquestionably domestic life is better than repelling intruders, but those who love their homes love them so much as to leave them, if needs be, in order to defend them. . . .

"Isolationism is both shortsighted and unfaithful. At the heart of isolationism will usually be found some trace of moral apathy or confusion. To suppose that we can believe in democracy, and at the same time remain neutral in our hearts and wills, as between democracies and their avowed enemies, is nonsense. To believe in democracy for ourselves, and at the same time be indifferent to its fate elsewhere, is absurd. . . . If we are concerned morally, we are concerned emotionally and we are concerned universally. If in the name of freedom or tolerance or democracy we cultivate detachment, indifference, suspended judgment, localism, relativism, or passivity on these very issues themselves, we shall end by becoming disloyal to them in our own hearts."

—RALPH BARTON PERRY, 1940

# THE BATTLE AGAINST ISOLATION, 1939–1941

When, in 1939, war came to Europe like the last act of a classical tragedy, a conflict broke out almost immediately over America's proper relationship to the struggle. To Professor Perry and those who thought as he did, the issue seemed clear: The Nazi ideology revealed a lust for conquest that threatened democracy everywhere in the world. All the elements that had weakened international stability since 1900—the restlessness of Germany, the rise of Bolshevism, the growing exhaustion of the democracies, and the ambiguity of American policy—had now combined to produce a titanic world struggle with strong ideological significance. Would America belatedly reverse her isolationist policies of the twenties and thirties and sway the balance of power once more toward the democracies? Or would the United States interpret her national interest narrowly and ignore the American stake in an Allied victory? "Recent events have proved," warned Perry, "that history is made by those who make up their minds; provided they exist in sufficient numbers, [and] provided they act promptly, resolutely, and unitedly. . . ."

### Days of Crisis: 1939

All through the months preceding the outbreak of war in September, 1939, Roosevelt maneuvered, largely in vain, to strengthen the nation's bargaining position and to prevent the impending catastrophe. In his message to Congress in January he hinted that he might seek repeal of the arms embargo which, he said, could "actually give aid to an aggressor and deny it to the victim." Then, in March, Hitler occupied Prague. The President sent a long appeal to both Hitler and Mussolini asking them to give assurance that they would not attack any one of some thirty designated nations. Hitler's reply was to ridicule his message before the Reichstag in a brilliantly satirical speech. Though fruitless, FDR's move may have nevertheless served to indict the Fascist nations more clearly before America and the world.

During the summer of 1939, Roosevelt went further. With the Polish crisis at hand, he strongly advocated repeal of the arms embargo. By now it was clear that Britain and France intended to honor their pledges to aid Poland should Germany attack, and this meant a general European war. In place of the arms embargo the President suggested a "cash and carry" policy that would require belligerents to pay for war goods on delivery and transport them in their own ships. But opposition, especially from Republicans, was strong on Capitol Hill. Representative Vorys of Ohio spoke for many of his colleagues when he said that "The President's policy is to use the threat of our power to preserve a balance of power

276

in Europe. Opposed to this is the traditional American belief that the way to peace is for us to be neutral." In desperation, Roosevelt called a number of senators to the White House and explained the strong probability of war. But Senator Borah of Idaho, a long-time leader of the isolationists in Congress, denied that war was imminent and told Secretary of State Hull that he had sources of information in Europe superior to those of the State Department. It became clear that Roosevelt lacked the votes to repeal the arms embargo. So, as World War II opened in September, the vulnerable and unprepared Allies were barred by law from buying a single cartridge in the United States.

*"IS 'E FRENCH OR GERMAN, BERT?"*

A British cartoon comment on the "phony war."

The war began over Poland, when Hitler demanded the return of the Polish Corridor and the free city of Danzig to Germany. England and France, groping for a way to stop Hitler, opened desultory conversations with the Soviet Union.

But neither the pair of them nor Poland was prepared to pay Stalin's price for aid against Hitler. The German Fuehrer, however, was prepared to agree, at least for the moment, to Russian hegemony in Eastern Europe. With his eastern flank secured by the Nazi-Soviet pact of August 23, Hitler defied the western democracies by announcing his intention to take over Danzig and the Corridor. When the Poles resisted, Hitler sent his troops across the border on September 1, 1939. Two days later, Britain and France declared war. Within three weeks the Polish armies were routed and Warsaw had fallen to the Germans. The twenty-year truce was ended and the nations stood once more at Armageddon.

### "Phony War"

After issuing proclamations of neutrality, Roosevelt moved swiftly to repeal the arms embargo. To a special session of Congress he confessed his regret that he had ever signed the neutrality laws and argued that repeal would be more likely to keep the United States out of war than an ostrich-like attitude of isolation. He suggested again that a policy of cash-and-carry be applied to all munitions and raw materials wanted by the belligerents. He fought hard to bring the public to his view, but opposition was strong. A poll in October showed that only 57 per cent of the people favored the change. In Congress the isolationist attack was heavy. Led by such senators as Robert La Follette, Jr., Gerald Nye, and Hiram Johnson, and supported by the ailing Borah, the opponents of repeal fought hard and long. If the measure were passed, said Borah, it meant moral commitment to the Allies; eventually, Borah warned, "you will send your boys back to the slaughter pens of Europe." Finally, at the end of October, the Senate voted 63 to 30 for repeal and the House followed a few days later. The vote ran ominously along party lines, foretelling future Republican opposition to the President's attempts to aid Britain.

The next six months were quiet as, following his victory in Poland and the division of the spoils with Stalin, Hitler paused before assaulting the western democracies. Hearing only quiet on the western front, some Americans dubbed the European conflict a "phony war." Only Stalin's ruthless invasion of Finland excited the American public during the winter of 1939-40. This Soviet move to secure the Baltic front against the Germans was fiercely resisted by the Finns and aroused the indignation of most Americans. Roosevelt denounced the "dreadful rape of Finland," but refrained from any action that might drive the Soviets and Nazis even closer together. As yet there was no real concern in the United States that Germany might win the war. Henry Cabot Lodge, Jr., grandson of Wilson's opponent, told the Senate that "the chances of England and France being defeated are slim indeed. The choice seems to be between a defeat of Germany on the one hand and a stalemate on the other."

Lodge and millions of others changed their minds swiftly in the spring of 1940. In April, Hitler's legions struck suddenly at Norway and Denmark. A month later the grey-clad German troops began storming across the Dutch and Belgian frontiers in the now familiar *Blitzkrieg* fashion. The lightning thrust caught the Allies unprepared as Nazi dive bombers wrought havoc behind the Allies lines and masses of tanks broke through the Allies defenses. As Belgium teetered on the brink of collapse, German forces pierced through the rugged Ardennes country and shot across northern France. Veering toward the Channel, the onrushing German armor pinned a half-million Allied troops into an ever-narrowing salient around Dunkerque. The miraculous escape of the bulk of the British armies from that trap between May 26 and June 3 did not mitigate the catastrophe of the Allied defeat, however. For on June 22, 1940 all resistance to Hitler on the western front ceased. France was defeated; Britain stood in mortal peril; only a further miracle could prevent Hitler from winning total victory in the west. The new British leader, Winston Churchill, told a hushed House of Commons in early June that

we shall defend our Island whatever the cost may be, we shall fight on the beaches, we shall fight on the landing grounds, we shall fight in the fields, and in the streets, we shall fight in the hills; we shall never surrender, and even if, which I do not for a moment believe, this Island or a large part of it were subjugated and starving, then our Empire beyond the seas, armed and guarded by the British Fleet, would carry on the struggle, until, in God's good time, the New World with all its power and might steps forth to the rescue and liberation of the Old.

## The End of Complacency

The hammer blows dealt America's former Allies resounded across the Atlantic. The United States now faced the prospect of living in a world dominated by totalitarians. If Britain fell, the Atlantic would lie open to German penetration and possible control, and America would stand alone. The seriousness of the crisis brought a dramatic alteration in the thinking of most Americans. Now the American stake in British survival became starkly clear. Of the heroic evacuation of Dunkerque, the New York *Times* wrote: "In that harbor, in such a hell as never blazed on earth before, at the end of a lost battle, the rags and blemishes that have hidden the soul of democracy fell away. There, beaten and unconquered, she faced the enemy."

Indignant and helpless, the President had watched the collapse of France. He had tried vainly to keep Mussolini from joining the war and when the Italians finally leaped on a dying France, Roosevelt declared at Charlottesville, Virginia, that "On this tenth day of June, 1940, the hand that held the dagger has struck it into the back of its neighbor." He outlined American policy in the same speech. "In our American unity," he said, "we will pursue two obvious and simultaneous courses; we will extend to the opponents of force the material resources of this nation, and at the same time we will harness and speed up the use of those resources in order that we ourselves in the Americas may have equipment and training equal to the task of any emergency and every defense."

There was no opposition to his defense proposals. Before 1940 was ended, Congress had appropriated more than $17 billion for military and naval programs. It had also approved the first peacetime conscription bill in American history And it offered virtually no opposition to Roosevelt's efforts to tighten hemispheric defenses. At Havana, in July, 1940, the American nations agreed to regard any act of aggression in the Western hemisphere as being directed against all and they agreed further to oppose any change in the control of European colonies in the New World.

But there was less accord concerning America's proper policy toward beleaguered Britain. That America would be gravely affected by a Nazi victory almost no one denied. But was the danger great enough to aid Britain even at the risk of war? Should the United States "go it alone" and possibly face Hitler later without friend or ally? Most Americans refused to make this choice; probably a majority of them wished to remain at peace and to aid Great Britain at the same time. As time wore on, however, more and more were willing to help the British even if it meant war. In answer to the question: "Which of these two things is more important for the United States to try to do—to keep out of the war ourselves or to help England even at the risk of getting into the war?" the proportion of Americans choosing the latter alternative climbed from less than 40 per cent in May, 1940, to more than 60 per cent a year later.

As the Battle of Britain opened in August, Roosevelt took the first major step to aid her. In exchange for several bases in Newfoundland and Bermuda and the lease of others in the Western hemisphere, the President turned over fifty destroyers, politely described as "over-age," to the hard-pressed British. On

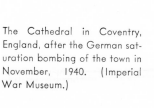

The Cathedral in Coventry, England, after the German saturation bombing of the town in November, 1940. (Imperial War Museum.)

behalf of his country, Winston Churchill pledged that the British fleet would never be surrendered to Germany. The exchange was widely applauded in the United States, though some critics assailed Roosevelt for acting without consulting Congress. Even the Republican candidate for President that fall expressed his guarded approval, though he agreed with the critics that FDR should have consulted Congress.

## Willkie versus Roosevelt: 1940

That Republican candidate of 1940 was a dark horse, Wendell L. Willkie from Indiana. As late as 1938 he had been a registered and voting Democrat. What was more surprising, he was a prominent figure in the unpopular utilities industry, had never run for office, and was almost completely unknown outside a small business circle. Why was he nominated? Primarily because, unlike the other leading contenders—Thomas E. Dewey of New York, Robert Taft of Ohio, and Arthur Vandenberg of Michigan—this Hoosier amateur semed acutely aware of the seriousness of the European situation. Alone among these leading Republican contenders, Willkie could be called an internationalist. In response to the fall of France, an early groundswell of Republican enthusiasm for Willkie had become a tidal wave by convention time and overwhelmed the delegates. He had other important qualifications besides internationalism. He was big, confident, and disarmingly frank; he had enthusiastic support from business and professional men in many parts of the country; even his amateurishness seemed an asset in the turbulent days of 1940. Though he disagreed with much of the New Deal, Willkie's criticism was tempered with appreciation for many of Roosevelt's relief and reform measures, and he refused to become a spokesman for blind reaction. In both domestic and foreign affairs he seemed to many to be the only candidate who could give responsible and effective opposition to the policies of Franklin Roosevelt.

Roosevelt meanwhile had come slowly to the decision to seek a third term as President. No serious competitor entered the lists as the convention in Chicago opened, for his silence on his intentions had driven most of the Democratic hopefuls from the field. Only Farley and Garner seemed to exert any efforts to attract support, while Hull simply appeared ready to accept the nomination if Roosevelt should tap him for the race. Across the nation, however, the vast majority of Democrats wanted Roosevelt. A number of the local machines, notably Mayor Kelly's group in Chicago and Mayor Hague's in Jersey City, saw in FDR their sole chance to elect their local and state tickets. Only Roosevelt, it was widely believed, could reverse the Republican tide that had set in since 1936.

When Senator Alben Barkley, as permanent chairman, began to read the President's message to the Chicago convention, a hush fell over the delegates. He had no wish to be a candidate again, the message read, and the delegates were free to vote for any candidate. But since he did not veto his renomination, the enthusiastic reception of Barkley's announcement left no doubt about whom the convention would choose. The President received 946 votes to Farley's 73 and Garner's 61 and a sprinkling for other candidates. The faithful Farley, now alienated from his chief over the third term and his own ambitions, moved to make the nomination unanimous. The next day, the only real opposition to Roosevelt's leadership broke out in a revolt against his selection of the liberal Henry Wallace, Secretary of Agriculture, as his running mate. But here, too, the Roosevelt backers were able to prevail.

The campaign was hard-fought. Wilkie

shocked right-wing Republicans by his endorsement of many Roosevelt policies, his rejection of isolationism, and his repudiation of the Republican tactics of 1936. His campaign theme became the effort to save American democracy from a dictatorial concentration of power in one man. His voice husky, his hair disheveled, he was seen and heard in thirty-four states as he carried his vigorous campaign across the country. But he was stacked against the greatest vote-getter in American history. Calm, seemingly unworried, Roosevelt ignored Willkie during the first month of the campaign. He made several inspection tours to national defense projects that critics charged were veiled campaign trips, but he made no political addresses until the closing days of the campaign. Then, shaken somewhat by the rise of Willkie support, he spoke in five major cities of the East and Middle West. In Boston, angry at Republican charges that he was a warmonger anxious to bring America into the war, he made a fateful statement that "Your boys are not going to be sent into any foreign wars." Like Wilson in 1916, he became the prisoner of a pledge which might not be in his power or America's interest to keep.

The verdict of 1940 was a hearty endorsement of Roosevelt. He captured the support of 27 million voters, or 54.7 per cent of those voting, while Willkie won 22 million votes. The President's labor and urban backing remained strong, and his margin of support from Jewish, Polish, and other anti-Hitler groups compensated for some losses in German and Italian districts. The farm vote, too, swung away from Roosevelt, apparently in response to both ethnic and economic motives. Throughout the campaign, Willkie had advocated an expanding economy in contrast to the New Deal stress on scarcity; this appealed strongly to farmers, who were growing increasingly restive under crop restrictions in a food-hungry world.

Basically, the victory was a personal one for Roosevelt—his party gained only six House seats, while losing three Senators. At stake, then, was not only the third term and Roosevelt's policy toward Britain but the leadership he had given the nation. More than any President since Jackson he seemed to draw down upon himself the love and hatred of great masses of human beings. No one, it was often said, could be neutral toward Roosevelt. But most Americans, surveying the change in the nation's spirit and economy since 1932, were willing to take a further chance on his leadership in yet another serious emergency.

### The Arsenal of Democracy

The election over, FDR turned again to Britain's critical situation. Since August, when the Battle of Britain had opened, British civilians had suffered indescribable horrors from the continual pounding of the *Luftwaffe*. Thousands of homes had been hit, large parts of many cities lay in ruins, and, worst of all, thousands of lives had been lost in the bombings. The game British response to this German onslaught stirred the admiration and respect of Americans. Churchill's government acted swiftly and, on the whole, effectively in these days of crisis. In the air, the Royal Air Force pilots fought brilliantly against their adversaries, destroying German planes at a rate of two to three times the British losses during the height of the battle. "Never in the field of human conflict," said Churchill for a proud nation, "was so much owed by so many to so few."

The British sorely needed help by the winter of 1940. Their funds for purchase of munitions in this country being virtually exhausted, many American feared to start again the loan policies that had left so bitter a heritage after the First World War. Roosevelt began to evolve in his own mind a plan that would meet

Britain's requirements and would also awaken Americans to the need for action. "Suppose my neighbor's home catches fire," said the President in an effective metaphor, "and I have a length of garden hose. . . . If he can take my garden hose and connect it up with his hydrant, I may help him to put out his fire." There should be no quarreling about how the hose was to be paid for when all that really mattered was stopping the fire. The United States, he said, should become "the great arsenal of democracy."

In January, 1941, Roosevelt supporters introduced into Congress the lend-lease plan, which authorized the President to sell, transfer, exchange, lease, or lend under whatever terms he thought appropriate the munitions and other things needed by Britain and other nations whose defense was vital to the security of the United States. There followed two months of passionate debate before the measure was finally passed. For no one doubted that the lend-lease bill committed the United States to the defeat of Germany. Its sponsors even argued that only help on a decisive scale could possibly tip the balance of force against Hitler. Many citizens still hoped that this might be achieved without the commitment of American men; but a growing majority by 1941 believed that America would ultimately join the war.

### The Isolationists In Extremis

Opponents of lend-lease charged that it meant certain war. It was difficult, of course, to argue that it would in no event bring the United States into the conflict. The choice lay with Hitler. Senator Barkley presented the case for lend-lease with clarity and force when he said that "the safest and surest way for the United States not to be compelled to be involved in war is to give such aid as will enable the countries which are now fighting Hitler to win." This did not mean, however,

"that under no circumstances in the future will we go to war; but I am certain that if England wins we shall be less likely to be required to go to war than if Hitler wins." Like most Americans, Barkley thought it more important that England win than that America should stay out of the war; but so long as there was any real chance that England might win without full-scale American intervention, then he favored a policy of "aid short of war."

The isolationists, beaten in the critical struggle over lend-lease, had passed the peak of their influence. Events made a mockery of their argument that America had no vital interests in Europe. Support for the isolationist view after 1940 drew heavily on traditional anti-British prejudices in certain ethnic groups and on strong partisan bias against FDR. The liberal idealism that had characterized so much of the opposition to American intervention in 1917 was far less important as a motive for isolationism in 1941. A few did express concern that another war might mean the extinction of democratic values at home and an end to domestic reform. Only a very few, however, continued to argue that no moral distinction could be drawn between the antagonists in the European struggle—the historian Harry Elmer Barnes, for one, could still write in 1939 that "There are not a few who prefer the forthright brutality and aggression of a Hitler to the smug double-crossing and sanctimonious hypocrisy of Britain's umbrella bearer"—and these few exerted virtually no influence.

In the fall of 1940 the America First movement had been organized by those who feared that Roosevelt's policies were leading the nation into a needless war. Made up heavily of Republicans, this group was led by such divergent personalities as General Robert E. Wood of the Sears, Roebuck Company, Charles A. Lindbergh, and Senator Burton K.

Wheeler of Montana. Though they brought up their heaviest artillery in the fight against lend-lease, they failed to halt the march of American sentiment. Basically, the America First position might be summarized as follows: The Axis victories in Europe had not jeopardized American security; Roosevelt's policy of aid to Britain, especially lend-lease, increased the likelihood of war; and even if Hitler should win, America would still be impregnable in its New World fortress. The security of Americans, leaders of the organization insisted, was not involved in England's tooth-and-nail struggle to survive.

Despite a considerable following, the America First movement never became truly national. It centered in the Midwest, particularly around Chicago, where the bulk of its members were found. Labor and farm organizations gave almost no support to the movement. Nor was it successful in raising the large sums of money necessary for a successful propaganda campaign. But it did exercise considerable influence during the year preceding the Pearl Harbor attack. Had it not been for the America First movement, the President would almost certainly have moved further and faster to help Britain against Hitler. But he feared the power of the isolationists in and out of Congress—some thought he exaggerated their influence—so he moved with extreme caution and often with indirection toward his goals.

### "The Irresponsibles"

While the America Firsters were mobilizing the forces of isolation, other citizens rallied behind the President. From the beginning of the world crisis, many had felt that the country was involved in the democracies' fight for survival, and they were now impatient with the President's equivocation and his concern over the strength of the isolationists.

"Why don't you tell our idol FDR to quit beating around the bush," a man wrote a friend of the President's in 1939. "Of *course* our first line of defense is the Maginot Line. Of *course* we cannot afford to let France and England get licked. Of *course* we should prepare to help them—first with munitions and then if that is not enough with everything we've got." He urged the President to stop stalling. "Why let these pussyfooting Senators kid the American people into the belief that we could stay out of another war?"

There were probably many who already felt as this correspondent did. They were joined by millions more in the terrifying spring of 1940. Some joined the Committee to Defend America by Aiding the Allies, which the old Kansas Progressive William Allen White helped to organize. The British, White told the nation, must be armed in order to give America time "to prepare for the inevi-

Charles Lindbergh and Senator Gerald P. Nye at an America First rally in New York, November, 1941. (United Press.)

table attack of the totalitarian powers upon our democracy, which must come unless Great Britain wins this war." White's Committee helped mightily in mobilizing the public behind the destroyer-bases trade, the lend-lease act, and other Administration measures.

Support for the President's policy came, too, from journalists, writers, and scholars who were alarmed at the growing totalitarian challenge to democratic values. Many leading newspapers, especially the New York *Times*, fought hard and long against the narrow nationalism that, they feared, was hampering effective American action in a time of danger. "There is no isolation," said the *Times* in a long editorial in early 1941, "there are only lines of defense." The real issue, the only issue, said the *Times*, was survival: survival of our culture, tradition, ideas, and way of life. A victorious Hitler would have the resources of twenty captive nations to pit against the last remaining democracy. "With Britain gone," the *Times* warned, "with all hope of resurrection denied to the little democracies that have contributed so generously to our civilization and our culture, with the hobnailed boots of an ignorant and obscene barbarism echoing in every capital from London to Athens, we should live in a new world, changed beyond all recognition."

Intellectuals, too, broke through the wall of indifference and cynicism that had surrounded their outlook on foreign affairs between the wars. They rediscovered the importance of power in the realization of ideals. The Fascist threat, many came to realize, could not be overcome by a denial of force and a refusal to meet evil head-on. Hemingway, symbol of the disillusioned spirit of the twenties, went to Europe to fight against the Spanish version of fascism. In *For Whom the Bell Tolls*, his idealistic hero gives up college teaching for a career as a dynamiter with the Spanish Loyalists. Surrounded by Fascist troops, he dies fighting, killing as many of the enemy as possible. Hemingway's title, taken from a sermon by John Donne, told the moral of his story: "No man is an Iland, entire of it self; . . . any man's death diminishes me, because I am involved in Mankinde; And therefore never send to know for whom the bell tolls; It tolls for thee."

American intellectuals, according to the Poet Archibald MacLeish in 1940, had been irresponsible to their high calling. Their cynicism, their attacks on idealism, their indifference to traditional values—these attitudes had weakened democracy and corrupted American ideals. Why, future historians would ask, had they not used their talents when there was still time to oppose the brutal tyranny of the totalitarians? Revolutionary gangs had perverted the thought of entire societies because those competent to answer them had remained silent. Writers and scholars, by cultivating objectivity and detachment even at the sacrifice of democratic values, had sought to free themselves of the personal responsibility that must go with freedom. "Why did we, scholars and writers in America in this time," the future would ask, "we who had been warned of our danger not only by explicit threats but by explicit action, why did we not fight while the weapons we used best—the weapons of ideas and words—could still be used against it?"[*]

The threat to democratic values from the advance of totalitarianism caused many intellectuals to reassess the relativistic assumptions on which they had based their thinking. The anthropologist Bronislaw Malinowski now contended that it was nonsense to argue that no universal moral judgment could be made of a political system like that of the Nazis. In the field of law, Karl Llewellyn of the Columbia Law School condemned the paralyz-

[*] A. MacLeish, "The Irresponsibles," *The Nation*, v. 150 (May 18, 1940), p. 618.

ing relativism that would make of law the mere expression of transitory mores. He reaffirmed in the spring of 1940 that "The goal of the law is justice, and judges, like other officials, are not free to be arbitrary." In other scholarly fields new interest sprang up in the principles and ideals on which American civilization rested. A spirit of nationalism issued forth in a burst of affirmative history, biography, and fiction centering on the American experience. "We wonder," wrote MacLeish in *Land of the Free*, "whether the dream of American liberty / Was two hundred years of pine and hardwood / And three generations of the grass / And the generations are up: the years over / We don't know."

### The Road to Pearl Harbor

No one really knew. The future of liberty never seemed more uncertain to thoughtful Americans than in those fearful months after the fall of France. Because of the strength of the isolationists, the President understated the danger of American involvement in the war and shrank from pursuing his policy with full vigor. Henry Stimson, who had been added to the Cabinet as Secretary of War in the summer of 1940 (along with Frank Knox, the new Secretary of the Navy) thought the President too timid and was disturbed by his failure to follow up his victory in the lend-lease fight. Roosevelt did agree, though, in early 1941 to secret discussions in Washington between American and British officers to outline a common strategy for making American aid effective and provide for future cooperation should the United States enter the war.

During the summer of 1941, Roosevelt moved gradually to align the United States even more firmly on the side of the Allies. In April, American troops occupied Greenland and, in July, Iceland, in order to prevent possible German control of

this critical area for Atlantic shipping. By mid-summer, American warships were convoying supplies as far as Iceland in the name of "hemispheric defense." In August came a sensational meeting between Roosevelt and Prime Minister Churchill off the coast of Newfoundland. After discussing lend-lease and other mutual concerns, the leaders of the two great democracies drew up an Atlantic Charter affirming their faith in self-determination, equality of trade opportunities, and an international system of general security. The significance of the Charter, however, lay as much in the cooperation it bespoke between the Atlantic democracies as in the statement of its principles. For the first time, an American president had set his signature in peacetime to a document that spoke of the "final destruction" of a potential enemy.

In the late summer, Germany stepped up her submarine warfare against Atlantic shipping. The need to take additional steps if lend-lease supplies were to reach the British became increasingly apparent. About September 1 Roosevelt made the decision to send naval escorts with merchant ships bound for the North Atlantic. After an attack on the destroyer *Greer*, which was radioing the position of a German submarine to the British, the President announced his intention to give protection to all merchant vessels in "waters which we deem necessary for our defense." American ships and planes would "no longer wait until Axis submarines lurking under the water, or Axis raiders on the surface of the sea strike their deadly blow —first." Congress took the final step short of war itself in November when, by a close vote, it gave approval to the President's request to arm merchant vessels and permit them to visit belligerent ports. This was hardly neutrality but, then, the United States had long since ceased to be neutral; now even the pretense was dropped.

Meanwhile, in September, Roosevelt had extended lend-lease aid to Russia following Hitler's invasion of that country in June. This astonishing gamble of Hitler's, undertaken while Britain, though prostrate, was still unbeaten, proved to be his greatest mistake. He had long coveted the mineral and food wealth of the Ukraine—he had boasted in 1936 how Germans would "swim in plenty" when Russia was subdued—and he feared to launch an invasion of Britain with the Red Army at his back. Now, though his legions hurled back the Russians and pushed to within sight of Moscow in November, he could not crush the fiercely resisting Russians.

The final explosion that brought America into open hostilities, however, did not occur in Europe but in the Pacific. During the long months when American relations with Germany were growing increasingly tense, Secretary Hull was carrying on involved negotiations with the Japanese. Since the invasion of Manchuria, Americans had watched with mounting apprehension the advance of Japanese imperialism in Asia. At stake, in the judgment of the State Department, were the Open Door policy, the China market, and the security of the Philippines. Following the Japanese invasion of North China in 1937, the United States strengthened the Pacific forces, extended a loan to China, and urged American manufacturers not to export planes to Japan. In August, 1939, the Administration renounced an American commercial treaty with Japan and six months later, when the treaty expired, halted the export of petroleum, scrap iron, and aviation gasoline to the Japanese. Almost half of the precious Japanese supply of these commodities had come from the United States. Surprisingly little opposition to these steps was raised in the United States. The isolationists' sentiments continued to be much more sensitive to strong measures in Europe than in Asia, a condition that was in harmony with the anti-European roots of American isolationism.

Relations between Japan and the United States became more critical following the fall of France. With that catastrophe the Tokyo government felt assured that an Axis victory was certain and that the European colonial empires in Asia were about to collapse, and it now sent Japanese forces to occupy northern Indo-China, a French colony. In September, 1940, Japanese diplomats signed a tripartite pact with Germany and Italy, a pact that, aimed clearly at the United States, bound Japan to come to Hitler's assistance (and vice-versa) in the event of an attack by a nonsignatory power. Tokyo followed this up with a strong protest against American restrictions on exporting gasoline and scrap iron to Japan, even suggesting that these could be considered "an unfriendly act." Hull told the Japanese ambassador that he was amazed that the Japanese government, "which has been violating in the most aggravating manner American rights and interests," should adopt such a position. The United States, he said, would not sit idly by and watch all of Asia become "Manchurianized," and he declared that it was "unheard of for a country engaged in aggression and seizure of another country to turn to a third nation and seriously insist that the latter would be guilty of an unfriendly act if it did not cheerfully provide some of the necessary implements of war. . . ." Clearly, by the fall of 1940, a serious impasse had been reached in Japanese-American relations.

What the United States feared most was a Japanese drive southward through French Indo-China and Malaya toward Singapore and the Dutch East Indies. Yet this was the very region, given the economic pinch they were feeling from the American embargoes, that promised most to the Japanese. In late

July, 1941, by overwhelming the rest of Indo-China, the Japanese presented a clear threat to British areas in the Far East and to the Philippine Islands. The American reply was the freezing of all Japanese assets in the United States, which meant in effect a complete embargo. The impact of this move on the Japanese was extremely serious; they were being forced to a choice between putting aside their conquests or facing war with the United States.

Four critical months of tension and diplomatic maneuvering followed. The risk of war was now plain to both sides, so they opened negotiations looking to an easing of tensions. But all negotiations foundered on three basic points: (1) Japanese refusal to withdraw from Indo-China, (2) Japanese commitments, under the tripartite pact, if the United States went to war with Hitler, and (3) the evacuation of China by Japanese troops. On these matters the militarist faction in Japan opposed any concession of a kind that would have satisfied Washington. The desperate Prime Minister, Prince Konoye, who was anxious to avert war, even proposed a meeting at sea between himself and President Roosevelt. Hull insisted, however, that some kind of previous agreement was necessary before such a conference could be held. Though Hull's position was perhaps too rigid, it is difficult to see how such a meeting could have succeeded without Japanese concessions that they had thus far refused and that the militarists violently opposed.

By the fall of 1941 an unbridgeable gulf separated the two nations. The Konoye Cabinet fell on October 16 to be replaced by a militarist government led by General Tojo. A final exchange of notes in November revealed the deep-seated differences in policy. The Japanese would agree at most to the evacuation of Indo-China in exchange for a free hand in China and the end of the economic embargo. Since the Japanese were bent on war if they failed to get their way, hostilities could be averted only by a surrender of principle on the China question. This Roosevelt and Hull refused to consider.

As December began, hopes for peace were faint. The Japanese, it was known, were readying an attack, though most authorities expected them to fall on the British and Dutch possessions in Southeast Asia. Japanese code messages, broken by the United States, made it clear that a large Japanese force was moving southward through the China Sea. What was its destination? What should the United States do if Hong Kong or the Dutch East Indies were attacked?

Almost no one thought of Hawaii. Routine warnings had gone to the American commanders there but few precautions had been taken. At Pearl Harbor, the long lines of battleships, all in port for the first time since July 4, made a perfect target as the first wave of Japanese bombers swept in at 7:55 A.M. on December 7, 1941. "The Japs are bombing us! The Japs are bombing us!" screamed the executive officer of the supply ship *Castor*. "The war is on, no fooling!" cried a man on watch aboard the submarine *Tautog* to the other crewmen; but many were incredulous—a fireman on the *Helena* thought the alarm was just another of the executive officer's bright ideas to get the crew to go to church. "I didn't even know they were sore at us," said a seaman on the destroyer *Monaghan*. In all, the Japanese sank five battleships, heavily damaged three others, and hit numerous lesser vessels. Of the 2403 Americans killed in the attack, nearly half were lost when the battleship *Arizona* exploded. Also, on the same day, the Japanese dealt smashing blows to Manila, Wake, Guam, Midway, and Hong Kong.

News of the attack stunned Americans everywhere. Radio announcers interrupted programs to give the sparse details; the

The battleship U.S.S. California settling into the mud after the Japanese attack on Pearl Harbor. (Library of Congress.)

crowd watching the Dodger-Giant football game at the Polo Grounds in New York got the news on the spot; and concertgoers at Carnegie Hall sang "The Star-Spangled Banner" a second time after they heard the report. "Others learned in other ways," writes Walter Lord, "but no matter how they learned, it was a day they would never forget. Nearly every American alive at the time can describe how he first heard the news. He marked the moment carefully, carving out a sort of mental souvenir, for instinctively he knew how much his life would be changed by what was happening in Hawaii."*

The next day, a solemn, angry Roosevelt stood before a joint session of Congress and began his brief remarks: "Yesterday, December 7, 1941—a date which will live in infamy—the United States of America was suddenly and deliberately attacked by the naval and air forces of the Empire of Japan." Within four hours,

* W. Lord, *Day of Infamy* (New York: Henry Holt and Company, 1957), pp. ix, 71-74.

Congress had passed a resolution of war, unanimously in the Senate, and by a vote of 388 to 1 in the House. On December 11, following a declaration of war by Germany and Italy, Congress also recognized a state of war with these countries.

Pearl Harbor was a major military disaster, probably the worst in American history, but at the same time it unified the American people in a way that would have seemed inconceivable a few days before. For the only time in the nation's history, there was no real opposition to the prosecution of a major war. Though a small band of postwar revisionists has sought to reopen the isolationist quarrel of 1939-41, and still others have charged Roosevelt, directly or indirectly, with responsibility for the Pearl Harbor disaster, the great body of Americans, then and since, including the vast majority of historians, has been convinced that the President's policies reflected both the nation's temper and by and large, its interest in these critical months.

## WAR FOR THE WORLD

The task confronting the United States was staggering. Unlike the struggle of 1917, the second great war of the century would be fought on a truly global scale. In Europe, not a single foot of soil on the continent was left in Allied hands; in the Eastern Hemisphere, the Japanese were free to roam and strike at will through vast areas of the Southwest Pacific. Before the United States and Britain could recover from the blows dealt them in December, the Japanese moved quickly into the Philippines, down the Malayan Peninsula, and against Singapore and the islands of the East Indies. The early months of the year 1942 were dark with discouragement and defeat as the Axis powers came to the zenith of their conquests. Manila fell to the Japanese on January 2, the Bataan Peninsula on April 8, and the last American resistance in the Philippines ended on May 6. Everywhere, from Manchuria and the Kuriles in the North to the Solomons and New Guinea in the South, the Japanese were victorious by mid-1942. A watery empire embracing millions of square miles was in their grasp. "In these hours," wrote George C. Marshall, Chief of Staff of the United States Army, "Germany and Japan came so close to complete domination of the world that we do not yet realize how thin the thread of Allied survival had been stretched."

### Ebb Tide: 1942

Americans grew accustomed to news of defeat in the first six months after Pearl Harbor. Not only in the Far East, but in North Africa, Russia, and the North Atlantic, defeat was the order of the day for the Allies. Under the "Desert Fox," General Erwin Rommel, the Germans drove the British across Africa to El Alamein, only seventy-five miles from Alexandria, in an effort to capture the Suez Canal and cut British communications with India. At sea, German submarines exacted a terrible toll in the early months of 1942, threatening the lend-lease pipeline to Britain and Russia. The Soviets, driven back into southeastern Russia and the Caucasus by a new German offensive, were urging Churchill and Roosevelt to launch an invasion of France. But the British, more alert than American leaders to the cost and peril of a cross-channel operation at this stage of the war, vetoed any suggestion of so risky a venture. Instead, the decision was made to invade North Africa in the fall of 1942.

Basic Allied strategy was agreed upon at the outset. At their very first meeting after Pearl Harbor, Churchill and Roosevelt decided to concentrate first upon the defeat of Germany. There were many persuasive reasons for this decision. The Germans, it was believed, were the more formidable adversary and more likely to increase their strength as time went on. All possible assistance should be given to Russia, lest it be added to the impressive array of states whose populations and resources were already under Nazi domination. The land and air forces necessary for the defense of Britain could not be spared for offensive operations in the Pacific until Germany was beaten. But once Hitler was overcome, Japan's demise, it was felt, would follow in short order. In the meantime, the Allied shipyards would hurry construction of the flotilla needed to fight the kind of war foreseen in the Pacific.

### The Tide Turns

Shipping was a vital Allied need to the very end of the war. At the start, the Nazi U-boats roamed all over the North Atlantic and even into the Gulf of Mexico and the Caribbean. As more than two hundred American coastal craft were sent to the bottom in early 1942 alone, a desperate race began between Allied construction and German sinkings of merchant vessels. As late as January, 1943, the U-boats were sinking more tonnage—nearly a million tons each month—than the shipyards of Britain and America combined could turn out. But gradually, through better methods of convoying, improved detection methods, and air patrols from carriers and land bases, the battle at sea began to turn against the Germans. The spring of 1943 brought a dramatic decline in ships destroyed and a sharp rise in U-boat losses. New construction, meanwhile, more than compensated for the sinkings. During the last two years of the war, losses dropped steadily. In the critical summer of 1944, in fact, not a single Allied ship was sunk by Nazi torpedoes in the North Atlantic. The maritime nations had once more proved their superiority at outproducing and outfighting the Germans in a naval war.

In the air the Allies also moved toward complete superiority during 1942 and 1943. After besting the *Luftwaffe* pilots in the Battle of Britain in 1940, the Royal Air Force had undertaken a number of night bombing sorties against German industrial and transportation targets. By mid-1942, the RAF was sending a thousand planes at a time against Cologne, Essen, Bremen, and other German cities to disrupt German industry. Then, the American Eighth Air Force joined the war in August, 1942, and played an increasingly important role. By March, 1943, the Allied forces were bombing Germany around-the-clock, the British specializing in night attacks and the American Flying Fortresses undertaking daylight raids. On October 14, 1943, however, the Americans lost so many planes in an attack on Schweinfurt that daylight raids were suspended for four months until long-range fighters became available. Still, by this time, no German city was safe from the demoralizing air attacks, and the damage to rail and highway communications had become ruinous. By the end of the war thousands of Allied bombers flew unchecked across Germany and struck almost at will at targets selected for them. The impact on German production, transportation, and especially morale was staggering.

On the ground, too, Allied forces saw their fortunes reversed in 1942. To save the Suez Canal and reduce the pressure on the beleaguered Russians, who were fighting furiously at Stalingrad, Britain and America undertook to wrest North Africa from Rommel's grip. On November 7, two weeks after the British Eighth Army, under General Bernard Montgomery, launched a powerful offensive from El Alamein, a combined Anglo-American force began landing along the entire coastline of French Morocco and Algeria. Marshal Pétain, head of the government of Occupied France, broke relations with the United States and ordered French troops in Africa to fight the invaders. But, following the movement of German troops into unoccupied France on November 11, General Dwight Eisenhower, in command of the invasion forces, was able to work out an armistice with Admiral Jean Darlan, Pétain's deputy in North Africa. A race now began for control of Tunisia. The Germans arrived first and poured in heavy reinforcements. Now American soldiers got their first taste of sharp fighting as Eisenhower's armies closed in from the west, while Montgomery continued his march from the east. As the vise closed about the Germans and their Italian allies in Tunisia between February and May, 1943, Hitler's hitherto invincible armies suffered their first crushing defeat in the west. In all, 350,000 Axis troops were killed or captured and a

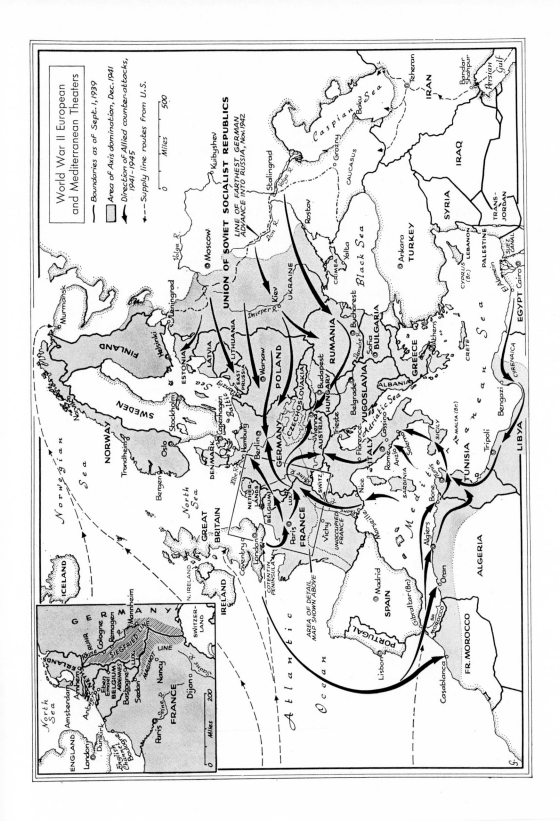

World War II European
and Mediterranean Theaters

Boundaries as of Sept. 1, 1939

Area of Axis domination, Dec. 1941

Direction of Allied counter-attacks,
1941–1945

Supply line routes from U.S.

Miles

0    500

LINE OF FARTHEST GERMAN
ADVANCE INTO RUSSIA, Nov. 1942

UNION OF SOVIET SOCIALIST REPUBLICS

Kuibyshev

Moscow

Volga R.

Leningrad

Murmansk

Helsinki

FINLAND

Stalingrad

Volga R.

Don R.

Rostov

Kiev

UKRAINE

Dnieper R.

Dnieper R.

CRIMEA

Yalta

Black Sea

Grozny

CAUCASUS

Baku

Caspian Sea

Tehran

IRAN

Bandar
Shahpur

Persian
Gulf

IRAQ

SYRIA

Ankara

TURKEY

SYRIA

LEBANON

PALESTINE

TRANS-
JORDAN

CYPRUS
(Br.)

SUEZ
CANAL

El Alamein

Cairo

EGYPT

Bucharest

RUMANIA

Sofia

BULGARIA

Danube R.

Belgrade

YUGOSLAVIA

ALBANIA

GREECE

Athens

CRETE

Mediterranean Sea

Bengazi

CYRENAICA

LIBYA

Tripoli

MALTA (Br.)

TUNISIA

Bone

Tunis

ESTONIA

LATVIA

LITHUANIA

EAST
PRUSSIA

Baltic Sea

Niemen R.

Warsaw

POLAND

CZECHOSLOVAKIA

Budapest

HUNGARY

AUSTRIA

Vienna

Trieste

Adriatic Sea

Cassino

Anzio

Rome

ITALY

Florence

Po R.

Nice

SARDINIA

SICILY

Salerno

Naples

Corsica

GERMANY

Berlin

Hamburg

Elbe R.

DENMARK

Copenhagen

SWEDEN

Stockholm

Oslo

NORWAY

Trondheim

Bergen

North
Sea

Norwegian
Sea

ICELAND

Rhine R.

NETHER-
LANDS

BELGIUM

LUX.

SWITZ.

FRANCE

Paris

Vichy

UNOCCUPIED
FRANCE

Rhône R.

AREA OF DETAIL
MAP SHOWN ABOVE

COTENTIN
PENINSULA

London

Coventry

GREAT
BRITAIN

N. IRELAND

IRELAND

English Channel

Atlantic Ocean

SPAIN

Madrid

PORTUGAL

Lisbon

Gibraltar (Br.)

Sp.
MOROCCO

Oran

Algiers

ALGERIA

FR. MOROCCO

Casablanca

Miles

0    200

North
Sea

G E R M A N Y

RUHR

Cologne

Rhine R.

Mannheim

Ramagen

SIEGFRIED LINE

SWITZER-
LAND

NETHER-
LANDS

Amsterdam

Arnhem

Elsen

Emael

BELGIUM

Bastogne

ARDENNES

Sedan

LUX.

MAGINOT
LINE

Nancy

Saône R.

Dijon

FRANCE

Paris

Seine R.

London

ENGLAND

Dunkirk

Boulogne

English Channel

large quantity of their tanks, airplanes, and ships was lost. The consequences of this first great Allied land victory of World War II were momentous. Europe now lay open to invasion from the South; the Italians had demonstrated they had no stomach for the war; the Mediterranean was open again to Allied shipping; and all the countries under Hitler's heel got a tremendous lift from his first great defeat.

While North Africa was being won, the Russians raised the siege of Stalingrad. After three months of terrible fighting in the fall of 1942, the Russian troops had held their ground against furious German assaults and now began to counterattack. In the spring of 1943 they pushed the whole German line back, in some places as much as 350 miles, and by fall they were deep into the Ukraine, ready to strike at Rumania. Not the least important factor in the growing might of the Soviets was the flood of American lend-lease supplies, which in value had reached a total of four billion dollars by the end of 1943.

In the Pacific, too, the tide of battle began to turn in 1942 and 1943. The threat to India and Australia was ended by stiffening British resistance in Burma and decisive naval encounters in May and June of 1942. In the Battle of the Coral Sea, May 7 and 8, American planes from the carriers *Lexington* and *Yorktown* halted a Japanese task force advancing on Port Moresby at the southeastern end of New Guinea. A few weeks later, the Japanese sent an invasion armada toward Midway Island, a strategic American outpost guarding Hawaii. Admiral Chester W. Nimitz, commanding the Pacific Fleet, had anticipated this move and on June 3 the Americans met the Japanese fleet in mid-Pacific. In a furious battle lasting four days, the Japanese suffered a crushing defeat, losing four aircraft carriers, a heavy cruiser, and three destroyers. The Americans lost only the *Yorktown*

and a destroyer. The entire conflict was fought by airplanes from the carriers and from Midway. Not a single shot was exchanged by the naval vessels engaged in this titanic struggle. The victories in the Coral Sea and at Midway halted the Japanese advance in the Pacific and conclusively ended the threat to Hawaii and the American mainland.

To protect Allied shipping in the South Pacific and prevent an invasion of Australia, American marines landed at Guadalcanal and Tulagi in the Solomon Islands in August, 1942. The Japanese resisted furiously in some of the bloodiest fighting of the Pacific war. Four Allied cruisers and a transport were sunk in a surprise attack off Savo Island. A six-month battle ensued for control of Guadalcanal and the sea and air around it. The marines were subject to heavy bombing attacks by land-based planes from the Japanese base in Rabaul. Finally, however, victory was won after several more encounters at sea and the landing of Army relief forces. On the night of February 7, 1943, the Japanese abandoned the island.

### Midstream

By early 1943, the Allies had clearly gained the upper hand. In January, Churchill and Roosevelt met at Casablanca to map the next phase of the war. The invasion of western Europe, they decided, must wait until 1944, though General Marshall still favored an earlier attempt. For now, from North Africa the Allies armies would move to Sicily in the most daring amphibious operation yet attempted. The Casablanca conference produced another critical decision. Under no circumstances, said President Roosevelt in a press statement, would the Allies accept less than an unconditional Axis surrender. This did not mean, he explained, "the destruction of the population of Germany, Italy, and Japan, but it does mean the destruction of the philosophies in those countries which are based on conquest and the subjugation of other people." Whether this decision to insist on "unconditional surrender" prolonged the war by stiffening enemy resistance has been vigorously debated. Churchill continued to believe, in any case, that any alternative plan, such as announcing specific surrender terms, would not have reassured the German people any more. "They might well have preferred," he wrote, "the vaguer terrors of 'unconditional surrender.'"

The invasion of Sicily brought the complete collapse of the Italian government. On July 25, 1943, two weeks after the British Eighth Army under Montgomery and the American Seventh under General George Patton went ashore in Sicily, King Victor Emmanuel III ordered the arrest of Mussolini and the opening of surrender negotiations. But the Germans moved swiftly. While armistice negotiations were in progress, they seized control of most of Italy. German parachutists rescued Mussolini, who was now put in charge of a new Italian "government" at Lake Como. Before the Allies could take Rome, as provided in the armistice, the Germans were in control of the city. So, in September, came the Allied invasion of Italy. In spite of fierce German resistance, the southern part of Italy to Cassino

was cleared by the end of the year. Deprived of decisive reinforcements—held off so that the build-up for the cross-channel invasion could proceed—the Allied troops in Italy engaged in some of the most desperate and bloody fighting of the war. Not until June 4, 1944, two days before the invasion of France, did Rome fall into Allied hands.

During October, 1943, the foreign ministers of the three major powers fighting Hitler met in Moscow to discuss mutual problems and prepare for the first meeting of the Big Three. There was little disagreement. Plans for the postwar treatment of Germany were discussed; Austria was to be once more an independent state after the war; and announcement was made of Allied determination to punish war crimes when the fighting was done. More important, Stalin told Secretary Hull that Russia would join the war against Japan after Hitler's defeat.

The following month Roosevelt left for Cairo and Teheran. At Cairo he and Churchill conferred with Chiang Kai-shek and the military commanders about the war in China and Burma, and particularly about the urgency of opening a supply line to China. Then from Egypt, Roosevelt and Churchill journeyed to their meeting-place with Stalin in Iran. As in Moscow, the atmosphere seemed cordial

Stalin, Roosevelt, and Churchill at Teheran. (Library of Congress.)

An American supply convoy climbing a stretch of the Burma Road with twenty-one switchbacks. (Imperial War Museum.)

this moment in the war, favored in varying degree the partition of postwar Germany. Roosevelt urged, too, that definite plans be framed for a United Nations organization after the war to prevent future aggression and preserve the peace.

Encouraging news was also received from the Pacific front during 1943. The growing might of the Allied fleet permitted a series of bold strokes against Japanese-held islands in the South Pacific and around the outer perimeter of the Japanese stronghold. From New Guinea and the Solomons the Allies began a pincers movement around the great Japanese base at Rabaul, on the island of New Britain, which had caused the marines at Guadalcanal so much discomfort. Ground forces under General Douglas MacArthur crept along the northern coast of New Guinea, while a series of amphibious attacks on New Georgia, Bougainville, and the Green and Admiralty islands cut Rabaul off from communications to the north. American air and naval superiority in the South Pacific was now complete.

Admiral Nimitz also took the offensive in the central Pacific. During 1943 and early 1944, American forces carried out decisive operations against islands in the Gilberts, the Marshalls, and the Marianas. The battle for Tarawa in the Gilbert Islands in November was especially fierce as Japanese defenders fought for every inch of ground. From the Gilberts the war shifted northward to Kwajalein, Eniwetok, and other islands in the Marshalls. Finally, in mid-June, American troops were in the Marianas with bloody assaults on Saipan, Guam, and Tinian. Only thirteen hundred miles now separated American bases from the Japanese home islands and invasion forces were being readied for the return to the Philippines.

While these epic victories were capturing the headlines, a forgotten war raged in Burma and China. An army of British, American, Chinese, and Indian jungle

and friendly. Roosevelt was pressed hard by Stalin, though, to set the date for the invasion of France. The Soviet leader seemed especially anxious that the supreme commander of the invasion forces be named as a token of American and British intentions. Enroute back to the United States, FDR told General Eisenhower that he had been chosen to command the great Allied effort in Europe. Plans for Germany's future were also discussed at Teheran. All three leaders, at fighters, supplied entirely by air, labored in northern Burma to reopen a supply route between India and China. The Chinese, isolated from Allied forces and fighting a desperate delaying action against the Japanese, were dependent on the meager supplies that could be flown over the "hump" of the Himalayas. In February, 1944, the campaign for Burma opened. Assailed by mud, disease, scorching heat, and loneliness, an unorthodox army of 100,000 men under such colorful leaders as Wingate, Merrill, and Stilwell engaged in arduous struggle against the Japanese. Finally, in January, 1945, despite new Japanese offensives and a falling-out between General Stilwell and Chiang Kai-shek, the Ledo Road was opened and Chiang's dependence on air supply for his hard-pressed armies was ended.

### Crusade in Europe

Of all the great events of 1944, America's third year at war, none exceeded in drama and significance the frontal assault on Hitler's *Festung Europa*. For more than a year the build-up of army and air forces in Britain had been going on. Plans for OVERLORD, the code name for the cross-channel attack, had been in preparation since 1942. To make available sufficient landing craft for the invasion, the target date for D-Day was postponed from May to June. Finally, after weeks of devastating air bombardment of French and Belgian targets, the invasion force was launched on June 6, 1944.

The invasion was aimed at the Cotentin Peninsula in Normandy. After heavy air and naval bombardment and the landing of three air-borne divisions, the armada approached the Normandy beaches in the early morning. As the first assault wave went in over barbed-wire entanglements, mines, and underwater obstacles German resistance was light in most places. But it was savage on Omaha Beach, where American assault troops suffered heavy casualties. "Order was

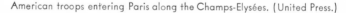

American troops entering Paris along the Champs-Elysées. (United Press.)

lost," reads the official historical account. "It seemed to the men that the only way to get ashore was to dive head first in and swim clear of the fire that was striking the boats. But, as they hit the water, their heavy equipment dragged them down and soon they were struggling to keep afloat. . . . Some drowned then and there. . . . Within 20 minutes of striking the beach A Company had ceased to be an assault company and had become a forlorn little rescue party bent upon survival and the saving of lives."

Despite the fierce resistance, five American divisions joined the other Allied troops who landed on D-Day. The fight for Normandy was intense. Fortunately, the German commanders, Rommel and Rundstedt, hesitated before throwing in their reserves out of fear the Normandy invasion might be only a diversion. In the first two weeks, a million Allied troops poured into France, the port of Cherbourg was captured, and the critical rail and highway juncture of Saint Lô fell before an American assault. The decisive breakthrough came on July 25. Patton's Third Army smashed its way into Brittany, isolating four German divisions, and then plunged eastward. For the Germans, all France was now in danger. On August 15, a new invasion force landed in Southern France and moved swiftly northward along the Rhône Valley. A month later, the battle for France was over; Brussels and Antwerp had fallen; and Allied troops had reached the Westwall, or Siegfried Line, between France and Germany. On the Eastern front, meanwhile, Soviet troops, in an offensive timed to coincide with the Western invasion, had smashed out of Russian territory and subdued the Germans on a front extending all the way from the Baltic to the Balkans. By February, 1945, the Red Army had reached the far shore of the Oder River, only forty-five miles from Berlin.

## Yalta

At Yalta, in the Russian Crimea, the war-time Big Three met for the last time in early February, 1945. The Red Army was close to Berlin while the Western allies were approaching the Rhine and preparing for the final thrust into Germany. Hitler's last desperate gamble, a sharp offensive in December against the center of the Allied lines in the Ardennes, had failed. It was now urgent that final plans be laid for postwar Germany. Concern was growing, too, over Russian policy in the countries she had conquered in Eastern Europe, especially Poland. In the Far East, plans had to be coordinated for Russian entry into the war and the final defeat of Japan. Though a few military men, particularly in the navy and the air force, believed that Japan would fall before sea and air power alone, most were convinced that only a massive offensive against Japanese land forces, including those on Japan itself, would bring victory. To avoid enormous American casualties, most political and military leaders warmly advocated Russian intervention.

The future of Germany occasioned the least debate at Yalta. Some dismemberment of German territory was deemed necessary by all participants. The northern part of East Prussia, it was agreed, should go to Russia, while Poland would be given the southern portion. The Soviets insisted, too, on their right to certain eastern Polish provinces that had been granted them by an Allied commission following World War I and then taken away by the Poles. As compensation for these losses, Poland was to receive territory in eastern Germany. The boundary between the new Poland and Germany was not set until the Potsdam conference in July, when the Oder-Neisse rivers were accepted as the demarcation line pending a final peace treaty. Beyond these territorial grants, the Russians insisted on reparations from the Germans in the amount of $20 billion. Roosevelt and Churchill refused to accept this figure but did agree to the establishment of a Reparations Commission to consider the whole matter. On the question of the postwar occupation of Germany, Stalin conceded a zone to the French on the condition it be carved out of the Anglo-American zones already drawn up.

Also discussed at Yalta was the proposed United Nations organization. Here the Russians seemed to make important concessions to the Anglo-American position. Stalin agreed that in the Security Council of the new organization the great powers should not have a veto over procedural matters; they could not, in other words, block the consideration of disputes to which they were a party. They could, however, veto *action* by the Council of which they disapproved. Stalin withdrew, too, a previous demand that each of the sixteen Soviet republics be given a seat in the General Assembly. A compromise was reached that only the Ukraine and White Russia would be given separate representation. Churchill, anxious that India and other nations in the Commonwealth and Empire be given separate status, readily assented. Roosevelt was promised that the United States, if it desired, would also be granted three seats in the Assembly. This offer was later rejected.

Doubtless the thorniest question at Yalta was the future government of Poland. With the Red Army in occupation of Poland, Stalin insisted that the Western Allies recognize a Soviet-sponsored government dominated by Communists. When Churchill and FDR refused, Stalin countered with the suggestion that the Soviet government in Poland be broadened to include a number of Polish leaders from the London government-in-exile, which was recognized by the United States and Britain. Only when Stalin pledged that such an arrangement would be temporary until free elections could be held did the President and Prime Minister reluctantly agree. In the other East European countries occupied by the Red Army, similar guarantees were made that free elections would be held as soon as possible. None of these pledges was subsequently kept, however.

To bring the Soviets promptly into the Pacific war, Stalin was promised the Kurile Islands, control of Outer Mongolia, and the return of certain territory and rights lost by Russia at the close of the Russo-Japanese War in 1905. In return, Stalin was to agree to the return of Manchuria to China and conclude a security treaty with Chiang Kai-shek's government. These concessions to Soviet military power in Eastern Europe, together with the secret Far Eastern settlement, were later to be savagely criticized.

Was Yalta a "sell-out" of America's allies? Did the Asian settlement constitute a "Far Eastern Munich," as some critics have charged? First of all, in the case of Poland, it is difficult to see how Roosevelt and Churchill could have extracted a firmer pledge than was actually given. That this pledge was not honored was due to Communist perfidy and the unwillingness or inability of the democracies to use force against the *status quo* in Eastern Europe. In the Far East, an error in judgment, it now seems clear, was made. Japan was far closer to collapse than Roosevelt's military advisers dreamed in February, 1945. Most experts anticipated a strong, fanatic Japanese resistance that would prolong the war for at least another year. Remember that at that time the atomic bomb had not yet been successfully tested. As a way to save perhaps a million American lives, Roosevelt thought, the Russian price for entering the war against Japan did not seem high. The Russians probably could not have been kept out of the war, in any case, as the end of Japan drew near and their opportunity became clearer. In the climate of early 1945, the Yalta conference seemed to promise a continuation of the cooperation between the western allies and the Soviet Union that had beaten Hitler. "The tragedy of Yalta," as the historian Foster Rhea Dulles has written, "did not lie in the agreements reached, but in the failure of Soviet Russia to honor her commitments." *

## Victory

A month after Yalta, the First Army, finding a bridge still intact at Remagen, crossed the Rhine and breached the last defenses of the Reich. Conclusive events now piled up swiftly. On March 24, the Allied armies began crossing the Rhine in force. A quarter-million of Hitler's troops were encircled and trapped in the Ruhr. Organized resistance to the Allied forces began to disintegrate. Berlin and Prague lay open and Churchill pressed for rapid movement eastward so that the western allies would be in a better bargaining position with the Soviets at war's end. Already, he knew, the Yalta agreements on Poland and the other East European countries were being cynically violated. General Eisenhower, however, resolved to move his forces against supposed German troop concentrations in southern Bavaria and Austria and then join the Russians on the Elbe River. Churchill appealed repeatedly to Roosevelt to override Eisenhower and press on to Berlin. When American troops reached the Elbe on April 11, Churchill was beside himself in anticipation. But Roosevelt, whose strength had been failing, died the following day. In the shock and unfamiliarity of the situation, the new President,

Harry Truman, was inclined to trust his military advisers and ignore the British Prime Minister's urgings. "As soldiers," General Bradley would write later, "we looked naively on this British inclination to complicate the war with political foresight and nonmilitary objectives." It was left to the Russians to capture Berlin on May 2, a few hours after Hitler's suicide had been announced. Three days earlier, Hitler's ally, Mussolini, had been captured and hung by Italian partisans. On May 8, 1945, the war in Europe came to an end.

The last year of the Pacific war saw a series of impressive but bloody victories. After American troops were landed on Leyte Island in the Philippines in October, 1944, the Japanese fleet made one last desperate attempt to stop the American advance. For two days a titanic naval struggle took place in the region of Leyte Gulf and, when it was over, the Japanese had lost virtually their entire force, including three battleships and four carriers. The conquest of the Philippines proceeded apace. Landings were made on Luzon in January, and on February 23, Manila was again in American hands. Meanwhile, air attacks on the Japanese home islands, including firebomb raids on principal cities, were exacting a heavy toll on Japanese morale. Closer and closer came the attacking force in the spring of 1945. Iwo Jima, only 775 miles south of Japan, was taken in furious hand-to-hand fighting in February and March. Then came the assault on Okinawa in the Ryukus, 350 miles from Japan, in early April. For eighty-two days the Japanese garrison, aided by suicide pilots who rammed American warships and transports, fought fanatically against the half-million invaders.

The end was now in sight. The Japanese had lost their navy and a large part of their air force; their German and Italian allies had surrendered; their cities and

* F. Dulles, *America's Rise to World Power, 1898-1954* (New York: Harper and Brothers, 1954), p. 218.

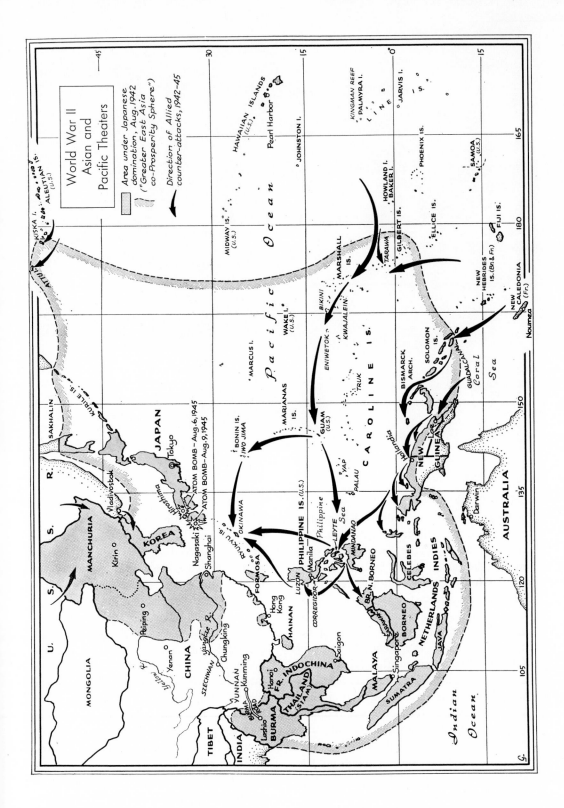

World War II
Asian and
Pacific Theaters

Area under Japanese
domination, Aug.1942
("Greater East Asia
co-Prosperity Sphere")

Direction of Allied
counter-attacks, 1942–45

Hiroshima after the atomic bomb. (United Press.)

factories were under continual bombardment. A faction within the Japanese Cabinet, supported by the Emperor, favored ending the war. But the military leaders refused to surrender. On July 26, 1945, following the successful testing of the first atomic bomb, Britain and America called upon Japan to give up or face utter destruction. When the Japanese Premier made a public statement that Japan would ignore the warning, President Truman made the decision to use the atomic bomb. On August 6 a bomb was dropped on Hiroshima that leveled the city and killed at least 80,000 persons. "The explosion," reads the official report of the United States Strategic Bombing Survey, "came as an almost complete surprise, and the people had not taken shelter. Many were caught in the open, and most

of the rest in flimsily constructed homes or commercial establishments. . . . Most of the industrial workers had already reported to work, but many workers were enroute and nearly all the school children and some industrial employees were at work in the open on the program of building-removal." Still the military leaders held out. Then came two decisive events on August 9: the Russian entry into the war and the dropping of the second atomic bomb on Nagasaki. The following day the Japanese government sued for peace. The formal surrender ceremonies took place aboard the United States battleship *Missouri* in Tokyo Bay on September 2, 1945.

The cost of the war was incalculable. Perhaps 80 million men and women throughout the world wore uniforms at

300

some time between 1939 and 1945; of these, 14 million lost their lives and many millions more were maimed or wounded. In addition, countless millions of civilians were killed or wounded as a result of the hostilities, while still others died from causes related to the war. The losses suffered by some of the belligerent nations, especially by Russia, Germany, and Japan, were staggering and unprecedented. England and France, too, were greatly weakened by the war. In the case of the United States, 407,619 Americans were killed or missing at war's end, while total casualties, including the wounded, went over the million mark. The financial cost of the war for all belligerents was estimated at more than a trillion dollars.

Victory had come through unparalleled governmental and military cooperation, especially among the Allies. Canada, Australia, and the other Commonwealth nations had joined whole-heartedly in executing the Anglo-American design for victory. The Latin American nations, too, had played a role, and by war's end all had joined the United States in the fight. Brazil became the first Latin American state ever to send troops to fight on European soil when she sent a division to the Italian front. Logistics had also figured importantly in the Allied victory. In the movement of supplies across thousands of miles of land and water, the Allies performed miracles against an enemy who continually enjoyed shorter interior lines of communication.

## THE WAR AT HOME

To win the war, the resources of the American nation had been mobilized on an unprecedented scale. No wonder that, in every area of American life, the impact of the great conflict was felt. For more than four years the Allied war machine hinged on the productive output of America's mills, shipyards, and factories. Organization on a vast scale was clearly necessary. Priorities had to be established; the armed forces must be given every possible man and weapon; Russia and Britain had to be supplied with the foodstuffs and armaments they needed to continue their valiant resistance; and morale must be maintained at a high level at home.

### The Role of Government

Government, of necessity, played a dominant role in organizing the nation's economy and manpower. Even before Pearl Harbor, the President had created a War Resources Board that had prepared a plan for industrial mobilization. In the Board's view, war production should be put under control of business leaders, who would be supervised by an economic "czar" with almost dictatorial authority. Critics of the scheme, including the President, were fearful that implementation of this plan would put the economy back into conservative hands and erase many New Deal gains. As the European crisis worsened in the spring of 1940, Roosevelt ignored the mobilization plan and, on the authority of a 1916 statute, created an Advisory Commission on National Defense. Dramatically, he called for the building of 50,000 planes a year, seemingly a utopian dream in 1940, although this figure was exceeded after America entered the war. The Commission, headed by William S. Knudsen, president of General Motors, was given responsibility for putting the defense effort into high gear.

Not until 1942, after much confusion and improvisation, did Roosevelt create an over-all economic authority. In January, a War Production Board was established under the leadership of Donald M. Nelson. Although intended to wield decisive authority, the Board failed to bring order out of the chaos of conflicting military and civilian demands. Finally, in October, 1942, Roosevelt asked James F. Byrnes, a Justice of the Supreme Court, to assume top command on the economic front as head of the Office of Economic Stabilization. Byrnes moved decisively to tackle the complicated problems of assigning priorities in steel, aluminum, and other critical materials. In 1943 Byrnes's powers and responsibilities were broadened into a super-agency called the Office of War Mobilization whose mandate gave him control over virtually all domestic war activity.

**The Battle of Production**

In the factories, the drive for full production got under way slowly, almost haphazardly. Some manufacturers, especially before Pearl Harbor, were reluctant to abandon lucrative civilian markets for the uncertain demands of war. By the latter part of 1940, though, a mild industrial boom had developed in response to defense orders. Still, many manufacturers continued to produce automobiles and other consumer items during 1941, while converting partially to war needs. After Pearl Harbor, an avalanche of war orders tumbled down on the manufacturers. Bottlenecks in production, which often took months to break, clogged many industries, and many producers were plagued by critical shortages of important raw materials, notably rubber. To this last problem, special attention was given. A Rubber Director, William M. Jeffers, president of the Union Pacific Railroad, was appointed to expedite the construction of synthetic rubber plants. By the close of 1943, these factories were producing more artificial rubber than the nation had consumed in natural rubber in prewar days.

Industrial output rose spectacularly during the war years. By 1944, American plants alone were producing twice as much as all Axis sources combined. Even so, war needs accounted for only a third of the nation's manufactures. Except for automobiles, electrical appliances, and other goods requiring critically short metals, civilian production remained high throughout the war. The war record of American industry was nonetheless staggering: nearly 300,000 airplanes, 2½ million machine guns, 86,000 tanks, and 75,000 naval vessels, cargo ships, and landing craft.

This wartime boom brought a rush of prosperity. The gross national product, which had stood at $91 billion in 1939, skyrocketed to $166 in 1945. Industrial production virtually doubled, war plants sprang up in all parts of the country, and unemployment virtually disappeared. Between 1940 and 1945 the average worker's wage, thanks in part to large amounts of overtime, increased from $25 to $43 per week. Farmers likewise enjoyed their greatest prosperity since World War I. In the same period, their net cash income quadrupled, farm mortgages were sharply reduced, and the amount of farm tenancy dropped in all parts of the nation. The spectacular rise in the wartime demand for food created a farmer's utopia in which prices and output rose simultaneously.

**Fighting Inflation**

The return of prosperity at a time when civilian goods were in short supply raised the spectre of inflation. Throughout the war the Administration viewed with serious misgiving the growing gap between disposable income and available goods and services. The Office

Shortages and rationing led to a certain amount of illegal trading during the war. Here a black-marketer selling hard-to-get foodstuffs set up shop on a street in Baltimore. The furtive customer in the foreground is hastening away with a bag of potatoes. (United Press.)

of Price Administration, created in 1941, at first lacked real power to halt the climb of prices and rents skyward. Prices were rising about 2 per cent each month during 1941. Then, in January, 1942, Congress granted to OPA the authority to fix maximum prices and to set rents in defense areas. After three months of piecemeal efforts at price stabilization and the rationing of scarce commodities, Leon Henderson, the OPA chief, froze the prices of consumer goods as of March, 1942. Rents, too, were frozen in critical housing areas. Food prices, however, continued to rise in response to the high parity ratio of 110 per cent set by Congress. Finally, as labor spokesmen assailed the rising cost of living, Congress passed in October, 1942, the Anti-Inflation Act, which enabled Roosevelt to freeze farm prices, wages, salaries, and rents everywhere in the country. Despite widespread grumbling and occasional inequities, the OPA managed to prevent a runaway inflation. During the last two years of the war, under the able direction of Chester Bowles, the agency held the rise in living costs to only 1.4 per cent. In all, the cost of living between 1939 and 1945 climbed about 29 per cent, or less than half the increase for the comparable period in World War I.

## Labor and the War

Of all the groups affected by the war, none experienced a sharper improvement in status than industrial workers. Nearly nine million men had been without jobs when war broke out in 1939. By 1941 this number had fallen to two and a half million, and after Pearl Harbor job vacancies consistently ran ahead of job applications. In size, the labor force climbed from 46 million in 1940 to more than 53 million men and women at the end of the war. Not only did the unemployed return to work, but large numbers of women, adolescents, and elderly persons found jobs as well.

Still, there was a manpower shortage. A total of fifteen million men and women donned uniforms at some time during the war. Local draft boards, manned by 200,000 workers and volunteers, sought to delay the call of married men with children as long as possible, but, owing to regional differences in the number of unmarried young men, many husbands and fathers were called. As more and more men were called up, critical labor deficiencies developed in important war industries. So in 1942 Roosevelt appointed a War Manpower Commission, charging it with responsibility for seeing that war industries did not suffer from lack of factory hands. Though the Commission had some success in barring war workers from leaving their jobs, it was unable to recruit needed help from non-essential industries. For Congress shrank back from ordering a complete mobilization of manpower that would have enabled the government to draft men for war work.

To deal with labor problems in wartime, Roosevelt created a War Labor Board in January, 1942. He was determined to stop strikes and block union pressures for wage increases that would promote inflation. The Board asserted its authority over wages, hours, and other disputed matters. Unions, for their part, agreed not to strike during the war. One of the hottest issues that faced the Board was the union-shop provision in many work agreements. Should new workers be required to join a union in wartime? Employers argued that this was unreasonable in a period of crisis when war industries were expanding at a fast pace and labor turnover was rapid. A compromise was finally reached. New workers were not required to join a union but unions retained control over old members and were granted bargaining rights for all workers under existing contracts. Even with the compromise, by war's end, union membership had climbed from nine million in 1940 to nearly fifteen million persons.

What to do about labor pressures for wage increases? Clearly, the cost of living, particularly in the early months of the war, was rising, and the pace was particularly hard for industrial workers to keep up with. In July, 1942, the Board finally acted by allowing a 15 per cent increase in wages in the Little Steel case. This formula was then applied in other industries. For a while there was peace on the industrial front until John L. Lewis defied the no-strike agreement in 1943 and called a strike of his United Mine Workers. Roosevelt seized the mines and later threatened to draft strikers if they did not return to work. Still, Lewis managed to get much of what he wanted before the crisis was over. An enraged Congress passed the Smith-Connelly Act, which gave the President the power to seize struck war plants and forced unions to wait thirty days before beginning a strike. But this weapon proved to be quite ineffective, since labor was often able to use the bare threat of a strike to reach its objectives. Throughout the country, in the war years, many states were beginning to pass laws against closed shops, mass picketing, and other union practices. Public opinion was clearly beginning to turn against unions, in part because of the highly publicized actions of a few irresponsible leaders.

### Basic Freedoms in Wartime

In most respects, the American public looked at the Second World War with far less zeal and passion than was the case in 1917. Many observers commented on the quiet restraint and lack of outward enthusiasm with which the war was fought. Most Americans seemed to view the war as a disagreeable task to be carried out as swiftly and efficiently as possible, and there was little hostility toward Germans or Italians who had made their homes in the United States. Almost no opposition to the war appeared. A small number of Nazi agents and native Fascists were jailed, but the trial of thirty leading seditionists, beginning in 1944, ended in dismissal. Conscientious objectors and others opposed to the war were dealt with moderately in comparison with the practices during World War I.

One serious exception must be noted,

however. On the West Coast, more than 100,000 persons of Japanese ancestry were herded by the Army into internment camps. Fears of Japanese sabotage, magnified by untrue stories of Japanese-American perfidy in Hawaii, were largely responsible for this action. Ten relocation areas were established in remote sections of the country. All Japanese-born and second-generation Japanese-Americans were removed from the westernmost areas of Washington, Oregon, and California, as well as from southern Arizona. More than two-thirds of the internees were American citizens. Ultimately, most were allowed to find new homes, if they chose, in other parts of the country, while a smaller group of about 18,000, whose loyalty was felt to be suspect, was sent to a special camp at Tule Lake, California. In 1944 a divided Supreme Court upheld the evacuation program, arguing that in wartime military leaders were justified in taking extreme measures to guard the nation's security. To many, this seemed like an important limitation on the civil liberties of all Americans. Especially noteworthy, in connection with the Japanese evacuation, was the fact that 17,600 Japanese-Americans served loyally in the armed forces and that not a single Japanese-American was convicted of sabotage or espionage during the war.

### End of the Roosevelt Era

The year of the Supreme Court decision was also the year of Franklin Roosevelt's last campaign. With the third-term tradition broken, he encountered little public criticism of his decision to run yet again. In a letter to the Democratic convention, he announced his intention to serve again if the American people ordered him to do so. The only battle at the convention, and it was a serious one, was over the vice-presidential nomination. Rumors of Roosevelt's ill health made this choice more important than in his previous campaigns. Henry Wallace, the heir-apparent, had failed to build widespread support, had quarreled bitterly with other Administration figures, and had given the impression of being an incurable amateur at the tough game of politics. Politicians close to Roosevelt warned that he could not win with Wallace, who enjoyed enthusiastic support only from union leaders and a small band of intellectuals. Who should be nominated? James Byrnes was often mentioned but he was anathema to the CIO because of his conservatism and his views on the race question. This left two compromise possibilities, Justice William O. Douglas and Senator Harry S. Truman. Of the two, the latter, because of his support among professional politicians and his prominence as chairman of the Senate War Investigation Committee, seemed the stronger possibility and proved to be the President's choice.

Against Roosevelt in 1944 the Republicans pitted the young and vigorous Thomas E. Dewey. After a highly successful career as a racket-busting district attorney, he had won election to the governorship of New York in 1942. Roosevelt, in contrast to Dewey, seemed old and worn as he used his previous tactics of ignoring the opposition candidate, making defense inspection trips, and delivering "nonpartisan" speeches. Dewey, on the other hand, seemed youthful and tireless as he stumped the country, castigating the "tired old men" who were leading the nation's war efforts. There were no real issues except the President himself. Finally, a month before election, the old campaigner responded with uncanny timing and effectiveness to the Republican charges against him. In a brilliantly sardonic speech to the Teamsters Union, he thrust at Republican libels against "my little dog, Fala." He made brief but strenuous tours through the

Northeast, climaxed by a day-long drive in an open car through the streets of New York City in a pouring rain. The old magic worked once more. His seeming vigor, his role as war leader, and his pledges to go back to the New Deal when the war was over converted thousands of wavering voters. On election day, 1944, Roosevelt won a fourth term by a margin of more than three and a half million votes. He garnered 432 electoral votes and carried thirty-six states. His party added twenty seats in the House, while losing only one Senate seat. It was a decisive victory, though on a less impressive scale than his previous triumphs.

Two and a half months after his fourth inauguration, Roosevelt was dead. On April 12, 1945, he suffered a massive cerebral hemorrhage at Warm Springs, Georgia, where he had gone to regain his failing strength. No one can describe the overwhelming sense of shock and loss that afflicted millions of Americans at the news. In Richmond, Virginia, a soldier ran outside to exclaim to his wife and neighbors, "My God, it's true." In a troopship at Cherbourg, France, a young infantryman said, "It's like somebody dying in your own family." And on Rivington Street, on the Lower East Side of New York, someone asked a Jewish housewife if she had heard the radio. "For what do I need a radio?" the woman cried out. "It's on everybody's face." "The greatness of Franklin Roosevelt," wrote Anne O'Hare McCormick on the day he died, was indefinable while he lived because it was a compound of many qualities, including the qualities of smaller men—and also because he did not make a point of it. No one was more aware that among the leaders of his time he occupied a great position as President of the United States, a role so fused with his own personality after twelve years that people in other countries spoke of him simply as "The President," as if he were the President of the world. But he did not pose as a great man. If he posed at all, it was not as somebody on an eminence, but as one who lived comfortably on all levels, a human being to whom nothing human was alien. He did not stoop and he did not climb; he was one of those completely poised persons who felt no need to play up or play down to anybody. In his death this is the element of his greatness that comes out most clearly.*

The odyssey that had begun on a cold, cloudy day in March, 1933, and had led through depression, domestic crisis, a perilous neutrality, and global war, was now over. It was a very different world Roosevelt left from the one he had first encountered as President in 1933. The cruel days of depression now seemed far behind; isolationism, at least in its old sense, was forever gone; a great war that claimed the lives of 400,000 Americans was nearly over; and at San Francisco, two weeks after Roosevelt's death, a meeting was to be held to organize a United Nations to prevent, if possible, a recurrence of the terrible catastrophe of war. Whether the new organization would succeed depended in large measure on whether the Big Three who had beaten Hitler and his allies into submission would continue their cooperation into the postwar period. Already there were signs that all was not well in the relations between the Soviet Union and the western democracies. To this growing tension and the disappointing aftermath of the greatest war in history we must now turn.

* B. Asbell, *When F.D.R. Died* (New York: Holt, Rinehart and Winston, 1961), pp. ix-xi.

# FOR FURTHER STUDY

*The books by Adler, Bisson, Hull, Ickes, Morison, Osgood, Sherwood, and Stimson and Bundy cited at the end of Chapter VIII continue to be especially useful for the topics dealt with in this chapter.*

## General Accounts

* W. Churchill, *The Second World War*, six volumes (Boston: Houghton Mifflin, 1948-1953). A brilliant and comprehensive account by perhaps the dominant figure in the Allied war effort.

F. Dulles, *America's Rise to World Power, 1898-1954* (New York: Harper, 1954). Contains three excellent chapters on the period of the Second World War and its immediate antecedents.

D. Perkins, *America and Two Wars* (Boston: Little, Brown, 1944). A brief but suggestive account of the parallels and contrasts in America's relation to the two world wars.

L. Snyder, *The War: a Concise History, 1933-1945* (New York: Julian Messner, Inc., 1960). A useful summary of the military and diplomatic phases of World War II.

## Special Studies

H. Barnes (ed.), *Perpetual War for Perpetual Peace* (Caldwell, Idaho: The Caxton Printers, 1953). An anthology of revisionist essays by men who are sharply critical of Roosevelt's foreign policies.

C. Beard, *American Foreign Policy in the Making, 1932-1940* (New Haven: Yale U. Press, 1946), and *President Roosevelt and the Coming of the War, 1941* (New Haven: Yale U. Press, 1948). These two books are from the pen of doubtless the most able of the revisionist critics of Roosevelt.

A. Bryant, *The Turn of the*

*Tide* (Garden City, New York: Doubleday, 1957), and *Triumph in the West* (Garden City, New York: Doubleday, 1959). The war as seen through the diaries and autobiographical notes of Field Marshall Alanbrooke, the top British army officer in World War II.

D. Drummond, *The Passing of American Neutrality, 1937-1941* (Ann Arbor: U. of Michigan Press, 1955). A competent summary of the period studied more intensively by Langer and Gleason (see below).

* D. Eisenhower, *Crusade in Europe* (Garden City, New York: Doubleday, 1948). The Supreme Commander's personal account of the war in Europe.

H. Feis, *Churchill, Roosevelt, Stalin* (Princeton: Princeton U. Press, 1957). The most important scholarly study of the wartime relations and diplomacy of the Big Three.

————, *The Road to Pearl Harbor* (Princeton: Princeton U. Press, 1950). A balanced interpretation of the prewar relations between the United States and Japan.

* R. Fenno, Jr. (ed.), *The Yalta Conference* (Boston: Heath, 1955). A useful compilation of excerpts from the conflicting accounts of such political figures as Hopkins, Byrnes, Churchill, Hurley, Harriman, Stettinius, and Bohlen on the significance of the conference.

J. Grew, *Ten Years in Japan* (New York: Simon and Schuster, 1944). Drawn largely from Ambassador Grew's diary and private and official papers for the years 1931-1941.

E. Janeway, *The Struggle for Survival* (New Haven: Yale U. Press, 1951). A good, brief account of America's economic mobilization during the War.

D. Johnson, *The Republican Party and Wendell Willkie* (Urbana: U. of Illinois Press, 1960). This book adds much to understanding of the 1940 campaign and its sequel.

W. Langer and S. Gleason, *The Challenge to Isolation, 1937-1940* (New York: Harper, 1952), and *The Undeclared War, 1940-1941* (New York: Harper, 1953). A careful and detailed study of these crucial years under the auspices of the Council on Foreign Relations.

W. Lord, *Day of Infamy* (New York: Holt, 1957). An entertaining, journalistic study of the events surrounding the Pearl Harbor attack.

* E. May, *American Intervention: 1917 and 1941* (Washington: American Historical Association, 1960). A brief survey of the literature concerning American involvement in the two world wars.

W. Millis, *This is Pearl!* (New York: William Morrow and Company, 1947). A well-written account of Japanese-American relations during 1941.

S. Morison, *History of United States Naval Operations in World War II*, fourteen volumes (Boston: Little, Brown, 1947-1960). A masterly study, detailed but interestingly presented, of naval activities during the war.

————, *Strategy and Compromise* (Boston: Little, Brown, 1958). A brief but suggestive little book on the major strategic decisions of the war, directed in part against Bryant's two volumes listed above.

F. Pratt, *War for the World* (New Haven: Yale U. Press, 1950). A useful little summary of the American military effort, 1941-1945.

B. Rauch, *Roosevelt from Munich to Pearl Harbor* (New

* Starred books are available in paperbound editions.

York: Creative Age Press, 1950).
Intended as a refutation of
Charles Beard, this volume
traces the struggle over Roosevelt's foreign policy through the
three critical years that followed
Munich.

P. Schroeder, *The Axis Alliance and Japanese-American Relations, 1941* (Ithaca: Cornell
U. Press, 1958). A monograph
focusing on the Tripartite Pact
and its impact on American
opinion and policy, which contends that American policy toward Japan from July to December, 1941, was "a grave mistake."

C. Tansill, *Back Door to War*
(Chicago: Henry Regnery Company, 1952). A revisionist interpretation that seeks to blame
Roosevelt and his advisors for
responsibility in bringing America
into war.

H. Trefousse, *Germany and
American Neutrality, 1939-1941*
(New York: Bookman Associates, 1951). An interesting study
of Germany's policies toward
the United States in the neutrality period.

* United States Government,
Bureau of the Budget, *The
United States at War* (Washington: Government Printing Office, 1946). The government's
official report on the mobilization of human and material resources during the war.

* G. Waller (ed.), *Pearl
Harbor* (Boston: Heath, 1953).
Another booklet in the Amherst
"Problems" series that presents
the pros and cons of Roosevelt's
responsibility for the Pearl Harbor disaster.

## Fiction and Drama

J. Cozzens, *Guard of Honor*
(New York: Harcourt, Brace,
1948). An important war novel
centering on an air base commander who has to deal simultaneously with the complex
problems of the base and a
personal problem involving his
whole future as an officer.

* N. Mailer, *The Naked and
the Dead* (New York: Rinehart,
1948). A study of the conquest
of a Pacific island, which describes with fidelity the ordeal
of the American troops, their
daily lives, their thoughts, the
monotony and deadliness of life
in such circumstances.

* J. Michener, *Tales of the
South Pacific* (New York: Macmillan, 1947). Stories that evoke
the mood, the scenes, and often
the lighter side of the Pacific
war.

* I. Shaw, *The Young Lions*
(New York: Random House,
1948). A long and brilliantly
contrived novel that brings together in war a German ski instructor, an American play producer, and a young American
Jew against the background of
their prewar lives.

* H. Wouk, *The Caine Mu-
tiny* (New York: Doubleday,
1951). A fascinating psychological study of the men aboard a
minesweeper called the *Caine*
and their mutiny against their
tyrannical commander.

## Films and Records

*Air Power* series (McGraw-
Hill, 29 minutes each, sound,
black and white). A series of
twenty-six films on such subjects
as "Target Ploesti," "Luftwaffe,"
and "Defeat of Japan," that
presents an excellent pictorial
history of the significance of air
power in the modern world.

*Appointment in Tokyo* (United World Films, 55 minutes,
sound, black and white). Produced by the United States
Army, this film is an historical
record of MacArthur's operations from the fall of Corregidor
in 1942 to the surrender of
Japan in 1945.

*Churchill: Man of the Cen-
tury* (Prudential Insurance Company, 58 minutes, sound, black
and white). An outstanding
documentary on the life of one
of the century's greatest figures.

*D-Day* (Prudential Insurance
Company, 58 minutes, sound,
black and white). A two-part
film record of the landings in
Normandy.

*FDR: Third Term to Pearl
Harbor* (Prudential Insurance
Company, 28 minutes, sound,
black and white). Another good
film in Prudential's "Twentieth
Century" series on Roosevelt's
troubled year prior to the Pearl
Harbor attack.

*How War Came to Asia*
(Educational Film Enterprises,
60 minutes, sound, black and
white). Depicts how the rise of
Japanese militarism led to the
attack on Pearl Harbor.

*How War Came to Europe*
(Educational Film Enterprises,
25 minutes, sound, black and
white). A film narrative of the
events surrounding the outbreak
of World War II.

1945-1949

# Triumph and Tragedy

## CHAPTER TEN

The Berlin Airlift, 1948.

THE MOOD OF THE TIMES

"We ask it in Manchuria. We ask it in Eastern Europe and the Dardanelles. . . . We ask it in Iran. We ask it in Tripolitania. We ask it in the Baltic and the Balkans. We ask it in Poland. We ask it in the capital of Canada. We ask it in Japan. . . . 'What is Russia up to now?' . . .

"It would be entirely futile to blink the fact that two great rival ideologies— democracy in the west and communism in the east—find themselves face to face with the desperate need for mutual understanding in finding common ground upon which to strive for peace . . . If this is so, Mr. President, I assert my own belief that we can live together in reasonable harmony if the United States speaks as plainly upon all occasions as Russia does; if the United States just as vigorously sustains its own purposes and its ideals upon all occasions as Russia does; if we abandon the miserable fiction . . . that we somehow jeopardize the peace if our candor is as firm as Russia's always is. . . .

"There is a line beyond which compromise cannot go; even if we have previously crossed that line under the pressures of the exigencies of war, we cannot cross it again. But how can we expect our alien friends to know where that line is unless we establish the habit of saying only what we mean and meaning every word we say? I have the deep conviction that this way is the dependable way to permanent peace and concord between us, with its inevitable effect upon the United Nations. Indeed, I have the feeling it is the only way. I have the feeling it is the best way to win Soviet respect and Soviet trust."

—SENATOR ARTHUR VANDENBERG, 1946

# YEAR OF DECISIONS

The great struggle against Hitler and his allies ended on a disquieting note. In Berlin, in Eastern Europe, in the Far East, in every place where Western power confronted the Red Army, strains of doubt and suspicion about Soviet intentions began to appear. Over the victory celebrations, at least in high places, hung an uneasy sense that the time of troubles had not passed. Even as American forces prepared to withdraw from Europe, Churchill warned of the future when only a handful of Allied divisions would stand opposed to the Russians' two or three hundred. Already, in the spring of 1945, he spoke of an "iron curtain" across the Russian end of the continent. It was vital, he told President Truman, "to come to an understanding with Russia, or see where we are with her, before we weaken our armies mortally or retire to the zones of occupation."

But the United States public in 1945 would countenance no firm stand against the Soviets. Though some Americans shared Churchill's apprehension about Soviet aims in Poland and elsewhere, few were ready to use American strength to force the Russians' hand. Many were suspicious that Churchill was simply reverting to Toryism in his anti-Soviet attitude; others were simply weary of war and unable to face the prospect of new conflicts; and over all the discussions of the future in 1945 hovered the fear of the atomic bomb. Cooperation

with the Soviet Union, the American government repeatedly declared, was the cornerstone of peace. President Truman, like most Americans, was unwilling to risk conflict with the Russians without some further attempt to reach peaceful solutions of the problems that had arisen.

The wartime friendship with the Soviets, which persisted, affected both official and private assessments of Russian actions. To turn from collective action with the Russians to opposition, as Churchill counseled, seemed to most Americans too Machiavellian a shift in policy. Let the West prove its good faith, it was argued, and the Soviets would cooperate in preserving the peace of the world. The mood of 1945 was perhaps best expressed by Harry Hopkins who remarked after the Yalta meeting that "We really believed in our hearts that this was the dawn of the new day we had all been praying for and talking about for so many years. We were absolutely certain that we had won the first great victory of the peace—and by 'we,' I mean *all* of us, the whole civilized human race." The Russians, in Hopkins' view, had proved their sincerity; there could be no doubt "that we could live with them and get along with them peacefully for as far into the future as any of us could imagine."

### Birth of the United Nations

The "era of good feelings" expected by so many was tied to extrava-

312

gant hopes for the United Nations. This new organization, it was believed, would enable the people of the world to guard against aggression and to pluck out the roots of war. The initiative behind its formation lay largely with the United States. From his first meeting with Churchill, President Roosevelt had pressed for a postwar organization to guarantee the peace. At the Dumbarton Oaks Conference in 1944 and again at Yalta, representatives of the Big Three had hammered out the main outlines of the United Nations organization. Now, in April, 1945, delegates from fifty nations met in San Francisco to draft a charter for the UN.

Learning the sad lesson of 1919, Roosevelt sought to avoid Wilson's error of binding the League to the Versailles Treaty by this time cutting off the new international organization completely from the peace settlement. And he tried to avoid another of Wilson's mistakes by sending leading Republicans, notably Senator Arthur Vandenberg, to San Francisco. The organization established at San Francisco, however, did not differ sharply from Wilson's League. The chief organs of the United Nations, as of the League, were to be a council, a general assembly, a secretariat, and an international court of justice. Most powerful of these organs was the Security Council. In this body of eleven members, five seats were permanently assigned to Great Britain, France, China, the Soviet Union, and the United States. In all but procedural questions, unanimity of these five powers was necessary for action. This provision reflected the belief of 1945 that only cooperation among the great powers could preserve the peace. Beneath the surface, however, strong tremors of disagreement between the United States and the Soviet Union had already began to rumble.

In settling disputes, the Security Council could recommend arbitration, judicial action, or other methods of peaceful settlement. Should these methods fail, it could suggest economic sanctions or "such action by air, sea, or land forces as may be necessary to maintain or restore international peace." An "international police force," foreseen in the charter, was never to materialize, however. Whenever military force was needed, as in Korea, Suez, or the Congo, it was recruited from member nations on a temporary basis.

The General Assembly was intended as a "town meeting of the world," a place where all states would have equal representation and voting power. Any matter threatening world peace could be brought before the Assembly and referred, if necessary, to the Security Council. But the growing cleavage between Russia and the West served to strengthen its powers ap-

During the organization of the United Nations in San Francisco, May, 1945, representatives of the Big Four nations read of the collapse of Germany. Left to right: Anthony Eden (Britain), Edward Stettinius (U.S.), V. M. Molotov (U.S.S.R.), and T. V. Soong (China). (United Press.)

preciably. In the event of a Security Council deadlock, according to a 1950 resolution, the Assembly might act to protect the peace. The steady growth in the size of the Assembly, particularly in delegates from newly independent and neutralist nations of Africa and Asia, tended also to increase its authority. More and more, as time went on, the moral and propagandistic strength of the United Nations came to rest in the General Assembly.

Other arms of the United Nations were established to eliminate the sources of conflict among nations. An Economic and Social Council was set up to promote cooperation in matters of international trade, finance, technology, health, and social problems. Numerous specialized agencies, such as the World Health Organization, worked closely with the Council under UN authority. One subsidiary unit of the UN—the United Nations Educational, Scientific, and Cultural Organization (UNESCO)—was charged with promoting better cultural understanding among the nations of the world. Other important branches of the United Nations were the Trusteeship Council, which had authority over the former League mandates and certain Axis possessions; the International Court of Justice at The Hague; and the Secretariat, headed by a Secretary-General, which was to perform most of the administrative tasks of the organization.

Who could oppose so beneficent an organization? That it was essentially merely an agency for international cooperation and not an instrument for international control seemed clear to all. But in the climate of 1945 this seemed to be sufficient. When the UN charter came before the United States Senate, there was almost no dissent. Indeed, only two votes were cast in opposition. The revolution in American thinking about foreign pol-

icy since 1919 was complete, and Americans were ready to take up where they had left off nearly thirty years before. Now that they understood that their everyday lives were certain to be affected by what happened beyond their national boundaries, isolation in the old sense was dead. But was the UN enough? Was the world of 1945 comparable to the post-Versailles world? Was the nation bent again on taking steps that would keep it out of the *last* war?

## Potsdam

At San Francisco, the rift between Russia and the West continued to grow. Violent quarrels between Russian and American spokesmen broke out over many points in the charter. On one occasion, only a personal appeal from Truman to Stalin saved the conference. In May, Truman sent Harry Hopkins to Moscow for frank talks about the deteriorating world situation. Stalin, who was bitter because of the abrupt termination of lend-lease aid at war's end, finally agreed to keep his Yalta pledge and admit noncommunists to the Polish government. Arrangements were made too for a final meeting of the Big Three at Potsdam, a suburb of Berlin, in July.

To confer with Truman and Stalin two men came to Potsdam to represent Britain—both Churchill and Clement Attlee, who were awaiting the outcome of a British election. When, midway in the conference, Churchill learned of his repudiation at the polls and surrendered his seat to Attlee, only Stalin remained of the original Big Three. The conference broke down into hopeless wrangling on almost every sensitive issue. After agreeing to send Japan an ultimatum demanding immediate surrender, Churchill and Truman joined Stalin in creating a Council of Foreign Ministers to draw up peace treaties for Italy and the Balkan states that had aided Hitler. But here the concord ended. On the future of Germany, especially the question of reparations, and on Stalin's pledge at Yalta concerning Eastern Europe, there was a sharp difference of view.

Russia had already turned over the administration of German territory east of the Oder-Neisse rivers to Poland without consultation with the Western powers. Confronted with this *fait accompli*, Truman and Churchill insisted that at least the final drawing of the German-Polish boundary must await the peace settlement. On occupation policy, the conferees reiterated and expanded the objectives discussed at Yalta. Postwar Germany was to be disarmed and demilitarized; her political, educational, and judicial systems were to be made democratic; her government was to be decentralized so far as possible; her war criminals were to be tried before a special tribunal; and her heavy industries were to be given a low priority in the reconstruction period. No final decision was reached on reparations, however. Russia persisted in her demand for $10 billion in German assets and industrial equipment. Though they refused to accept this figure, the Western nations did agree that each power should collect reparations from its own zone. Germany, the conferees agreed, should be treated as a single economic unit and capital equipment from the Western zones might be transferred to Russia as reparations in exchange for food and raw materials. An Allied Control Council, meeting in Berlin, was to carry out the basic directives of the victorious powers.

Disagreement was complete over the future of Poland and Eastern Europe. Stalin, denying all charges that he was violating his Yalta pledge, pressed for Western recognition of the Soviet-dominated governments in Hungary, Rumania, and Bulgaria. Truman bluntly replied that no recognition would be forthcoming until free governments were established "without pressure from beyond their borders." The Russians did agree to allow Western observers to move about freely in these countries in exchange for Western acquiescence in the Polish occupation of areas beyond the Oder-Neisse line. But this was small consolation. The Second World War had begun over Hitler's subjugation of Poland. Now, at Potsdam, the Western powers, war-weary, confronted with an accomplished fact, and unwilling to play the game of power politics, reluctantly concurred in a new kind of subjugation over Poland and Eastern Europe—one that was imposed by Stalin's rather than Hitler's bayonets. The extent of Stalin's triumphs to the time of Potsdam were summed up by the military writer, Major General J. F. C. Fuller:

Stalin . . . had been able to impose his messianic cult upon Estonia, Latvia, Lithuania, part of Finland, Poland, eastern and central Germany, a third of Austria, Czechoslovakia, Yugoslavia, Hungary, Rumania, and Bulgaria. Vienna, Prague, and Berlin, the vertebrae of Europe, were his, and, except for Athens, so was every capital city of eastern Europe. The western frontier of Russia had been advanced from the Pripet Marshes to the Thüringerwald, a distance of 750 miles and, as in the days of Charlemagne, the Slavs stood on the Elbe and the Böhmerwald. A thousand years of European history had been rolled back.

### The Victors and the Vanquished

To the west of Stalin's empire lay a prostrate Germany, smashed by war, dismembered by the Yalta and Potsdam agreements, and now cut up by her conquerors into four zones of occupation. How was Germany to be rebuilt and reformed along democratic lines? What punishment should be meted out to those who had done Hitler's bidding? When and how was Germany to be restored to the community of nations? Plainly, the tasks confronting the victors were stupendous. Millions of Europeans had been uprooted by war and were now left stranded in camps and communities hundreds of miles from home. Transportation had come to a standstill; manufacturing had virtually ceased in a hundred industrial centers; schools, courts, and local governments were either not functioning or were completely disorganized.

Measured against its staggering responsibilities, the Office of Military Government, created by the United States to administer occupied areas, performed its tasks with superb skill. Schools were gradually reopened in the American zone with faculties and books that had been "denazified." Local governments were quickly restored, often, unfortunately, at the price of employing former Nazi officials or sympathizers. Many of these, though, were purged in October, 1945, when stricter lines of procedure were laid down for the guidance of military government teams. Political parties, banned in the Hitler years, were back in operation within a few months of the end of the war. Furthermore, a number of newspapers were subsidized or encouraged by American occupation forces.

German heavy industry, in accord with the Potsdam agreement, was held down. A number of plants were even dismantled and sent to Russia as reparations. But conflict arose early in the occupation about how far this policy should go. The new Germany was clearly dependent on outside sources for part of her food, and to pay for essential imports some kind of industrial surplus would be necessary. Gradually, the restrictions on German industrial output were loosened, slowly at first, more rapidly as the boundary between the Russian and the Western zones began to harden. At Stuttgart, in September, 1946, Secretary of State James Byrnes declared against the policy of holding back German production so that reasonable standards of living for Germany were unattainable. The aim of the American occupation, he said, was not indefinite punishment but the rehabilitation of Germany along democratic lines. This was the first public reaction by an American spokesman to the growing impasse with Russia over the future of Germany.

There was little disagreement between Russia and the West over the Nuremberg trials, at least. Here, between November 21, 1945, and October 1, 1946, some twenty-two leading Nazi officials were tried for crimes against humanity and the plotting of aggressive war. The defense argued, not without some justice, that the accused were being tried for crimes that were not on any statute book at the time they were committed. The most controversial judgment of all was the execution of military officers for carrying out the orders of superiors. The prosecutors, including Justice Robert H. Jackson of the United States Supreme Court, countered that the defendants had violated international law as laid down in traditional practice and in such treaties as the Kellogg-Briand Pact of 1928. Only three of the twenty-two defendants were declared innocent. Eight were given prison terms, and eleven were sentenced to be hanged; but Hermann Goering, a leading Nazi and commander of the *Luftwaffe*, cheated the hangman by swallowing poison, and Martin Bormann, a top Hitler aide, was not apprehended. Over the whole proceedings hung a sense of foreboding that, however heinous their crimes, a precedent was perhaps being set that henceforth, in Churchill's words, "the leaders of a nation defeated in war shall be put to death by the victors." In addition to the leaders, 185 other leading Nazis were tried by special tribunals in the American zone, and more than half of them were executed or given jail sentences. In the Far East, another tribunal, after sitting for two years, found twenty-eight Japanese officials guilty of war crimes and sentenced seven of them to death.

In Japan, occupation policies were in American hands and the occupying troops were all Americans. Under the Supreme Allied Commander, General Douglas MacArthur, a thoroughgoing program of reform and democratization of Japanese institutions was undertaken. Political prisoners were turned loose; the press was unshackled; the general staff and the secret police were abolished; several industrial cartels were broken up; many of the great estates were divided; and a new constitution, modeled on Western democratic lines, was approved. Until the adoption of the constitution, MacArthur ruled through directives issued by the Emperor, who, according to surrender terms, was retained as head of the Japanese government. In the new constitution, the Emperor's powers were proclaimed as based on the will of the people and subject to cabinet approval in all matters of state. The constitution also renounced war and forbade the restoration of the armed services. Ironically, only a few years later, the United States would seek to eliminate this restriction and persuade the Japanese to share in the defense of Asia. Not until 1952 was a peace treaty formally signed ending the war with Japan. According to its terms, from which Russia dissented, Japan was to be limited to her home islands, all Japanese rights in China were renounced, and reparations were to be arranged separately with the victor nations.

Meanwhile, in 1946, peace treaties with Italy, Finland, Rumania, Bulgaria, and Hungary were hammered out after a number of stormy sessions. The unpredictable Soviets, rebuffed in a demand for the Italian colony of Libya, insisted successfully on keeping their troops in Rumania and Hungary in order to guard their communication lines to occupied Austria. Endless wrangling over procedural matters and speeches full of propaganda marked the formal sessions. Finally, in February, 1947, the five treaties were officially concluded in a session at Paris. All five of the defeated nations, save Bulgaria, lost some of their prewar territory. Italy was shorn of her whole African empire of more than a million square miles and lost additional territory to France, Greece, Albania, and Yugoslavia. Each of the vanquished states was to pay a modest amount of reparations, and each was required to accept a severe limit on the size of its armed forces and to assure "the enjoyment of human rights and the fundamental freedoms" of all citizens. Thus it was that almost two years after Hitler's Germany went down in defeat, peace was made with five of his former allies.

Hermann Goering, chief of the Nazi air force, makes a plea at the Nuremberg trials. Seated in the row with him are, from Goering forward: Rudolf Hess, Joachim von Ribbentrop, Wilhelm Keitel, and Ernst Kaltenbrunner. (United Press.)

## THE CRUMBLING OF BIG THREE UNITY, 1945–1947

### Dilemma in Germany

But there was to be no peace treaty for Germany. Discussions about the future of this strategic area of Central Europe, so crucial for the balance of power, foundered always on the question of the place of a reunited Germany in the struggle between East and West. Cooperation between Russia and the West broke down swiftly, first over economic matters, and then over the whole range of German policy. Soviet commanders ignored the Potsdam agreement that Germany should be treated as an economic unit. They took as reparations both plant equipment and current output, in defiance of the policies of the Allied Control Council. In addition, they never made food deliveries promised for the Western zones. In their Eastern sector, the Soviets moved swiftly to impose a communist-dominated government on a third of Germany. After finally halting the delivery of reparations to Russia, the Americans and British joined their zones economically in December, 1946. The French, though also concerned by the breakdown of Soviet cooperation in Germany, were not yet ready for so drastic a step. By the early months of 1947, four-power cooperation in Germany was dead.

At Moscow, in March, 1947, one last major effort was made to break the German deadlock. Truman was convinced that a final attempt at agreement was necessary before accepting the split of Germany as being beyond healing. He felt so because a divided Germany loomed as the most serious menace to future peace. Accordingly, the American delegation, led by Secretary of State George Marshall (who had just replaced James Byrnes), was instructed to be as flexible as possible in meeting any legitimate Russian demands arising out of fear for their security. But Stalin's negotiators made it very plain that they wanted no settlement in Germany or in Europe. Marshall interpreted the Soviet attitude to mean that they intended to play for time and delay a return to stable conditions in Europe as long as possible. From this time forward, the Truman administration was convinced that only a policy of realism would sway the Soviets to acquiesce in movements to restore stable world conditions. Within eighteen months of the end of World War II, the fateful decision was taken to begin anew the process of building American strength.

The decisive stand in the spring of 1947 ended a period of indecision and vacillation. In Europe, Truman had wavered between strong suspicion of Soviet motives and continued hope that Stalin might cooperate. In the Far East, he had been torn by doubts about Chiang Kai-shek's effectiveness and fears of a Communist victory in China. At home, he had called for universal military training but then surrendered to the irresistible urge to bring American soldiers and sailors home. As a result, the wartime force of perhaps twelve million men and women had melted away to little more than a million. Never had a great nation depleted its strength so completely in so short a time. Outside of pious hopes for the success of the United Nations and unrealistic expectations of Soviet-American cooperation, the United States could not be said to have had a foreign policy in these discouraging months that followed the joyous celebrations of 1945.

## Churchill's Warning

There had been warnings from several sources of what was coming. As tension rose in the spring of 1946, Winston Churchill, now out of office, had come to Fulton, Missouri, to deliver an urgent message. With Truman beside him on the platform, Churchill spoke bluntly of the dangers he foresaw. He pointed directly to the threat of Russian expansion and called for an Anglo-American alliance to halt it. "From Stettin in the Baltic to Trieste in the Adriatic," said the doughty Briton in words that were to become famous, "an iron curtain has descended across the Continent. . . . I do not believe that Soviet Russia desires war. What they desire is the fruits of war and the indefinite expansion of their power and doctrines. . . . I am convinced that there is nothing they admire so much as strength, and there is nothing for which they have less respect than weakness, especially military weakness."

Churchill's grim warning met with a chill reception. It was a measure of the nation's mood in 1946 that his speech was roundly criticized in many quarters as "provocative" and likely to destroy the UN. But it created far less stir than a speech by Henry Wallace later in the year in which the former Vice-President, now Secretary of Commerce, charged that American policy was too anti-Soviet. The United States, said Wallace, had gotten needlessly "tough" with the Soviet Union. Only friendship and understanding would produce peace. Churchill's alliance would lead to war, he insisted, concluding with the remark that "just two days ago, when President Truman read these words, he said that they represented the policy of his Administration."

Wallace's remark sparked a blazing controversy. From Paris, Secretary Byrnes sent a sharp message to Truman: "If it is not completely clear . . . that Mr. Wallace should be asked to refrain from criticizing the foreign policy of the United States while he is a member of your Cabinet, I must ask you to accept my resignation immediately." Vandenberg and other Senators scored Wallace's speech. Though Truman had seen the speech and told reporters he approved of it, he now retreated in the face of criticism, saying that he intended only to defend Wallace's right to express his ideas. A week later Wallace was dismissed from the Cabinet. No other incident of 1946 so confused and angered the American people as the President's inept handling of this affair. It seemed to symbolize the frustrations and uncertainties of that unhappy year.

## Russia and the Bomb

Meanwhile, American expectations for the United Nations were rudely thwarted on several fronts. Russia failed to join UNESCO and some other branches of the UN; she attacked the trusteeship system as a cloak for imperialism; there was sharp disagreement over the admission of new members with both Russia and the Western powers vetoing the applications of states thought likely to become satellites of the other; and soon Russia was using the big-power veto with a frequency that alarmed the Western nations and paralyzed the operations of the Security Council. All over the world doubt was growing whether the UN would be able to perform its primary tasks of preventing war and punishing aggression.

Yet there were some bright spots. For instance, the Soviets offered no objection to housing the United Nations on American soil and did not oppose American trusteeship for a number of former Japanese islands. The UN was instrumental, too, in securing the peaceful withdrawal of Russian troops from Iran, which had been occupied by British and Russian forces during the war. It succeeded also in arranging a cease-fire between Dutch and native troops in Indonesia in 1947 and putting an end to fighting between India and Pakistan over Kashmir the following year. Whenever the complaint involved the essential interest of a great power, however, as in Greece, where native communists were getting Soviet support, the UN was less successful in restoring peace.

No more vital question came before the UN in its first year than the control of atomic weapons. The danger to world peace and to civilization itself from the atomic bomb was by this time appallingly clear. In July, 1946, the American Navy carried out extensive bomb tests on the island of Bikini. The results were profoundly disturbing; a great leap forward in the destructiveness of war was clearly at hand, and even more advanced bombs were understood to be in preparation. Said one observer, who watched the sailors board the target ships at Bikini after the blasts, "they gradually became gripped by a strange, obsessive fear. 'Decks you can't stay on for more than a few minutes; air you can't breathe without a gas-mask but which smells like all other air; water you can't swim in; fish you can't eat; it's a fouled-up world,' they said."

The plan offered to the International Atomic Energy Commission in 1946 by the American delegate, Bernard Baruch, was an act of high statesmanship. Based on a brilliant report by Dean Acheson and David Lilienthal, it called for the creation of an international authority with a complete monopoly over the mining and use of fissionable materials.

An underwater test of an atom bomb at Bikini Atoll in July, 1946. At the instant of detonation, this dome of water rose above the test ships in the lagoon. (United Press.)

Under it, peaceful atomic activities could be carried on by individuals and governments only under license by the authority, which would have its own stockpiles of atomic materials that could be sold for safe commercial or scientific use. To check on all such activities, a rigid system of inspection would be established, and violators of authority rulings would be severely dealt with. In order that the authority might be able to cope with a recalcitrant government, its plants would be widely dispersed, so that a preponderance of atomic weapons could be manufactured, if necessary, to bring an offending state into line. No veto would be possible in the authority. As this system of control and inspection came into being, the United States would turn over by stages all its atomic facilities and secrets. When the system was complete, the United States would destroy its existing bombs and join in a general ban on all future manufacture of atomic weapons. "We are here," said Baruch in his speech to the Commission, "to make a choice between the quick and the dead."

But the American offer to give up its monopoly on atomic weapons was rejected by the Soviets. Though they were still three years away from exploding their own bomb, they resisted every crucial point in the Baruch Plan. Their counterproposals—destruction of existing stockpiles, outlawing of atomic weapons prior to establishing an inspection system, and enforcement in the Security Council, where the Soviets had a veto—were no less than an outright demand for surrender of American atomic superiority. Shrewdly, they made effective propagandistic use of their call to outlaw the bomb. They strongly denounced the inspection scheme, the provisions for punishment, and the American right to determine its own disarmament timetable in the Baruch plan. Why, the Soviet representative Gromyko shouted, should the Soviets trust the United States to disarm at the proper time when the Americans by their insistence on inspection showed that they did not trust the Soviets? Though the Baruch plan was endorsed in the General Assembly, the Soviets kept it from being adopted in the Security Council. After three years of hopeless wrangling, the International Atomic Energy Commission suspended further discussion of the subject in July, 1949. Two months later, the Soviets exploded their first atomic device. An atomic arms race, the most fearful prospect conceivable at the end of World War II, now rapidly became a reality.

## Soviet Postwar Expansion

American hopes of postwar cooperation with the Soviets, dampened in Poland, Germany, and the UN, were thoroughly drenched by the spring of 1947. In nation after nation in Eastern Europe, "people's democratic republics," dominated by communists and pro-Soviet in policy, had been smashed down upon populations totaling a hundred million people. The Yalta pledge of free elections in the liberated countries was now a cynical mockery. A ring of satellite states had been erected around the western borders of the Soviet Union in less than two years. From the Baltic to the Adriatic, as Churchill had declared, Soviet power was firmly entrenched. Behind the Iron Curtain lay Poland, Hungary, Bulgaria, Rumania, and Albania; while in Yugoslavia and Czechoslovakia a precarious independence was maintained under the shadow of Soviet power.

To the south and southwest of the Soviet empire lay the Middle East, the gateway to possible future expansion into Africa and Asia. And only the relatively weak states of Greece, Turkey, and Iran stood between the Soviets and an outlet to the warm water ports of the Mediterranean and the Persian Gulf. Heavy

Soviet pressure was applied to all three of these countries in the period just after the war. In the Azerbaijan province of northern Iran, for instance, the Soviets in 1946 established a puppet government, which collapsed only after the withdrawal of Russian occupation troops under strong American and UN protest. In war-ravaged Greece, guerrilla fighters were kept supplied by the communist nations on Greece's border in an attempt to over-throw the Greek government. Torn by civil war, weakened by poverty, the Greeks seemed an excellent target for Soviet expansion. In Turkey, the Soviets tried yet another stratagem, demanding naval and military bases in the Dardanelles Straits and a "friendship treaty" with the Soviet Union. Everywhere on the southern perimeter of Soviet power in the spring of 1947 were apprehension, fear, and uncertainty about the future.

## THE END OF INNOCENCE, 1947–1949

### The Truman Doctrine

A decisive shift in American policy took place in that spring of 1947. In February, the British government announced that it would no longer be able to bear the burden of aiding Greece in its fight against the communist guerrillas. Unless America acted swiftly, then, a Russian breakthrough to the Middle East was imminent. Now that Britain, exhausted by six years of war, was forced to give up her historic responsibilities in the eastern Mediteranean, would the United States assume them? Would America act to prevent a communist take-over in Greece and Turkey?

Britain's exhaustion brought Truman face-to-face with the central fact of the postwar world: America alone stood between the Soviets and the achievement of all their aims. The world was bipolar—no other nation could effectively intervene to protect the balance of power that shielded American security. Power, as Theodore Roosevelt had foreseen, meant responsibility; America might play her role reluctantly or naively but she could not avoid playing it. But how could this truth be explained to a public that was unprepared for it? "There's only one way," Senator Vandenberg, the architect of bipartisanship in foreign policy, said to Truman. "That is to make a personal appearance before Congress and scare hell out of the country."

Truman took his advice. On March 12, 1947, he asked a joint session of Congress for $400 million in military and economic aid for Greece and Turkey. "I believe," said the President in the heart of his speech, "that it must be the foreign policy of the United States to support free peoples who are resisting attempted subjugation by armed minorities or by outside pressures. . . . The free peoples of the world look to us for support in maintaining their freedoms. If we falter in our leadership, we may endanger the peace of the world—and we shall surely endanger the welfare of our own Nation."

This was the Truman Doctrine—a turning point in American postwar policy. Henceforth, we would give aid to those who were defending their freedom against communist subversion or Soviet pressure. The idea shocked many who had not yet thrown off the wartime mood of trust in the Soviet Union and faith in the effectiveness of the UN. Wallace and others on the left attacked the President for bypassing the UN and promising aid to corrupt and reactionary regimes; from the extreme right came anguished cries that the new policy would lead to bankruptcy and a series of global crusades; and many thoughtful Americans, deeply concerned by the turn of postwar events, asked where the Truman Doctrine would lead. Did it mean fighting communism everywhere in the world and finally a third world war? Truman's supporters assured the nation that the new policy meant only the assumption of limited responsibilities in areas where there was hope of success. So in the end the bill was approved in both houses of Congress by decisive majorities. Significant opposition came only from midwestern Republicans, who spoke for the old isolationist tradition.

## The Strategy of Containment

Behind the Truman Doctrine lay a new estimation of Soviet motives and intentions. Heretofore, even when opposing Soviet intransigence in Eastern Europe and the UN, there had been a disposition to believe in the "reasonableness" of the Soviet position. Arguments could always be found to justify each Soviet departure from just or honorable standards of conduct, as these were understood in the West. The Russians, it was argued, were understandably suspicious of Western motives; they were legitimately concerned for their own security; or they had experienced too much of British balance-of-power manipulations in the past. A little firmness coupled with patience and understanding, it was thought, would bring the Soviet rulers to see that they had nothing to fear from the West. The idea that Russia was a revolutionary regime bent on destroying the capitalistic institutions of the West was rarely heard in public discussions during the immediate postwar period. Only Churchill among major Western leaders had dared to speak out and he was largely repudiated.

But now, in the spring of 1947, a different view of Soviet motives began to gain acceptance. In a brilliant, anonymous article in *Foreign Affairs*, George Kennan, the State Department's foremost expert on the Soviet Union, reviewed "The Sources of Soviet Conduct." The Russian view of their relations with the West, he wrote, was one of fundamental antagonism. The world outside the Soviet Union, according to communist theory, was hostile; it was the Russians' duty to overthrow the political institutions beyond their borders. This Soviet hostility, Kennan said, was a constant factor in world relations; it would go on until capitalism was gone. From this world-view of the Soviets sprang many of the characteristics of their actions that Westerners found disturbing: their secretiveness, duplicity, unfriendliness, and suspiciousness. While Soviet tactics might change from time to time, their objectives would not be shaken. "There will always be Americans," he wrote, "who will leap forward with gleeful announcements 'that the Russians have changed'. . . . But we should not be misled by tactical maneuvers. These characteristics of Soviet policy, like the postulates from which they flow, are basic to the internal nature of Soviet power, and will be with us . . . until the nature of Soviet power is changed."

Plainly, then, the fight would be long, for the Kremlin was in no hurry. "Like the Church," Kennan warned, "it is dealing in ideological concepts which are of a long-term validity, and it can afford to be patient." Lenin himself had taught caution, flexibility, and deception as valuable qualities. Soviet power was "a fluid stream which moves constantly, wherever it is permitted to move, toward a given goal. Its main concern is to make sure that it has filled every nook and cranny available to it in the basin of world power." If blocked, it would back up and accept the inevitable. "The main thing is that there should always be pressure, increasing constant pressure, toward the desired goal."

How could such a resolute yet flexible enemy be stopped? Kennan's answer was that America should direct its strength and intelligence toward "a long-term patient, but firm and viligant containment of Russian expansive tendencies." This had nothing to do with "outward histrionics," with "blustering" or gestures of "toughness." On the contrary, too threatening an attitude might force the Russians into fighting despite their sense of realism. What America should do was to apply counterforce at every point on the Soviet periphery where expansionist tendencies appeared. By thwarting Russian expansion, the strains and stresses of Soviet society would be enormously increased. This would "force upon the Kremlin a far greater degree of moderation and circumspection than it has had to observe in recent years, and . . . promote tendencies which must eventually find their outlet in either the breakup or the gradual mellowing of Soviet power." The containment policy, calling for firmness, patience, and long-range planning by the United States, was an acid test of the capabilities of a democratic nation. It made the security of the American people "dependent on their pulling themselves together and accepting the responsibilities of moral and political leadership that history plainly intended them to bear." *

## The Marshall Plan

While this new view of Soviet conduct was being constructed, the plight of Western Europe, critical since the war, had become dangerous in the extreme. Crisis after crisis had wracked the governments of France and Italy; economic recovery had been slow and halting in all the Western nations; and grim talk of violent social upheaval became more credible with each passing day. Said Winston Churchill in May, 1947: "What is Europe now? It is a rubble-heap, a charnel house, a breeding-ground of pestilence and hate." Visitors returning from France and Italy warned that these countries might be next to fall to communist subversion. Only American · aid, some $11 billion worth in the months since V-E

* "X", "The Sources of Soviet Conduct," *Foreign Affairs*, XXV (July, 1947), pp. 566-582.

Gallery of makers of foreign policy in the forties: Dean Acheson, Secretary of State; George Kennan, State Department expert on Russia; Arthur S. Vandenberg, Senator; George Marshall, general, negotiator in China, Secretary of State. (All from New York Public Library Picture Collection.)

Day, had prevented starvation and complete collapse.

Kennan, who had been brought home from Russia to head the Policy Planning Staff in the State Department, favored a policy of massive American aid to Europe. Only such a policy, he believed, could restore Europe's productive capacity, cut the dollar gap, and bring about a return of political stability. The salvation of Western Europe, the Kennan group believed, was vital to the security of the United States. Since America could not supply the whole world's needs, it must, said Undersecretary of State Dean Acheson, "concentrate . . . emergency assistance in areas where it will be most effective in building world political and economic stability." This meant that the State Department, with Truman's approval, had decided that the recovery of Western Europe had a higher American priority than helping Chiang Kai-shek in his civil war against the Chinese communists.

On June 5, 1947, George Marshall spoke at Harvard University. "Our policy," said the Secretary, "is directed not against any country or doctrine but against hunger, poverty, desperation, and chaos." It was the American purpose to revive the sagging world economy, espe-

cially in Europe, in order to encourage the survival of social conditions in which freedom could flourish. More serious than even the visible destruction of European cities, factories, and railroads, said Marshall, was the dislocation of the entire European economy. The business structure of Europe had broken down and public confidence was at a low ebb. Indeed, barter had replaced money as the medium of exchange in many parts of the continent. City industries were not producing enough to trade for food and raw materials, so farmers were withdrawing fields from crop cultivation. "The modern system of the division of labor," Marshall warned, "is in danger of breaking down." Europe's requirements for the next three or four years, he concluded, "are so much greater than her present ability to pay that she must have substantial help, or face economic, social, and political deterioration of a very grave character."

To receive aid, Marshall told the Europeans, they would have to work out for themselves a comprehensive program of reconstruction. Russia, invited to participate, refused as did her satellites in Eastern Europe. Throughout the summer of 1947, however, sixteen West European nations drew up a set of industrial and agricultural goals, made plans to cooperate in reducing trade and currency barriers, and emerged with an over-all plan of reconstruction that would require $29 billion in American help over a four-year period. In December, Truman asked Congress for an appropriation of $17 billion to make the Marshall Plan a reality.

Vandenberg led the fight for the program in a Congress now controlled by Republicans. Without his stalwart leadership, the bill might well have gone down to defeat. Opposing him were an odd combination: the economy-minded conservatives and the anguished followers of Henry Wallace. But Vandenberg made

shrewd concessions at several points that won new support for the bill. He got Truman and Marshall to agree to an initial appropriation of $5 billion coupled with a recommendation that the program go forward in subsequent years. To meet Congressional criticism of the State Department, he recommended that an independent agency with a director of cabinet status administer the program. He accepted, too, a suggestion that the program's continuation "be dependent upon the continuity of cooperation among the countries involved." Before the bill came to a vote, even Senator Taft, leader of the economy bloc, said that he would support it.

Vandenberg was aided in his campaign by a new Soviet stroke in Eastern Europe. In the midst of the debate over the Marshall Plan, the communists seized power in Czechoslovakia. Nothing so convinced the American people and their representatives in Congress of the reality of the dangers that Vandenberg pictured as this bold coup in the most advanced democracy in Eastern Europe. The goals of the Marshall Plan, Vandenberg told the Senate on March 1, 1948, were "peace and stability for free men in a free world. It seeks them by economic rather than by military means. . . . It aims to preserve the victory against aggression and dictatorship which we thought we won in World War II. It strives to help stop World War III before it starts." When the votes were counted, the Senate had approved the bill by 69 to 17. Vandenberg, soon to undergo a serious operation, had won his greatest victory in a cause almost opposite to the one that had brought him fame as a crusader for isolationism in the thirties. His premature death in 1951 robbed the nation of its most effective Congressional leader in the immediate postwar years.

What may be said of the success of the Marshall Plan, or the European Recovery Program, as it was officially called? It seems, in retrospect, the single most imaginative effort made on behalf of a stable world order right after the war. It fired the imagination of peoples burned out by long years of war and misery. It set a course of action that stirred the self-respect and initiative of Europeans, as well as the idealism of Americans. And it worked so well so fast: By the end of 1949, levels of output of West European industry had surpassed those of 1939. Even the West German economy, following a stringent currency reform, began to rise at a phenomenal rate. By the end of the Marshall Plan in 1952, production of European industries had risen more than 35 per cent over prewar levels, while farm output was up 10 per cent over the same base period. The increase in production was valued at several times the $13 billion infused into the European economy between 1948 and 1952 by the Economic Cooperation Administration, the agency which dispensed the Marshall Plan appropriations. Trade among participating countries jumped 70 per cent and confidence in West European currencies climbed. Marshall called the result a "near miracle." Despite these material accomplishments, however, the greatest significance of the Marshall Plan, according to the British writer, Barbara Ward, was political and moral: "It found a continent shattered by war, divided between warring parties, fearful, uncertain, lacking the thread of hope and faith that all men need to guide them out of the labyrinth. Within two years it had created, if not a continent without problems, at least a community with a sense of promise and purpose. . . ."

### Blockade of Berlin

Soon after the passage of the Marshall Plan, Russia gave her answer to the American program of rebuilding Europe. New quarrels over the adminis-

Devastation after the war. The Cathedral of Frankfurt, Germany, with demolished bridges and buildings. It was conditions like these that led the United States to aid both victors and vanquished. (Underwood & Underwood.)

tration of Berlin in June, 1948, led to a Russian demand that Soviet-sponsored currency be used throughout the city. But the Western powers were already pushing for currency reform in West Berlin and were considering the creation of a constitution and government in the western zones of occupation in Germany. The Russians thereupon set up a complete blockade of all land traffic into Berlin. At stake were not only Berlin but also the Western position in Germany and Western Europe. If Britain and the United States could be forced out of Berlin, the Soviets would win a major battle in what was now beginning to be called the Cold War. "When Berlin falls," cabled the American commander, General Lucius Clay, "Western Germany will be next. If we mean . . . to hold Europe against communism, we must not budge . . . if we withdraw, our position in Europe is threatened. If America does not understand this now, does not know the issue is cast, then it never will, and Communism will run rampant."

Britain and America did not budge. Ruling out a military challenge to the Red Army as likely to bring total war, Truman decided upon an airlift to bring needed supplies to the city. A minimum of four thousand tons of food and fuel daily was deemed necessary to keep Berliners alive. By October, American and British pilots were flying in nearly five thousand tons each day. For 324 days the city was kept functioning by airplanes. At the peak of the effort in April, 1949, a plane put in at the Berlin airport every three minutes and the daily load was pushed to over twelve thousand tons. The besieged Berliners were actually eating more than when the blockade began. Finally, on May 12, 1949, the Russians capitulated to this magnificent display of determination and lifted the blockade. No other event of these melancholy postwar years so elevated the spirits of free men and women as this remarkable victory over Soviet expansion. "The position of the Soviet Union in regard to the struggle for the soul of Europe," said the new Secretary of State, Dean Acheson, "has changed from the offensive to the defensive."

### The North Atlantic Treaty

Meanwhile, as tensions built up over Berlin and the Czechoslovakian coup, Americans veered sharply away from their wartime mood of trust in the Soviets and faith in the UN. Was the Marshall Plan enough? Would European industry be restored only to fall into the hands of the Soviets? A genuine war scare stirred the country in the summer of 1948. "Cold fear is gripping people hereabouts," wrote a Chicago reporter. "Fear of what? Most people don't know exactly. It's not fear of Russia alone. . . . It's not fear of Communism in this country. . . . It's not fear of the atom bomb. . . . But it does seem to be a reluctant conviction that these three relentless forces are prowling the earth and that somehow they are bound to mean trouble for us . . . all winter, confidence in peace has been oozing away."

Europeans, too, were chilled by the events of 1948. On the continent, only a half-dozen Allied divisions stood opposed to the nearly two hundred divisions of the Red Army. Fear ran through the capitals of Western Europe in that eventful spring and summer. In March, Britain and France joined with the Benelux countries (Belgium, Luxemburg, and The Netherlands) in signing the Brussels de-

fense pact. All five nations, according to the terms of the treaty, would come to the aid of any signatory power who was attacked in Europe. Without American support, however, the Brussels treaty seemed a slender reed against the preponderance of Soviet power. In May, Senator Vandenberg introduced an important resolution calling on the Administration to begin negotiations with other nations for a system of collective defense. This laid the basis for an American alliance with the European powers, the first such peace-time treaty in the history of the United States.

From July, 1948, to April, 1949, negotiations for a North Atlantic Treaty continued. At the heart of the treaty, which eventually bound the United States, Canada, Italy, Iceland, Norway, Denmark, and Portugal to the five Brussels powers, was an agreement that "an armed attack against one or more of them in Europe or North America shall be considered an attack against them all." Joint commands of the military services would be established, as well as a permanent treaty organization, which eventually comprised a North Atlantic Council, a Secretary-General, and a Military Committee made up of the chiefs of staff of all NATO countries. Later, Greece, Turkey, and West Germany were to be admitted to the treaty group. The latter state was organized in 1949 by a West German constitutional convention, while the communists, in reply, set up a one-party state in their East German zone.

After two devastating world wars, America was now committed, *in advance*, to fight for Europe's freedom. NATO forces, particularly American troops, would act as a "tripwire" setting off air retaliation against the Soviet Union itself should the Russians attack. General Eisenhower was sent to Europe in 1951 to begin building the command organization and strategy to resist a Soviet offensive on the continent. Here was the culmination of Allied, particularly American, efforts to resist Soviet expansion in the immediate postwar era. No longer could the Truman Administration be charged with innocence concerning the aims and purposes of Russian communism. To Soviet accusations that the NATO treaty was aimed at aggression and war, Secretary of State Acheson replied that "This country is not planning to make war against anyone. . . . We have learned our history lesson from two world wars in less than half a century. That experience has taught us that the control of Europe by a single aggressive unfriendly power would constitute an intolerable threat to the national security of the United States. . . . We have also learned that if the free nations do not stand together, they will fall one by one."

### Defense of the Hemisphere

The totalitarian threat to Western Europe, as in the thirties, had important effects throughout Latin America. During the years from 1945 to 1949, as Soviet postwar aims became clear, the nations of the western hemisphere drew closer together for their mutual protection. Even before the end of the war, all the American nations save Argentina had agreed at Chapultepec, Mexico, to complete the transformation of the Monroe Doctrine into a multilateral treaty. According to the Act of Chapultepec, signed in March, 1945, as a war measure, any attack on the territory or independence of an American state, whether from outside or within the hemisphere, would be met by combined action by all of them. Argentina, which had remained friendly to Hitler during the war, finally signed the Chapultepec agreement and, at the last moment, entered the war against Germany and Japan.

But American troubles with Argentina were not over. In February, 1946, the United States government released a Blue Book strongly denouncing the militaristic clique headed by Juan Perón, which was accused of heading "a vicious partnership of Nazi and native totalitarian forces." This bold American intervention in Argentine affairs was followed, two weeks later, by the decisive victory of Perón in a presidential election. Tension between the two countries remained high for more than a year after Perón's election until Truman finally invited Argentina to participate in discussions for a Western Hemisphere defense pact. The world situation had so deteriorated by this time that Truman was convinced that American solidarity was more important than the continuation of his anti-Perón policy.

In August, 1947, spokesmen for twenty-one American nations met at Rio de Janeiro to implement the Act of Chapultepec. A treaty was drawn up which obligated the signatory states to break relations with any violator of the Chapultepec pledge, if two-thirds of the signers so voted. A security zone was established around the American continents, extending as far as Greenland, within which the treaty was to be operative. The Chapultepec principle thus became permanent policy. The following spring, at an Inter-American Conference at Bogotá, the Organization of American States was created. This was to be a regional association of the American republics, as provided in the UN charter, with regular procedures for conferences, consultations of foreign ministers, and a permanent headquarters in Washington. The Pact of Bogotá called for the peaceful settlement of all inter-American disputes, fair treatment of foreign capital invested in American states, and economic cooperation among the pact members. By May, 1948, when the Bogotá agreements were signed, Latin America was linked by numerous ties of defense and trade to North America and

Western Europe in the struggle against Soviet expansion.

Despite American concern over Latin America, the Good Neighbor policy began to deteriorate in the late nineteen-forties. Not only the aggressive American policy toward Argentina, but the growing American interest in European defense contributed to the decline. As American responsibilities grew in the late forties, Europe and Asia came to replace Latin America in the spotlight of American attention which it had enjoyed in the early Roosevelt years.

### Postwar Economic Policy

A large part of the United States's problem in Latin America was economic. The Latin Americans, like most of the people of the world, were unable to sell to the United States sufficient quantities of goods to pay for the imports they needed. Despite massive aid to foreign nations through the United Nations Relief and Rehabilitation Agency (UNRRA), a huge dollar gap began to appear in America's economic relations with other countries. This dollar gap was made worse by the abrupt ending of lend-lease, the cutting off of American contributions to UNRRA in 1946, and the rise in prices of American goods when price controls were abandoned.

Truman remained loyal to the liberal trade policies of the Roosevelt era. Diligently, he searched for ways and means of cutting the dollar gap and stimulating international trade. A conference was called at Geneva in 1947 to discuss mutual tariff problems. Out of this conference came the General Agreement on Tariffs and Trade (GATT), which cut American tariff rates about one-fifth in exchange for similar concessions from other nations. But the GATT accord had numerous weaknesses. American rates were still high; the former Axis nations and the Iron Curtain countries did not participate; quotas

continued to operate in the case of a number of farm products; and the administration of American customs was complex and baffling to the would-be trader. There was further concern because of the action of the Eightieth Congress in imposing "fees" on wool imports and advising the Tariff Commission, as it extended the reciprocal trade policy for only one year, to see that import duties did not fall below the "peril point."

America also supported the conference at Havana, in the fall of 1947, which sought to establish an International Trade Organization (ITO). Those who joined ITO agreed to negotiate tariff reductions, forgo export quotas and subsidies, and otherwise cooperate in expediting the flow of world trade. But ITO ran into strong resistance in the United States from economic nationalists and others who were suspicious of various features of the plan. Despite Administrative backing, the bill calling for American entry into ITO was buried in Congressional committees. There it remained despite President Truman's warning that America's trade policy could "lead the nations to economic peace . . . or plunge them into economic war."

Truman suffered few such defeats on issues of foreign policy in his first administration. In two swift years, he had gained Congressional approval for a series of radical departures from traditional American policy. He had brought about a major shift in American policy toward Europe and the Soviet Union through the Truman Doctrine, the Marshall Plan, and the North Atlantic Treaty. He had succeeded in building hemispheric solidarity and preventing a communist take-over in Berlin. Opposition to his policies at home had been weak and ineffective. The NATO agreements, for instance, were approved by a Senate vote of 82 to 13. His success was due in considerable measure, of course, to able Congressional leadership, notably from Senator Vandenberg, but it owed something, too, to Truman's own leadership and the change in popular attitudes toward the Soviets. By 1949, in any case, there were few Americans left who did not share the President's conviction that the threat of communist expansion was the gravest danger facing the nation.

## THE CHINESE PUZZLE

Curiously enough, however, most Americans were slow to recognize the danger of communist gains on the other side of the world. While Truman was struggling to rebuild European strength against the Red Army, communist forces in China were winning victory after victory over the armies of Chiang Kai-shek. By 1947, the year of the Truman Doctrine and Marshall's speech at Harvard, the contagion of defeatism was spreading through Nationalist China and victory for the communists began to seem possible. Why was it that communism triumphed in China between 1945 and 1949? Who was responsible? Why did America not act before it was too late?

### The Setting

From the turn of the century, China had been in constant turmoil. The weakened Manchu dynasty, protected by European rivalry and the American Open Door policy, was finally overthrown in 1911. A decade or more of chaos followed, marked by internecine conflict among the warlords controlling various provinces in China. Out of this conflict emerged in the nineteen-twenties the Kuomintang, or Nationalist Party, made up of intellectual and revolutionary elements headed by Dr. Sun Yat-sen. Upon Sun Yat-sen's death in 1925, his ablest general, Chiang Kai-shek, came to power. He soon broke with the communists, who heretofore had played an important role in the Kuomintang's success. For a decade Chiang struggled with only partial success to create a strong administration over China's scattered provinces. Then, in 1937, came the all-out Japanese effort to conquer China.

Even before Pearl Harbor, America sent aid to China and American sympathies were clearly on the Chinese side. And during the war, American supplies were flown over the Himalayas, while an American general, Joseph W. Stilwell, became chief of staff to Chiang Kai-shek. It was Stilwell's hope that Chinese resistance against the Japanese, split into communist and Kuomintang factions, could be stiffened. Unsuccessfully, he tried to reorganize the Chinese armies and foster cooperation between the two hostile groups. He was appalled by the low morale among Chinese troops, the corruption of the Nationalist regime, and the ineptness of Chinese military strategy. Furthermore, he took an intense personal dislike to Chiang, who returned his feelings in full. Finally, under intense prodding from Chiang supporters, President Roosevelt relieved Stilwell of his command in 1944.

Stilwell was replaced by Albert C. Wedemeyer, who was able to win Chiang's confidence but who accomplished no more than his predecessor in galvanizing Chiang and his staff into effective action. Wedemeyer found support for his policy of trusting Chiang in Patrick J. Hurley, who was FDR's personal representative and later ambassador to Chungking. Like Stilwell, Hurley tried to bring the Kuomintang and communist factions together in a coalition government, but he became convinced that his efforts were being undermined by foreign-service officers who were arguing that Chiang's regime was corrupt and that the communists were certain to prevail. Just after the war came to an end, with the question of China's future no closer to solution, Hurley resigned his post in a burst of indignation, charging the State Department and Embassy officials with the failure of American policy in China.

At war's end, hundreds of thousands of Chiang's troops were carried by American ships and planes to areas held by the Japanese, so that they, rather than the Communists, would be in control, and large amounts of American equipment were put into Chiang's hands. Thus, by the end of 1945, Nationalist troops were nominally in possession of most of China, except for Manchuria, which the Russians had occupied. As American forces now began their withdrawal from the Chinese theater, the stage was set for the last act in the tragic drama of China's fall to the communists.

### The Civil War

By November, 1945, Wedemeyer was warning of the consequences of a full American withdrawal. The abandonment of China, he prophecied, would mean the final victory of communism, for Chiang would never be able to unify his country and suppress his bitter foes. But few Americans believed this, and those who did were loath to become involved in a Chinese civil war on the side of an allegedly reactionary and corrupt regime.

The decision was taken to send General Marshall to China to seek a truce between Chiang and the communists and induce them to form a coalition government. He arrived in December, 1945. At first, he seemed to be succeeding in his task. A truce was arranged and plans were drawn up for a coalition regime. Even Stalin at this time apparently counseled the Chinese communists that a rap-

prochement with Chiang might be better than almost certain defeat at the hands of the Nationalists. But hatred, personal as well as ideological, ran deep between the opposing sides. When it became clear to the communists that the Nationalists were weaker than they had supposed, while dissatisfaction among the Chinese peasants and middle classes was more widespread than they had dared hope, violent quarrels replaced the relatively tranquil early sessions. Marshall became convinced that his task was hopeless and in January, 1947, gave up the attempt to restore peace.

The Chinese civil war now opened in earnest. The alternatives open to the United States, according to the American ambassador, John Stuart, were either to support the Nationalist government vigorously, or to withdraw completely, or else (he regarded this as the worst choice) to make a half-hearted effort to support Chiang. Yet it was this last course which the United States chose to follow. Though reluctant to abandon Chiang completely, the American government moved too late and too inconclusively to affect the march of events.

There were, to be sure, extenuating circumstances. The Nationalist armies of 1947 were better equipped and far superior in numbers to the communist forces. Few expected, therefore, the swift debacle that followed the withdrawal of American support from Chiang. Furthermore, during the crucial months when the battle turned decisively against Chiang, the Administration was busy with the important events in Europe which have just been recounted. The most critical period in the Chinese civil war, for example, coincided with the Berlin blockade.

Another mission, nonetheless, was sent to China in July, 1947. General Wedemeyer, at its head, concluded that it was dangerous to refuse aid to the Nationalists. A communist take-over in China, he warned, would imperil vital American interests throughout the Far East, for the Chinese communists were, in fact, merely agents of the Kremlin in its drive for world domination. The only recourse for the United States, he said, was to advocate putting Manchuria under UN authority and to inaugurate a program of American assistance to Chiang. Though Wedemeyer's recommendations, if followed, would probably not have forestalled a communist victory in China, they provided the only possible hope at this time. By the fall of 1947, the plight of Chiang's armies was clearly desperate.

But Truman did not ask for large-scale help for Chiang. He made only a very modest request for aid to Congress and a large part of the funds which were granted was earmarked for nonmilitary supplies. The President made no effort either to rally American opinion as he had done in the case of the Soviet threat to Greece and Turkey, or as he was to do during the Soviet blockade of Berlin. Perhaps Marshall, by now Secretary of State, was right when he said that the American government could do nothing to "make the present Chinese Government capable of re-establishing and then maintaining its control throughout all of China." But later critics did not forgive the Administration's failure to make the effort.

The communists completed their conquest of China in short order. By October, 1948, communists troops were in Mukden, capital of Manchuria, whence they swept down on the great cities of southern and eastern China. Incompetence, corruption, and runaway inflation marked the last days of the Chinese republic. The American ambassador learned, for example, that some of Chiang's top generals were hoarding thirty million silver dollars, while most of their troops went unpaid for months. In December, 1949, Chiang fled with his closest supporters to the island of Formosa, as the communists took over the shattered subcontinent of China.

## The Tragedy

Ambassador Stuart wrote a fitting epilogue for the tragedy of China. The choice before Americans in China, he said, seemed hopeless at the time. On

Victorious Communists march disarmed Nationalist troops down the main street of Shanghai during the civil war. (United Press.)

the one side were the shreds of demo-cratic idealism "perverted by bureau-cratic incompetence," while on the other was "a dynamic socialized reform vitiated by communist dogma, intolerance, and ruthlessness." Party members on both sides were but a fraction "of the huge, disorganized, inarticulate, amorphous pop-ulation." The great mass of the Chinese, he wrote, "cared for neither but were pow-erless to do anything about it." The Chi-nese people, wanting only "to be allowed to live their own lives with a minimum of government interference or oppression," were certain to lose no matter which party won. The tragedy of China, as it seemed to American policymakers, was that nei-ther faction seemed to promise a united, prosperous, and democratic future for the Chinese people. Political realism, it seemed later, should have dictated a pro-gram of strong resistance to a communist conquest of China. An American inter-vention on the scale of the Marshall Plan with the determination of the Berlin air-lift behind it might have saved China. But the price, in the still innocent years when the vital decisions were being made,

seemed too high. Was it even a feasible policy in the still changing political cli-mate of 1947 and 1948? It might well have interfered with the containment policy in Europe and almost certainly would have been unpopular in the United States. And even if America had intervened in strength, supporters of Truman's policy averred, it would have served only to prop up a fatally weak government that had lost the confidence of its own troops and citizens.

In any case, American intervention was not tried. And because it was not tried, it continued to haunt the minds of Ameri-cans in the years that followed. The fail-ure became an issue in partisan politics and set off one of the most intemperate political witch-hunts in American history. Further, to some it came to seem a debit in President Truman's otherwise brilliant record of leadership in the fight against communist expansion. And finally, it was to add to the general embitterment of American public life that took place in the early 1950's.

## FOR FURTHER STUDY

*The books by Churchill, Dulles, and Ferrell cited at the end of Chapters VIII and IX continue to be especially useful for the topics dealt with in this chapter.*

**General Accounts**

* H. Agar, *The Price of Power* (Chicago: U. of Chicago Press, 1957). A brilliant and forceful account of the main themes in American postwar history.
* W. Carleton, *The Revolu-tion in American Foreign Policy* (New York: Random House, rev. ed., 1957). A scholarly and interpretive review of American foreign policy from 1945 to the mid-1950's.

* Starred books are available in paperbound editions.

* H. Gatzke, *The Present in Perspective* (Chicago: Rand, Mc-Nally, rev. ed., 1961). A useful summary of the main events in world history since 1945.
* E. Goldman, *The Crucial Decade* (New York: Knopf, 1956). Covers American devel-opments from 1945 to 1955 in an informal way. The paper-bound edition by Vintage Books takes the story to 1960.
* R. Goldwin (ed.), *Readings in American Foreign Policy* (New York: Oxford U. Press, 1959). An exceptionally useful collec-tion of materials bearing on

the recent foreign policy of the United States.
* J. Lukacs, *A History of the Cold War* (Garden City, N.Y.: Doubleday, 1961). The author reviews the main events in the cold war, then analyzes the prin-cipal tendencies and develop-ments in Russian and American society.
   W. Rostow, *The United States in the World Arena* (New York: Harpers, 1960). An important evaluation of the American "na-tional style," how it developed, how it was affected by the Sec-ond World War and its after-

math, and what it means in the perilous world situation of today.

* J. Spanier, *American Foreign Policy since World War II* (New York: Praeger, 1960). This stimulating analysis has as its theme the idea that America's "separation of war and peace into two mutually exclusive states of affairs, and its divorce of force and diplomacy, have made it impossible to unite power and policy."

* W. Zornow, *America at Mid-Century* (Cleveland: Howard Allen, Inc., 1959). Intended as a supplement to textbooks in American history, this volume is to be revised from time to time.

## Special Studies

* R. Barnet, *Who Wants Disarmament?* (Boston: Beacon Press, 1960). An excellent review of the course of disarmament negotiations and thinking since 1945 that puts the Baruch Plan in proper perspective.

L. Bloomfield, *The United Nations and U. S. Foreign Policy* (Boston: Little, Brown, 1960). A thoughtful discussion of the relationship of the UN to America's security and national interest.

J. Byrnes, *Speaking Frankly* (New York: Harpers, 1947). The memoirs of the man who was Truman's Secretary of State from 1945 to 1947.

W. Davison, *The Berlin Blockade* (Princeton: Princeton U. Press, 1958). A full account of the blockade that is focused on such questions as how Berliners reacted under stress, the role of public opinion in a crisis, and how Soviet and Western diplomacy operated in the greatest crisis of the immediate postwar era.

C. Eichelberger, *UN: The First Ten Years* (New York: Harpers, 1955). A brief, sympathetic account.

H. Feis, *Between War and Peace* (Princeton: Princeton U. Press, 1960). A detailed and careful study of the events of the spring and summer of 1945 centering around the Potsdam Conference.

―――, *The China Tangle* (Princeton: Princeton U. Press, 1953). The best treatment of American policy in China from Pearl Harbor to the Marshall Mission.

W. Millis (ed.), *The Forrestal Diaries* (New York: Viking, 1951). Contains extracts from the private diaries of James Forrestal, who was Secretary of Navy under FDR and became the first Secretary of Defense in 1947.

G. Kennan, "The Sources of Soviet Conduct," *Foreign Affairs*, XXV (July, 1947), 566-582. The famous article by Mr. "X."

R. Payne, *The Marshall Story* (New York: Prentice-Hall, 1951). A popular, sympathetic, and largely uncritical biography.

H. Price, *The Marshall Plan and Its Meaning* (Ithaca: Cornell U. Press, 1955). An official history and evaluation of the Marshall Plan written under the auspices of the Governmental Affairs Institute.

H. Truman, *Memoirs*, two volumes (Garden City, N.Y.: Doubleday, 1955-1956). A full and forceful recounting of Truman's policies and problems as President.

United States Department of State, *United States Relations with China, with Special Reference to the Period 1944-1949* (Washington: Government Printing Office, 1949). The Truman Administration's "White Paper" on China, with an introduction by Dean Acheson.

R. Van Alstyne, *American Crisis Diplomacy* (Stanford: Stanford U. Press, 1952). An interpretation and a defense of the main developments in American policy in Europe and the Far East, particularly since 1939.

A. Vandenberg, Jr. (ed.), *The Private Papers of Senator Vandenberg* (Boston: Houghton Mifflin, 1952). Excerpts from the diaries, speeches, and other papers of this postwar champion of bipartisanship in foreign policy.

H. Vinacke, *Far Eastern Politics in the Postwar Period* (New York: Appleton-Century-Crofts, 1956). An excellent general his-

tory of Far Eastern developments between 1945 and 1955.

―――, *The United States and the Far East, 1945-1951* (Stanford: Stanford U. Press, 1952). A good, brief summary of American policy in the Far East from the end of World War II to the dismissal of General MacArthur.

A. Wedemeyer, *Wedemeyer Reports!* (New York: Holt, 1958). Chapter XXV deals with his mission to China in 1947.

* R. Winks (ed.), *The Marshall Plan and the American Economy* (New York: Holt, 1960). A booklet containing a number of conflicting views concerning the background, operation, and evaluation of the Marshall Plan.

## Fiction and Drama

* H. Habe, *Off Limits* (New York: Frederick Fell, 1957). A novel of Americans and Germans in complex human relationships against the background of the American occupation of Germany after World War II.

* A. Koestler, *Darkness at Noon* (New York: Macmillan, 1941). A penetrating insight into the working of the communist mentality.

* G. Orwell, *Animal Farm* (New York: Harcourt, Brace, 1946). A brilliant parody of a communist society in the setting of a barnyard.

* ―――, *1984* (New York: Harcourt, Brace, 1949). A much-discussed novel of what a completely totalitarian society might be like.

* V. Sneider, *The Teahouse of the August Moon* (New York: Putnam, 1951). A humorously satirical novel centering around a member of a government team sent to Okinawa, his commanding officer, and Plan B for the welfare of the natives.

## Films and Records

*The Cold Decade—Airlift* (Prudential Insurance Company, 28 minutes, sound, black and white). The film story of the Berlin Airlift of 1948-49.

*The Fall of China* (Prudential

Insurance Company, 29 minutes, sound, black and white). An outstanding documentary film on the events of the Chinese civil war from 1945 to 1949.

*I Can Hear It Now*—Vol. III: 1945-1949 (Columbia Records, edited by Murrow and Friendly). Another album of the sounds and speeches that made history between the end of the war and the lifting of the Berlin airlift.

*Nightmare in Red* (McGraw-Hill, 54 minutes, sound, black and white). A brilliant film reconstruction of the rise and expansion of Soviet communism from the "Project 20" series.

*1947—Year of Decision* (Teaching Film Custodians, 21 minutes, sound, black and white). Newsreel clips from this year of growing tension between America and the Soviet Union.

*The Nuremberg Trials* (Prudential Insurance Company, 29 minutes, sound, black and white). Another good documentary from the "Twentieth Century" series.

*The UN in a Revolutionary World* (National Educational Television, 29 minutes, sound, black and white). A televised discussion of the history of the UN and its role in maintaining peace.

# The Fruits
# of Frustration

## CHAPTER ELEVEN

Senator McCarthy with his aide, Roy Cohn.

THE MOOD OF THE

MR. WITHERS. Does the Senator think all the employees in the State Department are Communists?

MR. MC CARTHY. No. I think the vast majority of these employees are being done an almost irreparable wrong by having them painted with the brush of communism. . . .

MR. WITHERS. How does the Senator feel about attacking these men without calling names? How does the Senator feel the other employees who are straightforward feel about it, when he reflects on all of them, and does not call names?

MR. MC CARTHY. I think the condition today is so fraught with danger, I think we are in a period so definitely close to war, that even if we do damage some of the honest employees, I must take the only method I know of whereby I think we can secure a house cleaning. . . .

MR. WITHERS. The Senator simply tells us there are persons who are Communist but does not tell us who they are. Is that correct?

MR. MC CARTHY. . . . I have stated repeatedly that I would go before any Senate committee and divulge names. . . . I have dug out information which I think is of the utmost importance and I think we should get down to the job of trying to clean out these unusual people.

MR. WITHERS. Does the Senator indict or accuse or what is he doing in this speech? . . .

MR. MC CARTHY. I am not indicting those who are guilty. I am giving the Senate information about persons whom I consider to be Communists in the State Department.

—UNITED STATES SENATE, 1950

# THE POLITICS OF STALEMATE

By the time of China's fall, Harry S. Truman had begun his second term as President of the United States. Memories of the depression of the thirties, of Roosevelt's leadership, of the heroic days of war—these had begun to fade in the glare of the strange new responsibilities thrust upon the American people. The postwar world, it was by now clear, would bear no resemblance to the idyllic expectations nourished in wartime. Around the globe an aggressive communism threatened democratic liberties in a way more menacing, because more ambiguous, than Nazism had done. One form of totalitarianism had been crushed, only to give rise to another. The tides of the times were full with a new flood of frustration and disillusionment over the unhappy outcome of a great and victorious war. At the nation's helm, as the storm gathered in the late forties, was a man whose bumptious confidence and growing grasp of affairs contrasted sharply with his nervous and inexperienced leadership of 1945. Few people now asked, at any rate, as they did in 1945, "Who is Harry Truman?"

## The Man from Independence

Truman's administration began in a darkness that was real as well as figurative. It was late evening on the night of April 12, 1945, when a solemn Harry Truman took the oath of office.

His wife, beside him, seemed like a woman in pain. Outside the circle of klieg lights, Jonathan Daniels remembered thinking, the world beyond the White House seemed dark. "People everywhere," he wrote, "men in the streets, women who got the news by radio as they were cooking supper, soldiers in the Pacific, . . . Harry Hopkins in a hospital room in Minnesota, all had an individual and collective sense of the light going out like that at no other time in America since Lincoln had died in April exactly eighty years before." * Almost no one, in that hour of Roosevelt's death, thought of the great burden that fell on Harry Truman. Uninformed on the great matters of state that now confronted him, largely unknown as a political figure, he seemed pitifully inadequate to sit in Roosevelt's chair. "My God," said a soldier in southern Germany on that night of April 12, as the full realization of what had happened struck him, "Harry Truman is President of the United States!"

What manner of man was Truman? How had he been able to rise so swiftly from obscurity? What political forces thrust him to the forefront of American politics at this critical juncture in history? How did he view the office of the

* J. Daniels, *The Man of Independence* (Philadelphia: J. B. Lippincott Company, 1950), p. 258.

340

Presidency? These and other questions confronted political analysts who tried to explain how Harry Truman had become the leader of the free world.

A life-long resident of Missouri, Truman was born in 1884 in the little village of Lamar and grew up in Grandview, Independence, and Kansas City. He was a quiet, bookish, nearsighted boy who loved history and music. Denied admission to West Point because of his eyesight, he did not attend college but instead turned to odd jobs after his graduation from high school in 1901. After four years as a bank clerk in Kansas City, where he lived for a while in the same boarding house as Arthur Eisenhower, the brother of his successor in the White House, he was called back to the family farm at Grandview in 1906. There, for eleven years, the future President engaged in farming, dabbled in zinc mining and oil speculation, and got his first taste of politics. "It was on the farm," his mother said after Truman became President, "that Harry got his common sense. He didn't get it in town."

When war broke out in 1917, Truman worked hard to build a field artillery regiment in Kansas City. He went to France with his regiment and attained the rank of major by dint of hard work and outstanding leadership. Many of the men of his regiment later became his staunch supporters when he entered politics. "My whole political career," he once said, "is based upon my war service and war associates." After the war, he married his childhood sweetheart, Bess Wallace, and in Kansas City went into the clothing

Harry Truman taking the oath of office from Chief Justice Harlan Fiske Stone. Among those looking on are, in the front row, left to right: Secretary of the Navy James Forrestal, Secretary of Agriculture Claude Wickard, Mrs. Truman, Margaret Truman, House Speaker Sam Rayburn, wartime Director of Office of Economic Stabilization Fred Vinson, and Republican leader Joseph Martin. (United Press.)

business with a former sergeant in his outfit. He was wiped out by the sudden depression of 1921-22, which struck with savage force at this center of the grain belt. Though he lost about $28,000, he refused to go into bankruptcy. For years the claims arising from this failure hung over his head and cost him much anguish.

While depressed by this failure, Truman was offered the nomination for county judge by Mike Pendergast, the older brother of Tom Pendergast, who was the Democratic boss of Kansas City. To win this post, which was actually an administrative rather than a judicial office, Truman campaigned hard throughout his district. "I had kinfolks all over the county," he recalled, "and the people I was not related to Mrs. Truman was." Elected in 1922, he served one term and then was defeated two years later by a coalition that embraced the Ku Klux Klan and anti-Pendergast Democrats. He returned to political office in 1927 as presiding judge of the county court and proceeded to build a solid reputation as a road-builder, city planner, and honest administrator. Politically, too, he was growing in power and influence. "I controlled the Democratic Party in Eastern Jackson County," he said later. "In any election I could deliver eleven thousand votes and not steal a one. I looked out for the people and they understood my leadership. The vote-stealing in Kansas City was silly." *

By 1934 Truman was ready for bigger things. In that year, with the help of Pendergast, he won the nomination for the United States Senate. He went to Washington that fall in the amazing midterm Democratic sweep generated by Roosevelt's New Deal. Truman never denied the support he received from Pendergast, nor did he seek to disguise his own regard for him. Pendergast, he insisted, had never asked him to do anything dishonest. Tom Pendergast, according to Truman, "would stay with his friends straight or crooked, but when he found a man who was honest he would stand by him." When Pendergast was jailed in 1939 and FDR failed to support Truman in his re-election campaign the following year, it seemed that Truman's political career was over. But he conducted a furious campaign, rallying laborers, Negroes, and farmers to his side. Almost alone, as in a more famous campaign eight years later, Truman was confident of victory. By a small margin, less than 8000 votes, Truman was sent back to Washington.

Washington was a busy place in that winter of 1940-41. As the defense movement gathered momentum, Truman became concerned over the complaints by small businessmen that they were being ignored in the placing of military contracts. He was convinced, too, that there was much waste and duplication in the defense effort. From his knowledge of American history, he knew that a special Congressional committee had kept a watchful eye on the war effort during the Civil War. When, in 1941, a special Senate committee was set up to study the whole defense program, Truman was made its chairman. Over the next four years the Truman Committee won national headlines for its investigations of war spending, industrial contracts, and military efficiency, and was credited by some with saving $15 billion in unnecessary expenditures. The Committee's work made Truman a national figure and Roosevelt's choice for Vice President in 1944.

In the shifting political climate of 1944, Truman was the perfect compromise candidate. Wallace, the incumbent, was no longer acceptable to the conservative Democrats, whose power had been growing steadily since 1938. Yet a truly

---

* Ibid., p. 152.

conservative candidate would not have been acceptable to the Northern liberal-labor element that backed Wallace. In nominating Truman, says Samuel Lubell, the Democrats were buying time; they wanted to keep the line of succession from passing to either the Northern or Southern Democrats. Truman, eminently successful among the border-state "political brokers" who had prevented stalemate from turning into paralysis since 1938, could not break the deadlock between Congress and President. But that was not his task, says Lubell. His job, as Roosevelt's successor and later as President in his own right, was to raise all issues but to settle none. "The secret of Truman's political vitality," Lubell concluded, "is that he has shrewdly planted himself on the furiously dead center of stalemate to which irreconcilables must repair if they are to make a bargain." *

When he became President, many still knew little of Truman's background and character. Cheerful, modest, and unassuming, he seemed to many to be only a "caretaker President" who would preside at the White House until another election could be held. "You just sort of forget about Harry until he makes another mistake," ran a contemporary Washington observation. But he soon showed his intention to be President in deed as well as name. He mastered detailed reports of governmental operations; he broke with a number of Roosevelt's Cabinet members and replaced them with his own men; and he made it plain that he intended to make his own decisions. Courage marked many of his actions, as even his foes admitted. He made up his mind slowly, asking for all available facts and information, but once a decision was made, he said, "I did not worry about it afterward." He looked to

history both for his precedents and his justification. "Being President," he once remarked, "is like riding a tiger. A man has to keep riding or be swallowed."

And Truman did keep riding. Reporters noted a growing sureness in his manner after the first year or so. By the spring of 1947 he had grasped the reins of foreign policy and wheeled the country in a new direction with the Truman Doctrine and the Marshall Plan. He had also battled, with less success, to revive and extend the liberal domestic program of Franklin D. Roosevelt. He made it clear, too, that he intended to be leader of his party and seek election in his own right. Correspondents spoke of his "becoming President of the United States."

But he showed weaknesses, too, as a political leader. "Harry Truman, of all the Presidents I have known," an elder Democratic statesman remarked, "could do the big things in the biggest way and the little things in the littlest way." He could at times be willful, at other times petty, and not infrequently rash. His fierce independence was compromised by an unshakable loyalty to his political associates; his unquestioned honesty was marred by a willingness to shelter corrupt officials; and his courage in making the big decisions had to be set off against his pettiness in making the small ones. Further, some citizens thought he demeaned the Presidential office by such acts as calling a correspondent an "S.O.B." and writing a critic of his daughter's singing, "I never met you. But if I do you'll need a new nose and plenty of beefsteak."

As the shadow of historical perspective lengthens, however, Truman's reputation shows every sign of increasing rather than decreasing. Measured against his unreadiness for the task, Truman rose remarkably to a tremendous challenge. Given the American method of selecting Vice Presidents, the nation had no right

* S. Lubell, *The Future of American Politics* (New York: Harper and Brothers, 1952), pp. 20-24.

to expect so magnificent an effort from a man who could never have been President save by accident. "What matters about Mr. Truman," said the *New York Times* at the end of his administration, "are the qualities of character that he showed, which add up to something he need not be ashamed of; the times through which he lived and acted were prodigious in their effect on our lives; and the way in which he conducted the impossible office of President of the United States. . . . When the all-too-human side of Harry S. Truman has fallen out of mind, we think that for the high hopes he had and for the bravery with which he tried to realize them he will be remembered and respected." *

### Postwar Legacy

Truman's first problems as President arose from the swift collapse of America's enemies in the spring and summer of 1945. Few men in the government expected the final surrender of the Axis powers so soon; therefore, little thought had been given to the serious problems of reconverting to peacetime pursuits. The new President himself was unprepared for the important decisions that had to be made in that sphere. And there was uncertainty, too, about what Truman would do to honor Roosevelt's promises to revive the New Deal when the war was over.

Much of this doubt was removed when Truman went before Congress on September 6, 1945, for his first important message on domestic affairs. This was to be, he told Jonathan Daniels, his "declaration of independence" as President. In twenty-one specific recommendations, Truman called for a vigorous revival of the spirit and programs of the New Deal years. He asked for the expansion of social security, a full-employment law, a raise in the minimum wage to 65 cents

an hour, slum clearance and public housing legislation, a permanent Fair Employment Practices Act to protect Negro workers, and a host of other measures. This message, Truman said later, marked his "assumption of the office of President in my own right."

But Congress, previously uncertain about Truman's intentions, now sprang into action to block his program. Only two of his controversial proposals were even given serious consideration. Congress did agree to extend the President's powers over prices and wages during the reconversion period and did pass a Maximum Employment Act. This latter law, growing out of a wartime pledge of Roosevelt's, committed the federal government to help maintain full employment. A Council of Economic Advisers, made up of three experts, was to keep a close watch on the state of the economy, compile necessary statistics and information, and issue an annual report on the nation's economic health. A joint committee of Congress was to receive these reports and be responsible for measures aimed at "a full volume of employment and production." Though Truman had hoped for a much stronger law, one that would make explicit the government's role in maintaining full employment, this bill did recognize a new level of governmental responsibility for the planning and performance of the American economy.

The return to normal life after the years of war brought swift and overwhelming changes to vast numbers of Americans. Millions of men and women in the armed forces were discharged under a point system of priority within a few months of the end of the war. Many of them took advantage of the so-called GI Bill of Rights of 1944, which offered help to returning veterans seeking education, employment, loans, job training, or opportunities in business and farming.

* *New York Times*, January 16, 1953.

Emergency housing in Quonset huts for veterans attending the State College of Rhode Island under the G. I. Bill of Rights. Such temporary dormitories were commonplace at colleges across the nation in the first years after the war. (Wide World.)

Even as the veterans came home, however, most of the top military and civilian leaders were urging Congress to approve a system of universal military training for all young men on reaching the age of 18. "The day of the Minute Man who sprang to the flintlock hanging on his wall," Truman told the Congress in asking approval of this program, "is over." But Congress, reluctant to make so radical a departure from tradition, declined to act. As the postwar world grew more ominous, Truman was finally forced to appeal to Congress for the continuation of the wartime draft.

The reconversion of the economy was remarkably swift. The government cut back war contracts sharply after Germany's surrender and even more drastically following Japan's defeat, removed controls over iron and steel and hundreds of other commodities, sold war surplus materials, including whole factories, to private citizens and corporations at bargain prices, reduced taxes, and altogether abandoned the unpopular excess-profits tax of the war years. A number of the war agencies were quickly put out of business. And industrialists, eager to exploit the pent-up demand for civilian goods, turned with surprising speed to the production of consumer goods. By the end of 1945, more than 90 per cent of the war plants were producing civilian goods once more.

Most vexing of all the reconversion problems was that of controls over prices and wages. No one was certain, in those anxious months after the war, whether inflation or unemployment was the more serious danger to the economy. Many economists, remembering the many jobless citizens of the prewar years, feared that the return of millions of veterans to civilian life would precipitate a new unemployment crisis. But they failed to estimate correctly the speed of industrial reconversion and the tremendous demand that would develop for civilian goods. This demand, backed by heavy wartime savings, represented a serious inflationary danger unless the line were held on prices and wages.

But nothing was more unpopular in the postwar era than the continuation of wartime controls over the economy. A crisis quickly developed late in 1945 when the automobile workers, anxious over their loss of overtime pay as war contracts ended, struck for an increase in

345

their hourly rate to make up for the decrease in their incomes. The leader of the United Automobile Workers, Walter Reuther, insisted that General Motors could grant a wage increase out of its profits without raising prices. But General Motors denied this, arguing that wartime profits were over, and that a rise in wages would necessitate a rise in prices, which were still frozen by the Office of Price Administration. In January, three-quarters of a million steel workers also walked out, demanding a wage increase of 30 per cent.

Truman was in a dilemma. He considered price controls necessary during the transitional period before civilian goods became plentiful again. Rationing already having been abandoned, prices would rise swiftly once controls were dropped. To allow the auto workers and others to strike, however, would cut production at a critical time. The only solution, and it proved to be an unfortunate one, seemed to be surrender to the employers' demands for price increases to match wage increases. Both wages and prices were allowed to rise in a number of critical industries, thus inaugurating a price-wage spiral that became the standard economic pattern in the postwar years.

A new crisis arose in April, 1946. Nearly half a million soft coal workers led by John L. Lewis left their jobs when coal operators turned down his plan for an employer-subsidized health and welfare fund. Within six weeks, serious coal shortages developed in all parts of the nation, the steel and automobile industries being particularly affected. Truman seized the mines at the end of May just as a long-smoldering railroad strike hit the headlines. With attention diverted away from the coal crisis, the Administration arranged terms with Lewis that gave him much of what he wanted, including a welfare and retirement fund

jointly sponsored by the union and the coal operators. An exasperated Truman, meanwhile, was asking Congress for power to draft the recalcitrant rail workers, who were actually striking against the government itself. The railroad brotherhoods capitulated just in time to avert passage of Truman's bill in the Senate. The fight against the Senate bill was led, interestingly enough, by Robert Taft, who was soon to draft a new and controversial labor bill.

## "Had Enough?"

By 1946 the political currents were running against the Administration. Employers, landlords, merchants, and large segments of the public were strongly irritated by the paralyzing strikes, the freeze on prices and rents, and the continuation of wartime controls. Unionmen felt antagonistic toward Truman's strike bill, and consumers were dismayed by the continuing shortages of goods they wanted. The OPA had become increasingly controversial as the deadline approached for renewing its authority over prices and wages. Under tremendous pressure from businessmen who wanted outright repeal, union leaders who opposed any change, and farm spokesmen who sought to lift only the ceiling on agricultural goods, Congress framed a bill so full of contradictions that Truman considered it unworkable. He vetoed it as a "formula for inflation." With all controls off, prices shot up almost 25 per cent in less than a month. Congress moved quickly to pass a substitute bill, which Truman signed, though he regarded it as even more poorly drawn than the first. In fact, the measure proved incapable of braking the skyward momentum of prices in the following months. By 1947, the price level stood at 159.2 (1935-1939 = 100), compared with 128.4 in 1945. Prices, in other words, had gone up more in these two years than during the whole war period.

In the fall election of 1946, the Republicans hit on a slogan that expressed perfectly the nation's mood of angry frustration. "Had Enough?" queried thousands of billboards, leaflets, and campaign buttons. Truman, it seemed, was to be made the butt for the accumulated irritations of the postwar period. When the votes were counted, the Republicans had won Congress for the first time since 1928. With the help of Southern Democrats, they now had a commanding majority to push through the long-awaited "counter-revolution" to the New Deal. In deference to the voters' mood, Truman removed virtually all remaining controls except those on rent, and within two years the consumer price index stood at a towering 171.2.

## Truman and Civil Rights

A month after the Republican sweep of 1946, Truman appointed a special committee to investigate civil rights in the United States. Headed by Charles E. Wilson, president of the General Electric Company, the committee was charged with accumulating evidence and framing recommendations on the status of civil rights throughout the nation. In their report the following year, the committee called attention to a number of serious threats to the constitutional liberties of Americans, including lynching, police brutality, maladministration of justice, deprivation of voting rights, and discrimination in education, housing, and public places. On the basis of this report, Truman presented a strong civil rights program to Congress in early 1948. Among his recommendations were a permanent commission on civil rights, a federal FEPC law, and federal statutes against lynching, discrimination in interstate travel, and depriving citizens of the right to vote. He also announced that he had

instructed the Secretary of Defense to eliminate the remaining discrimination against Negro troops in the armed forces.

The message dramatized some of the continuing problems of American Negroes, though it resulted in little legislation. During the preceding fifteen years, the status of Negroes had undergone marked changes as a result of the New Deal, the war, continued emigration from the South, and a gradual rise in their economic and educational level. By the end of the forties, there were 15 million Negroes in the United States, of whom more than a third were living in northern communities. A decade later, only 52 per cent of the nation's colored population would remain in the eleven states of the old Confederacy. As Negroes came north, they found more jobs, more concern for their legal and political rights, and a greater degree of public acceptance. Meanwhile, in the South, the advance of industry and the diversification of farming, combined with a growing sensitivity to the South's treatment of the Negroes, operated to bring about a very gradual improvement in their position. During the course of the nineteen-forties, the Supreme Court set aside the white primary, declared racially restrictive real-estate covenants unconstitutional, and removed a number of barriers to educational opportunity for Negroes. But there were still serious restrictions on their rights as citizens and it was these which concerned Truman's committee. "It is still possible," the committee reported in 1947, "for a mob to abduct and murder a person in some sections of the country with almost certain assurance of escaping punishment from the law."

## That Eightieth Congress

Congress, however, was far more interested in other matters than in civil rights. Many Republican leaders, particularly, felt that the time had come to take a firm stand against any extension of the political and social programs of the Roosevelt era. Government, they argued, was becoming too strong for traditional American liberties to survive; deficit spending and unbalanced budgets had to be stopped; and labor must be disciplined and made as responsible as management for its actions. Some professed to see the advance of socialism under the administrations of Roosevelt and Truman. "I believe," wrote Robert Taft, leader of the Eightieth Congress in domestic affairs, "that we should battle the principles of communism and socialism and convince the world that true happiness lies in the establishment of a system of liberty, [and] that communism and socialism are the very antithesis of liberalism. . . ." Truman supporters feared that an instrument of reaction was being fashioned by the hands of Taft and his party. One political observer, noting the mood of the Eightieth Congress, was reminded of the Hoover years. "This Congress," wrote "T.R.B.," an editor of the *New Republic*, "brought back an atmosphere you had forgotten or never thought possible. . . . Victories fought and won years ago were suddenly in doubt. Everything was debatable again."

Labor policy, particularly, was "debat-

able again." Labor had made great gains since 1933, when fewer than three million workers belonged to unions and nine out of ten wage-earners were ununionized; by 1945, nearly fifteen million men and women were union members, or one of every three wage-earners. The greatest advances had been made among unskilled and semiskilled workers, who were largely unorganized in 1933. Almost 70 per cent of all production workers in manufacturing industries were union members by the end of the war. Only white-collar workers, who frequently identified themselves with "management," remained largely outside the union movement. This remarkable growth meant that organized labor had become an important agency in determining economic policy in the United States.

It was labor's strength, as evidenced in the controversial strikes of 1945 and 1946, that concerned the leaders of the Eightieth Congress. Had labor become too powerful? Was there need to offset the controls on management in the Wagner Act with similar restrictions on labor unions? Labor's defenders argued that the Wagner Act was intended only to guarantee workers' right to organize by preventing management from interfering with that right. The chief critics of the Wagner Act, according to labor spokesmen, were anti-union employers who remained unreconciled to the union movement. To charges that the National Labor Relations Board had shown favoritism and was concerned only with workers' prerogatives, defenders replied that the Board's only lawful purpose, in fact, *was* to protect the right to organize against hostile employers. Opposition to the Wagner Act, union spokesmen insisted, was actually opposition to the principle of collective bargaining.

Taft and other leaders of the Eightieth Congress did not think so. A new labor law, they concluded, was necessary to "equalize" the operation of the Wagner

"White Elephant" was the title of this 1948 cartoon, which summed up one view of the burden the Republican candidates were running under that year. (Herblock.)

Act. They were particularly concerned about abuses of the closed shop, jurisdictional disputes between unions over membership, and the use of picketing and boycotts to extend union membership. A grocer, for example, might be picketed because he sold goods produced by a nonunion manufacturer. And there was still a good deal of concern, too, about the dramatic wartime and postwar strikes that many felt were against the public interest. Unions, it was said repeatedly, must be made responsible to the public and workmen to their employers. Many Congressional spokesmen interpreted the election of 1946 as a mandate from the people to carry out labor reforms.

The Taft-Hartley law of 1947 was the most important labor law since the Wagner Act. It was designed to protect the rights of individual employees, neutral and interested employers, and the general public. Forced unionism, said Fred Hartley, co-author of the act, was "a tyranny more despotic than I could think possible in a free country." The new act barred unions from coercing workers to join up, outlawed the closed shop, and forbade contributions by unions to political campaigns. To protect the neutral employer, secondary boycotts and jurisdictional strikes were declared illegal, though in practice this ban often proved unenforceable. In their bargaining with employers, unions were made liable for breaches of contract and forbidden to exact "featherbedding" agreements from them; this latter provision also proved ineffective. The bill further guaranteed to employers a right to present their side during organizational campaigns. Finally, to guard the public interest, the Taft-Hartley law set a "cooling off" period of sixty days before the beginning of a strike and required union officers to sign affidavits that they were not communists.

Congress overrode Truman's stinging veto of the law on June 23, 1947. No act of the Eightieth Congress gave rise to such bitter and lasting controversy as the Taft-Hartley bill. It became almost immediately a political issue. Labor spokesmen denounced it as a "slave-labor" law, while employers praised it as a labor bill of rights. George Meany of the AFL charged that the law would have the effect "of jeopardizing, weakening, and even destroying the only instrument of self-defense that workers ever had, their own voluntary combinations, in other words, their trade unions." But despite labor's fears, the Taft-Hartley Act did not cripple the union movement, though it did have its debilitating effects. For one thing it weakened attempts to organize new industries, particularly in the South. Then, too, one of labor's most effective weapons in the past had been the refusal to work on goods manufactured by nonunion help, but this was now banned along with sympathetic strikes and other actions that had helped to win labor's battles long before the Wagner Act. In a number of ways, said Professor Edwin Witte, a specialist in labor-management relations, the unions were "in a distinctly less favorable position than if Congress had repealed the National Labor Relations Act in its entirety and let it go at that." The political impact of the Taft-Hartley law, in any case, was to confirm organized labor in the conviction that labor's future lay with Truman and the Democrats rather than with the Republican party. This was to have some importance in the 1948 election.

In other ways, the Eightieth Congress provided President Truman with campaign issues for the coming election. Truman's program for public housing, civil rights, federal aid to education, extension of social security, and a raise in the minimum wage was ignored or blocked on Capitol Hill. The President set a record for executive vetoes as he harpooned measure after measure sent by the lawmakers to the White House. Three times he vetoed tax bills that favored, in his judgment, the wealthiest segment of the population. And he castigated the Congress for cutting the agricultural budget and leaving farmers with insufficient facilities in which to store their surplus produce.

Less controversial were the National Security Act of 1947 and the measure authorizing the Hoover Commission to begin its monumental studies of the executive branch of the government. As for the latter, in all, the former President recommended more than 300 changes in executive departments to eliminate waste and duplication. The National Security Act, in many ways the most important action taken by the Eightieth Congress, authorized the partial unification of the armed services under a new Cabinet officer, the Secretary of Defense; created a National Security Council to coordinate all military, diplomatic, and domestic policies of the government; established a Central Intelligence Agency to bring all the intelligence activities of the federal government into one office; and set up a National Security Resources Board to advise on matters of manpower, strategic materials, and industrial mobilization. Each of these steps reflected a growing awareness that America could no longer carry its staggering responsibilities at home and abroad without a much larger degree of planning, coordination, and preparation than had ever before been given to the nation's security needs.

## A Large Dish of Crow

Truman's defense of unpopular causes and the Republican sweep of 1946 convinced most politicians that he had almost no chance of being elected for another term. He faced a formidable opponent in Thomas E. Dewey, who had just been swept into the governorship of New York by a 680,000-vote margin. Once again, the Republicans by-passed Taft, the spokesman of the Eightieth Congress, who seemed to many Republicans too conservative and tarred with prewar isolationism. Dewey's running mate in 1948 was the popular Earl Warren, governor of California, who had enthusiastic followers in both political parties.

The Democratic professionals not only despaired of Truman's winning—some tried to persuade General Dwight Eisenhower to become the Democratic candidate—but they shook their heads at the impending splinter of the entire Democratic party. Henry Wallace had already declared that he would run as an independent on a third-party ticket dedicated to better relations with the Soviet Union and more liberal policies at home. How many would follow the leadership of this quixotic idealist? Some analysts were predicting early in the campaign that Wallace might draw as many as five million votes. With communist support that grew as the campaign progressed, Wallace waged a vigorous campaign on behalf of disarmament, destruction of the A-bomb, equal treatment for Negroes, and repeal of the Marshall Plan. The very shrillness of his attacks, however, coupled to the obvious support from the Communist Party, hurt his cause badly and probably helped Truman to hold many voters.

At Philadelphia, the Democrats were further split when Northern liberals rammed through a toughly worded civil rights plank that caused a number of Southern delegates to leave the convention. A week later this anti-Truman wing of the party met at Birmingham to form a Dixiecrat Party in order to capture the Democratic electoral vote in as many of the Southern states as possible. Governor J. Strom Thurmond of South Carolina was nominated for President and Governor Fielding L. Wright of Mississippi for Vice President. Unfortunately for the Truman cause, these bolters had control of several of the state organizations in the South. Their real purpose was to defeat Truman, since they could have little hope of winning the Presidency.

The Democrats, meanwhile, had listlessly endorsed Truman and Senator Alben W. Barkley for the 1948 race. Though Truman delivered a militant speech, in which he called the Eightieth Congress back into session to "make good" on Republican platform promises, he evoked little enthusiasm. His situation seemed hopeless. Thurmond was sure to win a number of Southern electoral votes, while Wallace was expected to draw heavily in New York and other big cities of the North. Shot through with defeatism, the party did little to help Truman and party funds dwindled to a new low. The polls confirmed what everyone knew: Truman was certain to be defeated on November 2.

But Truman paid little attention to the polls. He became encouraged by the size of the crowds that met him at the whistle-stops he made across the country. He noted their enthusiasm when he struck out at the "do-nothing" Eightieth Congress, the worst, he said, in the history of the nation. In farm states he spoke of the Republicans having "struck a pitchfork in the backs of the farmers." Labor crowds he asked: "Do you want to carry the Taft-Hartley law to its full implication and enslave totally the workingman, white collar and union man alike . . . ?" When Dewey spoke of the Eightieth Congress having delivered for the future, Truman countered: "I'll say it delivered. It delivered for the private power lobby. It delivered for the big oil company lobby. It delivered for the railroad lobby. . . . That's what the Republican candidate calls delivering for the future. Is that the kind of future you want?"

Later, in writing his memoirs, Truman explained the technique that won him the most stunning upset in modern political history. "There were no special 'gimmicks' or oratorical devices," he wrote.

I refused to be "coached." I simply told the people in my own language that they had better wake up to the fact that it was their fight. If they did not get out and help me win this fight, I emphasized, the Republicans would soon be giving the farmers and the workers the little end of the stick again. . . . I talked to them as human beings with real needs and feelings and fears. I talked to them about their jobs, their homes, and the cost of living. I treated them not like crowds of people but like businessmen, tenant farmers, housewives, married veterans, laboring men, teachers—individuals with interests for whom I, as President, had a genuine concern.*

The election results appeared to surprise everyone but Truman. The Presi-

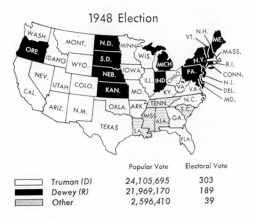

1948 Election

| | Popular Vote | Electoral Vote |
|---|---|---|
| Truman (D) | 24,105,695 | 303 |
| Dewey (R) | 21,969,170 | 189 |
| Other | 2,596,410 | 39 |

dent won 303 electoral and 24 million popular votes, while Dewey garnered 189 electoral and almost 22 million popular votes. Thurmond and Wallace polled a million votes each but only Thurmond made a showing in the electoral college with 39 votes. What had happened? "I don't care how the thing is explained," Taft fumed. "It defies all common sense for the country to send that roughneck ward politician back to the White House." But he was there and the analysts, many

* H. Truman, *Memoirs*, two volumes (Garden City, N.Y.: Doubleday and Company, 1955-56), II, p. 211.

of whom had predicted Dewey's victory, now tried to explain why. Some argued that the Republicans had been overconfident; others saw the labor support for Truman as crucial; still others pointed to the general prosperity, Midwestern distrust of Dewey, or the strong Democratic candidates for Congress as the explanation. But the noteworthy feature of the election was the surprising showing that Truman made in almost every section and class, east and west, farm and city. Except for Wallace, he might well have won New York and Michigan, too.

Almost all observers were agreed that an important shift had taken place in the farm vote during the campaign. Fear of another depression, according to Samuel Lubell, dominated the voting in 1948. The price of corn, which stood at $2.15 a bushel in June, 1948, had fallen to $1.20 at election time. For the first time in a decade, farm income was beginning to drop. To many voters, both on the farms and in the cities, Dewey seemed a radical intent on a "great house cleaning" in Washington. The public's desire to preserve and extend the social gains of the Roosevelt era, in Lubell's view, was basic to Truman's victory. In a sense, Lubell writes, FDR won his fifth straight victory in 1948.*

### The Fair Deal

Despite his surprising triumph, Truman was little more successful in winning Congressional approval for his program than in his first term. Though he now had a Democratic majority, the combination of Southern Democrats and Republicans was still strong enough to block most of his "Fair Deal" measures. He did

* Lubell, op. cit., pp. 158-178.

succeed in raising the minimum wage to 75 cents an hour and in amending the Social Security Act to cover some ten million more persons with appreciably increased benefits. He pushed vigorously, too, for a new housing act which, when passed, called for the construction of 810,000 low-cost units over a period of six years. But Truman went down to defeat on revision of the Taft-Hartley Act, civil rights, federal health insurance (the American Medical Association raised $3 million for a campaign chest to fight this), and a new farm program devised by his Secretary of Agriculture, Charles Brannan.

The Brannan Plan was a sharp departure from the parity system inaugurated by the New Deal. Brannan proposed that the prices of perishable farm produce be determined on the free market. Consumers would receive the full benefit of any lower prices that would result. The difference between these prices and a minimum standard, to be agreed upon, would be reimbursed through direct cash subsidies; the limit on the benefits to be received by an individual farmer was $20,000. The emphasis would thus be laid on high income for individual farmers rather than high farm prices. This would mean a shift in government benefits away from the large commercial farmers, who got the lion's share of benefits under the parity system, toward the smaller farmer whom the Brannan Plan was intended to help. But the Farm Bureau Federation and other spokesmen for the larger farmers savagely attacked the Brannan Plan and it got little support in Congress. Instead, Congress voted to maintain the old parity formula at 90 per cent with a gradual drop in support prices to 75 per cent at the discretion of the Secretary of Agriculture.

## THE POLITICS OF REVENGE

The frustration of Truman's Fair Deal was barely noticed in the charged emotional atmosphere of 1949 and 1950. During this time, the Truman Administration was under furious assault from many quarters because of the fall of China, the government's handling of the Hiss case, the outbreak of the Korean War, the growing fear of communist subversion, and the successful exploitation of these and other issues by Senator Joseph McCarthy. The President's triumph at the polls turned to ashes as a mood of vengeful frustration fired large numbers of the American population, and a flame of isolationist sentiment, differing in program but not in spirit from the prewar variety, swept through anti-Administration circles. By the time Truman left office, his Administration was under a cloud, his Secretary of State was under attacks so virulent they lacked historical parallel, and the President himself had been the subject of solemn talk about impeachment.

### Who Is Loyal to America?

What had happened? Why was Truman, leader of the anticommunist coalition in the free world after 1947, now the target of charges of appeasement and "softness" toward communism? The answer must be at once tentative and complex. Part of the answer probably lay in the rush of affairs, which created a sense of overwhelming disaster. Within a single nine-month period, from September, 1949, to June, 1950, China fell to the communists, the Soviets exploded their first atomic bomb, the second Hiss trial began, and the Korean invasion was launched. In that same period, significantly, came the first of Senator McCarthy's accusations that the State Department was riddled through with communists.

Why had events turned against the United States? Had another great war been won, only to have its fruits thrown away by bungling statesmanship? A long-stoked impatience, a smoldering discontent with the unhappy results of the war, now burst into public discussion. Revisionist historians found a wider hearing for their charges of Roosevelt's perfidy at Pearl Harbor and Yalta, and in the conduct of the Second World War. The fires were fed by political resentment of Dewey's surprising defeat and long-suppressed antagonisms to the New Deal and Fair Deal. They were fanned by widely publicized Administration blunders that seemed to confirm that there were flames under the smoke of suspicion. Truman, for example, referred several times to the Hiss case as a "red herring" and Acheson told a news conference after Hiss's conviction that he would not "turn my back" on Alger Hiss.

Frustration, fueled by doubt and political malice, inspired a search for explanations. Gradually a theory that fit the mood of the times began to emerge and gain a measure of acceptance. The plight of the United States in the postwar world, this theory held, was the result of a combination of, on the one hand, terrible mistakes dating back at least to Yalta and, on the other, communist subversion within the United States. The fall of China, the treachery of Hiss, and Soviet success in building an A-bomb were all linked together in a vast web of conspiracy. Hurley had warned of procommunist advisers when he quit his China post; Alger Hiss had been present at Yalta; Julius and Ethel Rosenberg and Klaus Fuchs, who had filched atomic secrets for the Russians, were representative figures in the giant conspiracy. The success of communism and the decline of American power were alike assignable to the work of a handful of disloyal men operating in sensitive areas of the United States government. Not errors of judgment alone, but treason was responsible for the frustration of America's hopes of 1945. McCarthy's unprecedented success, as Herbert Agar has pointed out, lay in this, that he squeezed the whole of postwar history into one disagreeable idea: "The reason we find ourselves in a position of impotency," said McCarthy, "is not because our only powerful potential enemy has sent men to invade our shores, but rather because of the traitorous actions of those who have been treated so well by this nation. . . . In my opinion the State Department, which is one of the most important government departments, is thoroughly infested with Communists."

There it was—the explanation for America's loss of omnipotence in world affairs. Throughout American history, thanks to the British navy and the European balance of power, the United States had indeed been able to "go it alone" and lecture the world on international morality. Now that the world was turning against us, the explanation must lie in our own incompetence, or the betrayal of American principles. Acheson, long identified with the policy of containment, symbolized the new turn of events. A graduate of Groton and Yale, a New Dealer, a friend of Alger Hiss, the defender of Truman's policy in China, he spoke a strange new language that embraced sophisticated terms like "limited war," "situations of strength," "containment of communism," and "indefinite crisis." "I watch his smart-aleck manner and his British clothes," blurted out Senator Butler of Nebraska, "and that New Dealism, everlasting New Dealism in ev-

erything he says and does, and I want to shout, 'Get out, get out. You stand for everything that has been wrong with the United States for years.' "

The crusade against disloyalty stirred a warm response in old isolationists, extreme conservatives, and those anxious to prove their Americanism. It got more support from Republicans than Democrats, more from Taft Republicans than Dewey followers, more from Catholics than Protestants, more from Midwesterners than Easterners, and more from recent immigrants and their children than from those with deeper roots. Among partisans of the extreme right the crusade was frequently tied to a violent disapproval of the welfare state, the income tax, organized labor, and the United Nations. It stirred a sense of vindication among isolationists who had opposed American entry into World War II, and who had favored fighting Japan rather than Germany first. "This constant raking over of the past," said Samuel Lubell, "is almost literally a raking over of the ashes of isolation in the hope that some embers of outraged memory can be provoked into flame again." *

That communists were active in the United States government, particularly during the New Deal and war years, almost no one denied. At a time when the Soviets were not our enemy, this seemed less consequential than it was to seem later. Soon after the war, following the revelations of a Canadian spy ring, President Truman appointed a commission to study the entire matter and make recommendations. In March, 1947, he issued an executive order that launched a sweeping investigation of the loyalty of all federal employees. Dismissal of every employee about whom "reasonable grounds exist for belief that the person involved is disloyal to the government of the United States" was promised. Those found to advocate overthrow of the government or to

* Lubell, op. cit., p. 152.

belong to any organization designated by the Attorney-General as totalitarian were subject to dismissal, along with those suspected of sabotage, espionage, or treason. Though the program was sharply criticized for its lack of judicial safeguards and its attempt to measure "potential disloyalty," it failed to halt the subsequent criticism by McCarthy and others that communists were still in the government. By 1951, of more than three million employees investigated, some 2000 had resigned and only 212 had been dismissed. Truman himself came to feel that the program had been too stringent and had resulted in the violation of the rights of a number of his employees.

Congress, however, felt that Truman had not been stringent enough. In 1950 it passed the McCarran Internal Security Act, which required all communist and communist-front organizations to register with the Attorney-General, barred communists from getting passports or finding employment in defense plants, excluded communists and other totalitarians from immigration quotas, and authorized the President in the event of war to imprison "each person as to whom there is reasonable ground to believe that such person probably will engage in, or probably will conspire with others to engage in, acts of espionage or of sabotage. . . ." In a ringing veto, which Congress did not sustain, Truman warned that the bill's provisions "are not directed toward the real and present dangers that exist from communism. Instead of striking blows at communism, they would strike blows at our own liberties. . . . Our position in the vanguard of freedom rests largely on our demonstration that the free expression of opinion, coupled with government by popular consent, leads to national strength and human advancement. Let us not, in cowering and foolish fear, throw away the ideals which are the fundamental basis of our free society."

Neither Congress nor the Supreme Court agreed with Truman's insistence on Holmes' old test of "clear and present danger" as the standard for freedom of speech. When the Supreme Court heard the case of *Dennis* v. *United States* in 1951, involving the conviction of eleven top communists for conspiracy to teach the overthrow of the government, the Court held by a margin of 6 to 2 that the defendants could be punished for conspiring to teach and advocate revolution. An attempt to overthrow the government, argued Chief Justice Vinson, even if doomed to failure, was a sufficient evil for Congress to prevent. In reaching his decision, Vinson drew heavily on the opinion of Judge Learned Hand of the Court of Appeals, who had interpreted the job of the courts in such cases to be the asking of the question "whether the gravity of the 'evil,' discounted by its improbability, justifies such invasion of free speech as is necessary to avoid the danger." In dissenting, Justice Douglas denied that America faced any real danger from domestic communists. "In America," he wrote, "they are miserable merchants of unwanted ideas; their wares remain unsold. The fact that their ideas are abhorrent does not make them powerful." But his plea for maximum toleration of free speech went unheeded.

What *were* the proper limits of freedom? Those who were appalled by the rise of communism and fearful of its future spread argued that a narrowing of the bounds of traditional freedom was necessary. Neither communists nor those sympathetic with them, it was sometimes said, should be allowed the full protection of American liberties. In line with this attitude, a number of Congressional committees conducted investigations of alleged communist infiltration into schools, churches, libraries, and the United States Army with the objective of rooting out communist influences.

Immigrants, too, came under the critical eye of Congress as it pushed the search for subversives. When the immigration laws were revised in 1952, Congress wrote into the McCarran-Walter Immigration Act a ban against the admission of potential subversives and a provision allowing for the expulsion of disloyal aliens. The Act retained the quota system of the Immigration Act of 1924 but removed the bar against the immigration and naturalization of Asiatics. "The basis of this quota system," Truman wrote in his veto of the measure, "was false and unworthy in 1924. It is even worse now. At the present time this quota system keeps out the very people we want to bring in. It is incredible to me that, in this year of 1952, we should again be enacting into law such a slur on the patriotism, the capacity, and the decency of a large part of our citizenry." But Congress ignored the President and overrode his veto.

Some Americans were deeply disturbed about the atmosphere of suspicion and distrust which the crusade against disloyalty helped to create. "We are busily engaged in adopting the most stupid and unjust of the ideas prevalent in Russia and are doing so in the name of Americanism," said Chancellor Robert M. Hutchins of the University of Chicago. These ideas Hutchins defined as the police state; the abolition of freedom of speech, thought, and association; and the notion that the individual exists for the state. "What is the new loyalty?" asked the historian Henry Steele Commager. It was no more, he concluded, than an uncritical acceptance of the status quo, a refusal to think or criticize or exercise independent judgment. "What do men know of loyalty," he queried, "who make a mockery of the Declaration of Independence and the Bill of Rights, whose energies are dedicated to stirring up race and class hatreds, who would straitjacket the American spirit?" Who were the truly dis-

loyal? They were, said Commager, those who subverted the Constitution, denied freedom of speech to those with whom they disagreed, pressed for their own selfish interests against the common interest, and "those who for selfish and private purposes stir up national antagonisms, and expose the world to the ruin of war." At the bottom of all true loyalty, he insisted, was the "realization that America was born of revolt, flourished on dissent, became great through experimentation." *

### Generation on Trial

But the tide was running strong against the libertarian views of Commager and Hutchins. January, 1950, brought an event that seemed to confirm the suspicion that communists had bored deeply into governmental agencies during the New Deal years. Alger Hiss, a former New Dealer, a secondary adviser at Yalta, and the organizer of the San Francisco conference, was convicted of perjury for denying he had passed government secrets to the Russians in the nineteen-thirties. Nothing that happened in these postwar years puzzled and shocked Americans more than the revelations that came out of the Hiss hearings and trials.

The case opened dramatically enough. Whittaker Chambers, an editor of *Time* magazine, told the House Un-American Activities Committee in the summer of 1948 of a list of alleged spies and communists which he had turned over to the State Department nine years before. Of all the men listed by Chambers, only Alger Hiss insisted on appearing before the Committee to protest his innocence. He denied categorically that he had ever known Chambers as a member of a communist ring in Washington. Who was lying? A dramatic confrontation between

* H. Commager, "Who Is Loyal to America?" in *Freedom, Loyalty, Dissent* (New York: Oxford University Press, 1954). The article appeared in *Harper's Magazine*, v. 195 (September, 1947).

Alger Hiss, right, and Whittaker Chambers, far left, meeting face-to-face at a session of the House Un-American Activities Committee, August, 1948. (United Press.)

the two men took place in a New York City hotel. Hiss even walked over to Chambers to examine his teeth in order to determine, he said, whether he had known him fourteen years before. He finally stated that he had known Chambers under another name but knew nothing of any communist activities. He challenged Chambers to repeat his charges of espionage outside the protection of the Congressional hearing. Chambers obliged by producing from a hollow pumpkin on his farm some State Department papers he said were copied by Hiss in 1938. Hiss was then indicted for perjury—the statute of limitations prevented his being tried for espionage—by the grand jury.

The Hiss case struck deep into American emotions. Many feared that anti-New Dealers were using the case to damn the integrity and loyalty of thousands of fervent men and women who had gone to Washington to launch the New Deal. Here was a "full-blooded New Dealer," as Alistair Cooke described him, come to justice at a moment in history when millions were looking for an explanation of America's failures. A verdict against Hiss,

some feared, would be a verdict against a whole generation. "The impulse that united everybody looking on," Cooke wrote, "was the impulse to see the New Deal on trial, and by association to expose or deny an old steady conspiracy with the Soviet Union." * On both sides, Hiss became a symbol of sharply conflicting reactions to the history of the preceding fifteen years. "How much more are we going to have to take?" demanded Senator Homer Capehart. "Fuchs· and Acheson and Hiss and hydrogen bombs threatening outside and New Dealism eating away the vitals of the nation. In the name of Heaven, is this the best America can do?"

### Enter McCarthy

No one understood the political implications of the Hiss affair any better than Senator Joseph McCarthy of Wisconsin. Already he had observed how the reputation of Congressman Richard M. Nixon, a member of the House Un-American Affairs Committee, had risen as

* A. Cooke, A *Generation on Trial* (New York: Alfred A. Knopf, 1952), p. 11.

357

a result of his work on the case. One month after Hiss's conviction in the second trial, McCarthy told the Republican women of West Virginia that the State Department was "thoroughly infested" with communists and that Hiss's friend, Secretary Acheson—"a pompous diplomat in striped-pants, with a phony British accent"—was the most dangerous man of all. In his hand, those present remembered him saying, he had a list of 205 names of State Department employees known by Acheson to be communists. In the resulting furor, he denied having used the figure 205, and referred in a speech at Salt Lake City to "fifty-seven card-carrying members of the Communist Party" in the State Department. Later, before the United States Senate, he reviewed eighty-one cases of State Department employees, past and present, whom he claimed were communists or sympathetic with communist purposes. Typical was Case No. 66, nameless as were the others:

This individual is also employed by the State Department as a music director in the Voice of America. He was listed on the draft classification as 4-F because of being a psychoneurotic. He and his mother, with whom he lived, provided a coffee kitchen for communistically inspired protest groups. He also worked for a time for a Communist-dominated organization. He studied for a time in the New School for Social Research under Hans Eisler, who, Senators recall, appeared before the House Un-American Committee. This individual is mentioned principally because he seemed to be representative of the group which accumulated around No. 81, whom I consider one of the big shots.

Under fire for his vague and anonymous charges, McCarthy finally agreed to name the man who was "the top Russian espionage agent" in the United States. He would, he promised, "stand or fall on this one." On March 30, 1950, he pointed to Professor Owen Lattimore as "undoubtedly the most brilliant and scholarly

of all the Communist propagandists" and "one of the top advisers on Far Eastern policy." In actual fact, Lattimore was not a communist, was not an employee of the State Department, and had only occasionally advised the government on Far Eastern policy. That some of his advice may have proved unsound did not alter the fact that McCarthy's charges were unsubstantiated. A Senate committee, headed by Millard Tydings of Maryland, gave Lattimore a clean bill of health and described McCarthy's charges as "the most nefarious campaign of half-truths and untruths in the history of the Republic."

The issue of "McCarthyism" divided the American people even more deeply than the Hiss case or the fall of China. Many were loath to believe that McCarthy's charges, which fit so perfectly the conspiracy theory, could be untrue. Support for McCarthy came from all the groups disaffected by the postwar turn in America's fortunes. Few dared to oppose him publicly lest they, too, be branded as disloyal to America. Senator Tydings, who had written the report criticizing McCarthy in the Lattimore case, was defeated for re-election in 1950, largely because of McCarthy's intervention against him with false charges of Tydings' associations with communists. Responsible Republican politicians encouraged him, or at least feared to challenge his authority. "McCarthy should keep talking," said Robert Taft, "and if one case doesn't work he should proceed with another." No Republican leader rose to dispute his charge that the period of Democratic rule had been "twenty years of treason." "The Democratic label," said McCarthy in a 1950 speech, "is now the property of men and women who have . . . bent to the whispered pleas from the lips of traitors . . . men and women who wear the political label stitched with the idiocy of a Truman, rotted by the deceit of an Acheson, corrupted by the red slime of a White." (Harry Dexter White was a former Assistant Secretary of the Treasury, who was accused by Chambers and others of being a member of a communist ring in Washington during the New Deal years.)

McCarthy's ultimate fall was due to his lack of restraint. Had he remained content to stir up suspicion of the loyalties of State Department employees, his appeal might have gone on unabated for years. But, instead, he broadened his accusations to embrace an ever-widening circle of institutions: universities, churches, newspapers, the United Nations, the Voice of America, and, ultimately, the United States Army. Finally, in 1954, after a television audience of millions saw him intimidate the Secretary of the Army and evade every query directed at him, his power began to fade. Senators long silent were now emboldened to speak up for traditional American procedures and values. In December, 1954, he was condemned by his Senate colleagues for bringing the honor of the Senate into disrepute. Three years later, Senator McCarthy, a broken and largely discredited man, was dead.

But McCarthy had come breathtakingly close to success. For nearly four years he had frightened senators and Presidents, cowed generals, and bullied hundreds of witnesses before his committee. He had nearly fulfilled Aristophanes' prediction for a coarse and vulgar sausage-seller in *The Knights*: "You shall trample down the Senate under foot/Confuse and crush the generals and commanders." He had seriously undermined the confidence of Americans in their civilian and military leaders and badly frightened America's allies in Europe. And the influence he exerted on the morale and confidence of federal employees, particularly in sensitive posts, was both devastating and lasting. Most surprising of all was the slowness and timidity of American leaders in reacting to this threat to democratic liberties. Perhaps Norman Thomas described best the halting and uncertain struggle against McCarthyism. "The struggle against demagoguery," he wrote, "scarcely fits the St. George-against-the-dragon myth. . . . Our democratic St. George goes out rather reluctantly with armor awry. The struggle is confused; our knight wins by no clean thrust of lance or sword, but the dragon somehow poops out, and decent democracy is victor." *

### Crisis in Korea

Four months after McCarthy made his initial charges in West Virginia, the United States was suddenly faced with its most serious crisis since World War II. On June 25, 1950, communist armies from North Korea launched an all-out invasion of the republic of South Korea. For five years the country had been divided at the 38th parallel as a result of a decision to divide occupation duties with Russia along this line. The cold war had made the division permanent; all efforts to end the split and unite Korea had failed. A special UN commission, denied admission to North Korea, had supervised elections in South Korea that had resulted in endorsement of a government headed by Syngman Rhee.

The lightning strike by the communists caught Truman unawares. Little military equipment or training had been given Rhee's forces out of fear that Rhee would carry out an oft-repeated threat to unify Korea by force. American strategists, furthermore, had made no allowance for any action short of all-out war with the Soviet Union. In such a war, Korea would almost certainly not be a battleground. Secretary Acheson, in a speech that was

* This quotation and other material in this section is taken from R. Rovere, *Senator Joe McCarthy* (New York: Harcourt, Brace & World, Inc., 1959).

heavily criticized later, had defined the American defense perimeter in the Pacific as running from the Aleutians to Japan, through the Ryukyus to the Philippines. Within this area, in the event of outside attack, America was committed to respond immediately. Beyond this American defense line, reliance would have to be placed on the peoples attacked and the United Nations. This strategy, reflecting the shrunken state of the army, an austerity budget imposed by Congress, and expectations that, should war come, it would be total war, was understandable in the light of current conditions; but there can be no question that its public enunciation gave encouragement to those planning the Korean invasion. Not Acheson's words alone, however, but the weakness and inflexibility that lay behind them were the real source of communist hopes that America would not defend South Korea.*

Truman faced another hard decision. Should America fight a "brushfire war" in Korea, for which the nation was poorly prepared, or surrender South Korea to the communists? As the President made up his mind, he thought how "Hitler, Mussolini and the Japanese had acted ten, fifteen, and twenty years earlier. I felt certain that if South Korea was allowed to fall, Communist leaders would be emboldened to override nations closer to our own shores. . . . If this was allowed to go unchallenged, it would mean a third world war. . . ." He decided to act. On June 27, he announced that American air and sea forces had been ordered to Korea and that Formosa would be "neutralized" by the American Seventh Fleet. The American action was backed by the UN, which called on its members to give all possible military help to repel the North Koreans. Three days later, on June 30,

Truman ordered General MacArthur, American Commander-in-Chief in the Far East, to throw American ground units into the war in order to halt the headlong retreat of the South Koreans.

At first, the war went well. After stubbornly holding a bridgehead around the port of Pusan against stiff enemy attacks, MacArthur struck boldly on September 15 with a successful landing behind the enemy lines at Inchon on the west coast of the peninsula. UN troops burst through the Pusan perimeter and pushed the communists out of South Korea. By October 1, MacArthur was back on the 38th parallel awaiting a mandate to push the attack into North Korea. Despite Indian warnings that an invasion of North Korea might cause Red China to enter the war, the UN Assembly, at American prodding, took the fateful decision on October 7 to convert the war into a drive for unification of all Korea. During the next three weeks MacArthur pushed rapidly northward, capturing the North Korean capital of Pyongyang, and mopping up the remaining units of North Koreans. Then, on October 26, American and South Korean troops began to meet the first Chinese "volunteer" troops. After several sharp encounters, MacArthur withdrew to the south to regroup and plan for a new offensive.

The war entered a new phase with Chinese entry into the conflict. America's allies in Europe feared that further attacks in northern Korea might mean a general war. Before these fears could influence American policy, however, MacArthur launched an "end-the-war" offensive on November 24 to reach the Yalu River separating Korea from China. A near catastrophe followed. Several hundred thousand fresh Chinese troops were waiting for MacArthur's armies in the mountains of North Korea. As the UN troops came within fifty miles of the Yalu, the Chinese struck, breaking the UN line, and

* Cf. J. Spanier, *The Truman-MacArthur Controversy and the Korean War* (Cambridge: Harvard University Press, 1959), pp. 17-21.

forcing the bulk of MacArthur's force back down the peninsula in a humiliating retreat. For a time it seemed that the UN troops might be forced into the sea but they rallied magnificently and stemmed the Chinese advance. By March, 1951, the battle line stood again at the 38th parallel, where the war had begun.

What should be done now? Should the United States go all-out to unify Korea by force, at the risk of a major war, or should it accept a divided Korea? Public anger and frustration at the turn of events in Korea were beginning to merge with other resentments of Truman's policy. The whole theory of containment of communism, which justified a halt at the 38th parallel, was coming under fierce attack. The war was becoming increasingly embroiled in the cockpit of American politics. MacArthur, under sharp attack for the blunder of his "end-the-war" offensive, sought to shift the blame to his civilian and military superiors in Washington, and he found ready allies in Senator Taft and other leading Republicans. The war, he insisted, should be pressed with full vigor to "severely cripple and largely neutralize China's capability to wage aggressive war." The means were already at hand, he argued: a naval blockade of China, air attacks on Chinese industrial and military targets, and use of Chiang's troops on Formosa. The Korean War, he told newsmen, was being fought under intolerable restrictions "without precedent in history."

Truman's advisers, both military and civilian, were convinced that MacArthur was wrong. The bombing of China, they felt, was almost certain to bring the Russians into the war in one guise or another. A large-scale war in Asia, even without Russian intervention, would lay Europe open to possible Soviet attack. America's allies were fearful of seeing the United States drawn into a war of attrition in China while Europe was still weak. A war along the lines counseled by MacArthur, in the later words of General Bradley, Chairman of the Joint Chiefs of Staff, would be "the wrong war, at the wrong place, at the wrong time, and with the wrong enemy." What this meant was that the United States had abandoned its policy of October 7 to unify Korea by force and returned to the original objective of halting communist aggression at the point where it began.

MacArthur, with strong support from Truman's enemies, continued to criticize the theory of a "limited war." Why should the United States, with its overwhelming superiority in atomic weapons, be fearful of the Soviets entering the war? Did not the Administration believe in its own

U.S. Marines resting during the retreat from the Changjin Reservoir area, December, 1950. Eventually they fought their way to Hungnam, where they were evacuated by boat (see map). (United Press.)

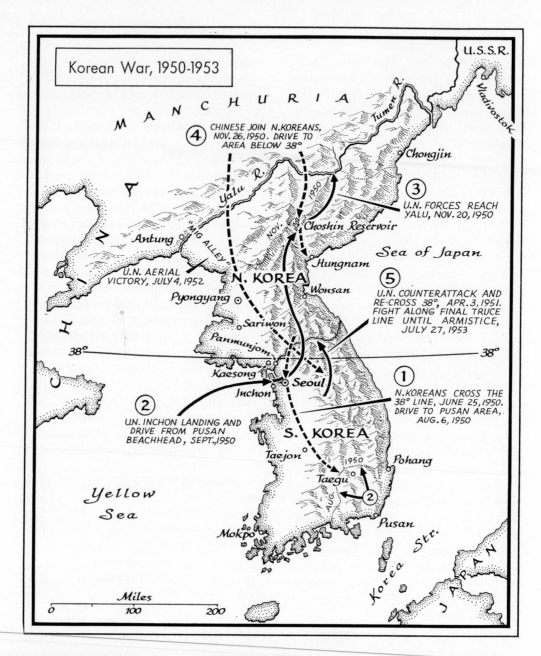

Korean War, 1950-1953

④ CHINESE JOIN N.KOREANS, NOV.26,1950. DRIVE TO AREA BELOW 38°

③ U.N. FORCES REACH YALU, NOV. 20, 1950

⑤ U.N. COUNTERATTACK AND RE-CROSS 38°, APR.3,1951. FIGHT ALONG FINAL TRUCE LINE UNTIL ARMISTICE, JULY 27, 1953

U.N. AERIAL VICTORY, JULY 4, 1952

① N.KOREANS CROSS THE 38° LINE, JUNE 25, 1950. DRIVE TO PUSAN AREA, AUG. 6, 1950

② U.N. INCHON LANDING AND DRIVE FROM PUSAN BEACHHEAD, SEPT.,1950

U.S.S.R.

MANCHURIA

Tumen R.

Vladivostok

Chongjin

Yalu R.

Antung

"MIG ALLEY"

Choshin Reservoir

Sea of Japan

N. KOREA

Hungnam

Wonsan

Pyongyang

Sariwon

Panmunjom

38°          38°

Kaesong

Seoul

Juchon

S. KOREA

Taejon

Pohang

Taegu

Yellow Sea

Mokpo

Pusan

Korea Str.

JAPAN

Miles

0    100    200

strategy which held that the Strategic Air Command would deter Russia from beginning a war? He took his case to veterans' groups and Truman's critics in Congress. Though strongly warned in December, 1950, against any further policy statements without Washington approval, he spoke out on March 24, 1951, against UN efforts to end the fighting. "The enemy," he wrote, "must by now be painfully aware that a decision of the United Na-

tions to depart from its tolerant effort to contain the war to the area of Korea, through an expansion of our military operations to its coastal areas and interior bases, would doom Red China. . . ." Truman wired the General that he was "deeply shocked." Before MacArthur could react, another of his messages, this one to Joseph W. Martin, Republican leader in the House of Representatives, was released. In it MacArthur called once more for use of Chiang's troops in an effort to crush communism in the Far East. "We must win," his message concluded. "There is no substitute for victory."

Truman could no longer ignore the challenge. His foreign policy was now under public attack by a popular general who had made common cause with the President's political enemies. The issue of civilian control over the military, basic to the American constitutional system, was, in his judgment, involved. On April 11, 1951, came the stunning news that Truman had relieved MacArthur of all his commands and appointed General Matthew Ridgway to replace him. "I could do nothing else and still be President of the United States," Truman wrote later. "Even the Chiefs of Staff came to the conclusion that civilian control of the military was at stake but I didn't let it stay at stake very long."

### The Great Debate

Though the Korean War dragged on for another two years until an armistice was signed on July 27, 1953, the firing of MacArthur was the most dramatic moment in the war. Shock and indignation ran through the public's reaction to Truman's announcement. Thousands of telegrams, the vast majority critical of the President, cascaded into the White House and Capitol. A group of Republican leaders met hurriedly and announced there would be an investigation of the Administration's foreign and military policy. "In addition," said House Minority Leader Martin, "the question of possible impeachments was discussed." Senator Richard Nixon proposed that Truman be censured and MacArthur restored to his command. Senator McCarthy called Truman a "sonofabitch" who had made his decision while drunk on "bourbon and benedictine."

Truman underwent his greatest torment as President during the days that followed. MacArthur returned as a conquering hero and told a hushed Congress that appeasement would beget only "new and bloodier war." "Why," he said his soldiers had asked him, "surrender military advantage to an enemy in the field? I could not answer." When the Senate debate on Far Eastern policy opened, General MacArthur was the first witness. Again he argued for a reversal of American policy in Korea by making use of a blockade, air bombardment, and Chiang's Formosan troops. But the Joint Chiefs of Staff, Acheson, and Secretary of Defense Marshall defended the Administration's stand against MacArthur. "Our position in Korea," General Marshall summed up, "continues to be the defeat of the aggression and the restoration of peace. We have persistently sought to confine the conflict

A view of the Truman-MacArthur debate. (New York Public Library Picture Collection.)

to Korea and to prevent its spreading into a third World War. . . . Our efforts have succeeded in thwarting the aggressors in Korea, and . . . given us some sorely needed time and impetus to accelerate the building of our defenses and those of our allies against the threatened onslaught of Soviet imperialism." The differences with MacArthur, said Marshall, stemmed from MacArthur's limited vision as a field commander as opposed to the Administration's responsibility for the total security of the United States.

The MacArthur hearings climaxed a series of foreign policy debates that had begun in the Senate in the winter of 1950-51. Truman, in responding to the new aggressiveness shown by the Kremlin, had decided to strengthen American ground forces in Western Europe. But a number of Republican spokesmen, following the first Korean reverses and Republican gains in the fall elections, had spoken out against this move. Herbert Hoover, in a radio address on December 20, argued strongly against too great a reliance on Europe, whose will to fight he thought dubious, and opposed any commitment of American ground troops there. In words reminiscent of prewar isolationism, Hoover declared that America's purpose must be "to preserve for the world this Western Hemisphere Gibraltar of Western civilization." Senator Taft also spoke against an American role in organizing the defenses of Europe, especially the assignment of an American commander to head NATO forces. Republicans, he said, were united in "all-out opposition to the spread of communism, recognizing that there is a limit beyond which we cannot go." This position was characterized by the New York *Post* as "the all-out, half-way policy." What bothered Taft most of all was the inconsistency he saw in risking war in Europe by aiding Greece and arming Europe, while refusing to be bold in Asia.

In January, 1951, the debate on sending troops to Europe came to a head. Senator Wherry of Nebraska introduced a resolution that "no ground forces of the United States should be assigned to duty in the European area for the purpose of the North Atlantic Treaty pending the formulation of a policy with respect

thereto by the Congress." A confused exchange followed about whether Congress had the constitutional right to limit the President's control over the armed forces as Commander-in-Chief. Finally, after Marshall, Acheson, and General Eisenhower argued the need for American leadership in Europe before a joint hearing of the Foreign Relations and Armed Forces committees, the Senate adopted a resolution on April 4, a week before MacArthur's dismissal, approving the sending of four divisions to Europe. But, significantly, the resolution called for specific Congressional approval of any further ground reinforcements. Behind the political skirmish between Congress and President lay a resurgence of isolationist feeling that found its outlet in distrust of the UN and collective security and in assertions of American power to "go it alone." It was at this hour of bitter questioning of collective security that General MacArthur, hero of the isolationists, returned to do battle for his principles.

## 1952: An Era Closes

As the 1952 election approached, it was clear that Truman's foreign policy would be a major issue. Disillusionment with the Korean War became intense as the armistice negotiations dragged on month after weary month. "Containment" became a term of opprobrium as Republican leaders called for a new policy of dynamic opposition to communism. The policy of containment, said John Foster Dulles, chief Republican adviser on foreign affairs, was "negative, futile, and immoral." The United States, following MacArthur's suggestions, should undertake to roll back the Iron Curtain, liberate the peoples in communist enslavement, and reassert America's moral mission to bring freedom by inspiration and example to the rest of the world. Not living *with* communism, but living *without* it should be the objective of American policy. There should be no more limited wars; America must either stay out of trouble spots or else fight through to victory. A clear line should be drawn on the map, Dulles believed, and if an aggressor crossed that line he should be crushed by "massive retaliation" from the strategic air force.

This was an appeal that sounded a basic chord in the American experience. It found immediate favor with most of the critics of Truman's policy. It seemed to promise action, boldness, reliance on American strength, and an end to the Cold War. It placed the blame for America's frustrations abroad, not on the Kremlin's drive for power, but on the machinations of blundering and disloyal statesmen at home. These blundering statesmen of the Democratic party, according to the Republican platform of 1952, had "traded an overwhelming victory for a new enemy and for new oppression and new wars which were quick to come."

The Republican candidate who best expressed these views in 1952 was Robert Taft. Midwestern political leaders were especially strong for the Ohio senator, who gave voice to their distrust of Europe, insistence on governmental economy, support for Chiang Kai-shek, opposition to the welfare state, and belief in the disloyalty of many federal employees. But an influential Eastern faction of the party, led by Thomas E. Dewey, Henry Cabot Lodge, Jr., of Massachusetts, and others, backed General Dwight D. Eisenhower, now NATO commander in Europe, for the nomination. This group was known to favor a moderate conservativism in domestic policy and a responsible internationalism in foreign affairs. Most of them believed in the importance of maintaining close relations with America's allies in Europe, and few accepted the thesis that domestic subversives were a greater danger to American liberties than the men of the Kremlin.

When the Republican convention opened in Chicago, Taft appeared to be in the lead. He had more delegates pledged to him than Eisenhower and, furthermore, his supporters controlled the national committee. This meant that the keynote speaker (General MacArthur) and the temporary and permanent chairmen would be Taft men. More important, the national committee would pass on the credentials of the seventy-odd delegates whose seats were in dispute. In Georgia, Louisiana, and Texas, Eisenhower men had backed their candidate with force in primaries and party caucuses and ignored the hand-picked Taft slates put forward by the party organizations. The party bosses in these states, all Taft men, had refused to recognize Eisenhower delegates to state and district conventions, sometimes claiming that these were not actually Republicans. The resulting split brought two sets of delegates from these states to Chicago.

In Chicago, the national committee duly awarded most of the disputed seats to Taft. The stage appeared to be set for a repetition of 1912, when Taft's father had steamrollered his renomination over the popular Theodore Roosevelt. But in 1912 there had been no television. This time, as the Taft-controlled credentials committee listened to the contest over the seats, millions of viewers witnessed the exposure of the Taft tactics in the South. The Eisenhower forces took high moral ground against the "vote stealing" in the South. On the critical vote on adoption of convention rules, the Eisenhower leaders proposed an amendment to prohibit delegations opposed by more than a third of the national committee from voting on the credentials of other delegates. After bitter debate, this motion carried. Then, on the specific question of the seating of delegates, the report of the credentials committee was rejected and the Eisenhower delegates were seated. Defeat for

Taft was now virtually inevitable. Eisenhower was named the Republican candidate on the first ballot and Senator Richard M. Nixon, who had played an important part in exposing Alger Hiss, was selected to run with him.

To oppose Eisenhower, the Democrats chose Governor Adlai E. Stevenson of Illinois. He had been reluctant to run and declared to the moment of his actual nomination that he was not a candidate. His only serious opposition came from Senator Estes Kefauver, who had headed a special Senate committee to investigate crime, but who had alienated President Truman and a number of local politicians. Stevenson's acceptance speech became something of a convention classic as he declared: "The ordeal of the Twentieth Century—the bloodiest, most turbulent era of the Christian age—is far from over. Sacrifice, patience, understanding and implacable purpose may be our lot for years to come. Let's face it. Let's talk sense to the American people. Let's tell them the truth, that there are no gains without pains, that we are now on the eve of great decisions, not easy decisions, like resistance when you're attacked, but a long, patient, costly struggle which alone can assure triumph over the great enemies of man—war, poverty, and tyranny—and the assaults upon human dignity which are the most grievous consequences of each."

Stevenson's campaign speeches touched a level of eloquence not heard in American politics since Woodrow Wilson. With wit and skill he defended the foreign policy of the Truman years, argued for repeal of the Taft-Hartley Act, and took stands on Negro rights and control of tidelands oil that were unpopular in the Democratic South. He embraced most of the Fair Deal program, including high price supports for farmers. And he spoke again and again of there being "no easy road to peace and security." With his running-

mate, Senator John J. Sparkman of Alabama, he waged an unexpectedly vigorous campaign.

But Stevenson faced impossible odds. On the Republican side were the mood of the country, Eisenhower's tremendous popularity, and virtually all the issues. Korea, communism, and corruption were the three most discussed topics in the campaign; Stevenson was on the defensive on all three. To make his burden heavier, Truman took to the hustings and pushed his Administration's record into the center of the campaign. The President blasted Eisenhower's "surrender" to the right-wingers in his party and warned that a military man would not make a good President.

Eisenhower worked hard to heal the breach in his party opened by the convention fight. He met with Taft and gained his pledge of support in return for a promise to cut government expenditures and end "creeping socialization." He shook hands with McCarthy and deleted a paragraph praising his old chief, General Marshall, from a speech he was to make in Milwaukee. He endorsed isolationist Republicans, as well as internationalists, on the ground that a Republican President needed a Republican Congress.

The General sharply attacked Truman for his "disastrous management" of foreign policy. "The seven years since the war," he said, "have been a record of catastrophe, with its climax in Korea." In Detroit, shortly before the election, he made the dramatic announcement that, if elected, "I shall go to Korea." Over and over again, he struck at the "mess in Washington," referring to revelations of influence-peddling in the Reconstruction Finance Corporation and tax-fixing in the Internal Revenue Bureau. Truman's inability or unwillingness to act decisively against these and other irregularities was a source of much discomfort to Stevenson during the campaign.

Nixon's role was to lay stress on the Administration's "softness" toward communism. He made much of a deposition that Stevenson had made as a character witness for Alger Hiss. He flayed Truman for his "red herring" statements during the hearings on communists in government. And he implied strongly that the State Department was still influenced by communists and other disloyal persons. Nixon himself came under fire when news was uncovered that he had been given $18,000 by wealthy friends to use for political purposes while he was a United States Senator. With public opinion running strongly against him, and with several influential papers demanding his resignation, Nixon went on television to fight for his political life. None of the money, he said, had been used personally but had gone into "exposing this Administration, the Communism in it, the corruption in it." He then detailed his life's story, including his war experience, his marriage and family, his mortgage and insurance policies, and the acquiring of the family dog, Checkers, as a gift ("regardless of what they say about it, we're going to keep it"). It was a dramatic and evidently effective performance. For as the wires poured in, 350 to 1 in favor of retaining Nixon, it became clear that he had turned a liability into a powerful asset. "The sophisticates . . . sneer," wrote Robert Ruark, but "this came closer to humanizing the Republican party than anything that has happened in my memory. . . . Tuesday night the nation saw a little man, squirming his way out of a dilemma, and laying bare his most private hopes, fears and liabilities. This time the common man was a Republican, for a change."

After the experience of 1948, the pollsters were cautious but the outcome should not have been in doubt. Eisenhower won the strongest victory of any candidate since FDR in 1936. Nearly 34

million persons voted for the General, while 27 million cast their ballots for Stevenson. Eisenhower swept thirty-nine states with 442 electoral votes, while Stevenson held only nine states and eighty-nine electoral votes for the Democratic Party. The President-elect ran far ahead of his party, which barely got control of Congress.

### 1952 Election

| | Popular Vote | Electoral Vote |
|---|---|---|
| Stevenson (D) | 27,311,316 | 89 |
| Eisenhower (R) | 33,927,549 | 442 |
| Other | 356,272 | 0 |

The twenty years of Democratic rule were over. They had been stirring years of trial and crisis, of tumult and controversy, of depression and war and anguished peace. During the last seven years, Truman had dueled with Stalin across the troubled boundary lines left by the military and diplomatic decisions of World War II. Each time that either sought to disturb the truce, as when Stalin threatened Turkey, or Truman ordered MacArthur across the 38th parallel in Korea, the other responded with force or the threat of force. Only China and Czechoslovakia had changed hands since 1945. But, as Eisenhower came to the White House in 1953, new influences were at work that would drastically alter the shape of the postwar world. The era of the H-bomb, of post-Stalin Russia, and of nationalist revolutions in Asia and Africa was at hand. Eisenhower had given voice to the mood of frustration of the American people in 1952. Would he be able to convert that frustration into positive effort in the frightening era just ahead?

## THE TEMPER OF THE FORTIES

The troubled postwar years left deep scars on the American psyche. The atomic bomb, the successes of communism, the revelations of corruption and disloyalty, and the collapse of familiar standards made it hard for many Americans to feel optimistic about the future. Even scientists, who were forced to wrestle with the moral implications of the atomic bomb, lost some of their old confidence. "Up to 1945," wrote C. P. Snow, British physicist and novelist, "the climate of science was optimistic. Now that unquestioning optimism has drained away from most of the scientists I know." In 1950, President Truman announced that an effort would be made to build a hydrogen bomb, whose explosive power would dwarf that of the A-bomb. Two years later, as the Truman era came to a close, the first hydrogen explosion was reported.

### The "Age of Anxiety"

A mood of quiet anxiety and resignation, a sense of powerlessness before the numbing forces moving modern life, seemed to pervade the thought of many sensitive persons in the 1940's. A feeling that something vague and indefinable was deeply wrong with the modern world was noted by some observers. "What is wrong with us?" queried the editor of the Cleveland *Press*, Louis B. Seltzer, in an editorial that was widely reprinted and discussed.

It is in the air we breathe. The things we do. The things we say. Our books. Our theater. Our movies. Our radio and television. The way we behave. . . . We abound with all of the things that make us comfortable. We are, on the average, rich beyond the dreams of the kings of old. . . . Yet . . . something is not there that should be—something we once had. . . . Are we our own worst enemies? Should we fear what is happening among us more than what is happening elsewhere? . . . No one seems to know what to do to meet it. But everybody worries. . . .

The "Age of Anxiety" some were beginning to call it. It was compounded of many things—the loss of religious certainty since Darwin's day, the humdrum quality of modern urban-industrial life, the terrible wars of the twentieth century, the urgency of the A-bomb, the tensions of the Cold War, the changing character of American society ("something is not there . . . something we once had"), and the fear that American civilization might have reached its peak and be on the road taken by Rome and lesser states. No important literary work of the 1940's excited more discussion than the abridgement of Arnold Toynbee's magisterial A *Study of History*, which found the key to the rise and flowering of the great civilizations of the past in a creative elite. Only a recovery of purpose, a new faith in Christian ideals and values, Toynbee seemed to say, could save us from Rome's fate.

There were other signs of a growing restlessness with the relativistic ideology inherited from John Dewey's generation. The theologian Reinhold Niebuhr called for a reaffirmation of historic Christian values and challenged sharply the naturalistic doctrine that men could find salvation through science and human effort alone. A group of Catholic scholars, drawn to the natural-law philosophy of St. Thomas Aquinas, pointed to the separation between the intellectual and the spiritual life as the major disease of the modern world. "Divorce and voluntary sterility," said Monsignor Fulton J. Sheen in 1943, "are not wrong because the Church says they are wrong. The Church says they are wrong because they are violations of the natural law which binds all men." A number of social scientists, too, showed impatience with the old strictures against value judgments and the insistence on the ethical neutrality of science. "My general impression," said the anthropologist David Ridney in 1952, "is that cultural relativists are so concerned to safeguard cultural differences that they fail to appreciate the polar requirement of a common core of objective values. There can be no mutual respect for differences when there is no community of values also."

But despite the appeals for greater certainty, the prevailing mood of the forties appeared to be uncertainty. Many who had never read Darwin or Freud or Niebuhr were aware of the cleavage in their beliefs. The sense of unsureness and the anxiety it entailed were all but universal. It lay at the root of the most common problems of everyday life—child rearing, marital relations, delinquency, the treatment of criminals. "The more the sense of quicksand came," wrote Eric Goldman in a perceptive account,

the more the disturbed citizen could find evidence of it on all sides. By the heavens, at least there was still such a thing as moral good and bad. But then, come to think of it, was there still such a thing? Hadn't the corrosives of all the old sure standards seeped even into this rock? . . . His denunciation of juvenile delinquents was inevitably followed by a news item in which an expert insisted that the fault should be assigned not to the delinquent but to a vague complexity called maladjustments in the home. Well, at least he was sure how to raise his own children. But then, matter of fact, was he really sure what closing hour to impose on his daughter's dates? And when he raised his hand to thwack Junior's bottom, the blows were unsteadied by a criss-cross of child-raising theories in his own mind.*

## Fiction and Values

This uncertainty about values had a crushing impact on the literature of the forties. Since World War I, literary men and women had become increasingly sensitive to the loss of stability and common values in American life. Writers of the twenties had taken refuge in symbolism (Gertrude Stein), in primitivism (Hemingway), or in the portrayal of the breakdown of values itself (Fitzgerald). In the thirties some writers had found unity and purpose once more in reasserting traditional values in the face of the economic breakdown at home and the threat of totalitarianism abroad. But now, in the forties, a new generation that had never known certainty, that had lost its illusions, that had been nourished on the angry, disenchanted novels of the twenties, began to write. What would they write about? The second World War was more catastrophic than the first, but who could feel freshly the loss of illusion, the disenchantment that had led Hemingway to write A Farewell to Arms? America was, even more than in Babbitt's time, a nation of materialism and gadgets and Rotarian boosters, but who could repeat Sinclair Lewis's performance of the twenties? Illusions once lost, wrote John Aldridge in a brilliant analysis, could not be relost. Insights into the nature of modern life, once made, were in the public domain and could excite no new interest.†

The writer's alternatives were limited. He could rely on brilliant technique and journalistic detail, or he could try to find new subject matter that writers of the twenties and thirties had overlooked. So

---

* E. Goldman, The Crucial Decade (New York: Knopf, 1956), p. 120.

† Much of this discussion is based on Aldridge's After the Lost Generation (New York: McGraw-Hill Company, 1951), especially pp. 87-106.

the novelists of the forties delved into homosexuality, dope addiction, racial and religious differences, and other neglected areas in an effort to chart new ground. In *Other Voices, Other Rooms*, Truman Capote constructed a homosexual fantasy that illustrated the new trend. Jewish characters now figured more importantly in the novels of the forties—*The Naked and the Dead, The Young Lions*, and others—frequently as heroic figures in conflict with an overpowering environment. Noah Ackerman, in Irwin Shaw's *The Young Lions*, for example, is a persecuted American Jew who fights bravely for life and honor against staggering odds.

The war novels, particularly Mailer's *The Naked and the Dead*, drew their strength from their journalistic attention to detail. Unlike Hemingway's novel of World War I, Mailer took as his canvas an entire army division and tried to follow it through a complex military maneuver in the Pacific war. With great vividness, he described the suffering and evil, the horrors and nightmares of war. He focussed down on the dilemma faced by men of character and integrity faced with the desperate conditions of battle. But the philosophical framework of the novel, designed to show how military ideology destroys human decency and moral values, proved less effective than his camera-like portrayal of scenes of conflict.

Other novelists of the forties sought to escape, though no more successfully, the dilemma of the modern writer. Alfred Hayes tried to repeat the Hemingway formula of World War I in his *The Girl on the Via Flaminia:* an infantryman on leave in Rome, a lonely Italian girl searching for love and companionship, and a background of futile and meaningless war. Irwin Shaw in *The Young Lions* attempted to portray the impact of war on three separate figures, a New York playwright, an American Jew, and a German ski instructor. Intended as a denunciation

of war and fascist tendencies in America, as well as a plea for religious tolerance, the novel was too patently a reassertion of values for which the dramatic action failed to supply support.

Of the dramatists, Arthur Miller and Tennessee Williams were most sensitive to the confusion of values at the heart of American life. The theme of Miller's *Death of a Salesman*, the most powerful social drama of the period, is the tribulation of a man who accepts at face value the hollow ideals of material success and blatant optimism that are dinned into his ear at every turn. The tragic downfall and defeat of Willy Loman, salesman, illustrates the failure of a way of life common to millions of Americans. His failure is the failure of all those who live on dreams and dare not face reality, dare not stand up to modern life. This was also the theme of Tennessee Williams' plays—*The Glass Menagerie, A Streetcar Named Desire, Summer and Smoke*—in which fragile personalities, often living in the past, are forced by relentless circumstance to confront the modern world.

Complaints were growing that novelists and dramatists were painting only the dark side of American life. There was too much of sex and violence and unnatural relations, these critics said, and too little of the wholesome qualities of modern life. But this criticism failed to penetrate far enough. The bizarre themes of so much of modern literature were a direct response to the uncertainty and emptiness within the writers themselves. "The main reason for this," wrote Professor Aldridge,

is that the artist today has no distinct attitude either toward his experience or toward the medium in which he works. . . . He is unable simply to look into his heart because he no longer knows where his heart is or whether he has one. He has been so thoroughly dissected and atomized that when he sits down to probe his conscience he has to summon into consultation a thousand disparate fragments of himself. . . . He is, in short, a man who knows too much to be knowing, who is too convinced of his own lack of conviction to be convincing, and who, therefore, lacks the basic requirement of the healthy artist—a dogmatic belief in his supreme power as an individual and a complete contempt for everything which stands in the way of its exercise. The absence of such a belief is largely responsible for the emptiness one senses in so much of the new fiction.*

### The Urge to Conform

Scarcely a writer of the nineteen-forties failed to comment on the growing standardization of American life. The continued expansion of industry, the more equitable spread of income, and the proliferation of mass communications, especially the advent of television in the late forties, seemed to speed up the process. The gap between styles of living of East and West, town and country, and rich and poor had clearly narrowed since

* Aldridge, op. cit., p. 256.

1929. No longer was it possible to pick the New York banker or the rural "hayseed" or the automobile mechanic out of a crowd by dint of their clothes or appearance alone. Mass advertising had made familiar all the common middle-class comforts from TV and electric washers to power mowers and outdoor cooking stoves. Middle-class standards of speech and manners were now all but universal. A casual style of dress and behavior and entertaining was becoming acceptable in all but a very few places. Even homes and automobiles showed less class differentiation than they once had. Though there was still much evidence of individual and regional differences among Americans at every hand, these were less talked about and certainly less praised than a few decades before.

The word "conformity" was now heard widely for the first time. As postwar housing developments pushed into the suburbs of many large cities, a pattern of liv-

Enormous, monotonous tracts of identical houses were one symptom of the conformity characteristic of the postwar period. (H. Armstrong Roberts.)

ing took shape that varied little from one part of the country to another. Informality, lack of privacy, similarities of taste and judgment, "keeping up" with the neighbors, and a growing intolerance toward unpopular or nonconforming opinions seemed characteristic of much of middle-class life. When André Siegfried returned to the United States a quarter-century after writing his successful book, *America Comes of Age* (1927), he was struck by the change in the national attitude.

The same type of train, the same hotels, restaurants, cooking, the same newspapers are to be found everywhere [he wrote;] and it is important to realize that this monotony is not only accepted but even highly esteemed. The American, who formerly appreciated eccentricity, has now become conformist in his habits, he prefers to be exactly like all his other fellow countrymen rather than individually distinctive in his appearance or his mode of life.*

The stress on conformity was clearly linked to the decay of common values and the general uncertainty of the age. The behavior of the group was becoming the one sure standard of guidance for the behavior of the individual. Parents no longer gave commands—they were confused or uncertain about what to command—but sought to impress upon their children the importance of "adjustment" to the group. In schools, offices, and factories, the same trend was noted; not commands, but persuasion was regarded as the best way to get things done. "Team" work, cooperation, and group rewards were frequently stressed. Most authority thus became external and anonymous, while the individual was, in David Riesman's term, "other-directed." And the mechanism through which this new authority operated, said the psychiatrist Erich Fromm, was conformity:

I ought to do what everybody does, hence, I must conform, not be different, not "stick out"; I must be ready and willing to change according to the changes in the pattern; I must not ask whether I am right or wrong, but whether I am adjusted, whether I am not "peculiar," not different. The only thing which is permanent in me is just this readiness for change. Nobody has power over me, except the herd of which I am a part, yet to which I am subjected.†

Though not all agreed that Americans were as conformist as these writers said, few observers denied that the standards of the group were playing a much larger role in determining the behavior of the individual than was true a century before.

### America at Mid-Century

It was thus a troubled and confused nation that found itself at mid-century the leader of the free world. Though strong beyond the dreams of the statesmen of 1900, it was torn by internal dissension, anxious about the future, and no longer so certain of its mission in the world. Americans were still free but unsure of the boundaries of freedom; they still believed, on the whole, in universal standards of right and justice but found it increasingly hard to say exactly what these meant; and they held more firmly than ever to their democratic system of self-government but were no longer sure that other peoples would benefit from such a system.

The war left the United States the most powerful industrial nation on earth. Despite tremendous exertions by Russian and West European factories and mills, the American economy easily outdistanced all the others. The gross national product, which had stood at $100 billion in 1940 rose to $213 billion in 1945 and would reach $284 billion by 1950. Of a population numbering 150 million in 1950, more than 56 million were gainfully employed.

* A. Siegfried, *America at Mid-Century* (New York: Harcourt, Brace and Company, 1955), p. 113.

† E. Fromm, *The Sane Society* (New York: Rinehart and Company, 1955), pp. 153-54.

One of every three working Americans now engaged in manufacturing, two in eleven were employed in trade, and only one in nine made his living at farming in 1950.

The population of the United States underwent sharp changes in the years of depression, war, and postwar. The rush to the cities resumed with the war so that, according to the census of 1950, urban dwellers (those living in places of 2500 people or more) accounted for nearly two-thirds of the entire population. Immigrants counted for little of this growth. The number of immigrants to the United States fell from four million in the twenties, the last decade of heavy immigration, to a half-million in the thirties and slightly more than one million in the forties. The population increase was largely due to a high birth rate which, following a severe decline in the depression years, rose spectacularly in the forties. But there were other important factors. The life expectancy of the average American rose as advances in diet, public health measures, and medical discoveries reduced the danger from disease. In 1900, the American's life expectancy was 47.3 years; this figure reached 62.9 in 1940 and 68.2 years in 1950. Most dramatic was the decline in infant mortality as the majority of childhood diseases were brought under check. Of all persons dying in the year 1900, sixteen of every hundred were under one year of age; in 1950 this number had dropped to three.

Surveying the American scene in 1950, the historian Henry Steele Commager concluded that the spirit within this pulsing, dynamic, ever-changing nation had not changed much since the eighteen-nineties. Despite the convulsive shifts in social and intellectual life, he found the American character "substantially the same." Many of the old qualities—optimism, materialism, and practicality—had survived with little change. Individualism remained an American ideal though in practice the nonconformist was likely to come under fire. Idealism was still strong in the American character, Commager believed, and words such as honor, courage, and liberty still evoked a meaningful response from most Americans. The most serious changes that Commager found in the American outlook were the growth of intolerance toward unpopular views, the decline of popular taste in literature and entertainment, and the atrophy of the creative instinct in the arts.

As the second half of the twentieth century opened, Commager posed a series of questions—which, he said, history rather than he would have to answer—about the meaning of the American experience. Americans, he said,

had created an economy of abundance; could they fashion a political mechanism to assure the equitable distribution of that abundance? They had become the richest people on the globe; would they use their wealth to prosper society or to display power? They were democratic in law; would they be democratic in fact? They were equalitarian by conviction; would they be equalitarian in conduct? . . . They had solved the ancient problem of liberty and order; would they succeed in maintaining order in a war-troubled world without such suppression of liberty as would change the character of their state? They had become increasingly like the peoples of the Old World; could they avoid the clash of doctrine and opinion, the conflict of church and state, of class and party, of race and section, that had for so long rent Europe with dissension and war?*

The whole world, said Commager, would be interested in the answers to these questions.

* H. Commanger, *The American Mind* (New Haven: Yale University Press, 1950), p. 442.

# FOR FURTHER STUDY

## General Accounts

The books by Agar, Goldman, Truman, Spanier, and Zornow cited at the end of Chapter X, and Johnson, *1600 Pennsylvania Avenue*, cited earlier, continue to be useful for the general themes of this chapter.

## Special Studies

* J. Aldridge, *After the Lost Generation* (New York: Mc-Graw-Hill, 1951). A brilliant interpretation of American writing of the forties.

A. Angoff (ed.), *American Writing Today* (New York: New York U. Press, 1957). This is the famous account of contemporary American writing that first appeared in *The Times* (London) *Literary Supplement*.

A. Barth, *Government by Investigation* (New York: Viking, 1955), and *The Loyalty of Free Men* (New York: The Viking Press, 1951). These are two of the most useful analyses of the loyalty-security problem.

C. Berger, *The Korea Knot* (Philadelphia: U. of Pennsylvania Press, 1957). A good summary of the origins of the Korean tragedy and its basic sequence of events.

W. Buckley, Jr., and L. Bozell, *McCarthy and His Enemies* (Chicago: Regnery, 1954). A defense of Senator McCarthy's record and an attack on his detractors.

M. Bundy (ed.), *The Pattern of Responsibility* (Boston: Houghton Mifflin, 1952). Made up largely of quotations from the speeches and statements of Dean Acheson, this book defends him against his critics.

W. Chambers, *Witness* (New York: Random House, 1952).

* Starred books are available in paperbound editions.

This classic in the literature of anticommunism is Chambers' personal story of the background of the Hiss case.

L. Chandler, *Inflation in the United States, 1940-1948* (New York: Harpers, 1951). A technical but lucid explanation of the origins, course, and significance of the inflationary spiral of the forties.

M. Clark, *From the Danube to the Yalu* (New York: Harpers, 1954). The story of the final days of the Korean War by the last commander-in-chief.

* H. Commager, *The American Mind* (New Haven: Yale U. Press, 1950), An important interpretation of American thought and character in the twentieth century, climaxed by an evaluation of "The Twentieth-Century American."

A. Cooke, *A Generation on Trial* (New York: Knopf, 1952). The fullest account of the events and significance of the Hiss case.

* M. Cowley, *The Literary Situation* (New York: Viking, 1954). An incisive series of essays on the war novels, the "new" fiction, literary criticism, and other features of the literary scene.

* E. Cronon (ed.), *Contemporary Labor-Management Relations* (New York: Holt, 1960). A good collection of materials concerning the Taft-Hartley law in pamphlet form.

J. Daniels, *The Man of Independence* (Philadelphia: Lippincott, 1950). Still the best available biography of Truman, Daniels' account is highly favorable to the former President.

* E. Davis, *But We Were Born Free* (Indianapolis: Bobbs-Merrill, 1952). An eloquent plea that America not forget its heritage of freedom in its anxiety to root out subversion and disloyalty.

R. Gabriel, *The Course of American Democratic Thought*

(New York: Ronald Press, rev. ed., 1956). A brilliant and optimistic interpretation of modern American thought whose closing chapters deal with the revolt against relativism.

* C. Glasrud (ed.), *The Age of Anxiety* (Boston: Houghton Mifflin, 1960). This is an extraordinarily good collection of materials bearing on the theme of anxiety in the modern world.

N. Graebner, *The New Isolationism* (New York: Ronald, 1956). An able interpretation of the confused currents of foreign and domestic attitudes of Americans in the early 1950's.

W. Hillman, *Mr. President* (New York: Farrar, Straus and Young, 1952). An informal pictures-and-text book of Truman's problems, policies, and private views as President of the United States.

S. Hook, *Heresy, Yes; Conspiracy, No.* (New York: John Day, 1953). Professor Hook makes a difficult but important distinction between tolerance of unpopular views and tolerance of a foreign-controlled conspiracy to subvert American institutions.

L. Koenig (ed.), *The Truman Administration* (New York: New York U. Press, 1956). Selections from Truman's papers and speeches bearing on his conduct of the Presidency, his views on domestic legislation, and his role as commander-in-chief and chief diplomat.

* S. Lubell, *The Future of American Politics* (New York: Harpers, 1951). Lubell's analysis of Truman's political strength and his election in 1948 is the most acute yet made.

H. Millis and E. Brown, *From the Wagner Act to Taft-Hartley* (Chicago: U. of Chicago Press, 1950). A very full, interpretive account of labor relations legislation from 1935 to 1948 that is sympathetic to organized labor.

W. Millis, *The Forrestal*

*Diaries* (New York: Viking, 1951). Contains excerpts from the diaries and other private papers of James Forrestal, first Secretary of Defense.

C. Mills, *The New Men of Power* (New York: Harcourt, Brace, 1948). A sociological study of the new type of labor leader produced since the nineteen-thirties.

* President's Committee on Civil Rights, *To Secure These Rights* (New York: Simon and Schuster, 1947). This is the final report of Truman's committee, whose chairman was Charles E. Wilson.

C. Pritchett, *Civil Liberties and the Vinson Court* (Chicago: U. of Chicago Press, 1954). An excellent analysis of civil liberties cases before the Supreme Court from 1946 to 1953.

* R. Rovere, *Senator Joe McCarthy* (New York: Harcourt, Brace, 1959). An analysis of McCarthy and his significance that concludes that his challenge to freedom "showed us to be more vulnerable than many of us had guessed to a seditious demagogy —as well as less vulnerable than some of us feared."

* A. Rose, *The Negro in Postwar America* (New York: Anti-Defamation League, 1950). A pamphlet that summarizes the Negro's postwar advances, problems, and reactions to new conditions.

K. Schmidt, *Henry A. Wallace* (Syracuse: Syracuse U. Press, 1960). A sympathetic and largely uncritical account of Wallace's 1948 campaign.

A. Siegfried, *America at Mid-Century* (New York: Harcourt, Brace, 1955). A translation from the French of a new evaluation of American civilization by the author of *America Comes of Age* (1927).

J. Spanier, *The Truman-MacArthur Controversy and the Korean War* (Cambridge: Harvard U. Press, 1959). A first-rate account that relates the controversy to the deeper strategic, political, and psychological factors involved.

G. Steiner, *Government's Role in Economic Life* (New York: McGraw-Hill, 1953). A careful analysis of the evolution of the problem and the contemporary pressures that make it urgent.

A. Stevenson, *Major Campaign Speeches, 1952* (New York: Random House, 1953). Fifty speeches by the most gifted political phrase-maker of the fifties.

R. Taft, *A Foreign Policy for Americans* (Garden City, N.Y.: Doubleday, 1951). A campaign document written to prove, said Taft, "that the freedom of the people of the United States is in serious danger from the foreign policy of the present Administration."

H. Truman, *The Truman Program* (Washington, D.C.: Public Affairs Press, 1948). Selections from Truman's campaign speeches of 1948.

* J. Wahlke (ed.), *Loyalty in a Democratic State* (Boston: Heath, 1952). A good collection of pros and cons on the loyalty controversy in the Amherst "Problems in American Civilization" series.

N. Weyl, *The Battle against Disloyalty* (New York: Crowell, 1951). A measured account of the loyalty controversy in historical perspective.

C. Whitney, *MacArthur* (New York: Knopf, 1956). A former aide's sympathetic account of MacArthur's career covering World War II, the Japanese occupation, the Korean War, and his return to America.

## Fiction and Drama

* L. Hobson, *Gentleman's Agreement* (New York: Simon and Schuster, 1947). A journalist, posing as a Jew to gather material for a series of articles on anti-Semitism, encounters a number of instances of discrimination.

* J. Michener, *The Bridges at Toko-ri* (New York: Random House, 1953). A short, somewhat bitter, novel of the Korean War revolving around Lt. Henry Brubaker, a family man, who is, as the author put it, "one of the voluntary men who save the world."

* A. Miller, *The Crucible* (New York: Viking, 1953). A drama of the Salem witchcraft trials of 1692 that parallels some of the contemporary injustices of the McCarthy era.

* E. O'Connor, *The Last Hurrah* (Boston: Little, Brown, 1953). A warm novel of the last stand of Frank Skeffington, Irish boss of an Eastern city, whose defeat symbolizes the passing of an era.

* I. Shaw, *The Troubled Air* (New York: Random House, 1951). The director of a popular radio program, ordered to fire five actors suspected of sympathy with communism, tries to clear their names only to find that no one is truly interested in justice for the accused.

## Films and Records

*Arnold Toynbee* (Encyclopedia Britannica Films, 30 minutes, sound, black and white). The author of *A Study of History* talks about his work.

*Arthur Miller* (National Educational Television, 29 minutes, sound, black and white). The playwright Arthur Miller discusses his views of the American theater, emphasizing the need for writers who can sense the themes of our age and make them understandable.

*The Cold Decade—Korean Stalemate* and *The Cold Decade—To the Yalu* (Prudential Insurance Company, 28 minutes each, sound, black and white). A two-part documentary from the CBS Air Power series on the Korean War.

*Henry Steele Commager: Part 3* (National Educational Television, 30 minutes, sound, black and white). Commager discusses with his guests the loyalty program and the problem of freedom and security in today's world.

*Korea, the Long Road to Peace* (March of Time, 29 minutes, sound, black and white). A documentary on the major political events of the Korean

War and the truce discussions.

*The MacArthur Story* (McGraw-Hill, 18 minutes, sound, black and white). The General's career is depicted from his service in France in World War I, through his role as Allied Commander in the Pacific in World War II, to his final post as UN Commander in Korea.

*Witness* (National Educational Television, 29 minutes, sound, black and white). A televised discussion of Whitaker Chambers' book, *Witness*.

# Conservatism Reborn

CHAPTER TWELVE

1856 · 1956
100 YEARS

PEACE

PROGRESS

PROSPERITY

*Centennial*

REPUBLICAN NATIONAL CONVENTION

Poster for Republican National Convention, 1956.

THE MOOD OF THE TIMES

"Inquiring reporters scurry about the country and note in wonder 'the new conservative trend.' . . . This public attention to the conservative philosophy is something new for our day. . . . But . . . the feeling for the values of conservatism has been abiding in the people all along. . . .

"In large part it was hidden by the cloak of language. Very vocal men equated it with 'turning back the clock' to McKinley's times, which no one wants to do any more. . . . So did our own Revolution long disguise the fact that it was wrought by men with a deep sense of conservatism. . . . And finally, we think, it was hidden by the fact that conservatism defies definition. . . . Unlike the brave new worlds and the promises of paradise, it cannot be coined into a political slogan.

"For conservatism is not a policy; nor is it a program to solve economic or political problems. It is hardly more than an instinctive belief that today's society is built on several thousand years and that in those years men have found things they should fasten to. Out of this grows not opposition to a change in political institutions or in economic methods but an awareness that in too hasty flight from the old we can flee to evils we know not of. . . . The instinct to conserve, we think, never left the American people."

—WALL STREET JOURNAL, 1955

# REPUBLICANISM RESURGENT

"In too hasty flight from the old we can flee to evils we know not of"—how well this expressed the attitude of most Americans in the 1950's! A new era had opened that was marked by political moderation, suspicion of social change, and greater caution in the worlds of intellect and culture. For the first time in twenty years, the word "conservative" was being used openly again. During the Roosevelt years and their aftermath, it had been a political drawback to be known as a conservative—even Robert Taft described himself as a "liberal"—but now the term began to lose its old sting of reproach. The new President himself, in a 1954 speech celebrating Lincoln's birthday, spoke of his program as conservative, then added, "And don't be afraid to use the word."

### Triumph of the Moderates

Dwight Eisenhower came to symbolize the national frame of mind in the nineteen-fifties. His very election as President owed a good deal to his popular image as a man above party and faction. After the sharp controversies and frustrations of the Truman years, Eisenhower seemed to promise a healing period of moderate but firm leadership and an end to bitter conflicts. Even a good many Democrats conceded that Eisenhower might have greater success than one of their party in dealing with such vexing matters as Korea, general corruption in government, or the menace of McCarthyism.

On most domestic issues, the two parties were still hopelessly deadlocked. Since 1938, when Roosevelt won his last domestic triumphs, neither party had been able to break loose from the slogans and deep distrusts of the New Deal period. The role of Eisenhower, according to the political analyst Samuel Lubell, was to act as substitute for the political alignment that had not taken place. His was the mediating function of presiding over an era of political transition. But transition to what? "If the Republicans triumph," Lubell prophesied before the 1952 election, "their victory, by itself, will settle nothing politically. What may develop after that, whether the Democratic majority can be broken for good or whether it will be restored, will depend on whether the Republicans can reorganize their own party after they have won." * This, then, was the task of Eisenhower and the Republican party: to transform the frustration and disillusionment of the early fifties into a permanent gain for their party and to make the nation forget the political wars of the New Deal and Fair Deal years. The issue, predicted Lubell, would not be decided until 1960, or possibly not until 1964.

* S. Lubell, *The Future of American Politics* (New York: Harper and Brothers, 1951), p. 226.

380

### Eisenhower: The Making of a President

Eisenhower, as all Americans knew, was not new to positions of responsibility or leadership. Since 1942, when Roosevelt made him commander of the North African invasion forces, he had been constantly in the public eye. As Supreme Commander of the invasion forces in France, Army Chief of Staff, then briefly president of Columbia University, and finally commander again of NATO forces in Europe, he had distinguished himself by his grasp of responsibility, his forthrightness and lack of pretension, and the confidence he inspired in others. Modest, friendly, even-tempered, and generous, he had few enemies and a host of friends. Unlike General Pershing, of whom it was said that four million veterans' votes would be cast against him if he turned politician, Eisenhower was well liked by most soldiers of World War II, who probably supported him in his political campaigns.

His rise to prominence was meteoric. Just eleven years before his great triumph of 1952, he was an unknown colonel at Fort Sam Houston. His entire adult life had been spent in the United States Army. There he had known the minor triumphs and heartaches, the loneliness and monotony, the masculine world of the professional soldier. Born in Denison, Texas, in 1890, he had grown up in the frontier town of Abilene, Kansas, which had long been an important outpost on the western border. Average as a student, athletic, cheerful, and self-confident, he was reared in an atmosphere of lower middle-class frugality and religious fundamentalism. In 1915 he graduated sixty-first in his class from West Point, where he made many friends, played football, and gained a solid grounding in military technology and discipline. He failed to get overseas in World War I but did do important pioneering work in tank warfare as an instructor at Camp Colt in Gettysburg, Pennsylvania. Then came the twenties and thirties, which were not a favorable time for an ambitious young officer to climb the military ladder, for the strength of isolationism and the economic depression kept outlays for military purposes at a low level. As late as 1935, when Eisenhower was 45, he had reached only the rank of major in an army of barely over 100,000 men.

But his fortunes changed in the fall of that year, when General Douglas MacArthur asked him to go with him to the Philippines. His assignment was to assist in the creation of a military establishment for the islands. During the next four years he gained valuable military experience, broadened his outlook on world affairs, and furthered his reputation as a diplomatic soldier who got on well with people. In December, 1939, after the outbreak of war in Europe, Eisenhower returned to duty in the United States. As the world outlook worsened, he hoped desperately for a command of his own. To Mark Clark in the War Department he wrote in the fall of 1940: "It is perfectly okay with me if the personnel section . . . is aware of the fact that I have an ambition to command one of the next armored regiments to be formed. They will probably think me a conceited individual, but I see no objection to setting your sights high."

His sights were not high enough. As Chief of Staff of the Third Army during the Louisiana maneuvers of 1941, he won wide commendation from his superiors. It is a measure of how slim his reputation was outside military circles at this time, however, that a press photograph of him was labeled: "Lt. Col. D. D. Ersenbeing." Five days after Pearl Harbor, Eisenhower was named assistant chief of the War Plans Division and soon began the first tentative sketches of a plan for a cross-channel invasion of France. In mid-1942 he was told by General George Marshall that he would command the European Theater of Operations. This assignment, which advanced him over hundreds of officers who were senior to him, was a measure of the confidence that Marshall and others had in him. The road to world fame and eventual leadership of the free world was now open to him.

Eisenhower, or "Ike" as he came to be known in the war years, was after 1942 the symbol of a nation that loved peace but fought vigorously in war. Decent, democratic, unpretentious, he seemed the very opposite of the hero-generals of history. He was typically American in his distrust of theories, his love for action and practical solutions, and his driving determination to win. These qualities served him well in peace as well as in war. As a political leader he showed himself to be a hard campaigner, a good organizer, and a man with a sharp sense of public relations. His actions as President were marked by a compromising, middle-of-the-road approach that aimed at solving problems by bringing divergent personalities together. And just as his flexible, undoctrinaire approach to military problems caused some of his fellow generals in World War II to deprecate his military judgment, so did his lack of fixed principles cause a number of political leaders to distrust his leadership in the 1950's.

Eisenhower's view of the Presidency was surprising for a soldier. He distrusted the concentration of power in the White House that had begun with Theodore Roosevelt; he did not believe that he should use his authority or popularity to impose his will on Congress or his own party; he preferred the role of chief of state to that of executive or party leader; and he insisted on the separation of powers between the executive and legislative branches of the government, allowing Senator Taft and later Senator Knowland to initiate policy on Capitol Hill. Con-

sistent with this position, he would not criticize McCarthy or his methods, though privately he detested them, because he felt he should not "interfere" with the Senate. "I am not one of the desk-pounding type that likes to stick out his jaw and look like he is bossing the show," he once said. The result was that Congressmen who had long smarted under the strong leadership of FDR and Truman were emboldened to oppose the President on foreign aid and other programs and even to move by means of the Bricker Amendment against the powers of the Presidency itself. By the middle of his first administration, critics were referring to him as a "Whig President."

Eisenhower's fundamental political ideas were the subject of widespread debate during his eight years as President. It was clear that he sought a "middle-of-the-road" position on most political questions and that he regarded himself as "basically conservative." Yet he came in time to accept most of the programs of the New Deal, including governmental responsibility for the nation's well-being. Even so, he was essentially nonideological in his approach to politics. His reactions were instinctive and emotional, rather than speculative or reasoned. He liked to describe himself as conservative on fiscal matters and liberal on human questions. But where did one leave off and the other begin? Suppose that a needed social program cost money, what then? Often he quoted Lincoln's statement that the legitimate object of government was to do for people what they could not do as well for themselves in their separate and individual capacities. But this was a principle to which Franklin Roosevelt could and did subscribe. The real questions concerned the interpretation of this principle. What *was* government's responsibility in the mid-twentieth century for better schools? highways? medical care? minimum wages? city slums? farm surpluses? social security? On these and other questions, Eisenhower, like most Americans, was pulled in two directions. If he was more inclined that his predecessors to bend toward the conservative side, he still failed to draw a clear line of demarcation between public and private responsibility. Like Harry Truman before him, he could not maneuver out of the political stalemate that was Franklin Roosevelt's legacy to the politics of the forties and fifties. "Eisenhower," wrote William V. Shannon in an article in *Commentary* in 1958,

is a transitional figure. He has not shaped the future nor tried to repeal the past. He has not politically organized nor intellectually defined a new consensus. When he leaves office in January 1961, the foreign policies and the domestic policies of the past generation will be about where he found them in 1953. No national problem, whether it be education, housing, urban revitalization, agriculture, or inflation, will have been advanced importantly toward solution nor its dimensions significantly altered. The Eisenhower era is the time of the great postponement. Dwight Eisenhower, the executor and trustee of the programs of his two Democratic predecessors, whose contemporary he was (Eisenhower is only eight years younger than Franklin Roosevelt and six years younger than Harry Truman), already looms in history not as the first great figure of a new Republican age but the last of an old Democratic generation.*

Eisenhower's place in political history, it seemed clear by the nineteen-sixties, would rest on his role as a symbol of unity in a strife-ridden era. After the tumultuous years of Roosevelt, war, and Fair Deal, Eisenhower restored a measure of tranquillity and moderation to American life. Amid the prosperity and fears of communist aggression in the fifties, he stood for level-headedness, security, and the homely virtues of turn-of-the-century Abilene. His success, measured against the standards of large segments of his party, was considera-

* W. Shannon, "Eisenhower as President," *Commentary*, XXV (November, 1958), p. 390. Copyright American Jewish Committee.

ble. By the time he left office, he had put the neo-isolationists in his party on the defensive, made support of the UN a bipartisan affair again, smashed the Bricker Amendment, quieted the smoldering controversy over "security risks," and made it clear that the New Deal was not going to be repealed. But Eisenhower's place in history will finally depend on his leadership in foreign affairs. Was domestic tranquillity bought at too high a price in faltering leadership at a critical juncture in history? Did the balance of world power shift fatefully away from the United States in the Eisenhower years? These are questions that will be considered, though not yet answered definitively, in Chapter 13.

### Finding the Middle of the Road

The task of a conservative administration, said Philip L. Graham, publisher of the Washington *Post*, would be "to show that there can be conservative social programs." Business would have to demonstrate that after its twenty years of opposition to federal housing, health, and social security measures it was actually opposed only to methods and procedure. Otherwise, he warned, "the tenure of this administration is going to be extremely brief." On the whole, Eisenhower and his advisers tried to follow this advice. After a cautious beginning, Ike backed programs for broadening social security, creating a federal Department of Health, Education, and Welfare, building a federal system of superhighways, clearing urban slums, creating defense scholarships, and continuing farm subsidies. These and other programs, representing extensions or departures from the New Deal and Fair Deal, were fitted within a close framework of fiscal concern.

It was Ike's fiscal policies that brought the first strong criticism. His Secretary of the Treasury, George M. Humphrey, a conservative Ohio industrialist, began a "tight money" program to counteract the serious inflation caused by the Korean War. Money became scarce and interest rates rose as Humphrey, aided by the Federal Reserve Board, forced through policies that tightened credit and made it increasingly difficult for private borrowers to get loans. The price and wage controls begun during the Korean War were suddenly terminated. A serious effort was made, too, to cut government spending—the Director of the Budget, Joseph M. Dodge, a Detroit banker, was instructed to go over planned expenditures with a fine-tooth comb. By the end of Eisenhower's first summer as President, he was asking Congress to postpone a tax cut and extend the excess-profits tax in order to keep the budget deficit as small as possible. Despite all his efforts, however, a deficit of nearly $4 billion remained.

When economic recession struck in the fall and winter of 1953-54, critics of the administration and some economists blamed the new fiscal policies. More likely, however, the impact of the Korean armistice of July, 1953, was being felt. As war orders were cancelled, industrial production fell off, farm prices began to drop, and unemployment approached four million. During most of 1954, steel mills, for instance, were operating at less than two-thirds of capacity. Alarmed Republicans began to fear a repetition of the disastrous Hoover years.

The handling of the 1953-54 recession by the Eisenhower Administration was revealing. Under the spur of political pressures, the government relaxed the tight-money policy, allowed tax cuts to go into effect, and temporarily abandoned all thought of balancing the budget. While Truman and other critics clamored for new public works expenditures, the President, while moving slowly, made it clear that highway and other spending projects would be accelerated if necessary. The influence of Dr. Arthur F. Burns, chairman of the Council of Economic Advisers, rose during the months of crisis. The issue at stake in meeting downturns of the business cycle, said Burns, was not whether government should intervene

Unemployed persons crowd the office of the Michigan employment security commission after 12,000 auto workers were laid off over a weekend. At the time, January, 1954, there were over 100,000 jobless in Detroit alone. (Wide World.)

but "rather the nature of governmental action, its timing and its extent." By the close of 1954, following a strong revival of the economy at mid-year, a White House adviser noted that "The President's changed, George Humphrey's changed—we've all changed since we came here."

During those first two years as President, Eisenhower groped cautiously to establish good relations with Congress. Though refusing at first to use the great weight of his office on behalf of his program, he did make public statements on legislation which he considered vital. In 1953 he approved legislation creating the Department of Health, Education and Welfare (first headed by Mrs. Oveta Culp Hobby), admitting 214,000 nonquota refugees, abolishing the Reconstruction Finance Corporation (under heavy fire because of scandals in the Truman era), and giving tidelands oil reserves to the states. This last measure involved the transfer to the coastal states of all rights to oil, gas, and other natural resources lying offshore to a distance of three miles (ten-and-a-half miles in the case of Texas and Florida). President Truman and conservationists had long opposed this transfer, but Eisenhower had pledged to make the move during the 1952 campaign. The following year Congress complied with Ike's request that social security benefits be increased and extended to some ten million new persons; and it also gave him a bill for slum clearance and urban renewal that included a modest provision for 35,000 low-rental housing units. To his chagrin, the President found that many of his legislative victories were made possible only by Democratic votes. According to the *Congressional Quarterly Almanac,* no less than 58 of Eisenhower's recommendations were saved by the Democrats in the 1953 session alone. Nor did Congress honor all his requests for legislation by any means. A number of his recommendations, notably those

calling for revision of the Taft-Hartley and McCarran-Walter acts, went completely unheeded.

One of the stiffest legislative fights of the opening years of the Eisenhower period concerned tax revision. Humphrey was intent on cutting industrial and corporate surtax rates in order to stimulate investment, while Democrats generally favored cutting taxes for the low-income groups. Senator Walter George of Georgia went so far as to sponsor a bill calling for a raise in personal exemption to $1,000 but he could muster little support. The new law, as finally approved in August, 1954, kept the old tax rates but greatly increased the variety of deductions. It granted businessmen faster tax write-offs and made it easier for them to get tax benefits over a long period in compensation for losses. Stockholders were given exemption on the first $50 of dividends, while tax rates on larger dividends were sharply cut. To offset these and other advantages to businessmen and corporations, further deductions were offered to working mothers, retired persons, heads of households, widows, and farmers.

### Freedom to Farm

Perhaps the most explosive policy of the new Administration was the decision to cut farm price supports. For twenty years farmers had been receiving government benefits to enable them to achieve incomes approaching the national level. Then the end of the Korean War widened the gap between farm production, which remained high, and farm income, which was declining. Large stores of corn, wheat, cotton, tobacco, and other crops were accumulating rapidly in government bins. The American Farm Bureau Federation, representing the larger and more prosperous farmers, had opposed Truman's policy of high support prices and now backed Ike's efforts to withdraw government gradually from the aid program. But the majority of farmers, who exercised powerful influence on farm-state Congressmen, fought hard to keep the price guarantees high.

Ezra Taft Benson, Secretary of Agriculture, was a strong believer in free agriculture. The farm crisis, he argued, had been worsened by unrealistic support prices and futile attempts to control production. The great bulk of farm income, perhaps 80 per cent, he pointed out, came from crops that were not supported or controlled. In 1954, under Administration pressure, Congress ordered a slight decrease in support prices for 1955 crops. The following year the President vetoed a Democratic bill setting parity prices at 90 per cent once more. But in 1956, as farm prices dropped and the national election approached, Eisenhower reversed his position and backed a "soil bank" for removing land from production and approved a level of price supports only slightly below 90 per cent. The unpopular Benson, who gave the impression of disliking all governmental subsidies to farmers, was criticized strongly by members of his own party.

The deadlock on farm policy continued through Ike's second term. In 1955, he asked for support prices of 60 to 90 per cent of parity but Congress reponded with a joint resolution "freezing" existing support prices and acreage allotments. Only corn was freed from the high-support formula, despite continued efforts at reform by Benson and wavering support from the President. In 1959, Eisenhower asked Congress to abandon the parity system altogether and substitute actual market prices in preceding years, but again he was ignored.

The farm problem was not solved in the nineteen-fifties. To some people, such as Secretary Benson, the only solution seemed to lie in returning to a free market and abandoning the "obsolete" parity

formula. Others were certain that this would mean a severe farm depression, similar to the one in the twenties, and sharp dislocations for a group of citizens who had long suffered disadvantages. Essentially, the farm problem was social and political, and not merely economic, in nature. Its resolution would depend as much on the social philosophy of the administration in power and the political

In this interpretation, the administration's farm program was inadequate to the farmer's needs. (Art Bimrose in The Portland "Oregonian.")

power exerted by farmers as on the strictly economic aspects of the problem. Viewed economically, agriculture was on the decline in America, a "sick" industry, as some called it. Since 1910, the number of persons engaged in farming in the United States had been falling rapidly; by 1955, America had the same number of farmers at work as in 1870—approximately eight million—though the population of the nation had quadrupled during this time. "In plain language," wrote Lauren Soth, editor of the Des Moines *Register and Tribune*, "there are just too many people to divide up the income which the American economic system allocates to food producers." * Only a relocation of a considerable number of farmers would, he said, solve the problem. But farmers were already leaving the farms in droves—could they be induced to leave faster? Would an end to price supports help this movement or only promote depression for all farmers? What were the social costs of this "flight from the farm"? Could America afford to pay them? What if war should come—would not a larger farm population then be beneficial? Who should make these weighty decisions? These questions were still being debated as Eisenhower left office and a new decade and a new administration began.

## Messrs. Dixon and Yates

Benson's farm policy highlighted the difficulty of finding a middle way between traditional free enterprise and the New Deal philosophy. Was not the welfare state itself, critics of the Administration asked, a middle way between conservative laissez faire and government socialism? Soon after his inauguration, President Eisenhower, in an informal talk at Custer State Park in South Dakota, tried again to define the conservative's feelings about the programs of the New Deal. "In the last twenty years," he said, creeping socialism has been striking in the United States." If the New Dealers were returned to power, he warned, "we very gravely run the risk, we've had our last chance." Asked later to cite examples of "creeping socialism," he named the TVA, thus provoking a new outcry over this most controversial of all New Deal programs.

The controversy came to center about the building of a new steam plant for the TVA in the Memphis area. By 1953, the TVA was operating in an immensely expanded grid of power sites and was selling electricity to thousands of customers, in-

cluding the Atomic Energy Commission, which owned plants at Oak Ridge, Tennessee, and Paducah, Kentucky. Having exhausted its potential for generating power from water, TVA had begun the construction of steam plants to meet the demands for cheap power. It was now asking Congress for funds to construct a plant at Fulton, Tennessee, near Memphis. This request was promptly struck out of the Truman budget by incoming Budget Director Dodge. So far, the actions of the new Administration were quite in line with Eisenhower's campaign promise to put a severe limit on governmental competition with private power producers.

But then the story became tangled. Dodge engaged Adolphe H. Wenzell, an official of a Boston security company, to make a study of TVA. His study, done in secret and without consulting TVA officers, recommended that private companies serve cities on the TVA periphery and supply TVA itself with any additional power needed, and that eventually TVA power units be transferred to a taxpaying corporation. Shortly thereafter, plans were begun to arrange for the construction of a private plant at Memphis, which would "replace" power needed by the Atomic Energy Commission. Eisenhower directed that the Atomic Energy Commission contract for the plant with Edgar H. Dixon, president of the Middle South Utilities, and Eugene A. Yates, chairman of the board of the Southern Company. The financing for the new plant was to be handled by the First Boston Corporation, the company for which Adolphe Wenzell worked. For a considerable period, it was established in later testimony, Wenzell represented both the Budget Bureau and his own business firm. A stormy controversy surrounded the whole Dixon-Yates contract, even before it became known that Wenzell was involved in a "conflict of interest." Fi-

* L. Soth, *Farm Trouble* (Princeton: Princeton University Press, 1957), p. 45.

nally, in June, 1955, the city of Memphis announced it would construct its own power plant and the President canceled the Dixon-Yates contract. Why the Administration had taken so devious a course—a New York *Times* reporter described it as going "around TVA, through the AEC, into a thicket of conflict of interest, all the while trying to cover up its tracks and dodging and equivocating when the trail was uncovered"—remained one of the impenetrable mysteries of the Eisenhower era.* Enemies of the Administration were certain, in any case, that Dixon-Yates proved the Republicans intended to restore private utilities to the Tennessee Valley.

The term that Eisenhower used most often to describe his power policies was "partnership." The federal government, he argued, should limit its projects to those too large for local enterprise alone. Flood control and irrigation programs obviously came within the purview of federal authority, but dams built for these purposes should be closely watched for competition with private industry. At Hells Canyon, between Idaho and Oregon, hopes for a federal hydroelectric project were dashed by Secretary of the Interior Douglas McKay, an automobile distributor and former governor of Oregon. He reversed the Truman Administration's policy of refusing to allow the Idaho Power Company, which was not, as its name suggested, a local firm, but a Wall Street organization, to go ahead with plans for three small dams in the Canyon. According to the Federal Power Commission examiner, only a high federal dam would produce maximum power development in the gorge, but the Commission, recognizing the improbability of Congressional support for a federal dam, endorsed the new Administration's rec-

* E. Kenworthy, "Dixon-Yates: the Riddle of a Self-Inflicted Wound," *The Reporter*, XIV (January 26, 1956), p. 19.

ommendations. Only the St. Lawrence Seaway, whose hydroelectric facilities were turned over to a New York State authority on the American side, added to the nation's major public power sites during the Eisenhower years.

## Dealing with Internal Security

Though Ike came to symbolize the new moderation of the American people after the excited partisanship of the Truman years, he did not succeed at first in quieting the storm over the loyalty of governmental employees. Indeed, some members of his own Administration exacerbated the mood of angry frustration incited by McCarthy and others. Soon after taking office, Eisenhower's Attorney General, Herbert Brownell, charged that President Truman had knowingly appointed a communist spy, Harry Dexter White, to a sensitive post in the United States government. The Republican chairman of the House Un-American Activities Committee went so far as to subpoena the former President to appear before the Committee to testify in the White case. Truman, while publicly denying the charge, refused to go before the Committee on the grounds that to comply with the subpoena would violate the historic doctrine of separation of powers and the independence of the Presidency. Eisenhower calmed that controversy when he replied to a newsman's question as to whether he thought Truman had knowingly put a spy in high office, "No, it is inconceivable."

New outbursts over the Administration's security program followed. In 1953 President Eisenhower abandoned Truman's distinction between those suspected of disloyalty to the government and those thought to be "security risks." Under Truman, in the case of disloyalty, a doubtful employee could be discharged, after a hearing, from any agency of the government; but "security risk" was a term applied only to those employed in sensitive agencies who, because of loose habits, garrulousness, alcoholism, or homosexuality, as well as subversive activities, were potential risks to the government. Eisenhower now extended the security program to all agencies of the government. A wave of firings under the new directive caused Administration spokesmen to speak of the hundreds, even thousands, of "security risks" appointed to federal office by the Democrats. Severe criticism came from the Democrats of what they called the "numbers game," as the Administration announced that first 1456, then 2200, and finally 9600 employees had been dropped at the President's order. Of 534 State Department employees fired by early 1954, for example, Department officials told a Congressional committee, only eleven were suspected of disloyalty and no actual communists had been uncovered. Eventually, more than half of those reported as fired for security reasons were Eisenhower's own appointees.

Criticism mounted in 1954 and 1955 as journalists, scientists, educators, and others joined in the outcry against the new program. A conservative Republican and former Senator, Harry Cain, whom Eisenhower had appointed to the Subversive Activities Control Board, carried on a personal campaign against the President's program, arguing that it was doing more harm than good. Many scientists protested when a famous atomic physicist, J. Robert Oppenheimer, who had played a major role in building the A-bomb, was classified by a special security board as a security risk and barred from government data, although the same board called him loyal and discreet, and commended him as a public servant whose contributions could never be repaid.

Despite the zeal of the Eisenhower Administration in tightening the security

program, Senator McCarthy was by no means satisfied. As chairman of the Permanent Subcommittee on Investigations, he sent his two aides, Roy M. Cohn and G. David Schine, to investigate the State Department's information program in Europe. Frightened officers in the information agencies concealed or withdrew many magazines and books which McCarthy's men might attack. Some books were actually burned. McCarthy tangled with the new Administration, too, over the appointment of Charles E. Bohlen as Ambassador to the Soviet Union (McCarthy called him a "security risk"), over communism as an issue in the 1954 elections (the "raw, harsh, unpleasant fact," said McCarthy, was that it would be an issue), and over alleged subversion in the Signal Corps at Fort Monmouth, New Jersey. This last attack on the Army, as noted in the last chapter, led to his swift downfall in the latter part of 1954.

The quarrels over loyalty and subversion in the Truman and early Eisenhower years continued to influence American public life for a good long time, a period in which timidity and caution seemed to characterize large numbers of writers, teachers, politicians, government employees, and movie and TV producers. In 1955, a sociological study of American attitudes toward communism and civil liberties showed that while there was no "quivering fear" or "anxiety neurosis" about the internal communist threat, many Americans, because poorly informed, were ready to believe demagogic leaders who exaggerated the danger.

When national figures say flatly that our schools and colleges are full of teachers of atheistic Communism [the study concluded], can we blame an average citizen who has no firsthand access to the facts if he comes to think a purge of the educational system may be necessary? When politicians for partisan advantage exaggerate the current spread of the Communist conspiracy, can we blame an ordinary person for supporting drastic measures to stop the supposed conversion to Communism of people in key positions in Washington or in our foreign service, armed forces, or defense plants?*

The fear and caution appeared to abate somewhat in the late fifties. The fall of McCarthy, confidence in Eisenhower, and a growing disgust at undocumented charges of disloyalty were all, doubtless, factors in the change. The Supreme Court, too, in a series of decisions in 1956 and 1957, moved to protect traditional guarantees of fair procedure against Congressional and executive violations. In the Jencks case, the Court held that if the government used testimony obtained by FBI questioning of witnesses, the defendant should be allowed to examine the FBI material to see if it were consistent with the testimony offered in open court. (The effect of this ruling, however, was limited by a Congressional statute of 1957 aimed at guarding the confidential nature of FBI files.) The Court also ruled in the Watkins case that a Congressional committee, in interrogating a witness before it, must limit its questions to those pertinent to the general area which the committee was authorized to investigate. Congressional committees, in other words, must investigate in order to frame appropriate legislation and not to convict or harass individual witnesses. In other cases the Court held that Eisenhower's "security risk" program applied only to sensitive posts in the government and not to menial employments; and it also narrowed the interpretation of the word "organize" in the Smith Act (1940), which had made it a crime to organize a group advocating the violent overthrow of the government.

* S. Stouffer, *Communism, Conformity, and Civil Liberties* (Garden City, N.Y.: Doubleday and Company, 1955), p. 223.

## "I (Still) Like Ike": 1956

As the end of his first term neared, Ike showed an increasingly firm grip on the presidential office. Despite a heart attack in September, 1955, which incapacitated him for several months, it became quite clear that he intended to run for a second term. He took more and more interest in legislation and became somewhat less reluctant to use his authority in Congress, especially in foreign affairs. His "chain of command," headed by Presidential Assistant Sherman Adams, former Governor of New Hampshire, functioned smoothly during his illness and played a major role in all his decisions as President. But he had little success with his domestic program in the Democrat-controlled Congress of 1955 and 1956. Among his major recommendations, only his proposal for a gigantic federal highway program met with success. The resulting Highway Act of 1956 called for the building of 42,000 miles of four- and six-lane highways over a thirteen-year period at a cost of at least $33 billion.

Though Democrats won control of Congress in 1954, Ike's own popularity remained undiminished. Both Eisenhower and Nixon had campaigned hard on behalf of Republican candidates in the 1954 elections but with little effect. Now, with the presidential election approaching, interest focused on the Vice Presidency, especially after Eisenhower suffered a second serious illness, an acute attack of ileitis, in June, 1956. Harold Stassen, head of the Foreign Operations Administration and former governor of Minnesota, led an anti-Nixon revolt that got nowhere at the Republican convention. Nixon was too controversial a figure, Stassen argued, one who would hurt the Republican ticket. At San Francisco, however, Eisenhower and Nixon were renominated by their party without opposition.

Earlier, in Chicago, Adlai Stevenson had also won his party's second endorsement. Only Governor Averell Harriman of New York, backed by former President Truman, gave serious challenge to Stevenson; but when the votes were counted, Harriman had garnered only 210 to Stevenson's commanding 905. The only real excitement in either convention was provided by Stevenson's surprise announcement that he would leave the choice of a running mate to the delegates. This step, it was reasoned, would contrast favorably with the coming cut-and-dried renomination of Nixon by the Republicans. After a night of wild campaigning, Senator Estes Kefauver of Tennessee and Senator John F. Kennedy of Massachusetts emerged as the front-runners. To head off Kefauver, who had strong farmer and labor support among Western delegates, many delegates from the East and South went to the thirty-nine-year-old Kennedy. But in a very close finish, Kefauver edged out his rival. The most remarkable feature of the voting was the support given Kennedy, a Roman Catholic, by the fundamentalist South—on the strength of this, some began to boom him already as a future presidential contender.

Stevenson attempted a more down-to-earth campaign than in 1952. Taking heed of criticism that he had talked over people's heads in his first campaign, he aimed at a simpler delivery and harder-hitting content. Against Republican claims of peace, prosperity, and confidence in Ike, he pointed to the role of Democrats in Ike's successes and the good times the President had inherited from Truman. Compelling issues were hard to find, though. Voters seemed uninterested in the questions of defense policy, conservation, education, farm problems, and foreign affairs that Stevenson sought to raise. His most dramatic suggestions—an end to the draft and joining with Russia to stop hydrogen bomb testing—evoked little support when Eisenhower threw his prestige against them. Eisenhower himself seemed impervious to assault. Although Stevenson charged that the President "has never had the inclination and now lacks the energy for full-time work at the world's toughest job," the direct attacks on Eisenhower in the campaign were surprisingly few. Often Stevenson struck at Nixon instead. In his final speech of the campaign, he warned that a Republican victory would "mean that Richard Nixon would probably be President of this country within the next four years."

Adlai Stevenson. (United Press.)

Few expected Stevenson to win. He was fighting the most popular figure of the decade at a time when domestic issues stirred little controversy and foreign affairs seemed in capable hands. Eisenhower, who had planned a late, brief campaign, was induced to make a number of earlier forays into most of the key states. Nixon, however, carried the brunt of the campaigning with three swings across the country. He hit hard at Stevenson, again and again contrasting his record of experience with that of Eisenhower's. When a serious crisis broke in the Middle East in the last two weeks of the campaign, following an Israeli attack on Egypt and British and French intervention in Suez, Nixon told a California audience: "This is not the moment to replace the greatest commander in chief America has ever had in war or peace with a jittery, inexperienced novice who is eager to have the job but who is utterly unqualified to make the great decisions demanded by the times." This note was struck repeatedly as election day neared.

Though the Suez crisis hurt Stevenson, it could scarcely have affected the result. On election day, an avalanche of votes for Eisenhower spoke strongly of his undiminished popularity. He beat Stevenson by nine-and-a-half million votes, the largest margin since FDR's great victory of 1936. He polled 457 electoral votes to Stevenson's 73 and carried 41 states. The nation had once again put its confidence in a man who stood for peace and prosperity, whose middle-of-the-road philosophy suited the temper of the times, and whose record as a military hero seemed important in a time of international danger. But the voters did an unprecedented thing in 1956: While endorsing Ike, they rejected his party. For the first time in modern political history, a winning president failed to carry the Congress with him. Most observers agreed that millions of Democratic voters had transcended party lines to vote for "Ike," while remaining faithful to their party in state and local races. The political deadlock between the major parties was thus continued. "The campaign," Walter Lippmann concluded,

has been clean and decent, but not enlightening or interesting. It takes two to bring on a debate, and the President refused to be provoked into debating anything. Since there was a great contented majority behind him, he did not have to admit that there was any issue to debate. . . . The correspondents, the commentators, and the pollsters have been essentially right in distinguishing between Eisenhower and his party. He has had an enormous vote of confidence. The Republican Party has not had one.*

## SIGNS OF SOCIAL CHANGE

Though Eisenhower restored tranquillity to the surface of American life, strong currents of change flowed beneath the surface. Vast shifts in the prevailing economic and social patterns of American life took place in the decade of the fifties. Inevitably, these changes would have an impact on the lives of most Americans in the second half of the century. Of the technological and social changes, any review would have to highlight the advent of guided missiles and H-bombs, the arrival of the jet era, the triumph over polio and the proliferation of "wonder drugs," the spread of television and air conditioning, the revolution in packaged and frozen foods, the building of superhighways and toll roads, and the rise of a whole new way of life associated with suburbs, ranch-type houses, shopping centers, and drive-in recreations. Never had the everyday features of life changed so utterly in so brief a time.

The nineteen-fifties, for all the talk of

* New York *Herald-Tribune*, November 8, 1956.

conservatism and moderation, was a decade of radical change in almost all phases of national life. According to the census of 1960, the nation's population had swollen to 179 million (a growth of 18.5 per cent in the decade), Negro population had reached 18,871,831 (up 25 per cent), the westward movement of the American people was accelerating, and family size was growing in every part of the country. Only the movement to the cities, among the major social trends of the century, showed signs of faltering—due largely to the flight to the suburbs around the major cities. The farm population, thanks to the decline of agriculture, was aging rapidly; by 1960, more persons 65 or older were living on farms than those between 25 and 34 years.

In the turmoil of rapid change of the fifties, those groups were most affected whose status was most uncertain—juveniles, Negroes, elderly or retired persons, white-collar workers, and the dwindling farm population. Young persons in particular were thrown into confusion. An unprecedented rise of adolescent crime, gang warfare, and teen-age brutality marked the decade, during which more than a million children each year were in trouble serious enough to warrant their arrest. In 1954, a special Senate committee investigating delinquency was told by Fillmore H. Sanford, executive secretary of the American Psychological Association, that "For every juvenile who actually engages in delinquent behavior . . . there are hundreds or thousands who may have delinquent tendencies or who fail in subtle and socially harmless, but still dreadfully crippling ways, to make a full and creative adjustment to life." By the end of the fifties, juvenile behavior had become a subject of nation-wide concern. What was the cause of delinquency? Why did adolescents commit brutal crimes? Behind all the theorizing of specialists and public officials was the growing conviction that something serious was wrong, that the cascading changes in American life were deeply disturbing to those growing up without fixed values and stabilizing influences in their lives.

### Separate but Unequal

No group experienced a more dramatic shift of status than American Negroes in the years since the thirties. Under the spur of the New Deal and the war, burgeoning prosperity, a favorable climate of world opinion, and the redistribution of Negro population, Negroes made greater social and economic gains in the quarter-century between 1935 and 1960 than in all the years since Appomattox. According to the 1960 census, forty-eight of every one hundred Negroes lived outside the eleven states of the old Confederacy, and the state with the largest Negro population, New York, was in the North. The income of Negroes, in dollars of the same purchasing power, was nearly four times in 1960 what it had been in the mid-thirties. And an ever-widening range of job and educational opportunities also opened up to them during the forties and fifties.

Nevertheless, serious problems of discrimination and inequality remained. Negro income was generally far below the white average; unemployment was proportionately much higher among Negroes than whites; and job discrimination remained a serious obstacle to Negro progress. Few Negroes, North or South, entered the professions (except for teaching) or attained positions of business leadership. Less than 1 per cent of the graduate engineers in 1955 were Negroes and only about 200 Negro doctors were graduated each year. Even at the lower levels of employment, discrimination was strong. In Omaha, an Urban League survey of 1960 revealed that of seventy-one jobs requiring no experience, 55 per cent were closed to Negroes and Indians, while another 30 per cent were open only on a limited basis. Housing discrimination, too, remained a serious bar to full enjoyment of the rights of citizenship. Thus, of approximately 25,000 new homes constructed in Omaha during the nineteen-fifties only 50 were available to Negro buyers, though Negroes accounted for nearly 10 per cent of the population.

Doubtless the most important event of the fifties, so far as Negro rights were concerned, was the Supreme Court's decision on segregated public schools. On May 17, 1954, Chief Justice Earl Warren, an Eisenhower appointee, ruled in *Brown v. Board of Education* that "separate educational facilities are inherently unequal" and violated the equal protection clause of the Fourteenth Amendment. In reaching this unanimous decision, the justices rejected a historical review of the intentions of the framers of the Fourteenth Amendment and a reliance on previous precedents alone. "In approaching this problem," Warren's opinion read, "we cannot turn the clock back to 1868, when the Amendment was adopted, or even to 1896 when *Plessy v. Ferguson* [which had held "separate but equal" facilities constitutional] was written." Instead, they relied on the "modern authority" of six psychological and socio-

logical texts which held that segregation retarded the educational and mental development of Negro children. "To separate them from others of similar age and qualifications solely because of their race," said Warren, "generates a feeling of inferiority as to their status in the community that may affect their hearts and minds in a way unlikely ever to be undone."

But school segregation did not end in May, 1954. Compliance with the Court's decision was slow and sporadic. The border states and a few states in the Upper South began to desegregate their schools under court order in scattered communities. Of 2909 biracial school districts in the South and border states, 802 had desegregated by the end of the decade. Approximately 140,000 Negro students were attending classes with whites for the first time. In the Deep South—especially in Alabama, South Carolina, and Mississippi—state officials stood firm against any change in their school systems. Violence occurred at several high schools that were preparing to admit Negro students. At Little Rock, Arkansas, the Arkansas National Guard was federalized by President Eisenhower in 1957 to preserve order and protect several Negro children after the state's governor had taken steps to prevent integration. A variety of laws—

National Guard troops, acting on orders of Governor Faubus of Arkansas, turn back Negro students trying to enter Central High School in Little Rock. (Wide World.)

some 200 in all—were framed to circumvent the Court's decision. In Virginia, however, in January, 1959, the state Supreme Court rendered unconstitutional a law empowering the Governor to close schools in districts where integration had been ordered. By the early 1960's, the schools of Atlanta had integrated, token integration had taken place in New Orleans, a major crisis developed over the admission of one Negro to the University of Mississippi, and pressures were mounting to accelerate the pace of desegregation. A new and aggressive attitude on the part of Negroes, as reflected in "sit-ins" by young people at lunch counters, libraries, bus depots, and other public places, was becoming increasingly effective in forcing the recognition of Negro rights. So much so that some 76 per cent of all Southerners, according to a Gallup poll of 1961, conceded that desegregation was inevitable.

The new political strength of Negroes was reflected in the passage by Congress of the first significant legislation on civil rights since Reconstruction days. When Eisenhower pushed for a mild civil rights bill in 1957, he broke the tacit alliance between Republicans and Southern Democrats that had long blocked Congressional action in this area. Congressional leadership, in the hands of moderate Southerners, was instrumental in getting Southern support for a compromise bill that concentrated on Negro voting rights. The Civil Rights Act of 1957 created a federal Civil Rights Commission, gave federal officers the right to obtain injunctions against anyone denying Constitutional rights to citizens, and called for the trial by jury of offenders in criminal cases, but without a jury in civil cases. A second civil rights law passed in 1960 strengthened the authority of the Civil Rights Commission and guaranteed Negro voting rights through a system of court-appointed referees. Though far short of

what champions of the Negro wanted, these laws represented an important breakthrough in civil rights.

## New Perspectives on Labor

Another group that found its position drastically altered in the new economic and social patterns of the fifties was organized labor. During the course of the decade it became clear that the process of automation (that is, automatic performance or control of many or all steps in manufacturing) was accelerating so rapidly that labor faced a major readjustment. In the late 1940's, it seemed clear in retrospect, a critical shift in the employment balance had taken place. Before then, those employed in the production of "material goods" in manufacturing, mining, and other industries had outnumbered those engaged in "service" industries, such as trade, finance, and government. But increasingly, during the fifties, the service industries began to outstrip the productive industries in employment until, in 1959, 32.4. million were at work in the former as compared with 25.4 million in the latter. As the result of automation, principally, a profound change was taking place in the structure of the whole labor force.*

A great surge of men and women into white-collar employments was thus a marked feature of the fifties. The significance of this was described at the beginning of the decade by the sociologist C. Wright Mills, who studied the changing character of America's working population. The typical member of this new middle class, Mills wrote, was a salaried office or sales worker, who met customers, filed papers, or pounded, turned, or fed an office machine. The occupational disease of the white-collar class was "status panic," a fear that the prestige it enjoyed

* A. Hansen, *Economic Issues of the 1960's* (New York: McGraw-Hill Book Company, 1960), pp. 71-72.

over wage-earners might be slipping away. As wage rates rose and industrial workers moved into the suburbs, the white-collar worker clung even more firmly to the one great advantage he had over wage-earners: his education. Indeed, no group in American society put greater store by a college education than the new middle class. Politically, the new class was both voiceless and frustrated; it felt itself to be politically impotent, said Mills, and the pawn of hidden manipulators. It was unorganized, split internally, and dependent on large forces beyond its control. Many of this class doubtless supported Eisenhower in his quest for a conservative, middle-of-the-road course.*

The domain of the white-collar worker seemed to some labor leaders the last great frontier for unionization. But the new middle class, it was found, was not anxious to join hands with organized labor. Many of its members were more concerned with fighting inflation than fighting employers, and they showed hostility to unions for their part in the wage-price spiral of the postwar era. Only a tenth of the employees in service, trade, and financial institutions had joined unions by the end of the fifties. Unions were making slower gains than at any time since the depression.

Labor suffered other setbacks in the nineteen-fifties. Nineteen states, most of them in the poorly organized South and West, had adopted right-to-work laws by the end of the decade. These laws, which usually forbade the union shop and other forms of compulsory unionism, were frequently sponsored by employers and organizations interested in attracting new industries and keeping down unionism and labor costs. In bitterly fought referendums in six states in 1958, labor turned back right-to-work movements in five states, including heavily industrial Ohio

* See C. Mills, *White Collar* (New York: Oxford University Press, 1951).

and California, while losing only in agricultural Kansas.

Probably the most serious issue facing unions in the late fifties was racketeering and corruption. Following the merger of the AFL and CIO in 1955, after twenty years of separation and jurisdictional battles, the ethical practices committee of the new organization asked the Teamsters Union to sever its relations with the International Longshoremen's Association, previously expelled from the AFL for corruption. Little was done, however, and in 1957 the Senate established a select committee under Senator John L. McClellan of Arkansas to investigate racketeering and corruption in the labor relations field. The committee, aided by the investigations of its chief counsel, Robert F. Kennedy, uncovered a trail of corruption in the Teamsters Union that led to the office of its president, Dave Beck. The Teamsters Union was promptly expelled from the AFL-CIO and Beck was jailed for income tax evasion and phone-tapping. As Beck's successor, the Teamsters chose James R. Hoffa, who had already aroused the suspicions and antagonism of the McClellan Committee. New hearings in 1958 brought Committee charges against Hoffa of violence, gangsterism, repression of democratic rights, and sharp financial practices. The courts, however, despite intense governmental efforts, ruled on several occasions that the evidence presented against Hoffa was insufficient to sustain the charges.

The upshot of the investigations of 1957 and 1958 was a new labor law. Ever since the passage of the Taft-Hartley Act in 1947, Congress had considered proposals for amending it. Now, in September, 1959, the Labor-Management Reporting and Disclosure Act was passed. It was essentially a compromise between a "tough" bill proposed by Representatives Landrum and Griffin and a milder bill supported by Senator John F. Kennedy. It called for new controls over union elections and finances, outlawed extortion picketing and most types of secondary boycott, and required all unions to file full annual reports of all their activities with the Secretary of Labor. Members of unions were to be protected in their right to free speech, a secret ballot, and participation in the formation of policy.

The new law marked the end of an era in labor history. By establishing detailed controls over the internal affairs of unions, it asserted the public's right to play a much stronger role in labor-management relations. Henceforward, it would be difficult for government to avoid intervention in any major labor dispute that threatened the public's convenience. The power of labor, despite the image it projected in the McClellan hearings, seemed clearly to be fading as the Eisenhower era ended. Not only was government taking a strong hand in controlling unions, but the AFL-CIO faced a difficult fight in holding its own in a growing labor force that was more white collar than ever before. The future of organized labor would appear

Robert Kennedy, counsel of the Senate rackets investigation committee, in conversation with James Hoffa (right), head of the Teamsters Union, and his attorney. In the background are charts showing the criminal records of officers of Teamster locals. (Wide World.)

to depend on its ability to unionize the last great areas of individual bargaining —agricultural workers, service employees, Southern industrial workers, and the less affluent professions—but the prospects for this did not seem bright as the decade of the sixties opened.

## THE NEW CONSERVATISM

The conservative upsurge in the fifties was widely felt. Not only politics and the labor movement, but almost every phase of American life and thought was affected. Everywhere there was evidence of a search for roots, a return to older values, and a quest for order in the chaos of modern life. In philosophy, religion, history, literature, and the arts there were stirrings that reflected the new mood. A nostalgia for the past, as seen in the boom of historical magazines, biographies, and Civil War accounts, gripped many Americans, including the President himself. Many conservatives seemed to want specifically to restore the values that had existed before 1929. Most of this group disliked the growth in strong government, welfare programs, and the power of the Presidency since 1933. Often they spoke of America in terms of the old virtues of industry, frugality, and self-reliance. They despaired of talk about "security" and joked of young men who inquired about pension plans in their employment interviews. They spoke disparagingly of the growth of federal bureaucracy and called for a revival of local government. And many of them agreed, in whole or in part, that American blundering and disloyalty had been responsible for the unfortunate shift in America's postwar position.

## The Road to Serfdom

Yet, such nostalgia to the contrary, the new conservatism was rooted in a search for security amid the frustrations and uncertainties of mid-century life. Its appeal was strongest among those disturbed by the currents of modern civilization, especially such streams as relativism, secularism, progressive education, and the growth of the welfare state. Frequently its spokesmen stressed such nineteenth-century values as limited government, constitutionalism, states' rights, fundamental law, fixed principles, and social order. They put great weight on private endeavor and responsibility. Yet they were often pessimistic about man's capacity to reform or improve himself. Still, in a time of bewilderment and anxiety, they reminded Americans of their heritage and traditions. At a critical hour in the nation's history, they stimulated pride in the glories and achievements of the American past.

Typically, the new conservatives looked to the past. The nineteenth century, particularly the golden age of Victorian liberalism, was the best of all times in which to have lived. Conservative writers recalled the joys of an era of small government, individual enterprise, unlimited opportunity, and private freedom. "One reason for my instinctive fondness for Switzerland," wrote William H. Chamberlin, "is that this country . . . has changed little in spirit since the nineteenth century." Chamberlin and others rejected completely the "middle way" of the New Deal as only a half-way station on the road to totalitarianism. Chamberlin, who had earlier been a radical, wrote now, in vocabulary reminiscent of Spencer and Sumner, that "Government by its very nature does not create wealth. All it can do when it goes into the business of subsidizing special interests is to rob Peter to pay Paul,

to pillage the thrifty for the benefit of the thriftless."*

Some conservatives rediscovered the writings of Friedrich A. Hayek, whose *The Road to Serfdom* was sometimes called the opening gun in the modern conservative revival campaign. In 1944, Hayek had openly challenged the Keynesian, welfare-state theories in vogue in Britain and the United States. He saw in the trend toward social security, full employment, and other welfare measures a repetition of Germany's disastrous course between the wars. The meaning of freedom, Hayek wrote, was being transformed from its nineteenth-century sense of protection against arbitrary action by government to the idea of protection against poverty and the tides of circumstance. This, he insisted, was only a modern scheme for realizing the old dream of a redistribution of the wealth by force. Planning and welfare laws led inevitably to dictatorship because they necessarily violated individual rights and the rule of law. "The guiding principle that a policy of freedom for the individual is the only true progressive policy," Hayek concluded, "remains as true today as it was in the nineteenth century." †

## Conservatism as an Ideology

Hayek's appeal to the conservative mind was direct and understandable. Like Spencer three-quarters of a century before, he buttressed with logical argument the businessman's instinctive preference for laissez faire. Like Chamberlin, James Burnham, Senator Barry Goldwater, and other political writers, his con-

---

* W. Chamberlin, *The Evolution of a Conservative* (Chicago: Henry Regnery Company, 1959).

† F. Hayek, *The Road to Serfdom* (Chicago: University of Chicago Press, 1944), p. 241. He later expanded these themes in *The Constitution of Liberty* (Chicago: University of Chicago Press, 1960).

servatism was narrowly political and largely confined to recent British and American experience. But other conservative writers, notably Russell Kirk, Peter Viereck, and Walter Lippmann, searched deeper into history for intellectual wellsprings and sought to create a system of values beyond politics. These were the conservatives who were troubled by a lack of firm standards in modern life, who saw relativism and secularism as more serious evils than the welfare state, and who regarded John Dewey rather than Franklin Roosevelt as the most dangerous man of the century.

Of the serious conservative writers of the fifties, Russell Kirk was probably the most influential. As editor of *Modern Age*, a conservative journal, and author of *The Conservative Mind* (1953) and *A Program for Conservatives* (1954), Kirk was often regarded as the intellectual leader of the New Conservative movement. He diagnosed the malady of modern society as arising not from welfare schemes or ambitious politicians but from the heart of man. Man's nature, he argued in opposition to liberal philosophers, was evil rather than good, his motives emotional rather than rational in origin. The historical watershed of modern man's problems was the French Revolution, which unloosed on the world the forces of political radicalism, secularism, and social leveling. Edmund Burke, who warned then against the evils of the Revolution, spoke directly to the modern conservative in his hatred of radical change, his love of order and tradition, his realization of man's depraved nature, his suspicion of reason, and his reliance on Divine Providence. But, later, liberal thinkers, especially Emerson, Mill, and Dewey, had ushered in the modern viewpoints of love of science, rejection of tradition, stress on man's rationality, and addiction to social planning. Given this mixed brew of ideas what was the essence

of an enduring conservatism? It was, said Kirk, belief in a divine order, suspicion of concentrated power, rejection of radical change, affection for human individuality, an end to democratic leveling, and a reliance on private endeavor in nearly every sort of activity with only contempt for collectivist reformers.*

There were others who, like Kirk, tried to take a broader view of man's dilemma and its causes. To understand modern man's quandary, said Peter Viereck, one must "think broadly and deeply and move out from parochial concerns into the dark places of history, political theory, and human sin." Viereck saw Prince Metternich of Austria as the most appropriate counselor for today's troubled world. Metternich had been a rock of stability, a defender of law and order, in a time of revolutionary change. True conservatism, Viereck wrote, made possible orderly change; it was not necessarily opposed to the welfare state or any particular economic doctrine. Its real function was to conserve the ethical values of Western Civilization amidst the chaos of modern history.† Walter Lippmann, too, called for a return to proven values to halt the decay of modern society. Only a society of fixed principles based on a fundamental law, he said, could repair the damage done by the rudderless democracies of the first half of the twentieth century. The failures of modern democracy, in his judgment, were due to the straitjacketing of elected officials by the masses who were themselves incapable of understanding the need for effective government or diplomacy. Dewey and the progressive intellectuals had freed man from the old public philosophy, which had held that general, objective criteria of right and wrong existed, and

* R. Kirk, *A Program for Conservatives* (Chicago: Henry Regnery Company, 1954), p. 41.
† P. Viereck, *Conservatism Revisited* (New York: Charles Scribner's Sons, 1949).

had left him no standards to which to conform. The result was chaos as the masses forced government to do things that were not rational or in the public interest. Only a return to a universe of fixed values, which Lippmann himself had helped to destroy nearly a half-century before, would, he now believed, halt the march toward oblivion.*

## The Conservative Mood

The new conservatism, then, was deeply pessimistic about human nature, coldly realistic about the potentialities of democracy and social reform, fearful of the growth of welfare-statism, and acidly critical of most liberal and humanistic thought since the French Revolution. Compared with American conservatism of the twenties, it was less individualistic, more tradition-minded, less optimistic, and more concerned with principle. Whether the new conservatism was a sharp new departure in American political and social thought, or only a passing mood, befitting the frustration of the fifties, only the perspective of history would reveal.

But the pervasiveness of the conservative mood could not be denied. It was felt in the religious revival of the fifties and in the popularity of Norman Vincent Peale, whose *The Power of Positive Thinking* was essentially a call for revival of the old American traits of optimism, self-confidence, and striving for success; it inspired a debate over America's national purpose, which led to the establishment of a President's Commission on National Goals; and it accounted for the success of Senator Goldwater's *The Conscience of a Conservative* (1960), which argued that conservatism was actually a spiritual theory, and not a shallow, materialistic creed ("Conservatism, we are told, is out-of-

date. The charge is preposterous and we ought boldly to say so. The laws of God, and of nature, have no dateline."). The new mood was heightened by the cautious atmosphere in the fast-growing suburbs (they grew six times as fast as cities in the fifties), where William H. Whyte, Jr., found a blend of political conservatism and a high degree of social conformity in his study of *The Organization Man* (1956).

Even the liberals were strongly affected by the new mood. "We are all more conservative than we were ten years ago," wrote Clinton Rossiter in 1955. "Even the liberal, the man with his heart in the future, speaks the language of tradition, loyalty, and preservation." † The historian Arthur M. Schlesinger, Jr., anticipated the tone of the fifties when he wrote that liberals have values in common with most members of the business community, especially their allegiance to the principles of a free society, and that they must fight together to hold the "vital center" against the opposing extremes of tyranny. Other historians showed the influence of the new conservative temper. Daniel Boorstin found the "genius of American politics" in the fact that America was born with a

† C. Rossiter, *Conservatism in America* (New York: Alfred A. Knopf, 1955), p. 172.

* W. Lippmann, *Essays in the Public Philosophy* (Boston: Little, Brown and Company, 1955).

complete set of political values, which shielded her against real political conflict and made liberals and conservatives more alike in America than either was to the warring, ideologically based parties of Europe. Similarly, Louis Hartz argued in 1955 that the conflicts of American history were illusory, since all Americans had escaped the divisive impact of European feudalism and shared a common tradition of Lockian liberalism. Both Hartz and Boorstin, like Schlesinger, stressed in a time of crisis the unity of America's past and the lack of conflict over basic values.*

### The "Alone Generation"

The conservative strain also found its echoes in literature and the other arts. Many of the attitudes of the new conservatives—the nostalgia for past periods, the desire for order, and the disdain of social conflict—were reflected in the novels, plays, and some of the paintings of the fifties. The new fiction, wrote Mal-

* A. Schlesinger, Jr., *The Vital Center* (Boston: Houghton Mifflin Company, 1949); D. Boorstin, *The Genius of American Politics* (Chicago: University of Chicago Press, 1953); and L. Hartz, *The Liberal Tradition in America* (New York: Harcourt, Brace and Company, 1955).

colm Cowley, was "aggressively nonsocial and nonpolitical." In Sloan Wilson's popular novel, *The Man in the Gray Flannel Suit* (1955), the hero, a rising young corporation executive, rejects the pursuit of wealth and power to embrace the conventional world of home, family, and suburban bliss. In *The Caine Mutiny* (1951), Herman Wouk upholds the principle of authority by convicting his hero of mutiny after he has relieved the tyrannical Captain Queeg of his command. And, in perhaps the most widely discussed novel of the decade, *By Love Possessed* (1957), James Gould Cozzens portrays a conservative, middle-class, snobbish community threatened with disruption that is saved by the decency and probity of the town's leading lawyer. These were all themes that were essentially undramatic, involving conventional people doing common things, but they upheld conservative values in a time of crisis.

The literary heroes of the fifties, wrote Alfred Kazin, were no longer superior men and women battling for principles against those who would deprive them of freedom. They were, instead, lonely men and women working out their individual prob-

Gallery of the fifties. Ezra Taft Benson, Secretary of Agriculture; Earl Warren, Chief Justice of the Supreme Court; Sherman Adams, Assistant to the President; James Bryant Conant, educator. (All from New York Public Library Picture Collection.)

lems with society merely a backdrop to their aloneness. "I am tired of reading for passion instead of pleasure," wrote Kazin.

In novel after novel, I am presented with people who are so soft, so wheedling, so importunate, that the actions in which they are involved are too indecisive to be interesting or to develop those implications which are the lifeblood of narrative. The age of "psychological man," of the herd of aloners, has finally proved the truth of Tocqueville's observation that in modern times the average man is absorbed in a very puny object, himself, to the point of satiety.*

Some of the trends noted by Kazin in literature were also seen in the world of art. Here, too, was the same rejection of social themes, the same glorification of individualism, and the same despair of recovering common values. "The overwhelming vogue of the abstract and the nonobjective," wrote the art critic Elizabeth McCausland in 1951, "clearly proves the retreat of much art-thought and artwork from reality." The crisis in values that plagued writers of the forties and fifties affected painters with similar results: a stress on technical brilliance, a new interest in the bizarre, and a journalistic concentration on detail. The social realism of Benton, Wood, and Curry, popular in the thirties, was now considered as passé as *The Grapes of Wrath*.

Art, to be sure, flourished in the postwar years as never before. In the latter forties, New York, with its school of abstract expressionism (or "action painting" as it was sometimes called), replaced Paris as the world center of modern art. This school had its foundations in the work of Jackson Pollock, Willem deKooning, Mark Tobey, and other painters who resided principally in New York. It was characterized by violence, anarchy of form, and an intense desire to project the

moment of physical action in the most direct possible way. It sometimes took the form of slapping on paint, dribbling it on the canvas, or throwing pigment onto the painting surface. By the end of the fifties, it had clearly outdistanced geometric abstraction, surrealism, and figurative expressionism as the dominant theme of American (and, indeed, Western) painting. What it portended for the future, however, no one was willing to guess, though it was clearly related to the confusion and immense variety of the modern world.

### Schools in Crisis

The tension and feeling of crisis that pervaded American thought and culture was brightly reflected in the great school debate of the nineteen-fifties. Serious criticism of America's schools came from those who argued that public school curricula no longer supported the traditional objective of education, that is, the cultivation of the mind to enable it to make wise choices among conflicting values. These critics, both professional and lay, charged that a deep and pervasive anti-intellectualism had invaded the schoolroom, disparaged traditional learning, made a cult of mediocrity, turned teachers into discussion leaders or babysitters, and tried to make society over in the image of the liberal political philosophers. The urgency of these criticisms was increased by a dramatic increase in school and college enrollment in the fifties, accompanied by an acute financial crisis, and by the launching of the Russian Sputnik in 1957. Science and education, warned a host of observers, had become the main battleground of the Cold War.

But what should be done? Though there was widespread agreement on the need for reform, most discussions of educational aims foundered on specific reforms. What were the proper aims of education? Despite the endless ferment in

* A. Kazin, "The Alone Generation," J. Fischer and R. Silvers, eds., *Writing in America* (New Brunswick: Rutgers University Press, 1960), pp. 14-15.

educational thought and practice, few new ideas pertaining to the basic purposes of education had been brewed since John Dewey began his work over a half-century before. And here, though few realized it, was the source of the sour taste in everyone's mouth: To advance beyond Dewey's experimentalism was difficult without rejecting the massive, liberal synthesis of modern thought from which his educational ideas sprang; while to abandon his pragmatic, relativistic, science-oriented approach to modern life and its problems was still for most Americans unthinkable. The educational ideas of conservatives, stressing "basic" subjects, philosophical absolutes, intellect and training, and a logically ordered hierarchy of studies, often struck Dewey's defenders as carrying a connotation of class and status. It was at bottom the same dichotomy that confronted the modern writer, painter, philosopher, political theorist, and scholar.

A great deal could be done, of course, within the old framework to satisfy the critics of modern education. "Basic" subjects were strengthened in many schools; students were grouped more often by abilities; and better qualified teachers and superior equipment were sought. In 1958, Congress enacted the National Defense Education Act, which made available funds for encouraging the recruitment of college teachers, expanding science and modern language equipment in high school and college, and identifying through counseling the talents of able students. But was this enough? Should the national government give still more assistance? In 1957 and again in 1959, President Eisenhower supported school aid bills that would have provided federal funds for school construction in needy states, but these and other bills were defeated by controversial amendments barring segregated schools from receiving help. Not unexpectedly, aid for school buildings and for teachers' salaries became a hotly contested issue in the 1960 election, with Senator Kennedy pledging support for both programs.

Meanwhile, James B. Conant, a former President of Harvard University, completed an important study of American high schools. In it he defended the conception of a multipurpose high school. The comprehensive high school, making available a variety of programs to meet the broad spectrum of the needs of youth, Conant called the unique feature of American education. Among his much-discussed recommendations were a reduction in the number of small high schools, a vast improvement in counseling, grouping by ability, special programs for the academically talented, and more stress on foreign languages and science.[*] This study, together with one published by the Rockefeller Fund on "The Pursuit of Excellence," stirred a lively interest during the late fifties in the future of American public education. Excellence, according to the Rockefeller report, was not incompatible with a democratic school system. "It is possible for us to cultivate the ideal of excellence," its authors concluded, "while retaining the moral values of equality. Whether we shall succeed in doing so is perhaps the fundamental issue in the development of our human resources."[†]

[*] J. Conant, *The American High School Today* (New York: McGraw-Hill Book Company, 1959), especially pp. 37-76.
[†] J. Gardner, *et al.*, "The Pursuit of Excellence and the Future of America," *Prospect for America: the Rockefeller Panel Reports* (Garden City, N.Y.: Doubleday and Company, 1961), p. 356.

## NEW REPUBLICANISM: FINAL YEARS

### "Lame-Duck President"

As Eisenhower began his second term, he told reporters that while he was "more conservative" than in 1952, he saw federal intervention as necessary in some of the urgent problems confronting the nation. Despite his huge electoral majority of 1956, however, he failed to get Congressional approval for much of his program. His proposals for federal aid to schools were blocked; he was forced to accept much less than he recommended in civil rights; he faced strong opposition to his foreign aid measures; statehood for Alaska and Hawaii, which he advocated, was held up until 1959; and he was vigorously criticized by his own party for failing to balance the budget. On top of his troubles with Congress, he wrestled in his second term with a growing Soviet diplomatic offensive, rapid advances by the Soviets in outer space and missile development, and a serious economic setback at home. Like FDR, he found that his most serious troubles came on the heels of his greatest triumph. But unlike FDR, he found his leadership further weakened by the Twenty-Second Amendment (ratified in 1951), which barred him from a third term.

Criticism of the President, almost unknown in the first administration, mounted after 1957. It centered largely on Eisenhower's indecisiveness and refusal to fight for what he believed to be necessary. After telling Congress of the need for a strong civil rights bill, for example, he later informed newsmen that he was not in full agreement with the proposed law. "The fiasco of his program," said *Life* magazine, "is in some part due to his own indecision and seeming unsureness in support of it." Critics leveled their sights, too, on the President's ineptitude, his ignorance of public affairs, and his subservience to business interests. Following the launching of the Russian Sputnik, the outcry became louder. *Newsweek* noted in early 1958 the "swelling tide of discontent with the way the White House is being run." The political analyst Samuel Lubell reported that many Eisenhower supporters were now saying: "Things are in an uproar, but what is Eisenhower doing? All you read about is that he's playing golf. Who is running the country?"

A sharp economic recession in 1957-58 added to the discontent with Eisenhower's leadership. Prosperity had swept back after the downward plunge in 1954 and by 1956 gross national production had soared over the $400 billion mark. But in 1957, due largely to a slowdown in defense spending and a reduction in exports to Europe, industrial production began to drop steadily. The stock market felt the impact of the recession in October. By June, 1958, more than five-and-a-half million workers were without jobs. Though the President was under heavy pressure to cut taxes and start new public works programs, he moved slowly and cautiously. The impact of the economic downturn was cushioned as before by the "built-in" stabilizers in the economy, especially unemployment insurance payments to the jobless. Further modest steps were taken to combat the recession by easing credit restrictions, cutting FHA down-payment requirements, and raising the amounts of defense spending in the areas with the greatest amount of unemployment. The Highway Act of 1958, which increased federal outlays for all classes of highways, also helped in the emergency. By late spring of 1958, Eisenhower felt certain that the worst was over and that the recession would end soon. Though some effects were still being felt in 1959, notably in the unusual number of chronically unemployed persons, the economy did seem to have made a good recovery and to be on the way to a new level of prosperity.

Eisenhower suffered another disappointment in the outcome of the elections of 1958. After taking to the stump to denounce the opposition as made up of "spenders" who would take the country further toward socialism, he was not prepared for the Democratic landslide that followed. The Democrats won 48 new seats in the House to give them their largest margin since 1936 and increased their Senate strength to 64 (including Alaska) against 34 Republicans. Many conservative Republicans, notably Senator William Knowland of California and Senator John Bricker of Ohio, went down to defeat, while Nelson Rockefeller, a liberal Republican, reversed the general trend by beating Averell Harriman for the governorship of New York. Eisenhower became the first President in history to face for six straight years a Congress controlled by the opposition.

What was the significance of the 1958 election? Walter Lippman interpreted the voters' action to mean that Americans wanted their government "to be alert and to show vigor . . . and not to dawdle along in the same old ruts . . . the President has lost touch with them and with their problems, and is living in the past." Certainly the Republicans were hurt by the recession, by strong labor efforts in the campaign, by Russian successes in outer space, by the ineffectiveness of the President's leadership, and by the revelation that Sherman Adams, the President's closest adviser, had taken gifts from a Boston textile producer. Adams resigned before the election but too late to affect the outcome. The President himself seemed perplexed by the election results. "The United States did give me," he told newsmen, "a majority of I think well over 9,000,000 votes. Now here, only two years later, there is a complete reversal; yet I do not see where there is anything that these people consciously want the administration to do differently."

## New Republicans and New Frontiersmen: 1960

As 1960 came closer, Republicans faced the question Lubell had posed eight years before. Had the Republicans under Ike's leadership been able to reorganize their party and convince the voters that they were the responsible party of progress? Was the Roosevelt coalition still intact? The Republicans had been able to win control of Congress only twice in thirty years. Eisenhower himself, the most popular Republican since Teddy Roosevelt, had been deprived three times out of four of a Republican Congress. Could the Republicans retain the White House without Eisenhower? Not only the succession to Eisenhower but the future of the Republican party was at stake. The resolution of the issue, Lubell had predicted in 1952, might be deferred to as late as 1964.

A new political generation dominated the politics of 1960. Although Hoover, Truman, Dewey, Farley and other veterans of past political wars were roundly cheered at the conventions, control of both parties rested with men who had matured in the years since the depression. Even Dwight Eisenhower seemed forgotten during long stretches of the campaign as younger men, veterans of World War II, struggled to break free of the slogans and emotions of the Roosevelt era. Like most Americans, they were conscious of a sense of urgency in seeking new solutions to the nation's problems. Change, new energy, new directions, new frontiers—these were the themes of both parties as the appalling dangers of the sixties took on sharper focus.

The Democratic nominee, John F. Kennedy, was freer to attack the recent past and to suggest new emphases. It was 1952 in reverse, with Richard M. Nixon now defending the record of the Administration in power. Kennedy had been nominated at Los Angeles in a convention shaped by the power of the young Senator's organization, the weakness of rival candidates, and the sentimental strength of Adlai Stevenson. Senator Lyndon Johnson, who ran second to Kennedy in the balloting, was chosen as his running mate. In his acceptance speech, Kennedy struck what was to be the dominant note of his campaign when he said, "Today our concern must be with the future. For the world is changing. The old era is ending. The old ways will not do. . . . The problems are not all solved and the battles are not all won—and we stand today on the edge of a New Frontier—the frontier of the 1960's—a frontier of unknown opportunities and perils—a frontier of unfulfilled hopes and threats."

In Chicago, two weeks later, Richard Nixon was nominated by the Republicans without opposition. The biggest fight at the Republican convention was over the platform. Earlier, Nelson Rockefeller had publicly accused the leaders of his party of being blind to the growing missile gap with Russia, of being indecisive in foreign policy, and soft on civil rights. The thrust of the Republican party, the New York governor insisted, must be in the direction of change and responsibility in a critical time. Nixon had flown to New York, spent an evening with Rockefeller, and then signed a statement indicating his essential agreement with Rockefeller on defense (hardening missile sites, raising second-strike capacity, and building a flexible force for brush-fire wars), foreign affairs, and domestic policy (economic growth, medical care for the elderly, and

civil rights). Though opposition was intense, Nixon's leadership at the convention, notably on the civil rights plank, produced a platform that liberal Republicans were able to accept. As his running mate, Nixon decided on UN Ambassador Henry Cabot Lodge, arguing that foreign policy represented the Republican's brightest issue. "If you ever let them [the Democrats] campaign only on domestic issues," he is reported to have said, "they'll beat us." In his acceptance address, Nixon, like Kennedy, stressed the gravity of the era ahead. "The major problem—the biggest problem—confronting the next President of the United States," said Nixon, "will be . . . to arouse the people to the mortal danger [the country faces] and inspire the people to meet the danger."

Kennedy's campaign began with a setback. In August, a special session of Congress, planned by Democratic leaders before the convention, resulted in a total failure of Kennedy's program. His three most important proposals—medical care for the aged under Social Security, federal aid to the schools, and an increase in the minimum wage—went down to defeat. His first campaign swing in September was likewise discouraging and Gallup polls showed him running well behind Nixon. Then his fortunes began to change. At Houston, on September 12, he met the issue of his Catholic religion squarely before the Greater Houston Ministerial Association by declaring his allegiance to the principle of separation of church and state and his intention not to accept ecclesiastical direction in matters of public duty. In late September his chances began to soar when he met Nixon in the first of four television debates. The TV appearances helped markedly to offset charges of Kennedy's immaturity vis-à-vis Nixon. They showed him to be serious, well prepared, and calm under pressure, while the Vice President, especially in the crucial first debate, was handicapped by fatigue,

Candidates Kennedy and Nixon, with moderator Howard K. Smith during a television debate in the 1960 campaign. (Wide World.)

unflattering lighting, and the impression that he agreed too much with his challenger. The polls revealed that a majority of the public believed that Kennedy had the edge in the debates.

In the final stage of the campaign, Nixon struck hard at Kennedy's inexperience, the cost of his welfare programs, and his attacks on America's declining prestige under Eisenhower. Kennedy, he said, was "running America down and giving us an inferiority complex." Defensively, he counterpunched at Kennedy's jabs at the Republican record on welfare legislation. Repeatedly, he told his audiences that he would continue the policies that had brought peace and prosperity under Eisenhower. The President himself entered the campaign in the last week. The impact of the Eisenhower personality was still prodigious; some felt that if he had been used more extensively in the campaign, the outcome might have been different. The Nixon campaign ended with a burst of television appearances in the final days, including an unprecedented four-hour telethon.

The election proved to be the closest in American history. Kennedy carried 23 states with 303 electoral votes to Nixon's 26 states and 219 electoral votes (Missis-

sippi's vote went to independent electors). The popular vote was 34,221,463 to 34,108,582. Because of minority-party candidates, Kennedy received less than 50 per cent of the vote. Nixon proved strongest in the farm, Rocky Mountain, and border states, while Kennedy's advantage was greatest in the industrial Northeast and the Solid South. Kennedy ran stronger among Negro voters than had been expected, due in part perhaps

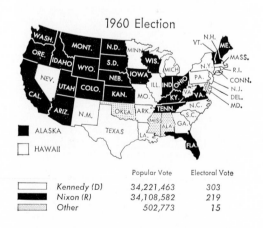

1960 Election

| | Popular Vote | Electoral Vote |
|---|---|---|
| Kennedy (D) | 34,221,463 | 303 |
| Nixon (R) | 34,108,582 | 219 |
| Other | 502,773 | 15 |

to a dramatic telephone call he made to the wife of the imprisoned Negro leader, Martin Luther King. The impact of Kennedy's Catholicism was more difficult to

407

measure. Without question, his religion hurt him in such states as Oklahoma, Tennessee, Utah, Florida, and Kentucky, while it helped him in the populous Northeast, especially in New York, Pennsylvania, and New England. Kennedy's basic strategy of concentrating on the Northeast, stressing civil rights, cultivating the big-city suburbs, and emphasizing issues with urban appeal, such as aid to schools, increase of the minimum wage, and medical care for the aged, had paid off. A surprising corollary of Kennedy's victory was a rise in Republican strength at the grass roots as reflected in a gain of 21 seats in the House of Representatives and other triumphs in state elections. The new Congress, elected to serve with a President pledged to move the country forward again, was clearly more conservative than its predecessor.

Lubell's prediction that the deadlock in American politics might continue to 1964 seemed fulfilled. Whether it could be broken would depend in large part on the new President—how well he marshalled his slim margin in Congress, how effectively he galvanized the will of a people torn by doubts and uncertainties, and how imaginatively he led the coalition of free states that alone protected the world from international communism.

## FOR FURTHER STUDY

### General Accounts

The books by Johnson, *1600 Pennsylvania Avenue*, and Zornow, *America at Mid-Century*, cited earlier, continue to be useful for the general themes of this chapter.

R. Rovere, *Affairs of State: The Eisenhower Years* (New York: Farrar, Straus and Cudahy, 1956). A useful journalistic chronicle that contains some shrewd insights into public affairs during Eisenhower's first term.

### Special Studies

D. Acheson, *A Democrat Looks at His Party* (New York: Harpers, 1955). A brief but able exposition of the tradition and principles of the Democratic party.

J. Aldridge, *In Search of Heresy* (New York: McGraw-Hill, 1956). Contains several interesting essays on the situation of the contemporary American writer.

D. Bell (ed.), *The New American Right* (New York: Criterion Books, 1955). An attempt by Daniel Bell, Richard Hofstadter, Peter Viereck, Talcott Parsons, Nathan Glazer, and Seymour Lipset to interpret the origins and significance of rightist movements of the fifties.

E. Benson, *Freedom to Farm* (Garden City, N.Y.: Doubleday, 1960). Eisenhower's Secretary of Agriculture defends his farm policies.

A. Berle, Jr., *Power without Property* (New York: Harcourt, Brace, 1959). An analysis of recent revolutionary changes in the nature of the capitalistic system, especially in the formation of capital and the aggregation of economic power.

A. Bestor, *Educational Wastelands: The Retreat from Learning in Our Public Schools* (Urbana: U. of Illinois Press, 1953). A sharp attack on modern educational practices by a well-known historian.

A. Blaustein and C. Ferguson, Jr., *Desegregation and the Law* (New Brunswick: Rutgers U. Press, 1957). A thorough analysis of the legal meaning and effect of the school desegregation cases.

M. Childs, *Eisenhower: Captive Hero* (New York: Harcourt, Brace, 1958). A mildly critical study of Eisenhower as general and President.

* J. Conant, *The American High School Today* (New York: McGraw-Hill, 1959). Conant's first report on his widely publicized investigation of American high schools.

R. Donovan, *Eisenhower: The Inside Story* (New York: Harpers, 1956). Written by a journalist who had unusual access to the men around Eisenhower and to materials concerning his presidency.

* J. Fischer and R. Silvers, (eds.), *Writing in America* (New Brunswick: Rutgers U. Press, 1960). Essays on fiction, poetry, and other literary features of the fifties that first appeared in a special supplement to the October, 1959, issue of *Harper's Magazine*.

J. Galbraith, *The Affluent Society* (Boston: Houghton Mifflin, 1958). Argues that the economic ideas which grew out of a time of bleak poverty are not suitable to the affluent society of mid-century America.

* B. Goldwater, *The Conscience of a Conservative* (Shepherdsville, Ky.: Victor Publishing Company, 1960). The best-sell-

* Starred books are available in paperbound editions.

ing popularization of conservative ideas, by an Arizona Senator.

S. Harris (ed.), *American Economic History* (New York: McGraw-Hill, 1961). An unusual textbook, written topically by a series of experts; contains a valuable chapter by Lloyd Ulman on "Unionism and Collective Bargaining in the Modern Period."

* F. Hayek, *The Road to Serfdom* (Chicago: U. of Chicago Press, 1944) and *The Constitution of Liberty* (Chicago: U. of Chicago Press, 1960). The books in which Hayek argues most strongly for a return to nineteenth-century liberal principles.

* J. Jessup, *et al.*, *The National Purpose* (New York: Holt, 1960). Essays, originally printed in *Life* magazine, by John Jessup, Adlai Stevenson, Archibald MacLeish, David Sarnoff, Billy Graham, John W. Gardner, Clinton Rossiter, Albert Wohlstetter, James Reston, and Walter Lippmann.

* R. Kennedy, *The Enemy Within* (New York: Harpers, 1960). Robert Kennedy's account of the investigation of corruption and racketeering in the labor movement.

E. Kenworthy, "Dixon-Yates: The Riddle of a Self-Inflicted Wound," *The Reporter*, XIV (January 26, 1956), pp. 19-25. A good account of the intricacies of the Dixon-Yates tangle.

* R. Kirk, *The Conservative Mind* (Chicago: Regnery, 1953) and *A Program for Conservatives* (Chicago: Henry Regnery Company, 1954). Two widely discussed books by the most philosophical of the New Conservatives.

A. Larson, *A Republican Looks at His Party* (New York: Harpers, 1956). A thoughtful exposition of the principles and views of the New Republicans.

* W. Lippmann, *Essays in the Public Philosophy* (Boston: Little, Brown, 1955). Argues that liberal democracy cannot long exist in a society which has lost the philosophy in which liberal democracy was conceived and founded.

S. Lubell, *Revolt of the Mod-*

*erates* (New York: Harpers, 1956). A stimulating interpretation of the origins and significance of the political conflicts of the fifties.

* C. Mills, *White Collar* (New York: Oxford, 1951). The most suggestive analysis yet made of the "new middle class," its origins, social concerns, politics, and place in American life.

W. Newman, *The Futilitarian Society* (New York: George Braziller, 1961). A critical examination of the ideas of the New Conservatives, especially in the writings of Peter Viereck, Russell Kirk, Walter Lippmann, and Daniel Bell.

* H. Pelling, *American Labor* (Chicago: U. of Chicago Press, 1960). A broad survey of the history of the labor movement.

* President's Commission on National Goals, *Goals for Americans* (Englewood Cliffs, N.J.: Prentice-Hall, 1960). The recommendations of the Commission and the "position papers" submitted to it.

M. Pusey, *Eisenhower the President* (New York: Macmillan, 1956). A warmly appreciative sketch covering only the first term.

* Rockefeller Brothers Fund, *Prospect for America* (Garden City, N.Y.: Doubleday, 1961). Includes the panel reports on foreign policy, defense, foreign economic policy, the domestic economy and social problems, education, and "the power of the democratic idea."

* C. Rossiter, *Conservatism in America* (New York: Knopf, 1955). This is a balanced, careful history of the course of American conservatism.

* J. Satin (ed.), *The 1950's* (Boston: Houghton Mifflin, 1960). A very useful collection of materials bearing on the mood and events of the fifties, including a section of statistical information.

* A. Schlesinger, Jr., *The Vital Center* (Boston: Houghton Mifflin, 1949). An early attempt to re-examine American liberalism in the light of postwar developments.

* C. Scott, C. Hill, and H. Burns, *The Great Debate* (Engle-

wood Cliffs, N.J.: Prentice-Hall, 1959). A good collection of views on the educational debate of the fifties.

E. Sevareid (ed.), *Candidates 1960* (New York: Basic Books, 1959). Essays by newsmen on Rockefeller, Nixon, Humphrey, Kennedy, Stevenson, Symington, and Johnson.

L. Soth, *Farm Trouble* (Princeton, Princeton University Press, 1957). An unusually lucid and perceptive account of the farm problem.

S. Stouffer, *Communism, Conformity, and Civil Liberties* (Garden City, N.Y.: Doubleday, 1955). The study done for the Fund for the Republic on the reactions of Americans to the communist danger, both internal and external.

C. Thomson and F. Shattuck, *The 1956 Presidential Campaign* (Washington, D.C.: The Brookings Institution, 1960). A careful step-by-step account of the 1956 campaign from the midterm elections of 1954 to the vote and its meaning.

P. Viereck, *Conservatism Revisited* (New York: Scribner's, 1949). Examines the "conservative way to freedom" via Metternich's Concert of Europe, which Viereck calls the "unacknowledged ancestor of our western union."

* T. White, *The Making of the President, 1960* (New York: Antheneum, 1961). A brilliant evocation of the moods and events of the 1960 campaign with some shrewd analysis of the significance of its outcome.

* W. Whyte, Jr., *The Organization Man* (New York: Simon and Schuster, 1956). A much-discussed book of the fifties on the ideology, training, neuroses, and living habits of the people who work for The Organization.

P. Woodring, *A Fourth of a Nation* (New York: McGraw-Hill, 1957). One of the best books to come out of the "great debate" on education in the fifties.

* B. Ziegler (ed.), *Desegregation and the Supreme Court* (Boston: Heath, 1958). Materials, pro and con, on the famous

school desegregation decision of May 17, 1954.

## Fiction and Drama

* J. Cozzens, *By Love Possessed* (New York: Harcourt, Brace, 1957). This novel portrays in flashbacks an entire American community as, in two eventful days, evidence of rape, theft, infidelity, suicide, and religious conversion come to light.

* A. Drury, *Advise and Consent* (Garden City, N.Y.: Doubleday, 1959). A realistic novel of Washington politics in the fifties that focuses on a Senate conflict over the President's appointment of a new Secretary of State.

* C. Hawley, *Cash McCall* (Boston: Houghton Mifflin, 1955). This is a novel of American business life centering on a specialist in big-business mergers, who finds that by acquiring a certain small business he can acquire a lever to gain control of a huge electronics plant.

E. Hunter, *The Blackboard Jungle* (New York: Simon and Schuster, 1954). An idealistic young man faces the bitter realities of being a teacher in the frighteningly brutal world of a big-city vocational high school.

* H. Wouk, *Marjorie Morningstar* (Garden City, N.Y.: Doubleday, 1955). A rebellious daughter of immigrant parents, finds, after she has been disappointed in love and thwarted in her career ambitions, that her comfortable middle-class life is not so bad after all.

## Films and Records

*Class of '58* (Prudential Insurance Company, 58 minutes, sound, black and white). A documentary on the educational and social problems of a typical graduating class of the fifties.

*Conservatism in America* (National Educational Television, 29 minutes, sound, black and white). A televised discussion of Rossiter's book, cited earlier, which stresses the book's coverage, themes, and ideological position.

*The Delinquents* (Prudential Insurance Company, 2 parts, 29 minutes each, sound, black and white). Traces the career of a typical delinquent in the first part and the modern rehabilitation of a delinquent in the second.

*The Face of Crime* (Prudential Insurance Company, 58 minutes, sound, black and white). Still another able documentary from the "20th Century" series.

*Generation without a Cause* (Prudential Insurance Company, 2 parts, 29 minutes each, sound, black and white). An attempt to portray the attitudes of today's youth.

*Portrait of Adlai Stevenson* (Spoken Arts Record). An hour of informal conversation with Stevenson at his Libertyville farm.

# The
# Wages of Strength

## CHAPTER THIRTEEN

Nike-Hercules ground-to-air missiles.

"Our people are not imbued with the righteous and dynamic faith which gives them a sense of mission and of purpose. The essential need is to recreate that. . . . No iron curtains of the despots, no cringing policies of the fearful, can prevent moral and spiritual forces from penetrating into the minds and souls of those under the ruthless control of the Soviet Communist structure. . . .

"[The] dictators keep their grasp on captive peoples partly by force, but also by providing a sense of momentous revolutionary movement. They claim to be leading to a new order of peace and social betterment. The very violence of their claim carries a conviction of sincerity and purpose which the free world lacks. . . .

"The situation will be totally different when our own conduct and example again brilliantly illumine the truth that men do not have to choose between freedom which is sterile and captivity which is purposeful; that freedom means, not idleness, not self-indulgence, but self-dedication to ennobling and creative ends. When we show, so that all may see, that freedom has that meaning, then the edifice of despotism will surely crumble, because free men will have broken the hypnotic spell by which the despots hold their masses."

—JOHN FOSTER DULLES, 1952

# A TIME OF REAPPRAISAL

"America has saved the world," said Winston Churchill in 1953. The long duel between Truman and Stalin that had raged for eight years over the northern half of the globe was stalemated. In Iran, Greece, Turkey, Berlin, and Western Europe the postwar ambitions of the Soviet dictator had been blunted by vigorous American action. Only Czechoslovakia and China, important though they were, had been added to the Soviet spoils of 1945. The military force of the United States and its allies, despite impressive Soviet gains, was still decisive. Though the American monopoly on atomic weapons had been broken, no one questioned the preponderance of nuclear strength on the allied side nor its lead in the development of hydrogen bombs. Everywhere, by the spring of 1953, there was hope that the checkmating of Soviet arms would produce an easing in the tensions of the Cold War.

## Framework of the Fifties

The spring and summer of 1953 were seasons of crucial events. Six weeks after President Eisenhower's inauguration on January 20, Josef Stalin was dead. The leadership of both camps in the Cold War thus underwent decisive changes at a critical juncture. Simultaneously with the change in leaders came a growing realization of the fantastic new pace in weapons technology. The Soviet Union exploded its first hydrogen bomb in August, 1953. Already there was talk of hydrogen warheads attached to guided missiles that could be fired from submarines or mobile pads. What were the implications for over-all strategy, for disarmament, for the utility of war itself? The atomic bomb, it had long been held, was the chief deterrent to Soviet aggression; what would happen if the Soviets closed the gap in nuclear weapons? Soon Winston Churchill was describing the new situation as "mutual terror," while J. Robert Oppenheimer, chief scientist in the construction of the first atomic bomb, likened the Soviet and Western powers to two scorpions in a bottle, each knowing it could kill the other, but only at the risk of killing itself, too.

The advent of hydrogen weapons was only one of the new factors in the international situation. Almost equally important in determining the course of diplomacy in the Kremlin and the White House was the revolutionary force of nationalism in southern Asia, Africa, and the Middle East. Most of the crises of the fifties involved the interplay of Cold War antagonisms with local nationalism in these parts of the globe. In Indo-China, Suez, Hungary, Lebanon, Cuba, Tibet, the Congo, Algeria, and other trouble spots the desire for national self-expression ran afoul of the interests of the great powers. No crisis could remain local any longer as every piece of national territory became a pawn in the power struggle; all nations were pressured to align themselves with either the communist or the anticommunist bloc, while those seeking neutrality were branded as "uncommitted" states.

The decisions taken in 1953 would affect Cold War diplomacy and strategy for the rest of the decade. How would the Kremlin and the White House respond to the new pressures that stemmed from the development of hydrogen weapons and from Afro-Asian nationalism? The answers were not long in coming. Following Stalin's death, Soviet strategy shifted from the military probing of Western defenses to a stronger emphasis on subversion, propaganda, economic penetration, and the exploitation of nationalist discontents with the West. Less was said of "banning the bomb"—the Soviet cry in the years of American monopoly—and more of the growing Soviet parity in offensive strength. Within the Soviet empire the gradual loosening of restraints after Stalin's death led to Khrushchev's dramatic denunciation of the former dictator in 1956 and the satellite revolts that followed.

Meanwhile, decisions of equal moment were being made in Washington. To meet the threat of Soviet military aggression, the Eisenhower administration proceeded to build up a system of military alliances in Southeast Asia and the Middle East. Because of the shift in Soviet policy, however, these new alliances proved far less effective in halting the inroads of communism than NATO had been in Europe. The Soviets were more successful than the West in supporting the nationalist explosions of the fifties and harnessing the energies behind them for their own purposes. Still, they, too, failed to achieve lasting dominance over the emerging Afro-Asian nations. In meeting the challenge of the hydrogen bomb, the Eisen-hower administration made the fateful decision to reduce conventional forces and rely on immediate hydrogen retaliation to check Soviet expansion. But the Soviets, now more intent on fomenting disorder and revolution among the emergent nations than on military aggression, presented the West with a long series of ambiguous challenges in Indo-China, Formosa, Suez, Cuba, the Congo, and other places. As the decade wore on, it seemed increasingly that Washington confronted a self-inflicted dilemma of beginning a war of atomic annihilation or watching new Soviet thrusts in impotent frustration. By the end of the decade, the national sense of being thwarted and facing possible defeat, of wrong decisions made and wrong roads taken, had grown so strong that it underlay much of the discussion of foreign affairs in the 1960 campaign.

## Realists and Idealists

What was wrong with American foreign policy? Where had the United States gone wrong in the postwar world? What principles guided American strategy? With increasing urgency these questions were asked in the nineteen-fifties. Scholars and statesmen joined journalists and others in debating the principles and conduct of American diplomacy. The past was ransacked to find explanations or prophecies of America's behavior as a world power. Were Americans patient and wise enough to construct a rational and effective defense of their vital world interests? Would the old impatience with Europe's power diplomacy prevent them from seeing clearly the best way to deal with the Soviet threat? "Americans naturally tend to rely on their old experiences," wrote an Italian journalist in 1953. "The temptation is always with them to rush into whatever there is to be done, do it, and get it over with. Who will tell them that the flames will never be extinguished and they will never go to bed? Can the Americans make the shift from the psychology of the emergency, which is what their historical experience has taught them, to the psychology of the long pull?"

The call for a more realistic foreign policy grew loud during the nineteen-fifties. From many quarters came the charge that Wilson and FDR, by their lack of realism, had needlessly sacrificed the fruits of two great world wars. What the United States needed, it was argued, was a policy based squarely on America's "national interest" and not on some vague abstraction called justice or international law. In a world of selfish, nationalistic states, it was suicidal for the United States to espouse unrealistic objectives or to embark on moral crusades. The failures in postwar policy, critics charged, signalized the bankruptcy of a national diplomacy based on sentiment, legalism, and utopian dreams of American omnipotence. "The intoxication with moral abstraction, which as a mass phenomenon started with the Spanish-American War," wrote the political scientist Hans J. Morgenthau, "is indeed one of the great sources of weakness and failure in American foreign policy." *

The realists, as they came to be called, shared a number of basic attitudes with the New Conservatives of the fifties. Both tended to distrust man's rationality and humanity when selfish interests were involved; both were suspicious of man's ability to avoid conflict and to build a peaceful social order; and both were deeply impressed by man's depravity and what was sometimes called the "tragic view" of history. Like the New Conservatives, the realists were strongly aware of the decay of absolute values in the modern world and of the need for authority

and positive action. Both regarded the liberal humanitarianism of the Jefferson-Wilson-Roosevelt school, with its visions of world peace and formulas for ending social conflict, with deep suspicion. Stop preaching, the realists seemed to say; stop worrying about what is right or just between peoples; instead, look to the vital interests of your own nation before all is lost.

Diplomatic realism as a body of doctrine was largely the work of five men—a theologian, a geographer, a political scientist, a diplomat, and a journalist. The theologian, Reinhold Niebuhr, early rejected the liberal view which held the use of force to be archaic and immoral. Coercion, he came to believe, was a vital element in all social relations, whether violent, as in war, or nonviolent, as in labor-management relations. Power, he argued, was never voluntarily surrendered but could be checked only by opposing power. The geographer, Nicholas Spykman, delved deeply into the foundations of national power and concluded that power politics were inevitable between nations. To ignore this fact, he warned, would be suicidal. "Political ideals and visions unsupported by force," he wrote in 1944, "appear to have little survival value." † The political scientist, Hans J. Morgenthau, was the acknowledged leader of the realist school of the fifties. Politics, he wrote on numerous occasions, was a quest for power; international life was a sea of uncertainty and disorder; security, such as it was, came only from the proper and realistic use of force. The fundamental error of American foreign policy, he wrote, was the assumption that national interest and moral principle were antithetical. In fighting World War II, the United States had tacitly accepted the old Wilsonian illusion that war could

* H. Morgenthau, *In Defense of the National Interest* (New York: Alfred A. Knopf, 1951), p. 4.

† N. Spykman, *The Geography of the Peace* (New York: Harcourt, Brace and Company, 1944), p. 3.

put an end to power politics and further war. This explained the simplistic faith of Americans in the UN and their shock at learning the details of the realistic settlement at Yalta. Even the Truman Doctrine and the Marshall Plan, he complained, were sold to the American people as humanitarian rather than realistic policies. "The illusion that a nation can escape, if it only wants to, from power politics into a realm where action is guided by moral principles rather than by considerations of power," he wrote, "is deeply rooted in the American mind." *

The popularizers of the realistic outlook in the fifties were George F. Kennan, former Ambassador to the Soviet Union and author of the containment policy, and Walter Lippman, long-time columnist and student of international affairs. In *American Diplomacy, 1900-1950* (1951), Kennan argued that the foreign policies of the United States had failed in the twentieth century because they were not based on "power realities" but on a "legalistic-moralistic" view of the world. An enlightened self-interest should be the only guide to American policy; the United States was not omnipotent and should husband its power and resources to attain practicable goals. And in hundreds of newspaper columns, Lippmann argued for a recognition of the roles that power and negotiation play in diplomacy and the need for democratic states to stop encumbering their leaders with crippling restrictions. American policies and commitments, he warned repeatedly, must be brought into line with American power.

Though the realists were fiercely attacked, they exerted a powerful influence on American thinking about foreign policy in the fifties. Defenders of traditional American policy arose to explain that moral principle had long been central to American diplomatic action and that this was the unique contribution of the United States to world politics. The Open Door policy, the evolution of the Monroe Doctrine, and American involvement in two world wars, it was argued, had all resulted from the American commitment to the ideal of the juridical equality and moral integrity of all states, large and small. The new realism, according to its critics, was in reality only the old power politics with roots in the antiquated policies of Richelieu and Bismarck. In its European form, it was held responsible by the critics for the wars and national decline of the European states over the preceding five centuries.†

Still other writers, however, saw the quarrel between realists and idealists as only a reaction to American failures since 1945. The rise of Soviet power, combining an ideological challenge with a threat to the world's power balance, had given rise to a feeling of contradiction between America's ideals and its self-interest in the Cold War. But ideals and self-interest, this mediating group argued, need not be mutually exclusive—a nation had moral as well as material interests outside its borders, and a policy of self-interest without ideals could only be self-defeating. The real contribution of the realists, it became clear by the end of the fifties, was their warning that American power was not omnipotent and that the undertaking of commitments beyond America's strength to deliver might endanger the nation's security and the survival of freedom itself.**

* H. Morgenthau, "The Mainsprings of American Foreign Policy: the National Interest vs. Moral Abstractions," *The American Political Science Review*, XLIV (December, 1950), p. 840.

† See F. Tannenbaum, "The American Tradition in Foreign Relations," *Foreign Affairs*, XXX (October, 1951), pp. 31-50.

** See the excellent discussion by Robert Osgood in *Ideals and Self-Interest in America's Foreign Relations* (Chicago: University of Chicago Press, 1953), pp. 437-451.

President Eisenhower flanked by United Nations Secretary General Dag Hammarskjold and Secretary of State John Foster Dulles. At Geneva, 1955. (Wide World.)

### Eisenhower and Foreign Policy

The favorite target of many realists in the fifties was John Foster Dulles, Secretary of State under President Eisenhower. Particularly did they resent the rigid, moralizing tone of his approach to world problems and his lawyer's emphasis on contractual agreements and points of law. The son of a Presbyterian minister, Dulles seemed at times to view the world in terms of a moral struggle in which the forces of anticommunism were ranged on the side of Heaven against the armies of satanic communism. A man of wide learning and strong personality, he was, in the words of Marquis Childs, "a mixture of sophistication and evangelism, of great knowledge and a weakness for glib slogans, of shrewdness and windy idealism, of harsh realism and

418

the most naive wishful thinking. . . ." [*]

Whatever his weaknesses or inconsistencies, Dulles exerted more influence on American policy than any Secretary of State since Charles Evans Hughes. Eisenhower was strongly impressed with his grasp of world affairs, his encyclopedic knowledge of detailed information, and the practical idealism of his approach to problems. Of all Cabinet officers Dulles alone had free access to the President's office. Though he cleared every move and decision with the President, he came to speak with virtually absolute authority on the policies and intentions of the United States. He became the prime mover of American policy, the source of American initiative in the Cold War, and the President's chief reliance in all discussions affecting America's relations abroad. Occasionally, Eisenhower vetoed or reversed a line of action which Dulles had initiated, but in the main the two men saw eye-to-eye on the diplomatic requirements and necessities of the nineteen-fifties.

The Eisenhower-Dulles diplomacy, particularly in the first term, bore the marks of the conflicting pressures within the Republican party. Foreign policy, as in the latter Truman years, continued to be at the mercy of domestic politics. The nationalist wing of the Republican party, which had leveled blistering attacks on Truman's Korean policy, the containment doctrine, the loyalty of State Department employees, and the Europe-first orientation of American strategy, had now to be convinced that a new era had begun. Eisenhower refused to use his enormous popularity to reorient his party in the direction of the liberal internationalists who had won him the Republican nomination. As in domestic affairs, he placed a high premium on party unity

[†] M. Childs, *Eisenhower: Captive Hero* (New York: Harcourt, Brace & World, Inc., 1958), p. 190.

and sought a *via media* between the internationalists and neo-isolationists in his party.

An attempt was made to appease both factions of the Republican party. Eisenhower made it clear that Truman's commitments to Europe would be honored but he also announced that "the Seventh Fleet [will] no longer be employed to shield Communist China." By implying that American forces had been used to protect the Red Chinese, rather than the Nationalists on Formosa, he pleased the "Asia-first" faction that had long called for American help in returning Chiang Kai-shek to the mainland. Yet at the same time Eisenhower asserted that his order entailed "no aggressive intent on our part." Similarly, when the President sent the name of Charles Bohlen to the Senate for confirmation as ambassador to the Soviet Union, the extremists rushed forward to attack him as Roosevelt's adviser and interpreter at Yalta. The impasse was broken only by the intervention of Senator Taft, who arranged a compromise—he and Senator Sparkman were to read Bohlen's FBI file—but he told the President that there must be "no more Bohlens." The right wing of the party was further appeased by Dulles' failure to appoint any leading Democrats to important posts, his unwillingness to defend the Voice of America from McCarthy's attacks, his dispensing with the services of George Kennan and several diplomats who had played a role in Truman's China policy, and his selection of a McCarthy supporter to be security officer in the State Department. Even the new defense policy of "massive retaliation" was a compromise of sorts between those who wanted a strong defense program and right-wing demands for governmental economies. The dilemma of the Administration was made more cruel by the dependence of the liberal Republican faction in Congress, which ostensibly spoke

for the President, on Democratic votes for support of Eisenhower's policies.

To increase the confidence of the Republican right wing that a new policy had indeed been launched, Dulles was forced to speak more aggressively about American policies than the Administration's intentions actually warranted. On numerous occasions he spoke of the new "dynamic foreign policy" under Eisenhower or of America's intent to work for the "liberation" of Eastern Europe or of the "massive retaliation" that would follow any Soviet aggression or of an "agonizing reappraisal" in Washington if France did not cooperate with plans for a European army. These expressions, as events demonstrated, were largely devoid of any concrete meaning. In actual practice, the Eisenhower-Dulles policies toward the Soviet satellites, toward new Soviet moves, and toward America's allies in Europe differed very little from the responses of Truman and Acheson in similar situations.

The fight over the Bricker Amendment was largely a struggle between the two wings of the Republican party. The Amendment, sponsored by Senator John W. Bricker, a conservative Republican from Ohio, gave Congress the power to regulate all executive agreements and denied the validity of any treaty in conflict with the internal laws of the United States. Nationalist organizations across the country rallied behind the amendment, which had the support of many right-wing Republicans, but Eisenhower was quickly convinced that it would seriously jeopardize the power of the executive branch of the government. To the Majority Leader of the Senate, William F. Knowland, he wrote in January, 1954, that "I am unalterably opposed to the Bricker Amendment. . . . It would so restrict the conduct of foreign affairs that our country could not negotiate the agreements necessary for the handling of our business with the rest of the world. . . . We cannot hope to achieve and maintain peace if we shackle the Federal Government so that it is no longer sovereign in foreign affairs." In the Senate showdown, the nationalists were barely defeated as seventeen Democrats joined fourteen Republicans to block a modified version of the amendment.

Eisenhower was most effective as a symbol of American unity and good will abroad. No President traveled so widely in the interests of peace nor spoke more eloquently of the purity of American motives and ideals. At Bermuda, in December, 1953, he met Winston Churchill and Premier Joseph Laniel of France in the first of a long series of conferences with the chiefs of foreign nations. Though the conference achieved little, it set a pattern of much closer personal relations with the heads of foreign governments than had been true in the Truman years. Following the Bermuda conference, Eisenhower flew to New York to make one of the most constructive proposals of his Administration, an atoms-for-peace plan to pool the atomic knowledge and resources of the major scientific nations for peaceful purposes. This idea was the germ of a new United Nations agency set up in 1957.

## The New Look

The defense policy laid down in 1953 proved the most controversial of all Eisenhower programs. Here again the pressures from within the Republican party played a significant part in determining the final decisions. Eisenhower had been elected on a platform that included strong criticism of the Korean War and of government spending. His Cabinet appointees, notably Charles E. Wilson as Secretary of Defense and George Humphrey as Secretary of the Treasury, were zealously concerned to honor the Republican campaign

pledges. The rapid arms build-up begun during the Korean War was now replaced by a policy of gradually building up strength over the long haul of ten to twenty years. "All this was largely euphemism," wrote Walter Millis later, "for a simple reduction in both the pace and scale of rearmament in the interests of economy and budget relief." *

At a time when nuclear war was coming to seem unthinkable, the decision was made to base American defense on the threat of atomic annihilation. The United States planned in the future, said Dulles in a speech on January 12, 1954, to rely on the threat of "massive retaliation" to "deter" communist aggression. The nation would thus be "getting maximum protection at a bearable cost." Local defense, Dulles admitted, was important, but the United States could not contain the mighty land armies of the communists by ground troops alone. A potential aggressor must know that he could not prescribe the conditions of battle, or else, glutted with manpower, he might be tempted to attack in confidence that he would be met only with conventional weapons. The basic strategic decision, then, was "to depend primarily upon a great capacity to retaliate, instantly, by means and at places of our choosing."

The massive-retaliation doctrine was a compound of revulsion at Korea, desire for governmental economy, and faith in air-atomic warfare. Herbert Luethy, a German journalist, called it a "lame compromise between the crusading spirit and the spirit of budgetary economy." The lesson learned from Korea was not the need for more conventional weapons with which to fight a limited war but the futility of all small wars. In its immediate effect, the new strategy called for a reduction in the size of the armed forces and a

* W. Millis, *Arms and Men* (New York: G. P. Putnam's Sons, 1956), pp. 339-340.

sharp increase in expenditures for the nuclear air force at the expense of conventional forces. The old Joint Chiefs of Staff were swept out and replaced by a new set of chiefs headed by Admiral Arthur Radford, known for his Asia-first orientation. These changes, deeply disturbing to the military, suggested that the Joint Chiefs belonged to the administration in power and were expected to abandon their nonpolitical role to champion the views of each new administration.

Criticism was sharp and constant throughout the decade. Only a President who spoke as a professional soldier could have commanded support for such controversial changes in military policy at a dangerous juncture in the Cold War. The military cuts were fought at various times by Democratic spokesmen, by Generals Matthew B. Ridgway and Maxwell D. Taylor of the Joint Chiefs of Staff, and even by Air Force champions, who felt that the budget was determining American military strategy, rather than the other way around. The sense of danger in relying so completely on weapons we were loath to use grew with the Bikini hydrogen bomb tests of 1954 and with the Administration's failure to invoke the threat of massive retaliation in the crises over Indo-China and Quemoy. By the end of the decade many Americans were deeply concerned that the new policy had made American power impotent and inflexible, while the Soviets had made alarming gains in their military strength.

## Falling Dominoes

The first test of the new policies decided on in 1953 came in the Far East. First, the war in Korea had to be terminated. As he promised in the campaign, Eisenhower had gone to Korea shortly after the election. Now he took steps aimed at convincing the Chinese that the United States would enlarge the war if an armistice were not signed. He strengthened American ground forces in Korea and moved a number of atomic missiles to Okinawa. Whether this psychological and military pressure, or the death of Stalin in March, was responsible for the subsequent turn of events is uncertain; but three weeks after Stalin's death, the communists accepted a UN proposal that sick and wounded prisoners be exchanged. Truce negotiations, resumed at Panmunjom, stalled once more on the question of the forcible repatriation of communist prisoners. Eisenhower, like Truman, stoutly resisted any suggestion that America surrender prisoners against their will. On May 22, Dulles hinted to Prime Minister Nehru of India that if the stalemate continued, American planes would blast Chinese bases in Manchuria. Three days later, with South Korea dissenting strongly, a "final" UN offer was extended. The last crisis came when Korean President Syngman Rhee released more than 27,000 North Korean prisoners on his own authority. Finally, after heavy American pressure, Rhee agreed to abide by a truce with the communists though he dissociated his country from it. On July 26, 1953, the war which had cost the United States 33,629 dead and 103,284 wounded came to an end.

After Korea, the test of communist strength in the Far East centered in French Indo-China. Here the French position had steadily deteriorated under the steady advance of the communist-led nationalist force of Ho Chi Minh. The crucial fortress of Dienbienphu was under communist siege by the early part of April, 1954. What action should the United States take? The French-backed regime of Emperor Bao Dai was clearly weak and corrupt; the French resistance, supported in part by American funds, was failing; and the communists were threatening to sweep through the rest of the country. As the French pleaded for desperate American measures, the Administration faced a formidable dilemma; to send ground troops to Indo-China would mean another Korea-type war, for which America was neither psychologically nor militarily prepared, while to use atomic bombs, even if they proved effective, might mean full-scale war without European support. At his press conference on April 7, the President implied strongly that he saw a vital American interest in Indo-China. "You have a row of dominoes set up," he said, "and you knock over the first one, and what will happen to the last one is the certainty that it will go over very quickly."

But what should America do? Admiral Radford wanted to launch bombers from aircraft carriers off the Indo-China coast but America's allies, together with other of the President's advisers, including General Ridgway, were strongly opposed. Ridgway was convinced that an aerial strike would lead inevitably to full-scale war. Further money and supplies were sent to Indo-China but no decisive action was taken. Finally, after the fall of Dienbienphu, the French agreed to a cease-fire and the partition of the Indo-Chinese state of Vietnam. Like Rhee at the Korean truce, the United States did not like the armistice but agreed in effect to accept it.

Indo-China was the first significant trial of Eisenhower's new diplomatic and military policies. The communists, by relying on nationalist hatred of France in a colonial country, had committed neither Soviet troops nor Soviet prestige, yet they had won an impressive victory. From this experience Dulles drew the conclusion, quickly challenged by critics, that to prevent the rest of Southeast Asia from falling to the communists a new military alliance similar to NATO must be formed. In September, 1954, after much prodding by Dulles, the Southeast Asia Treaty Organization (SEATO), comprising the United States, Britain, France, Australia, New Zealand, Pakistan, Thailand, and the Philippines, was established in Manila. But SEATO, unlike NATO, was aimed at a threat that in character was largely internal and nationalist, rather than external and military. Furthermore, it did not contain the leading noncommunist states in the region supposedly in danger, notably India, Burma, and Indonesia. Indeed, Nehru sharply attacked SEATO as an invasion of Asiatic affairs by one camp in the Cold War. The danger of communism in Asia,

On the island of Nankan, one of the Matsu group just off the China coast, Nationalist troops dig trenches in expectation of a Communist attack. (Wide World.)

Nehru argued, arose from sickening poverty and rising nationalism—and with these forces SEATO was incompetent to deal.

### Formosan Tightrope

The intent of Dulles' Asian policy, then, was to extend to Asia the wall of communist containment begun in Europe. But his policy overlooked the shift in Soviet strategy since Stalin's death. It ignored, too, the differences between Europe and Asia. The NATO agreements and the Marshall Plan had worked well in Europe because they were directed at a continent rich in industrial skills and ruled by reasonably progressive governments. In Asia, however, and later in Africa and the Middle East, American aid programs were directed at areas of extreme poverty, where governments were unstable and corrupt, and where industrial skills were almost unknown. Some states in Africa and the Middle East had, indeed, barely passed beyond the tribal stage of social organization. Complaints multiplied during the fifties of the ineffectiveness, impracticality, or military emphasis of much of the foreign aid program.

Again, in the fall of 1954, the communists presented the United States with an ambiguous challenge. The blow this time fell on the tiny island of Quemoy, five miles off the Chinese mainland, as the Chinese communists began an intensive bombardment of the Nationalist-held island. The bombardment, the Chinese leaders announced, was a prelude to the conquest of Formosa. A new crisis burst upon the Eisenhower Administration. According to a defensive pact which Dulles concluded with Chiang Kai-shek in November, the United States was committed to defend Formosa and the Pescadores. But what of the offshore islands, which were actually much closer to mainland China than to Formosa? What, specifically, of Quemoy and Matsu?

Dulles declared that America would fight for Quemoy and Matsu if their conquest seemed a prelude to a Formosan attack. Since this would be difficult to judge, Dulles was in effect leaving the situation purposely ambiguous, perhaps to deter the communists from launching an attack. In January, 1955, Eisenhower asked Congress for a resolution to grant him permission to use American forces to defend Formosa and the Pescadores. The offshore islands would be defended, he said, if their conquest were part of a general assault. Despite some criticism, chiefly from Democratic spokesmen, Congress approved the resolution without demanding any more precise definition of the commitment it was giving the President. Fortunately, the Chinese communists did not attack and Eisenhower was not forced to make the difficult decision whether a communist invasion of Quemoy or Matsu was more than it seemed to be. Chiang was permitted to retain his symbolic stepping stones to the mainland, though few now believed that he would ever return to rule over the Chinese people.

## YEARS OF HOPE

### "The Spirit of Geneva"

The first two years of the Eisenhower Administration had been a time of cautious reappraisal and wary testing of new policies. It was an interval of reassessment of Cold War strategy in the light of events—Stalin's death, the H-bomb explosions, and the restlessness of the non-Western world—that were certain to shake the world for decades to come. While both sides groped for new strategies with which to meet the new conditions, the wars in Korea and Indo-China were terminated and a new state of dormancy was achieved in the Formosa Straits. For the first time since World War II, there was no important fighting anywhere in the world. In Europe, West Germany was invited to join NATO in October, 1954, following the rejection by France the preceding summer of plans for an integrated European army (EDC). Though the level of NATO strength was far below that hoped for by American commanders, the threat of a Soviet attack on Western Europe seemed greatly reduced by 1955.

A new wind was blowing in East-West relations in the spring of 1955. Stalin's successors spoke in a tone of conciliation that had not been heard from Russian rulers in forty years. There was talk of raising the Iron Curtain and encouraging a flow of visitors into Russia and Eastern Europe. There were fewer, and less bitter, incidents between East and West than in the Stalin years. In May, a peace treaty was finally signed with Austria, a settlement which restored Austrian sovereignty and ended the four-power occupation of that country. For the first time since the war, the Russians and Americans agreed to withdraw their troops from a portion of Central Europe. Was the danger of a third world war receding? Were Stalin's heirs really intent on peace and a relaxation of tensions?

For several years Winston Churchill, who had returned to power in 1951 and was now nearing retirement, had been advocating a "summit meeting" of the Big Four. No meeting with the head of the Soviet government had taken place in ten years. The conviction was growing in the West that nuclear war was unthinkable and that perhaps the Soviets were sincere in desiring a reduction of Cold War tensions. So, under the pressure of popular interest, particularly in Western Europe, and the changing tactics of the Soviets, the Administration made the decision to seek a meeting with the Soviet premier.

In July, 1955, the first meeting between top Soviet and Western leaders since Potsdam took place in Geneva. The atmosphere was cordial as Premier Bulganin (accompanied by Khrushchev), Prime Minister Eden (Churchill had just retired), Premier Faure of France, and President Eisenhower discussed questions of disarmament, European security, and the future of Germany. Eisenhower created the most excitement when he offered to permit Soviet aerial inspection of the United States if the Soviets would reciprocate. This "open skies" proposal, intended to impress the Russians and the world with the sincerity of American interest in disarmament and peace, was politely received by Bulganin and Khrushchev but it gained no real acceptance. In fact no outstanding problems were solved at Geneva—the deadlock over Germany continued as Eisenhower insisted on free elections, while Bulganin advocated a provisional government of East and West German elements—but the climate of good will and friendliness did much to dispel apprehension. "The United States," the President assured Bulganin, "will never take part in an aggressive war," and Bulganin answered, "We believe that statement." The way seemed open to further negotiations and possible solutions to the great problems of postwar Europe. Nuclear stalemate seemed to have made both camps more cautious and willing to parley than in the Truman-Stalin era. In reporting to the American people, Eisenhower summed up the new hopeful mood which surrounded the Geneva meeting:

There seems to be a growing realization that nuclear warfare, pursued to the ultimate, could be practically race suicide. There is a realization that negotiations can be conducted without propaganda and threats and invective. Finally, there is a sharp realization by the world that the United States will go to any length consistent with our concepts of decency and justice and right to attain peace.

## Revolt in the Satellites

The mood of hopefulness grew stronger when Khrushchev delivered a blistering attack on Stalin in February, 1956. For four hours, the new Soviet premier denounced Stalin's abuses of power, charging him with brutality, duplicity, and the slaughter of thousands of innocent persons. He savagely criticized the purges of communist leaders in the thirties, the forced collectivization of Russian peasants, and Stalin's conduct of the Russian defense in World War II. The whole history of communism, Khrushchev cried, had been twisted and distorted to please Stalin's vanity. Within the Soviet Union, the rigid, brutal features of the Stalin era appeared to soften under the new regime. A mild amount of criticism was now permitted; a greater tolerance of unorthodox, even foreign, ideas was apparent; terror was no longer

the universal instrument for enforcing conformity; and the Russian people were encouraged to believe that "peaceful coexistence" with capitalism was possible.

One week after Khrushchev's epochal speech, Polish workers rioted against poor living conditions and the presence of Soviet troops in their country. At Poznan, in June, there were further "bread riots" and denunciations of conditions in Poland. That fall Poland was the site of mass disturbances as Wladyslaw Gomulka, who had earlier been purged for "Titoism," forced the resignation of Soviet Marshal Rokossovsky as Poland's defense minister. Gomulka was elected party secretary and moved swiftly to calm the rebellious temper of his people, lest the Soviets intervene with troops. The future of Poland, Gomulka declared, lay in loyalty to a Titoist communism and friendship with the Soviet Union. Though Khrushchev moved Soviet troops to East Germany and to Poland, he did not use force to put down this nationalist uprising. A measure of independence within the Soviet empire had been won by the Poles.

During the Polish uprising, the world's attention was diverted to Hungary, where

Hungarian rebels waving the national flag from a captured tank in front of the Houses of Parliament in Budapest. (Wide World.)

student riots began on October 20. As in Poland, resentment was intense at the low standard of living, the collectivization policy, and the anticlerical attitude of the communist government. Poland's success caused the Hungarians to demand the return of Imre Nagy, a Hungarian nationalist and communist, to power. Nagy, restored to the premiership, promised reforms and urged an end to the rioting. But the rioting students and workers, joined now by units of the Hungarian army, demanded the withdrawal of Soviet troops and a neutralist foreign policy. The rebellion spread beyond Budapest to the provinces. Unlike Poland, the revolt in Hungary now turned against communism itself. The hated political police, who had carried out the orders of the Stalinist regime, were savagely mauled. Nagy, prom-

ising free elections and a multiparty system, lost control of events. The Russians, who had countenanced anti-Stalinist and even anti-Russian sentiment, could not stand for the overthrow of communism in an important satellite. On November 1, Russian tanks began to move back to Budapest and other centers of revolt. The rebellion was ruthlessly put down and a new dictatorial regime under Janos Kadar was established. Nagy, who sought sanctuary in the Yugoslavian embassy, was later abducted and eventually executed. In all, more than 30,000 Hungarians were jailed, hundreds were executed, and 186,-000 fled to Austria and the outside world. It was a spectacular demonstration of the force upon which the Soviet system rested and of the festering discontent within the satellite nations.

## YEARS OF CRISIS

### Suez and Its Aftermath

Nationalists were in full cry in 1956. Not only in Hungary and Poland, but also in the Middle East, in Africa, and in Asia there were stirrings of native revolt against alien control. While the West pointed the finger of accusation at Russia for its handling of the satellite revolts, the Soviets were busy supporting anti-Western discontents in the Middle East. For the next several years American and Soviet policy came into conflict in the underdeveloped areas of the globe.

The sending of communist arms to Egypt sparked the major Western crisis of the fifties. Ever since World War II the Soviets had been probing for weaknesses on the southern flank of their empire. A Soviet foothold in the Middle East, it seemed clear to the Western powers, would jeopardize the West's lines of communications with Asia and outflank the

NATO powers in southern Europe. At stake, too, were the rich oil fields of this strategic region. Britain, whose influence in the Middle East had been dominant for half a century, lost much of her power after 1945. Her mandates over Jordan and Israel were withdrawn and British troops left the Suez Canal Zone. In Cyprus, Algeria, and other trouble spots native revolts threatened the remaining Western strongholds. Finally, a dangerous tension existed between the new state of Israel and neighboring Arab nations.

Dulles was convinced that a new approach to Middle Eastern problems was necessary. The Truman Administration, he believed, had been too partisan toward Israel and too little concerned with the military defense of the region. So he made overtures of friendship to the Arab world, and saw to it that Pakistan was included in the SEATO pact. After Egypt rejected Dulles' bid for a Middle Eastern military pact, the Secretary encouraged an alliance of the "northern tier" states of Turkey, Iraq, Iran, and Pakistan with Britain—the Middle East Treaty Organization (METO). This Bagdad Pact (1955), as it was called, proved ineffective and militarily impotent in the series of Middle Eastern crises that followed. Egypt, a rival of Iraq for Arab leadership, became more firmly anti-Western, while the pact itself offered no means of combating the new Soviet tactics of economic and psychological warfare.

A prolonged crisis began in September, 1955, when President Nasser of Egypt traded some of his nation's cotton for Czechoslovakian guns. In the following weeks, he concluded military treaties with Syria and Saudi Arabia. Tension between Israel and the Arab states now mounted even higher as both sought arms abroad. Russia, denouncing the Bagdad Pact, tempted the Arabs with further military and economic help. On July 19, 1956, Dulles, disgusted at what he regarded as Egyptian double-dealing, withdrew an American offer of aid to Egypt in building a high dam at Aswan. One week later, Nasser seized the Suez Canal, announcing that stockholders would be compensated and the canal kept open. The French and especially the British were ready to take strong measures, but Dulles counseled patience. A rift appeared between America and her principal allies following the failure of a Dulles-inspired attempt to arrange for an international organization to run the canal. Nasser was adamant in his refusal to compromise or negotiate; the UN appeared helpless as the Soviets vetoed further discussions; and Britain and France lost confidence in Dulles' ability to end the crisis.

The blow-up came in late October. Israeli forces launched on October 29, 1956, what they described as a "preventive attack" on Egypt. As their troops neared

Gaza, Egypt, the day after UN Emergency Force troops moved into the Gaza strip in the aftermath of the Suez crisis. Demonstrators carrying signs praising Nasser and condemning French and British leaders Mollet (misspelled here) and Eden (the name partly visible) demanded the return of Gaza to Egyptian rule. (Wide World.)

the Suez Canal, Britain and France, apparently by prearrangement, issued an ultimatum ordering the Egyptian and Israeli troops to withdraw from the canal to allow a British and French force to occupy it. Israel quickly accepted but Egypt bitterly denounced the ultimatum. On October 31, British and French planes started bombing Egyptian targets and five days later troops were landed at Port Said.

Eisenhower, in the midst of a political campaign and preoccupied with Hungary, was taken by surprise. Scenes of angry confusion followed in the White House, in the UN, and in Britain. The United

427

States joined with Russia in supporting a UN cease-fire resolution against its major allies, and, along with the Commonwealth countries and the opposition Labour Party in Britain, put strong pressure on Prime Minister Eden. As the Russians threatened to rain down rockets on London and to send "volunteers" to the Middle East, fear was widespread that the crisis would widen and provoke the dreaded major war. Finally, the British and French reluctantly yielded and the shooting was halted at midnight, November 6.

The heritage of Suez was bitter and lasting. The crisis ended with America's allies badly shaken and weakened, Nasser's prestige enhanced, and Russia in the role of champion of the small nations against the imperialists. The British and French, together with a number of American critics, blamed Dulles for the unhappy turn of events. His insistence on the Bagdad Pact, his vacillation toward Nasser, his abandonment of Allied interests, and his moralizing toward Britain and France after they had been stung to action were all major factors, said Dulles' critics, in the disaster at Suez. A crisis of confidence had split the Atlantic Alliance and created the most explosive conditions since World War II. Britain and France, humiliated by weakness and deeply hurt by America's action, were virtually finished as Middle Eastern powers.

To fill the power vacuum, Eisenhower asked Congress in 1957 for authority to begin a program of military and economic aid to the Middle East. This Eisenhower Doctrine, aimed at helping Middle Eastern nations that desired assistance, also empowered the President to use force to protect them "against overt armed aggression from any nation controlled by international communism." Again, as in the Bagdad and Manila pacts, the stress was on halting the spread of Soviet armies, though the imminent danger was still the skillful Soviet exploitation of nationalistic drives. American aid, of necessity, was funneled through the reactionary rulers who dominated most of these countries, which meant that reform movements were almost certain to be anti-American.

A new Middle Eastern crisis came in 1958 when a nationalist revolution in Iraq resulted in a complete sweep-out of the formerly pro-Western government. Lebanon and Jordan appeared to be next as anti-Western revolts and disorders broke out in both countries. The day after the Iraqi outbreak, American marines were ordered to Lebanon and British troops were soon flown to Jordan. In the UN the Arab states sponsored a resolution calling for noninterference in one another's internal affairs, which made possible an American and British withdrawal. The Arab pledge seemed to mean that Nasser had abandoned for the moment his program of uniting the Middle Eastern states in opposition to the West. A year later communist and Nasserite forces were in conflict in Iraq over control of the destinies of that country. Soviet policy, which had ridden with the nationalist tide throughout the fifties, was encountering increasingly stiff resistance by the end of the decade.

The prestige of John Foster Dulles reached its nadir in the two years following the Suez disaster. Soviet successes in the Middle East, accompanied by startling achievements in missiles and outer space, created a strong impression of rising Soviet power vis-à-vis the United States. The policy of massive retaliation seemed bankrupt after Hungary and Suez. American relations with Britain and France were at their lowest ebb since 1916. Dulles' boast of how America had averted war by daring to walk to the brink of catastrophe in Indo-China and Formosa now came back to haunt him. Like Acheson before him, he became the target for recriminations stimulated by America's loss of power and stature in the world since 1945. Throughout the world and even in America there were calls for his resignation. Leading Senators opined that Dulles had "outlived his usefulness." But the President never wavered in support of his Secretary. "The last person I would want to see resign is Mr. Dulles," he told a news conference in 1958. "I don't mind saying this: I believe he is the wisest, most dedicated man that I know."

### Guns and Diplomacy

On October 4, 1957, American prestige suffered further damage when the Soviets launched the first earth satellite. This event came on the heels of Russian announcements that they had completed tests of intercontinental ballistic missiles. Three days after the launching of *Sputnik*, Khrushchev told the New York *Times* that "I think I will not be revealing any military secret if I tell you that we now have all the rockets we need." The American missile and satellite programs, bogged down by insufficient funds and lack of Administration enthusiasm, suffered derision when the Vanguard rocket, which was supposed to send the first American satellite into space, exploded on its pad. Though the Administration argued that it still possessed adequate power with which to deter a Russian assault, criticism rose from all sides. The launching of *Sputnik*, said General James M. Gavin, long associated with American weapons evaluation, was "the most significant event of our time." "We are," he wrote in 1958, "in mortal danger. . . ." This was also the message of influential reports prepared by the President's Science Advisory Committee (Gaither Report) and by the Rockefeller Brothers Fund. Both recommended a radical increase in military expenditures, a reorganization of the nation's military

thinking, and a re-examination of basic American strategy.

Most military writers were convinced by the time of Suez and *Sputnik* that the New Look was bankrupt. To the criticism of the Administration's diplomacy was now added a serious challenge to its military policy. Almost no one argued in 1957 that the United States was as strong, compared with the Soviet Union, as it had been in 1953. The remarkable Soviet advances in jet planes, guided missiles, and now in outer space research had called forth no comparable spurt on the American side. On his retirement in 1955, General Ridgway had charged that the military outlay "was not based so much on military requirements, or on what the economy of the country could stand, as on political considerations." The Assistant Secretary of the Air Force, Trevor Gardner, resigned the next year, complaining of "short-sighted limitations" that were hampering jet and missile development. Yet in 1956 and 1957 Admiral Radford and Secretary Wilson, strongly opposed by General Maxwell D. Taylor, proposed further sharp cuts in conventional forces. After the launching of *Sputnik*, a host of critics charged that the American missile and outer space programs had been sacrificed to budgetary economies.

Had America's basic strategy in the fifties been wrong? Had reliance on air power and nuclear weapons weakened American strength in diplomatic bargaining? By the end of the decade, many observers thought so. The new weapons, they declared, had brought a revolution in diplomacy for which America was not prepared. As the horrors of nuclear war became starkly clear to both sides, the reluctance to use the ultimate weapons in their arsenals grew. After Bikini and the Soviet blasts, both Russia and America knew that a nuclear strike would bring devastating retaliation from that portion of the opposing force that was not destroyed. With near parity in atomic bombs, the advantage in war could go only to the side that struck first, or perfected new advances in the delivery of bombs, or found some means of blunting or surviving an atomic attack.

The impact of atomic stalemate on the diplomacy of the fifties was crucial. Diplomacy had rested historically on the willingness to use force to achieve national objectives. But by relying solely on the doctrine of massive retaliation to all Soviet thrusts, the Eisenhower administration sharply limited the alternatives open to American policy. Yet the Soviets, trusting in American reluctance to start a nuclear holocaust, exacted a kind of nuclear blackmail by presenting the West with a series of vague challenges clouded in anticolonialism and involving no Soviet troops.

The perplexities of nuclear diplomacy were skillfully portrayed by Henry A. Kissinger in an influential book in 1957. The inability to use decisive force, he wrote, would doom almost all disputes between the major powers to insolubility, since no nation would be willing to unleash atomic war in pursuit of its interests. The enormity of nuclear weapons made the thought of war repugnant, yet the refusal to risk war would mean giving the Soviets what they wanted. But when should war be risked? What was "worth" a war? "In the face of the methodical, almost imperceptible advances of the Kremlin, subtly adjusted so that no one of its individual steps seems 'worth' an all-out war," the problem seemed overwhelming. The all-or-nothing military policy of the Eisenhower years had played into the hands of the Soviet strategy of ambiguity, which was calculated to produce the maximum degree of uncertainty and hesitation. What was needed, Kissinger argued, was a new strategy that embraced a clarification of the actual military-diplomatic

threat confronting the United States and a graded deterrent to enable it to cope with limited as well as all-out wars.*

By the late 1950's, talk of limited war and "missile gap" drowned out discussion of almost all other problems of military strategy. Many competent observers agreed with Kissinger that the capacity for limited war, meaning a build-up of manpower and conventional arms and a vast increase in airlift capability, was the most pressing need in deterring further Soviet moves. "A thermo-nuclear-equipped B-52," wrote General Gavin in 1958, "can contribute little more to the solution of a limited local war than a 155-mm. gun can contribute to the apprehension of a traffic violator." † Gavin was alarmed, too, at the impending "missile gap," when the Soviet Union, presumably in the early 1960's, would have the power to obliterate SAC bases with intercontinental ballistic missiles, without fear of any overpowering retaliatory blow by the United States. In this period, wrote General Maxwell D. Taylor, former Army Chief of Staff, "the United States will be at a serious disadvantage in general atomic war regardless of how the first blow is struck." **

Only heroic measures, said Taylor, would enable the United States to evade the consequences of the situation. These included such steps as hardening missile bases, dispersing missiles on railroad cars and submarines, and improving anti-missile defense. Taylor advocated, too, a vast increase in conventional arms and a spurt in civil defense. During the 1960 campaign, Senator Kennedy showed the influence of the Kissinger-Gavin-Taylor line of argument in revealing the policies he would follow as President. The first requirement, he said in a Senate speech of

* H. Kissinger, *Nuclear Weapons and Foreign Policy* (New York: Harper and Brothers, 1957).

† J. Gavin, *War and Peace in the Space Age* (New York: Harper and Brothers, 1958), p. 128.

** M. Taylor, *The Uncertain Trumpet* (New York: Harper and Brothers, 1959), p. 134.

June 14, was to make invulnerable a nuclear retaliatory power second to none. This could be done, he argued, only through base dispersal, hardening bases, a stop-gap air alert, improved warning systems, and stepped-up missile development. "As a power which will never strike first, we require a retaliatory capacity based on hidden, moving, or invulnerable weapons in such force as to deter any aggressor from threatening an attack he knows could not destroy enough of our force to prevent his own destruction." He declared further that the United States must regain its ability to intervene effectively and swiftly in any limited war through an increase in conventional forces and weapons and an expanded airlift and sealift.* These were also the views which Governor Rockefeller pressed on Vice President Nixon in their famous New York meeting.

## Berlin Again

But before that election campaign got under way, new crises arose. Hungary and Suez were followed by clashes in Berlin, Cuba, and the Congo. The rhythm of crisis seemed to quicken and the note of perpetual tension to grow louder in the closing years of the decade. Dulles, who died in 1959, was spared the final round of critical events before the Eisenhower Administration left office. The preceding November, Khrushchev had elected to probe for the second time in ten years the strength and determination of the United States to remain in Berlin. He proposed that this beleaguered city, surrounded by communist East Germany, was to be turned over within six months to the administration of the East German government, and that West Berlin should become a demilitarized free city after the occupation troops left. The air and surface corridors from West Ger-

many into Berlin would be transferred from Russian to East German hands, according to Khrushchev's proposal, and Russia would conclude a peace treaty with East Germany and invite the Western powers to follow suit.

At stake, in the view of Eisenhower and Dulles, were all the issues dividing East and West in Europe. For the Soviets were seeking to incorporate Berlin into East Germany, thereby strengthening the communist position in Europe, and the fate of two million West Berliners, many of them veterans of the first Berlin blockade, thus hung in the balance. So, the United States, backed by France, Britain, and West Germany, took a strong position against any change in the status of

Premier Khrushchev and President Eisenhower cooperate in helping Mrs. Khrushchev step from a car when the Russian leader and his wife arrived for their tour of the United States, September, 1959. (Wide World.)

* J. Kennedy, *The Strategy of Peace* (New York: Harper and Brothers, 1960)..

Berlin. As the crisis continued into 1959, Khrushchev pressed for a meeting with the Western heads of government. Finally, after Dulles' death, Eisenhower invited Khrushchev to come to America for conferences and a tour of the country. Americans had the unique experience of watching the Soviet premier by television as he toured the nation. Most found an irresistible though unpleasant attraction in his blunt manners and repeated warnings, his pleas for peace and boasts of Soviet power. Though little was achieved in his Camp David meeting with Eisenhower, the atmosphere was not unfriendly and the Berlin crisis seemed temporarily to cool.

Just before the planned summit meeting of 1960, Khrushchev announced that a high-flying U-2 spy plane had been brought down over the Urals. The United States government, caught in a clumsy fabrication about the plane's destination and purpose, reversed itself and admitted the spying mission of the plane. Then, to the further chagrin of America's allies, Eisenhower and others declared that the spying flights would be continued. An enraged Khrushchev arrived in Paris for the summit meeting with a demand that Eisenhower apologize. Though the President now agreed to stop such missions for the duration of his term of office, he refused to apologize under Russian pressure. Khrushchev, violent in his denunciations of Eisenhower, refused to meet with him and cancelled the President's impending trip to Russia. After wrecking the conference, Khrushchev flew to East Berlin, where he made it clear that he would press no further with the Berlin issue until a new President sat in the White House.

### Crisis in Cuba

Meanwhile, a new crisis was building closer to America's shores. Throughout the fifties a slow deterioration of America's relations with its neighbors to the South had set in. Though aid to Latin America was greater than before the war, it was not accompanied by any increase in solidarity. Basically, the change reflected the new international position of the United States. During the thirties, when the Good Neighbor policy was in vogue, both North and South America had shared an isolationist sense of having interests different from those of Europe; it was hemispheric solidarity that was stressed in the memorable conferences at Montevideo, Buenos Aires, and Lima. But since World War II, the United States had become a global power with close ties to Western Europe and far-flung commitments in Asia and the Middle East; its ties to Latin America seemed less important than they once did, while many of the Latin American states remained isolationist in their approach to world problems. While the United States distributed aid to Europe, not to combat communism but to fight poverty and disease, according to Marshall, the Latin Americans knew that they suffered from a poverty far worse than anything known in Europe.*

The spur of nationalism and the humiliation at their colonial economic status were felt by people in Latin America as elsewhere in the southern half of the globe. Communism sought, largely unsuccessfully in the fifties, to exploit these feelings in Latin America as it did in Africa and the Middle East. A brief foothold was gained in Guatemala in 1954 when that small state came under a government willing to deal closely with the communists. When Guatemala received a shipment of arms from Czechoslovakia, Dulles rallied the rest of the American states behind a declaration condemning the spread of communism to the Western Hemisphere. He then gave encourage-

* L. Halle, "Why We are Losing Latin America," *Harper's Magazine*, v. 210 (April, 1955), pp. 48-54.

ment to a successful revolt of anticommunist forces launched by Guatemalan exiles from neighboring Honduras.

Resentments against the United States increased toward the end of the decade. American military and economic aid, as in the Middle East, was often channeled through unpopular dictators; this gave rise to charges that the United States was deliberately supporting autocratic regimes. Revolutionary movements, as elsewhere in the world, tended to acquire an anti-American bias. This tendency became more serious as a number of the dictators —Perón in Argentina, Rojas in Colombia, Jiménez in Venezuela, and Batista in Cuba—were overthrown in the late fifties. When Vice President Nixon visited some of these countries in 1958, he encountered violent anti-American demonstrations, including insults, heckling, spitting, and stoning. Never in American history had a high official of the United States government been treated with such disrespect.

The most serious of the Latin American disturbances was the revolution in Cuba. On January 1, 1959, a rebellion led by Fidel Castro succeeded in ousting the dictator Fulgencio Batista. Immediately, Castro launched a far-reaching program of land reform, industrialization, and nationalization of foreign holdings in Cuba. American reactions were wary but friendly; Castro himself got a warm reception in the United States in April. But relations steadily worsened as protests grew at the wholesale seizure of American properties, the summary execution of political opponents, and the indefinite postponement of free elections. Concern mounted, too, over the obvious influence of Soviet sympathizers on Castro. The anti-American tone of Castro's speeches grew more shrill in late 1959 and 1960. He blamed America for all Cuba's ills, while roundly praising the Soviet Union in official speeches and publications. He signed trade pacts with Russia, Communist China, and the satellite states. In July, 1960, Eisenhower retaliated against Castro's anti-American actions by stopping imports of Cuban sugar, the most important Cuban export. Castro then tightened his ties with the Soviet bloc and

Disturbing voices in the world of the sixties: Left, Cuba's Castro during one of his interminable harangues. Right, a Congolese addressing demonstrators during the chaotic, bloody first months of freedom; signs say "Long live confederation, long live the sovereign government of the Congo" and "Rather death than this traitorous government." (Both Wide World.)

Khrushchev promised to launch hydrogen missiles if the United States moved against Cuba. By the time the Eisenhower Administration left office, the Castro regime had taken on most of the trappings of a communist dictatorship on America's doorstep.

## The Necessity for Choice

The wind of nationalism that had blown through Southeast Asia and the Middle East and touched Latin America was sweeping across Africa at the end of the decade. In all Africa there had been only four sovereign states in 1950; ten years later there were twenty-six. Of the twenty-two new African states, no less than seventeen won their independence in the year 1960 alone. Though often ill-prepared for freedom, the fires of anti-colonialism burned deep in the classic colonial lands south of the Sahara. In the heat, the British and French empires of central and southern Africa disintegrated during the decade. In June, 1960, the Belgians, who had done little to bring the vast regions of the Congo to political maturity, suddenly released the Congolese to a confused and precarious freedom. Mutiny, riots, and anti-European outbreaks brought chaos within a few days. Only the intervention of the UN prevented complete disintegration as both Soviet and Western nations jockeyed for advantage in the confused situation in the Congo.

The world of the sixties would continue to be affected by the nationalistic upheavals and weapons revolution of the fifties. The force of nationalism, which had done so much to upset the 1953 calculations of Dulles and Eisenhower, was also disconcerting the Soviets as the new decade opened. Border troubles with the Chinese were causing a noticeable shift in Indian policy toward the West; Iraq was moving progressively away from communist influence; Nasser outlawed the communist party in Egypt and was making anticommunist speeches; Indonesia, despite its large Communist Party, dealt a severe blow to its domestic communists; and elsewhere in Southeast Asia and Africa, except for Guinea, none of the emerging states showed any wish to be included in the communist bloc.

The problem of weapons control was the most urgent diplomatic business bequeathed to the new Kennedy administration. In the grim statistics of the nuclear physicists, a single B-52 plane could carry enough destruction to equal twelve times the explosive power of all the bombs dropped in World War II, including atomic bombs. Enough weapons already existed in the American stockpile to exterminate every human being on earth. Since 1954, when the Baruch plan was withdrawn, tortuous negotiations on disarmament had dragged on in desultory fashion. It was clear by this time that no "foolproof" inspection plan, as envisioned in the Baruch proposals, was possible. The Eisenhower administration, furthermore, was now fully committed to its policy of nuclear deterrence. In any case, Russia had never shown the least interest in genuine disarmament accompanied by thorough inspection.

In 1955, however, the Soviets suddenly reversed themselves. They accepted the force levels originally suggested by the United States, admitted that concealment of atomic weapons was a serious problem, and agreed to the establishment of inspection posts at strategic sites in the Soviet Union. They further acceded to an earlier Western proposal that atomic and conventional disarmament go forward simultaneously. They also insisted on liquidation of America's overseas bases and a ban on nuclear tests. But the United States, forced now to re-examine its previous position, decided against any drastic reduction in armaments and pressed for more limited solutions. The American position was that "in the existing state of scientific knowledge, there could be no safe agreement to eliminate nuclear weapons."

After 1955 the stress in disarmament talks shifted to arms control rather than arms elimination. Interest centered on such topics as aerial photography (reflecting Eisenhower's "open skies" proposal), the prevention of surprise attacks, partial nuclear disarmament, and the banning of nuclear tests. For two and a half years, from August, 1957, to March, 1960, general disarmament negotiations ceased altogether. The Eisenhower Administration found it difficult to frame a policy that would meet America's security needs, please Western Europe, and still be acceptable to the Soviets. Paradoxically, the nuclear bombs seemed at once the chief stimulus to fear and the major deterrent to war. The United States government seemed to conclude that no system of inspection, no matter how efficient, could prevent the concealment of weapons for a treacherous strike. "To enter into a disarmament agreement dependent to any degree on 'good faith' with a nation of messianic ideas, implacable hostilities, and a deeply rooted belief that its ultimate survival depends upon the destruction of all its rivals," wrote Professor Richard J. Barnet, a close observer of the problem, "is more than a reasonable risk. It is an invitation to disaster." *

Hence the problem: How could the arms race be ended when Soviet intentions could not be trusted? Was there any alternative to constant acceleration in the struggle for weapons supremacy? If there was no alternative, was not the end result still likely to be war? Was there any way to enforce disarmament short of war it-

self? Proposals to reduce the size of conventional forces, to "disengage" in Central Europe, or to halt atomic testing represented efforts to reduce tensions without removing the capacity to attack. Nuclear testing, in particular, aroused worldwide concern in the late fifties as experts testified to the potentially harmful effects of polluting the atmosphere with radioactive particles, while disagreeing as to how much testing could take place before irreparable harm was done. A ban on testing was not negotiated in the Eisenhower years, but a voluntary suspension of nuclear testing was begun in 1958 that lasted until the Soviets resumed atmospheric testing of large bombs in 1961. A conference on the prevention of surprise attack in 1958 also broke up without agreement. By the early 1960's it was clear to most observers that disarmament proposals which sought to protect the United States against all conceivable risks were doomed to failure. "Any agreement for meaningful disarmament," wrote Professor Barnet, "requires an awareness of the risks involved, as objective an assessment of these risks as it is given to humans to make, and, ultimately, an act of faith."

It was Eisenhower's fate to be President at the most crucial stage in Soviet-American relations since 1945. In dealing with the post-Stalin world of hydrogen weapons and burgeoning nationalism, he had acted with dignity and calmness, if not always with resolution and purpose. The challenges he faced were complex and staggering in their implications; a wrong judgment or an error in military calculation could have meant the destruction of millions of human lives. He was forced to wrestle with the confused turns in Soviet policy following Stalin's death; he saw the American monopoly on advanced weapons of destruction fade and disappear; and he faced bewildering choices of policy in the emerging

* This quotation and other material in this section is taken from R. Barnet, *Who Wants Disarmament?* (Boston: Beacon Press, 1960).

nations of the Middle East and Afro-Asia. That he was a man of peace no one who saw his earnest manner and sober countenance in the years of crisis would deny. In the closing years of his Administration he made long good-will tours to the nations of Europe, Asia, and the Middle East, but was dissuaded from visiting Japan because of anti-American rioting led by leftist students and communist sympathizers. Everywhere else he was greeted by huge and enthusiastic crowds. In his foreign as well as his domestic role, Eisenhower sought instinctively the path of compromise, moderation, and decency.

But was it enough? Had the world struggle against communism turned decisively against the United States during his administration? Was American strength what it might have been under a stronger and more resolute leader? Could the wild beasts of colonialism and disarmament have been tamed more skillfully if they had been tackled with greater vigor and understanding? Did the NATO alliance atrophy during the Eisenhower years? Had the program of foreign military and economic aid been administered with discrimination and intelligence? These questions were asked by Eisenhower's contemporaries—and not only by his political critics. They would also be asked by historians.

As the decade of the sixties opened, America clearly faced a turning point in its relations with the outer world. Directly and urgently, America faced, in the words of Henry Kissinger, "the necessity for choice." The United States could not undergo another decline like that of the years 1945 to 1960 without becoming historically irrelevant. Whatever the causes, America's margin of survival had dangerously narrowed. The world of 1945, when America owned an atomic monopoly and communism ruled in only one country, had been replaced by the world of 1960, when hydrogen weapons were in the hands of the communists, who controlled a dozen important countries. Americans now lived in the consciousness that a single attack, lasting no more than a few minutes, could endanger their survival and that of all mankind. Militarily, wrote Kissinger, "we are best prepared for the kind of war most inconsistent with our values, our tradition, and indeed our national policy: a surprise attack against the Soviet Union." In the fields of arms control, NATO policy, diplomatic negotiations, and ideological conflict, American effort had been likewise fitful, rigid, and barren of new conceptions.

Though the margin of survival had narrowed, the possibility of choice remained:

We can still shape our future. The prerequisite, however, is that we give up our illusions. We are not omnipotent. We are no longer invulnerable. The easy remedies have all been thought of. We must be prepared to face complexity. . . . We must be willing to face the paradox that we must be dedicated both to military strength and to arms control, to security as well as to negotiation, to assisting the new nations toward freedom and self-respect without accepting their interpretation of all issues. . . . Our ability to master the seeming paradoxes will test even more than our ability to survive; it will be the measure of our worthiness to survive.*

This was the challenge of the sixties—no generation of Americans had ever faced a more difficult one.

* H. Kissinger, *The Necessity for Choice* (New York: Harper and Brothers, 1960), pp. 1-9.

# FOR FURTHER STUDY

*The books by Carleton, Childs, Donovan, Gatzke, Graebner, Rovere, and Zornow, cited at the end of the preceding three chapters, continue to be especially useful for the general themes of this chapter.*

## General Accounts

J. Davids, *America and the World of Our Time* (New York: Random House, 1960). A diplomatic history text concentrated on the twentieth century that devotes about a third of its coverage to the years since 1945.

* J. Lukacs, *A History of the Cold War* (Garden City, N.Y.: Doubleday, 1961). A popular, journalistic account that is sharply critical of Dulles-Eisenhower diplomacy.

W. Rostow, *The United States in the World Arena* (New York: Harpers, 1960). A brilliant interpretation of America's recent policies against a broad canvas of history, politics, and economic and social change.

* J. Spanier, *American Foreign Policy Since World War II* (New York: Praeger, 1960). A surprisingly compact account that is both factual and interpretive.

E. Stillman and W. Pfaff, *The New Politics: America and the End of the Postwar World* (New York: Coward McCann, 1961). A brief but trenchant essay probing the deeper reasons for America's diplomatic failures since 1945.

## Special Studies

D. Acheson, *Power and Diplomacy* (Cambridge: Harvard U. Press, 1958). The former Secretary of State criticizes massive retaliation, the handling of Suez, and other features of Eisenhower-Dulles diplomacy.

* R. Barnet, *Who Wants Disarmament?* (Boston: Beacon

* Starred books are available in paperbound editions.

Press, 1960). An excellent analysis of the history, problems, and prospects of disarmament.

J. Beal, *John Foster Dulles* (New York: Harpers, 1957). An uncritical biography concentrating on his years as Secretary of State.

L. Bloomfield, *The United Nations and U.S. Foreign Policy* (Boston: Little, Brown, 1960). A careful appraisal of American national interest in the UN in the light of critical developments of the fifties.

D. Brennan (ed.), *Arms Control, Disarmament, and National Security* (New York: Braziller, 1961). A highly-endorsed series of papers on arms control sponsored by the American Academy of Arts and Sciences.

B. Brodie, *Strategy in the Missile Age* (Princeton: Princeton U. Press, 1959). A review of the origins of air strategy, followed by an unusually lucid discussion of the impact of nuclear weapons on strategy.

* J. Campbell, *Defense of the Middle East* (New York: Harpers, rev. ed., 1960). A Council on Foreign Relations study that combines a historical sketch of the development of American policy in the Middle East with an analysis of the contemporary problems confronting the United States there.

R. Drummond and G. Coblentz, *Duel at the Brink* (Garden City, N.Y.: Doubleday, 1960). An anecdotal, journalistic survey of Dulles' conduct of American policy.

J. Dulles, *War or Peace* (New York: Macmillan, 1957). Originally published in 1950, this edition carries a new preface.

* T. Finletter, *Foreign Policy: the Next Phase* (New York: Harpers, 1958). A critical view

of American policies by a former Air Force Secretary who argues that the launching of the Russian *Sputniks* made mandatory a total rethinking of basic policy.

J. Gavin, *War and Peace in the Space Age* (New York: Harpers, 1958). Gavin, an Army general associated with defense policy, feels that the wrong conclusions were drawn from the experiences of the decade 1945-1955.

A. Hadley, *The Nation's Safety and Arms Control* (New York: Viking, 1961). A most useful book on arms control problems for lay readers.

* L. Henkin (ed.), *Arms Control* (Englewood Cliffs, N.J.: Prentice-Hall, 1961). Another book, growing out of an American Assembly meeting, on the citizen's stake in arms control, exploring the history of disarmament efforts since 1945, the implications of arms control for security and foreign policy, problems of inspection, and European and Soviet views on the subject.

* G. Kennan, *American Diplomacy, 1900-1950* (Chicago: U. of Chicago Press, 1951). Probably the most influential presentation of the "realist" thesis about American foreign policy since 1900.

———, *Russia and the West under Lenin and Stalin* (Boston: Little, Brown, 1960). An able attempt to view Soviet relations with the West since 1917 in historical perspective.

* J. Kennedy, *The Strategy of Peace* (New York: Harpers, 1960). A collection of Kennedy's speeches on foreign policy, edited by Allan Nevins, intended for use in the 1960 campaign.

* H. Kissinger, *The Necessity for Choice* (New York: Harpers,

1960). An important book on the dilemmas confronting American diplomacy and strategy in the sixties that presents Kissinger's own conclusions on strategy, limited war, NATO, arms control, and policy toward the emerging nations.

* ———, *Nuclear Weapons and Foreign Policy* (New York: Harpers, 1957). A much-discussed book of the fifties, dealing with the challenges of the nuclear age to American diplomacy and strategy and arguing the vital need of a strategic doctrine.

* E. Lefever, *Ethics and United States Foreign Policy* (New York: Meridian, 1957). This book, which "attempts to relate the insights and affirmations of Judaeo-Christian ethics to the problems and direction of United States foreign policy," echoes the realists' criticism of recent American policies.

G. Liska, *The New Statecraft* (Chicago: U. of Chicago Press, 1960). A pioneering attempt at a theory of foreign aid as an instrument of foreign policy.

* W. Millis, *Arms and Men* (New York: Putnam's, 1956). A review of American military history intended to throw light on the complex, if not insoluble, problems of war under modern conditions.

———, *Arms and the State* (New York: The Twentieth Century Fund, 1958). An important study of the now blurred line between civil and military elements in American policy.

* C. Mills, *The Causes of World War Three* (New York: Simon and Schuster, 1958). Argues that war has become absurd under modern conditions and that the drift toward World War III is the result of a lack of moral and political imagination.

H. Morgenthau, *In Defense of the National Interest* (New York: Knopf, 1951). The most closely reasoned statement of the realists' criticism of utopianism, legalism, sentimentalism, and neo-isolationism in American postwar policy.

* D. Price (ed.), *The Secretary of State* (Englewood Cliffs, N.J.: Prentice-Hall, 1960). Another American Assembly study

of the relation of the Secretary of State to foreign policy, the President, Congress, the Constitution, the public, and the Department of State itself.

* A. de Seversky, *America: Too Young to Die!* (New York: McGraw-Hill, 1961). Warns that unless we make sweeping changes in our concept of national security and exert maximum effort, war may come.

R. Strausz-Hupé, W. Kintner, and S. Possony, *A Forward Strategy for America* (New York: Harpers, 1961). Another sobering call for a reassessment of American strategy from the Foreign Policy Research Institute of the University of Pennsylvania.

M. Taylor, *The Uncertain Trumpet* (New York: Harpers, 1959). A sharp criticism of the New Look and the massive retaliation doctrine by the man who was Army Chief of Staff from 1955 to 1959.

K. Thompson, *Political Realism and the Crisis of World Politics* (Princeton: Princeton U. Press, 1960). Contains the most comprehensive account of the origins and ideas of the realist school of thought on American foreign policy.

* G. Turner and R. Challener (eds.), *National Security in the Nuclear Age* (New York: Praeger, 1960). Another incisive analysis of problems of weapons and strategy, limited war, NATO, and the army's role in modern war.

A. Wolfers (ed.), *Alliance Policy in the Cold War* (Baltimore: Johns Hopkins Press, 1959). The best study to appear to date on America's alliances since 1945, their origins, justification, problems, and strains.

## Fiction and Drama

* G. Greene, *The Quiet American* (New York: Viking, 1956). The story of intrigue in Saigon revolving around a skeptical British journalist, his Vietnamese mistress, and an eager but naive American.

* W. Lederer and E. Burdick, *The Ugly American* (New York: Norton, 1958). A much-discussed novel of Americans abroad, their

rigidity of approach, their insensitivity to native culture, and their insulation from local conditions.

* N. Shute, *On the Beach* (New York: Morrow, 1957). In 1963, following an atomic war that has wiped out life in the northern hemisphere, the people of Melbourne, Australia prepare for death at the hands of a steadily approaching radioactivity.

* L. Wibberley, *The Mouse That Roared* (Boston: Little, Brown, 1955). An amusing fantasy of the little Duchy of Grand Fenwick, which declares war on the United States, expecting good treatment following its defeat, only to win the war when its invading longbowmen seize the newly invented "quadium" bomb.

## Films and Records

*America's World Role* (National Educational Television, 29 minutes, sound, black and white). A televised discussion in 1959 of America's foreign policy, foreign aid program, and issues between the United States and the Soviet bloc.

*Ceiling Unlimited* (Prudential Insurance Company, 58 minutes, sound, black and white). A "Twentieth Century" program on outer space.

*The Red Sell* (Prudential Insurance Company, 2 parts, 29 minutes each, sound, black and white). A two-part program from the "Twentieth Century" series on Soviet propaganda methods and their effectiveness.

*Revolt in Hungary* (Prudential Insurance Company, 29 minutes, sound, black and white). An excellent television documentary on the 1956 uprising.

*Riot in East Berlin* (Prudential Insurance Company, 29 minutes, sound, black and white). Contains some wonderful shots of the East Berlin rioting of 1953.

*U.S. Foreign Economic Policy* (World Affairs Center, 29 minutes, sound, black and white). A 1957 discussion of American trade, foreign aid, and investment policies.

*U.S. Foreign Policy in the Middle East* (World Affairs Center, 29 minutes, sound, black and white).

# Dawn or Twilight?

CHAPTER FOURTEEN

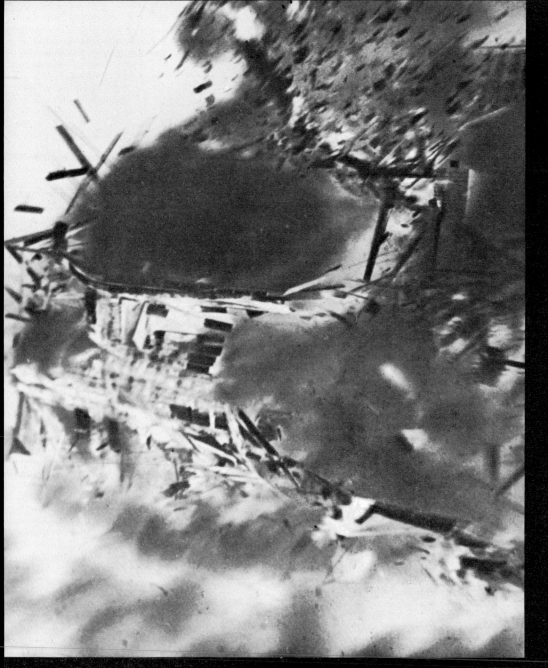

House disintegrating in atomic test.

THE MOOD OF THE TIMES

Here is a place of disaffection
Time before and time after
In a dim light: neither daylight
Investing form with lucid stillness
Turning shadow into transient beauty
With slow rotation suggesting permanence
Nor darkness to purify the soul
Emptying the sensual with deprivation
Cleansing affection from the temporal.
Neither plenitude nor vacancy. Only a flicker
Over the strained time-ridden faces
Distracted from distraction by distraction
Filled with fancies and empty of meaning
Tumid apathy with no concentration
Men and bits of paper, whirled by the cold wind
That blows before and after time,
Wind in and out of unwholesome lungs
Time before and time after.

—T. S. ELIOT

# HISTORY CLOSES IN

## The Triumph of Modernity

To Americans of the sixties, life had a sharply different taste from the savor it offered to those Americans who had welcomed in the new century three score years before. The unsettling forces of the latter nineteenth century, destined to provide so much challenge and opportunity to modern Americans, had clearly prevailed. The factory, the city, the immigrant, the new science, and the unstable balance of world power had together reshaped the outlook, attitudes, problems, and daily concerns of the average American. The way of life associated with urban industrialism—dynamic, restless, disciplined, secular, and highly organized—had become the standard pattern for 180 million people. Resistance to city ways and urban ideals had all but vanished. Mechanization was almost universally accepted as the tested route to comfort, power, success, and leisure. Organization was everywhere the key to effective performance in politics, government, business, education, and science. And the image of science that persisted, despite the pessimism of a few, was the nineteenth-century dream of new technological conquests, continually rising productivity, and increasing control over nature. The old antagonist of science, religion, now little more than a code of humane ethics, at least in its popular form, no longer viewed the march of science as necessarily hostile to its ideals and values.

What remained, then, of the ideals and values of Lincoln's generation? Well, democratic ideas were still deeply woven into the warp of American life, though many now questioned America's mission to transport them to other lands. Some feared for the future of freedom and self-government in an age that had cut loose from the anchor of a natural-rights philosophy. Most were still individualistic in principle, though the pressures of a mass society often produced uniformity of behavior in practice. By nineteenth-century standards, they seemed less restrained by traditional moral precepts, more controlled by external standards, less dogmatic in their religious beliefs, and more willing to accept organizational and governmental constraints. Such older national traits as generosity, practicality, materialism, and impatience still found a place in the American's make-up in the nineteen-sixties. And almost all Americans retained their faith that the central meaning of their historical experience was the "hope that they need not be locked into the boxes into which birth and inherited position had put them, that they can carve out their own careers, enjoy

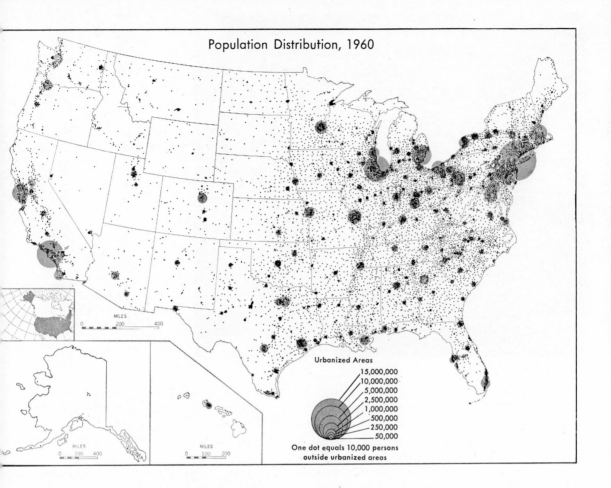

## Population Distribution, 1960

Urbanized Areas

15,000,000
10,000,000
5,000,000
2,500,000
1,000,000
500,000
250,000
50,000

One dot equals 10,000 persons
outside urbanized areas

what other men enjoy, reach their leaders and influence them, and live without deferring to a ruling group." *

### The Taint of Pessimism

In one profoundly significant way Americans of the sixties differed from their forebears of the nineties. Throughout their history Americans had been a strongly optimistic people; surrounded by broad oceans and weak neighbors, they had built a civilization of opportunity and hope in an environment free of many of the major tragedies of life. They had easily accepted doctrines of inevitable progress as they saw how easily nature and circumstance yielded

to American energy and imagination. They had swum with the tide of history as American ideas of freedom, self-government, and economic plenty coursed through other parts of the world. "This country," wrote the Britisher Denis Brogan, "was born in the age of progress, baptized in the religion of progress, created and peopled by men and women who believed in progress, in some amelioration for themselves, in more for their children." †

Now they had come to know pessimism. The first wisps of doubt appeared is 1914 as hopes of peace and inevitable progress faded into the smoke of war. Though Wilson appealed deeply to the aspirations of mankind with his pleas for

* C. Frankel, "The Power of the Democratic Idea," *Prospect for America: the Rockefeller Panel Reports* (Garden City, N.Y.: Doubleday and Company, 1961), p. 451.

† D. Brogan, *America in the Modern World* (New Brunswick, N.J.: Rutgers University Press, 1960), p. 6.

Automation, the newest wrinkle in industrialism, poses serious questions about the fate of displaced workers. Here is an automated bakery where only a handful of attendants are needed to watch the machines. (Courtesy Houston Chamber of Commerce.)

a just peace and his plan for a league of nations, the intellectual atmosphere of the postwar years was tainted by doubt and pessimism. The image of man constructed then by American and Western novelists bore increasingly the marks of despair and disillusion. Even the prewar revolt against tradition and formalism was no longer viewed with the same joyous sense of rebellion.

Then came the failure of the American economy in 1929. Though FDR revived the faith of Americans in democratic values and liberal government, the depression bit deeply into the confidence of Americans that history was on their side. After the depression came World War II, the rise of communist power, the Cold War, Korea, hydrogen bombs, *Sputnik*—twenty years of nearly continual emergency. The future of Americans seemed, for the first time, at the mercy of events beyond their control. "History less and less presents itself as something we *make*," as Robert L. Heilbroner expressed it, "and more and more as something we find made for us. . . . After a long voyage in which the favoring currents of his-

tory bore us in the direction in which we sought to navigate, we have emerged into an open sea where powerful contrary winds come directly into conflict with our passage." *

The "contrary winds" of Soviet expansion, hydrogen weapons, and explosions of population growth and nationalism blew in a climate of national unease that was new to America. It was galling for a people whose history had been uniquely sheltered and fortunate to admit the possibility of tragedy or the frustration of America's dream. That there might be no military "solution" to communist expansion, that the aspiring millions of Asia and Africa might reject Western or American answers to their political and economic problems, or that the course of world events might continue to go against the United States were ideas that, in the proper sense of a much-abused term, were truly "un-American" in that they found no echo in the American experience.

The feeling that "something was

* R. Heilbroner, *The Future as History* (New York: Harper and Brothers, 1959), pp. 55-58.

444

wrong" penetrated deeply into the American consciousness in the fifties. Most Americans outgrew the angry, troubled response of McCarthyism, which had sought explanation for all America's ills in disloyalty and blundering at home, but the mood of frustration and uncertainty remained. No one could argue in the sixties that Americans faced the future with the same confidence and sureness of their mission that they had felt in 1900, in 1940, or even in 1950. The brutal encounter with history induced a mood of pessimistic realism in some of the nation's most thoughtful citizens. Never in American history had a leading diplomat and scholar made so gloomy a statement about the future of the United States as George Kennan wrote in the *New Leader* at the end of the 1950's:

If you ask me . . . whether a country in the state this country is in today: with no highly developed sense of national purpose, with the overwhelming accent of life on personal comfort and amusement, with a dearth of public services and a surfeit of privately sold gadgetry, with a chaotic transportation system, with its great urban areas being gradually disintegrated by the headlong switch to motor transportation, with an educational system where quality has been extensively sacrificed to quantity, and with insufficient social discipline even to keep its major industries functioning without grievous interruption—if you ask me whether such a country has, over the long run, good chances of competing with a purposeful, serious, and disciplined society such as that of the Soviet Union, I must say that the answer is "no." *

### The Testing of American Civilization

The long isolation from the realities of world politics had hardened attitudes that still affected American performance in the 1960's. Power was evil, according to the American experience, and power politics was played only for

* G. Kennan, "A Proposal for Western Survival: Reflections on the Future of Democracy in the Light of Recent History," *New Leader*, XLII (November 16, 1959), pp. 10-15.

selfish and impure aims. When attacked, America had struck back in a righteous frenzy that had brought terror to the hearts of the wicked. Between war and peace there was no half-way house, for power and force inevitably corrupted those who employed them. At the heart of this American attitude was a conviction of American moral superiority to the rest of the world. Though the United States of the sixties had long since assumed the responsibilities of its power, its citizens still saw the world in starkly moral terms. Nations, like individuals, they felt, must be judged according to private standards of ethical behavior. Even the language of American politics, with its richness in terms like "crusade," gave testimony to the survival of this attitude. It survived, too, in American suspicions of diplomacy, in American views concerning the use of power, and in American policy toward the emerging nations.

Could America bring its undoubted strength to bear in a measured and intelligent way on the problems and aspirations of the world's peoples in the 1960's? No question was more urgent, none required more of the American people by way of transcending their historical experience. Would Americans be able to bridge the gap which the nineteenth century had opened between force and diplomacy? Upon the answer to this question, upon the way America deployed its strength to deter the expansion of the area of totalitarianism, depended the survival of Western freedom. Would Americans be able to advance beyond mere anticommunism in their policy toward the emerging nations? If not, future historians might well find the American efforts in these countries futile and irrelevant. And how would Americans resolve the dilemma of responding to colonial revolutions that tore at both America's revolutionary ideals and its self-interest in keeping its European allies strong? Other questions pressed for answers in this period of supreme testing of American civilization. Could America recover its vitality and sense of purpose? Could it free its foreign policy from the pressures of domestic politics? Could it make its own democracy work so effectively that it became once more a beacon for mankind's hopes? Could it find leaders who would lead? And would all these things be done swiftly enough to affect the present course of world history? If the answer were "no," a host of observers warned, the result might well be the end of American civilization. "The possibility of an American Götterdämmerung," wrote Professor John Spanier in 1960,

may sound fantastic to a people who have known an almost unbroken line of successes and achievements, to a nation which has never known complete defeat, conquest, or occupation, to a country which has reached the peak of its power and wealth. But the citizens of Carthage and Rome also once thought that fate had blessed their cities with eternal life. They, too, were confident that they could not make a mistake which their vast power could not rectify. They also dismissed the possibility that they might commit the one irrevocable mistake, and they condemned their critics as "prophets of gloom and doom" who had no faith in the Carthaginian or Roman way of life. But in the end, history proved the Cassandras to have been right after all. If the present-day Cassandras are also ignored, America's gravestone may someday bear these words: "Here lies the United States. Because of a misunderstanding of the nature of democratic leadership, she lost the cold war by default." *

## IN THE EYE OF THE HURRICANE

### The Politics of Crisis

The problem of leadership was vital. To galvanize effectively the efforts of the American people in maintaining peace in freedom would require a heroic blend of courage, intelligence, energy, and candor. The world was swept by revolutions; the dangers to American society were cruelly real; past experience was an insufficient guide; and the people themselves looked to their leaders for guidance and command. Above all, the crisis demanded truthfulness about the dangers ahead.

The voices that will serve this country, and indeed save it [wrote Walter Lippmann] will be those of stern men demanding hard things. They may not as yet do well in the Gallup polls. They will be listened to sooner or later. For they will shatter the belief, now so prevalent among us, that affluence is greatness. It is not. In the history of human society it has not seldom been the case that when riches were devoted to luxury it was the mark of their decline.

For a society with twice the productive capacity of the Soviet Union that could not match the Soviets in science, space, or weaponry, no excuses would long satisfy the friends of freedom abroad or in the United States itself.

The challenge was formidable. For almost a quarter-century neither party had commanded an effective majority in American politics. Too often this had caused both parties to accommodate foreign needs to domestic politics. Both were acutely sensitive to public opinion and too little concerned with leading and reshaping it. A kind of national Alphonse and Gaston politeness, as Professor Hans Morgenthau has noted, tended to characterize the relations between government and the people; the government stood back to wait for public opinion to be

* J. Spanier, *American Foreign Policy Since World War II* (New York: Frederick A. Praeger, 1960), pp. 218-219.

heard, while the public, in turn, waited for some sign of government leadership. Government by consent of the governed had given way in some degree to government by opinion polls and citizens' committees. At stake was not only America's ability to compete with communism but, more important, the adequacy of democratic government to the problems and complexities of twentieth-century political life. Was this political system, which was based on faith in human reason and entrusted power to the many, viable amid the conditions of modern life? The question went to the very foundations of American politics and history. Its answer might well be given in the American political performance of the 1960's.

### The Tensions of a Free Society

Many ancient questions took on a new perspective in the light of the continuing political crisis. What was the proper balance between private and public expenditures in a time of acute danger? How far should individual dissent be permitted to go when national extinction was a live option? How much delay in the achievement of full political and social rights for the Negro was possible in a world more colored than white? What were the implications for democracy of the vital strategic and scientific decisions necessarily being made in secret by men protected from full public responsibility? How could individual decision-making be freed from the stifling anonymity and timidity of bureaucratic advance?

In the 1960 presidential campaign there was extensive discussion of government spending, deficit financing, national debt, and economic growth in the sixties. The Democrats argued that the United States had been dangerously short-changing the public sector of the economy in favor of private consumption. Republican fears of inflation, they charged,

had caused them to allocate a shrinking share of the national product to such vital needs as education, roads, health, housing, and the rebuilding of cities. It was true that governmental expenditures for social welfare, as a function of gross national product, had declined precipitously since the thirties and continued to decline in the fifties. It was further true that federal expenditures for education, housing, health, and veterans' programs accounted for a much smaller percentage of governmental outlay in the late fifties than they had in 1940 or even 1950. But opponents of government spending countered that the level of expenditure for these purposes had risen sufficiently to meet all legitimate needs. What of the national debt? The gross federal debt stood at $269 billion in 1946 at the conclusion of World War II; it fell to $259 billion in 1952 at the end of the Truman administration; and it rose again to approximately $290 billion in 1960 following the recession of the late fifties. During these same years the federal debt burden on the individual citizen fell from $1832 to $1583; relative to national pro-

Many Americans were disturbed by the drift of military policy and the secrecy of decision-making. Here peace walkers in San Francisco protest nuclear testing. (United Press.)

duction, the debt dropped about 50 per cent. What all this meant, Senator Kennedy charged in the campaign, was that the Washington government had shirked responsibilities which it ought to have assumed by shunting them onto already overburdened state and local governments. The Eisenhower fiscal policies, according to Kennedy, had not only encouraged a dangerous allocation of the nation's resources but had stunted America's economic growth and failed to control inflation. Whether Kennedy would have greater success in stimulating economic growth, controlling inflation, and promoting a more equitable division of the national product between public and private projects in his own Administration remained to be seen.

The continuing crisis of the Cold War lent urgency to other familiar problems. The task of balancing individual rights of free expression and movement with the demands of national security remained acute. Though the McCarthyite rebellion against traditional American liberties was stilled, its echoes reverberated into the 1960's. The danger was heightened by the increased use of secrecy to protect scientific and military plans. "One of the most bizarre features of any advanced industrial society in our time," wrote the British scientist and novelist, C. P. Snow, "is that the cardinal choices have to be made by a handful of men: in secret." Frequently these decisions were made by men without scientific training who had to base their judgments solely on such intangible factors as personal confidence and trust.*

The mood of domestic distress of the late fifties owed a good deal to the virtual stalemate over school integration. In a world where the example of America, to have meaning, must kindle respect and admiration in the hearts of non-Caucasian peoples, the failure of the nation's political leaders in this area had world-wide ramifications. Most white Southerners, feeling that they were being hustled into a new age that was out of harmony with the values of their fiercely independent tradition, were loath to leave any stone unturned in building a wall against the process of integration; while the Negroes, impatient at the slowness of their white neighbors in yielding superior political and social privileges, looked to the national government to right their ancient wrongs. Of this tragedy for all Americans the Frenchman André Siegfried wrote in 1955:

* C. Snow, *Science and Government* (Cambridge: Harvard University Press, 1961), p. 1.

Negro sit-in demonstrators find the way barred to a lunch counter in a Memphis department store. These young people were among 100 who peacefully protested against segregation in Memphis stores. (United Press.)

Although progress has been made in the relations between the two races, any solution acceptable to both sides seems to disappear like a mirage as one gets nearer to it. Thanks to their voting power, Negroes will establish a place for themselves in American society, guaranteed by law, and finally, in the main, respected. Through international pressure, and also because they have come to merit it more and more by their personal achievements, the more distinguished of the Negroes will be treated with greater courtesy, and even admitted to important posts. But it is doubtful whether a colored man will ever be treated as an equal, except so far as his legal position is concerned, nor will he receive that recognition of his social dignity without which he will never feel fully satisfied. It was said ironically in Austria-Hungary, under the old regime, that no man below the rank of a baron need be considered as a man. In the United States, is the Negro really considered as a man? The American message to the world is thus weakened by not being entirely humane.*

If Siegfried were right, the prospects for American eminence in the world of the sixties and beyond were dim indeed.

## The Quality of American Culture

Siegfried was also concerned about the soul of American civilization. On this continent, isolated from Europe and the great civilizations of the Orient, Americans had reared a culture that gave free rein to their political and inventive genius. Their capacity for political innovation, for productive wizardry, for social organization was only remotely challenged by the great nations of history. But what of the *quality* of American civilization? What were the goals of American life? Would action always precede thought in the American scale of values? Was the American destined always to be a highly developed *Homo faber* rather than the *Homo sapiens* of the Greek ideal? Great civilizations of the past had left a high culture, great public monuments, and works of timeless beauty and

* A. Siegfried, *America at Mid-Century* (New York: Harcourt, Brace & World, Inc., 1955), p. 80.

worth. What standards of excellence permeated American literature, arts, crafts, and its popular life? What judgment would archaeologists make ten thousand years hence on the nature of American civilization?

No one questioned that the spread of leisure had permeated the quality of American culture. For the first time in the world's history the mass of men were free to develop their private interests outside the routine of daily toil. But the same organization and mechanization of society that set them free also offered them a mass culture aimed at the largest possible audience or clientele. The fare in television, radio, publishing, even museums, took account of popular fashions and tastes and stressed such universally appealing features as novelty, action, simplicity, and ways to enhance status and comfort. Critics railed at the low taste of Americans and their "status-seeking," while condemning, too, the commercial specialists who devised fresh means of appeasing popular standards. But there were defenders of popular taste, too, who argued that vendors of popular culture consistently underrated the capacity, if not the immediate desires, of the general public. A mass culture was a new phenomenon in the world's history and a population aspiring to a higher level of existence needed guidance and encouragement, not a cynical pandering to the lowest common denominator. As evidence of the upward striving of millions of Americans, defenders pointed to the vast "middlebrow" culture of paperbound books, high-fidelity recordings, book clubs, amateur theaters, and concerts. "Is not the truth of the situation perhaps something like this?" asked Frederick Lewis Allen:

Here is a great nation which is conducting an unprecedented experiment. It has made an incredible number of people, previously quite unsophisticated and alien to art or contemptuous of it, prosperous by any pre-

vious standard known to man. These multitudes offer a huge market for him who would sell them equipment or entertainment that they can understand and enjoy. To compare them with the people who in other lands have been lovers and students of literature and the arts is grossly unfair. They are not an elite, but something else again. Let us say it in italics: *This is something new; there has never been anything like it before.*[*]

More serious was the charge that America lacked standards of excellence. How

could America create an enduring literature and a great art if its creators had lost all sense of permanent and abiding values? "We can assert with some confidence," said T. S. Eliot, "that our own period is one of decline; that the standards of culture are lower than they were fifty years ago; and that the evidences of this decline are visible in every department of human activity." Was it true? Had the earlier smashing of standards in the progressive era and the contemporary preferences of the mass-man left nothing

* F. Allen, *The Big Change* (New York: Harper and Brothers, 1952), p. 277.

Is America developing a class or mass culture? Left, the elegant new Philharmonic Hall in New York City. Right, a magazine and paperback book stand. (Both Monkmeyer: left, Falk; right, Merrim.)

to cling to? One of the progressive reformers, J. Allen Smith, came to think so. "The real trouble with us reformers," he wrote, "is that we made reform a crusade against standards. Well, we smashed them all and now neither we nor anybody else have anything left."

The breakdown of the older order of values, particularly the abandonment of certainty, was the central theme of the American intellectual experience in the twentieth century. It affected writers, artists, ministers, historians, social scientists,

and virtually every sensitive man and woman who thought deeply about the meaning of modern life. In the twenties it produced a literature of disillusionment, nihilism, and primitivism; in the thirties and early forties it was deflected by the great human crises of depression and war; after 1945, it found expression in a literary mood of boredom, despair, and tired cynicism. "The change, in short," wrote John Aldridge, "has been from a stable and severe absolutism, in which what was possible was certain, to

451

an unstable and insecure relativism, in which everything is possible because nothing is certain." *

The quest for meaning was by no means abandoned, however, even among intellectuals. Man has never long been content with despair and disbelief as the reigning attitudes in his intellectual life. Since World War II signs have multiplied of a reconstruction in religion, a renewed interest in the Western tradition and its natural law, and a more hopeful approach to the human predicament. Such powerful religious thinkers as Reinhold Niebuhr and Paul Tillich have sought to make the Christian message meaningful for twentieth-century man in all his "estrangement" from God. Faith to Tillich meant "ultimate concern," a willingness to accept Nietzsche's pronouncement that the traditional Christian God was dead, but a determination to push beyond doubt to faith in the meaningfulness of life. The consequences of the fall of natural law for Western life and values were deplored by a host of intellectual figures.

"If what is good, what is right, what is true," wrote Walter Lippmann in 1955, "is only what the individual 'chooses' to 'invent,' then we are . . . back in the war of all men against all men." Lipmann and others called for the revival of a public philosophy that would once more put the central values of American life in a sheltered position. Still other writers threw off the mood of despair and pessimism that had gripped them earlier. Joseph Wood Krutch, for example, whose *The Modern Temper* (1929) was the most pessimistic book written by an American in this century, now attacked the cultural relativists who demeaned the significance of human choice and freedom. The findings of modern science, he argued, did not demonstrate that reasoning was only rationalization, that consciousness was only a behavioral "epiphenomenon," or that value judgments were merely the preferences that men had been conditioned to accept. "Perhaps," he concluded, "Hamlet was nearer right than Pavlov. Perhaps the exclamation 'How like a God!' is actually more appropriate than 'How like a dog! How like a rat! How like a machine!' " **

## VIEW FROM THE WHITE HOUSE †

This, then, was the civilization that confronted its greatest test in the years of the sixties: dynamic, restless, vital, troubled, committed to democratic ideals, confident of its strength, uncertain of its direction, moralistic, divided on the future of its Negro minority, and searching for leadership. The crisis was real; no less than the future of mankind hung on decisions made in this republic. Though Americans were not yet wholly sensitive to the dangers of this turbulent age— they still lacked the personal and painful immediacy of a flood or depression— their leaders knew that they could not escape responsibility.

The Presidency was the post that counted most in America's struggle to survive. Here was the place from which effective leadership could come, for only the President could seize the initiative,

* J. Aldridge, *After the Lost Generation* (New York: McGraw-Hill, 1951), pp. 232-233.

† This title and some of the material following are suggested by Theodore White's *The Making of the President, 1960*, especially pp. 366-382. Copyright © 1961, by Atheneum House, Inc., New York. By permission of the publisher.

** J. Krutch, *The Measure of Man* (Indianapolis: The Bobbs-Merrill Company, 1953), p. 32.

galvanize America's power, and impose a new design on America's policies at home and abroad. Great obstacles lay in his path—Soviet confidence and determination, the long-term political deadlock at home, and the myriad problems of race, education, economic growth, automation, and national complacency and apathy. But great problems meant great opportunities—after all, the great crises of the past had called forth America's strongest leadership.

No man since Franklin D. Roosevelt had yearned so hard to be President of the United States as John F. Kennedy, and none had shown greater insight into the nature and potentialities of the office. On January 20, 1961, he was given the opportunity for leadership which he sought. Around him he gathered advisers distinguished by their youthfulness, academic background, informality, and penchant for action. He made it clear that he intended to maintain personal control of the affairs of the Presidency, to keep the lines of communication open to all levels of government, and to use unstintingly the resources of politics and publicity to achieve his aims.

What were his aims? At home he pressed hard for new programs in housing, education, agriculture, minimum wages, urban renewal, and medical care of the aged. To the surprise of many, he succeeded, in part, in breaking the political logjam in Congress by forcing an increase in the size of the House Rules Committee and then marshaling narrow majorities for legislation on housing, urban renewal, depressed areas, and minimum wages. He sought also to broaden and strengthen America's defenses by increasing the invulnerability of the nation's missiles, appreciably raising the level of conventional arms, and rebuilding NATO strength. Abroad he pressed hard for a reconstruction of United States relations with Latin America and for a fresh approach to the

hard problems of arms control and a nuclear test ban. And to strengthen the image of the United States in underdeveloped lands, he suggested the creation of a Peace Corps of youthful volunteers who would serve at subsistence wages overseas as teachers, farm helpers, and public health workers.

But the high hopes of the first months of the Kennedy Administration were dampened by new Soviet moves in Laos and Berlin, and by an unsuccessful refugee invasion of Cuba. The Cuban invasion, encouraged by the Kennedy Administration, became a fiasco when the Cuban people, tightly controlled by Castro's police and armed forces, failed to rise in support of the rebels. The President, who took full responsibility for the decision to back the Cuban invasion, became the target of bitter questions about the wisdom and judgment of the new Administration. In Berlin, Khrushchev raised once more the crucial problem of the future of Germany. By threatening a separate peace with East Germany, closing the frontier between East and West Berlin, and halting the flow of refugees from communist rule, Khrushchev touched the vital nerve of East-West relations in Europe. He made these moves confidently, almost contemptuously, as if certain of his own strength and position. The counter-measures taken by Kennedy were vigorous and forceful, but they raised the question of whether they had come too late.

At home, Kennedy suffered new setbacks in his second year as President. Congress defeated his farm bill, blocked his proposals for aid to schools, gutted his tax reform measure (particularly the idea of withholding taxes on dividends and interest), and rejected in the Senate a compromise bill to extend social security to include prepaid hospital care for the elderly. To make matters worse, a sharp stock market collapse, the worst since

1929, raised serious doubts about the effect of Kennedy's economic policies on business. His one legislative victory in 1962 was the passage of the Trade Expansion Act, an important measure that greatly enhanced the President's power to raise or lower tariffs against foreign competitors, so that he might bargain with them for mutual concessions and advantages, particularly with the Common Market nations.

Criticism grew, too, of Kennedy's inaction in Cuba, where Castro was building a communist state with the help of the Russians. Matters came to a head in October, 1962, when the President learned from the Central Intelligence Agency that the Soviet Union was equipping its Caribbean satellite with missiles, manned by Russians, that could carry nuclear destruction to the United States. Kennedy's reply was a naval quarantine against ships carrying offensive weapons to Cuba. In an address to the nation he said that the United States had two goals: "To prevent the use of these missiles against this or any other country, and to secure their withdrawal or elimination from the Western Hemisphere." He warned that "any nuclear missile launched from Cuba against any nation in the Western Hemisphere" would be regarded by the United States as an attack by the Soviet Union and would bring full-scale nuclear reprisal against Russia.

Tension mounted as Soviet and satellite cargo ships headed toward Cuba. Would they change their course? Would Khrushchev risk war over Cuba? Finally, after several days of steaming toward the American blockade, the Soviet ships were ordered home. Then, as Kennedy stepped up the pressure for the withdrawal of the missiles, Khrushchev suddenly capitulated, announcing that he would stop building bases in Cuba, dismantle the offensive weapons, and return them to Russia under UN verification. Though the UN inspection was never carried out, due largely to Castro's stubborn refusal to permit it, American reconnaissance flights revealed that Khrushchev had indeed honored his commitments. Thus, in his first important confrontation of Soviet power, the President appeared to have won a significant victory.

The Cuban crisis affected the midterm elections in 1962. By acting with vigor and decisiveness, the President quieted much of the criticism of his Cuba policy, thereby removing one of the Republicans' strongest campaign issues. The outcome of the election was generally interpreted as a triumph for the President, though the margin was narrow. Four Democrats were added to the Senate, representing a clear-cut victory for him, while only four Democratic seats were lost in the House, the best showing for a party in power since 1934. It was clear, however, that the coalition of conservative Democrats and Republicans that had restrained Democratic administrations since 1938 would still have a controlling majority in the House on many domestic issues. Samuel Lubell's 1952 prediction that the deadlock on domestic policy inherited from Roosevelt might continue until 1964 appeared to have been fulfilled. The quarter-century between the Supreme Court fight and the 1962 elections looked more and more like a period of readjustment to the reforms and changes of the New Deal and war years, as well as a time of transition to some new age of national decision.

## PROLOGUE OR EPILOGUE?

### The American Mission in Violent Days

That perennial optimist, H. G. Wells, as he came close to death, wrote that the Western world was now jaded and lacked the power of recuperation. "Man must go steeply up or down," he said, "and the odds seem all in favor of his going down and out." This gloomy prophecy, when it was delivered in 1945, was still uncommon enough that it created something of a sensation; a decade and a half later it would scarcely have been judged worthy of comment. Pessimism and tragedy had begun to bite deeply into the Western soul, and Americans were inevitably affected by the sense of foreboding that came over the world after 1945.

But Americans were far from convinced that the *Götterdämmerung* had actually begun. They still had too much faith in their ideals, their history, and their own power to believe that the long night of oblivion could fall over their achievements or their hopes. For all the tensions, wars, and crises of the twentieth century, the American was still very much the child of the Enlightenment, a believer in human potentiality, a dreamer of dreams, a follower, despite all the evidence of history and science, of the idea of man's perfectibility and progress. Beneath the layers of cultural tissue was the gristle of animal faith that caused him to cling to the belief that human will counted in history and that it mattered what individuals did. This faith in man's capacity to move history, however exaggerated, had long given American life its peculiar transcendental quality; no one who knew Americans at first-hand in the 1960's

would deny that they retained a large residue of this faith.

### The Democratic Wager

The future of freedom was far from assured, however. Indeed, the whole faith in a free society, as Herbert Muller remarked, remained literally a faith. But it was this uncertainty, this plasticity, this possibility of error and destruction that also made possible man's grandest hopes and dreams. The immediate threat to free society was totalitarianism, but freedom had faced many enemies in its long history and there could be no assurance that communism would be the last.

Implicit in the American's faith in democratic freedom was the wager, as Charles Frankel called it, that the individual human being was improvable; and that the best way to improve him was to allow full scope to his individual efforts and talents. The ultimate measure of all man-made laws and institutions, the democratic theory held, was how well they served the individual, how they helped him to grow, to learn, to master himself and his environment.* In return for providing a fruitful atmosphere for his individual talents, the individual owed a moral responsibility to the whole community. Democracy entailed, then, a faith in the moral and rational faculties of mankind.

This was a powerful idea—that a whole society might draw its motive power from

---

* C. Frankel, "The Power of the Democratic Idea," *Prospect for America: the Rockefeller Panel Reports* (Garden City, N.Y.: Doubleday and Company, 1961), p. 406.

the energies and intelligence of autonomous individuals. It had once inflamed the world; it still attracted by its glow millions of unfortunate beings throughout the earth. No people who have ever known liberty and the blessings of a free society have willingly surrendered them to despots. Today, democracy faces a powerful challenge in a new social system that holds before mankind another dynamic vision of what the future could be like. If Americans were true to the best of their tradition, they would yet show the world what a free society could do.

## FOR FURTHER STUDY

*The books by Aldridge, Jessup, President's Commission on National Goals, Rockefeller Brothers Fund, Rostow, Spanier, Stillman and Pfaff, Thompson, and White cited at the end of the preceding two chapters continue to be especially useful for the topics dealt with in this chapter.*

### General Accounts

D. Brogan, *America in the Modern World* (New Brunswick, N.J.: Rutgers U. Press, 1960). A penetrating analysis by an astute British scholar of the current dilemmas of American life and thought.

R. Kirk, *The American Cause* (Chicago: Regnery, 1957). A conservative's view of the principles of American life, the claims of communism, and the American answer to them.

* M. Lerner, *America as a Civilization* (New York: Simon and Schuster, 1957). A massive book uniting historical and sociological insights into "the pattern and inner meaning of contemporary American civilization and its relation to the world of today."

H. Morgenthau, *The Purpose of American Politics* (New York: Knopf, 1960). A brilliant, critical, somewhat pessimistic, dissection of the contemporary crisis of American politics both at home and in its world aspect.

E. Morison (ed.), *The American Style* (New York: Harpers, 1958). A series of provocative papers and discussions on American values and performance in the recent past.

* H. Smith (ed.), *The Search for America* (Englewood Cliffs, N.J.: Prentice-Hall, 1959). Con-

* Starred books are available in paperbound editions.

tains papers by distinguished scholars and public officials on fifteen crucial problems facing the American people.

R. Spiller and E. Larrabee (eds.), *American Perspectives* (Cambridge: Harvard U. Press, 1961). Analyses by various authorities of the national image projected by American science, literature, politics, social science, and fine arts in this century.

### Special Studies

H. Agar, *A Declaration of Faith* (Boston: Houghton Mifflin, 1952). An eloquent statement of the heritage, traditions, and faith of the West as these have developed historically.

M. Agronsky, *et al.*, *Let Us Begin* (New York: Simon and Schuster, 1961). A pictures-and-text account of the first 100 days of the Kennedy administration, which includes suggestive essays by Eric Goldman, Barbara Ward, and others.

F. Bator, *The Question of Government Spending* (New York: Harpers, 1960). An economist argues that public expenditures have not been excessive, that inflation is not the inevitable result of government spending, and that the nation has committed too small a share of its wealth to such communal use as schools, sanitation, and urban renewal.

E. Burns, *The American Idea of Mission* (New Brunswick,

N.J.: Rutgers U. Press, 1957). Traces the American concepts of national purpose and destiny from the formative period to now.

S. Chase, *Live and Let Live* (New York: Harpers, 1960). A popular analysis of America's current situation by a famous social scientist who argues that the march of technology has made a shambles of our economic theories and made war unthinkable.

* The Editors of *Fortune*, *America in the Sixties* (New York: Harpers, 1960). Forecasts of economic and social trends for the 1960's.

* L. Freedman and C. Cotter (eds.), *Issues of the Sixties* (San Francisco: Wadsworth, 1961). Excellent selections from contemporary writers on such topics as the impact of science and technology, private groups and public policy, civil rights, coexistence, the emerging nations, and the changing American character.

* E. Fuller, *Man in Modern Fiction* (New York: Random House, 1958). The author believes that a corrupted and debased image of man has become widespread through the distortions of modern writers.

* A. Hansen, *Economic Issues of the 1960's* (New York: McGraw-Hill, 1960). Contains some provocative views on inflation, growth patterns, monetary and fiscal policy, trade cycles, and private versus public spending.

* R. Heilbroner, *The Future as History* (New York: Harpers, 1959). A brilliant analysis of the American encounter with history, the shock of recent events, the loss of optimism, and the need for realism in assessing America's position.

I. Hill (ed.), *The New Frontiersmen* (Washington: Public Affairs Press, 1961). Profiles of the men around Kennedy by reporters of the *Washington Star*.

J. Krutch, *Human Nature and the Human Condition* (New York: Random House, 1959), and * *The Measure of Man* (Indianapolis: Bobbs-Merrill, 1953). New and more optimistic views on freedom, values, and human nature by the author of *The Modern Temper* (1929).

* B. Morris, *Problems of American Economic Growth* (New York: Oxford U. Press, 1961). An attempt by an economist to popularize the issues involved in the "economic growth" argument of the early 1960's.

H. Muller, *Issues of Freedom* (New York: Harpers, 1960). A brief but eloquent statement of the origins, nature, paradoxes, and prospects of freedom.

J. Murray, *We Hold These Truths* (New York: Sheed and Ward, 1960). An important book on the Catholic relationship to the modern pluralistic society of the United States.

* W. Rostow, *The Stages of Economic Growth* (Cambridge: Cambridge U. Press, 1960). A much-discussed treatise on the stages of economic growth—the conditions for "take-off," the achievement of regular growth, the drive to maturity, and the stage of high mass consumption —that takes sharp issue with Marxist and communist theories.

* S. Opotowsky, *The Kennedy Government* (New York: Dutton, 1961). Popular essays on the launching of the Kennedy administration and the key figures in it.

* E. Schattschneider, *The Semisovereign People* (New York: Holt, 1960). Argues that conflict, competition, leadership, and organization are the essence of democratic politics and that the people are only partially sovereign in the textbook sense of direct control over government.

C. Snow, *Science and Government* (Cambridge: Harvard U. Press, 1961). A British scientist and writer uses the illustration of two highly placed British wartime scientists, to demonstrate that the most important choices today are made by men "who cannot have a first-hand knowledge of what these choices depend upon or what their results may be."

————, *The Two Cultures and the Scientific Revolution* (Cambridge: Cambridge U. Press, 1959). Snow argues in this book that the growth of modern science has led to the creation of two separate cultures, one literary, the other scientific, and that neither begins to understand the other.

D. Wolfe, *The Image of Man in America* (Dallas: Southern Methodist U. Press, 1957). An historical treatment of the view of man held by leading American thinkers from Jefferson and Emerson to Kinsey and modern American scientists.

## Fiction and Drama

* A. Huxley, *Brave New World* (Garden City, N.Y.: Doubleday, 1932). A satirical novel of a scientific and mechanized Utopia that has been denatured of all human striving and conflict.

* A. Koestler, *The Age of Longing* (New York: Macmillan, 1951). A literary analysis of how the will to resist totalitarian aggression has been affected by fear, apathy, and hatred.

* B. Pasternak, *Doctor Zhivago* (New York: Pantheon, 1958). A Russian physician, who has grown up amid the culture of prerevolutionary Russia, seeks to preserve his spiritual independence against the pressures imposed by a modern, totalitarian society.

* C. Snow, *The Affair* (New York: Scribner's, 1960). A novel of university politics, involving an injustice done a young scientist, that gives ample scope to the author's talent for dealing with struggles for power and the infighting between the literary and scientific cultures.

## Films and Records

*Are Americans Civilized?* (National Educational Television, 30 minutes, sound, black and white). A televised discussion, pro and con, of the view that American civilization is raw, materialistic, and mercenary.

*Democracy* (National Educational Television, 30 minutes, sound, black and white). Defines democracy, points out the differences between democracy and despotism, and discusses the question of equality in a democratic society.

*Freedom of the Individual* (National Educational Television, 30 minutes, sound, black and white). A discussion of individual freedom today, with emphasis on the scientist and the artist, between a physicist, Isidor Rabi, and an historian, Peter Viereck.

*Henry Steel Commager: Part 5* (National Educational Television, 30 minutes, sound, black and white). A well-known historian talks about the place of America in history and its contributions to technology, federal politics, social democracy, education, nationalism, and the separation of church and state.

*Readings on Freedom* (National Educational Television, 29 minutes, sound, black and white). Dr. John W. Dodds explores the concept of freedom as treated by Milton, Benet, Becker, Whitman, and others.

*The Revolution in Human Expectations* (National Educational Television, 29 minutes, sound, black and white). A documentary film on the underdeveloped nations, their needs and addiction to violence, which stresses the view that the eventual outcome of their struggle will shape much of the future.

*United States Responsibilities to the Rest of the World* (National Educational Television, 29 minutes, sound, black and white). A discussion of America's obligations in the world community.

# Index